TIMES
TO
REMEMBER

ROSE FITZGERALD KENNEDY

❧ ⟡ ❧

TIMES TO REMEMBER

❧ ⟡ ❧

1974

DOUBLEDAY & COMPANY, INC.
GARDEN CITY, NEW YORK

Grateful acknowledgment is made to the following for permission to reprint their material.

Column from the Worcester *Telegram*, Worcester, Massachusetts.

From *Markings* by Dag Hammarskjöld, translated by Leif Sjoberg and W. H. Auden. Copyright © 1964 by Alfred A. Knopf, Inc., and Faber & Faber Ltd., reprinted by permission of the publishers.

"Fratri Dilectissimo" by John Buchan, quoted by permission of the Tweedsmuir Estate.

From *Memoirs* by Arthur Krock, copyright © 1968 by Arthur Krock, with permission of Funk & Wagnalls Publishing Company, Inc.

From *Why England Slept* by John F. Kennedy, copyright © 1961, 1940 by Wilfred Funk, Inc., with permission of Funk & Wagnalls Publishing Company, Inc.

Library of Congress Cataloging in Publication Data

Kennedy, Rose Fitzgerald, 1890–
Times to remember.

1. Kennedy, Rose Fitzgerald, 1890–   I. Title.
E748.K378A37   973.9'092'4 [B]
Library of Congress Catalog Number 73–79682
ISBN: 0-385-01625-5

ACKNOWLEDGMENTS

I am most grateful to my children—Eunice Shriver, Patricia Lawford, Jean Smith, and Senator Edward Kennedy—and to my daughters-in-law —Joan Kennedy, Ethel Kennedy, and Jacqueline Onassis—and to my sons-in-law—Sargent Shriver and Stephen Smith—for their advice and counsel in all of the stages of this book. Without their thoughts, memories, anecdotes, and other contributions, my book would never have become a faithful portrait and history of our family. Robert Coughlan also deserves special thanks for his research, his editorial skills, and his fidelity to the main purpose of my endeavor. I also want to express my thanks to Sandy Richardson, my editor at Doubleday, for his sensitive guidance, advice, and support. To many others, who are quoted in these pages, my warm appreciation.

Never let success hide its emptiness from you, achievement its nothingness, toil its desolation. And so . . .
Keep alive the incentive to push on further, that pain in the soul which drives us beyond ourselves.

Do not look back. And do not dream about the future, either. It will neither give you back the past, nor satisfy your other daydreams. Your duty, your reward—your destiny—are *here* and *now*.

Dag Hammarskjöld
from *Markings*

All things have their season, and in their times all things pass under heaven.
A time to be born and a time to die;
   a time to plant, and a time to pluck up that which is
   planted.
A time to kill, and a time to heal;
   a time to destroy, and a time to build.
A time to weep, and a time to laugh;
   a time to mourn, and a time to dance.
A time to scatter stones, and a time to gather;
   a time to embrace, and a time to be far from embraces.
A time to get, and a time to lose;
   a time to keep, and a time to cast away.
A time to rend, and a time to sew;
   a time to keep silence, and a time to speak. . . .
For every man that eateth and drinketh, and seeth good of his labor, this is the gift of God. . . . Nothing is better than for a man to rejoice in his work, and that this is his portion. For who shall bring him to know the things that shall be after him?

Ecclesiastes is one of my favorite Books of the Old Testament, as it was also for my son President John F. Kennedy. Some of these lines were read during his funeral services in 1963.

Rose Fitzgerald Kennedy

This book is dedicated to my daughter Rosemary and others like her—retarded in mind but blessed in spirit. My vision is a world where mental retardation will be overcome, where we no longer mourn with mothers of retarded children, but exult and rejoice with parents of healthy, happy youngsters. Then, and only then, can we say, in the words of St. Paul: "I have fought the good fight. I have finished the course. I have kept the faith."

TIMES
TO
REMEMBER

Chapter One

❧❦

There have been times when I felt I was one of the more fortunate people in the world, almost as if Providence, or Fate, or Destiny, as you like, had chosen me for special favors.

Now I am in my eighties, and I have known the joys and sorrows of a full life. I can neither forget nor ever reconcile myself to the tragedies. Age, however, has its privileges. One is to reminisce and another is to reminisce selectively. I prefer to remember the good times, and that is how this book begins.

Before I began to write, I had to ask myself some hard questions, and the first was "Why do it?" And the second was "Well, supposing I do, then how? What is the best way?" I think that anyone who reads the book is entitled to have my answers.

Surely anyone who writes a memoir or autobiography must either believe that he or she is a rather special person with a special wisdom or body of experience, or has a contribution of some unique and valuable kind to make. If this were not so, history and literature would be lacking valuable (and less valuable) works that give us insights into times past and people and societies gone.

Millions and millions of words have been written about my family, collectively and individually, and if I were to make a guess about the contents of this mountain of print, I would think that most of it has, at best, been flawed by inaccuracies, misunderstandings, misinterpretations, and the worst has been mendacious and deceitful or even totally untrue stories that sound like pulp fiction and are often confused with history. For a great many years I tried to ignore everything, from the honest errors to the pure trash, for if I had allowed myself to care I would have been driven to distraction. There was too much; the flow was too heavy. I suppose it will continue at least awhile, so long as there are Kennedys in politics or somehow in the public eye; and I can do nothing about the errors and falsehoods that come off the presses. Nor can I possibly cope with all those that came off in the past. But, at least, in this book, I can deal with the major ones, and thus perform a service both to my family and to historians.

As for the second question, the best way to do the book, I was uncertain until, wonderfully enough, the question began to answer itself. I had diary notes that I had been keeping conscientiously since the time Joe was ambassador to England, and from these and various memorabilia I had worked up a thick sheaf of manuscript pages, some of which I thought were quite good. There were other resources, such as the black notebooks in which, for many years, I had been collecting quotations, interesting words, apt phrases, homilies, ideas and philosophical jottings and aphorisms, on all sorts of subjects, for potential uses in campaigning, other public speaking, and goodness knows what. There were other things, scrapbooks, clippings, notes, photographs, and so forth, along with a library of Kennedy books, some written by Kennedys. Still, somehow, with all these tools at hand, there did not seem to be enough resources to do justice to the theme. Neither my husband nor any of the children had written any substantial memoirs of the family; therefore this book would be—so far—the only book about the Kennedys written by a Kennedy, a large responsibility.

I will amend that now to take account of a rumor about the Kennedys that is quite true, and to supply what seems to me a happy ending for this first chapter. The truth is that the Kennedys cooperate with one another and that an individual's project is likely to become a family project. Everyone pitches in to help. I have been helped with time, energy, painstaking research, and encouragement by every member of the family. They have enabled me to find intrafamily letters, notes, and other artifacts that might help to fill gaps and add variety and a sense of life to this book. I asked if they would mind talking about me and our family, with a tape recorder nearby.

I was getting on in years, I said, and memories of long ago were hard to recapture, but I needed to do so. ("Good Lord!" said my daughter-in-law Ethel. "Twenty, thirty years ago? Remembering? Half the time I can't even remember things that happened yesterday afternoon! Who can?")

Extraordinary and beautiful things began to happen. Were there surviving letters? Hundreds and hundreds of them began to flow in, along with dozens of bits of childhood memorabilia, valentines, Christmas cards, second-grade scrawls, and fourth-grade poetic efforts, most of which I had long since forgotten, however much delight they had given me at the time.

I have my own, special memories of family and friends, but invariably their memories differ in some ways from my own. These add new dimensions, values, and insights to my memoirs. The letters and tape recordings were the missing elements, I now think, to the kind of book, historically true but with the full breath of life in it, that I had wanted to write.

Emerson: "Properly there is no such thing as history, only biography." This, then, to the degree that I have succeeded, is a book about my husband and myself, with something about our parents and a great deal about our children; in their settings, their humanity, their natures, and destinies.

With all the help I have received from so many people, and with all my thanks in many directions, this remains my own book, stuffed with my memories, especially memories of my children, and with my own thoughts and precepts and goals when I was raising them.

What I was able to pass on to them was, of course, in an indefinable but substantial degree what I had received from my parents, and they in turn from theirs.

Chapter Two

As with so many other American families of Irish descent, we begin with the famines that swept Ireland during the middle of the last century. Thousands of people died. Other thousands, younger and stronger and luckier, emigrated to the United States and a large share of these to the city and hinterlands of Boston. I have read that fare, including food, was about twenty dollars and that the voyage sometimes took as long as two months. With overcrowding, disease, and miserable and debilitating conditions, perhaps one passenger in ten died on the voyage. An Irish immigrant had to be both hardy and lucky to set foot at last in America.

My paternal grandparents, Thomas Fitzgerald and Rose Mary Murray, made that grim voyage in the 1840s. They both came from County Wexford, but they met and were married in Boston. Later, another son of Wexford, Patrick Kennedy, arrived in Boston. There he, too, met and married an Irish immigrant girl, Bridget Murphy. I have no direct memories of these four brave souls because each had passed away before I was born. But I know they arrived with scarcely more than determination and faith, that they worked hard, and raised their children in the love and care of God.

The Fitzgeralds had eleven children. Nine of them survived infancy; among these was John Francis Fitzgerald. He married Mary Josephine Hannon and they had six children—of whom I was the eldest. The Kennedys had four children including an only son called Patrick Joseph (known later in Boston political annals as "P.J."). He married Mary Hickey and they had three children. One of them, again an only son, was Joseph Patrick Kennedy.

The two family lines joined when Joseph Patrick Kennedy and I were married.

Grandfather Thomas Fitzgerald worked for a while as a farm hand at South Acton, a village twenty-five miles or so from Boston, just beyond Lexington and Concord, but later came back to Boston's North End, where he spent most of the rest of his life as a grocer. Thus it was in the North End (in a modest flat in an eight-family dwelling) that my father was born, raised, and felt most at home. And where in turn, after he and my mother married and had saved enough, they set up housekeeping in a modest house. It was there that I was born, on July 22, 1890, christened Rose Elizabeth.

The North End had been the center of colonial Boston: of all those mercantile, religious, cultural and political activities that made the city the hub of Massachusetts Colony and much of New England. In fact, it encompassed most of the city, which in those years had a population of only about seventeen thousand. As every school child knows, many of the causes, ideas, ideals of the American Revolution originated and were nurtured in Boston, and many of the first decisive acts of the Revolution happened there. So the old North End is full of historical buildings and sites—Faneuil Hall, the old North Church, and Paul Revere's house.

By the time he was in his late teens, my father was a fascinated amateur expert on Boston's history and was even conducting guided tours, with his own lectures. I remember as a child and as a young girl that it was a rare outing in Boston or anywhere in the area that did not inspire a discourse on historical names, dates, and incidents, delivered in a style that was informative, yet also marvelously interesting and entertaining. He made history come to life. Sometimes, a scene or event would remind him of Irish history and the migrations. He knew a great deal about them as well, mostly from listening to his own father. His conversation was wide ranging. From Boston's history to America's, Ireland's to England's, from these to the world's. From history to current events and from current events to their causes, which he would analyze and interpret and prognosticate about in a rush of thoughts and words, something like spontaneous combustion.

He talked to me incessantly when I was a child and young girl growing up: about everything in sight, but since so much in sight had some association with American history that is what I heard about more often than not. Naturally, this had an influence on me. Evidently, in fact, it was especially noticeable when it came to raising my own children. I believed they should know history and especially the history of their own country and, when they grew old enough to understand, I used to take them to the landmarks in Boston and the countryside, explaining what had happened there and discussing events with them so they would remember them.

I was determined about this, and I may have overdone it a little since there can be too much even of a good thing. My daughter Eunice says it seemed to her I was always dragging them off to Bunker Hill or Concord Bridge, and there were times when she thought of me as a schoolteacher. In any case they did learn, their interest developed with the years, and I suspect that this may be one reason why as adults they wanted to serve the country in public life. Jack, especially, was fascinated by history; he read it, wrote it, and lived it, and I think his sense of history guided his whole career and gave his presidency a quality of its own.

There is another family characteristic that I think derives from my father. This is a mixture of abundant energy, vitality, physique, quick reflexes, and a psychological or endocrinological "x factor." I refer not only to the touch football games, for instance, that became famous, but to the strenuous activities that were always going on. Of course, Jack's presidency is remembered, among many things, for its encouragement of increased physical fitness in the nation and calls for "vigor."

Elusive and incalculable as the influences of heredity and environment are, there is no way to assign shares, but it is clear to me that our children inherited these physical traits from both sides of the family. Joe was a superb athlete, and few men ever had such energy and stamina. And then there was my father.

Although he was only about 5 feet 7 inches, he was tremendously strong and agile. As he once recalled, speaking of his boyhood, "In those days we used to run on the sidewalks and cobblestones of Hanover Street, and I could always beat any of the boys." I remember also his telling us that he caught the greased pig at church picnics so consistently that he was declared ineligible to compete—and the next year one of his brothers caught it. At the Boston Latin School—the oldest and, at least in those days, perhaps the most prestigious public high school in the country—he managed and played on the baseball team, played football, and was team captain two years. He also edited the school magazine. There was no interscholastic athletic organization in Boston in those days; so, shortly after he graduated, he founded one and became its first president. Later, he developed a great fondness for riding. I should add that he also loved to dance as long as the music played, charming and beguiling his partners and talking a mile a minute between numbers.

His vigor, charm, and sheer joy in living were contagious. Many times I saw him walk into a room—a parlor, ballroom, the main lounge of an ocean liner—full of somnolent, inhibited people bored stiff with one another, and within five minutes have them smiling, attentive, active, having fun, perhaps even singing. He took charge of them and they loved it. And he did too. I think he felt it was a challenge to wake them up. Yet he also truly liked people and liked to see them happy.

As for his scholastic abilities, there was never any reason to doubt them. The Boston Latin School had high academic standards and he had done well there. He was accepted at Harvard Medical School and was already in his first year when Fate intervened to change his life.

His mother, Rose Mary Fitzgerald, had died three years earlier. Now his father, Thomas Fitzgerald, died. Both had been in their thirties. They left nine surviving children, all sons, of whom my father (then age eighteen) was third eldest; which, of course, left six more down the line from him, from teen-agers to toddlers. Thomas Fitzgerald had left a small amount of money but nowhere near enough to keep this large brood fed and sheltered very long, and obviously nothing could be spared for my father's expenses at medical school. He could have made his way through entirely on his own, I expect, but he felt a deep obligation to the memory of his parents and to what would have been their dearest wish, that the family stay together, despite the practical advice of the parish priest that the younger brothers be placed in foster homes. Consequently, he left school, took a civil service examination, and landed a steady job as a clerk in the Boston Custom House. (Incidentally, his top boss, the collector in charge of the Custom House, was Leverett Saltonstall.) I never learned why the two older brothers didn't take more responsibility, but the fact was that my father became the mainstay of the family and continued to be so until the youngest boys were ready to take care of themselves.

This marked the end of my father's formal education. I'm sure he regretted not having a chance to finish college. Yet, I have thought this was curiously to his advantage. So often, it seems, people get their college degrees and then are content to let mental facilities atrophy from disuse. My father, on the contrary, and perhaps because of being denied the credentials of an education, retained his appetite for knowledge and became an avid reader. He had wonderful azure blue eyes (I inherited the color but less optical quality) and boundless curiosity, so he read everything within reach: books, magazines, and, of course, many newspapers. Everything in print seemed to be grist for him—and when he found something that struck him as interesting, important, or in some way useful, he would cut the item out of the magazine or paper with a small penknife he carried. Then, to be sure he wouldn't lose it, quite often he would pin it (with a straight pin; he carried a supply) on his lapel or, when that area was filled, almost anywhere else on the front of his jacket. One of my earliest vivid recollections is of his sitting in a chair surrounded by newspapers, penknife in hand and neatly (always neatly, like a surgeon) excising something pertinent.

He kept on doing this all his life. Eunice says that one of her own enduring images of him—one of those impressions that somehow are selected and stored in the mind from among the many—was when he was well along in years, probably in his seventies. He was visiting us at Hyannis Port and was sitting in his favorite perch there, a chair at the far end of our big, bright, comfortable living room, with a sea view and the sunlight streaming in behind him. "There were masses of newspapers all over the floor around him, and he was clipping. He wouldn't get through a page or two without pulling out something. And he'd say, 'Now look at this! Look what the women are doing'—anyway, always he'd be finding something interesting."

And what he read, he remembered. He had a stupendous memory for facts and figures, points of law, historical facts, quotations, anecdotes, and, of course, anything to do with Boston—all of great advantage to him in his political speechmaking and in debating an opponent. He had a famous ability to talk about anything persuasively, cogently, and with swarms of facts seemingly produced from the thin blue. Someone put this verse in a Boston paper:

> *Honey Fitz can talk you blind*
> *On any subject you can find.*
> *Fish and fishing, motorboats,*
> *Railroads, streetcars, getting votes,*
> *Proper ways to open clams,*
> *How to cure existing shams;*
> *State Street, Goo-Goos, aeroplanes,*
> *Malefactors, thieving gains,*
> *Local transportation rates,*
> *How to run the nearby states;*
> *On all these things, and many more,*
> *Honey Fitz is crammed with lore.*

I expect that here again his character left some imprints on mine. I mentioned earlier my scrapbooks and looseleaf notebooks filled with useful facts and notable ideas and quotations, the gleanings of many years of clipping items from newspapers and magazines and transcribing favorite passages from plays and books. Also for years I have carried a small spiral-back notebook in my purse, which I use for jotting down similar treasures that I encounter on the go; and I'm sure I would feel rather lost and deprived without it.

The life of a custom's clerk could not contain my father's energies for long or ever satisfy his ambitious nature, so after three years of it he resigned and started an insurance business, with an office in the North End. He was already mixed up in so many civic, fraternal, social, and athletic affairs that he was widely known there, and with his natural gifts of salesmanship he soon was prosperous enough to marry the girl he had been in love with for years, Mary Josephine Hannon, daughter of Irish immigrants who had settled in the little town of Acton northwest of Boston. They married in 1889, and I was born the next year. Proverbially, a man wants his first child to be a son. But with nine boys in his family, and no female relatives in this country and none that he knew of in Ireland, my father was overjoyed to have a girl. According to my brothers, he seems to have regarded me as a miracle, an impression from which he never really recovered.

By the time I arrived he was already active in ward politics. Soon he was elected to Boston's Common Council. And then to the state Senate. And then—a meteoric rise—to the United States House of Representatives. He was one of the youngest men in Congress, the only Democrat from the whole of New England, and the only Catholic. He was re-elected twice, so his tenure in Congress lasted six years, from 1895 to 1901.

Meanwhile, our family was increasing. I had a little sister, Agnes; then a little brother, Thomas; and with three small children and the promise of more to follow, my father decided to vacate our small house and move us to a place in the country with space and a yard and fresh air. It was a big, old, rambling, architecturally hybrid but wonderfully comfortable house in West Concord, just a few miles from Acton, where my mother's parents lived on a hill. It was there that I spent the rest of my childhood.

They were wonderful years, full of the traditional pleasures and satisfactions of life in a small New England town. Years of serenity, order, neighborly human relationships, family affection: trips with horse and buggy to my grandparents' house, climbing apple trees and gathering wildflowers in the woods behind the house. I knew and remembered from year to year where the lady slippers were hidden, and where to look for the Solomon's-seal and all my other favorite spring flowers as they appeared, each in its time. The hand-cranked ice-cream freezer, and tantalizing visions of getting to lick the ladle—which never could be soon enough, because making ice cream was a big job, hard work, and it was only for Sundays, birthdays, and other special occasions. Warm milk fresh from the cows at a neighbor's farm. My memories seem to dwell on food. Fresh peas and salmon were Fourth of July for us and everyone else in the area (no one outside of New England, it seems, has ever heard of the idea), and peas in season were a Sunday staple. Baked beans and brown bread: Every household had a special, perfect recipe, and in all cases the smells were delicious every Saturday night, because that was the night for baked beans and brown bread. My father loved them. And, on Friday nights, lobsters brought in from Boston. I remember how happy he looked sitting at the table with his family and devouring lobsters, sucking the claws and pulling them apart with great gusto.

Except when Congress was in recess he could be there with us only for weekends. And these visits were feats of endurance. By the time he left his congressional office in Washington to board the train to New York and catch a train from there to Boston, and another from Boston to Concord, and ride in a carriage from Concord to West Concord where we lived, at least fourteen hours had passed. Then, to get back to Washington for the Monday-morning session of the House, it was all to do over in reverse.

He never complained or even commented on this outlandish commuting arrangement, so far as I can recall. To the contrary, it seemed to stimulate him. He loved excitement and every train connection was a gamble. As soon as I was old enough to handle the reins I was usually the one to go along with him to the Concord station and drive the carriage back home. He never wanted to leave until the last minute, and he would calculate it by having all us children look for smoke puffing up from the train as it approached—still a couple of miles away—through the woods to Concord. Then, depending on the report and what must have been some intricate mental arithmetic, he would regulate the speed of the horse. Now and then, not often, he cut his chances too fine or ran into delays and lost his bet with himself and missed the train. But that didn't seem to faze him. He accepted most things as they came—or went. He would shrug his shoulders and tell me he'd use his time getting a shave and reading the papers and a book or two he always had with him and wouldn't be missing a thing, no time really lost at all.

Losing time, wasting time, doing nothing—these were matters that really bothered him, so he always made sure there was something to do, something he could feel it was useful to do. And I think I have always been the same way.

I think there is truth in the idea that "opposites attract," because it was certainly true in the case of my parents. Father was an extrovert; Mother was innately rather shy and reserved. He would talk with anybody about anything. When she spoke, it was usually directly and to the point. Small talk bored her. He adored being with people—of all kinds, complexions, religions, attitudes, conditions, and ages, so long as they were alive and responsive. She was happiest with close friends and members of her family, yet she also needed time to be alone, in peaceful solitude for reflection and prayer. He loved being "on stage" and feeling the vibrations emanating from an audience. She could enjoy the show and the glamour, but as a spectator in the audience. When she was obliged to be on stage herself, as from time to time she was, she was likely to respond with a nervous uncomfortableness that she controlled somewhat stiffly and formally. When she was happy everyone knew it, and there were smiles and serenity, but when she was unhappy (she must have been sometimes; who hasn't been) she rarely showed it. She was unselfishly devoted to her husband and her family and to our welfare.

Mother was an immaculate housekeeper with a strong sense of the value of money and a sharp eye for any waste or any shortchanging. And a good thing; for my ebullient father's inclination was to cut a figure, bestow benefits, set a fine table, and think of the money a little later. But his nature and the nature of political life made him more spontaneous than frugal.

When I try to identify traits in myself that my mother may have had a special influence in forming, I would guess this is one of them. I grew up with the idea that one should be careful with money, that none should be spent without good and sufficient reason, and there should be something—tangible or intangible—to justify each expense. I have never changed in this belief, not even after money was no problem for us. Thriftiness is a famous Yankee virtue and I suppose I would have acquired it, to some extent, just from living in the Boston-Concord region, but my mother's example was probably decisive. This was a principle I tried to instill in raising my own children.

I also was influenced by her conviction that children need firm discipline. She, perforce, was the disciplinarian in our house because my father was not there most of the time. She brought us up quite strictly by today's standards. She made it clear we were to behave ourselves, study our schoolwork and our religious lessons, be punctual, neat and mannerly. If we didn't obey the rules, we were spanked.

A most precious gift that came in large measure from my mother was deep faith in the Church and its teachings and practices. My father was a devout and dutiful Catholic who took Holy Communion regularly and observed the holy days and obligations of the Church calendar. But he was so deeply involved in the affairs of the world that he took religion for granted without thinking much about it. Going to Mass was simply natural and normal and gave him the opportunity (I say this with love and without sacrilege) of communicating not only with God but with many of his friends and political constituents.

To my mother, however, the Church was a pervading and abiding presence, and she instilled these feelings in us. She drilled us in our catechism and other religious lessons, and talked to us about the fasts and feasts and special seasons of the Church. May was the month of the Blessed Virgin. There was a little shrine to her in our house, with her statue, and all month we kept it decorated with fresh flowers and offered a prayer there each night. Every night during Lent my mother would gather us in one of the rooms of the house, turn out the lights—the better to concentrate—and lead us in reciting the Rosary.

I'm sure my knees ached and that sometimes I wondered why I should be doing all the kneeling and studying and memorizing and contemplating and praying. But I became understanding and grateful. And in my own time I tried to pass on to my own children this precious gift of faith.

Yet along with these qualities of dutifulness and piety and austerity of temperament my mother also knew how to enjoy life. She went on vacation trips with my father, leaving us children (two more, John F. Jr. and my sister Eunice, were born in these Concord years)

in the care of a nursemaid and housekeeper. One year they went to
one of the spas that were so much in fashion in that era, and came
home with a matched pair of beautiful black horses, Black Hawk
and Maud. My mother loved riding and excelled at it. One of my
most vivid memories is of her riding sidesaddle at a gallop on one of
these black horses, its mane and tail flying, and her own long, thick,
lustrous dark brown, nearly black hair—fallen loose from the hairpins
—streaming behind her. She was magnificent and, it seemed to me,
perfectly beautiful.

She had dark Irish looks, with a fine complexion, and a small, lithe,
trim figure, which she never lost. From the time she married to the
end of her life (at the age of ninety-eight), her weight seldom varied
much from 115 pounds. She was fine boned and finely proportioned,
standing only about 5 feet 3 inches but seeming taller because of the
dignity of her bearing. Even in her last years her hair was only partly
gray. She liked clothes and dressed with instinctive taste.

My father was enchanted with her and very proud of her. When
both were old, and someone asked him to look back and name the
happiest day of his life, he said: "When I got the girl I wanted, Mary
Josephine Hannon. We've lived together now for forty-five years.
The first time I met her, I knew."

We lived in Concord when I was between the ages of seven and
thirteen. There were many good times and many warm memories.

I remember the sweet and peaceful Sunday afternoons when,
after morning Mass and a bountiful country-style noontime dinner,
we got into a carriage or two and—still in our Sunday best—clattered
away in the countryside for an airing. Naturally, there was an
ultimate destination, a purpose: most often my grandparents' house,
sometimes a farm where we children could admire the animals and
chickens and my father could do a little political pulse-taking with
the farmer. He could tell him a few remarkable facts about the origin
and proper care of guinea fowl or something. Or sometimes it would
be a swimming lesson in a nearby fresh-water pond.

How I remember the lessons! We children would scatter into the
bushes to change into our bathing suits. There was a makeshift raft
at the water's edge: That was my father's headquarters for the ses-

sion. He had put together a contraption consisting of an old-fashioned cork circular lifesaver into which we were tied, the lines leading to a strong fishing line, in turn attached to a strong bamboo fishing pole, which my father grasped in his hands as he stood on the raft. Then I, or one of us, was in the water . . . shouts of instruction, "Kick your feet" and "Move your hands and arms" . . . and shouts of encouragement . . . and, whenever I or the contraption went out of kilter, a swift yank from the pole to the line to the ropes and the lifesaver and me, putting everything temporarily right. That is how I learned to swim. And, although I never got much beyond the "dog paddle" and breast stroke, swimming has been one of the abiding pleasures of my life; and to this very time, when the weather permits, I swim every day.

Those Sunday outings became even pleasanter when my father bought a two-horse carriage that was half-moon shaped, like a truncated bay window or part of a theater box on wheels, a congenial design big enough to hold us all—parents, children, and grandparents—side-by-side but in view of one another. As we jounced along, behind our spirited Black Hawk and Maud, we chattered back and forth and sang our favorite songs.

By the time I was twelve or so I had my own rig—a gentle horse and small carriage—of which, of course, I was quite proud. I used it for all kinds of errands and explorations, but I remember best the summer days when school was out and time was heavy and I used to drive back and forth to the Concord Library for books. I loved to read, another enthusiasm I inherited mainly from my father. Yet I was far more interested in fiction than fact, especially "romantic fiction." Most of the authors, titles, and plots have long since faded from memory, but I'm sure that in the spirit of the age they were, without exception, moral, inspirational, and sentimental. A usual theme, as I do recall, was that love (aided by virtue and hard work and pluck) somehow conquered all. I attribute to this my later girlhood conviction that I must, absolutely, marry only for love. The books I remember best were those by Louisa May Alcott. She had lived and written in Concord and was one of the famous literary names of the region, along with Emerson, Thoreau (we used to have church picnics at Walden Pond), and numerous others who brought about the literary "Flowering of New England." The library had her complete works, and I'm sure I read them all. *An Old-Fashioned Girl, Little Men,* and others, but her most popular book was also my own favorite: *Little Women.*

Every summer, then and later, our family spent two or three weeks at the seaside at Old Orchard Beach, Maine. It was a pleasant place for both old and young, but especially attractive to my parents because so many of their friends went there. Not surprisingly, practically all of them were Irish Catholics from Boston and my father's congressional district, and many of the men were involved in politics. They all knew one another. They came with their families, and visited back and forth and picnicked together while the children played. It was nothing at all like a conclave: The attractions were as simple as they seemed, salt water and sunshine and congenial company, and families came and went without discussing any topic more serious than the weather. Yet mixed with the salt air was often the whiff of politics. One of the men who came there fairly regularly, with his family, was a greatly respected businessman and political leader from East Boston, Patrick Joseph (P.J.) Kennedy. Needless to say, he and my father knew each other well.

So it was at Old Orchard Beach that my future husband and I first saw each other. Neither of us had the faintest recollection of that "historic" encounter until, many years later, someone turned up a yellowed clipping from a Boston newspaper: A group photograph of the Fitzgeralds and Kennedys and a dozen or so other families lined up for the camera on a part of the beach, with a caption identifying everyone. And there was Joe, a rather spindly-looking nine- or ten-year-old and there was I, not so much to look at either, but apparently taller though two years younger.

Chapter Three

❧❦

Boston politics of this era was not unlike that in Ireland before the Anglo-Norman conquest. The Irish had their local chieftains, who often warred against one another for fancied glory and advantages for themselves and their followers. They made unstable alliances that could find one year's ally another year's foe. Yet they produced especially strong leaders, superchieftains who reigned as kings over large regions, in turn allying and defecting and forming new constellations as the winds blew. Occasionally one would be successful enough to claim the status of "high king" but never without challenges, direct or brewing, against his authority.

The Democratic Party was predominant in Boston. It was less a party than a number of leaders representing neighborhood and district interests. They were often in contention, with alliances of convenience quickly formed and broken. Around 1900 there were four men who used-to meet regularly, usually in a private room of the fine old Quincy House hotel, and iron out differences and make plans over luncheon and coffee. They were nicknamed the "Strategy Board." One of them was my father. Another was my future father-in-law, P. J. Kennedy.

My father's position as congressman for a district that took in all of Boston was obviously reason enough for him to be included as one of "The Big Four" on the Strategy Board. But why Patrick Joseph Kennedy? I must now digress briefly to bring this part of the story up-to-date.

As I have said, his father, Patrick, migrated from Ireland during the Great Famine and settled in the region of Boston harbor now known as East Boston. There he made his living as a cooper; married Bridget Murphy and had a family of four; and there he died nearly penniless at the early age of thirty-five—the same age that death took my grandfather Thomas Fitzgerald. His widow opened a little "stationery and notions" shop and managed to eke out a living. Her children helped as they grew old enough. Patrick Joseph, the youngest, worked in the store, ran errands, found innumerable odd jobs around the waterfront and, when he was big and strong enough, became a stevedore. Because of the family's grinding financial need he had to drop out before finishing grade school; but he, like my father, was a great reader, with a special interest in American history.

After several years of scrimping he saved enough money to buy a neighborhood saloon. He prospered and put his profits back into his business, which expanded until he had partnerships in other saloons as well as a retail, wholesale, and importing trade. He went into the coal business, too, and into banking. His was a second-generation immigrant American success story.

In Ireland, as in England, the neighborhood pub was "the poor man's club" and the tradition also existed in Boston. As bartender, host, and proprietor, P. J. Kennedy found himself in the middle of East End news, gossip, celebrations, hopes and fears, troubles and tragedies. He was a good listener, knew how to keep confidences, and had a compassionate spirit. He helped people with loans, gifts, and advice. Often he passed the word on to somebody that so-and-so needed this or that and P. J. Kennedy would appreciate it, asking nothing in return but good will. Everyone knew that he was an honorable man, and everyone respected him. He was 5 feet 10 inches, with a brawny physique, blue eyes, a rain-washed, rosy complexion, reddish hair, and a handlebar mustache that swooped gracefully, adding to his air of composure and dignity. Predictably, he became a political force in East Boston. And before long, he was the most influential figure of that whole region of the city.

He served a term in the Massachusetts House of Representatives and another in the state Senate, and was a delegate to three national Democratic conventions. But elective office, with all its demands for public appearances and speeches, was not his style. He preferred to work quietly, behind the scenes, which ideally suited him to the work of the Strategy Board.

He and my father had been friends, or at least close acquaintances, for a long time. Temperamentally they were opposites, and I suppose they must have grated on each other's nerves at times. But they had many things in common too: their immigrant background, the early deaths of their fathers, the personal determination, foresight, hard work that raised them to their positions and, of course, a sophisticated understanding of politics. I'm sure they understood each other and each in his way liked and admired the other.

I am reminded now of the analogy with which I began this chapter. And of a comment my son Jack once made about political relationships as he encountered them in his own career and described with his succinct wit. He said: "In politics you don't have friends. You have allies." He cited a book by Frank Kent, one of the best political reporters early in this century, called *The Great Game of Politics*, a title that conveys a lot about the necessity of teamwork, of allies— and the possibility of upsets—and, finally, the desirability of handshakes after the "game."

My father had first run for Congress and won in 1894 against the opposition of the Strategy Board, of which he was not yet a member, though P. J. Kennedy was. (A fabled independent chieftain, Martin Lomasney, was his strong ally. "My political godfather," my father said.) A few years later, when my father came onto the Board, the past was smoothed and he and P. J. Kennedy became allies.

But in 1900, as my father was ending his third term in Congress and expecting renomination and re-election, there were seismic movements, shifts, realignments. I had no idea at the time what it was all about. In any case, P. J. Kennedy and the other Board members (and a new mayor with whom my father disagreed) blocked his renomination. He might have won against them in the primary as he had the first time, but a look at the odds persuaded him not to try.

His congressional career ended in 1901.

My father then bought a moribund little weekly newspaper called *The Republic*, which he managed to pick up for only five hundred dollars. He thought he could turn it into a money-maker, which was urgent because he no longer had his congressional salary. But he also knew the power of the press in politics, and in *The Republic* he saw a potentially valuable instrument for advancing his political career. He was both resilient and audacious, and his goal was to become mayor of Boston.

He had no experience in newspaper publishing, but he had many friends on Boston papers to give him advice, and he learned quickly. He knew what was interesting and how to present it in an appealing way. He was also shrewd.

As he said later: "I knew the success of a newspaper depended on its advertising revenue, and that advertisers look to women, who spend most of the money in the big stores that did most of the advertising. I accordingly made the paper more readable to women . . ." Although women did not yet have the vote, he was aware of their power. I think he influenced some of the campaign strategies Jack would adopt when he entered public life.

With his ideas and energy and salesmanship, my father soon made a success with *The Republic*. After a few years he was said to be clearing five times his congressional salary. True or not, I do know that by 1904 he could afford a fine, spacious fifteen-room house in the Boston suburb of Dorchester.

Dorchester was outside of the Boston city limits, and my father was preparing to run for mayor of Boston. Yet his legal address, his "voting residence," had continued and still continued to be in the old neighborhood, Ward Six, the North End. He was always in touch with the voters there, as well as the solid dependable lieutenants who were the foundation of his strength. He was the "boss" of Ward Six and, if not yet the "boss," at least the leading political chieftain of the whole North End.

He was a very sentimental man. When he talked about the North End, it was "the dear old North End." When he ran into some former neighbor or acquaintance who had gone to another part of the city or region, he was inevitably moved to reminisce about "the dear old North End." Here is a sample of his manner and style, as he once described a visit to the old neighborhood:

"As I came up old Hanover Street this morning—up the dear old North End—every man and child had a smile for me. It seemed as if the very paving stones rose up and greeted me. I met old Johnny

Doolan on the corner. 'God bless ye, little Johnny Fitz,' he said to me, 'you deserve to win.' "

Someone, probably a newspaper reporter who heard the phrase often, contracted it to the generic term "Dearos" for all who lived in the North End or had ever lived there and had any association at all with my father. The name caught on, and it became one of those trademarks that can be useful in politics. He was the king of the Dearos, who became part of the language of Boston politics.

Despite my father's love for the dear old North End and his Dearos, he preferred his own family to have the fresh air and open spaces of small-town and suburban Dorchester. Indeed, Concord had been some twenty-five miles from the nearest border of his congressional district, which caused some of his critics to call him a "carpetbagger."

We lived in Dorchester very comfortably and happily for a good many years. Another baby, my youngest brother, Frederick, was born there: the last of us six. I went to the Dorchester High School, where I soon made many friends while managing to do well in my studies. I was in the college preparatory curriculum and had my eye set on Wellesley College, where in fact I was accepted in my junior year. I resumed the dancing and piano lessons I had begun in Concord, both of which I liked, and am everlastingly grateful to my parents for providing me with them. I was also rather interested in boys, and they seemed interested in me. But our relationships were predictably strained and giggly.

My mother went on serenely and conscientiously with her domestic and motherly duties. My father, despite the proximity of Boston and Dorchester, was no more, and perhaps even less, visible in the household than he had been in Concord. He was busy with *The Republic* and actively preparing his campaign for the mayoralty. He attended meetings, banquets, church parties, parish reunions, clubs, societies, and sodalities. There were hundreds of speeches to make, thousands of hands to shake, jokes, songs, warm glances, and cheery smiles, patient listening, good advice and favors to grant. It was a rare night he was home to have dinner with us.

I was certainly not happy about that, at the time. I'm sure none of us were, especially my mother. Yet I have come to realize this is a price that members of a "political family" have to pay. I watched my own sons and their wives and children go through the same strains and disappointments.

But there was a compensatory side to my father's infrequent presence at home. Modern candidates seem to have to live with political matters all the time. I noticed with my sons that key supporters and assistants were practically part of the family; that there were reporters and photographers often around the house; that strategy meetings and staff consultations frequently took place in the living room. In short, public and private life had become inextricably mixed.

In my father's time a politician's home was still his castle. The planning, consultation, horse trading, and persuading took place in political clubhouses, hotels, and campaign offices. Home was a place for peaceful rest and quiet, away from the fray. This is what my father wanted. My mother did much to give him a healing balm to his spirit and refreshment for his energies.

We children had only a hazy idea of what was happening when, in 1905, he announced his formal candidacy for mayor of Boston and began his campaign. Of course, there were some posed pictures taken of us, and our schoolmates looked at us with a new curiosity. We also saw pictures of my father and articles about him in the papers and we were excited. Yet the sounds of the battle seldom reached us.

As I learned later, from reading and from hearing my father and some other old combatants reminisce about it, it was one of the most hard-fought, noisy, complex political melees ever seen in Boston, which says a good deal.

Again the Strategy Board opposed him in the primary. Further, his former mentor, the independent chieftain Martin Lomasney, whom my father had been counting on for support when he decided to run for mayor, switched to a temporary alliance with the Board members and declared to the press that if elected my father would be the worst mayor in Boston's history. The outgoing mayor, close ally of Lomasney, also denounced my father. An awesome combination.

But my father adroitly turned events to his advantage by making the main issue of the campaign "Down with the bosses! The people, not the bosses, must rule! I want a Bigger, Better, Busier Boston!" He had his picture and his slogans all over town on billboards. He toured the city in a gleaming red horseless carriage, followed by a caravan of supporters and reporters—the first time such an automobile caravan was used in a Boston election. His Dearos were everywhere, cheering and working hard for him. He averaged ten speeches an evening. On primary election eve, with his red horseless carriage to speed him from meeting to meeting, rally to rally—a technological break-through—he managed to visit all twenty-five wards of the city and deliver thirty speeches, emphasizing that: "I am making my contest singlehanded against the machine, the bosses and the corporations."

And so, through foresight and long and careful planning, through indefatigable attention to the needs of others and the establishment of personal relationships, through energy, ingenuity, and boldness (and, I should add, some timely defections from the "machine" by several ward leaders and rising younger politicians), my father won the nomination.

That night, after a proper celebration at his Ward Six headquarters, he visited other wards to thank his supporters and begin the job of fence-mending needed to unify the party for the general election. At East End headquarters the place was full of rather somber-looking election workers. My father moved around the room, shaking hands, and as P. J. Kennedy remarked, with the unblemished admiration of one pro for another pro's fine performance, "He knows them all. I don't know half of them, even though they are in my district."

My father made his way to P.J. and said, "Now that the fight is over, let's get together."

They shook hands on it and that was that. They were allies once again.

His opponent in the general election was Louis Frothingham, a distinguished member of an old Yankee family. It was quite a campaign. Martin Lomasney—a fine friend but a fierce foe—bolted the party and swung his support to the Republican.

Nevertheless, my father won.

On election night there was such excitement, with such crowds of celebrants that my father could not even get inside the Quincy House to attend his own victory party. His shouted remonstrances, "I've just been elected mayor and they're all waiting for me. I'm John F. Fitzgerald," were to no avail, such was the crush of his admirers outside the entrance. Suddenly some of those nearest him saw a solution, seized him and boosted him up to an iron awning above the doorway: There, ten feet in the air, he made his victory speech to thunderous rounds of cheers.

Chapter Four

And so in January 1906, not far from his birthplace in the dear old North End, my father was inaugurated mayor of Boston. His one regretful thought, he said, was that his parents were not alive to see the day. "It would have been a great delight to them. . . . I am the first son of foreign parents to become mayor of Boston, thus my parents were the first persons of immigrant stock to have a son a mayor."

As for us at home, back in Dorchester, his new status made little difference in our lives. Later on it would, but not then; we were all so young.

Although he was very busy, he made all the important family decisions and a good many less important ones. Among the latter, I particularly remember one. There were Saturday-afternoon dances at our high school. They were "mixers" with the boys and girls allowed to invite friends from other schools in Boston and the region. It was all quite decorous, but I was never allowed to go. My father was a great innovator in public life, but when it came to raising his daughters no one could have been more conservative. When you put the "Yankee ethic" and "Irish Catholic ethic" together, the results are formidable. Which was sad. After all, you're only young once and young people should be able to get the most from those special years which last such a short time. But my father was adamant. He believed I was too young to be going to public dances and that was the end of it. I never thought of remonstrating with my father.

In those days, at least in Dorchester, high school consisted of three years with a fourth, postgraduate, year for those who were going on to college. So, in the spring that I was graduated from the three-year program, I was still fifteen, which my father interpreted as another indication of extraordinary talent. He officiated proudly at the graduation ceremonies, handing out the diplomas and, as a news article noted, ". . . much interest was manifested by the audience when he called forward 'Rose Elizabeth Fitzgerald,' his daughter, and handed the prized certificate to her." Then, through one of his journalist friends, he arranged to have a big picture of me published with a big black headline, MOST BEAUTIFUL GIRL GRADUATE? and a caption saying that I had graduated with honors (that was factually correct) and moreover ". . . her schoolmates are unanimous in their declaration that she is not only the youngest and most beautiful girl graduate . . . but that her attractiveness surpasses that of any other girl graduate of the state."

When I read that, I wept. I was sure it was the worst thing that could happen to me, and all my friends would hate me. As it turned out they didn't, probably realizing that my father the mayor had a hand in this florid tribute.

I took the fourth, postgraduate, year and so actually left high school at age sixteen. Although I would have been seventeen the next fall, my father decided that I was still too young for Wellesley and insisted I take an extra year at the Convent of the Sacred Heart in downtown Boston. I was disappointed, but it turned out that I liked the school and did well there. I also took piano lessons again but in a more serious way, with enrollment and regular attendance at the New England Conservatory of Music and an hour and a half of practice a day.

It was still a time when some skill in music, playing or singing, was considered a social adornment and almost *de rigueur* for any proper young lady, so I was encouraged in my musical studies by my parents. But I also truly enjoyed them. I had a good ear, and still have. In those years, as I tried to look ahead and imagine what I would be doing until that future time—unknowable, unpredictable, beyond the horizon, but surely there someplace—when I married for love and devoted myself to a husband and family, I thought very seriously of becoming a music teacher. That didn't happen. But my ability to play the piano turned out to be a wonderful asset, then and for a great many years to come, in ways I couldn't have guessed.

Also, as events turned out, I never did go to Wellesley—and that is something I have regretted, for I'm sure it would have been an interesting and rewarding experience. However, I had another experience of greater value.

The mayoralty term in Boston at that time was two years, so in 1908 my father came up for re-election. Once again, there were new outbreaks of factionalism. This time the Strategy Board—with P. J. Kennedy still a member and a strong ally of my father—worked hard for him. But there were others who didn't. A decisive factor was a third party sponsored by the Good Government Association ("Goo-Goos," as they were nicknamed) that cut deeply into the regular party vote. My father was defeated by a plurality of a little more than 2,000 votes, and a Republican took office.

Although I'm sure the defeat was a sore blow to my father, there were few signs of it in our household. Election night, when someone asked him about his future, he replied: "We held a conference a little while ago and began our planning for the next election."

Meanwhile, he apparently decided to enjoy a respite from the political arena. He and my mother spent a winter vacation in Palm Beach, where they had been going for the past few years. Then in that summer of 1908, they took my sister Agnes and me along on a trip to Europe.

There were crowds of Dearos and others, friends and relatives and well-wishers of all sorts, to see us off when we sailed in July from Boston harbor. It is worth remarking that the only one from the Strategy Board was P. J. Kennedy.

With flags flying and music playing, handkerchiefs waving, we were in a sea of smiles and shouts, and the smoke of photographers' flash powder. There were confetti, balloons, and all the marvelous trappings that used to make sailing on a big liner such an exciting and glamorous experience.

In my school studies I had learned a little about the countries and peoples of Europe and the British Isles, some of it superficial, I suppose, and some clogged with dry facts and statistics; yet I became entranced with the idea of seeing these places. On many a Saturday afternoon I had sat enthralled in Boston's Symphony Hall listening to Burton Holmes—whose illustrated travelogues were among the famous and popular entertainments of the era—and envying his experiences, wishing I could visit some of those places. These were the beginnings, I expect, of a lifetime wanderlust and global curiosity that to this point have taken me to every continent but Antarctica. In July of 1908, with an excitement one can imagine, I was setting out on the fulfillment of a girlhood dream.

We went to Ireland, England, Belgium, France, Switzerland, Germany, and Holland, all in about two months, which in those times was a rather hectic schedule. Agnes and I loved it, though both of us had a little trouble keeping up with our energetic father, who liked only about five hours of sleep a night and could go twenty-four or thirty-six hours without signs of fatigue.

I remember that as we walked through Phoenix Park in Dublin, laced with paths and full of flowers, my father pointed out the place where a member of the underground Irish republican army had assassinated the British Chief Secretary for Ireland, Lord Frederick Charles Cavendish on May 6, 1882. Among many things I could not have imagined was that someday I would have a daughter, Kathleen, who would marry Lord Cavendish's grandnephew, Billy Hartington.

We went on to England and visited Stratford-on-Avon. Mind you, my father had read Shakespeare and revered him and sprinkled his speeches with quotations. Nevertheless, he took twenty minutes to gallop our rented horse and carriage from the railway station to the village of Stratford. Thirty minutes to get us through Shakespeare's house and garden and the village and tell us more than we knew about them. Another twenty minutes to force the horse back to the station again in time to connect with our train to Scotland. As I said, he didn't like to waste time.

I remember that in Germany he was impressed with the neatness and discipline, the warmth and companionability, and, above all, the vitality and forceful energy of the people. He said to us that the area they were in, about as big then as our own state of Texas, could not contain them and they would burst out sooner or later and there would be a war. It occurred six years later practically to the month.

I remember also that wherever we went he was comparing the countries to the United States and the cities to Boston, almost always to the advantage of our native country and city. But the problems of city government, and the solutions and attempted solutions that he saw, were especially fascinating to him. The slogan "A Bigger, Better, Busier Boston" was to him less a political catch phrase than a summary of a grand design. The ambition of an immigrant son who wanted to repay thricefold his city and his country.

Toward the end of that summer, it was decided Agnes and I would stay on for a year of school. In those times, it was considered a great advantage for a young person to have gone to school "abroad" and I find myself still in agreement with this. The place my parents chose was a convent boarding school called Blumenthal (a German word translatable as "Valley of Flowers") in Holland, near the German border and Aachen or, as the French call it, Aix-la-Chapelle, the ancient capital of Charlemagne.

I would have preferred going to school in France, because I had been studying French (preceded by years of Latin), and I knew the best way to improve my skills would be to live there. However, as the result of a crisis between church and state, the teaching convents in France had been closed. Since Bismarck, the teaching orders of nuns had been banned in Germany. Yet the government of Holland was tolerant, and Blumenthal was haven for a number of French nuns and even more nuns from Germany. It was a little Franco-German-and-much-mixed Roman Catholic enclave in the peaceful Dutch landscape. Girls enrolled from many countries (the majority were from Germany) with classes conducted in both French and German.

So, I was able to polish my French after all, as well as my German, to which I had already devoted three years of study in Boston. A great arrangement. I became proficient in both languages and they have been assets all my life.

Because a convent education was impossible in France and Germany and many Catholic families in both countries wanted one for their daughters, Blumenthal's students were predominantly German and French and mainly from the aristocracy or at least the well to do. No distinctions were made, no talk allowed about titles. But a number of the girls were from some of the oldest and noblest houses of Europe, including such other nations as England and its then-dominion, Ireland, as well as a share of well-connected gentlefolk here and there. Agnes and I, Miriam and Margaret Finnegan from Massachusetts, and two or three others were at that time the American delegation.

We all seemed to get along together quite well, managing to communicate across language barriers in our fractured French or German or English. I seemed to have a degree of natural facility (or determined interest) in languages, so one of the things I remember from that time is sitting in a group and translating back and forth, in and out, English and French and German for girls who had not yet acquired the "ear," to help keep some of those schoolgirl conversations going, and classroom duties accomplished.

Actually, though the atmosphere was religious, as at all convent schools, Blumenthal's curriculum was unusually concerned with the practical things of this world. It was assumed that the girls when they married would be devoting their lives to *Kinder, Kirche, und Küche* (children, church, and cooking) and needed to prepare for all the duties implied in that expression. It was further assumed that as wives of *Offizieren* they would have servants to do all the actual work, but in order to instruct and supervise the servants and to run an efficient household they should be proficient in what has been called "domestic science." So at Blumenthal we were all coached in cooking, sewing, and the other arts of housewifery.

Another forte of the school was music, with excellent choral and instrumental instruction, so I was able to continue my music lessons to great benefit. Further, wonderful music, wonderfully well played, was practically as much a part of the surrounding scene as church spires. In Boston I had been allowed to go to the Friday-afternoon concert rehearsals of the Boston Symphony and, for fifty cents' admission, sit in the balcony at Symphony Hall. Although they were called "rehearsals," I cannot remember a time when the conductor stopped the orchestra to correct a badly rendered passage. Whereas at a similar afternoon rehearsal in Aachen with Richard Strauss conducting, I remember Strauss halting everything in mid-flight four or five times and putting instrumentalists, or sections, or the whole orchestra through the music again, demanding nothing less than perfection.

Because so many of the nuns and girls at Blumenthal were German and the border was so near we could drive across to small towns or to the city of Aachen to buy our toiletries and little gifts to send home, I had a chance to observe "the German character" and learn to appreciate its virtues. For instance, their industry, ambition, and ready acceptance of hard tasks; their respect for learning, and the way the children paid attention to their studies, especially foreign languages. (I wish more American children would do the same.) I admired the respect children had for the authority of their parents and the deep sense of spiritual responsibility parents felt for their children, demonstrated in such a lovely, open way. I often saw the sign of the cross made on a child's forehead when he and his parents met after a separation.

At the beginning of this book I mentioned that many family letters had been saved through the years and had turned up when I sent out a general alert for help in writing this book. To my amazement they included scores of letters I had written home to my parents from Blumenthal and some places we visited (under scrupulous care of a chaperone from the convent) during holidays. I will not put them here verbatim. Most of the contents are, of course, just as inconsequential as those of practically all schoolgirl letters: lovingly written and lovingly read at home at the time, but of faint interest, if any, to posterity.

However, looking at them sixty-odd years later—I think that excerpts from them can be useful in conveying some of the flavor of that scene and those times, and the warmth and closeness of our family relationships. They reveal something about my own outlook on life and my own character at eighteen, when I was leaving girlhood and becoming a young lady.

But before quoting from the letters I should tell you a little bit about my sister Agnes. She was very pretty. When I was seven and she was five, and our father a congressman, he took us to Washington, and to the White House to meet President McKinley. The President was an imposing man but warm and friendly. He liked my father and my father was very fond of him, despite their difference in political parties. He handed me a carnation from a vase on his desk, and then one to Agnes, and said to her: "This is for the prettiest little girl I have ever seen in the White House." I thought it was a wonderful thing for him to do, and through the years I told the story often, until by the time Jack was a teen-ager I guess he had heard it often enough. He looked at me, his face a perfect mask of innocence, and asked, "Why didn't he say it to you, Mother?"

As for temperaments and tastes, Agnes and I were as complementary as in coloring. I was the one with lots of ideas. I would be the one to say, "Let's have a party." She would think that was a marvelous inspiration, and would plan the menu, set and arrange the table, and I would invite the people. I would say, "Let's take a trip to so-and-such"; again marvelous, and she would pack our bags. I liked one kind of beau. She liked another kind. So there was never really any reason to argue, nor any jealousy between us.

The letters from Blumenthal were addressed mostly to "Dear Mother," but were meant for both parents. I might make a remark directed specifically at one or the other, which caused them no confusion but might cause some for the present reader without this word of explanation.

Here, then, are the collected and much abbreviated letters in rough sequence and by the month.

"September

"Well, here we both are safely packed away at last in Blumenthal. We have a dear little room just above Miriam's and after we put our rugs in, and the pictures on the walls, I am sure it will look real homelike. The nuns are simply lovely to us, and do all in their power to make everything as agreeable as possible. We have our milk or our cocoa—in fact everything we can wish for in the line of edibles.* The girls talk German nearly all the time. Then all the recommendations are given in French, and we have French stories and French conversations while we are walking in the garden. Give my best love to everyone who asks for me. With many many kisses and hugs and my dearest love to all, believe me ever. Your daughter, Rose."

"Well, our first week of school is over. I am glad, because I think the first week is always the longest. We had an hour's instruction this week in politeness. We do not take gymnastics, because I thought

* We were also offered beer every day.

it would take up our time too much and Agnes did not seem to favor the idea *at all*. My music lessons have begun. I am to play twice for the celebration in November. The singing teacher said I had a good voice, and told me the hoarseness in my throat would soon disappear. The bell has rung. Good-bye. Much love and kisses to all and my dearest for you and Papa. Rose."

"Another new pupil arrived, a girl of about twenty, who comes here to study German in order to prepare for entrance examinations to Dublin University." (This was Mary Magiore, future Mary Colum, wife of Padraic Colum.) "She has to take examinations in Ireland, too. Oh yes! She is very much interested in politics, so I think I shall be able to learn a great deal about Ireland from her. I should like it very much if you would send me a *Sacred Heart Review*, a *Republic* and a *Transcript* about once a month. Please send wrapped inside them the songs 'Are You Sincere,' 'Take Me Out to the Ball Game,' and one or two more of the very latest. Our very dearest love and kisses to you and dear Papa. Rose."

"Your pictures are standing on our writing tables, so whenever we raise our eyes from our books there you are. I have a splendid one of Pa with Vice-President Fairbanks and all the nuns are very much interested in it. Our black uniforms are all made and really are not *very* repulsive looking after all. This morning we had a fitting for the white ones, which we wear on feast days. Wait till you see them. Our hair we wear straight back from our forehead and braided down with two ribbons. We had it shampooed a week ago and you should have seen the rubbing and scrubbing it got. This operation is performed every three weeks. This afternoon we are going to make a pilgrimage (on foot of course) to some shrine about an hour's distance from here. By the way, there is a German countess staying here now for a few days. She is only about nineteen but wears her hair up, and looks about twenty-three. Miriam says they all look much older than they really are. Agnes is quite happy, I think. She and I both hope everyone at home is perfectly happy. Very dearest love to you and Father and the rest. Rose."

"We had a very exciting time here entertaining the sisters, who had their feast day, with five or six short plays. You should have seen Agnes. As she cannot speak German, she took the part of a bell and chimed. I played the part of a child who did not want to go to church. I told the girls that it was mean to 'give me away' like that. It is time for lunch now. I know Father will be glad to hear that I usually succeed in being on time here. Dearest love. Rose."

"October

"School has started in dead earnest. We have not wasted a second. I am rather glad, for when I have a great deal to do the time goes more quickly, and I feel as though a year ought not to be very long in passing, and then I can go home, and never have to go away again. We try to talk together at night when we are getting ready for bed. We do not have much opportunity during meals for we have conversation only during breakfast time for a few minutes. During dinner there is German reading, and during supper, French reading, and we are silent. I am used to this regulation now, but at first it was very hard. The bell has rung. I enjoy the *Republic* more and more every day. So glad Pa is not bothering with politics. Love to all and my dearest and best to you and Pa. Rose."

"November

"The Americans entertained at recreation by singing "Yankee Doodle Boy" and "School Days" and quite a few others. My singing lessons are going along well. The teacher said that the hoarseness in my throat would disappear after a short while. Everything is marked out for a certain period of time and we have hardly any free periods. Do tell me soon who is President. I did not realize Election came off so soon. Dearest and best love and kisses. Rose."

"We just received the loveliest box of candy from home, and we have been having a regular little party to celebrate Agnes' birthday eating it and talking about what we would be doing a year from today, etc. The little pin was very pretty, too, but unfortunately we wear no jewelry whatever. You should just see how *demure* we are in our plain black dresses with our little black aprons on. I should like to see a *Ladies' Home Journal*. Any number will do. Vera wrote me that Taft was elected. Dearest love. Rose."

"Well, another week has gone by. As I am an angel" (a neophyte in the sodality) "I arise at six o'clock (fifteen minutes earlier than the others) and go to meditation nearly every morning. So you see my picty is increasing. If I am extremely angelic, I may become an aspirant for the Children of Mary; later I may become a Child of Mary. That is the highest honor a child of the Sacred Heart can receive. So I shall have to be a model of perfection for the next few months. My French and German are coming along fairly well, I think. It is such a funny combination here. The French girls wish to speak German or English; the Germans want to talk English or French, and the girls from English-speaking countries want to speak French or German. My dearest love and kisses for you & dear Pa. Rose."

"Dearest Father,

"I have something very important and exciting to tell you so I hope my words will be persuasive and you will say 'Yes.' Christmas is coming and there is to be a fifteen-day vacation, from December 23 till January 8. We love Blumenthal very dearly, but we do not at all relish the idea of spending our vacation here, when all the others are home, having a happy time with their families. We can take a two-week round trip from Aachen to Hanover, to Berlin, to Dresden, to Leipzig, to Cologne and back to Aachen, with room and board and incidentals, for about $140. This amount seems very large, but I hate to get away and not have enough. The cities we want to visit will prove interesting. They contain famous picture galleries and churches. An opportunity would also be afforded us to go to the theater, and see some of Goethe's and Schiller's plays. We would get a chaperone, so we would be perfectly safe. The mothers here at school approve of our plan and will write ahead and engage room and board in convents. We could see the Celtic Art Collection too, about which the *Republic* spoke. We do not want to spend the holidays here. It would make us too lonesome. I do hope Mother will approve. If I could only talk to her I am sure she would. We will think of you when you cut the *Turkey* tomorrow. Dearest love and kisses to you and Mama. Rose. (If you send money send it to me in check for bank at Aix-la-Chapelle.)"

"December

"Dearest Mother,

"I was delighted to hear that your whist party was such a great success. Of course I knew it would be. I am glad, for your sake, that it is over, for it is apt to cause you a little trouble and care. What did you think of the letter I wrote Father? By this time, he will have received one also from Mother Esterhazy. I had her write Father, because I thought you would be better satisfied about the chaperone. Now do let us go. While we are in Europe it is worthwhile to travel, for we can see new places and things, and perhaps we shall never have a chance to see them again. My dearest to you and Papa. Rose."

"Your letter just arrived. To think of anyone saying that we really ought to stay here at least two years. It is very nice for girls who are used to boarding school life, but I prefer to be home in America. Everything points to the approach of Xmas now. Miriam heard from Rome today and has the names of some dandy pensiones, and the mother of one of the nuns knows of a convent where we can stay in Berlin. So you see all we are waiting for is a word from you and then we can trot off. Send us a cablegram and just say 'Yes.' We would understand what you mean. Your affectionate daughter. Rose."

"Father's letter arrived and how we jumped and talked and laughed when we received it. It was just lovely of you both to give us the permission to go. We both were so happy and vowed you and Pa were the best and the dearest father and mother in the world. We shall both think of you at the midnight Mass, and pray for you. We have a great deal of opportunity to pray here. Happy New Year. Your loving and devoted daughter. Rose."

"January

"The Reverend Mothers and Mother General stayed up to welcome us back again. We have been kept busy talking about our trip ever since. We seemed to have seen everything. New Year's Night in Berlin we heard *Tannhauser* and it was truly wonderfully beautiful. We had to wear 'décolleté' gowns and you should have seen us. We took the yokes out of our light dresses, and threw veils over our heads and there we were. The Kaiserin and Crown Princess as well as other members of the royal family had a loge directly below us . . ."

"This evening the retreat begins. Three days of complete silence will be quite an experience for us all. Of course the retreat is a great blessing. There is hardly any news except the Kaiser's birthday. At dinner each nation stood up and wished the Kaiser a happy feast. The French did not like it very well; they were the last ones to wish the Kaiser well and they would not stand up during the singing of the German national anthem. . . ."

"I was so rushed about the retreat that I forgot to tell you and Father about what we sent him for his birthday. We received permission from the Mother General to make fudge. It really tasted very good when it left here. It may have been hard when it reached Pa, but he knew we thought of him anyway."

"April

"We went to Aachen for shopping, and Agnes and I bought two captivating little black hats, just the kind you and Pa like, plain and small but oh! so coy! I hear they are wearing huge ones at home, but I prefer something small and serviceable. After our shopping we had afternoon tea and cakes. Here abroad people, even men, have afternoon tea and cakes . . ."

"Father's and your letter arrived. It would be too much of a sacrifice for you and for us to remain away another year. If I did not *love* you all so *madly*, I might consider another year or two. But I often think, how could I ever forgive myself if anything should ever happen to you or Papa while we are over here. Mother seemed to say that Pa would run for mayor. How I hope he will not use all his strength and tire himself out, bothered with politics. It is so much better to have him in good health and free from worry . . ."

"I must go directly and practice the piano. You see I am the orchestra for the play which we are going to give, so I shall be kept quite busy. Jeanne d'Arc is what is going to be presented, and a French girl is to play the part of the heroine! It lasts about two hours and promises to be quite grand . . ."

(This was Schiller's version of Joan of Arc and was titled *Die Jungfrau von Orleans*.)

"May

"We had quite a celebration here after the news came of the birth of Holland's little princess. We sang the Dutch national song, and made speeches at dinner, telling how glad the representatives of the different nations here were that the Queen had a little successor."

(That "little princess" was Juliana, who succeeded her mother as Queen in 1948. She herself is the mother of four daughters and several times a grandmother. Recently, at a dinner party, I found myself with a Dutch noblewoman and told her I had been in Holland and helped celebrate the birth of her Queen. She looked at me with astonishment as if thinking, "How can you—or anybody—be that old?")

"We are wild to see you and dear Papa again, besides Eunice and the boys. We are wondering if you all look the same. Miriam's father wrote her that his hair was turning gray, but of course our father is too young to meet with any such catastrophe."

"I received my medal for the Child of Mary today. As I told you before this is the highest honor and blessing a Sacred Heart girl can get and one which we all strive for. We are supposed to be a model and a help in the school, and someone to be depended upon, etc."

"The Finnegans are going to Liege for clothes and I thought we might go with them and buy a new suit. We have not a thing to wear. . . ."

"June

"This is the Feast of the Sacred Heart and I could tell you a great deal about it and a great many other feast days which we have been having lately. First I must finish the important things. I had a fitting on my white dress yesterday. It looks too pretty for words, and I am so pleased with it. I got slippers for my dress and they match beautifully. I am going to be St. Peter in a French play at Graduation so I got black suede slippers, too."

(In mid-June we had a letter from our father saying he had decided to run for mayor again. And that if we wanted to we could come home, at least for the summer. But, in that case, he would come to escort us on the journey.)

"We just received Father's letter and it seems best to us to come home & home we shall be. It seems like some lovely dream. I would not have Father risk the mayoralty fight for the world just to see us. It is not for his sake alone, but for the sake of the whole party—the men who work and sacrifice so much in order to help him. They might not think it was the honorable thing to do, to rush off in the middle of the campaign almost. Write to the captain and tell him to take care of us. We know how to behave ourselves anyway I think. We shall need no extras in wardrobe—something stunning to land in, that's all. . . ."

"July

"I am telling the nuns that you are so well acquainted with the captain on the boat that it is perfectly natural for us to return alone. I suppose we shall offer the same explanation to people at home. I do not dare to think about home much because my imagination runs away with me . . ."

My father cabled that he was coming over on the next boat. He met us with tears and open arms.

Together we went sight-seeing in Holland and in Belgium, and went on to Paris too. Agnes and I did a little shopping for "something à la mode in gay Paris." I remember, especially, that we bought two large velvet hats and two white ostrich plumes to put in them. That was our idea at that age of "something stunning to land in." Also, if we wore them they would qualify as used clothing and we wouldn't have to pay duty on them.

On the way back we stopped off in England for a few days and were at Cowes at the time of one of the great boating regattas. My father had earlier become a warm friend of Sir Thomas Lipton, the famous merchant and yachtsman who used to bring his ocean racers (the sequence of boats numbered, but all named *Shamrock* in honor of his mainly Irish ancestry) to our waters to race for the America's Cup. We had entertained him in Boston. He was always full of compliments for us, and of invitations to visit him. We had already been aboard his big seagoing residential yacht *Erin* several times, so she was a familiar enough sight. And so, as my father related the story:

"Rose sighted Lipton's *Erin* in the distance and we went down to a wharf, hoping to find a motorboat that could take us out to the *Erin*. There was no boat there, but we noticed the King's launch and thought one of the members of the royal family was aboard. The launch came up to the wharf where we were, and the skipper looked around and was about to start away when the officer in charge came up to where I was and asked if he could be of any service, seeing that I was anxiously looking about. I told him I was a friend of Sir Thomas and was looking for a boat to carry us to the *Erin*. The officer graciously said the King's launch was at my service.

"As we approached the *Erin*, Sir Thomas saw us through his glass, and figuring it was some member of the royal party, possibly the King or Queen, he had all his crew brought forward on the deck to receive these eminent guests. Among his guests were some Americans, and they were all anxiously asking Sir Thomas as to the etiquette to be followed immediately upon the approach of the King or Queen. Sir Thomas was busily explaining when the boat arrived and as I popped my head over the rail he nearly fell on the deck, so great was his surprise. 'My heavens,' he said, 'it's my friend, John Fitzgerald of Boston, with Rose and Agnes.'"

In his own memoirs, Sir Thomas told the story from his viewpoint on deck, and added a few touches:

"You could have knocked us all sideways with a feather," he wrote, "so great was our astonishment and bewilderment.

"'My word, Fitz,' I exclaimed, 'but you have arrived in great style.'

"'What do you mean?' he asked blandly, 'I took the best boat I could see available to bring me over to you.' Then he went on to say that being in London, he had decided to run down for the day and give me a call. Arriving at the sea front of Cowes he and his family had strolled along to 'that building over there,' pointing to the sacred steps of the Royal Yacht Squadron, and had 'hired the only launch he could see idle at the moment!'"

Apparently, there was a small crisis when the King and Queen arrived to find their launch gone and "nowhere to be seen" while they were "waiting impatiently on the jetty." But there was a happy ending. Sir Thomas explained everything. King Edward VII was not irritated but amused.

In August, we were back in Boston and Dorchester. Our mother greeted us with tears in her eyes. She had been terribly lonely. It was decided we would not go back to Europe for another year's study. Instead, Agnes went to the Sacred Heart Convent at Providence, Rhode Island, a rather short distance from Boston, and I went to the Sacred Heart Convent at Manhattanville, New York, farther away.

Meanwhile, my father won the nomination for mayor. As I think my letters from Blumenthal indicate he had not even been sure he wanted to run again; but once in the race he was sure to run hard. J. J. Storrow was as worthy a rival as he would ever meet, a patrician of old proper Bostonian stock, Harvard crew captain and graduate and overseer, successful in business and enormously wealthy, a patriotic political independent, leader and benefactor of good causes from the Boy Scouts to the beautification of the banks of the Charles River. He and my father had always got along well together. But then came this political encounter, head to head so to speak, and things became noisy and acrimonious and bitter.

All but one of the Boston papers had lined up on Storrow's side. I would awaken practically every morning to find my father accused in headlines of being guilty of nearly every sin short of murder. Storrow's managers also ran a series of large advertisements, each headed in screaming type FITZGERALDISM, followed by some fervid accusation against my father and "the Fitzgerald ring." "Never," according to a leading historian of the Boston political scene, J. H. Cutler, "was character assassination more brutally practiced in a Boston campaign."

Heretofore, I had been too young to pay much attention to my father's earlier campaigns. This, in fact, was the first political campaign of any sort of which I was fully aware—the first one that I clearly remember. When the mud began flying, my instinctive reactions were shock and outrage; I seethed. But my father seemed to take it more or less for granted. Some of the accusations and personal slurs undoubtedly angered him, but outwardly, at least so far as I could see, he was unperturbed. I remember bringing the morning papers in to him at 9 A.M., when he would be waking up from a hard day and evening's campaigning. He would sit up in bed and go through them with great interest, and now and then would reach for his penknife and excise an item he wanted to make use of or to rebut, but with no more visible emotion than my mother might display when, for instance, cutting out a recipe or an advertisement for a bargain at Filene's department store. Sometimes, after catching up on the latest news of his alleged infamies, he would drop off peacefully for an extra catnap before rising and returning to the battle.

And so, taking my cue from his example, I calmed down and began to accept the idea that gossip and slander and denunciation and even vilification are part of the price one pays for being in public life. As Jim Farley once commented, "You have to have the hide of a rhinoceros to stay in politics." It is a lesson that is hard and unpleasant but necessary to learn: For unless one does learn it and knows what to expect and is prepared to cope with it emotionally, life in a "political family" such as ours could become miserable.

This was on my mind when my sons married. They all had had a taste of it, one way or another, from a fairly early age and could take the penalties more or less in stride. But neither Ethel nor Jackie nor Joan had been brought up in a political atmosphere. Jackie had some knowledge of political life because of having worked on a Washington newspaper, but even so that is another side of the matter. Writing about someone is different from finding oneself written about. So each time, in turn, Ethel, then Jackie, then Joan, I made sure to warn them in advance of what they were in for: that they might be hearing and reading all sorts of scandalous gossip and accusations about members of our family, about their husbands, and for that matter about themselves, and eventually even about their children; that they should understand this and be prepared from the beginning, otherwise they might be very unhappy. They took the burden with the blessing, and all three have managed well.

When Jackie married Ari Onassis, she endured all sorts of false "rumors" and irresponsible "exposés." Press and photographers followed her every movement. Jackie and I were talking about this not long ago, because she was feeling the pressures. I wanted to give her the best advice I could, but what it came down to in essence was what I had told her before and had been telling myself for many decades:

"You're bound to have publicity of that sort, the world being as it is, so why pay attention to it? Don't waste the time. We're a strong family unit and we can face it in confidence and go on with our lives. Not only for ourselves but for the sake of the children: We must do whatever is important for them. There are people in this world who have to gossip, it seems. There are people who chronically want to believe the worst. Yet most people are kind and sympathetic. So you can always hope for the best in humanity and expect it."

I was at Manhattanville while Father's campaign roared along through the final weeks—perhaps mercifully for my feelings, since the mudslinging increased. I understand that up to within a few days of the election the Storrow forces were sure of victory, and that most of the signs, such as public opinion polls, pointed that way. But my father put on one of those whirlwind finishes in which he was a specialist. There was the biggest turnout of voters in the city's history, about 95,000, and when the count was over my father had upset the predictions and squeezed through by a plurality of 1,402 votes.

In thanking his supporters, he said: "No man could ask for a greater victory. My family appreciated the triumph especially, because there had been so much injustice in the attacks made on me— so much misrepresentation and vilification. For the sake of my boys and girls I wanted to win the election as a vindication."

My school year at Manhattanville passed peacefully and productively. I was able to get home on school holidays and for weekends a few times. Old friends were able to visit me; there were excursions and diversions; the months went by quickly. In June of 1910 I received my graduation certificate, listened to the advice of the saintly nuns and then departed, at last, for Boston. I was no longer a schoolgirl. In fact, I was on the verge of leaving girlhood, for I was to be twenty years old the next month, and the following winter I would be making my debut, the rite of passage that would make me a full participant in adult life and the perils and excitements of the world.

Chapter Five

"There is a time to laugh and a time to dance" and those next few years were such times. I was "the mayor's daughter" again but now old enough to enjoy the attentions and participate in the pleasures that came my way. Further, with a change in the city charter, the mayoralty term had become four years instead of two. My father could relax a bit, which relaxed us all. I myself was, as they said in a term of that day, "in the bloom of youth and beauty." My spirits were further uplifted by the fact that Joe Kennedy and I were in love and knew we wanted to marry.

Yet it was not all fun and frolic. Aimless frivolity has never appealed to me. What does anyone get out of it? A life of partying and socializing would have bored me to death. I took afternoon courses at Boston University in French, German, and art. I kept up with my music and studied the history of piano at the New England Conservatory. I joined a "little theater group" and appeared in a play and some musicals. I conducted catechism classes and taught Sunday school. I sewed for the poor and did settlement work. I went to educational lectures. I was the youngest member of the Public Library Investigating Committee, whose principal function was to recommend books and make reading lists for Boston children. (Needless to say, I stanchly supported Louisa May Alcott's works.) I was a member of the French and German friendship and cultural associations, the Alliance Française and Deutsche Gesselschaft and attended and contributed to their meetings.

I even founded a club composed of young women who had been to school abroad and were interested in studying and discussing world-wide current history and meaningful current events. Thanks to my father, we were able to get all sorts of visiting dignitaries to address us. One of the first was the Reverend Bernard Vaughan, S.J., himself one of the most distinguished English clerics and brother of Cardinal Vaughan of London. He was also a man of keen wit. Knowing that Boston was full of clubs of all kinds and degrees, proliferating in all directions, I asked him for a suggestion as to what to call ourselves, and he said: "Why not 'The Ace of Clubs'? Meaning the first and the foremost and the most important of all clubs." The motion was seconded and carried with enthusiasm. Rather soon, inevitably I suppose, even among serious-minded young women, the club sprouted some social activities, notably an annual charity ball (for years, as president, I led the grand march), and became quite fashionable, with a long waiting list. One result of that was that some reporters and quite a few readers made mental slips and miscalled it by such names as the Ace of Spades or Ace of Hearts Club, and as I recall there were some who thought of it as a gambling club. But it was the Ace of Clubs and it had a truly serious purpose.

My debut was not lavish, at least by the standards of those times. It was a beautiful reception and tea at our home in Dorchester. Though it was the dead of winter, my parents had turned the house into a bower of roses for me. There were other flowers too as accents, and ferns and palms and garlands, but roses were the motif of the day. I wore a white satin dress with a short train; the bodice and skirt were embroidered in white, with just a touch of yellow silk ribbon showing through the embroidery along the hemline. Long white kidskin gloves; no jewels or ornaments except a bit of white ribbon in my hair; a corsage of violets and lilies of the valley. With my mother in black Chantilly lace and my father in cutaway and winged collar, I received the guests in the drawing room. I was so excited by the occasion that I felt no fatigue standing three or four hours and shaking hands and chatting with more than 450 people, among them the new governor, two congressmen, and numerous other dignitaries, including the entire Boston City Council, who had accepted my father's invitation and closed down for the day. In fact my debut—thanks to my father's boundless enthusiasm for the event—was treated as a municipal celebration, with yards of photographs and write-ups in the newspapers. There were messages from far and wide, including one from our dear family friend Sir Thomas Lipton who cabled: "I extend my heartiest congratulations to you on the occasion of your coming-out. I suppose that in a short time I will be sending congratulations for another occasion of great joy. Before that occurs I hope that you pick out a man who is the equal of your father."

In my heart, I had already done that. Joe was there. So were a couple of would-be rivals and a number of other young men and girls, all good friends. After the older people had left, we went upstairs to a room festooned with ropes of roses, where we had a sit-down dinner and sang and joked and laughed and danced. No champagne, no alcohol in any form, for none of us used it so far as I knew, and certainly on that evening none of us needed anything for a good time but our own high spirits.

Actually, there were two societies in Boston. One of them was almost entirely Protestant and was mainly of English descent, though with admixtures of Scottish, Scot-Irish, and even some Irish, plus a soupçon of French and others; in any case, all descended from colonial or early American settlers, blended into the general breed called Yankee or old American or (in a term coined later) "proper Bostonians." Their main citadel and symbol was the region known as Back Bay where wealthy and distinguished families such as the Cabots and Lodges lived serenely amid ancestral portraits and mahogany sideboards and silver tea services in spacious houses on large grounds. With the advantages of inherited wealth and status and close-knit interfamily ties, they controlled the banks, insurance companies, the big law firms, the big shipping and mercantile enterprises, and almost all the usual routes to success, and thus were a self-perpetuating aristocracy. They had many admirable qualities. But they were a closed society.

The other predominant group consisted of Irish Catholics, descendants of those impoverished hordes who had fled from the great famines of the 1840s to 1860s. Through hard effort and much ingenuity, often by way of politics but in every other way open to them, large numbers of these second- and third-generation offspring had achieved prosperity, and many had achieved a cultural level fully equal to that of the Back Bay Brahmins.

Between the two groups feelings were, at best, suspicious, and in general amounted to a state of chronic, mutual antagonism.

The reasons are too much a part of familiar history to need any exposition, but I will mention just a few. One of them, anachronistic but nonetheless powerful, stemmed from the ancient unhappy relationship between England and Ireland. Despite having broken away from England, most of the old Yankee families had strong cultural roots there and shared many of the ancestral biases, such as anti-Catholicism and a diffuse image of the Irish people as being inferior and troublesome; whereas the Boston Irish, of course, had their ancestral image of the English as a callous coldhearted breed of apostates, exploiters, and oppressors. The old biases might have died away in the new land, but instead were reinforced by the circumstances of the mid-nineteenth-century migrations. Children of the immigrants heard at their parents' knees the dreadful stories of mass suffering and death while the English absentee landlords, the English Government including Queen Victoria, and presumably the English people in general, had remained unconcerned except for a few tokens of sympathy during the potato famine, and a good deal of fretful worry that their usual sources of income and tax revenues in Ireland were shrinking.

On the Yankee side, precisely because the immigrants were so poor and distressed and came in such sudden great numbers, there were natural fears of being inundated, swamped, and overwhelmed by a tide of unfriendly, uneducated, uncouth aliens with customs and a religious belief at odds with their own. In their alarm and disdain they gave the Irish nicknames such as bog trotters, clodhoppers, Micks, Harps and—because so much of the pick-and-shovel labor of digging ditches and canals, leveling hills and filling in swamps and oozy tidal flats was done by Irishmen—"blacklegs" and "muckers." They worked long hours at backbreaking work for any subsistence wage they could get, and many businessmen exploited them for every penny to be gained from their sweat. There were others who could not abide them even to exploit them. In the "Help Wanted" columns of the classified ads, or even in large lettering on cards in shop windows, those feelings were put in such cold blunt terms as "No Irish Need Apply."

All this overt hostility had fairly well died down by the early part of the twentieth century. On both sides, nevertheless, mistrust and resentment remained. The two coexisted, having as little as possible to do with each other. In fact, it was so difficult to find a common meeting ground that my father and James Jackson Storrow and other men of good will got together and founded a club, the City Club, to give prominent leaders of both elements a chance to meet in a neutral and socially relaxed atmosphere.

I'm sure both sides were to blame. Both being too myopic, too preoccupied with old grudges, too little able to realize that there were new circumstances that appropriately needed fresh and different responses; too little, by far, of the quality of mercy and the capacity to forgive and forget and go on. I remember, for instance, that when my father appointed an old-line Yankee Protestant, Charles Cole, as Boston's fire commissioner, there were Irish Catholics who grumbled to me, "Why didn't he appoint one of his own kind?" And later on after Joe and I married and had our first child and I asked my obstetrician, of Irish Catholic descent, to select the best pediatrician he knew to take medical care of our baby, and he chose a doctor of Scot-Irish descent and Presbyterian faith—oh! what a commotion there was then among some of my friends and the doctor's other patients. Why was this, they wanted to know! Why an "Orangeman" even if he was supposed to be one of the best pediatricians in Boston?

And what a scandal when this same doctor called to attend an ill little boy, the cardinal's own nephew, on St. Patrick's Day—wearing an orange tie!

With such "cultural lags," still widespread then in Boston, I suppose it was inevitable and even in some atavistic way "natural" that there would be two societies. And so there were. Separate "society columns" were published in the newspapers, one about them, one about us.

In later years people who know me and my personal background have asked me what my reactions were. Well, the fact is, at the time I really just took it for granted. I was aware that there was an incongruity, but I don't think it occurred to me to be surprised. I had known since young girlhood about the social division, had grown up with it, and accepted it as one of those elementary facts of life not worth puzzling about. I knew that was Boston: That's the way it was. I would not be mixing with the Back Bay set. None of them would be mixing with ours. I had neither feelings of exclusion nor inferiority because I knew some of the Back Bay girls well enough to know that we were similar in talent, manners, and interests.

The two social sets did more or less the same things in the same ways at the same times, often at the same public places, dressing and behaving and enjoying themselves in ways so nearly the same that to an observer from London or Paris or Berlin or outer space there would have been no discernible differences. They had their Junior League, we had our Cecilian Club, equally dedicated in principle to unselfish good works. They had their benefits and bazaars and charity balls under various labels, and we had ours under different ones. There were some advantages to the arrangement. They all knew one another, and so did we, so in each environment there were minimal needs for explanations and defenses and the best of chances for spontaneous conversations about common interests. Catholic young men were extreme rarities at their parties, just as Protestant young men were at ours. For example, although our Abbotsford Club gave three subscription dances a year, and for several years I was at all of them, I can't recall meeting a Protestant at any of them. The principle was wrong, of course, but the practical effects were to help prevent romances leading to "mixed marriages" with the eventual unhappiness that sometimes awaited such a marriage in the world as it was. As for the separate society columns, there was an advantage to that contrivance, too, in fact quite a convenience. We always knew exactly where to look for the news of our friends.

I think I have made it clear already that my father was a "natural performer." The political arena was his stage. And like any skilled performer he achieved rapport with his audience and played to it not only in his manner of delivery, which ranged from the hortatory, pontifical, and inspirational to the merriest laugh, but also in the content of his script, which ranged from the most serious issues of statesmanship to song and dance.

Indeed, he did a great deal of singing instead of speechifying. A favorite song of those times, "Sweet Adeline," became one of his political trademarks. Since I played the piano well and often accompanied him on his rounds during those years, I was a participating partner in some of his musical productions.

"Sweet Adeline" is as inseparable from his legend as Al Smith's "The Sidewalks of New York" or Franklin D. Roosevelt's "Happy Days Are Here Again," probably more so. I have played it a few thousand times.

My father sang it at the summer White House for President Taft. On a trip to Central America he sang it so often, with such feeling, to such applause that years after, when President Franklin D. Roosevelt was on a good-will tour of Latin America, he was met in one country by a band playing "Sweet Adeline" which was believed to be the U.S.A.'s favorite anthem—an incident that FDR related later to my father with the greatest delight.

The song became so closely identified with him that I must mention that he knew others—at least one of which I can document from my scrapbook of those years. News clippings describe a visit to Boston by a large group of students from Germany, and related how my father entertained them with a banquet and "informal musicale" at the Hotel Somerset. The German students burst into song at a certain point (one reporter used the word "inevitable"), and my father, after words of appreciation, responded in kind. "The mayor did not let the chance of singing what he termed 'the municipal hymn, "Sweet Adeline,"' go by and insisted that the visitors should join in the chorus." But also, as the news story goes on to say, he sang "Love Me and the World Is Mine." It's true. I was there. "Miss Rose Fitzgerald . . . made a short speech in German, in which she welcomed the visitors to these shores."

Since my father spoke no foreign languages, he asked me to speak to dignitaries from abroad who came to Boston and needed some form of official greeting or hospitality from the mayor, or wished to talk with him. My mother also certainly did her part and did it well, and my father and our friends were very proud of her. I remember that at one reception a reporter who recognized me asked me to point out Agnes for him. Then he said: "And the very slim one in blue—which of the daughters is she?"

"Her name?" I laughed. "Why, don't you know her? Her name is Mother!"

For reasons not only of temperament but of time, Mother had a limited capacity for the official social whirl. She still had young children at home who needed her. Moreover, as she declared to one interviewer, "I want my home to be a place of inspiration and encouragement to all my family. I am a home woman in every way, and my one ambition is to make the home the most happy and attractive place for my husband and our children."

Frankly, I don't think any woman, however gregarious and heedless of other duties, could have kept up with my father on a regular basis. His strength and energy were just overwhelming. On his fiftieth birthday, in 1913, he announced to the press, "I feel no older than I did twenty-five years ago." His schedule was a whirligig of dedications, cornerstones, receptions, banquets, picnics, parades, orations, rallies, greetings, grand marches, and ceremonials—from attending important wakes and funerals to crowning beauty queens—besides other things that popped into his head spontaneously. When she was out with him, my mother never knew what to expect next. Once, when they were the guests of honor at a dressy party at the Dorchester Club, he brought her home on a fire engine, sirens howling through the night.

Obviously, my mother appreciated my cooperation and I was happy to give it. We reached a perfect arrangement.

I was his companion, hostess, and assistant on a good many of the trips he took. He loved to travel, and as mayor he could always find a good official reason for a jaunt of some sort, and at least a plausible reason to take me. I was with him in Chicago for an international meeting of municipal executives. And in Baltimore for the 1912 Democratic Convention where Woodrow Wilson was nominated. On some of the trips, Agnes was along. One winter my father led the Boston Chamber of Commerce to Panama to ponder the possible effects on Boston of the recently opened Panama Canal. I was along as hostess-companion-helper. Another time, for the same purposes, he took a Chamber of Commerce delegation to Europe to examine the big ocean port cities such as Hamburg and Brussels and the highly developed systems of inland waterways that carry such a large traffic of goods to and from those ports. Agnes and I accompanied him, and with our fluent German and French, and our basic knowledge of Europe, we performed valuable services for the group; while also having a fine time in our own ways with our own interests, which had less to do with rivers and harbors per se, and more as places to sail around on, preferably with some young beaux.

During most of the trip we were joined by Hugh Nawn, an attractive young man a year or so older than I. He was the son of near neighbors and close friends of my parents in Dorchester. His father, Harry, was one of the leading contractors of the region, successful, and a man of charm and other attractive qualities. He was a great pal of my father's. In fact, on many a night when my father came back to Dorchester after a hard day-and-evening's campaigning he would head first for the Nawn house, and—I have heard—Harry would pour some milk or cocoa and whip up some peanut-butter sandwiches, of which my father was excessively fond, and the two would sit in the kitchen trading jokes and discussing the affairs of the day and nation and world. Hugh Nawn, after graduating from Harvard, had joined his father's firm with clearly foreordained prospects of someday owning it. Thus, he had the soundest prudent business reasons, having just come to the end of a European tour on his own, in joining our Chamber of Commerce inspection of rivers and harbors for good ideas for a busier Boston.

He and I had been good friends for a long time, and we were quite fond of each other. He was the proverbial "boy next door." In later years we were at many parties and dances together. Sometimes he was my escort. We had lots of fun, we were congenial, and it would be easy to imagine that our relationship could blossom into romance and marriage. There were signs that my father thought so and so did Harry Nawn. But that did not happen.

Anyway, Hugh joined our group at Ostend and was along for the rest of the time, and that was great good luck for Agnes and me. One

of the beautifully happy memories of my young life was a night we
sailed from Vienna down the Danube and Hugh and I danced on an
open deck in the moonlight to the strains of "The Blue Danube"
waltz.

Chapter Six

❧❦

I want now to tell you about Joe Kennedy, the boy I fell in love with, the man I married, the father of my children, and the architect of our lives.

We saw each other again about eight summers after our first meeting at Old Orchard Beach, Maine. During the few days we were together, we became friends, then affectionate friends, and later began to think of ourselves as sweethearts. At least I did.

Joe Kennedy was tall, thin, wiry, freckled, and had blue eyes and red hair. Not dark red, orange red, or gold red, as some Irish have, but sandy blond with a lot of red lights in it. His face was open and expressive, yet with youthful dignity, conveying qualities of self-reliance, self-respect, and self-discipline. He neither drank nor smoked, nor did I. He was a serious young man, but he had a quick wit and a responsive sense of humor. He smiled and laughed easily and had a big, spontaneous, and infectious grin that made everybody in sight want to smile, too. Even then, he had an aura of command, an attitude of being competent to take charge of any situation. At Boston Latin School, from which my father had graduated, he was captain of the baseball team, player-manager on the football team, captain of the tennis team, a star on the basketball team, colonel of the all-Boston prize-winning school regiment, and president of his class.

The autumn after we had met as teen-agers at Old Orchard Beach, he invited me to the first dance of the season at Boston Latin. My father refused to let me go. He disapproved of a girl of sixteen going around to dances in strange places and meeting people who might cause trouble. This didn't seem logical to me since it was his school and he was proud of it. He knew Joe and the Kennedys, and besides it was an afternoon dance, so I would be home before dark. I also knew my way around Boston on the street-cars and took them often. But my father made the rules. In politics he was known sometimes as "The Little Napoleon"—and he could be Napoleonic in matters of home and family as well. Argument would have got me no place.

So Joe asked somebody else, after first telling her she was his second choice. I thought that was very honest of him, and I admired him for it.

The next spring, when I was finishing my postgraduate year at Dorchester High, there was a big graduation dance there. I was still sixteen but soon to be seventeen; the school was nearby; the time was afternoon. It was a sentimental occasion, so after some pondering my father let me attend. Obviously, I invited Joe Kennedy.

Formal "dates" were very rare events among my age group in those days. Regular dating was taboo and "going steady" was completely out of the question. This was a serious problem for Joe and me, and one we had to work out, as best we could, through "innocent" stratagems.

For instance, could anyone object if by coincidence we happened to be at the same place at the same time? Joe was captain-manager of the Latin School tennis team. When I went for a weekend visit with an aunt of mine in Concord, he arranged a match between Concord High School and his team, at Concord. We spent quite a few hours together that day.

We also met at informal get-togethers with friends at somebody's house, usually in the afternoons and always, of course, with a responsible adult on the premises. We would push back the parlor furniture, lift the breakable bric-a-brac out of the way, make lemonade or punch and cookies and fudge, and someone would play the piano. We gathered around and we sang and we danced. Joe and I had many mutual friends. If I were invited, he would just drop in.

We also met at lectures, the library, and walked part of the way home together. (That was the beginning of a good habit. For many decades Joe and I took long walks together, not for dutiful exercise but for pleasure. I still take a walk, by myself, almost every day.)

It took teamwork and conspiracy, because we needed reliable allies.

Some were girl friends of mine in Dorchester and the area, their parents known to my parents. They gave more "drop-in" parties— well planned ahead—than they would have otherwise. Another ally was my father's chauffeur. He was a very good man. He was devoted to my father. But he was also a sentimentalist, and was fond of me, and liked Joe, and knew young love when he saw it. He helped to smooth the way. Sometimes, when he picked me up in the car he would ask what route I might prefer, and I might give him a round-about one. And there to the surprise of neither of us would be the recognizable figure of Joe Kennedy waiting for a trolley, or lurking on a bench, or strolling along. This would suddenly remind me that there was something I wanted to speak with that young man about, so would the driver take the car to the end of the block and wait a few minutes? The minutes might stretch to half an hour. Then Joe would take me to the car, open the door, greet his benefactor, and I was sped home, dutiful as usual. There was always a faint smile on the chauffeur's face.

During that last year at Dorchester High and the following year, when I was commuting to Sacred Heart in Boston, Joe and I managed to see each other rather often. Less often than we would have liked, but more often than my father was aware of, and enough in any case to reaffirm in our hearts how deeply we cared for each other.

But then I went to Blumenthal, an ocean away. I could only write and wait. When I came home again, it was only for about six weeks. At Manhattanville, we exchanged more letters and made a few visits back and forth. When I returned to Boston to stay, I became involved in public functions and far-flung travels with my father.

Scarcely had the roses from my debut faded when my father announced that in honor of my new status in the world he would take me on a winter vacation to Palm Beach. I was thrilled by the prospect of southern sunshine instead of a Boston February of snow and slush, of exciting new scenes, new friends; to say nothing of summer frocks and evening dresses. Palm Beach was even then known as a center of style and fashion. But then I discovered that the trip con-flicted with the date of the Junior Prom at Harvard. Joe had invited me, and to make it easier for me to get my parents' permission he had even arranged for one of his college roommates to invite a girl who was one of my best friends.

It was an awkward choice to make, but a clear one. I thanked my father gratefully but told him I had already accepted an earlier in-vitation, to the Prom. My father replied that he would hear of no such thing and I would be going to Florida.

I didn't argue with my father since, as I have said, I wouldn't have dreamed of doing so; but I was visibly upset, downcast, teary, and melancholy. My father began to show signs of weakening. But then my mother, with all the firm common sense of her character, told me to stop being foolish, for I might never again have a chance to go to Palm Beach. (Fate is so ironic, because since then I have been to Palm Beach every year, but I have never been to a Junior Prom.)

So I sniffled a bit and submitted and boarded the train for a trip of some twelve hundred miles, each of which I heartily regretted. I kept hoping for a major disaster in Boston. Nothing that would kill or injure people, of course; just something like a two-foot snowfall or a fire that would burn down a few acres of the port and warehouse area, enough that the mayor of Boston would feel duty bound to go back home and I could feel free to go to the Harvard Junior Prom.

In 1911, Florida was still sparsely populated, with only about 800,-000 people in the whole state compared with the many millions now. There were few cities of any size, and Palm Beach itself was hardly more than a village, with a population of less than a thousand. Today airplanes make the trip in a few hours, but early in the century it meant two days and one night on the train from New York to Palm Beach, plus more hours in carriages or taxis and on the ferryboat. Getting there was a tiring adventure. But having arrived, one could see why people made the trip. For, behold, there indeed were the palms and the beaches, and balmy breezes and white clouds in limit-less skies, and beautiful blue-green water just the right temperature for swimming. A couple of splendid hotels with every convenience, and a dozen fine private homes in large grounds by the sea. In short, an aquamarine gem in a perfect setting.

We had a wonderful visit, full of fun and razzle-dazzle and high spirits, with lots of sun and sea and blue skies. If it hadn't been for missing the Prom I think I would have enjoyed it immensely.

A few months afterward, my father and Agnes and I and our Chamber of Commerce cohorts sailed off on the *Franconia* (my father serenading dockside friends, and an honor escort of Hurrah Johnny Cadets in small boats, with you-know-what song) to look at the European port-and-river systems.

And so it went. Europe, Central America, Palm Beach, Kansas City, St. Louis, Chicago, Baltimore, and here and there, meeting many people, including a certain number of attractive, eligible young bachelors along the way. Did my dear father have a plan?

Did he object to Joe? He did not. How could he? There was nothing to object to. The only fault that anyone could find with him was that he had to take an extra year at Boston Latin to make up some languages; furthermore, when a few acid-tongued acquaintances remarked that with those low grades he must be "dumb in school" my well-founded reply was, "I don't see how he has time to study at all, he's so busy with all those sports and leadership activities and winning all those high honors and awards." And he ended up with an academic record good enough to be admitted to Harvard: one of the few Boston boys of Irish descent in that era to go there.

He played football, but baseball was his favorite sport. My father and I saw him the day he won his "H," when he made the winning play against Yale. He was widely popular and respected. He was elected to Hasty Pudding Institute of 1770 and to one of the best fraternities, Delta Upsilon. He was involved in all sorts of things but still did well in his major studies, history and economics, and graduated with a creditable average. During his senior year he made money as coach of the freshman baseball team. I doubt this escaped my father's notice, for much as he valued academic achievement, he placed a high premium on popularity and respect, athletic skills, physical fitness, energy and ambition. All of these were obviously part of Joe's equipment and credentials.

It has been said that my father objected to Joe Kennedy because of his political feuds with P. J. Kennedy. Yet I never heard, then nor later, either say an uncomplimentary thing about the other. They were never meant to be close personal companions—and they never were—because of their different temperaments. But they could be friends and from all outward signs they were. Their paths crossed amicably in many places, including holiday resorts such as Old Orchard Beach. There is a photograph of them taken at Asheville, North Carolina. They are on horseback and ready to take off on a fox hunt, of all things.

In those days, a debut meant, as it still does, that a girl was introduced to society. It did not mean that she was suddenly to make up her mind about marriage, but rather that eligible young men and young women were aware of her presence as a woman in their social milieu. If a couple became engaged directly after the debut or worse, already had a "secret understanding," it was considered foolishly romantic. People were likely to say: "Think of all the fun they missed before they settled down." The accepted opinion was that when ardor had cooled and nostalgia had set in, they would suffer marital discontent. Or worse.

Also, my father had extravagant notions of my beauty, grace, wit, and charm. As I entered young womanhood these delusions deepened. I suppose no father really thinks any man is good enough for his daughter. But my father was a hopeless case. Therefore, believing that I could take my pick of any beau, and happy that through his own hard-won success he could give me the opportunity to meet a large cross section of suitable admirers on several continents, he didn't want me to make the rash, shortsighted, and ungrateful mistake of pledging my heart prematurely to any young man, however attractive and brilliant he might be.

My father never said any of this to me explicitly. There were no "scenes" and no lectures. Actually, his temptation to issue Napoleonic orders gave way to sweet reason. He pointed out that I was fortunate enough to have unusual advantages and opportunities. Therefore, I shouldn't say yes to the first man who fell in love with me and wanted to marry me. I should take my time and look around. This theme was often repeated and endorsed by my mother.

So there I was wobbly and often tearful in private, as I tried to find an equilibrium of my own. I adored Joe. I also adored my parents, and knew how much I owed them. I didn't want to be ungrateful, and certainly didn't want to offend or deceive them. Thus it was with pangs of conscience that I began to see Joe more often than I was supposed to.

As the years went along I found myself a willing accomplice and imaginative coconspirator in stratagems we devised to be together.

Some of them were really rather funny.

Our finest hour in clandestine meetings, as Joe and I later agreed, came on a walk one day when we thought we saw a newspaper reporter. We were just then passing a church, so we quickly went inside and sat in a rear pew, rather breathlessly, not paying close attention to our surroundings for the moment. Then we looked at the literature in the pew racks and discovered we were in a Christian Science church. As Roman Catholics we were not supposed to be there. But we immediately decided to accept that and answer for it later. Anyone else who came in and thought we looked like Rose Fitzgerald and Joe Kennedy—scions of well-known Catholic families— would have to assume this an interesting example of coincidental resemblance, since we could not possibly be who we really were. After we were married, Joe and I drove past that church many times, and in fact Joe would go out of our way to do so. He said that as soon as he could afford it he would make a contribution to the church for blessings received in a time of need. And when he was able to, he made an anonymous gift, for he wanted no personal notice or thanks.

Another conspiracy concerned the important dances of the year. At the beginning of the season Joe would say to me: "Now remember, you are invited to the Cecilian Club dance, the Newman Club dance at Harvard, the Ace of Clubs dance, and any other dances I can't think of now—remember that I invited you to all of them." I agreed cheerfully, while knowing, as he did also, that most of the time he would be my escort only in theory. For my mother, as the mayor's wife and leader of Catholic society, was a chaperone or "matron" at many of the dances, and when this occurred, I was expected to go with her and come home with her instead of being escorted by a man.

Yet all was not lost because there were "dance orders" in those days. I understand the practice still exists in a less formal way, in some places. What it came down to was that no matter who invited whom to a dance, once the couple arrived there each person was a free agent. Customarily they had the first and last dances together, and one or two in between, but otherwise any man was free to ask any girl "for the honor of a dance." If she accepted he wrote his name or initials next to the appropriate number on the girl's "program" or "dance order," a card or little booklet she carried, usually on a ribbon at her waist or around her wrist. The most popular girls had their cards filled within minutes at the beginning of the evening. The least popular had dances to spare and became "wallflowers." The system had its cruelties, both for girls who didn't get asked for dances and for boys who asked and got turned down. But the general effect was to add excitement and variety and let people circulate, instead of couples being stuck with each other all evening. For most people it was really quite a good idea. But not for Joe and me. We didn't need excitement and we didn't want to circulate and we did want to be stuck with each other all evening. What to do?

Joe's solution was bold and elegantly simple. Forgery. Well, not forgery literally because he didn't sign the names of real people on my card, but instead names and initials that he made up out of thin air. He had half a dozen or so that he liked best and used often, mixing them up and scrawling in different handwriting. His favorite one, though, and mine too, was "Sam Shaw" or just "S.S." for short.

Since I was not supposed to be dancing with Joe all the time and since my mother usually was there as one of the matrons sitting at the side of the dance floor, one may wonder how our deception worked. Shrewdly, Joe would leave a couple of dances open for Hugh Nawn or other beaux. At those times I contrived to dance in good view of where my mother was, and perhaps wave to her or even stop to chat with her for a minute or two. As the man who had invited me, my official escort of the evening, Joe was entitled in her eyes to the first, last, and a few other dances. The others, we "sat out," vanishing amid the potted palms or into the arcades and verandas of the hotel or country club, and in fine weather onto the terraces and paths. Some of my sweetest memories are of music floating in the night air, and the distant sounds of gaiety and laughter, while I took walks hand in hand with "Sam Shaw."

After Joe graduated from Harvard in 1912 there was less need for subterfuge, and finally there was none. Part of the reason, I suppose, was that my father, with his capacious sense of realism in political and public matters, finally became realistic about our romance, faced the facts, and adapted himself to them. Another reason was simply that Joe had a Harvard diploma, a symbol of respectability and capability; and for a boy or young man, college graduation was a rite of passage, rather like a girl's debut, both signifying that the person was ready for adult relationships and responsibilities. Furthermore, there soon were signs that Joe had special talents in certain activities where the prizes were tangible, practical, and, to my father's pragmatic parental eye, quite impressive.

Joe was as fascinated by the world of finance and business, with its infinite variety and possibilities, as my father was with the world of politics. Soon after graduation he took the examinations to become a state bank examiner. They were difficult and exacting. He passed and received his appointment, and during the next year and a half visited banks all over eastern Massachusetts. The job was still another factor to limit our time together; but also it was highly educational for him—he learned far more about finance than he had in all his Harvard economics courses.

I mentioned earlier that the financial institutions of Boston were controlled by "proper Bostonians." They sat on their fortunes like broody hens on fertile eggs, and intrusions into their hen houses were met with resentful cluckings. I remember my father telling of an encounter he had with one old-line Boston banker. "You have plenty of Irish depositors," he commented. "Why don't you have some Irishmen on your board of directors?" The banker replied, "Well, a couple of our tellers are Irish." "Yes," said my father—the indignation still in his voice long later—"and I suppose the charwomen are too."

As a result of this oligarchical control over finance and credit, P. J. Kennedy, together with a few other of the more prosperous Irish businessmen, had founded an independent bank in East Boston called the Columbia Trust Company. After nearly two decades it was still a rather small bank, but it had grown large enough that one of the big Boston banks wanted to absorb it, and offered the stockholders a good price. Most of them—holding a majority of the stock—

wanted to accept. P. J. Kennedy did not. He wanted to preserve the bank as an independent, neighborhood institution under local control. He hadn't enough money of his own to buy out the others and block the deal. So he called on his son Joe—who by then had grown wise in the ways of banking and knew allies to seek and moves to make—to lead the fight against the take-over.

It was quite a battle. It caught the imagination of financial reporters on the Boston papers, and there were practically blow-by-blow accounts as a young David defended his people against the financial Goliath. When the tumult and shouting had stopped, Joe was the victor. Columbia Trust was saved intact and secure. And Joe Kennedy was its president. He was then twenty-five years old: the youngest bank president in the United States, probably the youngest one in the world. The Boston financial writers were enchanted, not only with him as a financial prodigy but as an appealingly fresh face and colorful character in a scene that for so many years had been colored in tones of gray. Within the financial community, and in the general community of Boston Irish, he was no longer just P. J. Kennedy's son but suddenly well known in his own right.

My father now had to agree that if any young man were worthy of my hand in marriage, Joe Kennedy would be a good choice for me.

The Columbia Trust battle occurred during the latter part of 1913. We waited nearly a year more before we married. This may seem strange to some people. There was Joe with a fine job and fine prospects; both families had money enough to spare to give us a good start in our married life, so why wait? The answer lay in an attitude of the times: Before a couple married they should be sure they could stand on their own, without financial gifts or subsidies. The man should have a secure job with a certain income. The woman should be able and willing to live on that income. Until that came about, they waited. To us, it was a matter of personal pride, dignity, self-respect.

In those days we unquestioningly believed that life was meant to have certain basic forms and structures. We felt that "To everything there is a season, and a time for every purpose." There was courtship, there was the discovery of love, there was engagement, there was marriage, there was parenthood: Each in its season and marked by traditions and rituals which, believe me, were sources of strength to young people then and I hope will continue—in some way—to be for others for a very long time to come.

Having said this I now find myself slightly embarrassed because in that procession of events, each of which should be engraved in my memory, there are two that I can't quite remember. Try as I will— they are absolutely gone. One is the time Joe asked me to marry him. The other is the time he gave me my engagement ring.

I feel fairly easy about the first, because I don't think he ever *did* ask me, not just straight-out. That's not the way it was. It was less a matter of "Will you marry me?" than of "When we get married . . ."

As a matter of fact, while on the topic of proposals, the only direct one I ever had was from Sir Thomas Lipton and was neither meant nor taken seriously. Sir Thomas was a perennial bachelor, and one of the most eligible bachelors in the world. Consequently, there was much speculation about the lady he sooner or later would choose, and good-humored joshing by his friends about his hesitation. One evening when he was in Boston, and at a private dinner party my father gave for him and some friends at one of the hotels, this banter started again and it was demanded he speak out at last and declare his intentions.

He looked over at me, and said:

"If you want to know who Lady Lipton is going to be, she is right here in this room. Come along, Rose, we'd better let them in on our secret. Stand up, Rose!"

"I won't accept you, Sir Thomas," I replied with what I hope was not too much of a blush. "I think you are altogether too fickle!"

"Well," he said, when the laughter subsided, "now I know how it feels to be jilted!"

From that bit of byplay the rumor spread that Sir Thomas wanted to marry me (or in other versions, my sister Agnes), and in time, as so often has happened, this began to be transmuted into "fact" and turned up as such in articles and books. The truth is that of course I loved Sir Thomas, as I would a grandfather, and that he loved me too, as he would a granddaughter, for we were just about that far apart in age.

Joe gave me the engagement ring, I'm certain, during late winter or early spring of 1914. Also, I remember his telling me he had bought it through a Harvard college friend, Arthur Goldsmith, who had graduated and gone into the family jewelry business in New York. Further, I am practically certain that he gave it to me one evening in my home. Beyond that, everything is hazy: no dialogue, no details, not even the general scene. I can hardly believe it myself. But there it is. Perhaps I was too excited by the event and perhaps also a bit stunned by what I saw: For when I opened the ring box I found a two-carat stone, pure white, flawless, superb.

The summer of 1914 was, of course, a time of high drama and crisis in Europe. The assassination of the Austrian archduke in June was followed by political and diplomatic storms, the mobilizations of armies, and the outbreak of war in August between the Allies and the Central Powers. Warfare between Germany and France, the countries I loved best and admired most after my own United States, was deeply distressing to me. Joe was saddened too; for only the summer before he had gone to Europe for the first time, with a group of Harvard friends. They traveled in Germany and France, and he had come home with fine memories of both countries and peoples.

Nevertheless, we were young and in love and the Atlantic lay between us and that tragedy. President Wilson declared America's neutrality. We could assume that the war would be settled by somebody, and somehow fairly soon, since all the nations had intelligent leaders, and intelligent men could not fail to look for and find some reasonable compromise before events became too serious. We assumed that it would all be done with, peace restored, before it could possibly affect our own life together in any direct way.

Thus that summer of 1914 passed for us in much the same way that earlier summers had passed. We went to the Boston "Pops" concerts and loved the music and ate ice cream. Usually on Friday nights some friend was having a small party; one or two dozen of us would gather around the parlor piano and sing old favorites and new hits, and some of us danced. On weekend afternoons, at one of the clubs or good hotels, there was likely to be a tea dance with an orchestra. Between numbers we chattered with one another and drank tea or lemonade or one of the new, popular soft drinks such as Moxie.

We always had good times at these little soirees, partly because I loved dancing and Joe was such a good dancer. He always knew all the current steps: the waltz, of course, as the perennial favorite, but others such as the two-step, the turkey trot, the tango (the last two considered rather wicked), and the latest rage then, a dance called "the boston." It had come along very recently, during his senior year at Harvard, and he hadn't had a chance to master it until he discovered that one of the young novitiates into Hasty Pudding was greatly adept at it. There was "hazing" for new members, certain duties the upperclassmen assigned to them, and Joe plucked this boy out and gave him the full-time special duty of teaching him the boston. The boy worked hard, and Joe learned well.

It goes without saying that we talked a good deal about ourselves, our plans for our wedding and honeymoon, where we would live, what kind of furniture we should have—all that. And I'm sure we exchanged special hopes and dreams about our future together.

Joe and I were married that October of 1914 in a service attended only by our families and close friends—neither of us wanted a public fiesta—in the private chapel of Cardinal O'Connell, who officiated. Agnes was my maid of honor. Joseph Donovan, an old friend of Joe's from boyhood through Harvard, was best man.

We had a beautiful honeymoon trip of two weeks at the Greenbrier in White Sulphur Springs, West Virginia. Then we returned to Boston, to the home we had selected and had already furnished so it would be waiting for us.

Chapter Seven

꧁ ꧂

Most of our young married friends lived in rented apartments, and as a place to start our life together an apartment would have been perfectly fine for me. But not for Joe. From the very beginning, "home" was the center of his world and the only place that really, finally, counted in his plans, no matter where those plans took him from time to time. Moreover, despite all his capacities for persuasion and leadership—tête à tête across a table, or as a team captain, or as administrator of vast enterprises in business and government, as he would be in years to come—he had a strong need for privacy, for independence, for being able to choose the people he wanted to be with in close association. In later years when he became a leading figure in Wall Street he was known as a "lone wolf." These traits of temperament were manifested in the first big decision he made for us. Home could not be an apartment but had to be a house. I gladly seconded the motion.

We looked around that summer before we were married and found one we both liked and decided would suit our needs. It was a nice old wooden-frame house with clapboard siding; seven rooms, plus two small ones in the converted attic, all on a small lot with a few bushes and trees. It would have blended perfectly into most of the main streets of America. It was in the Boston suburb of Brookline, yet only about twenty-five minutes from the center of the city by trolley, the usual means of transportation in those days. There was a sense of openness in the neighborhood, with a vacant lot on one side of us and another across the street, and fine big shade trees lining the sidewalks. It is built up now and to my eye seems rather congested and drab. But our house, our first home, is still there at 83 Beals Street.

It is now a public museum, part of the National Trust, and is visited by many thousands of people a year. The house has been restored with most of the original furniture, some of which Joe and I had saved through the years and some we had lent or given away, but which could be traced and collected. It is good, solid, serviceable, conservative furniture in the taste of the times. The muted color scheme is set off by reproductions of the great masterpieces I had seen and especially admired during my travels in Europe. We have done our best to put it all back together the way it was, including the beloved Ivers and Pond grand piano that was a wedding present from two of my uncles, and the set of teacups and saucers, blazoned with shamrocks, that Sir Thomas Lipton gave us that were like the ones he used on his yacht.

Tastes change. Nowadays I use a lot of bright colors in our houses at Palm Beach and Hyannis Port; but at the time, the Beals Street house seemed to us just right, beautiful and comfortable, a dream realized, even if seeing it now reminds me a little of a museum. I had no way of knowing that eventually women from all over the country, and for that matter most of the world, would be forming their opinions of my taste while looking into my parlor, dining room, and kitchen, and the second-floor bedroom that was Joe's and mine, and the adjoining two rooms that became nursery and bedroom for our children. The center of attention in the nursery is the small bassinet that in succession held all nine of our children.

I think our worldly ambitions as a young married couple were about the same as those of other young couples then and now. With a home of our own and furniture of our own, the next goal was to have a car of our own.

Only a few of our friends had cars, so it wasn't as if we felt deprived. Most of us took the trolley cars or, if we were in Boston, either the trolleys or the subways.

One of the great thrills of my life was the day my husband drove home in our very own brand-new, gleaming black Model T Ford. No Rolls has ever seemed so beautiful to me. Naturally, Joe was proud and excited about this surprise he had brought into our lives and was eager to take me out for a drive. And immediately after supper, in the summer twilight, off we went heading toward a neighborhood shopping center called Coolidge's Corner. That very afternoon I had walked there to buy a few things and on the way had noticed workmen digging a ditch preparatory to laying some water pipe. They had left two or three kerosene lanterns to mark the excavation. But these produced only dim light in the dusk. Joe was occupied with the challenging job of steering our new vehicle. I was so excited that it slipped my mind entirely to mention the excavation, and by the time I saw the lanterns and shouted a warning it was too late, and into the ditch we went.

There was a terrible lurch and bounce; noises of metal grinding on pavement, motor racing, rocks and dirt flying, yells from Joe and from me; total confusion. But Joe went to full throttle, gripped the steering wheel while I gripped the side of the car with one hand and his coattail with the other, and with another great bounce, seconds later, we were up and out and upright on the other side.

Neither of us was hurt except for a few black-and-blue bruises. And our beautiful car was relatively undamaged. They made tougher springs in those days. Joe had no loss of nerve. I expect he saw I was a little pale and decided for my sake to turn around and get us back home to Beals Street.

Except that Joe and I had a house and a car a little sooner than most of our friends, and a few other blessings that came our way, there was little to set us apart from our peers. There is a time for everything. And one of the lessons of my life is that people have a better time at any interval of their lives if they stay with friends who have similar backgrounds, interests, and resources, and are contemporaries in age, and thus have experiences together. I continued as president of the Ace of Clubs. Joe's time was his own, as it had been and always would be: School and college had once taken much of it before, and now it was business that did so. We shared as we had before, except more so. I loved music, especially the classical composers, and since Joe had not been exposed to serious music in his earlier years, I suppose I had something to do with introducing him to this great pleasure. Yet the natural taste was there, as his mother sang in the church choir, and one of the joys of his life remained the collection of classical records we accumulated. Years later, it was primarily Joe who enabled Arturo Toscanini to leave fascist Italy and live in the United States.

He also introduced me to pleasures I might otherwise have missed. While he was at Harvard he had become a great admirer of Professor Copeland of the English Department. "Copey," as he was known with affection by generations of students, was famous not only for scholarship but for showmanship: His "readings" from the classics were literary feasts in which he enabled his audiences to savor all the drama of plot and nuance of character. Joe was entranced by his readings from Dickens.

Joe loved football. He had roomed in his senior year at Harvard with Bob Fisher, the team captain and All-American, who by this time had become the Harvard coach. The combination of interest, school loyalty, and his great friendship with Bob was enough, of course, to make Joe want to turn out for every Harvard game he could possibly get to, and he wanted me to be with him at Harvard Stadium on Saturday afternoons. Being there in the middle of huge excited crowds, the pennants and pompons and banners and bands and noise, sharing as best I could in Joe's enthusiasm, hoping the best for the team and for our dear friend Bob, was something special and thrilling, and I had a great time.

The great new experience we shared, which affected our thinking about everything else in life, was parenthood. Since most of us had married at more or less the same time, we were having our children at about the same time. I don't recall that there was any great amount of conversation about them, or comparing notes about bottles and safety pins. Certainly not on my part, at least: For me, there was always a multitude of things more interesting to think about and talk about than whether one brand of talcum powder might or might not be slightly better than another for diaper rash. Yet we were all interested in each other and hence in each other's families; in fact, taking us as a group, we had some resemblance to an "extended family"; and without boring one another with sentimental details, we felt profound new meanings and grand new dimensions in our lives. We were aware that God had given us incalculable blessings and responsibilities.

Joe Jr., Jack, Rosemary, and Kathleen were born during the years we lived at Beals Street.

They arrived in a space of less than five years, counting from Joe Jr.'s birth to Kathleen's. The nursery was becoming cramped and on the verge of overflowing, since I was soon pregnant again.

True, there were the two small rooms on the third floor but they were occupied by live-in help. We had started out with a maid of all work who cooked, served, cleaned, laundered, with an afternoon a week and every other Sunday off, all for seven dollars a week, the usual wages and conditions in those days. When the babies began coming we added another helper, a hospital-trained nursemaid; as I recall she was paid three dollars a week, the going rate. With the fifth child on the way I couldn't do with less help and probably would need more, at least for a while, and obviously I needed more space. This was equally clear to Joe. So we began looking for another house. As always, my primary concern was that it be near good schools, good transportation, and a good shopping area. It also must be in a quiet, uncongested area with plenty of fresh air and play space for the children. We found what we needed in our same neighborhood: a bigger and better house for our busier family, only about a five-minute walk from Beals Street, at 131 Naples Road. Consequently, early in 1921, Joe sold the Beals Street house, bought the one at Naples Road, where Eunice, Pat, and Bobby were born.

When Patricia, our sixth, was born, Joe had to be in New York on complex and time-consuming financial operations involving Wall Street and the Hertz-Yellow Cab interests and couldn't get back home to Boston until about two weeks later. When he did, the five older ones all wanted to greet him at the station and were driven down in the limousine to wait for his train. So when he came onto the platform (he loved to tell this story) and looked around, there they were, the five of them ranging from ten to two, all hanging their heads out the car windows and waving and yelling and laughing: "Daddy! Daddy! Daddy! We've got another baby! We've got another baby . . ." And as the other arriving passengers saw and heard all this and saw Joe walking toward his children with his arms outstretched and a big grin on his face, their faces were a study in mixed emotions. Joe related: "They were smiling, they were mellow, but with a touch of perplexity and maybe sympathy, as if they might be thinking to themselves, 'What that fellow there certainly doesn't *need* right now is *another baby.*'"

Joe always gave me a special present of some kind to celebrate the birth of each child. After our eighth, Jean, arrived he turned up at my bedside with three diamond bracelets, which he had taken on approval so I could have my choice. A girl friend of mine had dropped in to visit. I put all three bracelets on at once, the better to compare them—and to say the least it was a glittering sight. My friend's eyes opened wide, and she turned to Joe and gasped, "What can you possibly think of to give her next if she has the ninth baby?" Joe glared at me. "I'll give her a black eye," he said gruffly, and broke down with laughter.

We did have the ninth, of course, and Joe gave me something more enjoyable than a black eye. I can't remember quite what it was (a trip to Europe?). He loved giving me things and any pretext or none would do. In any case, Teddy himself has been treasure enough. He is the only son I have now, and is my joy and support and solace.

Thus with Bobby's arrival I had had a child on the average of once every eighteen months and by then had seven children, the eldest of whom was only a little more than ten years old. I must say that even I, now that I stop to do these calculations, find this arithmetic rather amazing, even though it didn't seem particularly unusual in the decade, 1915–25.

And, of course, Jean and Teddy were still to come. By then we had left Boston for New York. I came back for each of them, partly because I had such confidence in my obstetrician there, so both Jean and Teddy were born in Boston, in St. Margaret's Hospital.

And as I think any mother who cares deeply about her children, and their individual welfare and development, will know—as any good father will know, too—much as I welcomed and counted on help from maids and nursemaids I was extremely busy.

And sometimes, distracted or excited or tired, feelings familiar to parents of young, active children, I was also happy, optimistic, and proud. I had made up my mind to raise my children as perfectly as possible. What greater aspiration and challenge are there for a mother than the hope of raising a great son or daughter?

Chapter Eight

People who have admired my children often ask me about "early influences," with an implication that I must have found and applied some private formula to make them turn out so well. This is flattering and I do wish I could claim original discoveries in the field of child rearing, but I must confess there would be nothing to support it. When they were old enough to understand the rules of right and wrong, to learn responsibility, and to have their interests broadened and channeled from those of babyhood to childhood and thence to youth—my methods with them did depart somewhat from the norm, but practically always in the direction of the old-fashioned rather than the newfangled. As for the earliest influences, those of birth and infancy, they could hardly have been more old-fashioned since I followed the customs of my time, which also had been those of my mother and my forebears.

Women had their babies at home, wherever and whatever "home" happened to be. And so did I, except for the last two. Women nursed their babies during early infancy. I nursed many of them, though later the pediatric fashion was fast changing to bottle feeding almost from birth. (I am amused at such reversals of scientific fashion among great and famous experts: Breast feeding is now once more highly recommended, and there is even a noticeable trend toward giving birth at home.)

When Joe Jr. was born on July 28, 1915, home temporarily was a cottage we had taken for the summer at Hull, a pretty town near Boston on a sandy hook of land that curves far out into Massachusetts Bay. Many of our friends had houses there and Father had a house in close proximity. I expect that Joe rented the house because he thought the fresh sea air would be good for me and for our first-born. He was fully as excited and reverent about this incipient miracle as I was.

Once my obstetrician, Dr. Good (whose fee for pre- and postnatal care and delivery was about $125), had confirmed pregnancy, the next important step was to engage a trained nurse for the expected time. Since babies show their individualism from the beginning by arriving on their own schedule and nobody else's, during the last week or fortnight she stayed at her own home "on call" around the clock, until I telephoned her that I was feeling contractions or other signs that the baby was coming, and she hurried over. From then on she lived in the house, available at any time of the day or night to care for me and for the baby, until I was up and feeling fit and the baby was making the usual healthy gains, generally a period of a few weeks. For these responsibilities she had a salary of twenty-five dollars a week. Meanwhile, at the same early signs of labor, Dr. Good was notified, and soon he arrived with an assistant, whose main job was to administer the anesthetic, which was ether. (His fee was twenty-five dollars.) Meanwhile, too, my bed would have been moved next to the sunniest window, if this was daytime, or if at nighttime to the best sources of light, because I did want Dr. Good and all concerned to be able to see exactly what was happening and what they were doing. Meanwhile, the housemaid and nursemaid would be busy with all sorts of paraphernalia and supplies—fresh sheets, towels, ice bags, or anything the doctor ordered, especially pots and kettles of hot water.

The rest was up to me. I put my faith in God, accepted directions and encouragements from Dr. Good and the others, and tried to sublimate my discomfort in expectation of the happiness I would have when I beheld my child.

For any normal woman in normal circumstances there is bound to be a special excitement and joy and gratitude to God when she holds her first baby in her arms. It was so with me when the first tiny, amazing creature in swaddling clothes, Joseph Patrick Kennedy, Jr., was presented to me. But with each one it was a new thrill and joy, and I have cherished all of them equally.

It may seem unusual, but I did not think it was vital for my husband to be on hand for the birth of the babies.

I knew he worked hard for us, went on working hard even when he wasn't feeling well or sometimes when he was in severe pain. Yet there was nothing that he could do to help me in bearing a child, just as there was nothing I could do directly in helping him bear the burdens of business. Nonetheless, indirectly, I could help. If he was away on business I would not insist that he be home for the birth of our new baby. Yet he was always exultant and happy when he arrived to see his new child for the first time.

This was another aspect of the "synergistic" quality of our marriage. We were individuals with highly responsible roles in a partnership that yielded rewards which we shared.

In the same spirit and for the same reason, as the years went on and our children grew and went through the inevitable period of childhood accidents and diseases (though the latter were more frightening then than now), I saw no point in mentioning these to Joe if he was away and telephoned me for the local and family news. There was little or nothing he could do to help the situation at a distance, so why worry him? How could he do his own work well if his thoughts were preoccupied with concern for a beloved child?

I remember once, for instance, when he was in California and telephoned me within a matter of minutes after I arrived home from a car accident that had put a good-sized gash in my forehead. I was feeling shaky. In fact, when the call came I was lying on my bed pulling myself together and drinking coffee. But I spoke naturally, gave him news of the children and told him what a fine day it was: a perfect day for golf. Then I drove to the hospital where the doctor took five stitches in my forehead.

Characteristically, the family chauffeur decided that news of the accident and my injury would be on the radio and Joe would quickly learn of it. He felt it was his duty to telephone Joe first. After he got the call, Joe called back in a state of great anxiety. I then had to convince him it was just a minor accident. No one was hurt seriously, including me. He was not to worry.

Thus, nothing was gained from his knowing about my accident and something was lost: time and energy that both of us—he out there, I back East—could have put to good use and really couldn't spare, because both of us were very busy.

Joe was delighted and enchanted with his children from the time each child was born. He spent as much time as he could with them. Yet those times soon became scattered and unpredictable. Early in 1917—with only Joe Jr. born and Jack still on the way—he turned Columbia Trust over to his father to run and became assistant general manager of Bethlehem Steel's huge Fore River shipyard at Quincy, Massachusetts. With America's entry into World War I, he was under such pressures that, except for Sundays, he came home just long enough to sleep. The shipyard broke all production records. And Joe developed an ulcer.

It was during those times that he became acquainted with Franklin D. Roosevelt, who was then Assistant Secretary of the Navy.

After the war, Joe went into the brokerage business, and later into the private banking business, which enabled him to spend much more time at home. But, as always with Joe, one idea easily sparked another; he was quick to see opportunities and to seize them before others did. Before long he was in all sorts of enterprises that kept him busy, traveling more and more. For instance, he formed a syndicate to buy control of a chain of New England movie theaters. This led him into movie distribution as well as exhibition, and thence into movie production, which in turn led to studio ownership and operation. This required a lot of time in New York, which was the financial center of the movie industry, and in Hollywood, the production center. He worked away from home for days, weeks, or even months at a time. He telephoned me nearly every day; and each Sunday at noon he called and spoke with the children. I had them all lined up and waiting, in the order of their ages, so that even the smallest could hear his voice. To them he never seemed far away. His influence was felt in our house even when he was away. When he was home he was deeply involved with our children. Yet for quite a few years I was responsible for most of the child rearing.

Eunice and I were talking recently, trying to come to a definition of the roles Joe and I had in their lives. She states things clearly and directly, a quality I admire, and she puts it this way: "You were in charge of us and raised and trained us while we were children. And then, when we began turning into young people, Dad took charge the rest of the way." I think perhaps this was so.

"As the twig is bent, so the tree inclines"—an elementary home truth that apparently psychologists of most schools now accept. I now realize that I had a considerable part in forming the characters of our children. Naturally, I had very good material to work with. Yet I knew what I wanted from them. I didn't always succeed in all my aims, but it was never from lack of effort. I looked on child rearing not only as a work of love and duty but as a profession that was fully as interesting and challenging as any honorable profession in the world and one that demanded the best that I could bring to it.

I was more fortunate than most women in having the domestic help and money that I required. On the other hand, with nine young children the needs were extraordinary and demanded not only personal efforts but a lot of planning, organizing, and supervising. I learned to become an executive.

I did little diaper changing, but I had to be sure there were plenty of good-quality diapers on hand, and that they were changed as needed and properly washed and stowed for use. One of my continuing memories is of two decades of rows of diapers hanging up to dry on the back-yard clotheslines. In the winter they often froze stiff and then had to be thawed and further dried before being put away. I learned that the best method was to put them on the steam radiators —and I remember all those radiators, sizzling away, draped in white.

There were also the daily supply of bottles and nipples to be cleaned and sterilized. I didn't do much of it myself, but I had to be sure it was done properly, and on a schedule that wouldn't interfere with another vital schedule. If nursemaids were in the kitchen boiling bottles and nipples and preparing "formulas" and pureeing vegetables (there were no canned baby foods then) when the cook needed the stove and some of the same utensils to prepare supper, there could be a kitchen crisis, sharp words and bruised feelings and, from a management point of view, a precipitous drop in morale and efficiency.

In passing, I would like to pay tribute to whoever invented zippers. In my times all we had were snap fasteners, hooks and eyes, and buttons. Primarily buttons, buttons, and more buttons. In warm weather with light clothing the button problem was only moderate. But in winter, whenever the young children were outside they were dressed in long leggings, and I can't begin to calculate the hours the help and I spent buttoning and unbuttoning them. Also, no matter how strong the thread or how well sewn, it was forever pulling loose or wearing thin or breaking. With daily inspection and some luck we spotted loose buttons while they were still dangling. With less luck they were lost and had to be replaced from the button box, with its collection of spares of miscellaneous sizes and colors, from which it was a problem to find something to fit if not quite match.

I liked sewing, so this was a job I often did myself. There was a little room on the second floor at Beals Street that I fixed up as a combination sewing room and office: a desk on one side for correspondence and record keeping, my sewing gear on another side. I spent many hours there seaming, sewing, mending, and darning. In those days children wore long stockings; in winter they often managed to wear holes, particularly in the knees, which were always tearing.

Having deplored old-fashioned inconveniences, I want to praise an old-fashioned convenience, the front porch. Nearly all houses had a front porch in those days: It was almost as much taken for granted in home architecture as walls and windows. In my experienced opinion the front porch is one of the greatest arrangements ever imagined for the benefit of mother and child.

Young children need fresh air, exercise, and activities that stimulate their interest, some of which I could supply by taking them for a daily walk. Most mornings, while the domestic chores were getting under way, I would put the current toddler in a kiddy car and, with one or two older ones on either side, set off to the shopping center. I didn't buy much—perhaps a box of talcum powder or some other household item that needed replenishing—but it was an interesting adventure for the children and good for me. Sometimes we went into the five-and-ten, and that was especially exciting for them. Almost always, on the way home, we stopped in at our parish church. Part of the reason was that I wanted them to understand, from early age, that church isn't just something for Sundays and special times on the calendar but should be part of daily life.

So the walks were fine and full of fun but they weren't enough, and the front porch thus became a blessing. With a folding gate to block the entrance, the children could play there in fresh air and in full safety and, moreover, with the full panorama of neighborhood life to entertain them. Cars passing by, people walking along (many of them acquaintances who waved), the letter carrier, the milkman with his wire basket loaded full as he came to our house and empty as he left, the policeman passing by on his patrol, the grocery boy, tradesmen, visitors, and friends of all degrees and kinds—everybody with a smile and cheerful greeting for the children.

Imagine Naples Road, with its big front porch, in 1925. Joe Jr. and Jack by then were nine and a half and soon to be eight, respectively, and playing (in their buttoned leggings) someplace in our yard or nearby where I tried to keep track of them while keeping an eye on activities on the front porch. There, probably—or outside with the boys—would be Rosemary, by then about six and a half, Kathleen, five, Eunice, three and a half, Pat, a year and a half, and in the baby carriage would be three- or four-month-old Bobby.

With that many children—seven, counting Joe Jr. and Jack, who would be in and out—we discovered it was a good idea to divide the porch into sections with folding gates: two, three, or four of them as the situation at the time indicated. That way they could be with each other and entertain one another for hours at a time with a minimal risk that they would push one another down or stick one another with something sharp or perhaps pile heavy objects inside or on top of the baby carriage.

With all our children and all the statistics that needed to be remembered each week, month, year, and for years ahead, I found my head beginning to spin. One day, therefore, while passing a stationery store in our shopping area, I stopped in and bought a supply of file cards and index tabs and set to work cataloguing names, dates, and events in a systematic way. I continued to do this for many years.

As each new baby came along, he or she was indexed and the card contained all the primary vital statistics such as date and place of birth, church of baptism, names of godparents, and any other pertinent data. In due course I added the date and place of Confirmation and First Communion. Meanwhile, there were entries on anything of importance concerning health and physical welfare. The child was weighed each Saturday night and if there was loss of weight two weeks in a row I took measures: perhaps a richer diet and less exercise until the scale went up. Vaccinations, Schick tests and results, eye examinations, dental examinations. Everything went onto the cards, including dates and notations of childhood diseases and aftereffects, the names of the doctors in case of relapse or complications or the need of more information later on. Thus, I maintained a health summary on small cards, literally at the reach of a finger tip.

When Joe became ambassador to the Court of St. James's and we all went over there the English press treated my card file as a phenomenon of the magnitude of Henry Ford's assembly line. My dutifully kept box of file cards thus became a symbol of "American efficiency." Actually, it had just been a matter of "Kennedy desperation."

But I must say that it is really impossible to convey what it meant to me and to Joe, when I wrote those brief notations. I think any mother will understand what I mean.

Each card evokes a biography.

Joe Jr. was a healthy infant and child, big and strong for his age, and there are few notations about him in the early years.

Jack was a healthy infant too, but then, as noted on his card: "Has had whooping cough, measles—chicken pox," childhood diseases that were expectable in those days but that of course caused worries about him.

Then: "Had scarlet fever—February 20—1920." Scarlet fever was a dreaded disease, fairly often fatal, quite often crippling in aftereffects; heart, eyes, ears; there were various possibilities that were awful to think about. It was highly contagious, and Rosemary was only a year and a half, and Kathleen had just been born.

Joe rarely discussed finances. In fact, I expect that one of the rare times he ever mentioned money was when Jack got scarlet fever. It was a terrible time for us and, above all, a time for prayer. Kathleen was only a few days old; and with that very contagious disease in that small house on Beals Street there were fears that Joe Jr. and Rose-

mary would get it, and that the new baby might also, and so might I.
And yet there was no place in Brookline where Jack could be taken
—the hospital wouldn't admit patients with contagious diseases—
and our family wasn't eligible for use of the Boston hospitals because
we didn't live in the city. Finally, through my father's influence Jack
was admitted to the Boston City Hospital, which had a special ward
and facilities for these diseases. By the time he got there Jack was a
very, very sick little boy. Joe was in church praying for him, and in
his prayers he promised that if Jack were spared he would give half
of all his money to charity. When Jack did recover, Joe fulfilled his
pledge by giving a check to the Guild of St. Apollonia, which had a
program of taking needy children to dentists and doctors for good
care but lacked money for a bus for the purpose. Joe's contribution
was, I expect, just about the right amount. His check was for $3,700
—which was exactly half his "fortune" at that time.

The others didn't get the disease, and Jack recovered without
serious complications. Yet that was only the beginning. Almost all
his life, it seemed, he had to battle against misfortunes of health.
Perhaps this gave him another kind of strength that helped him to
be the great man he became.

I know that there are few simple answers to anything. In our
family, in sickness and in health, we were all involved with one another, all in the same life, a continuum, a seamless fabric, a flow of
time.

Chapter Nine

File cards show the milestones in the lives of our children when they were young; but, of course, life isn't a matter of milestones but of moments. They tick away like the heartbeat of time itself, and as we begin to think of the last tick-tock we can look back and count the years and remember them, but how do we cherish the moments, minutes, hours that make them whole? A child's smile or tears, a first tooth, a funny little expression or remark, a good or naughty deed as he discovers the world for himself and grows into it in his own way, developing his own personality. Impressions, feelings, sights, sounds, and smells—of a snowfall or a sea breeze—bits of life soon gone and, unfortunately, relegated to the recesses of one's memory as life goes on happening. Becoming.

Our home at Hyannis Port is a big, old-fashioned house with a big rambling attic that has served us well as storage space for the memorabilia that became too bulky to keep around the house, but too precious to give away or throw out. I'm sure all families know the problem.

My daughter Pat said recently: "That's a memory of mine, and of all of us, growing up, that Mother was in the attic, putting things away. And now that we're grown up she's *still* up there, taking things out."

True. It is time for the collection to be dismantled and the parts sent to the places they best belong: to family members and friends, to Jack's presidential archives, and to the files I have been building to help me with these memoirs.

For example, I found that I kept a diary during 1923.

I had started diaries before, during childhood and girlhood, but they have not survived. My nephew Joey Gargan, who spent many summers with us, recalls: "One of my memories of Aunt Rose is her saying we ought to keep diaries, because they would be so interesting for us later. But we didn't quite get around to it. And now, all these years later, of course I'm sorry. I wish we had taken her advice." I wish that I had taken my own advice; for the fact is that I did not keep a full diary until the time of Joe's ambassadorship.

Yet, let us now be thankful for small blessings, among them the 1923 diary. I must have begun it in the spirit of a New Year's resolution since it starts on January 1 and continues in almost unbroken sequence through January 21, with the entry: "Stormy day. Could not go to church. Children in all day." Thereafter, the entries tend to become scattered, lasting into December. Thus, the diary does cover most of a typical year in Brookline.

My diary summons all sorts of memories. Disordered memories. Bits of time I remember.

"January 1, 1923

"Came up to Poland Springs December 27th with Joe Jr. and Jack and Mary Moore. Eddie and Joe Sr. came later. Two horribly snowy days and boys had to stay in the house."

In those times "winter sports" as we know them now—the ski lifts and long manicured ski trails, the artificial snow, the sheltered hot-water pools, the chalets, hotels, motels—the whole huge business didn't exist. But there was Poland Springs, a well-known spa that stayed open in the winter. We had been going there for some years, beginning about 1916, and enjoyed ourselves thoroughly. Sleighs met us at the railroad station and we were bundled into raccoon coats, with blankets over our legs, and taken to the hotel with bells jingling and steel runners crunching in the snow. We reveled in the adventures of skiing the gentle slopes and coasting on the snow and skating on the ice rink. Our skates had to be screwed onto the soles of our shoes with a key and secured with leather straps bound around our shoes and ankles, an irksome job that gave uncertain results. The skates were likely to come loose and fall off, and we were likely to trip on the straps and slip and slide and fall down. But that is how

Joe Jr., Jack, and some other children learned to skate—the numb fingers, lost skate keys, bumps, and fun.

The Mary Moore and Eddie mentioned in this first diary entry were Mr. and Mrs. Edward Moore.

Eddie Moore was a devoted friend to my father and had worked for him as secretary and confidential assistant during the years of the mayoralty. He knew our family well. When my father left office he joined Joe in a similar role but, in a sense, even more so. For, as I have said, Joe had a rugged individualist's need for privacy; there were very few men he liked, trusted, and could relax with entirely. Among these Eddie Moore became his closest friend, someone he trusted implicitly in every way and in all circumstances. His wife, Mary, became an equally great friend, confidante, and unfailing support for me.

They were older than Joe and I, and we felt the full affection and confidence and unquestioning mutual acceptance that might be felt for a beloved aunt and uncle.

They had no children; so they turned to ours, in love and duty, bringing their parental emotions to them, and rejoicing with us in every childhood triumph and sharing in every sorrow. The children adored them. When our ninth child, and fourth son, was born, we named him Edward Moore Kennedy.

"January 2, 1923
"Joe Jr. and I went home on afternoon train leaving Jack and Mary, as I think Jack needs a few days longer. Train ½ hour late. Jack said he had to put his hand over Mrs. Moore's mouth last night, because she was humming (she really was snoring)."

"January 5, 1923
"Ace of Clubs dance—wore blue and silver Hickson dress."

I was still president of the Ace of Clubs, as I continued to be until we moved away from Boston, so I was still responsible for the general arrangements, including those for our annual gala ball. That accounts for the first part of the notation. As for the second, the "Hickson dress," that really was quite special.

I'd been brought up to dress well. My mother had a fine sense of style: nothing frilly or fancy, always an emphasis on quality and cut and fit and simple, classic lines, little or no ornamentation, everything just right to set off her special beauty. My father had the same sense of what was right. My friend Mary O'Connell Ryan remembers, somehow, a special prudence of mine about hats:

"Rose liked millinery. And she would take a hat home—whatever she would buy—and she would study it and think about it some more; and then, if she decided she didn't like it, as happened fairly often, she would take it back and exchange it. She was always a careful shopper. And always cautious, never extravagant about money."

I had been buying most of my clothes off the rack in Boston and Brookline shops and having them fitted. Others had been run up by local seamstresses working with patterns and my own ideas. But never had I splurged on the total luxury of *couture*: a dress made by a famous designer—as Hickson was—one of its kind, fabric chosen with only me in mind, design inspired by his artist's vision of what I should look like. It was wildly expensive: something like two hundred dollars, as I remember. But it was much complimented at the Ace of Clubs ball and much admired by Joe.

Joe always wanted me to dress well. It pleased him, in fact it delighted him, to have me turn up in something quite special.

"January 10, 1923
"Children's nursemaid came back tonight. Rose home from school on account of grippe epidemic, though she is feeling okay."

Rose here is Rosemary, our third child and first daughter, who by this time was about four and a half; the school mentioned is, of course, a kindergarten.

"January 11, 1923
"Eunice went back to Saranac . . ."

This was not my daughter Eunice but my younger sister, for whom she was named. She had fallen ill with tuberculosis, and Saranac was a leading center for treatment.

"January 13, 1923
"Went to Harvard-Princeton hockey game, then to Brunswick with Mab and Joe O'Connell. Big gay crowd there."

Joe O'Connell was one of my Joe's oldest, closest friends . . . godfather to our first-born, Joe Jr. . . . brother of Mary O'Connell (Ryan) who was one of my own closest friends; the two of them, respectively, nephew and niece of Cardinal O'Connell, who had married Joe and me in his private chapel.

"January 16, 1923
"Joe Sr. left on 5 o'clock for Palm Beach with Eddie Moore and a couple of other friends who joined them in New York."

Joe wanted to get down to Florida with three reliable pals to make a golf foursome, and he needed the rest and sunshine and could arrange his business affairs to be away at that time. I couldn't be away, for obvious reasons—children with bad colds and worse, at the worst time of the year for more colds and complications—so I sent him off with loving blessings. Partly, of course, or shall I say largely, because it was already well understood between us that soon I would have a trip of my own, accompanied by someone I wanted as a companion, to someplace I wanted to see. And that, of course, is exactly what happened, with his loving blessings to me.

Moreover, I would have been bored by going to the same place every year for a holiday. I was eager to travel to other parts of this country and of the world. Joe wanted and needed rest, and found waiting for trains and boats irksome. He felt that his businesses required enough travel, and preferred sun and golf in Palm Beach.

"February 14, 1923
"Eunice walking alone and talking a lot. Best little talker of all. Also tries to take a bow and say, 'Little Partner, dance with me,' etc. . . ."

She was only one and a half then, but I think these jottings foretold something about the girl she became. Wonderfully well coordinated and with quick reflexes, one of the best athletes in our active family. A "talker" with a special way of expressing herself in a pithy and witty manner that made her one of the livelier participants in our family conversations. But she was also a good listener, and marvelously generous in her interest in others, especially her brothers and sisters, but including waifs, strays, and anybody who needed her. And so through vigor, candor, wit, and comprehending sympathy she endeared herself to all of us. A special girl, no one like her.

What could be more interesting for a woman than to watch one's very own child grow and develop, or more rewarding than to guide the child, with understanding, imagination, patience, perseverance, to bring out the best that Nature has given? As I found out from raising our nine, all of whom have shared some qualities and traits, yet also have been so different from one another, each child is a continual surprise. Each baby is truly "born to be different." None should be compared with another, for each has God-given potentialities which depend for full realization on influences in his or her environment. In the early years, this depends primarily on the mother. I mean the guidance, the imagination, and the "emotional climate" a mother can provide.

"February 20, 1923
  "Kathleen cut her cake . . ." (And a notation two days later) "Kathleen goes out now in her little sleigh."

She was three years old, a beautiful and enchanting child, with the soft, high coloring and beautiful skin of her Kennedy grandmother. Although we delighted in her, I don't think we could have spoiled her if we had tried.

"February 23, 1923
  "Joe Jr. went inside altar rail today at early Mass at St. Aidan's to practice being altar boy, but has not been one yet. Has cassock all ready."

He was seven and a half, a very young age to be an altar boy. But he was responsive and responsible, energetic and full of initiative. A manly, straightforward, visibly intelligent little boy, quick to smile and laugh, and yet with a certain forcefulness of character that marked him as a natural leader. That was a quality we all recognized in him early. Kathleen once wrote that "somehow we all looked up to Joe and everything he did." And my father, his grandpa Fitzgerald said, "No sweeter personality ever lived. . . . He loved life. He liked to meet people. His sincerity was apparent when he shook your hand."

Yet he also got into his share of mischief.

"February 25, 1923

"Joe Jr. and Jack have a new song about the Bedbugs and the Cooties. Also a club where they initiate new members by sticking pins into them."

I believe this needs no comment from me.

"February 28, 1923

"Their aunt Agnes sent boys alligators from the South. They named them after their best friends Jerry and Charlie. Charlie has a dog whose name is Brandy, because his father is a bootlegger."

"March 30, 1923

"Jack did not care much about wishing for happy death, but thought he would like to wish for two dogs.

"Joe Jr. went to Stations of the Cross all dirty."

"April 1, 1923

"Easter. All went to Winthrop, except Jack who had a little cold. Eddie and Mary Moore over to dinner."

Winthrop is a town near Boston where the elder Kennedys lived. Patrick J. was sixty-five by then and in semiretirement: still a political power but in the role of elder statesman. He took great pride and satisfaction in Joe's accomplishments, of course, and for his own part Joe was a very affectionate and dutiful son. So, in the months of good weather, we often used to pack the children in the car and drive up to spend Sunday afternoon with them. We would pay Sunday-night visits to my parents and my brothers and sisters.

"April 3, 1923

"Jack said, 'Gee, *you're* a great mother to go away and leave your children all alone.' "

He was then nearly six. As I have indicated, he was a rather frail little boy. Not small for his age but with a tendency to be thin, so I was perpetually concerned that he got enough of the right things to eat. At family meals, if there happened to be an extra portion of food, or perhaps some rich gravy left in the bottom of the pan, I would usually tell the cook to give it to Jack because he needed it. He had a rather narrow face and his ears stuck out a little bit and his hair wouldn't stay put, and all that added, I suppose, to an elfin quality in his appearance. But he was a very active, very lively elf, full of energy when he wasn't ill and full of charm and imagination. And surprises—for he thought his own thoughts, did things his own way, and somehow just didn't fit any pattern. Now and then, fairly often in fact, that distressed me, since I thought I knew what was best. But at the same time that I was taken aback, I was enchanted and amused. He was a funny little boy, and he said things in such an original, vivid way that I felt they were worth recording, as these diary entries show.

As for the one just noted above, it was brought on by the fact that I was about to leave with my sister Agnes on a trip to the West Coast. Having an insatiable curiosity about the world, I managed, in those times and later on, to get away every year or two to a place I hadn't seen before. In this country I hadn't been to the far West. Joe arranged his business plans so he could be in Boston, or within easy reach, while I was away; and so, with Mary Moore always ready to lend a helpful hand in any emergency, I could travel without undue worries about the children.

I must say that Jack's comment made me feel I was a little hardhearted. And the next day, April 4, when I said good-bye to the children on the porch, I felt miserable. They looked so forlorn, and when I kissed them good-bye I had tears in my eyes. After I was down the street a way I suddenly realized there was something I had forgotten and I came back—to find them all, laughing and playing on the porch, apparently not missing me much at all. I resumed my journey with an easy conscience.

That little scene illustrates something too about the benefits of a large family. They take care of, and are good company for, one another, and in those respects it seems to me the bigger a family, the better for everyone. That is a theme I will have reasons to illustrate in a number of ways in other parts of this book.

Agnes and I were gone for about six weeks, during which I made

almost daily diary notes. Reading them now I must admit there is
not much in my jottings that could fascinate others.

While we were in the Los Angeles area we visited Hollywood, as
most tourists did, for by that time the movies had become a national
habit and Hollywood was established in the public mind as a glamorous and fabulous place. That same year, Cecil B. De Mille released
The Ten Commandments, one of the first of the silent superepics,
advertised as having cost the then-staggering sum of more than a million dollars and "with a cast of thousands." The star system was then
coming into its glory too and many a girl, I'm sure, sat in front of
her mirror wondering if she might possibly resemble Mary Pickford
or one of the reigning movie queens.

Besides the movies, California seems to have impressed me most
for its oranges, to judge by my notes: "Countless orange groves, with
wonderful fragrance . . . stopped at Sunkist factory . . . Pasadena
—Orange Grove drive . . . mountainous country and orange groves,
most attractive." But we did all the sights up and down the Coast,
from Catalina to the redwood country, with side trips to Yosemite
and elsewhere.

Back in Brookline, I was met with joy and learned that there had
been an epidemic of measles in the house. Joe hadn't told me because he didn't want to worry me and perhaps cause me to cancel
part of my trip. Mary Moore was there, we had a good doctor, good
household help, and he managed. They all recovered without aftereffects.

"June 7–8, 1923
"Moved to beach, cool but pleasant. Joe Jr. and Jack at Mc-
Elwain's with pony."

The "beach" for us was not yet Hyannis Port—that came a few
years later, and meanwhile we tried several places along the extraordinarily long, convoluted coastline of Massachusetts. For a while
we were at Hull, where, as I mentioned, Joe Jr. was born, and my
father had bought a big and rather elegant old Victorian house
where he and my mother and the younger children summered. By
this time we had taken a place a few miles farther south of Boston,
on the way (as it turned out for us) to Cape Cod, at Cohasset. In

any case the whole Boston-Cape Cod region is fairly compact, with good roads even in those days, so we were within reasonable driving distance of my parents' summer home and that of Joe's parents', farther down at the village of Sagamore. Hence there was a lot of visiting back and forth.

"June 13, 1923

"Down to Sagamore with Kennedys . . ."

"June 15, 1923

"Joe up all night on business. Boys now down here for rest of the summer."

"June 19, 1923

"My sister Eunice going back, cannot sleep here . . ."

"Going back" must have meant back to Saranac to the TB sanatorium. She had responded well enough to treatment to be released for a while, but she had relapses.

She was a beautiful young girl, intelligent as well as attractive, with very lively ways, much of the spunk and spirit and wit of my father, which made it seem all the more cruel that she should be stricken by this wasting disease.

"June 21, 1923

"Celebrated my birthday by trip to Cape. Men golfed at Wianno, we went to Hyannis. Joe gave me blue and gold vanity case from Cartier's."

My birthday was a month away, on July 22, but Joe had to be gone then on business so we celebrated early. Not for the first or the last time, and I expect it has happened to quite a few millions of other couples, especially in these days when so many men have to travel away from home so much.

"October 26, 1923

"Boys went to store and saw 'No dogs allowed in this Restaurant,' and they put in front of dogs, 'Hot.' "

"October 28, 1923

"Boys stole false mustaches from shop."

"November 21, 1923

"Boys were down cellar collecting milk bottles to sell when I found them."

"December 5, 1923

"Jack said, 'Daddy has a Sweet Tooth, hasn't he? I wonder which one it is?' His teacher is coming over to tell on him. He says, 'You know I am getting on all right and if you study too much, you're liable to go crazy.'"

It was at about this time—with a few other episodes such as finding one of the boys, Joe Jr. I believe, on the roof of a neighbor's garage, and Jack in one or another state of quixotic disgrace—that I decided to take the boys out of the local public school and enroll them in a nearby private school, Dexter, where there would be afterschool supervised play. Their father and I had both gone to public school, and we appreciated the advantages of public school education. But I think the above makes it clear why I was driven to my decision.

My 1923 diary entries end in early December, I imagine, because our family was already deeply involved in preparations for Christmas, always the greatest event in our house.

We always had a Christmas tree selected with care by Joe or some of us together, but as big as our living room would allow.

Meanwhile, someone, usually Mary or Eddie Moore, after many whisperings and long preparations, would have taken each of the children to the five-and-ten at Coolidge's Corner, where they would choose presents for one another and for us and others in the house. From the age of five they had an allowance, beginning as I remember at ten cents a week, an amount that was to cover not only their lollipop expenses but leave something for birthday and Christmas shopping. Each had a little bank. Some of them were more frugal than others and had their reward at the five-and-ten when they could afford something that took their eye for someone they loved. A storybook with large colorful pictures—what could Jack like better than that? Or a bubble pipe for another one, or a little wind-up toy or, for the baby of the moment, a rattle or teething ring or set of jingle bells. For their father perhaps a fancy pencil holder, for me perhaps a gay red and green cloth penwiper as we used pen and ink in those days.

Then the wrapping, getting the edges stuck down with seals full of elves and holly wreaths and smiling Santas and flying reindeer, and trying to fix ribbons and festive fancy bows, and hiding everything away in the most unlikely places because everything had to be secret until Christmas Day.

When Joe Jr. was three years old, we had our first crèche. We would tell him about the star in the East guiding the Wise Men to the manger at Bethlehem. We would talk of the shepherds tending their flocks and of the Christ Child in the manger. We spoke of the joy of His birth, and what it meant to the world because the Christ Child was a baby, as Joe was, and he was fascinated by it. Each year, with the passage of time, other little Kennedys heard the Christmas story. They saw the crèche at church, and prayed there and at home, as well. The Christmas story is endlessly fascinating to children, and one they can identify with. I have such happy memories of them singing "Away in a Manger." I often think of the warmth and delight of our family Christmas.

It was exciting to the children on Christmas morning to open the wrappings and see what Santa had brought and what each had given to the others, each child opening his or hers in turn according to age, with exclamations of wonder and delight.

Chapter Ten

꧁ ❦ ꧂

I have always felt that the more experiences a child has and the more things he sees and hears the more interested in life he is likely to be, and the more interesting his own life is likely to be.

On the whole I think my conviction that my children should have many "learning experiences" and should use their minds to the fullest capacity, discovering the world for themselves through personal encounters with the world outside, worked out well and perhaps had something to do with their curiosity, their enthusiasm for new adventures, their confidence in knowing that life was exciting. But I am frank to admit that there were some miscalculations.

I remember, for instance, the time I decided it would be a rewarding experience to take the children out to pick blueberries. In those days wild blueberries grew in profusion on most parts of the Cape; and the wild blueberries have a much fuller flavor than the big plump cultivated kind. So I loaded five children in the station wagon and set off over sandy rough roads with everyone bouncing and jouncing and laughing, until we were about ten miles into the wilds and saw a big, sunny patch of bushes with ripening berries and the Cape's multicolored wildflowers.

Each child was given a little tin pail, the accepted receptacle for berry picking. Soon they were all busy trying to find the bushes heaviest with berries, calling back and forth, vying to see who could cover the bottom of a pail first. They were having a marvelous and memorable time.

Suddenly Eunice came running up with a piercing shriek. A bumblebee had stung her on the arm. We had no ointment with us to allay the pain. As the others stood around watching her they all began imagining they felt bumblebees alighting on their arms and legs, even if it were only a mosquito.

When Eunice's suffering and their apprehensions lessened, they all went back to berry picking. Eunice was still sniffling a little, but being brave.

Minutes later Jack ran up to me yelling and waving his arms. He had been sitting on the ground, presumably to get at the lower berries on a bush, and had sat on an anthill. Ants were swarming all over him. We took off his clothes and shook them. The ants departed.

Then, with a small harvest and my deflated educational ideas, I repacked our little darlings into the station wagon and we drove off toward home, stopping on the way to buy three quarts of blueberries at a neighborhood store.

I never mentioned picking blueberries again.

Some outings were more successful. We liked family picnics, usually at one of the excellent Cape beaches. The menu tended to become standardized. We filled a big thermos jug with creamed chicken and bought a big container of ice cream at a drugstore on the way, along with a package of crispy cones. We always brought lollipops. And all sorts of fresh fruit. And, as the crowning glory and favorite of all, a chocolate cake: a white cake iced with thick, gooey chocolate frosting.

The most popular dessert was a luscious concoction called Boston cream pie, a light fluffy cake with custard cream in the middle and a firm chocolate frosting on top. These pies were easier to transport than the cakes, since they survived jostling and never ended in a chocolate mess. We always took them on our longer trips. After we moved to Bronxville and had to travel to the Cape and back, a trip that also involved a couple of large automobiles and a long train ride, a Pullman drawing room or two and some aisle space became our temporary home. Rather than go to the dining car it was much more fun for the children if we packed a picnic lunch and spread it out on fold-down tables. The climactic display, the cutting and serving of the Boston cream pies, always anticipated and cheered, helped make our sooty, cindery, often hot and humid trips not only endurable but also memorable. We often served this same confection at home. The children associated it with good times together, and now so does the next generation.

Most of the grandchildren are at Hyannis Port at least for a while each summer. They come and go, in and out of our old house, as informally and freely as their parents did. There are so many now I can't keep track of them. But once or twice a week I have a few over for lunch, in groups of the same age so we can discuss things suitable to their age and experiences—as I did with their parents. Naturally, as I see them sitting there in the dining room, often in the same chairs where long ago their parents sat, I want them to get a little sense of family history, our family life—where they are, where they came from, what it was like, what good times there were. I give them the old reliable menus, the things their parents liked best. Not long ago I had a "t.l." from Jack's little boy, John Jr., who was down to the Cape with his mother and sister, Caroline. Somebody asked him if he liked coming to lunch with me and he said: "Yeah, she has really good food! She has very good creamed chicken and Boston cream pie."

Except for picnics, where informality is half the fun, our family meals were subject to definite rules of procedure. First, everybody should come to the table on time, neither sooner nor later, no nibbling, and no loitering. There were practical reasons for this, one being that in a family of our size, and with increasing numbers of friends and relations and drop-ins, meals really had to be timed with some precision to avoid near chaos, resulting in disgruntled cooks and exhausted kitchen help packing their bags and leaving us to fend for ourselves from the icebox. Second, mealtimes were the only times we had a chance to sit down together and find out what each of us had been doing. Moreover, Joe and I believed strongly that time is a precious commodity. There's only so much of it, never enough to do all the things that need doing. Thus, promptness was a self-evident virtue. "Promptness is a compliment to the intelligent, a rebuke to the stupid."

Our reasoning was so obviously sound that it should have worked to produce the logical result: promptness from all. Alas, this did not turn out to be the case. Again, one of the interesting things about having a large family is the gradual discovery of the various responses the same influences can elicit. Most of our children were reasonably prompt. But among them Jack was generally at the bottom of the class.

We frequently went to a beach club a few miles from Hyannis Port—a station-wagon load of children, ten or a dozen, counting visiting cousins and friends. The rule was to reassemble at the car at twelve forty-five so we could be home for one o'clock lunch. Jack usually was nowhere in sight. So, in an effort to teach him a lesson, I would drive off without him. He always managed to "hook a ride," as he said, with somebody else and would show up cheerfully at the luncheon table ten or fifteen minutes after the rest of us had sat down. By then the first course was gone and we were partly through the second. I had made it quite clear that tardiness meant starting in the middle of the meal—no asking for a first course. Just potluck. Jack knew better than to ask for an exception, so he frequently had a meager lunch.

Afterward, he would slip into the kitchen and charm the cook into filling him up. I knew what he was doing. And he knew that I knew. But I let him get away with it, despite my theoretically inflexible rule, because he was so skinny I felt he needed the nourishment more than the discipline.

If Jack was the worst about remembering to be prompt, I think Bobby was the best. Or at least the most spectacular. While they all knew what was expected of them, Bobby really worked at it.

Perhaps this had something to do with his position among his brothers and sisters. He was the seventh child, which is supposed to be lucky. On the other hand, by then even the most enthusiastic parents may feel less excitement about "another baby." We were all happy he was a boy baby, after four girls. It was wonderful for the girls. And for us. Our next child was our sweet and beautiful daughter Jean. And by the time Teddy arrived in 1932, Bobby was already more than seven years old. So there he was, with two older brothers and one very much younger, none of whom was much use to him as boyhood pals, playmates.

I don't think I worried much about this situation, but I remember my mother did. "He's stuck by himself in a bunch of girls," she would say. "He'll be a sissy."

But of course this didn't happen. He never did become tall but he became strong, muscular, fast—a fine athlete, in fact, a rather famous varsity football player, an end at Harvard. I think this was the result of raw will power. When he was grown up and in politics, reporters wrote about his toughness and said he was ruthless. I think this is mistaken. He was determined, dedicated, loving, and compassionate. He was a thoughtful and considerate person. He always had the capacity, and the desire, to make difficult decisions. Those who loved him saw this in him, and understood. As I did, as we all did. And he was probably the most religious of my sons.

And, as the family knows, Bobby was prompt. Sometimes even to the point of rashness.

Our daughter Pat remembers an episode soon after we moved to Bronxville, New York, into a big house with a lot of rooms and corridors and alcoves, and still weren't quite used to where things were. That was 1929, so Bobby was not quite five years old; but he was already working hard at being dutiful. Pat says:

"There was a large living room, and that's where Bobby was when the call came for supper. We had been brought up to be prompt, *very* prompt—one had to be on time. Dad was extremely punctual, and he said he didn't keep people waiting, so why should others keep him waiting? He really impressed the idea on us. So Bobby was in the living room, and between it and the dining room there was a passageway under a sort of a grand staircase, and in that was a big heavy sheet of glass. I suppose it slid back into a groove in the wall, to join the rooms, but it was closed then. When the call came Bobby took off and ran right into it and smashed it. And the pieces cut his head and he fell down and there was blood all over the place, a horrendous scene. It turned out to be not nearly as serious as it looked, no effects on Bobby after he'd had some stitches taken. And none on me. But I'm always still on time. I guess it's just habit."

Pat collected personal reminiscences from many people about Bobby after his assassination and made a book, *That Shining Hour*— privately printed for our family and friends—from which several exccrpts are adapted here for this book. One is from James Noonan, a good friend of Bobby's at Hyannis Port for many years.

He recalled an episode that matches the one above, at least for eagerness. It was during the summer of 1948—when Bobby was twenty-two—and Bobby stopped by one day and invited him out to crew for him in his fine sailboat, of the class known as a Wianno Senior, "although Bobby knew only too well my knowledge of sailboats was limited.

"As we cruised along, he mentioned that most of his family was at the Cape and that his father had arrived the previous evening. As was the custom, when Mr. Kennedy was at home" (especially then!) "luncheon was served at an appointed time and all members were expected to be prompt. Time slipped by quickly. Bobby realized it was later than he thought. He came about and headed for the 'Compound.' As we approached the shore, to my complete amazement, Bobby stood up and dove into the water. He yelled back that mooring the boat was up to me. *He* was expected to be on time for lunch. In desperation I tried to hail any passing boat. Finally, a power boat came alongside and helped me to a safe mooring. That evening I could hardly wait to tell Bobby of my ordeal. But it was obvious his moments of concern had long passed—*he* had made lunch on time. To him my story was comedy. His reaction was—'Terrific, but we've got to do something about your sailing!' "

We certainly wanted him to be prompt. But not that prompt.

I don't want to give an impression that our lives somehow revolved around meals and mealtimes, but the fact was these were about the only times for Joe and me to talk with the children and, more important we both felt, to encourage them to have their own ideas and learn to speak up for them. I also had a bulletin board someplace the children were sure to see it, which meant a place on their way to meals, and I would clip items from the papers and magazines and pin them up there. The girls and boys who were at the age of reading and reasoning were supposed to read or at least scan these in order to be able to say something about the topics of the day—opinions, comments, questions, objections, or confessions of sheer confusion or bewilderment or disbelief, or at least something about current events during the mealtime conversations. Surprisingly these were spontaneous conversations. They were fun. Yet they were certainly not meant to be pointless chatter, and I led them and popped in questions or made comments according to the flow of talk.

A few examples:

A Florida item could cue me to ask how the state got its name. What does the word mean, what language is it from? Think of Spanish names of towns there. Sarasota, Tampa—no, not Miami, that's Indian. Where else in the country are there a lot of Spanish names? Yes, California. What about San Francisco?—what does that mean, who was it named after? You know about that from church? Think of some other saints' names out there. San Diego, San Gabriel, Santa Barbara. And what about Los Angeles? Do you know how to spell it? L-o-s, meaning "the." And A-n-g-e-l-e-s—what do you suppose that means? And why is our part of the country called New England? Think of English names *in* New England. New Hampshire, New London, New Bedford, Acton.

And they would become very interested in this educational game. At first, some of them wouldn't know many answers. Yet they would the next time the subjects came up.

Easter is coming. Why was the priest wearing those special pink vestments last Sunday? Why do we have Lent? Does Easter come the same time every year? What's the term the Church gives to something that changes like that? It's a "movable feast." How is the date calculated? It's the first Sunday after the first full moon after the vernal equinox. What does "equinox" mean? What does "vernal" mean? The days are getting longer now—why is that? When is the longest day of the year? The shortest? When are daylight and dark exactly even? Why is that?

Or, at Thanksgiving, I would remind them that the Pilgrims came to these shores for religious freedom. They had endured the hardships of a long and slow ocean voyage. And the first Thanksgiving was a celebration of their successful harvest. Plymouth was only a few miles from our home. The children understood the cold winds of the Cape Cod autumn and were, therefore, able to feel the same chill that the Pilgrims felt in the sharp November air.

With our large family there couldn't be family conversations that would interest all the children at the same time. Or older ones would give quick answers and the younger ones would never have a chance. After all, there were seventeen years between the eldest and the youngest; which meant, for example, that by the time Teddy was six and learning to read, Joe Jr. was twenty-three and a Harvard graduate, and more. As the years went along we decided to have two tables and servings. The small table, for the little ones, would be in the nursery or perhaps a breakfast room or alcove; away from the main table. I would sit with them, usually at supper. The conversation would be adjusted to fit.

I would tell them that when they saw a big Christmas tree outdoors in a public square or park or village green, all decorated with lights and ornaments for everyone who passed by to enjoy, *that* idea had begun with their grandfather Fitzgerald. He felt sorry for people who couldn't afford a Christmas tree. Perhaps they didn't have a home, or had to be away from home. So their grandpa had a big tree put up in the middle of Boston Common, a Christmas tree for everyone. And the idea spread, until thousands and thousands of cities and towns and villages all over the country have public Christmas trees every year.

Thus at "the little table" as at "the big table" everyone had the chance to learn and converse at his own level of understanding. Nevertheless, I had to make sure that an older or more mentally agile or more assertive child didn't monopolize a conversation or try to put down the others by interrupting them in an intimidating way. For the silent, it could lead to shyness, diffidence, a sense of inferiority, and self-doubt. The main point of our conversations was to encourage precisely the opposite qualities.

If a child is encouraged to have ideas and speak up for them, with no fear of ridicule, in an atmosphere of mutual respect for others and their ideas, not only are wits sharpened but his confidence grows. So, with practice, does a child's ability to communicate. In my notebook, I have written a notation, "The destiny of the world is shaped by those persons who get their ideas across—for better or for worse."

Later when I heard the children stand up and speak before large audiences—thousands of inquisitive, often skeptical people—and speak well and directly and reasonably, and perhaps have to defend their statements against vigorous challenges from an opponent, as in Jack's televised debates with Nixon in the presidential campaign, I liked to think that those spirited discussions when they were young contributed to their effectiveness.

If children are to develop into effective people the process must begin when they are small. They can't suddenly as teen-agers, for instance, bloom into remarkable conversationalists or speakers or suddenly acquire the mental quickness, emotional poise, and the breadth of knowledge that is needed. It doesn't happen at fourteen or fifteen or sixteen without preparation and effort that begin, at the latest, at age four, five, or six. We've heard a lot from psychologists in the past forty or fifty years about the importance of early childhood influences. In my years as a mother of young children Dr. Freud was only a name to us, and Dr. Spock was a boy.

Bringing up children isn't easy. Mothers get tired, or feel unwell, or become inundated in obligations and demands. Also, children can be uncooperative. Or worse: shirk, interrupt, show off, rebel. Break into arguments among themselves. Punch one another over the table and kick one another under the table. So it isn't now nor was it then as simple as I may make it sound. But almost always there are ways to overcome the problems, and the results are worth the efforts.

I don't want to leave the impression that these mealtime talks were mental drill sessions, because they weren't. There was nothing cut and dried at all. It was spontaneous, natural; there would be mistakes, wild guesses; no one was graded or rated—it was a game. People told jokes, made wisecracks, hurled friendly insults, and hooted and hollered at silly mistakes. They joshed and kidded and made faces and fooled around (within limits) and talked about things that popped into their minds: things that had happened at school, news of friends, opinions, likes and dislikes, a certain amount of chatter and gossip: the stuff of life, well spiced. I enjoyed listening to them talk. I could be sharp with them, I could be quite sharp, but I could laugh with them too, and there was no lack of laughter or fun.

There was another game that I learned from my father and used to spring on them to help them with their arithmetic. I still do it with my grandchildren. My father called it "Examples," and my grandchildren have for some reason decided to call it "Snakes." This is the way it goes. I would say:

"Five times three, add one, divide by four, times eight, take away two, divide by three, divide by two. What's the answer?"

I had so much training from my father in these gymnastics that I could do them as fast as I could say them. Finally, one after another, the children began writing down "Examples" I had given and brought them to me. It was good practice for them: They really learned arithmetic. So this game worked well.

The children don't know this—or won't until they read this page in my book—but when Teddy was just old enough to know arithmetic, around fifth grade or so, I had gone through two of these "Examples" with him and shown him how they worked and what the answers were. The first answer was 4, and the second was 2. I would reel off the numbers to the others, and while they were still groping, Teddy could spring up and say, "That's 4" or "That's 2." They all thought he was amazingly smart at math. He supplied an incentive: They wanted to catch up to the little brother. So that worked very well too.

Nor should anyone think these multiflavored encounters and activities were limited to mealtime. On a trip, the children might form two teams and compete to see who could spot the most animals on either side of the road. (And identify them, and thus learn a little more about animals.) Or there would be guessing games and charades—we always loved those, and Jack usually was the best at them.

If we were passing through a pretty little New England town where so much American history took place, and I happened to know the historical significance of, for example, Salem (witchcraft) or Sandwich (glass), I would bring that up, tell them some interesting facts, quiz them a little, and try to lead them on to think about what they had just seen. I did this for many years and do it still—whenever I get the chance—with my grandchildren.

My daughter-in-law Ethel was asked about her recollections of the first time she met me, her first visit to Hyannis Port. She was Jean's roommate at Manhattanville, a great friend, and that's how she met Bobby and started going with him. They came to Boston—they and a

My father, John Francis Fitzgerald.

My mother, Mary Hannon Fitzgerald.

Joe's father, Patrick J. Kennedy.

Joe's mother, Mary Hickey Kennedy.

Joe, with sister Loretta, 1892.

An early Fitzgerald family photograph. Left to right are Mother, Eunice, Agnes, Father, and I. In front, John F. Jr., and Tom.

JOE AND ROSE ON PICNIC AS CHILDREN

This ___ to of Fitzgerald and Kennedy families and their friends was taken at Old Orchard Beach about ph 895. John F. Fitzgerald is seated on post at left, his daughter, Rose, beside him. Joseph Patrick Kennedy, in plaid blouse and cap, with finger in mouth, is in center of second row beside his aunt, Mrs Katharine Hickey. Behind them, is Joe Kennedy's mother in black silk and Keck and white bonnet. The man in white shirt and cap with heavy mustache, second on Mrs Kennedy's left, is Patrick J. Kennedy, father of the future Ambassador, with his daughter, Joe's sister ___ ld r, Loretta on his knee. She is now Mrs George Connelly of Winthrop. Mrs John F. Fitzger- ___ r on white ___ with sea gull and leg o'mutton sleeves stands by post at extreme right, holding ___ aughte-

Joe and I first met at a family picnic. I am second from the left standing beside my father, who sits on the post. Joe is in the second row center, to the left of his aunt in white dress.

3

My father, the mayor of Boston, presented my high school diploma to me in 1906.

In 1909 I was graduated from Blumenthal. I am in the last row, seventh from the right.

Aboard Sir Thomas Lipton's yacht. Agnes sits below Sir Thomas, I sit beside him.

My father, then mayor of Boston, with President Taft in 1912.

Joe and I are married, 1914.

Joe and I skating, Poland Springs, Maine, 1915.

Rosemary, Jack, Joe Jr., and I, 1919.

Joe and I, Palm Beach, 1925.

few other friends of theirs—and I went up from the Cape with a car and driver to collect them and their baggage. Ethel says:

"It was a big chauffeur-driven limousine, but there were a bunch of us, so the car was crowded. Very, very crowded. And it was raining. That gives the general picture: a pile of kids and luggage, driving for two hours in a closed car on a rainy day. Mrs. Kennedy spent practically the whole ride giving us a history lesson—and she was great. It was October 31, Halloween, so there were jack-o'-lanterns on people's porches and in windows, and that's what started her off. She said, 'Now why do you suppose people have jack-o'-lanterns, how did that custom ever begin?' That led back to All Hallows Eve and witchcraft and all that, and then to the Church and saints' days, and then up into American history and Pilgrims and pumpkins and superstitions and autumn harvest and protect the crops and pumpkin pies and apple cider and . . . anyway, I thought she was fascinating, she knew so much, and twitted us a little if we didn't know perhaps as much as we should've, and she got us all involved and probably all of us did learn something and pretty soon the trip was over and we were at Hyannis Port.

"And I remember arriving at the Cape and going to Jean's room and thinking how everything was so well thought out for the happiness of children and guests. There were fresh flowers. There were interesting books on the bedside table. It was all so comfortable and pleasant and beautifully done—all those niceties that can make life so pleasant. She had thought of them all. Nothing showy, just very nice."

Obviously, I didn't do too much damage to the romance because they were married while Bobby was still in law school. I had misgivings about that. But I have always been glad he married Ethel. She was a wonderful wife to him, and was and is a wonderful mother to their children. Some years after their marriage they bought a house next door to our house at Hyannis Port, and Ethel still comes there every summer, and most of the children are there too for at least part of the time, which is a joy for me.

Everyone knows that reading is the most important instrument of knowledge, so naturally a parent is gratified if a child reads early and enjoys books, and worries if the opposite happens. I was most concerned that my own children learn to read well, enjoy it, and have the right books. When they were preschoolers I read them bedtime stories. A bit later on, when they were sick and needed to stay quiet in bed but also needed some entertainment, I read to them, often hours at a time. And I was careful about the books, selecting them from the P.T.A., Boston Women's Exchange, and library lists for their educational and inspirational values—not only entertainment, but books with useful ideas and artistic design and illustrations. They were never chosen hit or miss.

We also always had a governess who had been a schoolteacher so we were assured she always spoke correct grammar to the children, was well acquainted with literature, had advice about what to read, and was aware of current events.

A good time for the children to read was after lunch. An orthopedic doctor also told me that an after-luncheon rest period is good for growing children and it was quite simple as everyone in the house rested, including my husband and me.

Jack and Bobby, as youngsters, were very different in their reactions to my well-laid plans. Bobby just didn't care about reading. If I gave him books he was likely to skim them and put them aside. I said, "Well, why don't you go to the library and pick out some books for yourself," and with enough urging from me he would; but even then he wouldn't spend much time with them. Yet, in later years, he became an assiduous reader in the fields of law, political science, history, and sociology.

He became a wonderfully well-educated man. He had traveled and seen and learned things for himself, with his own eyes, in his own way, and had developed great intellectual curiosity. He had been swept up in ideals of service and excellence that his father and I had communicated to our family. He had matured, "found himself" and his own goals, and from then on spent his life running hard to achieve them.

On the other hand, Jack was a "natural reader." The fact he was so often sick in bed or convalescing in the house and needed entertainment only encouraged what I think was already a strong natural bent. He gobbled books—not necessarily the ones I had so thoughtfully chosen for him from the P.T.A.- and library-approved lists. When he was little his greatest favorite was a book called *Billy Whiskers*, the fictional adventures of a billy goat, of all things. It seemed to me very, very poorly illustrated, with the pictures in brash flamboyant colors. I wouldn't have allowed it in the house except that my mother had given it to him. Jack adored it. As I recall, Billy married, and he and Mrs. Whiskers had twins—twin "kids"—and the goat family had many adventures in a series of books, all of which Jack found vastly interesting, and I felt were a waste of time. However, one day he came to me to ask, "Mother, where are the Sandwich Islands?" I confessed I didn't know but said I'd find out, as I did, and then showed him in the atlas. "Those are the Sandwich Islands but the name is changed and now we call them the Hawaiian Islands. Why are you interested—are you studying about them at school?" He said, "No, but Billy Whiskers had stopped at the Sandwich Islands on his way across the Pacific." So it is really difficult to predict what may awaken a child's interest and imagination in constructive ways. Billy Whiskers, after all, was teaching him some geography and history; and, in this case, teaching some to me, too.

Another favorite, when he was a small child, was the series of little stories about animals—fictionalized and with a continuing cast of characters with such names as Reddy Fox—mixed up in an endless series of simple, but I guess exciting, adventures. They were written by Thornton Burgess and appeared for many years in the newspapers. Jack never forgot the pleasures he had from them when he was a little boy; and many years later, when he was President, he was delighted to receive from Mr. Burgess, who by then was quite elderly, a specially inscribed copy of *The Adventures of Reddy Fox*.

As he grew older his tastes broadened and began to include a number of the books I thought he should read. He liked stories of adventure and chivalry, such as Sir Walter Scott's *Waverley* novels and biographies of famous or interesting people and, in general, subjects having to do with history, so long as they had flair, action, and color. He had a strong romantic and idealistic streak. In fact, he was inclined to be somewhat of a dreamer. I often had a feeling his mind was only half occupied with the subject at hand, such as doing his arithmetic homework or picking his clothes up off the floor, and the rest of his thoughts were far away weaving daydreams. I was deeply touched but not surprised to learn long years later (after his assassination) that Jackie had taken Camelot as a small, personal, private symbol of their romantic and glorious life together. I remembered him in his boyhood reading and rereading his copy of *King Arthur and the Round Table*.

Many people have asked me about the books he read when he was a boy. With the help of various friends and family members I have been able to put together a list of most of the books for children and young people that we owned as part of our own library. I expect all the nine children read some of them, and some, especially Joe Jr. who loved books, read most of them, but my strong guess is that Jack read almost every one of them. Here is the list, in the same order I had written in my notes:

Arabian Nights
Billy Whiskers series
Kidnapped by Robert Louis Stevenson
Treasure Island by Robert Louis Stevenson
A Child's Garden of Verses by Robert Louis Stevenson
King Arthur and the Round Table by A. M. Hadfield
Lays of Ancient Rome by Thomas Macauley
The Jungle Book by Rudyard Kipling
Kim by Rudyard Kipling
Bambi by Felix Salten
Uncle Tom's Cabin by Harriet Beecher Stowe
Peter Pan by J. M. Barrie
Black Beauty by Anna Sewell
Story of a Bad Boy by Thomas B. Aldrich
Wing and Wing by James Fenimore Cooper
Biography of a Grizzly by Ernest T. Seton
At the Back of the North Wind by George MacDonald
Pilgrim's Progress by John Bunyan
Wonder Tales From East and West, Introduction by Maud
    Wilder Goodwin

There were others, I'm sure, and books borrowed from friends and libraries, and story books and history books and others that were part of school instruction, but these are enough to give the general flavor. Some of them are still there at the Beals Street house, others are in his presidential archives at Harvard, and others have been passed on to the various grandchildren, as I'm sure a great many parents do if the books happen to survive. I know that Caroline and John Jr. have several of Jack's favorites.

With reading aptitudes and skills and enjoyment there would come, I fondly supposed, both facility in using words properly and effectively and mastery of the essential mechanics of written expression: grammar, penmanship, spelling. After all, any good craftsman respects and relies on his tools, the farmer or fisherman or carpenter or writer, as I pointed out to them. So if they wanted to write such things as they would want to read they must master the tools.

To my distress, most of them seemed to be afflicted with deafness about the proper uses of "who" and "whom," "I" and "me," "shall" and "will," "may" and "can." They split infinitives with abandon, and put in commas or left them out as the spirit (an evil spirit) moved them, and they ended sentences with prepositions. Eventually, with continual reminders and repeated explanations of the really very simple rules governing these matters, they did absorb proper usage, and in later years some of them went on to become extraordinarily good writers. Bobby's mature writings, for instance, were admired for their fluency, force, and precision of meaning. There are scholars who have ranked Jack as one of the masters of modern prose.

Here, line for line, is a letter he wrote to his father. It is undated, but I think he must have been about ten years old:

A Plea for a raise
by Jack Kennedy
Dedicated to my
Mr. J. P. Kennedy

Chapter I
   My recent allowance
is 40¢. This I used for areoplanes
and other playthings of childhood but now I am a scout
and I put away my childish

things. Before I would spend
20¢ of my ¢.40 allowance
and In five minutes I
would have empty pockets
and nothing to gain and
20¢ to lose. When I am
a scout I have to buy
canteens, haversacks, blankets
searchliagts ponchos things
that will last for years
and I can always use it
while I cant use a
chocolate marshmellow
sunday with vanilla ice
cream and so I put in
my plea for a raise of
thirty cents for me to buy
scout things and pay my
own way more around.
                    Finis
          John Fitzgerald Francis
                    Kennedy

I should add a couple of notes about this letter. I don't know why he included "Francis" in his signature. Perhaps it was to invoke the blessing and help of that gentle saint.

His father, after brief deliberation and consultation with me—since I was the one who handed out the allowance money to them once a week—granted the raise. So Jack didn't have to write a "Chapter II."

Clearly, we did keep a close rein on their finances. And that, too, was part of their education. We wanted them to know the value of money, the foolishness of squandering it, and the painful consequences of heedless extravagance—as painful, let us say, as not knowing at age five where your next gumdrop is coming from. As I mentioned earlier, that was the age at which they began receiving weekly allowances of ten cents. Usually their first thought was of the candy store. At Hyannis Port, two short blocks from our house, there was a tiny "variety store" with a rather amazing variety of goods, including a rich, colorful, tantalizing assortment of penny candies. There would be a temptation to spend the whole dime at a swoop—but that would not leave the penny or two that ought to go in the bank for Christmas shopping. Then, whatever the amount bought, the temptation to gobble it all up in the first few days, leaving nothing but sorrow and regrets for the rest of the week until next allowance day.

This was fully as important for the girls, I felt, as it was for the boys; for, after all, when girls grow up and marry it is ordinarily they who actually spend most of the family income on food, clothing, and other necessities. They have to know how to budget, keep track of the dollars, how not to waste. I have always felt sorry for a couple when the wife is heedless about money, piling up bills, forcing the husband into debt or to work harder and harder to provide the means. It must be very disappointing and discouraging if he finds he has to follow her around pointing out unnecessary expenses. Constant argument about money leads to all kinds of other quarrels and difficulties; and, as I have often read, this is one of the most common roots of marital discord and thus of a great many broken marriages.

We followed the same principle in our Christmas, birthday, and other special-occasion gifts to them. When they were little they had their share of the things children like: the dolls and gocarts, the train sets and cap pistols, the parcheesi games and wind-up cars and stuffed animal toys and the rest that most parents want to give and manage to afford. But we made it a point that these were not particularly expensive, just the normal toys, and that they came only a few at a time. None of those elaborate crisscrossing toy railway systems full of switches and semaphores that fill a big table, and no menageries of stuffed toy animals that fill a closet or a couch. Galsworthy said, "Variety of choices leads to confusion of the mind," which I think is likely to be true in adulthood as well as childhood. People need some simple certainties in their lives, more solutions and fewer problems.

As a general guideline in all such matters—allowances, gifts, perquisites and privileges, clothes, and, in due course, clubs, boats, cars, travels, and other things involving a degree of mature responsibility—we wanted the children to have whatever was needed for them to fit in normally, naturally, easily with their environment. As the environment changed, so did the needs. It is a long distance in more ways than one from Beals Street, Brookline, to Ocean Boulevard, Palm Beach.

Within the family, we didn't talk about money. It wasn't a forbidden subject, but simply didn't meet the criterion that if you want to talk, have something interesting to others to talk about. If you need or deeply want something special then discuss this privately with your father or me. We wanted them to learn the value of work, of efforts and rewards, and to respect it for its own sake—the idea of "the dignity of work."

Bobby had a paper route. That pleased us, of course. The "paper boy" is practically an American symbol of boyhood spunk and ambition. Then, after a while, I found he had talked the chauffeur into driving him. There he was, riding around all over Bronxville—making his deliveries from a Rolls-Royce. Needless to say I put a stop to this at once. Shortly afterward something interfered, perhaps he came down with summer flu, and Bobby was out of the newspaper-delivery business.

When some of the children went into politics and public life, it was said that their father was spreading around his money and influence and had more or less bought and paid for their successes. This was rubbish. When the children were growing up, they neither had nor expected any privileges whatever. They lived at the level of their "peer groups." Being intelligent and observant they realized at some point in their maturation that although we lived on a lower scale than some families we lived on a higher one than others, and they realized that was because their father was successful at his work. They knew as they grew older what this work was. They did know, for a period of years, that some of his work had something to do with the movies, because there was visible evidence.

When he came home from his trips to Hollywood he brought souvenirs or mementos. One time, I remember, he came back with "Tom Mix" cowboy outfits for Joe Jr. and Jack. Anyone old enough to remember Tom Mix can understand what a sensation those caused with the boys and among their friends.

Gloria Swanson was our house guest for a couple of days in Bronxville and brought along her small daughter, who was about the age of our Pat, who was about ten. The two got along well together, and Pat took her down to show her the Bronxville public school and meet her classmates and perhaps show off a little, as she did by introducing her as "Gloria Swanson's daughter." Nobody believed her. They all just grinned, thinking it was a joke. After all, Gloria Swanson was, to them, practically a supernatural being, so she wouldn't be in Bronxville and wouldn't have a daughter, and Pat was just doing some silly spoofing. I can't recall the exact details but I do remember how completely indignant Pat was when she and Gloria's little girl came home and told us.

At Hyannis Port, in what used to be part of the basement, we installed a little theater, which still exists much as it was. I do mean "little": fixed chairs—the old-fashioned kind with iron legs and fold-up-down wooden seats—for an audience of about two dozen, with space for others to sit or recline on the steps and sidelines, maximum uncomfortable capacity for a hit show on a wet night for as many as forty or, with standees jammed in shoulder to shoulder, for a super-hit, maybe even fifty. It had a little stage for the children's theatrical productions, but primarily it was a movie theater. Because of Joe's position in the industry he was able to borrow practically any film from practically any studio, which of course was useful to him as an exhibitor and producer, but which also gave us an inexhaustible supply of home entertainment. Naturally, anything shown for our young audience was recommended or checked by someone in advance as being suitable for family viewing. If there was a slip-up and the plot became lurid, the projector was switched off and the audience was sent out. But that seldom happened. Consequently, our summers at Hyannis Port took on something of the character of a modern movie festival, with a different film shown three or four evenings a week. Everyone in the house, including the staff, was invited, and almost always the children would have some of their friends over too, so there was always a large, appreciative audience.

Well, now, obviously not everybody in the world has two very nice houses, a couple of boats, a tennis court, a swimming pool, and a Rolls-Royce or two in the family. The children realized their father enabled us to afford all this. But they had no real idea that their father was "a rich man" and that we were "a rich family" until Joe entered politics and public life.

That began in 1931, when he became one of Franklin D. Roosevelt's strongest supporters and chief advisers in the campaign for the Democratic nomination and the presidency. Thus, he was suddenly in the national limelight and the press took an interest in him.

He was already something of a celebrity in the movie industry and the stock market, but the stories about him usually appeared in trade journals or on the financial pages and dealt with specific deals or operations in which he happened to be involved. Now the political reporters got to work on him and raked up all sorts of information from all quarters and put it into news and feature stories—especially, of course, in the Boston papers. Usually there was mention of his wealth. He was "Movie mogul and stock market operator Joseph P. Kennedy."

Thus, the time came when we had to tell the children that their father was well to do. We were careful to emphasize that money brought responsibility. I used to quote from St. Luke to the children, "To whom much has been given, much will be required." Money is never to be squandered or spent ostentatiously. Some of the greatest people in history have lived lives of the greatest simplicity. Remember, it's the you inside that counts. Money doesn't give you any license to relax. It gives an opportunity to use all your abilities, free of financial worries, to go forward, and to use your superior advantages and talents to help others—at school, in the neighborhood, and later in working for social gains in the community and in government.

Once again in that spectrum of attitudes, undoubtedly Jack held the championship. The others offered challenges, but he was beyond reach. For example, Jack might be traveling around someplace and have no money with him. He had simply forgotten to bring any. It hadn't occurred to him. Several of his old friends—friends during his grown-up years—have remarked about this. They would be having lunch together, let's say, and when the time came to pay the check Jack would fumble around and then say with an apologetic smile that he hadn't any money along to pay his share, so would the other person take care of it and he'd square accounts later. His attitudes about dress and appearance were apt to be equally offhand. We have a snapshot of him at the time he graduated from Harvard, in his black academic gown, with a suitably serious expression, but with his feet in a pair of worn brown-and-white saddle shoes, reproduced in this book.

While I didn't mind him and the others dressing like roughnecks for play I did want them all to look brushed and neat at school, church, and in public. I bought them good clothes, and very often dressed them alike when they were children: There would be identical sailor suits, which were the fashion, for Joe Jr. and Jack, and identical middy blouses and skirts for Rosemary, Kathleen, Eunice, and Pat, in descending sizes. On school days I was always with them at breakfast, partly to be sure they were properly groomed and dressed. On Sundays before church I would be at the foot of the stairs to inspect them as they came down, making sure they had their prayer books and rosaries.

As Joe Jr. and Jack often had similar outfits, it would happen from time to time that Jack would absent-mindedly help himself to Joe Jr.'s clothes, even though they were too big for him.

Joe Jr.'s temperament was different from Jack's in many ways, one of which was a better defined sense of neatness and order. Another was a strong sense of ownership and responsibility for his personal possessions. A third was that Joe Jr. had a quick temper. The consequences were predictable. There were times when I had to pry them apart.

Being brothers and less than two years apart in age had its advantages and its disadvantages. Generally, they were good pals and playmates and shared all sorts of experiences and adventures together, including getting into mischief. But I suppose it was inevitable that they were also rivals. With their different temperaments, this brought flare-ups that included personal combat.

I remember, for instance, one time when they were very young and sitting across from each other at their little table in the dining room at Beals Street, with Joe and me at the big table, and suddenly there was an awful outcry which brought us to our feet. Once we sorted things out we discovered what had happened: It was dessert time, we had one of those favorite cakes with the rich gooey chocolate icing, and Joe Jr. had taken off the top icing of his piece and put it aside to save for last. When he wasn't looking, Jack reached over and took it and gobbled it down. Joe Jr. gave him a whack, and Jack let out a big yell and hit back. Joe and I spoke sternly to both and sent them off to bed.

Did justice triumph? The punishment is supposed to fit the crime. Was it worse for Jack to have stolen his brother's chocolate icing or for Joe Jr. to have given his brother an angry punch? And if assault and battery are more serious than petty theft, should Joe Jr. actually have been punished more severely than Jack, even though Jack had provoked him? I'm sure that throughout history mothers have faced similar conundrums and have puzzled over the right answer.

In any event, during the earlier years of their boyhood there were fights, few of which I saw but some of which I have been told were real battles. Joe Jr. was older, bigger, stronger, but Jack, frail though he was, could fight like fury when he had to. He had wonderful physical coordination. Thankfully, they probably fought no more than other brothers so close in age do and, in fact, possibly less.

On one occasion, when they had brand-new, matching bathing suits, Jack, by mistake, put on Joe Jr.'s. Joe Jr. was furious. I quieted him and assured him that it would *never* happen again. Four days later, however, Jack made the same terrible mistake. Joe Jr., this time, was up in arms.

I was out at the time, so I didn't witness the scene, but I learned that Joe Jr. exploded and took off after his brother. Jack looked back over his shoulder momentarily and then sensibly took flight, across the lawn, through the marsh, and down the beach. He then ran along the old breakwater.

Joe Jr. was gaining on him when, thank goodness, Eddie Moore arrived on the scene. He realized instantly that Jack had done something wrong and Joe Jr. was chasing him for it, but this time the situation could be dangerous. He shouted: "Stop that! You two get yourselves back here! Right now!" They did, but it chilled me to think what could have happened if Eddie hadn't turned up at the right time. I daresay Jack thought about it, too.

The friendly enmity between those two veered this way and that during their childhood and early youth. But as the years went on their affection and understanding for each other deepened, and in maturity, as young men, they had a very deep bond—tacit but evident —of love, loyalty, and confidence.

After Joe Jr.'s death, Jack made a collection of essays about him, by people who had known him well. They were privately printed for family and friends in a book titled *As We Remember Joe.* Jack began the foreword, saying: "My only hesitancy in collecting these essays was that I doubted that Joe, if he had had a voice in it, would have approved. But I have disagreed with him before, so here they go." Jack himself wrote the first essay in the book. He headed it simply "My Brother Joe," and wrote, in part:

"Joe did many things well, but I have always felt that he achieved his greatest success as the oldest brother. Very early in life he acquired a sense of responsibility towards his brothers and sisters, and I do not think that he ever forgot it. Towards me, who was nearly his own age, this responsibility consisted in setting a standard that was uniformly high. I suppose I knew Joe as well as anyone and yet, I sometimes wonder whether I ever really knew him. He had always a slight detachment from things around him—a wall of reserve which few people ever succeeded in penetrating. I do not mean by this that Joe was ponderous and heavy in his attitude. Far from it—I do not know anyone with whom I would rather have spent an evening or played golf or, in fact, done anything. He had a keen wit and saw the humorous side of people and situations quicker than anyone I have ever known. He made friends with admirable ease, and wherever he went, his popularity was assured.

"He would spend long hours throwing a football with Bobby, swimming with Teddy, and teaching the younger girls how to sail. He was always close to Kick" (our family nickname for Kathleen) "and was particularly close to her during some difficult times. I think that if the Kennedy children amount to anything now, or ever amount to anything, it will be due more to Joe's behavior and his constant example than to any other factor. He made the task of bringing up a large family immeasurably easier for my father and mother, for what they taught him he passed on to us, and their teachings were not diluted through him, but rather strengthened."

Jack was being modest about his own contributions. He did his share of pitching footballs and teaching sailing and swimming, and other activities were projections of his own interests and personality. His love of reading, his fascination with history and great events, and his rather romantic approach to life impressed his brothers and sisters. The open, friendly, disarming, and wholly charming way he had about him helped form that unique quality he had when he was President that has been called "a special grace."

Eunice says:

"I'm sure it's normal for girls to look up to older brothers with some admiration and sense of dazzlement, but in our case it was fairly extreme. To us they were marvelous creatures, practically God-like, and we yearned to please them and be acceptable. Not that any of us would necessarily show it in any overt way, and nothing sugary, which would have turned them off and wasn't our style anyway. But we had this great feeling about them—as they did about us—as we all did about one another—and part of it was that they were such fun to be with. They treated us in a loving but offhand way, occasionally sternly bawling us out, but most of the time considerately and humorously, and affectionately."

In later years people remarked about the unity of the family, the close bonds of loyalty and faith among the members and their spontaneous understanding of each other. There was talk of "the Kennedy clan," a term I dislike. The idea of "clannishness" has, for me, connotations of narrowness, exclusivity, and suspicious rejection of other people and indifference to their interests. This is diametrically opposed to the ideals of our family, and those which they brought with them into public life. I can see one merit in the expression, however: In a clan there is a pervading body of common beliefs, customs, modes of acceptable behavior, community of interest and purpose, so that members know what to do without having to ask or explain themselves to one another. And, in truth, this fairly describes our family.

For parents who have or expect to have a sizable family, my strong advice would be to work hardest on the eldest, for in the direction they go the others are likely to follow. Children are naturally imitative, and although at first they tend to imitate their parents' examples, as the years pass they tend to imitate those set by older children, especially those in the family. And the elder ones, in my experience and in my observations of other families, enjoy the responsibility of setting an example, of correcting missteps, of deserving the confidence of the parents and the respect of the younger ones.

Indeed, if they are properly encouraged to take an interest they will begin taking over functions that in a small family might be thought of as parental—and do so not only willingly but in many instances more effectively than the parents themselves could. If one of the girls, say, at age seventeen was using too much lipstick and I spoke to one of her older brothers and had him express his disapproval to her, she was sure to listen. Or, again, if she was going out with a beau of the wrong sort, some remarks from a big brother would be a hundred times more effective than a speech from us.

This also applied to the boys. Bobby wanted to be like his two big brothers and strove with all his might and main to be. And the three of them profoundly influenced Teddy.

I haven't said much about Teddy so far in these pages, for the reason that until quite late in the period I have been describing he hadn't been born. He arrived on February 22, 1932. With my own July 22 (1890) birth date, I was exactly forty-one and a half at the time.

After Bobby was born in 1925, some of my best friends had begun indicating delicately but unmistakably that he should be the last one. When Jean, our eighth, arrived, the broad hints turned to admonitions.

And if I was with new acquaintances and they learned I had eight children they tended to regard this as a phenomenon and wanted to discuss it with me.

Finally, I evolved a stratagem. If a conversation turned toward family and children I would quickly ask if the person had children and, if so, what ages they were. Usually I would be able to say I had children of just about those same ages, and at those ages—say, of five or ten or fifteen—children are fascinating. Then I'd change the subject.

Mary Sanford is an old and close friend of mine who was also a friend of Joe's—she was Mary Duncan of the movies before she married "Laddie" Sanford, the great polo player and racing stable owner —and who for many years lived down the road from us at Palm Beach. She was saying some things about me, bringing back some memories for this book, not long ago, and said:

"She used to go to the polo games with me. Laddie was playing a lot of polo, and Joe Kennedy wasn't so famous then, and this must have been at least forty years ago when she had all those children, you know. And I would take a delight in introducing her to someone and then mentioning she has eight children, or whatever she had at the time, because she always looked like a young girl. She's always had a beautiful figure. I never happened to see her when she was large with child: I suppose she must have put on weight then. Anyway, she would say, 'Mary, please don't talk about how many children I have.' And I said, 'Why not? I think it's so fabulous because you look like such a young girl and you have all these children.' She said, 'Thank you, but . . . it makes me . . . well, just don't do it, don't bring that up.'"

Then I learned I was to have another baby.

So I made a firm resolution that this was not going to be any disadvantage to me or to the baby. None, none whatsoever. The baby, boy or girl, would always know it was a welcome and cherished member of our family, always feel loved, and would grow up knowing the profound meaning of love: in joy and confident service and happy relationships with others.

When Teddy was born I went out of my way to make sure that these resolutions—for me and for him—were kept in every way I could do so.

There were many factors that counted in the formation of his special character and personality. During Teddy's later boyhood and his youth he was more exposed to his father's direct and frequent hearth-and-home influence than his older brothers had been. This was a great source of inspiration and strength. I suppose the fact that he was the little brother of them all got him more attention— and affectionate indulgence—than the older ones would have been inclined to give one another. I expect if the next elder had been a brother there would have been rivalry. Girls, however, tend to be protectively fond of little brothers. Pat had a special empathy with

Bobby. Jean has always had a special relationship with Teddy. They were a pair; they trotted around together; she sometimes admonished him and sometimes scrapped with him but mainly was his valiant friend and big sister, as she still is, though he is now nearly twice as big as she is. They shared a lot, including a quirky sense of humor. When they were teen-agers we sent them on a trip to Europe together—taking care of each other—but with a scolding note saying they had been spending too much money and should be more careful. From London we had a cablegram, which I'm sure they worked out together: "After reading your letter I decided to travel tourist and I put Jean in my duffel bag. Lucky no one weighed the duffel bag. [Signed] Teddy." Which reminds me of another we had from Teddy from the Riviera: "Having barrels of fun. Send more money for more barrels."

When Teddy was about six, he came to me one day with a solemn request. Could he please punch a schoolmate named Cecil? Asked why, he explained: "Well, he's been hitting me every day, and you tell me I can't get into fights because Dad is the ambassador." The request was taken up at the dinner table, and after some discussion the ambassador gave Teddy permission to fight back without fear of causing an international incident.

Teddy always was big and strong for his years. Who knows where this came from? There were athletes on both sides of the family. From someplace in his ancestry, no doubt on both sides, Teddy got the right genes to give him all the physical attributes a boy needs to excel at sports and the spirit to go with them.

His father was, of course, delighted. His older brothers were, of course, delighted too, as well as amazed, amused, and challenging. This was fine, provided the little brother could respond and live up to the challenges. Teddy could and did, or at least he always tried his best. Sometimes at the risk of life and limb.

I remember an incident on the Riviera at Eden Roc, a beautiful hotel with grounds that end abruptly on a twenty- or thirty-foot cliff with the Mediterranean below. The water below is deep, so it is a great place for high diving, provided one knows how to do it. And I remember Teddy up there on the cliff and Joe Jr. and sometimes Jack yelling up to him to jump in. And he did. To my consternation and concern he kept doing it, egged on with great applause. I didn't interfere because the big brothers wouldn't be putting him up to it unless it were safe. And he seemed to be having a great time. I think he had confidence in Joe Jr.'s confidence in him. And that is something I did not want to disturb by being a solicitous mother.

I knew each of them would have to work things out for himself, and each would need all the pluck and experience that circumstances could provide. There are, therefore, risks that a parent must take, nervous though some may make one feel.

Eunice was recently talking about the differences among the boys. She said:

"Teddy had a different physical constitution from Jack. He's always had enormous physical energy. He could do all the sports and do them well. Jack was, in a sense, envious of that. Or 'envious' would not be the right word—more like 'admiring,' and because Jack was so much older and Teddy wanted his admiration it made him more, say, extroverted and more interested in doing all those things Jack wished he could do, but couldn't because he had an injured back. In a sense, Jack did the best on all the intellectual things and sort of monopolized them, and so the younger boys looked for something a little bit different. Probably all of them were more or less equally bright. I've never understood why one child will develop in a certain way and another quite differently. Mother treated us all the same. She did not play favorites."

Teddy's brothers and sisters took care to build his character. Here is the best piece of direct evidence imaginable, which I am taking verbatim from Jack's book of essays about Joe Jr. The first lines, those in italics, are Jack's introduction to the essay by Teddy (age twelve), which then follows.

"*One day last fall, Eunice and I were discussing this book when Teddy interrupted and said that he wanted to write about Joe, too. Eunice started to explain how Teddy should write and tell 'how wonderful and strong and calm' Joe was, when Teddy burst in with, 'But he wasn't calm; he threw me in the ocean.' So I told him to go ahead and write about that, and here it is with capitals and periods falling where they may, just as Teddy wrote it.*"

"I recall the day the year before we went to England. It was in the summer and I asked Joe if I could race with him. He agreed to this so we started down to the pier, about five minutes before the race.

"We had our sails up just as the gun went for the start. This was the first race I had ever been in. We were going along very nicely when he suddenly told me to pull in the jib. I had know Idea what he was talking about. He repeated the command again, a little louder tone, meanwhile we were slowly getting further and further away from the other boats. Joe suddenly leaped up and crabed the jib. I was a little scared, but suddenly he zeized me by the pant and through me into the cold water.

"I was scared to death practully. I then heard a spash and I felt his hand grab my shirt and then he lifted me into the boat. We continued the race and came in second. On the way home from the pier, he told me to be quiet about what happened in that afternoon. One falt Joe had was he got very easily mad in a race as you have witnessed. But he always menat well and was a very good sailor and swimmer."

Teddy had a wonderful sense of humor. In our family solemnity would have been intolerable. We were serious about serious things, but we liked laughing at things that weren't, including, sometimes, some of our own foibles. Humor is a necessary part of wisdom; it gives perspective; it frees the spirit. Here is a verbatim letter from Teddy to his father.

"Dear Daddy,
"I have been to the Worlds Fair today with jimmy Murphy. I went into the swimming pool with my clothes on but the pool was empty.
Write to me soon.

"Love fram
"Teddy"

Speaking of Teddy's boyhood leads me to his first cousin, Joey Gargan, my sister Agnes' son. During most of the summers of boyhood and youth they were together at Hyannis Port and became such great pals and inseparable companions, sharing all sorts of adventures together. We were so glad to have Joey with us, as he was a wonderful pal of Ted's. Ted had no brother near his own age.

Bobby was seven years older and was advanced in sailing, tennis, and football. So Joey found a warm welcome with us.

Agnes had married Joseph F. Gargan, originally of a Lowell, Massachusetts, family. He had graduated from Notre Dame, had been a captain in the Marine Corps, had returned for a law degree, and by 1929 was a lawyer practicing in New York City. By Agnes' choice their wedding was a private ceremony, as mine and Joe's had been. I was her only attendant. It was a fine, happy marriage, soon blessed with three children: Joseph Jr., "Joey," Mary Jo, and Ann. They were still very young when Agnes died suddenly in 1936.

Along with my deep feeling of personal loss, I was concerned about her children, knowing how the thought of leaving them would have grieved her.

There were many letters of condolence, all of them appreciated beyond measure, but perhaps they can be represented by one that came from the president of my alma mater, the College of the Sacred Heart at Manhattanville. Reverend Mother Donnalley wrote:

". . . May God comfort you . . . I know how much your faith sustains you at this moment. How do those bear sorrow who have not that hope? I remember dear Agnes as such a charming, lovable, beautiful character. God is rewarding her now with unlimited joy for all she did for Him during her full life and she will watch over and protect from Heaven those poor little children who cannot have her visible care."

One of the benefits of being in a large family is that in tragedy there are always many people who care deeply and can be counted on to rally to do whatever must be done.

My husband and I took the children into our home. After many consultations with their father and the relatives, it was decided, because my husband had become a high official of the Roosevelt administration and trouble shooter for the President, making our own family plans unpredictable, that the children should live in Lowell with their father's brother and his wife. But, of course, the rest of us continued to have them in our thoughts and to do everything possible for them. In the years following, as Joey, and Mary Jo and Ann grew older they began to spend summers and some of their school vacations with us. This lasted many years, and in a real sense they became members of our own family.

Although I have said a good deal about education, I am far from finished with the topic. For I feel it has meant not only the formal categories of knowledge—history, literature, grammar, and the rest —but also education in the simple social graces. On the subject of good manners, the children were taught to speak politely to the servants, not to yell at them. For instance, they were to ask the chauffeur when it was feasible to take them into the village, not to demand that he drop everything and take them. I also stressed that punctuality was important and that first impressions are highly so.

I was just as rigorous with Joey Gargan in such matters as I was with his pal Teddy—and with all the others—and a few decades later he has recalled:

"Aunt Rose wasn't severe with us but she certainly, almost constantly, supervised us. Appearance and conduct. Don't wear white socks with dress suit. Wear dark shoes with blue or gray suit, not brown shoes. Suit sleeves short enough so shirt cuff hangs below suit sleeve one inch. Don't say 'Hi' to people when addressing them, but particularly don't use it when greeting Cardinal Cushing, James Forrestal, Arthur Krock, or the like.

"We got the natural instructions at the dinner table about good table manners in eating, and right forks and so forth and deportment, such as proper seating and 'ladies first.' That reminds me of a classic scene with Aunt Rose and Jack.

"They had a wonderful relationship, but at the same time they were often in a way at cross purposes so far as household disciplines were concerned because he didn't fit into them too well. Aunt Rose, for instance, would always be seated at the far end of the table. And, of course, the idea was, when a meal was over, the ladies and particularly Aunt Rose were to leave the dining room first. That was good manners. But very often Jack would forget. He would have been having an interesting conversation, or his mind was on something else, or someway he would unintentionally forget the order of departure. This happened so often that when a meal was over Aunt Rose would start quickly for the door. And then, quite clearly, it could be a race between her and Jack as to who was going to make it.

And she would frequently mention this to Jack and he would say, 'Oh, yes, Mother, I'm sorry'—and they would both kind of chuckle —but a couple of days later it would happen again. The rest of us all knew what was likely so we would sort of stand by our chairs or move toward the door slowly—to give her a chance to get out first."

I remember those episodes quite well. Joey is telling the truth. One thing he hasn't mentioned is that during those Hyannis Port summers I chased him around a lot making *him* behave. He goes on to say:

"She was always very much aware of where we were going and what our activities were, whether going to a movie on a rainy day down at Hyannis (we rode our bikes, about three miles each way, and we were given just the price of admission, no extras) or going out in a boat— particularly the boat or anything to do with the water. If we were sailing she wanted to know where we planned to be, what time we were coming back, and we were always to watch the flagpole in front of the house. If she wanted us to come in for some reason she'd take the flag down and that was her signal. Sometimes she'd ask Wilbert, the gardener-caretaker, to handle this, but if he wasn't in sight she'd just do it herself. Ropes and pulleys didn't faze her. She was especially concerned to know if we were taking any other children with us and, if so, who they were and did their parents know—so that the parents wouldn't miss them and start wondering and worrying about them. She was *very* conscious, always very aware and considerate, about the feelings of other parents, and she was in touch with them about all the activities of our group of friends. When we were older and going to dances and driving cars, she had to know the names and addresses of our dates—just so she could be in touch with the parents in case of any problems that could involve not getting the girls home on time. The club dances ended at midnight in those days. We were supposed to take our dates directly home and be back at the house ourselves about twelve-thirty. And if we missed by more than ten minutes or so, we'd hear about it from her the next morning. That went on until we were well up into our late teens."

I have always been a rather light sleeper, so I would hear them when they came into the driveway and put the cars away in the parking space in back of the house. If they were later than they should have been they drove in very slowly, with the least possible noise, turning the headlights off, and careful not to slam the car doors or the back door of the house. They would take their shoes off and sneak upstairs in the dark to their rooms. But I knew what was happening. I asked Pat to keep vigil one night, but she fell asleep herself.

Joey's sister Mary Jo says:

"The rules were a little different for the girls than for the boys. If I stayed out an extra fifteen minutes I could expect to see Aunt Rose looking for me. And that is the absolute truth. She had a little blue car—and she'd come looking. We'd always have told her where we planned to be, and there wasn't much of any place to go anyway. We could be at the golf club or down by the post office and variety store. But if we weren't home on time she'd come out and find us and say, 'Dear, it's time to come home,' and home we'd go. And everyone recognized her headlights on the little blue car and knew she was coming. She was, for us, even then a very strong personality. I think she knew us all very well—she had had an awful lot of experience raising children.

"But I can't ever remember her putting anybody down. That was one of my biggest memories of her about raising children. She probably would remind you of what you had done wrong. If I was late or something, and she had gone out after one of us, there'd be a note on that person's pillow: 'The next time be sure to be in on time.' She made herself clear and that was it: You were never chewed out. And over a period of time, this method really worked, it got to you.

"After I stayed awhile there at Hyannis Port with her and Uncle Joe I became very close to her, because I liked her very much. And loved her, really. And I think that when you feel that way about somebody, you don't—even if you're quite young—want to hurt them by doing things they would consider wrong. And this was especially so with Aunt Rose. There's something about her. She believes in people. You just didn't want to do anything to disturb her or make her upset. If she said, 'This is the way I think you should do it,' you probably would find yourself thinking, well, I would kind of like to do it that way. And usually it did turn out her way was the best in the end."

I sent Mary Jo to the Convent of the Sacred Heart, where I had been a pupil, and she graduated from Manhattanville, as had my daughters. Joey was sent to Notre Dame, where his father had studied. Later, my husband arranged for all our nieces and nephews —forty-five of them by now—to receive college expenses. It has been a pleasure that all of them have responded so willingly and with appreciation.

I do think that a parent who has a child's love and confidence has the most effective of all instruments, in the long run, for shaping character and good behavior. But there are times when even they are not enough, particularly when children are very young and their physical safety depends on learning certain lessons soon and clearly. For instance, if I found a child playing with my sharp scissors I would take them away, explain how dangerous they could be and then, to make this immediately clear, stick the points against a finger or arm just enough for him to feel some pain and to understand. Or, again, if I found him too near a hot stove I would hold one of his fingers close enough to the flame or the oven door for him to feel the heat uncomfortably, and thus realize what it could mean for him if he weren't careful.

People have asked me if I ever spanked Jack when he was a boy. I suppose it is part of the mystique surrounding the presidency that anyone who occupies the office is endowed with qualities that are extraordinary and he must have passed through childhood in a glow of virtue. I can state that this was not the case with Jack, nor was it with Bobby or Teddy or any of the others, and whenever they needed it they got a good old-fashioned spanking, which I believe is one of the most effective means of instruction.

I should add that if a spanking is necessary it ought to be a parent —not a baby-sitter or nursemaid—who gives it. Since Joe was away from the house much of the time that duty fell to me. And I saw it as a duty, never to be done in anger or a fit of irritability. I also believe that physical punishment should not be the first choice of instruction but the last. Nevertheless, there are times and situations in which some solid whacks may be the only thing a very young child understands.

I kept a ruler in my desk and used it for measuring out punishments. After a few times of being whacked on the hand or the britches, the mere mention of the ruler would have a healthy effect on a child's behavior. Since justice should be both sure and swift, fairly often I didn't even wait to get to the desk but took the nearest thing at hand, which was likely to be a wooden coat hanger. With our big family there had to be a lot of clothes and therefore of closets and hangers—they were always within reach. A hanger didn't hurt any more—probably less—than a ruler, but it is a rather unusual implement for this purpose, and as adults the children have liked to rag me about how "cruel" I was to "beat" them with coat hangers. (They weren't beaten, they were spanked—just hard enough to receive the message.) The coat hangers have become a part of our family lore. When Eunice was having her fifth child some few years ago I went down to help with her other children and the household while she was in the hospital, and I found that my reputation had preceded me. Her boys had taken all the coat hangers in the house and put them down the laundry chute. It may have been a joke, but I've never been too sure.

In any case, when my children were grown up and married and faced with their own problems of child raising, they accepted the idea of corporal punishment with perfect equanimity. Teddy says:

"One of my memories of when we lived in Bronxville was walking home one day from kindergarten, which I wasn't supposed to do, and getting spanked by Mother. There was always someone to meet me in a car and bring me home, and Mother's point was that the person wouldn't know where I was and she wouldn't either—and something might have happened to me—and I had caused needless worry to others. So she spanked me. I think it was a ruler or hairbrush or maybe a coat hanger. Whack!

"And she was right.

"I think that if discipline is immediate and direct and responsive in proportion to the size of the mistake, then physical punishment can be good. If the mistake is dwelt on and there's a sense of accusation around—that's no good. When I was nine I went to boarding school at Fessenden. The school had sent a notice to all the fathers of the entering boys for permission to paddle their sons, and my father was the first one to send it back, approved. In four years there

I was paddled thirteen times. (That may not be good campaign material for a U.S. senator, but there it is, thirteen.) Sometimes we'd even be paddled just before going out to do our best for the school in an athletic event. But I never resented it, because if I broke a school rule I knew I was supposed to be corrected and it was a matter of preference. The boys whose parents hadn't given permission would have to stay over during Thanksgiving, get days cut off from their Christmas vacations, or couldn't come to the school's 'Saturday Nights,' or had to spend hours writing repentant slogans on blackboards. The disciplinarian did most of the whacking, but I didn't hold that against him at all, and after I was out of there I used to go back to see him and visit with him. I considered him a good and trustworthy friend: He was that kind of man. And, of course, this is a tremendously important factor, the personality, the character, of the individual on both sides of the equation. With some kids an experience of corporal punishment would be absolutely horrendous. Bruise very badly, psychologically. Anyway, as for Mother, I never felt I was getting more nor less than justice from her, although it was a justice tempered by mercy and love. You knew those qualities were there. Even when—after the exercise of her motherly duty—your behind was sore."

I do remember that some of the boys, knowing they had been naughty and would be punished, would, if there was time, stuff a pillowcase into their pants to lessen the anguish. Those were vintage years for the Sunday "funny papers," including the "Katzenjammer Kids," who were always in mischief and being spanked and trying to pad their britches in advance; perhaps that's where our small sinners got the idea. I was seldom deceived. But sometimes I'd let them get away with it.

I believe that while a child is still very young the parents should let him know he is not to "have his own way" and is not to say "No." He should have this explained—and soon should understand—that his parents love him very much and are advising him on everything for his own good. And he is not to contradict them.

This idea worked so well that I can remember only one instance in which a child said "No" to me directly, even though I realized, sensibly, that some of them were probably saying "No" to themselves and didn't always do as they were told. The exception was our eighth, Jean, who one day in Florida announced that *No!* She was not going to a swimming lesson. After I recovered from the shock I said to her, "*Every little Kennedy goes to the Bath and Tennis Club and takes a swimming lesson, so you just run along like your brothers and sisters!*" Perhaps she sensed something in my tone of voice. Anyway, she went. (It was only during my research for this book that I discovered she went to her room instead of to the club.)

Jean disapproved of my telling anybody about her rebellion, because, as she said, it made her seem like the black sheep of the family. Yet she is now amused by it, perhaps because it gave her a unique place in our family history or because rebels are popular.

Eunice says:

"We were really organized. It was an extraordinary thing the way she had us all . . . I guess the word is disciplined. We went to dancing lessons once a week, which bored us, but we did turn out to be good dancers. She wanted us to swim and play tennis and golf properly, so schedules of lessons were laid out, which sometimes were a drag, but we did develop the skills and they've been assets. In fact, if Jack hadn't been such a good swimmer he probably couldn't have come through alive—let alone rescue crew members—after his boat was sunk in the Pacific.

"A lot of Mother's things have paid off, both in general and in special ways. For instance, that so-called 'flashing Kennedy smile' that got to be part of the trademark after we grew up and some of us entered public life. You don't flash unless your teeth are good. Mother monitored our intake of sweets. She kept a box of assorted candies in her bedroom, and after dinner each of us was allowed to pick a favorite piece. One piece, and that was it. This got to be such a custom or habit that we would hardly have dreamed of asking for a second.

"Then the toothbrushing. After every meal. Dentists have always recommended it but we actually did it. I remember it as part of the morning drill. She'd always come down, in her robe, for breakfast with us, to make sure we had the right food and ate it and then brushed our teeth. There was a downstairs bathroom and we'd file in and out one by one. Then stand inspection for spots on our clothes and general neatness. These things get to be a habit—if you're brought up that way you think it's natural.

"And then also we had our teeth straightened. All of us. Mother is a perfectionist, so every three weeks five or six of us had to hop in the car and be driven about an hour down to New York to a super-dentist. We'd wait our turn, and go to the chair, and be driven home with our braces tightened. I remember doing this for five years. With the age spread in our family there must have been close to twenty years of continuous tooth straightening among us, with Mother keeping tabs on it all the way."

Eunice's mention of habits, good and bad, reminds me of some we tried to discourage such as the use of tobacco and alcohol. Joe never smoked. As a schoolboy and college athlete—and as a fit, trim, enormously vigorous sportsman until the vascular accident that led to his death late in life—he knew that smoking was bad for wind and health. Besides, his whole nature rejected any idea that he could become dependent in the least on anything but his own physical and mental resources. He had a drink or two now and then, before dinner or on social occasions, but never before an important meeting. He always said he wanted his mind completely clear.

As for me, I never thought of smoking. When I was a girl and young wife any woman who smoked a cigarette was typed as a scarlet woman. Drinking? In my young married set we knew that some of the men took a nip, but any overindulgence or visible inebriation was considered shameful. My father, by the way, though he might have a drink with friends in private, never drank anything in public; for he believed it would contribute to the caricature of "drunken Irish politicians—a glass of whiskey in one hand, a pipe in the other." He resented deeply the Boston Brahmin image of the Irish and wanted to dispel it. Times and outlooks change. Tea dances gave way to cocktail parties, and sometime in the early 1930s, in Florida, I tried my first cocktail, an Orange Blossom. I found the sensation pleasant. It made me feel quite hospitable. However, I found that the only alcoholic beverages to which I am not allergic are products of the grape, and among those the only one that really agrees with me is champagne, in small quantities. So through the first half of my life I was "teetotal" and for the rest of it I have been abstemious, except for an occasional glass of champagne.

Joe and I both realized that as the children passed through their teens they undoubtedly would be exposed to provocations and temptations. We had always believed in rewards for good behavior as well as penalties for bad; in encouragement, praise, recognition, prizes, such as the silver cups and trophies they accumulated. I therefore had a flash of inspiration when I read that the Rockefeller children, not many years older than our own, had been given a thousand dollars each for not smoking or drinking until they were twenty-one.

I am not, in fact, certain as to the amount. Governor Nelson Rockefeller told me he remembered it as three thousand. However, sitting next to his elder brother, John D. III, at the opening of the John F. Kennedy Center in Washington, I asked him about that figure. He said, "Well, I think it was only one thousand. Perhaps when Nelson and the other younger ones came along my father raised the amount. But I think I got one thousand." In any event, Joe and I agreed upon a thousand dollars for not smoking, another thousand for not drinking, to each child if he or she on his or her honor made it all the way to age twenty-one. This was not a "bribe" for good behavior because they already realized they would come into money when they reached that age, since Joe had arranged trust funds for them. Rather it was an interesting and enticing trophy. From age twenty-one onward they were presumed to be adults in command of their own futures.

I think it worked as well as we could have expected and perhaps even a little better. Joe Jr. went through his twenty-one years without faltering and got his prize. One or two of the girls did begin to smoke because, they said, it helped them cut down on sweets and they were afraid of losing their figures. I didn't approve but I could sympathize. In general, the no-smoking prize was more successful than the no-drinking reward because of circumstances. All the children were abroad at one time or another during their late teens; and, of course, beer and wine are considered staples of life in most parts of Great Britain and Europe and are served as part of a meal.

Actually, the overwhelmingly favorite beverage in our house always was and still is—milk. Sometimes with some cocoa or other flavoring but essentially just milk. Mary Jo says:

"After coming back from a dance or a party we drank milk or

cocoa or whatever was there but not beer. A couple of boys in our age group did drink beer and one is now the headmaster of a country day school: We kid him about how bad he was. I didn't drink at all. The boys in the family told me I shouldn't. It was never anything for them until they were old enough, around twenty or twenty-one. But the one who impressed it on me the most was Pat. She was a beautiful girl and just had everything, so far as I was concerned. I was seventeen or eighteen and starting in college and she told me not to drink because, she said, 'You'll have a much better time if you don't'—and Pat was my idol."

Ethel has a memory of a later time—this would be December of 1960, just before Jack's inauguration, and a lot of us were at Palm Beach, and in and out were as large a variety as one could imagine, from Cabinet appointees to grocery boys. A very busy and exciting but slightly disheveled period when days ran into nights. She says:

"I remember going into the kitchen and there were several of us there, talking about whatever we were talking about, past, present, future, with glasses in our hands. And Oleg Cassini joined in and he couldn't *believe* we were all standing around drinking *milk*."

Joe was absolutely devoted to his children. He loved them and he let them know it, realize it, absorb the understanding of his love from their earliest childhood and in the most outgoing demonstrative ways. In business and politics many people found him "hard-headed" and "tough," but they should have seen him at home, warm and gentle with the little ones. He would sweep them into his arms and hug them, and grin at them and talk to them, and perhaps carry them around. Also, as each one became old enough to talk—had enough vocabulary and understanding for a simple conversation, which would be roughly at about age two and a half or three—he would want that child in bed with him for a little while each morning. And the two of them would be there propped up on the pillows, with perhaps the child's head cuddling on his shoulder, and he would talk or read a story or they would have conversations. These were on any topic whatsoever that the child wanted to talk about. He would be responsive, understanding, amused or mock-horrified, always affectionate but if necessary corrective, with advice or plain declarations of Yes or No and Good or Bad. Even when they were that young he treated them, in a sense, as equals, respecting each one as a unique and wonderfully interesting individual and trying to bring out whatever that individuality was. Except to adjust his vocabulary to theirs, he never "talked down" to them, never patronized them from the lofty holier and wiser attitude that I have seen some parents take. He said what was on his mind and in his heart. There was a marvelous combination of sternness and warmth, severity and great good humor, the greatest of expectations along with a knowledge of human frailties and a very deep sense of justice. I think children understand parental qualities and attitudes: They just soak them in. Ours grew up with feelings of awe and reverence and respect and friendship and camaraderie and love and duty toward their father.

Physical punishment was not his style at all. (It wasn't mine either once they were old enough to be reached by the power of reason.) He may have, and probably did, give some of them a paddy-whack at one time or another, but I can't remember a single time that he ever spanked any of them. Instead, he enforced his ideas by the sheer strength of his personality—an almost physical emanation of energy and power and mental quickness and forthrightness. He did not, in the phrase, "suffer fools gladly" and if there was foolishness going on the culprits knew it, and usually all it took was a look. He had bright blue eyes with a remarkable range of expression. They could change, at a moment, from sunny affection and merriment to one that—as a young house guest who was there to see it happen a few times described at a later time—"was ice-cold steel blue, piercing right into and through you and stripped you to the soul; and you felt naked, shriveled." That may be a little elaborate. It was known in the family as "Daddy's look." Mary Jo recalls:

"I can't remember him raising his voice. Or even thinking of doing anything. But he had a way of putting his glasses down and *looking* at you over the glasses. I never found out what was beyond that, but I really never felt that I wanted to find out. It was just one of those things. The fear of God was there and why tamper with it."

Her brother, Joey, says:

"He didn't have to say anything to you. All he'd have to do was look down the table rather sternly over the top of his glasses and that was enough to indicate it had better not happen again; and it very rarely did. At the same time he was very kind and, I always felt, extremely understanding. If you did get into trouble—with a car or a boat, say, even foolishly—he would make it clear he was upset about it, and the person should have had better sense; it was unnecessary. Once he'd made it clear that he was unhappy and hoped it would never happen again, the subject was not mentioned again. It was a past incident, you had learned an important lesson and life went on from there.

"Once, when I was old enough to drive, he called me in Boston and asked me to bring his new Cadillac down to the Cape. On the way, a truck came out of a side road and hit the left front fender. The car went off the road and into the trees and one of them crumpled the right front fender, so now there were smashed fenders on both sides of his new Cadillac. The car was still drivable, so I took it on to Hyannis Port and into the parking area back of the house. Bobby and the chauffeur, Dave, both saw it, and of course were horrified, and suggested I take it to a garage for repairs before Uncle Joe saw it. I decided to be brave. So, with my face the color of cement, I went in and told him what happened. He said, 'Let's see the car'—which was a mess. Instead of tearing me apart he said, 'Joey, you're lucky to be alive,' and that I should take it back to Boston on Monday to get it fixed and, meanwhile, just then, I ought to get into the touch football game that had begun out front on the lawn.

"There was often a little good-natured ragging going on in the household. And if somebody was in trouble with Uncle Joe all the others were delighted it was that person who was in a hot spot, not they, and they might even bait Uncle Joe a bit and encourage the situation—just to see the fireworks. That evening at dinner Jack, who was a congressman then, began this operation by remarking very innocently, 'Dad, I hear Joey had a little accident with the new car.' At that, Uncle Joe put his glasses down a little, peered at Jack with that special 'look' and said: 'Joey and I have discussed the car, and I don't want to hear it mentioned again.' And it never was. In fact, a week later he asked me to drive Aunt Rose to the airport. It was his way of telling me and showing others that he still had confidence in me."

When any one of them got into trouble (I didn't say "if" but "when"), his first approach was to demand all the facts. He would say: "Tell me the truth. Tell me everything about it, the whole truth. Then I'll do everything I can to help. But if you don't give me the truth, I'm licked." Painful as truthtelling might be in some situations, they all understood what he meant and, I think, almost always brought forth the truth as they saw it. (Sometimes giving themselves the benefit of the doubt, I daresay.) Then, if on the basis of the facts he decided they had been in the wrong he would tell them so, straight out, logically, emphatically, and carefully explain why they had been wrong and how they could and should guard against getting into that sort of difficulty again. If he thought they needed a stronger speech he would give it, and if there was some really serious lapse he would give them blue blazes. But then, as Mary Jo and Joey have indicated, when it was over—it was over completely. He had made himself entirely clear. He assumed they understood and realized, and had made their own vows to themselves, that they were not to engage in any such nonsense again. Teddy remarks:

"When I got into that mess at Harvard in my freshman year at eighteen and was suspended, and called to tell him, his initial reaction was very calm. What exactly was the situation I'm involved in? What impact could this have on my life and relationships? And then about eighteen to twenty-four hours later, after he had got a 'feel' for what it meant, he was absolutely wild and went up through the roof. For about five hours. From then on he was calm. It was just 'How do we help you?' And he never brought the thing up again."

Many years later in 1964, after Ted had his nearly fatal airplane accident and while he was in the hospital recuperating, he collected essays from family members and friends about his father, and these were published in a privately printed book that he titled *The Fruitful Bough* after a passage in Genesis (49: 22, 24): "Joseph is a fruitful bough, even a fruitful bough by a well, whose branches run over the wall . . . his bow abode in strength, and the arms of his hands were made strong by the hands of the mighty God." Here are excerpts from the essay that Teddy himself contributed to that book:

"My first consciousness of how important Dad was to me began when I was allowed to crawl into bed with him in the morning and listen to him read Donald Duck.

"From our earliest days, I think all the Kennedy children were made to feel that our father's principal interest in life was his family. As the youngest, it appeared to me that the family was his only interest.

"I have always felt the greatest gift Dad gave to each of us was his unqualified support. His purpose was to encourage and to sift the relevant from the irrelevant. His criticisms were always positive and constructive and made sense. His guidance was for our own good and the family's. Perhaps we might not agree with his conclusions, but the final decision was more sound because of discussions with him.

"Even when he was away from home, he made sure to get reports on our conduct. At a very early age each of us realized the need to speak to Dad frankly and forthrightly. 'Applesauce' was not for him, and he wanted no 'monkey business' at school or at home.

"When Dad was away from home, he kept up with everything going on in the family. The children who were away at school reported to him regularly by letter and phone. No matter how busy he was, he seemed to have a moment to listen and to encourage us.

"Dad wanted us to be natural and able to smile no matter how tough things were. He wouldn't let any of his children feel sorry for himself. 'I don't want any sour pusses around here,' he would say. Yet he was quick to scold a child who tried to smile too readily or to charm his way through life. 'Remember,' he would say, 'a smile and a dime can only get you a ride on a streetcar. You are going to need a lot more than that to get somewhere in life.'

"Clarity, frankness, and honesty were basic parts of his character. He was never afraid to state his case. Typical expressions were 'He doesn't have the brains of a donkey,' or 'Enough brains to find his way out of a telephone booth.' One whose personal honesty or ethics might be in question was described as one who 'would take a red hot stove.'

"Although we loved him as a father, we also admired him as a man, who was eminently successful, extraordinarily knowledgeable, and thoroughly enjoyable. His handshake was strong and firm, and he looked you straight in the eye. His broad smile and wholehearted laugh were infectious. His welcome was warm and genuine—a special one for each of us.

"He was generous to a fault, but woe unto him who made the mistake of taking advantage of it. Dad was a taskmaster, too. He was also quick to admonish us for errors. He tolerated a mistake once, but never a second time. Because he was interested, because he did care, because he wanted to help, he brought out the best in each of us. We were ashamed to do less than our best because of our respect and feelings for him."

Ted's last remark brings up a question that has often been asked of me: "What has made the Kennedy children strive so hard for individual excellence?" The answer is a combination of elements.

Superior achievement or making the most of one's capabilities is to a very considerable degree a matter of habit. This was the reason why Joe used to say to the children, "We don't want any losers around here. In this family we want winners." They were encouraged to be winners, leaders, and victors in whatever they set their hand to, and to develop the habit. "Don't come in second or third—that doesn't count—but win." If they lost in a sport—or lagged in school or other activity—the reasons were analyzed. If these turned out to involve some negligence or lack of effort or "monkeyshines," that was dealt with in very clear terms. Eunice has recalled:

"Mother and Dad put us through rigorous training in athletics. Dad wanted his children to win the sailing and swimming races (I remember racing fourteen times a week when I was twelve years old!)."

Joe's attitude has been much written about, particularly after the boys went into public life with such conspicuous success. Journalists and others pondered what had caused the so-called "Kennedy phenomenon." The main point of the whole exercise was not "winning" per se. It was rather that we wanted them to do their absolute best. Always give their maximum effort. "From each according to his abilities and to each according to his needs" might be one way of saying this. Another could be "God wants a different thing from each of us . . . which only we can do and for which we were created."

Joe and I knew they were not perfect. We knew they were each different, yet we wanted each to develop his or her individual abilities and to do the very best that was in them to do.

Bobby, in his essay in *The Fruitful Bough*, said:

"He has called on the best that was in us. There was no such thing as half trying. Whether it was running a race or catching a football, competing in a school—we were to try. And we were to try harder than anyone else. We might not be the best, and none of us were, but we were to make the effort to be the best. 'After you have done the best you can,' he used to say, 'the hell with it.'

"Most importantly, he has been there when things went badly. Our opponents became his opponents, our problems his problems . . . and he was there to help. In bad times it has been he, more than anyone else, who has seen the bright side. 'Call up Dad, he will be cheerful,' my older brother used to say. The greater the disaster, the brighter he was, the more support he gave.

"And so it has been this interesting combination—his demand that all his children strive for excellence—strive for it, perhaps not achieve it, but continuously strive for it; and—what made this demand tolerable and in fact enjoyable—the interest and support we felt we always had from him."

I think the most important lines in these paragraphs of Bobby's are: "After you have done the best you can, the hell with it." I was saying the same thing to them, more sedately.

The other more pertinent remarks are about his father's invariable support in times of troubles and the infectiously optimistic reassurance he could always manage. How many times I have heard him declare: "That may be one of the *best* things that ever happened to you!" And sometimes it really was. I can remember when Joe was quite discouraged about the support of a key Democratic governor for Jack's presidential candidacy. Yet when Jack called his father to express his own worry, Joe would immediately brighten up and reassure Jack warmly that everything would be all right. Jack would then take courage from his father's optimism.

Another of Joe's statements that everyone in the family heard often enough was: "We don't want any crying in this house."

It too was picked up by some of the writers and misunderstood or misused in a way to make him seem hardhearted or as if he were trying to convert the children into Spartans and stoics. What he really meant was that there was to be *no self-pity*, and no burdening of others with any personal misfortunes by making a commotion about them. He knew that for almost everyone life is likely to hold many knocks and bruises, and that people had better get used to that idea at an early age.

I have a favorite passage from Dag Hammarskjöld's *Markings:*

"Keep alive the incentive to push on further, that pain in the soul which drives us beyond ourselves."

And another that I jotted in my notebook, regrettably without noting the author:

"A healthy attitude can change a burden into a blessing, a trial into a triumph."

One especially appropriate example was the way Jack happened to write his book *Profiles in Courage.*

Ever since the war and his injuries during the PT-109 ordeal he had a serious problem with his back. He was seldom if ever really free of pain, although he bore it with such few outward signs that nobody but his doctors, the family, and a few close associates realized his condition. Meanwhile, he had plenty of reason to think about courage. Finally, during 1954, the problem became so bad that he had to be on crutches; and rather than face going through life as a cripple he agreed to a spinal operation. Not only was it a failure but an infection set in. He nearly died: he received the Last Rites of the Church. But he did pull through, and after the danger was past he was flown— on a stretcher—to our Palm Beach house for recuperation in the warm climate. In a few months he was "healthy" enough for the doctors to try the operation again. If he wanted it. He did. So it was back to the hospital in New York, where the second operation was successful (relatively speaking, for he was always afterward in discomfort, which he ignored), and then back again to Palm Beach for more months of recuperation. It was there, during those times, that he did most of his work on *Profiles in Courage.* He had, as I said, been fascinated since boyhood by history and biography. In his own life, and from life in our family, he knew the meaning of courage. The theme of the book was a natural one for him. He worked on it most of the time during the long period of trial and risk and suffering—in his hospital bed, with a writing board propped in front of him, in bed at the Palm Beach house; other places—but my vivid memory is of him sitting in a wheel chair and later in a comfortable camp chair out by the sea wall.

There is a little promontory, about the size of a big bay window and shaped like one, that protrudes from the wall, with beach and ocean on three sides. On calm sunny days this was an office and studio for him. Literally an office because all the most important mail and messages and items of Senate business were sent down to him from Washington. Literally a studio because Jackie got him interested in painting, as a good relaxation, and sometimes he would be out there with easel and palette trying his hand at seascapes and beach scenes or, for practice, copying a painting he had taken off a wall someplace in our house. (Rarely with a by your leave to me. Not that we have any valuable paintings, but still . . . ! And he would say, "Oh, yes, Mother, sorry," and then I'd find another one gone.) And literally an office-studio-library—or whatever the best term is for the working habitat of a writer—because so many times I remember looking out from the house across our sturdy green lawn and past the tall royal palms toward the tropical sea, the aquamarine white-capped ocean and blue sky and passing clouds and ships in the distance, and there was Jack in his sea-wall alcove with his writing board and a thick writing pad clamped to it, and a folding table or two piled with books and notebooks and file folders—paperweights or perhaps some rocks from the beach to hold things down against the sea breezes—and his head would be forward, and he would be writing away on that book. From full heart, mind, and spirit.

It turned out to be a very fine book. One he could take satisfaction in for several reasons: first, because it expressed ideas and ideals he believed in and believed were very important in the life of this nation; and also because he realized he had expressed them well—and as I said, before he happened to go into politics, his ambitions had revolved around writing, journalism, teaching.

Furthermore, its excellence was recognized and rewarded. It received a Pulitzer Prize. It was admired by historians and influential figures in government and journalism and other "opinion makers" of the so-called intellectual establishment—whose good opinion in political life in this country usually has been and hopefully always will be of great importance. After publication of the book Jack was no longer just an interesting, attractive, but relatively inexperienced and comparatively unknown junior senator from Massachusetts, but was someone discussed and weighed and measured nationally. He was chosen to give Adlai Stevenson's nomination speech at the next Democratic Convention, in 1956, and he himself came within a hair's breadth of becoming nominated for the vice-presidency. From the force of that momentum he went on to the presidential nomination and election in 1960. Quite obviously there were many complex elements. An early and important and possibly even crucial one was Jack's own response to his own misfortune and sufferings back in 1954–55: a positive, affirmative, constructive response that—to an extent that I'm sure he never even faintly imagined at the time—did "change a burden into a blessing, a trial into a triumph."

This is one example. There have been others, both in his life and the lives of others in the family.

I think the spirit of endurance and affirmation can be overdone sometimes, and in particular I am thinking of an incident about Bobby as related by Kenneth O'Donnell, sometime classmate and ever afterward close friend of Bobby's, and later a campaign assistant to Jack and his appointments secretary in the White House. Since this has to do with football, I should mention that, as a senior, he was Harvard's football captain. In Pat's book about Bobby, *That Shining Hour*, Kenny O'Donnell recalled when Bobby came back to Harvard in the fall of 1946, after serving as an enlisted man in the Navy:

"By this time, the GI bill allowed even the poorest of boys to seek an education in our best universities and Harvard was overflowing with the finest collection of athletes . . . with transfers from all over the United States—most of the boys had played some one or two years at Notre Dame, Wisconsin, etc. Because of Bobby's size the coach exhibited very little interest in him, and consigned him to sixth or seventh squad. By the middle of fall he had been promoted to the Varsity. By the end of the season, Robert Kennedy was a member of the Varsity Club, admired and respected. In 1947 he started the opener against Western Maryland. We defeated Western Maryland 47 to 0, and Bobby caught his first and only touchdown pass of his collegiate career. A week later, we were scrimmaging and he and I were playing side by side, missing block after block. The coach was raging at me, and I was raging at number 86. After nearly half an hour, Bob collapsed on the field. He had been playing with a broken leg all that time. . . ."

That, needless for me to say, was over and beyond the courage and fortitude that Joe and I wanted to instill. Even so, it had an ultimate and unexpected reward for Bobby, for as Kenny goes on to say, even though that "ended his football career, he did play briefly in the Yale game to earn his letter," which is the Harvard player's dream, and which I suppose was the coach's way of recognizing and rewarding Bobby's extreme bravery and dedication.

In training them for excellence, Joe and I always worked toward the same goals, although not necessarily in quite the same ways. Nor even the same times. Eunice remembers:

"It was not one of those things where the father commutes and goes away in the morning and comes home at night. He was away a lot. When he was there, it was his personality that dominated. Our mother was articulate about everything but more so when he wasn't there—when he was home she let him sort of take over. By the time I got to know my father really well it was later, because he was around so much more when I was eighteen or nineteen. He made it possible for us to do things, but I think the terrific drive—for me—came much more from my mother. That more so for the girls than for the boys, because he took charge more of the boys, but she was the one who was there.

"And she could be quite stern. She knew there were certain ways to behave. It wasn't a great emotional thing with her, as it is with some mothers, she was more a teacher and an inspirer. She was interested in whatever you were doing, reading or taking skating lessons. I remember she would take us ice skating in Bronxville, and you just wouldn't go skating off into the blue yonder: She'd say, use your right leg or use your left leg better; again it was this terrific drive, she wanted everyone to do their best. There was quite a little pressure around. If you weren't doing very well there weren't any excuses for it. She'd say, you just get along there, don't be stupid about it, or something like that. Never, oh you poor thing, you may not feel well today. She wouldn't excuse you. Oh, you can't do Latin well and that's too bad, so drop Latin and take another subject—no, you go in there and you learn Latin, and she made sure you did. She would do homework with me, and if I couldn't do it right she'd get cross and say you just learn this and you sit there and learn that verb.

"And she was always very energetic and expected us to be. Today, children stay in and watch television or listen to radio or records, but we were packed up and out we'd go, no matter what the weather was. On the porch, or sled riding or ice skating, or playing tennis. I suppose if we were really sick we stayed in, but so far as I can remember the first time in my life I ever stayed indoors was when I was in my thirties and had a baby and had to stay in. And I walked around in the hospital and thought, How odd, some people stay in and read all day . . .

"This may make her sound like she was sort of an ogress, but actually none of us felt that way in the least. We always understood she wasn't doing any of these things for her sake, but for our sakes. You felt that she felt you had more in you than you thought. She always assumed you did. She was a great believer in opening up many opportunities for us. Some of the things were difficult, but she'd say, well, you ought to try them. Such as taking trips on our own while we were young. And encouraging my father to let us go. At first he might say an idea we had for some trip was no good, but she'd talk him into it. I can remember that very well when I was sixteen and my sister Rosemary and I wanted to go to Switzerland. Dad's first reaction was no, it was too risky. We went, and there were no problems. Mother believed we could do it and believed young people ought to be exposed to lots of experiences."

In any case, something seems to have had a lasting effect on Eunice because I have known few people in the world to match her for initiative and energy and drive. I was looking over her schedule during the 1972 election when she was out helping Sarge in his campaign for the vice-presidency.

On one typical day she flew from New York City to Utica, New York, met and talked with county Democratic leaders, addressed an assembly at a local high school, took part in a rally at the state office building with Democratic officials and candidates, attended and spoke at a big fund-raising luncheon, spent an hour at a day center for senior citizens, was interviewed on a radio show, took part in a television panel show, flew back to New York, and was there in time for dinner and an evening of other activities. In three months, either on her own or with Sarge, she traveled thousands of miles, attended several hundred meetings, rallies, political breakfasts, luncheons and dinners, gave innumerable talks or "remarks," gave dozens of interviews on radio and television, visited scores of schools and centers and other institutions, and was introduced to and shook hands with thousands of people. Meanwhile, she was also attending to various important projects and duties that are part of her normal life, and also, and by no means incidentally, attending to the health and welfare of Sarge and their five energetic children and to the operations of a large house and staff in Maryland. She thinks I have a lot of energy, but she amazes me.

Jack once remarked of me that I was "the glue that held the family together." I'm not so sure I like the metaphor but the sentiment is all right. Bobby once wrote that I "was the stabilizing influence, performing all the functions that a mother can for children." Pat has said she remembers a lot of "care and interest" and that I was "very solicitous and kept up with whether one was doing well or not"; adding that, as for my praising her, "Well, she must have, though that's not one of my strong memories." Eunice, writing in a sentimental mood, remarked on "Mother's compassion, and ever present, ever constant love and example of goodness and faith." Teddy, in an interview about me, spoke of "gentleness and understanding, and support and encouragement that made the high family standards livable and perhaps reachable."

I am indulging in these quotations, making a little mosaic of them, because together they may help illuminate a question that naturally could come to people's minds after what has been said about our aim to bring out the best in each of our children. It is true, as Eunice put it, that in this sense "there was quite a little pressure around." But we had a child who was retarded. Rosemary, our eldest daughter.

People who have read the preceding pages may well wonder how she fitted into the scenes that have been described, and about her personal relationships with her brothers and sisters, and the ways in which Joe and I adapted our aims to her needs.

I'm sure it will be understood this is not an easy matter for me to write about but I will do my best, while also drawing on the memories of others in the family circle.

After Joe Jr. and Jack, it was of course a special joy for Joe and me when our third was a girl, a daughter for us and little sister for them. She was a very pretty baby and she was sweet and peaceable and cried less than the first two had, which at the time I supposed was part of her being a girl. I delighted in her. And because the nursemaid was so busy with the two boys, still very young and needing a lot of attention, I took care of her most of the time myself. Physically she was very healthy, and there were no signs I recognized that anything might be wrong. She crawled, stood, took her first steps, said her first words late, she had problems managing a baby spoon and porringer— and yet, as everyone knows, babies always have their own individual rates of growth and of acquiring skills, so I was patient, concerned, beginning to be a little apprehensive, but not worried, partly, I suppose, because of wishful thinking.

It became apparent that Rosemary was born a retarded child. No one knows why—there are only hypotheses. Eunice, though several years younger, even in childhood, was particularly good and attentive and helpful with her, encouraging her to do her best; and later on, because of this loving and unremitting interest in her older sister, she became a lay expert in the field of mental retardation and is director of the Joseph P. Kennedy Jr. Foundation.

Rosemary was a pretty baby girl, and it was only slowly, as she grew to be a toddler and beyond, that I began to realize she might be handicapped.

She was slow in everything, and some things she seemed unable to learn how to do, or do well or with consistency. When she was old enough for childish sports I noticed, for instance, that she couldn't steer her sled. When she was old enough to learn a little reading and writing, the letters and words were extremely difficult for her, and instead of writing from left to right on a page she wrote in the opposite direction. She went to kindergarten and first grade at the usual ages, but her lack of coordination was apparent and as time went on I realized she could not keep up with the work. In the Brookline school system intelligence tests were given to all the children very early. I was informed that Rosemary's I.Q. was low, but that was about all the concrete information I received, and it didn't help much. This was in the early 1920s, the tests were still quite new and unrefined, and neither those who created them nor those who used them could say, really, how accurate they were or what the scores meant except in a general way. Joe and I looked for experts in mental deficiency, at Harvard as well as in hospitals, and I talked with some of them. They were not very helpful. They could venture certain theories to account for her condition—"genetic accident," "uterine accident," "birth accident," and so forth—but when I would ask, "What can I do to help her?" there didn't seem to be much of an answer. I was frustrated and heartbroken.

There were a few private schools, in those days, that offered living facilities and care and training for children with neurological defects, and it was suggested we put Rosemary in one of those. Much as I had begun to realize how very difficult it might be to keep her at home, everything about me—and my feelings for her—rebelled against that idea, and I rejected it except as a last resort. In the inevitable atmosphere of such a place, living in a population of neurologically maimed children, gaited to their pace, she would soon realize and feel deeply her difference from her brothers and sisters, and that might remove the incentive for her even to try her best to learn. We decided that care, understanding, encouragement, and tutoring would be the way to bring out the best in her and develop her capacities to their fullest, whatever they turned out to be. Eunice has written:

"My mother had carried the main responsibility for Rosemary—taking her to doctors, educators, and psychologists. My father supported her, but he was much more emotional, and was easily upset by Rosemary's lack of progress, her inabilities to use opportunities for self-development.

"His belief in family loyalty, however, was again an influence. When psychologists recommended that Rosemary be placed in an institution he said, 'What can they do in an institution that we can't do better for her at home—here with her family?' So my sister stayed at home. He believed that Rosemary should have every opportunity that the rest of us had, even though she could not make the most of such opportunities."

This did, of course, involve a good deal of time. The less progress Rosemary seemed to make, the more time I would spend trying to bring her along—time that had to be subtracted from that spent with the other children. Kathleen, the next youngest in the family line, was such a beautiful and lively and outgoing child and girl that I became convinced she never felt at all neglected. I was less sure about Jack. He was the next eldest, and as I have said he was rather sickly and therefore needed attention: perhaps more than I gave him, in my worry and distraction about Rosemary. In the later years I sometimes wondered if he had felt neglected by me. Not long ago I asked Jackie if he had ever mentioned this to her. She assured me he hadn't, or had indicated it in any way. But the thought still bothers me a bit that he may have when he was a little boy, and only realized later on why I spent so much time with Rosemary.

Joe and I, knowing we wanted her to be brought up and treated in the most normal way possible, steeled ourselves as best we could and did not indicate either within the family (except as necessary, and then casually and indirectly) or outside that there was anything extraordinary about her. I think there were only very few outside the family circle to whom she seemed noticeably "different" from the others in our family or other children. Mary O'Connell Ryan, one of the dearest and closest friends during the Brookline years, and a dear friend still, who has been quoted here earlier, recalls:

"I had small children of my own and loved to sew and design clothes for them, so I opened a children's shop, and Rose was one of my first customers and was a steady one until the family moved from Brookline down to New York. She would bring her children in— four or five of them, then—all beautiful children, and Rose didn't treat any of them differently from the others. She kept all of them on the mark. Oh, yes, always right on the mark! But she never showed the slightest difference with her affection and attention. I remember Rosemary as a little shy, but nothing was made of it at all. There is a mutual friend of ours, Miriam Finnegan—she was a schoolmate of Rose's at the Blumenthal convent in Holland, and later one of our charter members when Rose founded our Ace of Clubs—and, of course, she saw Rose and her family from time to time, and she noticed that Rosemary seemed a rather shy little girl. Miriam, I remember, mentioned this to me and said: 'I think there's so much made of Kathleen'—that's 'Kick' as they called her later, and there was a lot made of her, for good reasons, she was so vibrant and alive and everything—'that Rosemary is a little conscious of that and feels a little bit in the background.'

"So that's the way it was, nothing to indicate that Rosemary had any special problem, because I'm sure lots of little girls could feel inhibited by an especially beautiful baby sister. And on Rose's part, nothing, nothing at all. Nothing was ever said even to very close friends. No one outside that family—except I suppose some doctors —knew or suspected that Rosemary's condition was that unusual. I didn't know anything about it for all those years, not until 1960, when Joe gave an interview explaining she had been a retarded child. That was when Jack was running for the presidency, and I suppose there were rumors around and the family decided to quell them by putting the cards face up on the table."

I felt that if Rosemary could acquire enough of the basic skills in reading, writing, and arithmetic, a little history and geography, and sports and dancing, at least well enough to participate and enjoy them, she would manage to be happy. If she was attractive and well groomed and well mannered, she would be able to have a reasonably satisfying life. With special attention, which we arranged at the schools she attended, and with great effort on her part, she did achieve reasonable performances in all these matters.

Yet, success bred its own problems from time to time. Since we treated her in every possible way as if she were normal she couldn't understand why, for instance, she couldn't take a rowboat out alone in the harbor the way other children did. In fact, she couldn't manage the oars. She resented having someone always go with her to the station when she took the train to her school. Because, she said, other girls went to the station alone. Sometimes she would run away from the person accompanying her.

The other children in the family must have realized that she was different from them and from children of her age group, but Joe and I tried hard to minimize this. They were merely told that Rosemary was "a little slow" and that they should help her and encourage her. When she did something well, tell her so. If she made a joke, laugh with her, don't give her a quick retort. If she has on a pretty new hair ribbon or blouse say something about that; but don't talk about her lack of tennis skills. If there is some activity going on, let her participate, invite her to be involved. All of them were very understanding and cooperative. Eunice recalls:

"Rosemary was never hidden away or anything, she was pushed right on with the rest of us. Even though she was slow she was always given every opportunity that everybody was given. As I said, we took a trip all over Switzerland together; I was sixteen, she was nineteen. There was no tension in the family about her, and she didn't cause scenes. There was never any bursting into tears or running to her room. She laughed and she was always rather jolly. We all had the feeling she was just a little slow, so jolly Rosemary along. But my mother spent a lot of time with her, a lot of effort and concern. If you were going down the hall on the way to swimming she'd call out to ask, 'Will you take Rosemary?' And she would say to me, 'Will you play tennis with Rosemary?' She wasn't very good, Rosemary, but I played tennis with her. Or she would say, 'Will you take her sailing, racing?' I was quite good at racing in those days and I could handle a boat all right by myself, so I'd take Rosemary. Then I'd tell my mother she had done well on the boat, and Mother was pleased —it meant a lot to her. But the situation never depressed her. Then, also, the boys were always very good with her. Like Jack would take her to a dance at the club, and would dance with her and kid with her and would make sure a few of his close pals cut in, so she felt popular. He'd bring her home at midnight. Then he'd go back to the dance."

I'm sure that the children who were old enough to sense the need (Teddy, so many years younger, says he thought of her as "just a very sweet, much older big sister") and those such as Agnes and the Moores and others who were in the inner family circle, and thus knew or sensed the problem, always did things to help her along without mentioning or even thinking much about them at the time. It was a conspiracy of kindness.

About this time I changed my handwriting. I was brought up to write "a fine Spencerian hand" with all the letters of a word gracefully flowing and connected one to another. It was called the Palmer Method. Yet, because of Rosemary's neurological problems in recognizing written letters of the alphabet and in being able to reproduce them with a pen or pencil, or to read them, she was taught to use the printed forms: Thus the words in a book would look like those words as she would write them and so they would be easier for her to read. When she was old enough to receive postcards or little notes from me when I was away, I took up this same method so she could read my messages and so that she wouldn't think my way of writing was different from hers. It became a habit with me, and my writing has ever since been more printed than written. Of course, much later on, this form of "cursive" handwriting came into fashion and millions of people use it today.

Rosemary was an affectionate, warmly responsive, and loving girl. She was so willing to try to do her best, so appreciative of attention and compliments, and so hopeful of deserving them. I have been looking through letters from and to and about her, and perhaps a few passages from these may tell a good deal.

October 1934, from the Sacred Heart Convent at Providence, Rhode Island, where she spent the school year of '34–'35, when she was sixteen, and where Joe had visited her:

> "Dear Daddy
> "I had a lovely time on Saturday.
> Thank you ever so much
> for coming down to see me.
> Sunday I also had good
> time.
> "I would do anything
> to make you so happy.
> "I hate to disapoint
> you in anyway . . ."

That same year, in a letter to Joe and me. Examination time; and she wrote,

"Pray very hard that I will get someplace, I tried as hard as I could."

A letter to us in the winter of 1936, when she was seventeen:

Our 1927 Christmas card.

Bobby, Jack, Eunice, Jean, Pat, Kathleen, Joe Jr., and Rosemary on the beach at Hyannis with Joe and me and our dog Buddy.

Rosemary at fifteen.   Jean.

Lady Astor and I on the SS *Aquitania*, 1928.

Joe Jr. by the pool in Palm Beach while I take my daily swim.

Mother and I, Palm Beach, 1938.

Justice Reed swore Joe in as Ambassador to the Court of St. James's, as President Roosevelt witnessed the occasion.

Kathleen, Bobby, Ted, Pat, and Jean are with me as we depart for England, 1938.

Bobby, St. Moritz, 1938.

Keystone

Jean, Teddy, and I, St. Moritz, 1938.

Sleigh riding in St. Moritz. Eunice, Bobby, and Rosemary face Jean, Teddy, and me.

nedy Family Collection

Teddy wanted to be the first to snap Joe's and my picture as we emerged from Buckingham Palace after paying our respects to King George VI and Queen Elizabeth.

". . . Thursday, I went to Girl Scouts. I am taking Nature up . . . Sunday, Joe and Jack, and I, Grandma, Grandpa, went to Aunt Agnus for lunch, then Jack took Grampa, Grandma, and I to St. Joseph Cermtory. Also Grandma took me to the movies . . . Jack is taken me to the next dance. He is going to take me in his new car. . . . I gave Jack 1$ he diddn't ask for it either. 2 cents I paid for his papper. . . . Lots of love kisses your darling daughter."

She adored her father, and he was wonderful with her: joking with her, congratulating her warmly for achievements, chiding her forthrightly—as with all the others—for unseemly behavior or carelessness about her personal appearance. She tended to become overweight, for instance, so Joe gave her a kind but firm talking-to about watching her diet and getting exercise—for these were things that lay within her own competence to do for herself. After war broke out in September 1939, Joe, while of course staying at his ambassadorial post in London, sent the family home, except for Rosemary. We had her in a small school deep in the Hertfordshire countryside, safely remote from any military target, and she had made such exceptional progress we decided to leave her there for another term. Joe was especially attentive to her during that time, supervising everything from her studies to her pocket money and dental care, and writing to her often, and visiting the school. Which accounts for the following correspondence (she was twenty-one).

Joe to Miss Gibbs, a headmistress and also Rosemary's special tutor-companion:

"I was more than pleased to see Rosemary Sunday. She was looking very well and seemed to be in excellent humor. I do feel that she is getting altogether too fat and I told her so in no uncertain words. So I wish, if you could, you would try to build up the idea that she should lose weight. I told her that her mother would be very disappointed and also that I could not have her picture taken for America if she remains as stout as she is. Both these arguments seemed to make some impression. It really makes me very happy to see the great improvement she has shown and I can never thank you and Mother Isabel enough . . ."

Miss Gibbs to Joe:

"You *must* have made a big impression on Sunday—because when she was showing a new lot of snapshots today she remarked, 'Yes, my figure does look fat, doesn't it?' Thereupon she said, 'What do you suggest I can do about it?' So we can proceed peacefully, and we will."

Rosemary to her father:

"Many, many thanks for coming to see on Friday. You were darling. I hope you liked every-thing here. . . . Mother says I am such a comfort to you. Never to leave you. Well, Daddy, I feel honour because you chose me to stay. And the others suppose are wild."

She came to the United States the next spring, 1940, and in her first letter to her father included the proud news that:

"The Saks man wanted to hear about my trip. And he things I am the best looking of the Kennedys."

Her following letter was to tell him she had a job as a junior counselor at a summer camp for girls and was teaching arts and crafts to the younger girls.

"Another girl, Alice Hill, has the bigger girl in Arts and Crafts, so the two of us run it. They were looking for somebody else to teach it. And they have me now. Mother went to talk to the Sullovan's girls about it and Judge Sullovan's daughters run it. But isn't it interesting. But me being a Junior Counsellar the first year."

Joe wrote to her:

"I couldn't have been more surprised to hear you had gone up to camp as a junior counselor. It looks to me like all the rest of the Kennedys are still going to school, including the boys, while my eldest daughter is out working. Good for you!

"We go occasionally to Windsor" (where we had a country house) "when it is a nice weekend, but I am living regularly at the embassy. There are so many things to be done in the office all the time. I certainly miss those weekends with Eddie, Mary, and you, and we haven't had any good laughs since you left."

"Incidentally, I have gained four or five pounds myself and am starting on a diet right now. I guess while you were here I was so busy trying to keep you thin, I didn't have a chance to eat and have been making up for lost time.

"Give my love to all and keep right on working and setting a good example for your brothers and sisters."

Joe always made it possible for me to have a nursemaid or governess to help in caring for the children. There were several during the years, young women of fine character, intelligence, and education, who really became part of the family and were trusted by us and loved by the children. None was more efficient or delightful than Elizabeth Dunn (later Mrs. Anderson) who came to us at Hyannis Port in the summer of 1936. I asked her for some recollections:

"One of the first things that I remember on arriving at your home was the regular noontime swims with the family down at Taggart's pier. The children all looked forward to being with you and displaying their swimming and diving ability and how they improved. It was great fun when you and Mr. Kennedy would form a big circle with the older children, and then Teddy, Jean, and Bobby would swim first to the one nearest them and gradually work up to the one farthest away. Of course, the first summer Ted could only do the dog paddle from you to Mr. Kennedy, or from me to one of the older children who was closest, but you always made him and Jean a part of the group. They had no fear of the water, and when it was time for you and the older ones to have your swim, he and Jean would put their arms around my neck and one of the older ones and we'd swim back to the pier steps where they were very content to dog paddle and watch the rest of you play ball or have water fights.

"They all had the same color bathing hats so you could identify them in the water.

"The children ate with the family and any guest who might be present, which enabled them to meet many dignitaries and benefit from grown-up discussions of world affairs. This aroused their curiosities and interests and made them more conscious of what was going on around them than the average youngster. It also awakened their interest in history.

"After lunch they all were required to have a rest and be quiet for a while—when they couldn't sleep, they were allowed to read quietly.

"You read to them a good deal, and they looked forward to you telling them stories of when you were in school, growing up, and going on different trips with your father when he was in politics, and particularly loved hearing you tell of Sir Thomas Lipton and his boat.

"I also remember that you encouraged them to play with their puzzles and you would work on them with them, often at the Cape.

"In the early evening after dinner at the Cape, the children looked forward to your playing the piano for them and they loved singing some of the old songs, as well as the new ones you'd teach them. It was funtime for them and they had much fun with the musical games.

"They all wore navy coat sweaters with name tags inside to identify them. Each spring the girls had navy dress coats, navy shoes and purses, and white gloves. They weren't too clothes conscious—just always wanted to look well—and didn't borrow one another's clothes too much, mostly sweaters.

"During schooltime, it was a bit of a ritual after breakfast to check children's nails and spots on uniforms and sweaters."

Faith in God and His wisdom and mercy and goodness and in the teachings of the Church had been instilled in me from my earliest years. One of my nephews became a priest. A niece, Ann Gargan, youngest of Agnes' children, was training to be a nun when illness forced her to leave that vocation. So, religion was "in the family."

I didn't think of myself as being particularly "religious." One of the strange stories that was printed about me much later was that at the Blumenthal convent I used to spend an hour at a time at Confession. Another was that after I was home again I moved to the attic to "mortify" my flesh and spirit. This is nonsense. You already know from the Blumenthal letters that I was a lively young lady who chafed more than a bit under convent restrictions and found some of the ceremonials rather tiresome. I'm sure I never had a "holier-than-thou" attitude because it would never have occurred to me that I was any "holier" than anybody I knew. I was just an ordinary, stanch, believing Irish Roman Catholic.

This also meant that my faith and my Church had great importance for me; that I realized their values; and that when I had children of my own I wanted to pass those beliefs and values on to them as they had been passed to me.

Rosemary's misfortune did not incline me in the least toward doubt; but rather, if anything, strengthened my belief and sheltered my spirit from despair. I asked myself endlessly why this had to happen to her. I felt it was so unfair for her to have so many handicaps and the others to be so blessed. The more I thought, the clearer it became to me that God in His infinite wisdom did have a reason, though it was hidden from me, and that in time, in some way, it would be unfolded to me. "God wants something different from each of us."

Religion was never oppressive nor even conspicuous in our household, but it was always there, part of our lives, and the Church's teachings and customs were observed. We went to Mass on Sundays, holy days, First Fridays. We said grace before meals. I would choose a different child each time to say grace. At Sunday dinner after the Mass, we generally had a little discussion of what the sermon had been about, what the Gospel message meant, so the children would pay attention during Mass. If it was a holy day or a favorite saint's day, we discussed its meaning and asked what the saint's life could teach us. At Easter, of course, we asked the meaning of the Resurrection and Life Everlasting. Why did Jesus accept crucifixion and suffer and die for us? What was He doing for us, and by His example telling all of us? Faith, I would tell them, is a great gift from God and is a living gift, to sustain us in our lives on earth, to guide us in our activities, to be a source of solace and comfort, so we should do everything we can to strengthen its roots, to nourish it, and to help it grow and flourish, and try never to lose it. Many of the institutions of the Church are meant to help us in this way, and of course do. Catechism: I would hear them recite their lessons every week before Sunday school. I also encouraged the idea—in youth and adulthood—of making a yearly retreat, spending a weekend away from the world in a quiet, wholly religious environment of devotion, instruction, and contemplation.

When they were little they accepted their religious training with few questions; the normal, innocent, curious questions. As they grew older, toward and into adulthood, they responded and questioned or accepted in their individual ways.

Dave Powers, a close friend and political associate of our family for many years, Boston Irish Catholic born and bred, has a story about Teddy:

"This is at Hyannis Port and Mr. Kennedy and I and young Ted —he's a big, strong, very healthy boy or youth of maybe sixteen, anyway old enough to be driving—are having breakfast together that morning and Ted is telling his father about the weekend he's got planned for sailing and racing. They're sailing up to Edgartown from the Port, and he's talking about the crew and how they're going to race. Just then his mother—who had just returned from Mass and Holy Communion—walked into the room and when the discussion had slowed a bit she said, 'Ted, I made arrangements for you to attend retreat up at Lawrence.'

"And I looked at him, thinking what I might have said to my own mother in a situation like that. He said, 'Yes, Mother, I'll be ready to go.'

"And then she went upstairs to change. His father, realizing how Ted must have felt after all those plans and all that, said, 'Ted, you can drive my new car up to the retreat.' Ted thanked him, and a minute or two later he left the room.

"His father was gazing at him as he went. And then Joseph P. Kennedy turned to me and said, 'Dave,'—and those blue eyes were a little misty—'Dave, you know, he's a good boy.'"

I wanted all of the children to have at least a few years in good Catholic schools, where along with excellent secular education they would receive thorough instruction in the doctrines of their religion and intelligent answers to any doubts or perplexities. A child thus educated, I maintained, would have more poise, more peace of mind, more confidence about settling the problems of everyday living, and a better concept of his duties toward his God, his neighbor, and himself. This was one of the very few instances in which Joe and I were in disagreement. He said that a child learned faith and morals at home, and that for the boys, in particular, when they grew up they would be dealing with people of all faiths or none, and he wanted them to meet all men on their merits without consciousness of religious factors, which were matters of personal belief. As a consequence, all the girls had some years at convent school, but the boys were educated almost entirely at secular schools. Joe Jr., in fact entirely. Jack, part of a year at Canterbury, a Catholic prep school. Bobby had a year or two at Portsmouth Priory in Rhode Island, and Teddy had a term there when he was very young and another at Cranwell, a Jesuit school in western Massachusetts.

Yet, in retrospect, it's clear I needn't have worried. The boys as well as the girls seemed to have deep religious convictions, though as usual each manifested them in his or her own individual way. Eunice says:

"I don't remember any of my grandparents or aunts or uncles being intellectually or emotionally superdevout. Mother was, always was within my memory, and where it came from I don't know. Of course, I was fifth in the family, so by the time I was old enough to understand anything a lot had already happened and obviously I wouldn't know. I do have clear impressions later, and I remember we were doing all the First Fridays and all that and Joe Jr. was quite serious about it. He was in the St. Paul Catholic Club at Harvard and later on, when he was training for naval aviation at Jacksonville, he was head of the Catholic club there. Bobby was really quite religious. He was at Communion on Sundays all the time. He was very strong on this."

Pat says:

"I remember Bobby wanting to be an altar boy, that would be at St. Joseph's Church when we lived in Bronxville. I suppose they all were altar boys, but he was next youngest to me and for some years there he was the little brother, so I was conscious of this ambition and how much he worked at it. My room was between his and Mother's. I used to go into his room to hear his Latin. Then Mother would come in, or he'd go into her room, so he could show her how much he'd learned. He worked hard at it.

"We always had a rosary on our beds; and then, of course, she'd hear our bedtime prayers and do our Catechism with us every week for Sunday school. But I don't recall any abnormal pressure at all."

I felt that each should have at least one summer, at a summer camp away from the seashore, so they would know about camping and life in the fields and forests. I must add in all candor that by the time Pat and Bobby, the sixth and seventh, came along, the idea had begun to seem even better to me, since it meant I would have one or two fewer children to struggle with during the summer. However, this turned out to be one of my least successful ventures in child rearing. Most of the older ones went, as I recall, for short times but didn't really care for the experience at all and said loudly and clearly they would rather have been at home with the family at Hyannis Port. With Pat and Bobby my plan nearly led to disaster. The summer when he was twelve and she was barely fourteen, both went to camp and both became dangerously ill: she with acute appendicitis requiring an emergency operation. She was joined at the same hospital a day or two later by Bobby, another emergency case, with pneumonia. Neither knew the other was there.

Pat says:

"They told me at the hospital that there was a little boy down the hall who really liked Cokes and comics and things, but they didn't say who it was—they thought I'd be so upset. I think we traded a few comic books and sent a few oral messages back and forth, but it was days before we realized we were doing this with each other."

It was in this ordeal—and needless to say Joe and I were terribly worried—that we had the great good fortune to meet and know Luella Hennessey. She was a special nurse at the hospital and was put in charge of Pat's care; and knowing Pat's brother was down the hall, she was in and out to see him too. It was she who delivered the messages and comic books, and I think it was she who broke the news to them about each other. In any case, both children became extremely fond of her, with the result that she became an integral part of our family life. I now have twenty-eight grandchildren, and she has been on hand to take care of twenty-seven of them from birth. (As it happens, the exception was Pat's own first born, Christopher Lawford: He came a few days early, and I was visiting Pat and Peter at that time, so I took charge and took care of him.) Luella wrote in Pat's book about Bobby:

"I suspect that Bobby and Pat connived to have me go to Hyannis Port with them; and then later, to England with the family at the time their father was Ambassador to Great Britain. Thus, it may very well be that these two young people conspired to alter the course of my life. . . .

"Even at twelve, Bobby was 'people-minded.' People interested him, and the problems and troubles of people concerned him deeply. Not only were his eyes quick to see, but his heart and mind were prompt to follow through.

"At the Brompton Oratory"—our church and parish house in London—"Bobby noticed that each priest had to supply fuel for the fireplace in his room. He also observed that when his priest friend was short of funds, he was also short of fuel! He spoke to his father about this predicament, and Mr. Kennedy arranged for a year's supply of wood to be sent in. This deep love for people made me think that perhaps Bobby would be the Kennedy who would one day enter a seminary and follow the religious life. But it was not to be so; he was a lay apostolate."

And what about Jack, who was destined to be the first Catholic President of the United States? Eunice goes on to say:

"He tended to be casual about religious rituals and observances as in a lot of other things. I personally felt so strongly about them that when I was at college at Manhattanville I used to call him up, and he must have thought I was crazy—here I was nineteen years of age and calling and asking him why he wasn't going to church on First Fridays. But he went to Sunday Mass. I lived with him a long time while he was a congressman in Washington, and he always hustled off to Mass. People who were with him on his campaigns and travels say he always did, wherever he was. With his inquiring mind I think he was always a little less convinced about some things than the rest of us. But that didn't make him less truly religious. He prayed. Lem Billings, his roommate through prep school, has said: 'Never can I remember Jack not saying his prayers on his knees every night before going to bed.' And this lasted right on through. One night when Dad was visiting at the White House, it was late and he started into Jack's bedroom to mention something he had just thought of. Then he stopped short and left without being noticed—because there was the President kneeling by his bed, saying his prayers.

"So the training Mother put us through and her own unquestioning strong belief made an impression that lasted. She was successful in instilling firm faith in all her children."

I always felt the children should have as much continuity as possible in their education. At best, changing schools is disquieting, moreover, since curriculums and textbooks are not standardized from one school and locality to another, a transferring student may find himself at a serious academic disadvantage. For that reason I stayed on in Brookline with the children a couple of years after Joe's first big venture in the movie business obliged him to spend his work weeks in New York City. Only when he was certain that this business was solidly successful and would be taking most of his time in the foreseeable future, did I consent to move from our Boston suburb to a New York suburb, with the proviso that it be a place with excellent schools, preferably within walking distance of home.

Walking to and from school is healthful exercise; it is fun in good weather and teaches perseverance when the weather is bad. It teaches punctuality and responsibility by making the child accountable for lagging and tardiness; and in the coming and going he becomes acquainted with all the children of different ages living in his neighborhood. Eddie Moore was put in charge of the housing problem and produced a good temporary solution in a large and handsomely furnished house, formerly the home of Chief Justice Charles Evans Hughes, in Riverdale, on the Hudson, a small, quiet, pleasant community that lies just north of the city and has an excellent day school for boys and girls.* Meanwhile, Eddie kept on looking and found a rather ideal spot and situation for us a few miles farther north. This was Bronxville, a very attractive village of only a few thousand people, whose average per capita income, however, was among the highest in the country, so they supported an outstanding public-school system. There were also a private school for girls and a private kindergarten. Yet the village was only a mile square, which put the schools and churches within walking distance.

We bought a big house set in six acres of grounds: a property well scaled to the needs of our increasingly large and energetic family. Joe Jr. and Jack continued at Riverdale, riding the school's bus that made the rounds of the area; they had adjusted to the school and were doing well. We didn't want to uproot them so soon again, especially since they were old enough (fourteen and twelve) and

* We lived there two years.

obstreperous enough so that we foresaw we soon would be sending them off to boarding school. All the others, including Jean and Teddy when they came along, had a portion of their schooling in the schools of Bronxville, which remained our home and main base of operations for nearly thirteen years.

We debated whether the children should stay at home and go to day school until ready for college, or at some point in their teens go off to boarding school. If the latter, which school? At what age?

Joe and I had agreed that the responsibility for education of the boys was primarily his, and that of the girls, primarily mine. My conclusions were easier to reach.

I sent Kathleen off to Sacred Heart at Noroton, Connecticut, when she was thirteen. She was quite pretty and was getting altogether too popular with boys, which she enjoyed. She was on the telephone with them for hours at a time and was being distracted from her school-work and other duties by boys inviting her to the Saturday-afternoon movies and so forth. My answer to the situation was to send her away to school.

Eunice never liked this story because, she said, by comparison it made her seem like a wallflower. At that age Eunice was never distracted by the boys, so I never had this problem.

As usual, things did not always work out according to my ideas and plans. In writing this book, I have learned many things I may have suspected but never fully understood until now. Recently Pat was talking about life in Bronxville and her school days.

"That was my first home, at least the first I have any real memories of, because we moved there when I was five and stayed until I was seventeen or eighteen. We had very, very happy times there. Particularly on weekends when Jack and Joe would come down from their schools, usually with some friends along. We had a big lawn. The boys would be playing football or kickball or something, and they would always let us join in. There would be five or six big boys and a small mob of younger children, because each of us probably would have a friend or two over.

"Joe and Jack were terrific with us and of course we thought they were marvelous. To us they were heroes, young gods. It was Mother's idea of having the older children bring the younger ones along. Then all of us, and the school friends, would be together, with Mother and Daddy, for a big, Sunday lunch, which was a very happy time. A very happy house.

"We always had dogs—I remember especially a wirehair terrier named Skippy. We'd skate on the ponds and go sledding and tobogganing, because there were a lot of hills and open spaces. I liked that town. Even the tradespeople were especially nice. There was a drugstore on a corner, just up from the public school, and it had a great soda fountain, so that's where the kids congregated at noontime and after. It also had great gum and Life Savers, and the trick was to get in there and steal the gum and Life Savers without being caught. The owner knew what was happening and kept a sharp eye on all of us. But I guess he charged up a few gum and mint losses to normal cost of doing business in a place like that full of kids. Anyway, he never turned any of us in to our parents, which was kind of him, because they would have been very upset, my mother especially. I liked the school, the people, my friends, the whole scene. So when the family came back from England in 1939 I was returning to a place I was happy to be in.

"But then a question about schools. I was fifteen and a half and would be going into my junior year of high school. Kick and Eunice had both been to Sacred Heart at Noroton and Mother felt it was time for me to go too, and graduate from there. But from being away in England—some different subjects there and taught in different ways from those at home—she thought I might possibly have to repeat a year back here. And if that happened I would stay home during that time and go to day school. But the only way to know would be for me to go up to Noroton and take the exams.

"So I went there and they asked me the date of the Battle of Hastings, and I said it was 1740.

"They asked me about the Declaration of Independence and I said it was 1812.

"They asked me to recite the Apostles Creed and I recited the 'Our Father'—something like that.

"I came home and they called Mother up and said, 'This child really has to stay back.'

"Mother then put me in a convent school at Maplehurst, which is about a fifteen-minute ride from Bronxville. Of course, within a matter of about two weeks they put me up to junior year there. But by then Mother decided it was too late to send me off to Sacred

Heart at Noroton, because everything would have started and I'd be behind, so she settled for the other, which is also a very good school.

"So that's how I could stay home. In fact, I never went to boarding school until college.

"I never told her what I had done."

Pat was so bright that I suspected there might be something unusual—possibly even a little fishy—to account for her poor performance on that exam. Now the truth is out.

While the children were young I always felt I could manage the boys in their little escapades and their schooling and everyday problems, but as they became teen-agers I was increasingly uncertain; and it was at this point that I was especially grateful for my husband's experience, sympathy, and judgment.

Joe was a perfect father in dealing with our teen-age sons, not only because he had their love and respect but also because he took every bit of time needed, in all circumstances, to think about them and their needs and what was best for each of them. In the matter of schools, he decided for well-considered reasons they should have their college preparatory years at boarding school, and that the school should suit the boy. A big one such as Andover or Exeter would be right for a boy with a certain temperament, ability, and interests; a smaller one with a different atmosphere might be much better for a boy with a different personality and interests. Joe did a lot of investigating, thinking, and discussing. For a time his chief adviser was Mr. Pennypacker, who had been headmaster of Boston Latin, and who became dean of admissions at Harvard. I wanted a school nearby, so that the boys could visit us on weekends. But these plans never materialized.

It was decided to send Joe Jr. to the Choate School, in Connecticut, and after finishing grade school at Riverdale he was enrolled there. It was a fortunate choice. The school suited him, and clearly he suited the school. His grades were excellent. He entered enthusiastically into school activities and demonstrated qualities of leadership that brought high praise from his masters and, of course, made Joe and me very proud of him.

As Joe noted later, in the introduction to Jack's book *As We Remember Joe:*

"At Choate he played end on the undefeated football team of his senior year, was vice-president of the St. Andrews Society, editor of the yearbook, and won the Harvard football trophy, 'awarded to that member of the Choate football squad who best combines scholarship and sportsmanship.' "

He wanted to go to Harvard and was accepted there, which of course deeply pleased his father, a loyal alumnus. However, Joe and I wanted the children to have a year of study abroad. The question was, should this come after college or before? The decision for Joe Jr. was before. Which country, which school? There were many consultations. Finally, we had a long talk with Felix Frankfurter, the Harvard Law professor and later Supreme Court Justice, who at that time was on an exchange professorship at Cambridge University. Joe then decided to send our eldest son to the London School of Economics to study under Professor Harold Laski.

Professor Laski was one of the best-known theoreticians and leaders of British socialism, and interpreters and scholars of Marxism in its various forms.

I must say I was rather taken aback by this choice. I asked Joe why he chose the London School of Economics in favor of sending Joe Jr. to Oxford or Cambridge to study under renowned professors at those great and famous places? After all, Joe was by that time—1933—quite a well-known capitalist. His answers, which puzzled me then, make perfect sense now. The United States and most of the Western world were in the grip of the Depression, and there were many revolutionary currents and ideas—Marxist and semi-Marxist—in the political atmosphere. Roosevelt had taken office and the New Deal had barely begun. It was still unformulated, and no one could be sure whether the new Administration would succeed in restoring stability and a sense of confidence in the free-enterprise system. Therefore, he wanted our son to understand the challenges he might be facing as put forth by a brilliant challenger, Professor Laski. He already had the same plan in mind for Jack. For after all, he said, "These boys are going to have a little money when they get older, and they should know what the 'have nots' are thinking and planning." As he said later in an interview, speaking of Professor Laski: "I disagreed with everything he wrote . . . But I never taught the boys to disapprove of someone just because I didn't accept his ideas. They heard enough from me, and I decided they should be exposed to someone of intelligence and vitality on the other side."

It is interesting to know what Professor Laski thought about this youth of barely nineteen, who arrived in the autumn of 1933 to attend his extremely sophisticated classes in economics.

When Jack was doing his book about Joe he asked the professor for any comments or memories he might have about his brother. I am going to quote from those pages, beginning with Jack's own lines of introduction to them:

"When Professor Laski was asked to write about Joe, he wrote back, 'Joe is one of the most vivid memories among all of the students I have had, so that I am glad, indeed, to do what you ask.' The year that Joe spent with Professor Laski was a decisive year for him, and under Professor Laski's encouragement, a career in Public Service became Joe's dominant ambition."

Professor Laski wrote:

"A large part of every teacher's life is in the students for whom he feels a special affection; and when they die, something in him, I think, dies too. Joe came to work with me at the London School of Economics and Political Science in 1933–34, for the year before he entered Harvard. He was adorably young and still more adorably unsophisticated. He went to some seven or eight lectures each week and did a weekly essay for me; and he accompanied my wife and me when I went to lecture at the University of Moscow in the summer of 1934.

"Three things, above all, stand out in my recollection of young Joe in that year. Above all, his astonishing vitality. He was interested in everything and only disturbed by the limitations of twenty-four hours which Nature has put on the day. And, second, there was his astonishing capacity for enthusiasm. What he liked, he liked with all his heart. He had nothing of the cynic's pose which sometimes affects the undergraduate. He gave all of himself to what he did with immense energy and eagerness. The third thing was his profound interest in politics. He had set his heart on a political career; he had often sat in my study and submitted with that smile that was pure magic to relentless teasing about his determination to be nothing less than President of the United States.

"At the stage when Joe worked with me, of course, his mind was only just beginning to discover the enchantment of thought. But his essays were written with great care, and he took criticism with a disarming friendliness. He never stopped asking questions. I had him join a seminar of mine which was intended for third-year students; and I can see now the quick shift of his attention as the argument moved from one undergraduate to another . . . He was very popular with the other students. He was so simple and so frank and so forthright. They loved to tease him about his American ways, and I think he enjoyed being teased if only because the process enabled him to affirm, with that special kind of laughter that has intense conviction behind, his love for America . . .

"He never posed. He was always anxious to know. He repaid one's efforts with a fidelity of heart that was deeply moving . . . I am glad I knew Joe. . . ."

The combination of famous professor and young precollege student, of London and Boston, of Jewish descent and Irish descent, of erudite scholarship and eager curiosity, of deeply compassionate interest in the welfare of humanity by both and a mutual desire to do something to better it, was one that I think few men but my husband, in his situation and at that time in history, would have ventured—and then stepped back to see the consequences. And then if necessary, to take his own stand with his son, defend his own beliefs in his own way. I have always felt that this was intellectual honesty and courage of the highest order.

It has been said that when Joe Jr. came back from his studies with Professor Laski and that summer with the Laskis in Russia, he and his father had heated arguments about the comparative merits of capitalism and communism, that emotions became high, and that at least one time Joe Jr. "bolted from the table" and another time Joe Sr. "stalked away." Well, all I can say is that I was there and nothing of that sort happened.

I do remember a couple of incidents within that context. Joe Jr. did come home well immersed in the idea and ideals of socialism, and he did declare himself in favor, for instance, of all people sharing equally in the world's wealth. I suggested that in that case he should give up his boat and just fish off the pier or play baseball or do other things that most people do for recreation. Joe Jr. objected to that vigorously, for, he said, one person giving up one boat would not make enough difference in the social objective of sharing the wealth. Joe often said, "If I were their age I probably would believe what they believe, but I am of a different background and must voice my beliefs."

Another time, after one of these Sr. and Jr. debates, I remember Jack—then around sixteen or seventeen—commenting to me, "Joe seems to understand the situation a little better than Dad." I mentioned this later to their father and he said:

"I don't care what the boys think about my ideas. I can always look out for myself. The important thing is that they should stick together." That thought dominated him and them all their lives. Bob and Ted had the same philosophy. Very important.

As Jack went on to record in his book about Joe:

"The following year he entered Harvard, and his success was immediate. He played football and Rugby for four years, was a member of the Freshman Union Committee, chairman of the Smoker Committee, on the Student Council for three years, and was chairman his senior year. He managed the financial end of his class yearbook, was elected chairman of his Class Day Committee, was a member of the Pi Eta, Hasty Pudding, and St. Paul Catholic Clubs, and in 1938 graduated *cum laude*. . . .

"Though a glance at Joe's record shows that he had great success, things did not come particularly easy for him. I think his accomplishments were due chiefly to the amazing intensity with which he applied himself to the job on hand. I do not think I can ever remember him to sit back in a chair and relax. Even when still, there was always a sense of motion forcibly restrained. And yet, this continuous motion did not have its roots in restlessness or nervousness but rather came from his intense enthusiasm for everything he did and his exceptional stamina. . . ."

Thus, for Joe Jr., this combination—Choate, the London School of Economics and Political Science, and Harvard—evidently came close to being ideal.

In 1945, when Jack was writing these words about his brother, it was before he entered politics or had any clear idea of what he wanted to do with his life, or whether he would ever amount to much. Yet I expect that in the back of his mind he may have been thinking how different his own academic career had been in so many ways, with the same opportunities and at most of the same institutions.

Many people have asked me about Jack's teen-age years. Did he like school, did he do well, what were his favorite subjects, what didn't he like, did he have any "adolescent problems," and so forth.

The best way to tell that story is to let it tell itself through a series of letters, with such comments and explanatory notes as may be needed from me to supply the missing links.

Jack went through his fourth, fifth, and sixth grades at Riverdale Country Day School and did reasonably well; I think it leveled out to around a B— average. Meanwhile Joe Jr. had gone to Choate and was doing so well there we decided it would be a good place for Jack, too, so we put in his application the spring of 1929, in advance, for enrollment in the fall of 1931. We were advised that he should first have a year away, at some other boarding school, so he could mature and become accustomed to boarding-school life. As I have said, I wanted each of them to have at least a while in a Catholic school, so it was decided he would go to the Canterbury school.

It was not one of his better years. As I look back over his letters home—I discover that his spelling remained peculiarly his own ("I learnt how to play baggamon to-day . . ."), that his right eye was bothering him ("I see things blury even at a distance of ten feet"), that he had a sledding accident ("The hill is all ruts and all icey for ½ mi. You go from 35 mi. to 40 mi."); and that "my Latin could stand improving"; and, P.S., that "We have Scott's 'Lady of the Lake' in English." Then, during Easter vacation of 1931, with his bad luck in health he was stricken with appendicitis and had to have an operation. By the time he recovered, the school year at Canterbury was nearly ended, so there was no point in his going back. Instead, we engaged a tutor to work with him at home, in the hope that with concentrated study he could pass the entrance examinations for Choate that summer, and thus still join his elder brother there that fall.

I see that on July 3 I wrote to Choate's headmaster George St. John, from Hyannis Port:

"Jack and I were delighted to hear that he passed the English and Mathematics. His tutor and he were extremely doubtful about the Latin—so he was not too disappointed. I am arranging for him to work down here every day with an experienced teacher, and I hope and I will make sure that by the end of September he will know his first-year Latin. As a matter of fact, he hates routine work but loves History and English, subjects which fire his imagination.

"Again let me thank you for your interest and patience with Jack. He has a very attractive personality—we think—but he is quite different from Joe, for whom we feel you have done so much.

"Sincerely yours,
"Rose Kennedy"

After intensive drill during the rest of the summer he took the Latin exam again. He passed. And that fall entered Choate, for which we all were thankful.

As usual and for a long string of reasons—from scarlet fever when he was two to the appendicitis when he was thirteen—I was concerned about his health, and I see from correspondence that I was in touch fairly often with the school about that, usually with Mrs. St. John, who, as wife of the headmaster, stood *in loco parentis* for the mothers of all those boys and, I expect, heard from quite a few of them. I see that Jack was soon afflicted by a bad cold or virus that gave him some badly swollen glands, and I wrote to her with some of his medical history. He'd had the same trouble before. My next letter was:

"Dear Mrs. St. John,

"I understand from Jack's letter that he is much better, and he also said something about eating in the Tuck Shop in order to get 'built up.' I was a bit worried at that suggestion because the Tuck Shop usually means sweets to me, and Jack has no discretion; in fact, he has never eaten enough vegetables to satisfy me.

"I do not want to bother you, but will someone please investigate this matter a little? . . . I do want him to go along the right track.

"How is his weight? My records show 114½–115 in January—after supper.

"Sincerely yours,
"Rose F. Kennedy"

And in due course, as the years went along, messages from me such as:

"I received your letter regarding the condition of Jack's feet. It is probable that his fallen arches are the cause of the trouble. He has inherited that weakness in his feet and he has persisted in wearing cheap, rubber-soled shoes during the last two or three years.

"I shall be interested to hear whether or not he finds relief when his shoes are built up. Please write to me. . . . Let me thank you for your interest and attention."

And:

"Dear Mrs. St. John,
"I should like very much to hear about Jack's knee. . . ."

And so it went. At least once he was hospitalized with a football injury. Despite his proneness to illness and injury he went ahead with activities in several sports including football. Or at least tried to. He wasn't nearly heavy, nor strong, nor healthy enough for the varsity. But one of his teammates spoke of him later as "a tiger on defense." And the coach has said:

"The most burning thing I can remember about Jack was that he was a fighter. You take Joe, he was a real athlete. But Jack made up for what he lacked in ability with his fight."

I was often anxious about his physical health in those years; and so was his father. Yet by that time, I suppose, both of us were accustomed to the idea that every now and then he would be laid up by some disease or accident. What concerned us as much, or more, was his lack of diligence in his studies; or, let us say, lack of "fight" in trying to do well in those subjects that didn't happen to interest him. Like practically all the old, established eastern prep schools in those days, Choate had a highly "structured" set of rules, traditions, and expectations into which a boy was supposed to fit; and if he didn't, there was little or no "permissiveness." Joe Jr. had no trouble at all operating within this system; it suited his temperament. But Jack couldn't or wouldn't conform. He did pretty much what he wanted, rather than what the school wanted of him.

After his first year there, with a poor set of marks, it was decided he should stay on for the summer session to improve his standing. Mr. Steele, the director of the summer school, wrote to my husband:

"You may count on us in every way to do everything in our power to stabilize Jack this summer and make him appreciate not only the necessity but the advantage of consistent and well-balanced effort. . . ."

But Mr. Steele was doomed to disappointment. The more pressure that was put on Jack, the more he seemed to find ways to frustrate and annoy those in charge. One winter I sent him a crate of oranges from Florida, and he amused himself by pegging some of them out his window at friends who were passing by below. It was a silly thing to do, and one of the masters caught him at it. He received another demerit. Once he collected all the pillows from all the rooms in his dorm and put them in some boy's room, filling up the whole room top to bottom, so that when the boy came back from a class and opened his door there was just a solid mass of pillows. At the end of his second year, his housemaster Mr. Maher filed a despondent report with Mr. St. John.

"I'd like to take the responsibility for Jack's constant lack of neatness about his room and person, since he lived with me for two years. But in the matter of neatness, despite a genuine effort on Jack's part, I must confess to failure.

"Occasionally we did manage to effect a house cleaning, but it necessitated my 'dumping' everything in the room into a pile in the middle of the floor. Jack's room has throughout the year been subject to instant and unannounced inspection—it was the only way to maintain a semblance of neatness, for Jack's room was a club for his friends.

"I regard the matter of neatness or lack of it on Jack's part as quite symbolic—aside from the value it has in itself—for he is casual and disorderly in almost all of his organization projects. Jack studies at the last minute, keeps appointments late, has little sense of material value, and can seldom locate his possessions. . . ."

Hoping against hope, or perhaps grasping at straws, Mr. Maher did go on to say in conclusion:

"Jack has had a thoroughly genuine try at being neat according to his own standards and he has been almost religiously on time throughout the (last) quarter. I believe Jack . . . has and is trying to be a more socially-minded person."

The outstanding talent Jack had demonstrated in school—as Mr. Maher indicated—was a talent for making friends and enjoying friendships. He had, it began to seem to me, innumerable friends, for during vacations and special weekends when he came home he invariably had at least one, usually two, three, four, or more school friends with him. We never knew whom to expect or how many. It became a joke in the family, a little shorthand expression that evoked a lot, "Jack's surprises." After a while, though, it was no surprise to see LeMoyne ("Lem") Billings, who became Jack's best friend and finally his roommate. They had great rapport; and they sparked each other to various pieces of nonsense including one at the expense of the long-suffering housemaster Mr. Maher, who certainly deserved a better life than he had with those two around.

"It was shortly after Jack returned to school from his summer vacation"—Lem relates—"and we were dragging his trunk down the stairs to store it in the cellar. We were making a good deal of noise. Our housemaster, Mr. Maher, came out of his room. He reminded us this was during study period and the noise was a distraction for people who were trying to work. He ordered us to take the trunk back up and bring it down to storage the next morning instead. So Jack and I got up at 6 A.M. We dragged the trunk out and down the stairs, bumping all the way down. Mr. Maher came tearing out of his room, in his bathrobe, wild-eyed, and demanded to know what we thought we were doing. 'But Mr. Maher,' Jack said innocently, 'you *told* us to take it down in the *morning*.'"

Besides talking things over with Jack at home and writing to him, his father was having correspondence with Mr. St. John. It seems to me the headmaster showed a great deal of forbearance and understanding. In Jack's junior year he wrote:

"The fact of the matter is that I cannot feel seriously uneasy or worried about Jack. The longer I live and work with him and the more I talk with him, the more confidence I have in him. I would be willing to bet anything that within two years you will be as proud of Jack as you now are of Joe.

"Jack has a clever, individualist mind. It is a harder mind to put in harness than Joe's—harder for Jack himself to put in harness. . . . A more conventional mind and a more plodding and mature point of view would help him a lot more right now; but we have to allow, my dear Mr. Kennedy, with boys like Jack, for a period of adjustment. All that natural cleverness Jack has to learn how to use in his life and work, even to cover it up at times, how to subordinate it, and all the rest. I never yet saw a clever, witty boy who at some stage in his early development was not considered fresh . . . the final product is often more interesting and effective than the boy with a more conventional mind who has been to us parents and teachers much less trouble.

". . . By and by, when Jack is in college, and especially when he can choose his own subjects, his academic output will correspond more nearly with his high I.Q."

Considering how much Joe wanted for our sons and how much he wanted them to respond to their opportunities, his response to Jack's peccadilloes was, I should think, a model of reasonableness.

"Now, Jack," he wrote in one of his letters, "I don't want to give the impression that I am a nagger, for goodness knows that is the worst thing a parent can be. After long experience in sizing up people, I definitely know you have the goods, and you can go a long way. Now aren't you foolish not to get all there is out of what God has given you?

"After all, I would be lacking even as a friend if I did not urge you to take advantage of the qualities you have. It is very difficult to make up fundamentals that you have neglected when you were very young, and that is why I am urging you to do the best you can. I am not expecting too much, and I will not be disappointed if you don't turn out to be a real genius, but I think you can be a really worthwhile citizen with good judgment and understanding."

By the end of the first quarter of his senior year, Jack evidently was beginning to see the light clearly, for he wrote to his father:

"Dear Dad:

"I thought I would write you right away as LeMoyne and I have been talking about how poorly we have done this quarter, and we have definitely decided to stop any fooling around. I really do realize how important it is that I get a good job done this year if I want to go to England." (To study under Professor Laski, as Joe Jr. had done.) "I really feel, now that I think it over, that I have been bluffing myself about how much real work I have been doing. . . .

"I really feel that we will get something done this quarter as Le-Moyne seems to feel the same way as I do.

"Love,
"Jack"

Nevertheless, it was about the same time, or a bit later, that these two characters formed a little enterprise to pull the headmaster's leg—that nearly pulled the roof down on their heads.

Mr. St. John often addressed the student body assembled for convocations or at chapel. His remarks were designed to inspire, guide, if necessary chastise, and in general to expound the ideals of the school and the kind of responsible citizenship he expected from the students. Any boy who did not uphold those ideals, behaved irresponsibly, disrespected the aims and disciplines of the school did not belong at Choate, and he had a descriptive term that summed up all such unworthy qualities. The term was "mucker." "Muckers" were everything that was not wanted at Choate.

Lem Billings, at my request, wrote me a letter recently explaining—close to forty years later—just how it happened that he and Jack organized a "Muckers Club."

"In those times part of the daily schedule at Choate was compulsory evening chapel, starting about twenty minutes after supper.

And in those times, seniors were the only students allowed to have combination radio-phonographs—and Jack and I had a very good one. As it happened, our room was directly above the dining hall, and with the stairway close by it was very convenient for us to get down and back for meals—and also, of course, very convenient for other boys to get from the dining hall up to our room, and with those twenty minutes to kill they were coming up by the dozens to listen to the radio-phonograph. The congestion became so bad that sometimes Jack and I couldn't get into our own room. So we decided to form a club—and only club members could be in the room during that period.

"We chose thirteen of our best friends as members. All of them were top athletes of the school; but there were none representing student government.

"There was nothing wrong so far: The unfortunate thing was the name we chose. Mr. St. John used the word 'mucker' as the epitome of the worst element. Therefore, in our juvenile way we found it amusing to call our group the Muckers Club. We even had little gold charms designed in the shape of shovels and engraved 'Choate Muckers Club.' I don't know whatever happened to Jack's, but a couple of Christmases ago I gave mine to Caroline.

"Naturally, I suppose, rumors began to spread. The worst things Jack and I ever did at Choate were to keep a messy room and be late for classes. Some of our members, I expect, did break the school code of conduct by going into town and smoking, drinking, and so forth. Anyway, the rumors centered on our room because that's where the club met nightly. The school gossip reached Mr. St. John, and when he heard the name of the club—he saw red. He was furious.

"Jack and I were the prime targets of the wrath.

"He called my mother—my father had died two years before—and she had to come all the way from Pittsburgh to have a session with him and me about my part in the Muckers Club. She decided it was much ado about very little.

"He called Mr. Kennedy in Washington and asked him to come up to Choate to discuss Jack's part. Mr. Kennedy was chairman of the Securities and Exchange Commission and there were many important matters to occupy his full time and attention in Washington. But he came up anyway."

Many years later Mr. St. John was asked to recall this episode and meeting for a book about Jack, *John Fitzgerald Kennedy . . . As We Remember Him*, and he said:

"He was the chief mover in the group. . . . They weren't wicked kids, but they were a nuisance. At one time, it came to the point where I was saying to myself, 'Well, I have two things to do, one to run the school, another to run Jack Kennedy and his friends.' And they weren't bad, you know, but they had to be looked after. In other words, they just weren't maturing. So I wrote to Mr. Kennedy, and I said, 'I think you and Jack and I ought to have a three-cornered talk, Mr. Kennedy. Could you come up here. . . .' We held nothing back. I was angry. . . . Psychologically I was enormously interested. I couldn't see how two boys from the same family as were Joe and Jack could be so different. But Mr. Kennedy and Jack and I sat together, in my study, and I rehearsed the chapter and verse of things that had happened. . . .

"Well, we reduced Jack's conceit, if it was conceit, and childishness to considerable sorrow. And we said just what we thought, held nothing back, and Mr. Kennedy was supporting the school completely. I've always been very grateful to him.

"There are lots of boys who go through a period like that, and the greatest kindness is some severity. Jack's father didn't hold back. In fact, he spoke very, very strongly, and also with Irish wit. You know, in dealing with Jack, you needed a little wit as well as a little seriousness. Jack didn't like to be too serious; he had a delightful sense of humor, always. His smile was, I think, as a young boy, when he first came to school—well, in any school he would have got away with some things just on his smile. He was a very likable person, very lovable."

The final outcome of the Muckers escapade was that both boys graduated with their class at Choate, in 1935, in no disgrace. Jack, in fact, though his cumulative grades placed him slightly below the middle of his class, was voted "most likely to succeed."

Lem went on to Princeton, did well there, and afterward has made an interesting and successful life for himself. He remained Jack's lifelong close friend, confidant, sharer in old memories and new experiences. He has continued to be to this day for all our family, a wonderful friend to all of us, in all weathers, in all times. Lem is always there whenever he feels help may be needed. He has really been part of "our family" since that first time he showed up at our house as one of "Jack's surprises."

As for Jack, I think that this silly episode of the Muckers may well have been a turning point in his life. I'm sure he didn't like that confrontation with the headmaster and his father, that "three-cornered talk." Something certainly soaked in, and deeply. There would be no way to measure the influence of this embarrassing necessity to talk things out—and to have a good talking-to, in open forum, from his father. Probably it was also, or even more, as Mr. St. John has indicated, a matter of "passing through a phase" and thus of getting a little experience leading to adult maturity and perspective. At any rate, his life took on a new momentum from then on.

Chapter Eleven

꧁ ꧂

As Joe's wife and hostess, and with his expanding activities in so many fields of business and government, I found there was seldom a dull moment. I was involved, for example, in the golden age of films because Joe very soon became one of the leaders of the movie industry. Others such as Louis B. Mayer, Jesse Lasky, the Schenck brothers, and Adolph Zukor were shrewd entrepreneurs and showmen. So was Joe—but he had the advantage of knowing the world of stocks and bonds and corporations. When he went to Hollywood there were predictions that this Boston Irishman soon would be sadder and poorer. Instead, in less than three years after entering film production, he headed or controlled three studios, and had merged them with Radio Corporation of America to form a major new studio—RKO—contending with Paramount, Metro-Goldwyn-Mayer, Fox, Warners, Universal, and other large studios of the period. Consequently I knew a number of the stars, some of whom visited us at Bronxville or Hyannis Port.

One who thrilled our children especially was Fred Thompson, a handsome and highly intelligent Princeton Ph.D., who with his horse Silver King (highly trained and, for a horse, very intelligent) was one of the popular heroes of the Westerns. Joe paid Fred fifteen thousand dollars a week. When not carrying Fred around through quicksand gullies, Silver King enjoyed a life of ease in a mahogany-floored twenty-five-thousand-dollar stable.

There was so much money to be made in the movie business in those days the stars began to feel that, even with their huge salaries, they were not being paid a share commensurate with the profits generated for the studios. Douglas Fairbanks, Mary Pickford, Harold Lloyd, Charlie Chaplin, and others, therefore, decided not to renew their studio contracts but form their own companies to produce their own pictures, taking the financial risks involved but also reaping the potential great gains. Gloria Swanson wanted to do this, too. While she could earn twenty thousand dollars a week on contract at Paramount, it followed that if she could have the right business advice and management, she might earn even far more in independent productions.

Obviously the best adviser-manager-financier in Hollywood was Joe Kennedy. I knew few of the details of his business ventures, whether buying and selling an office building, or stocks and bonds, or movie properties, but I do know that Gloria wanted his advice and he did help to set her up as an "independent," under the label of Gloria Productions, Inc., and he became the managing director of this additional enterprise.

Gloria was grateful. She told me she was in a financial morass. Mary Pickford had her mother to advise her. Harold Lloyd had his brother; everyone seemed to have a fully trustworthy adviser, but she had none and really needed someone like Joe. She was married to the Marquis Henri de la Falaise de la Coudraye. But although "Hank" (as his Hollywood friends called him) was a very attractive, charming, witty, and delightful man, a perfect consort for Gloria, he knew little about business, finance, or the complexities of film production.

Among the films Joe made for Gloria Productions, I have special personal memories of *The Trespasser* (1928). Joe felt it had potentialities of becoming a great box office hit, and to that end he decided on a campaign of international publicity with successive premières in Paris, London, New York, and Los Angeles, building to a tremendous climax when the film was released to the general public.

Joe, his sister, Margaret Burke, and I therefore sailed in June 1928 for France, and were joined by Gloria in Paris.

There was a lot of excitement, fun, and crises.

Much of the excitement revolved around clothes. Gloria and I both needed some things to wear. Gloria had to have something not only becoming, but spectacular, something that would draw gasps and ohs and ahs and would photograph well. Since there would be four different premières, she needed four different outfits. And she was not easy to dress, because she was small. Tall women have more options in dress than short ones; and while I am short, less than five feet three inches, Gloria is smaller.

The leading couturier of Paris in those times was Lucien Lelong. We went to his salon. I had bought some clothes in Paris when I was a schoolgirl traveling with Agnes and our father and later traveling with Joe, but this was my first full exposure to the *haute couture* at the height of its dazzling elegance. I sat fascinated as the beautiful mannequins slinked and slithered the length of the ornate salon showing M. Lelong's creations. And, of course, being with Gloria magnified the experience, for the *vendeuses* and management hovered around her, attentive to her every whim; and both the girls and the customers kept stealing glances at her. She was the great celebrity. I, by comparison, was a nobody, just the wife of the producer. But it was fun being with her and sharing in the excitement she generated.

My own special interest in clothes developed during this period, not just from this episode but from the general circumstances of which it was an especially vivid part.

During Joe's years in the movie industry he was surrounded daily by some of the most beautiful women in the world, dressed in beautiful clothes. Obviously, I couldn't compete in natural beauty, but I could make the most of what I had by keeping my figure trim, my complexion good, my grooming perfect, and by always wearing clothes that were interesting and becoming. And so, with Joe's endorsement, I began spending more time and more money on clothes. Eventually, I began landing on some lists of "Best Dressed Women." Eunice wrote recently:

"We'd go shopping together in New York, and I'd pick out something and she'd be terrific; I always liked to go with her because she always had better ideas than I had. She'd suggest a dress or two for me, and it was always very nice, the right dress. But if I found another one a bit prettier, I'd find she had already picked that one for herself and she'd have it off, in a corner.

"Or in Paris, we'd see some beautiful dress and I would refuse to buy it because it cost so much; but then she'd buy it and give it to me. She has always been very generous, in addition to her other wonderful qualities. She's fantastic with her children, but she's got her own thing, too."

Pat has a comment:

"I remember in Bronxville when she'd go out at night with Daddy—I remember her coming to kiss me goodnight, and she was always so beautiful. My room was dark and this vision just sort of appeared, smelling absolutely marvelous with her perfume.

"I was fascinated by the perfume, we all were, and as we girls grew older we'd ask her what it was. But she wouldn't tell us. She didn't want even her own daughters to have it. We'd sneak in and try to find it, but we never could. Finally when she was seventy-five she told us. Now we all wear it; it's our favorite perfume.

"Even Ethel took it over.

"But when we all started to smell alike, Mother changed hers to something else."

Eunice continues:

"She has a wonderful sense of color. I was with her lately and we were looking at some dress materials. I picked one out, and she picked one afterward and said 'I would get this one if I were you,' and I looked at it and it was definitely better. She can always do that. She'll do it with me and with my sisters. She has a fashion sense that none of us have ever had. We had the same resources she had, not as much but it was enough, in other words we could afford, but we just never . . .

"I suppose it goes back to the fact that she really likes clothes and likes design—and she likes to look very, very well whenever she goes out. She goes to Mass every morning. I was at Palm Beach and at church, and saw her, and afterward—putting her on a bit—said, 'A joy to see you at Mass.' But I had been sitting back there in my slacks which were too tight and she was up in front with a French dress on."

We went up to Deauville for a few days, back to Paris for our fittings, and everything was going well, with that mounting nervous euphoria that happens before an "opening night."

At this point, unexpectedly, Gloria told Hank (the Marquis de la Falaise) and Joe, and all of us, that she was suing for divorce immediately and Hank could not escort her or be seen with her at the opening night in Paris—just a few evenings away—or any of the other openings.

Joe was flabbergasted. Hank retreated to other quarters in the hotel. Gloria's attitude was one of cold, regal rage. Joe's sister, Margaret, and I were, to say the least, concerned and perplexed. There were two or three close, trusted members of Joe's staff who were there to see that everything went gloriously well, and these seasoned veterans of show business and publicity and studio diplomacy were also in a state of high commotion.

When emotions had cooled enough, we began to take stock. Joe had a lot of money in the movie, and of course so did Gloria—since he was not, after all, subsidizing her but acting as her financier—and he wanted at least to make a profit. So we sat around for long hours discussing the problem. Would it be better "box office" if Gloria were involved in a sensational divorce (as this one was bound to be) or would it cause a boycott of the movie? Some of the sessions at the Ritz reminded me of what it must be like to negotiate a complex international treaty among friendly and unfriendly powers. After hearing all the accusations and arguments and suggestions, Joe finally brought everything back into focus by declaring that he had put money and time and effort into this picture, and so had other people, and these were *not* going to be lost just because of a disagreement between a husband and wife. He proposed that Hank and Gloria *act* out the relationship they had before the trouble began. Until the premières were finished they were to appear in public as a devoted, happy, and glamorous couple.

And that's what happened. Gloria, of course, was a wonderful actress, and Hank showed that he was quite an actor himself. At the Paris opening they walked hand in hand, all smiles. The movie was a grand success and Gloria's performance was greeted with great demonstrations. Lavish bouquets, congratulatory telegrams, parties, and banquets were given with speeches and gallantly phrased toasts to the star.

There was a similar scene in London, and then again in New York. Except that in New York the crowds were more boisterous—perhaps because of the advance publicity from Paris and London—and Gloria, riding with Joe and me in our car, was afraid that someone might break the windows and her face would be cut. That had once happened to a friend of hers. I realized her face was more valuable than mine, but I got rather nervous myself.

After Paris, London, and New York I decided to get back to our children in Bronxville. And I did.

Not long after the Los Angeles opening, and *The Trespasser* was well along to being the great hit that it became, Gloria and Hank were divorced. Later he married Constance Bennett. He was divorced from her and married a wealthy Latin-American girl. I saw him from time to time in the later years, at Capri, Eden Roc, Paris, New York; the same smiling, urbane Marquis Henri, whom we had all enjoyed so much.

Gloria's next picture, after *The Trespasser*, under the flag of Gloria Productions was *Queen Kelly*, which achieved enduring fame in Hollywood as one of the great disasters of all time. Briefly, this is the story:

Following a rash of scandals among Hollywood celebrities and a trend toward salacious movie scenes that caused denunciations of Hollywood as a capital of wickedness, the leaders of the industry had formed the Motion Picture Producers and Distributors of America, Inc., and hired Will Hays, the former Postmaster General and a greatly respected public figure, to take charge of the moral contents of films. The "Hays Office" established a strict and precise "Code." It reviewed all new films and if there were scenes that violated the Code, they had to come out. Otherwise, the film would not be handled by any reputable distributor or exhibitor. Joe was a firm supporter of the Hays Office and moreover became a close personal friend of Will Hays.

The second element of the *Queen Kelly* fiasco was that Joe and Gloria engaged Erich von Stroheim as the director. Von Stroheim was considered one of the great directorial geniuses of films and was one of the very few who could demand complete "artistic control," including "improving" the script as he went along. This time he altered the story in ways Joe would not have dreamed of. From Von Stroheim's fertile mind came a graphic scene of a convent girl being seduced. And another, of a young priest giving the Blessed Sacrament and Last Rites to the madam of a house of ill repute who was dying.

Gloria naturally had begun to worry a good deal about all this, and one day she called Joe, who then was back East to tell him, "There's a madman in charge here. The scenes he's shooting will never get past Will Hays."

At this point, however, Joe was in an emotionally heartrending situation. His father was very ill and, according to the doctors, might die any day. Joe felt he couldn't leave. A round trip to the Coast meant at least a week just in travel time. So he stayed on and supervised the production as best he could by telephone, with Gloria becoming more upset and Von Stroheim more stubborn; while his father faded and rallied again and again as the days and weeks went by. Finally, Joe decided to take a chance and go to California.

While he was away, his father died. Joe couldn't even get back in time for the funeral; a matter that to him, with his very deep family love and loyalty, I know, was a source of painful regret for the rest of his life.

While he was on the Coast, he saw the twenty thousand feet of film that Von Stroheim had shot, realized that the personal vision of the story by the great director wouldn't pass the Hays Office and, even if it did, could not be presented under his own aegis as a "Joseph P. Kennedy Production." So he dismissed Von Stroheim and engaged another fine director, Edmund Goulding, who saw no way to salvage it except by reshooting a large part. Costs were already around $700,-000, the price of a great "epic" in those days. After trying various remedies, while costs rose to $800,000, Joe decided the only rational thing was to cut the prospective losses and scrap the whole venture. That is precisely what happened. Thus ended the sad saga of *Queen Kelly*. Almost.

Many years later, when both Gloria and Erich von Stroheim had retired from the movies they came back to star, with William Holden, in a remarkable film called *Sunset Boulevard*. Gloria played the part of a former great star. Von Stroheim played the part of her former great director, who was now her butler. During one episode, when the former star was entertaining guests by showing films of herself in some of her great roles, with the projection machine being run by her former director, there was a sequence of *Queen Kelly*. Time heals enough, so that by then it could be taken as an "inside joke."

Gloria and Joe made one other picture together, called *What a Widow*, which was a hit and quite profitable. He had an advisory role in Gloria Productions for a while longer. During 1929–30 he liquidated all his movie interests except for his chain of theaters and a few minor properties.

I didn't see Gloria again until a long time afterward, just a few years ago, when I was lunching at the Ritz in Paris and recognized her at another table with a woman who turned out—when I was leaving and stopped by to say hello—to be her daughter: that former little girl whom nobody at the Bronxville school could believe was "Gloria Swanson's daughter" and who now was expecting a child of her own. We chatted together a couple of minutes, recalling old times. I gave the daughter a Kennedy half dollar as a keepsake for the baby. I haven't seen Gloria since.

From 1929 on, for the next couple of years, Joe was at home with us in Bronxville. That is to say, generally he commuted to his office in New York City during the week, as did most of the men of that suburb, and ordinarily was home at nights and during weekends. This was a golden interval for me and for the children. He and I were able to play a good deal of golf together, and also able to resume those long, conversational walks that had been so much a part of our life in Boston and Dorchester and Brookline. Pat says:

"I remember every Sunday afternoon, after lunch, Mother and Daddy would go down the long driveway together and way up Pond-field Road around that whole area, which has a lot of hills and by-ways. Sometimes a couple of us would start out trailing behind them, but they walked so fast or so long, we'd get tired and go back home. We weren't included, they weren't talking with us, they were talking to each other. And they walked: Those Sunday afternoon walks were *their* walks. It indicates something about their relationship. They were interested in each other, they enjoyed each other, they wanted to talk with each other."

While Joe had been active in the movies he had also continued to be substantially involved in the stock market. Part of his genius was an amazing sense of timing: his ability to analyze a situation in the most clearheaded way, refusing to be swept along in tides of opinion, and to reach the hardheaded, rational answer at just the right time. There was no better example of this than in that boom-and-bust year of 1929.

While the stock market was soaring and the newspapers were full of statements from famous political and business figures about "limitless prosperity" in a "new era," Joe took a long hard look at the scene and decided this was a bubble that was bound to burst. He began taking his money out of the market. By the time of the famous crash of 1929, nearly all of his major assets were in cool hard cash in safe banks (as again I know from reading; he didn't tell me). Thus, not only had he saved his wealth from the disaster but was in a position to "sell short." Consequently, he made money as the market went down.

Years later when Jean was of an age to be going out with young men, one of her escorts remarked to her that during the market debacle of 1929–31 her father had been a famous "bear."

Jean wasn't too clear about the meaning of the term but the image struck her as hilarious, and when she came home she said to her brothers and sisters: "Did you know that Daddy used to be a big bear on Wall Street?" They were enchanted by the idea, and when Joe appeared that next evening they all gathered around and joined in the refrain, "Daddy is a bear, Daddy is a bear!" Joe was momentarily perplexed, but then caught on and laughed and began giving them all bear hugs.

So Joe's "bearishness" became another part of the family lore, something to tickle the fancy and elaborate on in poems and playlets and valentines and birthday cards and joking pseudo *sotto-voce* asides in family conversations. One of those really "inside" jokes that gets better with the years because it evokes so many scenes of silliness and kidding and laughter and banter from the past; hard to explain; one would have had to be a part of it.

While Joe took normal satisfaction in the way his judgment was confirmed, he was at the same time becoming increasingly worried about the state of the nation. The market collapse did not "cause" the subsequent general economic disaster, but it did cause widespread loss of confidence among businessmen, and the secondary effects spread as bankruptcies and unemployment and mortgage foreclosures rose and the "recession" became a "depression" which gave way to the Great Depression. As hardships increased, seemingly with no end in sight, people began losing faith in the whole structure of the American system of government and economics. There were powerful voices raised for radical changes—Norman Thomas, the Socialist; Father Charles E. Coughlin, the "radio priest" with his message of "social justice" and audience of millions every Sunday, and others to the left of them who were fomenting revolutionary change.

Joe had never been directly concerned with politics, and was not particularly interested in the political processes except as, from time to time, they directly affected his own interests. But with the same analytical intelligence that had enabled him to see through the pronouncements of a "new era of prosperity," he now saw that the country was heading toward a potential explosion.

Joe admired and liked President Hoover, and continued to; in later decades, they worked closely together on the "Hoover Commission" to improve the efficiency of government. But, regretfully, Joe decided Hoover was not temperamentally suited to the role demanded by this extreme emergency. The times required bold decisions, made by someone who, through force of personality as well as reason, could command the confidence of the country, restore a sense of optimism, unite disparate elements in a common effort for the good of the nation.

Who could this man be? I remember Joe turning this over in his mind, discussing it at dinner with experienced political figures including my father (who at first thought Al Smith was the man who . . .), as well as with influential leaders in business and journalism such as Bernard Baruch and Herbert Bayard Swope.

Joe had been manager of the Bethlehem Steel Company's shipyards at Fore River, Massachusetts, during the First World War while Franklin D. Roosevelt was Assistant Secretary of the Navy with responsibilities for shipbuilding. Both were strong characters who were giving their best to their jobs, which resulted in arguments and misunderstandings, but also in a good deal of mutual respect. Joe had had very little contact with FDR for at least a decade, though each had enjoyed remarkable success. Roosevelt had become governor of New York State, a key state in any national election. His name, therefore, came up in any conversation about the Democratic nomination and the national election of 1932. I think it was Henry Morgenthau who brought them together again, for mutual reappraisal and exchange of ideas. Joe and Morgenthau went to Albany for a talk with Governor Roosevelt. Joe returned with his mind made up that Roosevelt was the man who could save the country.

Once Joe had decided on his goal—in this case the nomination and election of Franklin D. Roosevelt in 1932—he worked ceaselessly to achieve it. I won't go into details of that campaign. But I do know that Joe was one of the earliest, most ardent, and most effective of FDR's supporters. By then he had contacts throughout the financial community from New York and Boston to Los Angeles and San Francisco, and he knew how to talk with financiers in ways they would understand and respect. Indeed, he knew people in influential places all over the country, and if he didn't know them personally he knew people who could pave the way for talks with them.

One of his friends was William Randolph Hearst, the powerful publisher. In 1930, Joe began to persuade him to back the Roosevelt candidacy. Hearst decided to wait, however, and let the field of candidates develop, before making a choice. Meanwhile, he supported John Nance Garner, then Speaker of the House, who consequently came to the Convention with the votes of the Texas and California delegations, both actually under Hearst's control. After the first three ballots it was evident there was a stalemate between the forces of Roosevelt and those of Al Smith, and unless it was broken the Convention would settle for some minor, "dark horse" candidate. Many people were trying to reach Hearst by telephone in California, but Joe's call was one of the few accepted. Arthur Krock, the political reporter-commentator of the New York *Times* was with him in his hotel room when the call went through, so he heard that end of the conversation.

As Krock recalled in his *Memoirs:* " 'If you don't take Roosevelt,' " Kennedy warned Hearst, " 'you'll get Newton D. Baker,' perhaps the nominee least acceptable to the press lord at San Simeon." And as Krock declared, it was Joe's "successful intervention by telephone with William Randolph Hearst, Sr., that clinched Roosevelt's victory on the fourth ballot."

Mr. Hearst had plenty of advice of various sorts from other men, I daresay, and in my later reading about the era I would come across names of those credited with influencing his decision, and I asked Joe. The best evidence he had, he told me, was a symbolic act that nevertheless had a very clear meaning: When Hearst made his financial contribution to the Democratic presidential campaign, it was through Joe he channeled it. "I'm the one who got the Hearst check and gave it directly to Roosevelt," Joe explained, "and in politics that meant I was the one who had 'delivered Hearst' at the Convention. W.R. meant it that way and FDR understood it."

Joe was closely involved throughout the course of the campaign, though not in a conspicuous way. He always preferred to "work behind the scenes." This was one of the reasons he declined FDR's invitation to serve on the campaign's Executive Committee. Another was that it would involve working closely with Louis McHenry Howe, a wizened, brilliant, vindictive little man, who had spent most of his life as Roosevelt's personal assistant and political secretary and who was utterly devoted and jealously resentful of anyone he thought might be a rival as chief confidant and lieutenant. Joe had long since been aware of Howe's suspicions and animosity, and didn't want to arouse him.

He did, however, accept an invitation to go along on the train in which the candidate—with other advisers, speech writers, secretaries, organizers, and members of the press—toured the country during the last six weeks or so of the campaign. Usually, when the train stopped long enough at some town or city, he would go off on his own to seek out the local financial and business leaders and explain to them why Roosevelt was the man to save the nation, and perhaps get some pledges from them for much-needed campaign funds. During that time also, traveling and living with that aggregation, he made many friends who not only were pleasant but also cooperative in the years ahead.

Joe was elated when the election returns showed that Roosevelt had swept the nation. He naturally expected to be a part of the new Administration in a role commensurate with his efforts and abilities.

To him this meant appointment as Secretary of the Treasury. He felt he could do that job as well as anybody in the country. He wanted the post and let people know that he did. Instead, to general surprise, Roosevelt appointed William H. Woodin, a competent businessman (president of American Car and Foundry Co.), but rather colorless and certainly more pliable and submissive to White House wishes than Joe would have been.

Joe was keenly disappointed. He was as much or more so when Mr. Woodin retired because of health two years later and President Roosevelt again passed him by and appointed Henry Morgenthau— uncritically devoted friend and Dutchess County neighbor—to the Treasury. Meanwhile, he and the President had a friendly, though more or less remote, relationship. There were exchanges of greetings and good wishes and invitations to drop in at Hyde Park or at the White House any time we were in Washington—and from us to President and Mrs. Roosevelt if their travels happened to bring them near our houses, which by mid-1933 included the one we bought at Palm Beach.

There, and at Hyannis Port and Bronxville, we entertained many of the friends Joe had made during his years in Washington, among them Raymond Moley, the founder and chief recruiter of the "Brain Trust," and Arthur Krock. Thus, Joe kept in touch with the Washington scene, and while he had been offered several positions during this period, none interested him.

The outstanding personal experience for me during that interval was when Joe and I, and Jimmy and Betsy Roosevelt, went to Europe together in 1933. Jimmy, the oldest of the Roosevelt boys, had been his father's closest attendant during the campaigning, and thus circumstances had brought Joe and Jimmy together. They became fond of each other and established great rapport. Jimmy and Betsy, and Betsy's sister Mary Cushing (they were daughters of the famous brain surgeon Harvey Cushing of Boston) were visiting us later at Palm Beach, and we had such a good time together that when Joe had to go abroad on business it was decided we'd all go and make it a party.

Joe's reason for the business trip was yet another example of his sense of timing. Foreseeing that the Prohibition Amendment would soon be repealed, he felt that anyone franchised to distribute the good British and Scottish brands of liquor was bound to prosper. Thus, he decided to go to the sources of supply and negotiate agreements with the heads and owners of the big distilleries. They were mainly family firms; the families were of old lineage, with titles and castles and lodges and mansions galore, and they entertained us (and Jimmy and Betsy) as if we were, at the very least, visiting nobility.

Joe, knowing we would be entertained at the houses of some of these people and that it might be embarrassing if I came up with a question such as how does Scotch whisky differ from Spanish sherry, gave me a cram course in elementary terminology and genealogy on the boat going over. It was, if I may use the term, like a daily catechism. Joe said if I got in difficulty, it would be a good idea to discuss our children.

The trip turned out to be another business success for Joe. He secured the U.S. franchises for the distribution of the products of Haig and Haig, Ltd., and John Dewar and Sons, Ltd.—who I had learned were among the most highly esteemed manufacturers of Scotch whisky—and also those of another well-known firm, the Gordon's Dry Gin Company, Ltd. I mention this because I want to make a point. In later times there was a story that Joe had used his official position, as U.S. ambassador to Britain, to get these contracts. In fact, he got them as a private citizen and quick-witted businessman, years before it had even occurred to him and others that he might become ambassador. I don't know the origin of such stories. Anyone who wanted access to the facts could have found them in the records very easily.

Soon afterward Joe returned to New York because of some emergencies there. The rest of us went on with our itinerary to Rome. And, as any tourist with an eye for beauty and a sense of history would be, I was fairly overwhelmed by its grandeur, past and present. We had an audience with the Pope, then Pius XI. This was a tremendous event for me. It was my first opportunity to see St. Peter's, the Vatican, the papal chambers, the attendants, the marvelous works of religious art, and I think I must have been deeply impressed because about all I really remember are my feelings of beauty and majesty and awe and reverence.

In the summer of 1934, more than halfway through President Roosevelt's first term, Joe finally was appointed to a job in the New Deal that challenged and excited him.

During the electoral campaign he had contributed many ideas for reforms that could help restore health and vigor to the country. Few were as specific and complete as those for reforming the rules (or lack of rules) by which financial institutions operated, particularly holding companies and the commodity and stock exchanges. Joe handed these suggestions to Ray Moley, and they became the basis of one of Roosevelt's most powerful speeches and, subsequently, a solid starting point for New Deal legislation, culminating in a new arm of government, the Securities and Exchange Commission.

Who should be the chairman, the guiding spirit? Moley wanted Joe because, as he wrote the President, ". . . of executive ability, knowledge of habits and customs of business to be regulated and ability to moderate different points of view on the Commission." There were objections from others who considered him too much an "insider" and adept "professional" in the stock market's operations to enforce the new rules firmly. Joe, naturally, took this as an affront to his honor. There was to be a decisive meeting in Washington. I well remember that as Joe left our house that morning he said to me, "I'll probably be back tonight because I'm not going to be on the Commission unless I get the chairmanship."

There was a full confrontation that evening at the White House with the President, Joe, Ray Moley, and Bernard Baruch. Joe had been heavily attacked by the Scripps-Howard chain that very day, with a declaration from Roy Howard there would be more to come if Joe were named chairman.

The President nevertheless said he wanted Joe as chairman.

I'm indebted to Ray Moley's memoirs for the following account:

Joe said: "Mr. President, I don't think you should do this. It will bring down injurious criticism."

Ray Moley said: "Joe, I know darned well you want this job. But if anything in your career in business could injure the President, this is the time to spill it. Let's forget the general criticism that you've made money in Wall Street."

Moley goes on: "Kennedy reacted precisely as I thought he would. With a burst of profanity he defied anyone to question his devotion to the public interest or to point to a single shady act in his whole life. The President did not need to worry about that, he said. What was more, he would give his critics—and here again the profanity flowed freely—an administration of the SEC that would be a credit to the country, the President, himself, and his family—clear down to the ninth child."

I think Ray may have been exaggerating the "profanity." Around the house at any rate, Joe never used anything but the mildest swear words. But I do know he didn't come back that night, because he had been appointed to the chairmanship of the Securities and Exchange Commission.

Once again we had a decision to make about our family. Should we move to Washington? That would mean changing schools again for the younger children, changing the parish, the doctors and dentists, uprooting the life we had established by then in Bronxville. We decided not to move. For one thing, Joe would be spending some time in New York City, since it was the financial capital of the country and the securities and most commodities exchanges there dominated exchanges elsewhere. For another, Joe hoped and believed he could have the whole SEC apparatus set up and running well within a year's time; then he planned to give his resignation. Actually it took exactly sixty-six days longer, at which point he did resign, leaving behind a great record of accomplishment within the Administration and one of the enduring monuments of the New Deal.

That September of 1935, Joe and I, accompanied by Jack and Kathleen, sailed for Britain and Europe. Jack had graduated in reasonably good standing from Choate, and the time had come for him to take his year with Professor Laski in London. Kathleen was fifteen and old enough to get something out of a year of schooling abroad, which I wanted her to have in a French convent so she could absorb French culture and language. And Joe needed some rest and relaxation, and he and I wanted time together free of pressure, after the long high-voltage demands of his SEC job. So there was a combination of worthwhile purposes.

I seem to have a reputation in some quarters as a planner and organizer. But as the poet Burns observed, "The best-laid schemes . . . Gang aft a-gley." Joe and I traveled in Britain and France and had a delightful, marvelous time. On the other hand, as an ex officio but still intensely loyal member of the Roosevelt-New Deal team, he undertook (at the President's request) a private survey of the European political and financial scene, talking at length with such figures as Sir Montagu Norman, head of the Bank of England ("The smartest banker I ever met," he commented to me), and formed extremely pessimistic judgments about the chances for economic stability and chances for peace. All of which he reported to the President, and which I'm sure was useful to Mr. Roosevelt, but not good for Joe's ulcers.

Further, the convent school where I had placed Kathleen turned out to be so severe in its rules and so remote from the general life of the country that she felt forlorn. So I had to change that plan and put her in a more sophisticated convent school in the Parisian suburb of Neuilly, where she stayed a year and did have a pleasant and rewarding experience.

The thing that really went wrong was that Jack developed hepatitis, or "jaundice," and had to drop out of the London School of Economics after only a month.

He felt well enough by the time we were home again and thought he could manage all right at an American university. The place he wanted was Princeton, because his Choate roommate, Lem Billings, and several other good friends were there. Joe, of course, as a Harvard man, was not happy about that. But after he and Jack had a full discussion and each made his points he let Jack have his choice without argument.

Jack was accepted at Princeton even though classes had started a few weeks earlier. He was always bright enough so that he could catch up whenever he really needed and wanted to. He did well and liked the school. I remember Jack's being in a bit of a quandary at the time of the Princeton-Harvard football game. His father was a former Harvard athlete who always rooted hard for all Harvard teams.

His brother Joe Jr. was on the Harvard football team. Jack said: "I'm not sure who I want to win the game."

However, after he had spent less than two months at Princeton, his hepatitis flared up again and put him out of commission once more.

I think it was around that time that someone in the family—probably Bobby, who would have been ten or eleven—made a bon mot that the other children took up and made a family joke. He said, "If a mosquito bit Jack Kennedy, the mosquito would die." Jack took that sort of joshing in very good spirit. Even when he was laid out flat in bed from some new accident or disease, with his face thin and his freckles standing out against the pallor of his skin, he could always smile or grin about his own bad luck, as if he had been victimized once again by some absurd joke that he should have been on guard against. He never mentioned his ailments until he had to, and even then he didn't accept them. He went along for many years thinking to himself—or at least trying to make others think—that he was a strong, robust, quite healthy person who just happened to be sick a good deal of the time.

Writers have sometimes portrayed Joe as a relentlessly demanding, Spartan father. This was not true. He worried about Jack. He was tender with him—very tender in his own masculine, "bearish" fatherly way, as I think can be shown quite well in a letter he wrote soon after Jack had enrolled at Princeton:

"Dear Jack:

"I had a nice talk with Doctor Raycourt . . . and we have decided to go along on the proposition as outlined by Dr. Murphy and see how you get along until Thanksgiving. Then, if no real improvement has been made, you and I will discuss whether or not it is best for you to lay off a year and try and put yourself in condition.

"After all, the only consideration I have in the whole matter is your happiness, and I don't want you to lose a year of your college life (which ordinarily brings great pleasure to a boy) by wrestling with a bad physical condition and a jam in your studies. A year is important, but it isn't so important if it's going to leave a mark for the rest of your life. So let's give it a try until Thanksgiving and see if you are showing any improvement, then you and I will discuss what's best to do.

"You know I really think you are a pretty good guy and my only interest is in doing what is best for you.

"Love,
"Dad"

Jack left Princeton a few weeks after Thanksgiving. We sent him out West to recuperate. Most of the rest of that school year of 1935–36 he spent in Arizona, since the sunny and dry climate there was said to be good for health and especially good for asthma, because he had that also. Joe Sr. had it too, and several others among our children had it, and some of our grandchildren do also, so apparently it is congenital. The form it takes with us evidently has some connection with allergies.

Nineteen thirty-six was a busy year for Joe.

David Sarnoff, the head of Radio Corporation of America, requested that he reorganize the entire financial structure of RCA.

Then, at the request of the board of directors of Paramount Pictures, an ailing giant of the movie industry, he reorganized that company from top to bottom, both the financial and studio operations.

Then William Randolph Hearst asked Joe to study the financially troubled Hearst publishing empire, and he produced a plan that resulted in drastic changes there.

That year, 1936, was also a presidential campaign year, with Roosevelt running for re-election against Governor Alfred M. Landon of Kansas. In his first four years the President had alienated many important persons and special groups in the country, and the resentment against him among business and financial leaders was wide and deep. Joe, though often at odds with these men, was still highly respected and accepted by them. He knew that Roosevelt needed him, and responded by writing a book titled *I'm for Roosevelt*, in which he showed that the New Deal was not the enemy of business but, in fact, by its reforms, had saved capitalism and the free-enterprise system in America. He then went on to take a very active part in the presidential campaign, right up to Election Day. He was happy when the returns came in, showing the greatest landslide in U.S. political history.

Somehow, despite all the things he was doing—an incredible list as I contemplate it now—we managed to have more time together than we had had for many years. There was time for opening nights of Broadway shows, usually preceded by dinner at the Colony. Joe had many friends and acquaintances in show business; and we would always encounter a number of them in the restaurants and theater lobbies, and everybody was called "darling." It was, "Oh, darling, so marvelous to see you!" and "Oh, darling, when did you get back East?" I got used to that. There was one situation, however, in which I didn't. Joe gave me a mink coat, and it seemed unusual to me when the furrier who designed it and was doing the fittings kept addressing me as "dearie." (That wouldn't have happened in Boston.)

Another vivid memory came directly after the election. Cardinal Eugenio Pacelli, who was then the Vatican's Secretary of State—and later became Pope Pius XII—was visiting this country and before returning to Rome wanted to consult with President Roosevelt. Bishop (later Cardinal) Spellman, who was a close friend of Cardinal Pacelli's, and Joe worked out an arrangement for him to do so, informally, at Hyde Park, since the United States did not recognize the Vatican as an independent state and had no diplomatic relations with it.

The President invited Joe, as one of the nation's leading Catholic laymen, and me to join Cardinal Pacelli's entourage in New York and ride up to Hyde Park in the private railway car. On the car we were presented to His Eminence. I was struck by his appearance. He was a tall thin man of rather dark and sallow complexion and dark eyes behind rimmed spectacles set on a Roman nose. He was not a handsome man, yet his eyes shone with such intensity and compassion, in his bearing there was an unearthly sense of important purpose that I truly felt I was in the presence of a mortal who was very close to God.

At Hyde Park there were cars waiting to take us the additional few miles to the President's home. This was early November, and it was one of those flawless autumn days, crisp and bright and fair,

The coronation of Pope Pius XII, March 1939. Kathleen, Pat, Bobby, Jack, Teddy, Eunice, Jean, and Rosemary are with Joe and me.

King George VI and Queen Elizabeth return from a trip to America, June 1939.

At the American embassy, London, 1939.

man Parkinson

Teddy.

Joe opened the twelfth annual British Exhibition and sold me the first doll. The items for sale were the work of war veterans in London.

national News Photo

Associated Press of Great Britain, Ltd.

Lady Astor gave a fancy dress party in 1939. Kathleen took the Statue of Liberty (Jean) and a Pilgrim (Teddy).

Jack and Bobby on the balcony of the embassy. From this vantage point, they watched parades and the changing of the Guard.

Planet News,

Dinner at the embassy.

Bobby and Teddy, England, 1939.

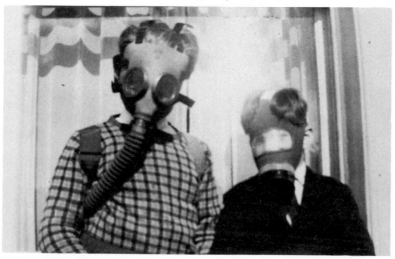

In 1938, I was presented at court.

Dressed for the inaugural ball, 1961.

Bobby, Jack, Joe, Teddy, and Joe Jr. in 1939, Antibes, France.

with the sky blue and most of the colorful foliage still on the trees. Suddenly, about halfway there, there were hundreds of children—from local and nearby parochial schools—lining the road, all rosy cheeked and excited and waving their little U.S. and papal flags. The cardinal could have waved and smiled and passed by; but instead that humane and godly man stopped our caravan, left his car and—with the red robes of his cardinalate moving with the shift of the autumn breezes—passed among the children, smiling and patting heads, and with his right hand making the Sign of the Cross or raised in a gesture of benediction. I shall never forget the future Pope Pius XII striding in his robes among those children on a rural roadside near the Hudson River in apple-and-pine tree country in New York State. It was such a happy and spontaneous gesture.

There were quite a few people at the Roosevelt house at Hyde Park. Eleanor Roosevelt was not there. I remember that FDR's mother, Sara Delano Roosevelt, was quite an imposing person, a handsome and impressive *grande dame,* whose appearance and attitude clearly demonstrated that she was in charge of the household.

On the way back to New York City the cardinal left his special railway car and came to take tea with us at our house in Bronxville. It was a most unusual gesture on his part. The visual memory that stays most clearly in my mind is of His Eminence sitting on a sofa in our living room, and of Teddy—then four years old—being deeply interested, and liking him very much, and finally going over to sit on his lap. Whereupon, of course, Teddy got a good, close look at the pectoral cross the cardinal wore on a long chain and was fascinated, took it and gazed at it, and turned it around and gazed some more. The cardinal accepted all that with smiles and complete understanding; he had a wonderful way with little children, and he loved them, I believe, as Jesus did. I have regretted that we didn't have a camera in the house at the time to record the scene. But I have kept that sofa ever since, through many moves and changes, and it is now to this day—along with so many other souvenirs of our lives—in our house at Hyannis Port.

The third particular memory I have of that extraordinary year, 1936, was of a trip to the Soviet Union. This came in the late winter of the year, and Joe had finished his analysis of RCA's financial problems but was already deep into the far greater ones of Paramount; which meant he would be busy in New York and on the Coast. Kathleen's school in France allowed an Easter vacation of several weeks, and inasmuch as I wanted to see her and thought we could have a good time together during her holidays I sailed from New York early in April. But then what? Both our imaginations had been considerably fired by Joe Jr.'s impressions of the Soviet Union and the sometimes warm discussions these had occasioned at home. So Kick and I agreed it would be a wonderful idea to go and see for ourselves.

In those days, to most people, the Soviet Union seemed as remote and mysterious as the other side of the moon, and when I made the arrangements in Paris for the two of us, mother and young daughter, to travel there on our own, everybody seemed to think I was slightly out of my mind. However, I knew that once we were in Moscow we could stay at the embassy, and that Ambassador William Bullitt would take charge of us and arrange for us to see everything that was open to foreigners.

Actually, the most exciting part of the whole adventure was simply getting there, for the European commercial airlines went only as far as Latvia, where we were to change to a Soviet plane. While we were waiting for it at the airport I saw a small old-fashioned plane being trundled across the field. It had a pair of ropes looped around the back, evidently to hold the fuselage and wings together. Imagine my consternation when, a few minutes later, I saw our luggage being carried out and put aboard.

It was our airplane, all right, and in fact it was all ours, for there were only four seats, including two for the pilot and copilot. The other seat remained vacant. Anyway, we got in, Kick and I in back, the pilot and copilot in front, and strapped ourselves firmly to the seats, and as I recited Hail Marys silently to myself and thought of my other children at home, perhaps so soon to be motherless, the plane went yawing down the runway and with a convulsive shudder lifted off and we were airborne.

More or less, that is, for we were seldom more than a few hundred feet off the ground. I don't know if there was anything but a compass in the way of navigation equipment, but if so the pilot apparently wasn't using it—perhaps he was too proud or wanted to show off his skill—because he flew by visual landmarks, now and again tipping a wing so he could peer down. I can't imagine what he saw that could help him, because to me it looked like nothing but an endless expanse of dark, dense, impenetrable forest, which for variety was sometimes obscured by fog or low-hovering clouds, in which case he would dive down to treetop level for a closer look. The landscape kept looming up at us. The pilot would then pull out the choke, pull back on the rudder or whatever it was, and we would rise sharply—leaving our stomachs, Kick's and mine, back on the latest cloud.

Actually, the pilot was very friendly and solicitous. Often, after one of these near misses, he would take his eyes off the terrain altogether while the copilot took over and would turn to us and give us a smile and a wave, indicating that despite the extreme turbulence everything was just fine and we should have complete confidence. I'm sure he must have been a very good pilot. After some hours we landed safely. Neither Kick nor I had become airsick. Probably because our normal reflexes were paralyzed.

Anyway, Ambassador Bill Bullitt was a perfect host. We saw everything there was to see, so to speak, both in Moscow and in Leningrad, the old czarist St. Petersburg. We went to the ballet and the museums (which included many of the palaces and churches built by the old regime and taken over by the new). We visited schools and hospitals; and Lenin's tomb on Red Square, of course, and the famous Moscow subway where every station is a work of art in marble and mosaic.

We saw the former private apartments of Nicholas and Alexandra, the deposed and slain czar and czarina. While reflecting on that human tragedy I also noticed in their bedroom—where a great many of their personal things remained, just as they had left them—that they had had twin brass beds, with icons on tables next to them.

I remember, too, that in the living room of the royal apartments, down at one end of the room, was a secret door that would open and close, leaving no sign of itself, and this led to a hidden staircase that in turn led to the outside of the palace. And this, in case of betrayal or attempted *coup d'état* or assassination, none of which were in the least uncommon in imperial Russia. In turn, this reminded me of something Sir Thomas Lipton told me one day about a cruise

Nicholas and Alexandra had taken with him on one of his yachts. Alexandra evidently was having a happy and reposeful time, and she said to Sir Tom that this was one of the few days of her life since she married Nicholas that she felt safe from assassins. Otherwise, she said, in Russia she was haunted by the idea that at any time someone might try to kill her and her husband and their children.

Bill Bullitt told us on our arrival that if we made any telephone calls from the embassy we should be discreet about what we said because the switchboard operator—a pleasant, efficient woman who was fluent in English, and I suppose French and German also, besides her native Russian—was a spy and would be reporting everything to the authorities. He told us we would be under surveillance all the time, and this turned out to be true except that there was nothing "secret" about it; any time Kick and I left the embassy to drive somewhere, there was a little car parked down the street with two plainclothesmen in it and they would trail along—to see where we went and what we did. On our visits to the factories and schools, I, of course, was curious about many things and was asking questions. But soon one of the embassy people told me I mustn't do much of that, because if our guide-translator interpreted the answers or made comments in ways that didn't quite fit the official doctrines, other guides might report these lapses, and our guide would be in trouble.

Bill said there was no escaping the police-spy apparatus so we might as well get used to it, and told us a story about himself when he was on a visit to the Black Sea, the Russian southern resort area. Bill was a strong athlete, a confident swimmer, so he swam far out in the water and was floating there on his back and looking at the azure sky and thinking peaceful thoughts such as that, finally, for a while, he was free of the police "shadows" who always trailed him. Suddenly he was aware of gurglings and splashings from another swimmer, and turned to see the familiar face of one of his customary NKVD followers, who had surfaced about a hundred feet away and was nonchalantly pretending to look the other way as if he were out there just because he liked long-distance swimming.

For a Soviet citizen suspected of disagreeing with government policies it must have been very difficult, nerve-racking, and dangerous. Yet I could understand why the broad masses of the people would accept the communist system. Not just because there was no alternative or because of the incessant propaganda that was dinned into them, but also because the masses really were better off in a good many ways than they had been under the czarist system.

I remember, for instance, talking privately with one of our guides, a very nice and attractive young woman, who told me about her life. She had been educated by the state, she said, and now had a good well-paying job, which she enjoyed. Her husband was finishing higher education, in college, at state expense. They had a young child who was being educated and taken care of during the hours she worked by a state school and child center, and who in turn would be assured of opportunities for advancement and ultimately of a job—since all able-bodied people worked, and there was no such thing as involuntary "unemployment." She said that none of these advantages could possibly have come to her or her husband—their families lacking money or influence—under the old regime; so naturally they liked the new one—and why shouldn't they?

I remember, too, a day when another of these attractive young guides was showing us around one of the big libraries and said proudly: "We can read any book in the whole library that we want to." I was touched by her naiveté, because, of course, in the United States we all are so accustomed to our public libraries and to perfectly open access to books, and, besides, books critical of communism or contrary to its doctrines had been purged from the Soviet libraries. Still, that left a large part of the world's literature, including many of the familiar American classics: the works of Thoreau, Emerson, Hawthorne, and others dear to my childhood (I forgot to ask about Louisa May Alcott, but I suppose she was there; I hope so), and Poe and Whitman and Mark Twain, Dreiser, and, of course, Jack London (a favorite in Russia), and numerous others. So in this case, too, I saw that ordinary citizens had much greater opportunities to educate themselves and better themselves, and that they appreciated this.

So, although there were many things I saw that dismayed me—one which I need only mention, without elaboration, being the official doctrine of atheism—I did see why the Soviet system could be acceptable to the people of the U.S.S.R.; moreover, that many of its aims, if not many of the methods, were worthy of respect and discussion and study in some of our Western societies. I did, at least, understand a lot better what Joe Jr. had been talking about, which was bound to be of some satisfaction to a mother with a very bright eldest son, on whom many hopes rested.

Eunice has always been one of the most faithful correspondents in the family. I had a letter from her in Paris on my way home, in the late spring of 1936. It gives a flavor of the family news at that time:

"Dearest Mother,

"We are awful glad your coming home. Bob has sold 4 rabits at 75¢ each and so is doing very well. Dad called up yesterday and said Jack was staying in Cal. with him and he also said he would be home the end of the week or the 1st of next week. Jack wrote and said he is having a wonderful time out West. Smokey" (Jack's then-current dog, a shepherd dog of some sort) "is out there with him now. School is just the same and I am certainly anxious to get to the Cape. It is very warm here. Well thats all.

"All my love
"Eunice"

And here is another, dated "about Jan. 20th" which I must have received in Florida, having stayed down there awhile after the children went back north to school after the Christmas holidays.

"Dear Mother,

"I suppose you are having a wonderful time. My exams started today and get over in two weeks. Bob went to Boston today and was very excited as he is planning to see Joe, Jack" (Joe was at Harvard; Jack hadn't yet gone West) "Grandpa and Grandma and he wont have to go to school tomorrow. Yesterday the lights went out about four thirty over most of New York and it was terrible. . . . How do you like this writing paper. Mrs. Moore gave it to me. Please excuse this letter but Teddy is running around my room shouting like a manic, as he put a huge piece of gum in his hair and Kicko" (the resident nursemaid) "is trying to get it out but has not succeeded and

Pat is practicing so I cant think straight. Well I hope you come home soon as we all miss you *loads*.

"Love from us all
"Lots and Lots of Love
"Eunice

"P.S. Have a nice time."

Active as Joe was in 1936, busy accomplishing things that many talented businessmen would have considered the climax of a career, he soon began feeling uncomfortable at being out of the thick of things in Washington.

Consequently, the following year, 1937, he accepted FDR's request that he head up a new federal agency, the Maritime Commission, which was supposed to bring sense and profitability into the chaotic, fast-declining U.S. merchant marine. The long skein of circumstances, beginning back in 1916 when FDR was Assistant Secretary of the Navy and Joe was manager of the Fore River shipyards, had made Joe the President's first and logical choice.

Joe took the job, re-leased the same house he had had near Washington during his SEC chairmanship. I visited now and then, as I had before, and he managed to take every weekend back in Bronxville. The heavy demands of his new job and his determination to keep a reasonable semblance of home and family life put a heavy strain on him, vigorous as he was. First the SEC, now the MC, both important, no doubt, but the New Deal was teeming with "alphabetical agencies," all of which presumably had some important reason for existing. I felt that Joe deserved something better, something really special, in the government and I told him so. We discussed the situation at home and with close friends in the Administration and with trusted and knowledgeable friends in the press, such as Arthur Krock.

What Joe had always wanted, as I mentioned, was to be Secretary of the Treasury, but there was no chance left for that after FDR appointed Henry Morgenthau. The President wouldn't have removed Morgenthau even if he had been otherwise inclined to, because Mrs. Morgenthau and Eleanor were such great friends, and dispensing with Henry could have resulted in friction not only in the Dutchess County neighborhood but in the Roosevelt home. FDR had enough problems without adding that. The other Cabinet-level jobs were of little or no real interest to Joe. A high-level ambassadorship would, of course, be another and attractive possibility. But Joe spoke no foreign language and had no "ear" or natural facility in languages. Thus the suitable possibilities really were reduced to only one post, that of being ambassador to Great Britain. That was occupied by Robert Worth Bingham, a most competent and respected man. However, it was rumored and rather soon confirmed that Ambassador Bingham was seriously ill and would have to resign.

When Joe came home for weekends, I would ask him, "What has the President said? Couldn't you tell him what you want?"

Joe said to me, "Well, I can't just walk into the office of the President of the United States and say 'I want to be ambassador to England.'"

Through other means behind the scenes, however, eventually it was understood that if he did his usual excellent job at the Maritime Commission the next step beyond would be the ambassadorship. He was confident enough of this that in the fall of 1937 he told not only me but Joe Jr. and Jack so they could make their plans too. Arthur Krock broke the news on an unofficial, "well-informed sources" basis in December, and early in 1938 it was confirmed by the President's official appointment of Joe as his ambassador to the Court of St. James's.

Chapter Twelve

❧❧

Somehow Joe had the knack of being in the center of great historical change. For example, if President Roosevelt had made Joe Secretary of the Treasury, as Joe had hoped, he would have missed the challenge of building and running the Securities and Exchange Commission. Also, if Joe had become ambassador to the Court of St. James's in 1932 he would not have been in England during the dramatic years preceding World War II.

The political and diplomatic history of that time has been written about from all sorts of national and personal viewpoints. What I can add are only some footnotes—interesting ones, I hope—from the viewpoint of the American ambassador's wife, official hostess, companion, and mother of his numerous children, who were transported from a more or less "normal" American environment to the complicated world of diplomatic London.

I was sure this would be an important experience for them, and indeed it was. In fact, in retrospect, it probably put Jack on the first rung of the ladder to the presidency. However, there was also the immediate, practical matter of schools for them.

It was decided that Bobby, who was then thirteen, and Teddy, who was six, would live with us at the embassy residence but go to day school in London. Eunice and Pat and Jean would go to a Sacred Heart boarding school near London similar to the one at home. Rosemary, because of her condition, would go to a special school, as I have described earlier. Kathleen, who had graduated by then from convent school and had been going to Parsons in New York to learn design and decorating, would drop out for a while and live with us at the residence, helping me a bit with my duties as hostess and also having her debut in London. Joe Jr., who was in the last semester of his senior year at Harvard, would stay on to graduate and then come over to gain embassy experience as a very junior secretary to his father, and to travel on the Continent as his father's unofficial but bright observer of the troubled scene.

As for Jack, who when last mentioned in these pages had hepatitis and asthma and had dropped out of Princeton for the academic year of 1935–36, he would also stay on at Harvard to the end of the semester. Meanwhile, he had recovered enough health so that he could go to college again and this time had chosen Harvard, to his father's hardly concealed pride and joy, and entered there in the fall of '36 for the academic year of 1936–37.

He had done well. A letter from his father in February 1937, from Palm Beach, is evidence of large change:

"Dear Jack:

"I am impressed with the almost complete turn around you have made in yourself in the last year. You know I always felt you had great possibilities and I think now you are starting to avail yourself of them. You are making a great hit with the older people and they are very much impressed with your discussions and looking on you with a great deal of respect. For your own satisfaction this is really worthwhile.

"I talked with your mother on the phone last night, she is coming down this week. Said she had a wonderful time in Boston and was more than pleased with you and Joe. Rosemary had a marvelous time also and really does not require many gestures like this to make her life worthwhile.

"My golf is completely gone, I can't beat anybody . . . Good luck to you on the swimming and as to football, remember to be as good as the spirit is. You ought to weigh somewhere about 170.

"Love,
"Dad"

Jack had run for class president that first year and had been swamped. The next school year, 1937–38, he ran for student council and lost. I think that this was his last venture into student politics.

He continued during those years to show rather more interest in social activities and sports than in grades. He went out for swimming, football, and golf.

He was a strong contender for the varsity swimming team, in the backstroke, but as the crucial meet with Yale approached he came down with a hard case of influenza and had to be in the infirmary. He made a secret pact with his roommate Torbert Macdonald, who remembers:

"Guts is the word. He had plenty of guts . . . he had the flu, but he was set on making his letter. So every day I'd sneak into the infirmary with some food for him." (Lots of steaks and thick malted milks, to keep his weight from dropping.) "As soon as he'd eaten, we'd slip out the back door, and I'd drive him to the indoor athletic building, where he'd doggedly practice his backstroke. Then I'd drive him back to the hospital."

Alas, in spite of all that valiant foolhardy effort he lost in the trials for the meet (to Richard Tregaskis, who later on became a well-known journalist, author, and broadcaster). As for football, he tried out for the varsity although he weighed only 149 pounds, which again showed a lot of courage but not much sense. He dropped back to the "junior varsity" and was doing a good job there until one day in practice he was hit by a hard block or tackle and landed at the wrong angle and ruptured a spinal disk. This injury ended his football days and marked the beginning of troubles with his back that were to haunt him the rest of his life.

Between his first and second years at Harvard, the summer of 1937, he and his pal from Choate and Princeton, Lem Billings, had traveled around Europe together, and as Lem has recalled:

"I went over with very little money because my father wasn't alive. This is another side of Jack's character: He was perfectly happy to live at places for forty cents a night, and we ate frightful food . . . but he did do it, and that was the only way I could go with him. We had a terrific time." (The two toured France, Germany, Holland, Italy, Spain, and parts of England.) "London was last . . . and Jack broke out in the most terrible rash, and his face blew up, and we didn't know anybody and had an awful time getting a doctor . . .

Food poisoning of some kind." (Probably it was an allergic reaction.) "This was just before the war, and Jack decided to report to his father what he was finding out—he was constantly asking questions. . . ."

When he came back to Harvard in the fall he decided to major in government. He still had no particular idea of going into politics himself, or participating directly in government. His ambition inclined toward journalism, and studies in political science and government would be very useful background for him in that profession. In any case, his new curiosity and interests were reflected in improved marks and also, fortunately, helped prepare him to be an intelligent observer of events during his father's ambassadorship.

Joe went to London in February of 1938. My travel plans and preparations were interrupted by an inconvenient attack of appendicitis. There was nothing to do but have the thing out, so without informing anyone but Joe, the Moores, and the help—why worry the children?—I did so. When I was ready to leave the hospital someone told the newspapers and my exit was made in a commotion of photographs and interviews.

Eunice wrote from Sacred Heart at Noroton:

"Dear Mother,

"Of all the surprising things that occurred in the Kennedy family within the past few months the greatest shock came when I heard that you had your appendix out . . . we are praying for you up here so I am sure you will be up and even running around dear old England in no time. . . ."

Actually, it didn't take long. I was able to sail by early March, bringing Kick, Pat, Bobby, Jean, and Teddy with me. It was an exciting and slightly hectic sailing, because so many friends of all ages were there to wish us bon voyage and a marvelous time in England, to say nothing of a great many members of the press. Among these was our old friend Mary Pickford, pretending to be a reporter because she was about to play the role of one in a movie and wanted to get a little practice in an authentic scene.

Our first port on the other side of the ocean was Cobh, Eire, and this brought back some memories. I had been there with my father in 1908 when I was eighteen—Kick's age—and it was Queenstown, Ireland, and I remembered the sight of young men and women on the quays saying emotional farewells to relatives and friends before sailing off to America, more than likely to Boston. In similar scenes and far worse circumstances my ancestors and Joe's had departed. Now our family returned, momentarily, in circumstances that could hardly be more dramatically different. There were many thoughts in my mind that day.

As I approached London, the embassy, and the Court of St. James's as the wife of the American ambassador, I freely admit to feeling a bit nervous.

The British press seemed fascinated by the idea of a large and lively Boston Irish family descending on the London diplomatic scene. There had already been a good deal of advance publicity about us, and once there we became practically public property. I almost began to feel that we had been adopted, as a family, by the whole British people. Wherever we went, we were greeted with smiles and waves and bright looks—a spontaneous outpouring of human warmth that I shall never forget.

This was all very stimulating, but the pressing need was to attend to the business of settling in. The embassy residence stood six stories high and was part of a long row of similar, connecting houses fronting on a street called Prince's Gate, in one of the pleasantest parts of London, almost opposite the beautiful park called Kensington Gardens. In back, it shared a large enclosed expanse of lawn and garden with the other houses of the block. It had been given to the United States Government by J. P. Morgan. It sounded like a nice location.

Although I supposed it would be furnished in silk and damask and precious objects, I had inquired through Joe's office at the State Department if there was anything I should bring or have sent over. With our large family, I was also curious about the sleeping arrangements.

A letter soon arrived from "Department of State: Division of Foreign Service Administration," initialed "BK," from which I will quote:

"There are no bed linens and no dining room linens of any description; no towels of any kind; no bath mats.

"The only dining room silver consists of 4 solid silver sauceboats. A list of the Lenox and other china is attached.

"There is a sewing room which does not seem to be equipped with a Government sewing machine."

As I read further, I found some good news: "A careful comparison of the attached lists with the inventory cards indicates that the Embassy residence is quite completely furnished with high grade furniture." However, BK continued, "Of course I have no way of ascertaining the present condition of the various pieces . . ."

More good news: "Curtains and drapes appear to be adequate for the whole building, as well as rugs and lamps.

"There are mattresses and springs for all beds.

"In 1931 the Department paid $506.52 for 68 blankets.

"There are eight baths and three servants' baths.

"There are eight bedrooms, 2 single and 6 double. All appear to be well furnished. For the servants there are 13 bedrooms, 19 beds."

How on earth was I going to fit our family into the residence? We were eleven people and there were only eight bedrooms. Double everybody up, one may suggest. But this would have left no privacy for the older children; and even then would have left no space for guests. And the beds for three bedrooms were in storage. I solved this problem in a practical way. We certainly didn't need nineteen live-in servants in thirteen bedrooms, which occupied the entire two top stories of the residence, so we poached on that territory and had rooms enough for ourselves and for our guests, as necessary. With three of the girls at boarding school, Jack at Harvard about half of our time there, his and Joe Jr.'s trips to the Continent, it all worked out.

Andrew Mellon had, of course, been one of the great art collectors of this century, and during his tenure at the residence the walls were hung with masterpieces. Upon endowing the National Gallery in Washington, however, he had transferred all his art treasures there, leaving the walls of the residence practically bare. In the interval no one had seemed to have ideas about what to do with the bare walls. Fortunately, Joe and I knew another fabulous art collector, William

Randolph Hearst. He owned a castle in Wales, with many fine paintings, and Joe arranged for a number of them to be loaned to the residence.

The staff that lived in, or came daily to the residence—butler, chef, secretaries, maids, and others—was almost wholly British and wonderfully well trained and proficient. I also was able to call on the services of the embassy staff. I have been asked how I could know quite what to do in such a delicate but important matter as the order of precedence in seating people at a large formal dinner at the residence.

The answer is that I didn't know, but there was always someone on the staff to whom I could turn for guidance and, in fact, confidently entrust with nearly all the arrangements. Almost invariably everything came out just right.

There were three American staff members, though, who had come along with us and, within the family, had far higher ratings than any new acquaintances could possibly achieve. One was Luella Hennessey, who by this time was the person we looked to first when any one of us needed skilled and loving nursing care. She was, by turns, nurse, nursemaid, companion, and friend to the children.

Another was Elizabeth Dunn, governess for the younger ones. The third indispensable American was our cook, Margaret Ambrose, who kept the family supplied with creamed chicken, strawberry shortcake, and Boston cream pie.

Another item of interest:

Our six-story residence had an elevator—a "lift." It was a large fancy cage that went up and down smoothly and majestically on a system of hydraulics involving a couple of enormous weighted steel pillars that alternately pushed or gave way: a most impressive and fascinating machine. In no time at all Bobby and Teddy discovered it and how to make it run and decided it was the greatest thrill in the world to get inside and work the controls and go gliding up and down, up and down. The butler discovered them at the game and tried to coax them out but, poor man, he wasn't used to small American boys, and it was I who ordered them to disembark and never again to treat this useful machine as a toy.

Those first months passed in a whirl of introductions and social and official events. This was compounded by the fact we had arrived at the beginning of the London spring "season," when gentry arrive from far and near for a round of balls, parties, and court functions. This is also the season for English girls to make their debuts. Kick, being eighteen, had reached the customary age for "coming out" and it was logical she should do so in London. There were many preparations to make. For instance, I had to be introduced to the mothers of all the other debutantes. Unless they had met me personally, etiquette would have forbidden Kick to be invited to the parties they gave for their daughters. There were many other formalities through which to tread my way. A pleasant but exhausting one was to call on the wives of all the other ambassadors and introduce myself. It was interesting seeing the other embassy residences, meeting these women and getting a sense of who was who in the diplomatic colony. The list was long, and it took me months to work my way through it.

The first protocol visit came only two days after my arrival while I was still unpacking and getting my bearings.

Ambassadorial wives—accompanied by their husbands—were always "received" by the Queen, a gracious form of welcoming them to the country. So, on March 18, Joe and I arrived at Buckingham Palace, and precisely to the minute of our appointed time were ushered into a beautiful and very comfortable sitting room, where Queen Elizabeth came forward to greet us.

She had such a happy, natural smile and friendly manner that I felt at ease with her at once. She indicated I should sit beside her on a small sofa near the fireplace (in which a cheerful, warming, and most welcome fire was flaming) and that Joe sit in a big, comfortable-looking chair opposite us. She and Joe had already met, so they chatted a bit about Anglo-American relations, but she soon wanted to hear all about our children, their ages and school plans, their feelings about coming to England, and so forth.

I found it a great conversational convenience that ours were spread over such a range of ages, because the two eldest royal children, Princess Elizabeth (the present Queen) and Princess Margaret Rose, were about the ages of two of our youngest, Bobby and Jean. Her Majesty and I could compare notes and agree that these were remarkably interesting ages in child development.

Soon afterward Joe and I received a royal invitation to spend the weekend of April 9–11 at Windsor Castle. The other guests were Prime Minister and Mrs. Neville Chamberlain, Lord and Lady Halifax (he was the new Foreign Minister), Lord and Lady Elphinstone (she was the Queen's sister), and, I suppose as an "extra man," Major the Honorable Sir Richard Molyneux.

We came up from London in an embassy car to Windsor, and through a large and beautiful park, to arrive at the castle at 7 P.M. There we were met by the master of the household, Brigadier-General Sir Hill Child, who conducted us to our rooms. They were in one of the towers, with a lovely view of the park, and the furniture was upholstered in red damask; there were accessories in gold and white. In my bedroom was a huge bed, also upholstered in red damask and set high, so that one had to use a stepstool to get into it. There were numerous servants in evidence, in full livery; soon one of them brought us sherry. Another, who also wore a peruke, was especially appointed to attend us and lead the way whenever we left our suite.

After a few minutes of contemplating the scene, Joe turned to me and said, "Rose, this is a helluva long way from East Boston."

That weekend at Windsor was one of the most fabulous, fascinating experiences of my life. I took many diary notes. These are excerpts which I hope will be interesting to others:

"At 8:20 the footman came to escort us to the Green Reception Room. At 8:30 the King and Queen came in and greeted everybody by shaking hands. All the ladies curtsied, and the men bowed low. Dinner was announced and the King and Queen walked ahead . . . they sat opposite each other at the middle of the table, I at the King's right and Mrs. Chamberlain on his left. The Ambassador sat on the Queen's right and the Prime Minister on her left. Lord Elphinstone was on my right and was extremely agreeable. I talked a good deal to the King about my children.

"On the wall behind the Queen was a portrait of Queen Victoria with the ribbon of the Order of the Garter. Conversation led to this and to the story that Queen Victoria had declared the ribbon was not painted the correct hue and had one sent to the artist so he could do retouching. He somehow thought he was being decorated with the Order, and when after correspondence and dispute he learned this was not the case he refused the royal wish—so the color was never made right."

(I learned that there are two versions of the origin of the Order of the Garter. The first holds that Edward III, at the Battle of Crecy, ordered his garter to be displayed as a signal for the beginning of the fight. Another, and perhaps the correct version, holds that during a dance at which a lady's garter fell to the floor, causing laughter, the King rebuked the court by picking up the garter, putting it on his arm, and saying, *"Honi soit qui mal y pense."*

In the present day, the Order of the Garter is designated by a blue ribbon. The Order itself consists of the sovereign and twenty-five knight companions. Since 1805, the Prince of Wales has been a hereditary member of the Order. Women, including Her Majesty the Queen and Sovereign of the Order, Elizabeth the Queen Mother, and Queen Wilhelmina of the Netherlands, wear the Garter on the left arm between the shoulder and elbow. The Garter is dark blue, edged in gold.)

"Table decorations consisted of high flowers, which made it difficult for the King and Queen to see each other and caused some good-natured teasing when he could not communicate to her that she should rise, the signal to leave the table.

"After dinner, the Queen stood in front of the fireplace in one of the drawing rooms. Each of the men bowed to her, then went into an adjoining room to talk with the King, the ladies remaining with the Queen. She talked with me first for about fifteen minutes, then Lady Halifax brought up each of the other ladies in turn. Joe told me that the same procedure took place with the men, in regard to the King. Meanwhile, a Scottish piper walked through the rooms, piping away. The Queen is of Scottish descent. We are of Irish descent. The pipes are equally Scottish and Irish; so this was a congenial touch. I found it very difficult to accustom myself to saying "Ma'am" when addressing the Queen and she told me not to bother, putting me at my ease. She has a very pleasing voice, a beautiful English complexion, great dignity, and charm; is simple in manner, stands very erect and holds herself well, and is every inch a Queen. We talked, among other things, about the difficulty of sleeping in London, and the Queen was very much amused that I put wax in my ears.

"After a while the King and the men came back, and after mixed conversation the King and Queen showed us some of the treasures of the castle, in a room off the drawing rooms. There were jewelry and trinkets worn by Mary, Queen of Scots, and the original blue garter from which the Order of the Garter has its name.

"At 11:00 the Queen said good night and shook hands again with all. In bed, but before sleep, we heard the sounds of the Changing of the Guard, and the clock striking in the tower."

I lay in bed thinking I must be dreaming that I, Rose Kennedy, a simple, young matron from Boston, am really here at Windsor Castle, the guest of the Queen and two little princesses.

I had unlimited admiration for Queen Elizabeth when we were there, as I now have for her daughter, Elizabeth II. Their obligations are multitudinous and unending. They constantly meet people from different countries and must be briefed on the political, social, and ideological ideas of those countries. They must always be punctual for royal appointments and must always greet their guests with a smile.

In the United States, when people in government choose politics as a career, they can retire at will, but royalty is born to all these obligations and they are never away from the relentless glare of publicity. Before the war, I had seen Queen Elizabeth at a demonstration of war planes. She appeared genuinely interested, even in the splicing of a wire, and she was just as courteous and involved in the technical aspects as she would be if she were talking to the French ambassador about international relations. I recall on Sunday at Windsor that the little Princess Elizabeth was seated between Prime Minister Neville Chamberlain and my husband, the ambassador from the United States. I suppose this was a pattern of regular procedure—associating with older people even when she was very young (at this time she was thirteen). Of course, there are many advantages to this way of life but also many restraints on the natural inclinations of a normal youngster, those tendencies toward fun and frolic.

The next day, April 10, was Palm Sunday. My diary notes continue:

"We had breakfast in our sitting room. Then went to Mass in the town of Windsor, where the priest met us at the church door. On return we saw the Changing of the Guard—very impressive—then walked in the park that surrounds the castle and ran into Princess Elizabeth hiding behind the shrubs. She had on a pink coat and was hatless, and she smiled at us. Walked around the private golf course and had a lovely view of the castle.

"At luncheon the Queen wore a bluish-green dress, no hat, and an aquamarine bracelet. The princesses were in rose dresses with checked blouses, red shoes with silver colored buckles, white socks, and necklaces of coral and pearl. Princess Margaret had a ribbon in her hair. She sat next to her mother, and Princess Elizabeth sat next to Joe. I sat on the right of the Prime Minister and had Viscount Gage on my left. I told the Prime Minister he was very much like my husband, with his business background and both of them so fond of music and walking. (Joe later told me I could compare him with any-one I wanted to, but to keep such opinions private.)

"After lunch there was a band concert. Then it was arranged for us all to take a walk, very informally, with the King and Queen and the two little princesses. Everybody changed into comfortable shoes and tweeds. We walked to Frogmore, one of several mansions that monarchs have built in Windsor Park as domiciles for visiting family members and guests. It is very stiff Victorian, with yellow damask curtains, though the entrance hall is rather sweet in white delicate chintz. The King told us that his parents—with their large family— had used it as a schoolhouse and he had studied there. We also saw many of the natural and cultivated beauties of the park such as the mulberry bushes. Margaret Rose was very much interested in a California pine tree of great height and said it made you giddy to look up to the top and she thought that was funny."

We left at mid-morning the next day, and were back at the embassy residence in time to have guests of our own to lunch there.

For various reasons of state, British and American and others, we were to find ourselves associating with the King and Queen fairly often in the many months ahead. And, indeed, with many other royalties and members of the highest nobility, both foreign and domestic. Within two weeks of my arrival, as I see by my diary (March 29), we were "received" by Dowager Queen Mary at Marlborough House. My notes of the day read:

"Ushered into a sitting room where we met Dowager Countess Airlie and another lady-in-waiting. The ladies-in-waiting are always peeresses, usually serve two weeks at a time and may go home nights except at Windsor . . . Met Her Majesty in a small sitting room. She was dressed in gray wool crepe with silk dots scattered. She wore a small diamond and coral pin. She sat very straight, was meticulously groomed. As usual, discussion was of children."

In May, we gave a "coming out" party for Kathleen, actually, a joint debut for her and Rosemary, who was also of an appropriate age. As I have said, we always wanted Rosemary to participate, as fully as possible, in the activities of the family and of her general age group. On such an occasion as this—a big, somewhat confusing scene with much music and dancing and lots of people who didn't know— we naturally had a few apprehensions. But she looked quite pretty, she was happy, and everything went well. Rosemary went to some parties, but as she was rather shy we always had one of the men from the embassy escort her to see that she had dancing partners and wasn't left too long with one partner. I say this because parents who have a retarded child may be discouraged and think their child could not undertake a social occasion. We made special provision to see that Rosemary was included.

Also, that same month, Kick, Rosemary, and I were presented at court, one of those British royal ceremonies that has since disappeared but at the time was glamorous beyond belief. Being presented was one of the most utterly simple and intensely complicated events imaginable.

The simplicity consisted of the act itself. One went to Buckingham Palace, sat awhile in a reception room, and on cue from a functionary of the court entered the Grand Ballroom, at one end of which on a dais sat the King and Queen and two or three other members of the royal family. One walked out in front of them, curtsied to each, then walked to the side of the room and stood there, or perhaps sat on an available gilt chair. Others would have been doing this before you, others would do it after, there would be several hundreds of girls and matrons at any given session of court, of which there were four that year, and literally that's all there was to it: a couple of brief curtsies to the enthroned monarchs.

Not only were the selected debutantes presented, but also the wives and daughters of the diplomats and of visiting dignitaries from far parts of the British Empire, and anyone else who had the means to get to London and could somehow wangle an invitation, a process that in most cases involved the various embassies.

The pressure on the U.S. ambassador, from socially ambitious American women, to arrange presentations for them had been intense for many years. Joe decided to put a stop to that, and he did so forthrightly by announcing that the only Americans presented in his ambassadorship would be wives and daughters of men attached to the U.S. diplomatic mission or of American families who for other reasons were actually residing in England. That caused some heartaches at home, but Joe had secured approval in advance from Washington—where senators and State Department officials and others were glad to be rid of the pressures. Officials of the court told Joe, too, privately, that they thought it was a very good idea because the competition for presentation was getting to be too fierce. After all, even the facilities of Buckingham Palace are limited.

It was decided that about ten of us who were associated with the embassy—we three, the wife of the military attaché, the wife and daughter of the naval attaché, several others—would go to the first evening of the first of the four court presentations. As there would be matrons and girls from other embassies, as well as many members of the British "ruling classes," we wanted to do our best to represent our embassy and country properly; and this was especially incumbent on me and the girls.

An important matter was proper gowns. Our British friends, and ladies of the embassy who had been presented in earlier years, said they should be by a British designer since he would understand the exact needs, including the dimensions of the train. I went to Molyneux, the foremost British designer of the time (who also had a salon in Paris) for my dress of white lace beautifully embroidered in tiny silver and gold beads. For Rosemary, we selected a white net trimmed in silver. Kathleen's dress was from Paris, selected at Lelong during a long weekend, and was also of white net and trimmed with silver croquettes. (I was amused afterward to see in the British press that my gown and Rosemary's were described in detail and credited to Molyneux; whereas Kathleen's very lovely one was also described, but the designer's name was omitted, leaving an inference that it too was a Molyneux.) The girls and I had decided in advance that we should be in white, or else a very light pastel shade of ivory, because this would look best with the white plumes, which every woman presented wore in her hair.

I as a matron would wear a tiara in my hair. I didn't own one. It had simply never occurred to me before coming to England that I would ever need one. My new and sympathetic friend Lady Bessborough lent me hers, and it proved to be most flattering and magnificent. It fitted well and had many brilliant diamonds, including a gorgeous marquise diamond in the front. With a few temporary adjustments and arrangements, it was perfect. I was so grateful to her for the thought. I remember that my children—Bobby and Teddy as well as the girls—were extremely impressed.

We at the embassy who were to be presented had many discussions about all the paraphernalia. And we also had rehearsals. To save time and strain the matrons and girls would be presented together in pairs. It was important that there be carefully calculated equal space, not only for harmonious design, like a ballet, but to ensure that we would not become entangled in or tread on one another's trains. Precision was a crucial matter also in curtsying. It would have been awkward to have one lady bobbing up while the other was bobbing down. After all, the eyes of the court and the diplomatic corps would be upon us. So we practiced, though we had had years of curtsying at the convent, like all Sacred Heart girls.

The great night arrived.

I had already been to the hairdresser that afternoon and my hair was done in a way to receive Lady Bessborough's tiara. I had an early supper on a tray in my bedroom. I was carefully inserted in my lovely embroidered gown by a covey of enchanted, murmuring maids. The man from Molyneux came over to check details and to pin and secure the white plumes of the Prince of Wales at the proper angle, as I had no idea as to how this should be done. A hairdresser was there to place the tiara on my carefully constructed coiffeur. The maids helped me draw extra-long white gloves almost all the way to my shoulders. My jewels were added.

I viewed the complete picture in a long mirror and was perfectly amazed at myself. I had never dreamed of looking this way and being part of such magnificence. I felt a little like Cinderella.

I ran into my husband's room to show him my elegance. He wasn't quite finished dressing, but he turned and looked at me, and his blue eyes lit up, and he grinned in the most loving way and said—as he *would* say—"You're a real knockout," which was the highest compliment I could ever want.

The girls meanwhile had been having their own special attentions and in a few minutes, fully as excited or more so than I, came running in to see us and be seen. More exclamations all around. Then downstairs to be viewed by the younger children, who were duly impressed, then to stop in the hall for the staff to see us, then followed by a session with photographers, and then in large cars off to Buckingham Palace. As we neared it we saw people who had gathered hoping to catch a glimpse of glamorous ladies in their court gowns and gentlemen in their regalia. They waved to us; we waved to them.

The rest was a gigantic theatrical. The Palace illuminated; the Guards resplendent; the Beefeaters in costume with maces, lining the Grand Stairway; passing through anteroom after anteroom attended by footmen in full livery; at last the ballroom and a sight of the royal dais, and being ushered to our place among the diplomatic corps—our place determined by length of tenure (everything governed minutely by protocol), which put us after the Chinese ambassador but before the German ambassador—and looking around at the grandeur of the room with its vaulted and frescoed ceilings and its walls of murals and gilded pilasters and elaborate details, and looking around also at the others there, the men immaculate and in their "decorations" and the women striking and regal in their beautiful gowns and jewels. I won't ever forget the beautiful embroidered dress worn by the wife of the Chinese ambassador.

It is a strange aspect of human nature—or perhaps a saving grace— we tend to expect the best and discount the possibilities of the worst, even though experience shows that the worst often happens. Humans seem to have been designed to be optimistic. Otherwise, why would anyone have children, plan for their future, while realizing that every day is problematical, and that for all of us, as individuals or even nations, there may be no future?

I am led to these thoughts because, while all the pomp and circumstance and romantic storybook traditions that I have described were continuing with hardly a ripple to blemish them, events were, in fact, building toward the general disaster (and for us, very personal disasters) of the Second World War.

"May 17

"Gave dinner in honor of Foreign Minister Lord and Lady Halifax. Had shad roe sent over from America, which arrived frozen and in very good condition and tasted delicious. Surprised how many people were familiar with it and enjoyed it.

"After dinner we had a moving picture, *Test Pilot*, with Myrna Loy and Clark Gable. Colonel Charles Lindbergh, who sat next to me, said the aeronautical display was very authentic. He came with his wife and mother-in-law, Mrs. Dwight Morrow. This is the second time I have met him—first being at Cliveden, home of Nancy Astor. He acts very shy, smiles in a boyish sort of way, and seems to retire to a corner where he stays most of the time. Anne is all poetry and light, simple, natural, and lovable, with an enchanting smile.

"Mrs. Morrow is an alert, keen, pleasant woman who pleased me enormously by saying that even though she is a Republican she is glad to see Joe here."

"May 19

"Photographers from *Vogue* and also two women interviewers.

They inquired again about the cards. I mean the file where I keep the list of the children's illnesses, dentist visits, eye examinations, etc. This idea has created a furor in the press."

"May 25

"Dinner for Mr. and Mrs. Henry Luce. A gift, a beautiful gold and jeweled clip, arrived later with a note from them, reading:

" 'We wanted to send you flowers when we left London. But you seemed to have so many that we decided to send these frozen ones instead. The clip, they tell me here, are the flowers of the Empire—the rose for you—and England—the thistle and the clover for luck—and the shamrock for Joe of course. Again thank you for all your sweetness to us.

" 'Love,
" 'Clare and Harry.' "

"June 1

"Went to Epsom Downs to see the Derby with about fifty of Lord Derby's guests. Took a train down. Joe and I rode with Lord Derby, who is the jolliest, the most cordial of the Englishmen I have yet met; gray mustache, stocky in build, has a ruddy complexion and a ready smile."

I knew this race had originated with his family, had become one of the most famous of such events in the world and was the progenitor of others, such as our own Kentucky Derby. So I asked him about the history of the race, and the next day I received a very long letter from him, written in his own hand, telling me all about the Derby. I was honored and flattered, and, most of all, impressed by such personal thoughtfulness.

Of course, he was part of the Victorian-Edwardian era of good manners and graceful living, in which personal correspondence was regarded as important and almost as an art form. I have often wished our society had retained more of that feeling: So much correspondence nowadays comes off a typewriter and lacks the personal qualities of handwriting; and, of course, there is such a great deal of telephoning now, instead of writing, and the words spoken are lost forever.

"June 14

"Arrived at Ascot about 12:45. Met Sir John Monk who told us to be on hand after the first race to dine with the King and Queen. We walked up the curved stairway with its white rails and a bronze balustrade, and on arriving in royal box met the King, Queen, Dukes of Gloucester and Kent, and Duchesses, and Princess Royal, and former Queen Ena of Spain. All the ladies wore long dresses of lace except the Duchess of Kent, who wore a short white crepe. It was the most perfect day, warm, bright sunshine . . . an atmosphere of contentment, of joy, of interest and satisfaction. . . . When we went to lunch, I was escorted by the Duke of Kent and on my other side was the Maharajah of Rajpipla, who had on a sort of black homespun coat with five buttons of diamonds and rubies and a turban of a mixture of green with yellow stripes swathed around his head. . . . Joe escorted the Duchess of Gloucester. Marvelous view of race track, straight and completely made of grass. In the United States our tracks are almost oval and made of dirt."

"June 16

"Gold Cup Day at Ascot. Said to be the day when women wear their finest, most luxurious dresses, hats, etc. Beautiful day. In early afternoon came the procession of the carriages containing the King and Queen and all their royal guests from Windsor. It starts at the beginning of the long green race course which seems miles off in the distance, and we see a faintly moving colorful something advancing. Promptly at 2:10 the first carriage, containing the King and Queen, arrives, followed by the others, and all proceed down the course and then around in back of the grandstand, where all alight and proceed up the stairs to the royal box. There are vast throngs to see them and to view the carriages, which carry two footmen in back and two in front, dressed in navy blue coats with scarlet trimmings. The carriages are open barouches.

"When Joe first saw the royal procession, he commented, 'Well, if that's not just like Hollywood!'

"I wore black organdy dress and black hat, more unusual than lavenders and pinks and other pastel shades of the crowd. It came from Patou."

"June 22

"After luncheon at Lady Abingdon's, returned home to greet Mother and Father, just arrived from America on the *Manhattan*."

My father was then seventy-five, my mother seventy-three, and both were healthy and active, and really had no trouble at all about making the trip. Naturally, I wanted them to see us in our rather amazing setting and to participate in the life we were leading.

That year in February, on my father's seventy-fifth birthday, there had been a testimonial dinner for him by the Boston Chamber of Commerce, with seven hundred and fifty guests and with Charles Francis Adams—the most patrician of all Back Bay Bostonians, descendant of two U.S. Presidents, former Secretary of the Navy, a man of immense and diverse talents—as the featured speaker. I am going to quote the gist of his speech:

"It is a pleasure to testify to the good Irish qualities that are in you, John. And I am glad to thank you personally for what you have done for us and the city of Boston.

"At times in your past, you, John F., have found it politically expedient to say things about my class that have sometimes hurt. You have even called us degenerate sons of splendid ancestors. Quite possibly that is true. But it takes a man of supreme gifts to tell us a thing like that without arousing rancor. Yet, it was said so pleasantly, with such good humor, that no one could take offense, or long be angry with a man of the charm of John F. Fitzgerald. In everything you have done and in every way you could, you have tried to develop Boston and to improve our community. Even today you are sweating your heart out to bring this port back to what it was, to make it what it should be."

My father replied in his special way, saying among other things:

"I told Charley recently that I might go abroad pretty soon to meet the King and Queen . . . and asked him for tips. You see, Charley Adams' great-grandfather and his grandfather were ambassadors to Great Britain in times of great stress, too. Before I go, I'm going to get some pointers from him."

They stayed at the embassy residence with us for several weeks: "us," at that period, meaning mainly me and the younger children

because Joe had returned to the United States briefly, for consultations with the President and to be present at Joe Jr.'s graduation
from Harvard (*cum laude* and chairman of his Class Day Committee), and to bring both Joe Jr. and Jack back with him. They arrived, appropriately, on July 4.

I showed my parents London and made sure they had a good time.
We did not have a long time together because they also wanted to
tour England, Scotland, and Ireland once they were on our side of
the water. I see from my diary notes that on June 27 we went out to
Cliveden, the huge and beautiful estate of Lord and Lady (Nancy)
Astor. Although the Astors didn't happen to be there at the time, we
could wander as we liked in the magnificent house and around the
endless gardens and grounds.

Another day Mother and I went off to Wimbledon for the tennis
matches. (Helen Wills Moody, Helen Jacobs, Sarah Palfrey Fabyan,
Alice Marble, Donald Budge, and other "immortals" of tennis.)
Dowager Queen Mary was there, and in passing up the aisle between
matches saw me, stopped to speak, and so was introduced to Mother.
Queen Mary at once recalled that she had heard my parents were
to be visiting me and she wanted Mother to feel welcome in England. It was a heart-warming example of how well trained the royal
family has been to remember such things, which are so important in
public life, as I used to remind my sons. She then invited us to have
tea with her group of dignitaries and royalty; a most welcome and
exciting invitation. And so we joined them.

There were other memorable occasions, but I think the one that
gave my father the greatest thrill was having tea at the Prime
Minister's residence. My diary notes say:

"Mrs. Chamberlain very charming. Seems to have time for all of
her guests, has a quiet leisurely manner and a very calm unruffled
expression. Told Father her family was Irish. In fact, Fitzgerald was
their name, which quite pleased him."

Naturally my father, during that visit, could not help but indulge
his sense of humor and his sense of politics. One day he went down
to a secretary's office, helped himself to engraved ambassadorial in-

vitation cards—which had the blank spaces to be filled in, in handwriting, as to the occasion and the hour people were to arrive—and mailed them to great numbers of his pals in Boston, inviting them to the embassy at teatime five days later. As he knew perfectly well, by the time they received the invitations it would be impossible for them to get to London, even if in some delirium they had wanted to cross the ocean for a tea party.

When Joe heard about this he was considerably annoyed. But my father was not in the least disturbed. He thought it was a nice gesture, one that had made many people happy, and that he had been quite clever to think of it.

Anyway, Father and Mother had a very good time. And we could enjoy it together, three generations, because they didn't leave until the latter part of July. By then Joe Jr. and Jack were there, the girls had come down from boarding school, and Bobby, Jean, and Teddy were on hand, so it was a full assemblage. I was happy to know my parents had lived that long, unimpaired in their capacity to enjoy life, and that they could be with us at that time; because I know it was a great pleasure for them.

I spent most of the next two months near Cannes, the younger children with me and older ones floating in and out, and Joe dropping over from London when he could get away from his duties.

"July 27

"At Eden Roc for bathing. Saw Elsa Maxwell at lunch so I introduced her to children, who later saw her walking with Marlene Dietrich and they requested her autograph.

"Am trying to inspire Pat and Eunice to be interested in collecting autographs. Begged three of Anthony Eden the night of our July 4th dinner. Marlene is gracious, animated, pleasant to meet, seems to be taking a holiday with her hair thrown to the winds and no worry about make-up."

"August 3

"Joe and Kathleen flew down from London. Kathleen had been house guest of the Duchess of Devonshire a few days at the end of July."

"August 4

"All lunched at Eden Roc Casino, which is quite good, with a special *plat du jour*. Laughed at waiter yesterday who did not charge for Teddy, saying the little fellow did not eat much, though he had a full course."

"August 5

"Joe has told Jack that though the milk has a peculiar, to us, sour taste, it is really the flavor that milk has which is not pasteurized. He says he drank that sort of milk in Wales for three or four days—at Mr. Hearst's castle. Jack is more resigned."

"August 7

"All went to church. Priest told Eunice that he was most appreciative of all the francs we give him as usually there are only the smallest coins in the collection. Says Mass very quickly. Mass and Benediction are finished in twenty-three minutes."

"August 13

"Almost go mad listening to discussion of diets, as Jack is fattening, Joe Jr. is slimming, Pat is on or off, and Rosemary (who has gained about eight pounds) and Kathleen and Eunice are all trying to lose."

"August 17

"Joe planning to send Joe Jr. to Paris as it looks as though there would be a crisis in the government at any minute and if he is on the spot it would be a wonderful opportunity for him to see history made."

"August 28–September 13

"Joe Sr. flew to Paris. I took train up at night . . . luncheon next day at the American embassy, which Bill Bullitt (ambassador to France) gave in honor of Senator Barkley (majority leader of the Senate) and Mrs. Barkley and some other Americans. Joe Jr. in Paris, and see him every day . . . Joe's birthday (Sept. 6) and phoned him in London; party for him at embassy. . . . Paris rather chilly and I will be glad to go back to Cannes again and to the sunshine tomorrow. . . . Shops here filled with Americans as usual. No one seems to enjoy it all, and both agreed that it is difficult to weigh actual advantages and experiences of his stay in Europe. This year will be an accumulation of meeting and seeing men who are shaping the world's destiny.

"Arrived at Cannes from Paris. Rainy day . . . Margaret preserved dozens of yellow peaches which have the most delicious flavor in the world and grow here in great profusion. . . . Ted has a bad cold, and it is so damp we have kept him in bed all day. . . . Teddy adores pedal boats which he can run when he does not swim. . . . Went to church in a modern good-sized church. No Communion and though I wanted to go I was afraid the priest would shout at me as the one did at Eunice at Valbonne, so I desisted. . . . Beautiful day. Ted is so much better that I have decided to send him to London by air in the morning, with Jean and Miss Hennessey. The other children, Rose, Eunice, Pat, Bob, with Miss Dunn, started on a week's tour of Scotland. . . .

"When Joe phoned at night, he said things were terribly agitated in London and perhaps I should have to leave in the morning."

"September 14

"No seat on the plane so I am going by sleeper to Paris tonight. I think I should be in London as Joe has Teddy on his mind and, also, there are these crises in world politics. Everyone fearing war. The French all took part in the last war and are almost frantic at the specter of another one."

As I wrote that, I had in my mind a heartbreaking conversation a couple of weeks earlier with a Frenchwoman I had met. She said: "My grandfather was killed in the war in 1870 against the Germans. My husband and brother were killed in the war in 1914, and my cousin was blinded. And now they are asking me to send my son to war in 1938. I cannot, I will not." I was terribly moved.

"September 15

"Arrived in Paris about 9:30. Was told that Chamberlain was on his way by air to Berchtesgaden to talk to Hitler. First air flight of Prime Minister, who is almost seventy years old. Position much more acute and more urgent than P.M. had realized. Hitler determined to march in and risk a world war if Sudetenland Germans do not get the right of self-determination."

"September 18

"Church at Brompton Oratory. Children brought back ties, etc. from Scotland with the Ireland Kennedy colors in the plaids, also some Beleek china for me, which I love.

"The telephone rings constantly and insistently for Joe. Sometimes from London and sometimes from U.S.A.

"Telephoned to Father and Mother. They were fine and it is their forty-ninth anniversary."

"September 22

"Prime Minister went back to Germany, to Godesberg, which is a more convenient place than remote Berchtesgaden. . . . Profound shock when he was told the original proposals were to be replaced. . . . Memorandum and map received, which was an ultimatum the Prime Minister felt would profoundly shock public opinion. Hitler to occupy Czechoslovakia October first. Hence, the urgency of making all plans.

"Bobby and Teddy return to Gibbs School, a day school."

"September 23

"Scotland, Gleneagles Hotel.

"Days are usually rainy and wet in the morning. Have ordered a high pair of rubbers, the like of which I have not worn for years. . . . They were quite shocked at the hotel when one of my compatriots asked for pheasant yesterday, as they expect all the world to know that one does not start shooting pheasants until October.

"Shoots:

"Grouse shooting	August 12
"Partridge shooting	September 1
"Pheasant shooting	October 1"

"September 24

"Foggy and drizzly.

"Prime Minister back in London with memorandum which was transmitted to Czech Government.

"President Roosevelt sent two messages to Hitler, also messages around the world to try to get all the people to exert moral support against aggression."

"September 25

"Czechs say demands absolutely unacceptable. . . . Chamberlain seems hopeful. Mike Scanlon phoned from London, said trenches were being dug in Hyde Park and sandbags were being put up around the air ministry building."

"September 26

"Cannot seem to find quiet walks here in the woods or surrounding country like we have at home. There also do not seem to be any specially attractive places to sit out of doors. . . .

"French ministers informed us if Czechs were attacked, France would support them . . . Speech of Prime Minister on radio. His voice filled with sadness, with loathing of war, with discouragement as to result of his efforts, but still urging people to keep calm, to cooperate quietly and with confidence, and not to give up the last shred of hope."

"September 27

"Today, individual, brooding silence was general, as were unsmiling, unemotional faces. Everyone unutterably shocked and depressed, feeling from the Prime Minister's talk that his hopes for peace are shattered and that war is inevitable.

"Went to launching of the *Queen Elizabeth*. Queen came without King as the times are so uncertain. She was dressed in gray with a smart small hat and looked much thinner than in the spring. Little Princess Margaret Rose saw me in the group, smiled, told her sister, Princess Elizabeth, who immediately told the Queen, who looked over and bowed."

"September 28

"Joe phoned this morning. Said I should come back tonight, as we must make some sort of plans for the children because war is imminent. Everyone here depressed and sober. . . .

"Lunched in rather a subdued atmosphere as few people are at hotel, though the races are on at Perth. Took ride to Perth and visited Frazer's tweed shop, said to be the last word for tweeds. While there, the proprietor told us that the four great powers were to go to Munich to discuss peaceful ways of settling the controversy.

"Everyone immediately felt a vast relief and unspeakable emotion. From the depths of despair we were moved to a new hope. . . . I decided to stay on at least over the weekend."

"September 29

"Joe called. Said everything was packed, though nobody wants to go except Teddy, because he thinks if he has his tonsils out back home he can have all the Coca-Cola and ice cream he wants.

"Talked to Kathleen who went to the horse races at Perth yesterday. Called at Lord Forterrot's castle yesterday and saw her for a moment as she was just returning from a cocktail party after the races. . . .

"Everyone expects Prime Minister's visit to be crowned with success, though preparations for war are still being carried out. Trenches are being dug and gas masks fitted. . . ."

"September 30

"Everyone feels relieved and happy. Chamberlain arrived home last night, and he was given a wonderful reception by the people and received a tremendous ovation when he appeared with the King and Queen.

"We all feel that a new psychology for settling issues between countries has been inaugurated and that henceforth war may be out of the question.

"Chamberlain's words, from Shakespeare's *Henry IV*: 'Out of this nettle, danger, we pluck this flower, safety.' The result of the Munich settlement, he said, would be 'Peace in our time.' "

In the end it was an illusion. But everyone clung to it until the Nazis broke their pledge six months later and took over the rest of Czechoslovakia. As Jack wrote in his book *Why England Slept*:

"The situation came to a head in March when Hitler invaded Prague. It now became evident to all that the hope of a permanent peace for Europe was doomed. The invasion of Prague meant the end of the Chamberlain policy of appeasement; and, it meant, in addition, the desertion of the traditional policy of refusal to make commitments in Eastern Europe. The Government realized that something would have to be done to build back British prestige, to bring to the world a realization that from this time on appeasement was officially dead, and that England now was really determined to resist German attempts at Expansion. . . ."

Jack was an observer and even to some degree a participant in those events that finally led to war. After the summer and early fall of 1938, he went back to Harvard for his junior year. However, his father, realizing that momentous history was being made in London, Paris, and the other capitals, and that it would be infinitely more instructive for Jack if he were on the scene, suggested he defer his second semester and rejoin us. He could help in the London embassy and, by arrangement with Bill Bullitt, in the Paris embassy, and also do some traveling in other parts of Europe.

So he came over in February 1939 and was there the rest of the time, seeing it happen with his own eyes. So was Joe Jr. The boys helped their father and not least by the reports they sent to him on their impressions—from very broad cross sections of society—during their work and their travels.

Here are other notes—from my diary, from letters—that convey the tension of our lives during the period that remained for us in England.

Teddy had his tonsils out on October 3 (1938) in a London hospital, and everything went well, but he was disappointed in his hopes for endless Coca-Colas and ice cream. . . .

Kathleen and I investigated a couple of colleges for her in London, with the idea that while helping me at the residence and having her social life she could also be continuing her education with part-time courses. The trouble is that so very few English girls went to college then and few arrangements were made for them. That was especially true of the girls of the "upper classes" and aristocracy— the debutante set—who in the fall and winter stayed in the country, at the ancestral places, and went shooting and riding, and would give and go to house parties. (I'm sure this has changed, but that's the way it was then.)

I had as good an opportunity as anyone to observe Joe's reaction to the European crisis, from the time we arrived in England until that fateful day in the fall of 1939 when the war began. Joe despised everything about Hitler and naziism. But along with all people of sanity and good will he prayed that somehow war could be avoided. Knowing the terrible destructive power of modern weapons, he realized the widespread death and suffering another World War would bring. As he said a little later in a letter to Teddy, written during the London blitz:

"I hope when you grow up you will dedicate your life to trying to . . . make people happy instead of making them miserable, as war does."

Joe was also concerned about what the waste and destruction of a war might do to America's economy and system of government. The country was still trying to recover from the great Depression; over ten million workers were still unemployed. World War I had been followed by two world-wide depressions. He could imagine the fabric of American life falling to pieces in the aftermath of another World War.

As ambassador he was supposed to represent the viewpoint of the United States Government and the American people, and he could do so in perfect conscience. A short time earlier, in 1935, Congress had passed the Neutrality Act, forbidding our government to send arms in any foreign conflict. And only a month before Joe arrived in London, the House of Representatives almost passed a really radical populist bill (failing by a minuscule 21 votes) that would have prevented any congressional declaration of war from taking effect until the people had approved it in a national referendum. Although President Roosevelt was strongly sympathetic to the British cause and was under pressure from some of his advisers to take action against Hitler, the chief aim of his foreign policy (and he left no doubt with Joe about this) was to keep the war from beginning. It is a fact—a fact very little known, and I feel I should make it better known—that at the time of Munich, Roosevelt sent a personal message of congratulations to Mr. Chamberlain. Joe was supposed to deliver it.

He did so, in Mr. Chamberlain's office, but instead of handing it to the Prime Minister he read it to him, then put it back in his pocket. Because he had a feeling, as he remarked later, that the message might prove to be an embarrassment to the President and Joe wanted to protect him.

In November 1938, Joe was asked to give the principal speech to the Navy League in London on Trafalgar Day. He chose his words carefully, to make sure they reflected both American policy and public opinion. The speech was cleared in advance by the State Department in Washington. The part that was widely quoted said this:

"It is true that the democratic and dictator countries have important and fundamental divergencies of outlook, which in certain areas go deeper than politics. But there is simply no sense, common or otherwise, in letting these differences grow into unrelenting antagonisms. After all, we have to live together in the same world, whether we like it or not."

In terms of the world of today, and the policies we are following toward China and the Soviet Union, this thought can't seem at all startling. Of course, the idea isn't viable unless those concerned do believe in "live and let live." No one knew then that Hitler was criminally insane and had no intention of living by humane standards except his own demented ones, and that his promises meant nothing to him.

In the Trafalgar Day speech, though without commenting specifically on the wisdom of the Munich agreement, Joe had expressed his—and thus his government's—belief that common sense demanded peace in the world. In his introductory remarks, in order I suppose to warm the audience a bit with a personal note, he said he had discussed some of his views about war and peace with me. Among the repercussions was an acidulous message from the U.S. State Department about me. I find that on October 22 I have a diary entry:

"Joe received note from State Department saying if I were going to write his speeches, there were several suggestions which it would be wise to send."

"(Should like to send for them.)"

That was the beginning and the end of my entire career in international politics.

Something else Joe did at this time, and for which he has never been given proper credit, concerned the plight of the Jews in Germany. Hitler's anti-Semitism had caused some Jews such as Albert Einstein to leave Germany soon after Hitler came to power. However, the full extent of the horror did not really appear until after the Munich Pact was signed (September 30, 1938). On the nights of November 9 and 10, 1938, under pretext of taking reprisal for the assassination of a German diplomat in Paris, Hitler loosed destruction upon the Jewish neighborhoods of German cities. Two hundred synagogues were destroyed and thousands of innocent Jews were beaten and arrested, and many were killed.

It became clear to Joe that the Jews had to escape from Hitler's Germany if they were to survive. From that point on he was active, behind the scenes, in helping many individual Jews escape. Further —a matter of saving millions—he devised what became known as the "Kennedy plan" to find new homes for all Jews trapped under Hitler. British policy prohibited large-scale Jewish immigration to Palestine, which then was under British mandate from the aftermath of World War I. Joe proposed the Jews be granted asylum in settlement areas in South America, Lower (Baja) California, and Africa. For months he poured much of his energies into developing this plan, getting the permissions, transportation, facilities, trying to cut through the endless red tape and details, trying to get the vast amount of money needed from governments and philanthropies for this exodus of millions. But before the plan could be worked out, war began. The rest is one of the most tragic chapters in world history.

The fogs and gray skies and chill of the English winter were beginning to stimulate my wanderlust. Therefore, not long after Joe Jr. and Jack were re-ensconced at the residency, I left on a southern tour that took me to the Riviera, to Genoa and Naples, Athens, and the Greek islands, Turkey, Palestine, Egypt. Then back to Italy—because Pope Pius XI had died, and I received word that President Roosevelt wanted Joe (and thus, informally, me also and our family) to represent him at the coronation ceremonies for the new Pope. This was the first time an American President had sent an official representative to such an occasion. And the new Pope, Pius XII, was our gracious friend Cardinal Eugenio Pacelli.

There were a lot of logistics involved, with our family spread in several locations, but we managed to assemble by the date of the coronation, March 12, except Joe Jr. He was in Madrid. The Spanish Civil War was at a climactic stage and communications from Spain to the rest of the world were so chaotic that he didn't receive his father's message in time.

Joe Sr. and Jack came down on the same train with the Duke of Norfolk, the leading peer of the realm (a Catholic), whom the King sent as his representative. Joe and I had time before the ceremonies to move around Rome a bit and pay official respects to dignitaries who had come from all over the world. It was a special joy for us to talk with Cardinal O'Connell of Boston, who had known both of us since our teens and who had married us. He had been deeply interested in us and our family all these years. He was now about eighty and becoming feeble, yet he retained his kindness and wisdom.

The next morning His Holiness received us in private audience. First, he and Joe were alone awhile, talking, I daresay, about the state of the world and the prospects for war or peace. Then I came in from a reception room, and we reminisced a bit about his visit to Hyde Park and Bronxville. Then came the children, with Elizabeth Dunn and Luella Hennessey, and Mary and Eddie Moore. The Pope seemed pleased to see everyone, especially Teddy, whom he remembered fondly as the little boy on his lap who had been so curious about the crucifix.

I noted in my diary:

"Miss Hennessey must have had twenty dozen rosaries to be blessed. In fact we had to carry a small suitcase to hold hers and the rosaries of all the children."

Two days later, March 16, I have another note:

"Teddy received his First Communion from Pope Pius XII."

Then we returned to London:

"April 4

"Lunch at 10 Downing Street, Prime Minister and Mrs. Chamberlain, plus their married daughter. Joe and P.M. did all the talking. Prime Minister looks very worn down compared with last spring, but does not look his seventy years as he has plenty of hair. Is not overoptimistic as he cannot tell what Hitler has in view. I asked him if Hitler died would he be more confident about peace, and he said he would.

"I said I wondered at lack of knowledge of British Government about preparations in Germany. He said there . . . were reports. They must be analyzed. . . ."

"April 7

"Everyone away for holiday extending over Monday. Played golf with Joe and when we finished, about one o'clock, he had a tense look as he had just received word the Italians had marched into Albania and it might mean war. He came home, went to Foreign Office. Chamberlain is in Scotland for a much needed rest. . . . Feel so sorry for the Prime Minister as Mrs. Chamberlain said he was so looking forward to the long holiday. Now a plane is waiting to bring him back. . . ."

"April 23

"At Cliveden, home of Lady Astor.

"Nancy Astor has the most amazing energy of anyone I have ever seen. She went to Christian Science church, had huge lunch with about twenty-eight to thirty, went off to play eighteen holes of golf. . . . I like her because I think she is inherently good, works hard to help out others, strives to do the right thing, is passionately devoted to her family (her own children, her nieces, etc.). I have heard someone say she dominated her own children too much so it's difficult for them to be around her. She is great fun anyplace, talks about everything, anything, intelligently and with gusto and with an inexhaustible sense of humor. Also she is a clever mimic, and when she puts in a pair of false teeth she changes her whole facial expression and is marvelous."

"May 4

"Very busy all day preparing for the dinner for the King and Queen. The flowers arrived from Paris about one-thirty. As we found we could get more unusual flowers there and much less expensive, Offie had them flown over by plane. Everyone was rather nervous until they arrived because it always takes quite a long time to arrange them, and get the right colors for the right rooms. The flowers for the table were particularly lovely. They were like baby orchids, some white and some orchid color. They were called moth orchids, or *phalaenopsis*. I did not want the press to get the idea that I was decorating the table with orchids, which would sound too nouveau riche or too extreme, so I called them *"phalaenopsis"* to the press. As we had old-fashioned strawberry shortcake, the strawberries also came from Paris by plane, as we thought they would be better. Everyone seemed very calm and confident, but I know everyone in the house was terribly excited, including myself and the ambassador.

"During the day men from Scotland Yard came up to interview our butler to find out who the men were who were helping out in the evening. The butler, who had been in London for a long time, had chosen men who had all served at Buckingham Palace, so Scotland Yard was reassured, and there were no detectives present. I suppose they are especially careful at this time because of the Irish terrorists in the I.R.A.

"We were all ready at about eight o'clock when the two ladies from the embassy arrived who were going to assist me in receiving the guests, Mrs. Michael Scanlon and Mrs. Butterworth. We all wore tiaras, of course, in honor of the Queen. I gave them last-minute instructions, and the guests started to arrive about ten minutes past eight. The British are always on time, especially when they are to meet royalty. Mr. Bullitt arrived, very elegant, and very happy-looking, as usual. We served cocktails while we were waiting, as all the guests knew one another quite intimately; they were all close friends of the King and Queen.

"Just before eight-thirty, the ambassador and I went downstairs in the hall, and the footmen all waited. About twenty-seven minutes of nine, they told us the automobile was approaching. There was quite a little gathering outside of men and women to see Their

Majesties, and we heard a cheer go up. The ambassador had already descended the steps, as one is supposed to meet the sovereigns at the foot of the steps, when they are honoring a house or an embassy. As they entered the hall, my own maid took the Queen's coat, which is a prerogative to the personal maid of the hostess.

"We bade them welcome and then the Queen and the ambassador went up the stairs first, the King and I following. We were told the King preferred the Queen to go ahead of him. (Although I remember in France that the President of France and I as hostess entered the room before the President's wife and Mr. Bullitt.) They were received in the French room upstairs, which is Louis XVI, overlooking the garden, where a circle had already formed. Mr. Bullitt, as the only American guest, was in the line first, and the other people had arranged themselves, and we passed from one to another. The children had been told to be at the end of the circle and they were all there together.

"We invited the King and Queen to have a cocktail which they declined. I remember at Windsor, they had never drunk cocktails with the guests, but I was told that sometimes they liked to have one before dinner, and so we made the gesture. The Queen seemed to feel the same way I do about them. She said they never lifted her, and I always feel when I want to be lifted up they are apt to make me sleepy and when I want to be sleepy, they are apt to stimulate me.

"We chatted informally and dinner was announced in two or three minutes, when we went downstairs. The guests were all seated by Sir John Monk, who usually has that responsibility at big occasions. Mr. Bullitt was on the Queen's right, as he was the only one she hadn't seen for a long time. Of course, when the King and Queen are present, they take the place the host and hostess usually have in the center of the table, and, as usual, are opposite each other. Our table has one advantage in that it is narrow so that we can see across and chat across it, which makes things much less formal than a very wide table. We naturally used the embassy china and the glasses. The King, unlike Queen Mary, did not seem to have any favorite wine.

"The six youngest children were seated at a small table at the end of the room. The conversation was naturally quite informal. I told the King about the shad roe which we had had sent from America for a big dinner last year and which had not arrived on time as the boat was twelve days late. Therefore, at the last minute I had to substitute fillet of sole. As the menus had already been printed for shad roe, we had had to leave them. And one English lady was quite astonished to find that shad roe tasted so like her own fillet of sole, and so I had to explain the difficulty.

"We also talked about the King's coming visit to America.

"At the end of dinner the Queen and I left the table, I giving a slight curtsy as I left the King; and as the ladies left the room, they each curtsied toward the King. We then went to the French room. The Queen and I went upstairs to my bedroom for a minute to powder. I showed her my reflector mirror, something she had never seen before. She asked me if I got up in the morning to see the children off, and I said I used to in what I called the good old days, but that now I was usually up late at nights and rested in the mornings. To my astonishment and humiliation, she said she usually got up, half dressed, to see her children, and then went back to bed again.

"When we joined the ladies for coffee, she chatted with two or three of them, and I brought up two or three of the American ladies with whom she chatted about seven or eight minutes. We followed the regular procedure of the hostess, bringing up different ladies to speak to her for a few minutes each. Lady Halifax, who was lady-in-waiting, had already told me in advance with whom she would chat. After about twenty-five minutes, we were joined by the gentlemen, and we went into the Pine Room which had been arranged for the cameramen and had two pictures taken, one serious and one laughing.

"Then we went to the back room for the film. We had two of Walt Disney's and *Goodbye, Mr. Chips*, which was long, as it had not been cut—to use moving-picture parlance—but excellent and marvelously acted. I think it was an American film made over here. It was quite sad, and after it was finished, it was very plain to see that the Queen had had a little weep, as had most of the people.

"After that we stepped into the hall where we had something to drink. Again they chatted with a few of their friends and then went downstairs. They shook hands with almost everyone as they left. I said good-bye in the hall and the ambassador went to the car with them. After a minute's interval, the other guests said good night and the party was over."

"May 5 and 6

"It was so nice to receive letters from several people who wrote saying they had enjoyed the party and that they thought everything had gone off so well. . . ."

Early in May, the King and Queen left England for a tour of Canada and the United States. Inasmuch as Joe and I had talked with them and their staff a number of times about their itinerary, and Joe, of course, had many consultations about the visit with our State Department and others back in Washington, it seemed useful and almost necessary that I should be there at the same time they were.

Here is one "memorable" entry concerning that visit:

"Great argument on whether it is befitting for the President to serve hot dogs at a picnic to the King and Queen. . . ."

That was at Hyde Park. The President did serve them, as a "typical American delicacy," and Their Majesties were delighted, and it all caused a great sensation in the press.

Just a few more social notes. Because very soon there will be no more at all.

"June 22

"Met Joe and went with him to Waterloo Station to meet the King and Queen who arrived at 4:50. All the members of the Cabinet were there, and it was the first time I ever saw Joe look small; he was standing talking with Lord Halifax (6 feet 5 inches). . . . The King and Queen drove off in their coach with the famous gray horses with a rider in front. The Queen and the princesses wore dresses of light shades so that they could be readily identified by the people and the photographer, even at a distance. They received a wonderful ovation all along the route. . . .

"That night was Eunice's debut party. She wore a peach-colored dress from Paquin. . . .

"About half-past two they all started doing the Big Apple, a new dance, and everybody got very gay. I was quite surprised and even a little shocked. However, I was assured by some of the chaperones that the party was a huge success. . . . The Duke of Marlborough had asked if he might come, although the fathers don't usually come to the debut parties. He was one of the leaders of the Big Apple."

"June 27
"Four of the children, Joe, Jack, Eunice, and Kathleen, went to a reception at the Prime Minister's at 10 Downing. They were shown through the house and went into the room where the Cabinet meets."

This reminds me of when Jack first came over to London, and I was showing a few of the sights and we drove past the Prime Minister's residence. I pointed it out to him, and he was so excited that he leaned over to my side of the car in order to see better. Then he asked me with awe and almost reverence, "Is that really *Number Ten* Downing Street?"

"July 3
"The papers are full of war; many articles about evacuation schemes and lists of supplies which should be stored at home. The Duchess of Marlborough and Lady Astor are getting their houses ready and the people on their staffs organized so they can turn their houses into hospitals or homes for children in the event of war."

"July 4
"We had the Fourth of July party and received in the dining room. . . . The entire group was very attractive and quite representative, I thought, of an American gathering. There were quite a number of people from Boston.
"That evening, at a large official dinner, I sat next to the Duke of Kent, who accidently told me he had seen Kennedys at every table at the 400 Club, which is supposed to be rather gay and not a place for Kathleen. Joe reprimanded Kick for being there." (A few nights later, the Duke apologized to Kick for telling on her.)

"July 12
"We went to court. . . . Joe stood next to the German ambassador

(protocol, as before) who remarked that it was much easier now than in the days of the previous King, George V, who used to insist on the diplomatic corps going to four or five courts. He said Queen Mary is much less shy now and much less difficult than when King George was alive. She now has time to go to things which she enjoys.

"The German ambassador considers the whole court procedure a waste of time."

"July 13

"We gave a small luncheon for the Prime Minister. Mr. Lamont, a banker from New York, Justice and Mrs. Felix Frankfurter, and Mr. and Mrs. Joe Patterson, New York newspaper people, were present. It was a small luncheon so that Mr. Chamberlain might get his point of view over to the men.

"All the Americans feel that they may be seeing some of their English friends here for the last time as everyone feels that war is more or less imminent. Although many people think that since it has been delayed so long there is still a chance, or a way may be found, to put it off."

"August 1

"Now there seems to be a bit more confidence, though no one really knows. But everyone in this country is possessed of an ardent hope that war may still be avoided."

"August 12

"Jack and Torb Macdonald leave for Germany. They would like to go to Prague, but we are told no one is allowed to go there."

"August 16

"Reports keep coming that war is imminent and August 29 seems to be the date, as the harvest in Germany will have been reaped and all the reserves have been called."

And that is the last entry in my diary. There was too much to think about, too many plans to make. The war didn't break out on August 29. The estimate was off by three days. On September 1, the Nazi armies invaded Poland. Two days after that, September 3, the British Government fulfilled its pledge and declared war against Germany.

Joe Jr. and Jack and Kick and I were there in Parliament to hear Mr. Chamberlain's heartbroken, heartbreaking speech (the text of which the Prime Minister had shown to Joe a few hours earlier) with its tragic lines:

"Everything that I have worked for, everything that I have hoped for, everything that I have believed in during my public life has crashed in ruins."

While we were on our way home from the House of Commons the air-raid sirens began to howl, and we ran for refuge into the nearest shelter we could find—which was not a bomb shelter but happened to be the basement at Molyneux. I thought later, what an ironic way for a woman to begin her war experiences. At the time I was simply scared for us all. As I recall, there were no bombs dropped on London that day—the raiders were turned back—but it was a vivid experience and a premonition of what soon would be happening in deadly earnest.

It was time to get our children back home.

That wasn't particularly easy. Space on American and other neutral ships was jammed. The seas suddenly were dangerous for ships of any combatant nation. On the fourth day of the war the British ship *Athenia*, heading for Canada with fourteen hundred passengers including three hundred U.S. citizens, was torpedoed and sunk. The survivors were landed in Scotland and brought to Glasgow. Joe sent Jack up there to interview the Americans—most of whom had survived—and to file a report to the embassy on the circumstances of the sinking, and also to do for them whatever was possible to do, within the powers and resources of the embassy, to help them with food, clothing, shelter, funds, and other transportation. Joe trusted him to do a proper job, though he was only twenty-one. He did it well and it was a wonderful experience for him.

All but two of us were back in the United States by the end of that month. As I have explained earlier, we decided to let Rosemary stay on awhile because she was doing so well at her special school, which was far in the countryside and almost surely safe from any bomb damage. The other missing member was Joe, who was duty bound to stay at his post, and did so for more than another full year; save

Joe and George Bernard Shaw.

Joe Jr., Kathleen, and Jack, September 3, 1939—the day
Neville Chamberlain declared war on Germany.

Eunice, Jack, Rosemary, Jean, Joe, Teddy, Joe Jr., Pat, Bobby, and
Kathleen at the embassy in 1939.

Joe watches air drills near Windsor Castle with Princess Helen (daughter of Queen Victoria) and Neville Chamberlain, June 1939.

At the embassy, 1939.

King George VI and Queen Elizabeth at the embassy dinner in their honor.

Jack, Eunice, and I at Sugarloaf Mountain, Rio de Janeiro, 1941.

Joe Jr. received his commission from father, May 1942.

Teddy with Joe and me after his confirmation, March 15, 1942, in Palm Beach.

Jack at Harvard graduation; his scuffed-up saddle shoes made their appearance.

Captain Frederic L. Conklin awards Navy and Marine Corps medal to Lieutenant John F. Kennedy, 1944.

Joe served on the Hoover Commission. President Hoover presented him with this photograph inscribed "To Joseph P. Kennedy, the greatest of our members."

for trips home for rest and consultations and to help President Roosevelt in his bid for a third term.

Jack resumed his undergraduate studies at Harvard and by taking extra courses was able to graduate the next year, in the class of 1940. He decided to do his senior thesis on the reasons why the British Government, under Stanley Baldwin and then Neville Chamberlain, had not armed the nation sufficiently to meet the growing power of Hitler's Germany—thus making the Munich Pact necessary. The title he chose was "Appeasement at Munich." Naturally, he and his father had a lot of correspondence about the subject matter. The thesis was rated *magna cum laude,* which enabled Jack to graduate—despite his fragmented collegiate career—*cum laude.*

Chapter Thirteen

When the war broke out, the use of the transatlantic telephone between the United States and England was limited to high priority messages. At first, Joe was told that he couldn't call us at all. Finally, he was allowed ten minutes every Sunday. As there were ten of us, arranging for each of us to have a budgeted minute or minute and a half required precise organization. Everything had to go like clockwork. I stayed in the living room, by the telephone, with two of the older children to act as escorts for the younger ones, who were waiting in the nearest room. When a child had finished his turn, he was hustled out while another child was being hustled in. Thus each got to hear Joe's voice, and he got to hear theirs.

Obviously there was no time for any real exchange of news and views; and so all of us fell back on that old-fashioned method of communication, letter writing.

A great many of the letters survived. In reading them after all these years, it seems to me they form a remarkably complete and vivid family narrative of our life during that time. It was a crazy time in the world—outrageous and frightening at first, then exasperating as the war fizzled into what was called the "phony war." Then, terribly and suddenly, the Nazis swept through Denmark and Norway, the Low Countries and France; and began massing their forces for the defeat of England.

From the great number of letters exchanged I have selected excerpts from a few dozen; not because they are "important" but because they seem interesting. Some of the dates are missing, but the letters are in approximate chronological order. I have added notes as needed.

Eunice to Father:

"September 17, 1939
"On Board S.S. *Washington* to the U.S.
"It is really amazing the number of people they managed to get on board. People are sleeping in the lounge, swimming pool, gymnasium, in fact everywhere thinkable, but it is all great fun. Nobody has their bags, and Kick and I wear the same costume for breakfast, lunch, and supper but then, so does everyone else. . . .

"Bob is rushing around trying to get Tilden, Budge, and Montgomery's autographs, but today two people asked him for his, so at present he is feeling very important.

"Hope to see you soon, Dad, and don't work too hard. Everyone we have met on the boat, even the young people, think you have done and are doing a marvelous job . . ."

Kick to Father:

"September 26
"Bronxville, N. Y.
"Well, we have been home a week. I can't believe it, even though everything is just the same. That's the amazing thing when one's been away, one expects things to have changed & they haven't—

"I have been to the World's Fair twice . . . I went to the polo game on Sunday with Peter Grace who was playing on Tommy Hitchcock's side & he played very well. I went to the theater with him last night. He's just the same . . .

"I couldn't get into Sarah Lawrence so I am going to Finch's in New York. It is a junior college and one can get a diploma, which is something.

"Everyone is just the same. Eunice is working hard & comes home every night. Jack is taking out Frances Ann this weekend so we can all hardly wait."

("Frances Ann" was Frances Ann Cannon, an attractive girl in whom Jack seemed to be quite interested at that time, and evidently she was interested in him too. At least Kick seemed to be implying that some "announcement" was in the offing.)

Eunice to Father, postcard from Richmond, Virginia:

"September 29

"We have had a marvelous day and everyone is talking about how well Mother did. She made two marvelous speeches . . ."

People, particularly women's groups, were interested in my experiences as wife-hostess-consort of the American ambassador at that time, so I was invited to speak at a number of places. I prepared a few talks on nonpolitical subjects, and usually they did seem to go over well. Richmond has a large population of English descent, so I expect people there were especially receptive, and I was encouraged to accept other invitations. Perhaps, indeed, I was made a bit giddy by success. I remember later speaking to a group of predominantly Irish Catholic women in Boston and saying something like, "Now, of course, you're all familiar with Windsor Castle . . ." I heard a woman in the front row turn to a friend next to her and whisper loudly, "What does she *mean* we're all familiar with *Windsor Castle!*" And I didn't blame her a bit. She was right, I had been wrong, and I was careful not to make any more such remarks.

Pat to Father, from Bronxville, early in October:

"We are all thinking of you on your anniversary." (October 7, 1914.)

"Mother is up visiting Bobby at school this weekend. I haven't been to the Fair yet but I am going . . . How are you and Rosie? Don't work too hard. Teddy is going to Lawrence Park West and loves it there. Jean goes into the convent every morning with me. She likes it very much." (Teddy's school was a few minutes from Bronxville; Pat and Jean's was Maplehurst, of which we heard here before.) "Miss Hennessey went away for the week and Teddy is getting away with anything, but Miss Dunn is coming today so he will be under control . . ."

Father to Pat, from London:

"November 3

"You are doing yourself proud on letters. I certainly think that you are having a much gayer time there than you possibly could have had over here. . . . I still go out to the country every night" (at Windsor Park, near London), "and between you and me it is pretty lonesome. I live alone except for the weekends when Rosie and the Moores . . . come out. Work hard, dear, have fun and think of me. Love."

To our joy Joe returned in December for consultations with President Roosevelt and U.S. officials most concerned with the war, and later was able to join us at the Palm Beach house for Christmas. Rosemary did not come with him. Transportation was difficult and tiring, at best, the best being a four-engine Pan American flying boat that came from England by way of Portugal, the Azores, and other way stations on this side. It would have been an unpleasant trip for her, possibly a complicated one for Joe. Also, as I have said earlier, she was making encouraging progress at her special school in England, so all in all it seemed wise that she stay there and miss this one Christmas with us.

From the time Joe bought the Palm Beach house in 1933 we had been spending the Christmas–New Year holiday time there. Most of us traveled from Bronxville in a Pullman car and we filled several drawing rooms. Meanwhile, two or three automobiles would have started south, occupied by household help and vast amounts of personal luggage, and tied and bowed Christmas presents.

The logistics were formidable. There were eleven of us, and there was a present from each to each of the others and (eleven times eleven) that accounted for 121 presents. In addition, there were presents from grandparents, aunts and uncles and cousins and friends such as Mary and Eddie Moore, and from other close associates and assistants, and also presents to the young from Santa Claus. We had lots of ornaments, many that the children had made in times past, many we had collected in our travels and had saved through the years. With the small mountain of gifts under the tree, it was an ideal gathering of a united and happy family.

Joe wished he didn't have to leave the family and go back to London. But the President wanted him to; and so he returned to London early in 1940.

Thus the family correspondence continues.

Teddy to Father, from Bronxville:

"January 1940

"Mr. Santa Claus

"J. P. Kennedy

"Dear Santa Claus,

"Thank you very much for the toys you gave me. You can give some more any time you want too. I liked the watch best. Thank you again. Lot of love. Happy New Year."

Bobby to Father, from Palm Beach:

"January

"Joe has a pretty good sunburn but the newest bulletin is he thinks he is going to peel. He has been giving all his speeches around here." (Joe Jr. was about to run as a delegate to the Democratic National Convention of 1940.) "They are pretty good. Last week Jack told us all about himself, now Joe is telling us about himself.

"Grandma and Grandpa are still down here and are fine. I am sorry but I have run out of ink . . .

"I have been playing quite a bit of tennis and swimming a great deal but I only went fishing once when I caught 2 or 3 small fish.

"Teddy flew back yesterday. He is as fat as ever and rising steadily in weight.

"My report was much better Miss Dunn said, but I'll have to do better in my marks I think.

"This is about all the news. Give my love to Mr. and Mrs. Moore and Rose."

Jack to Father, from Harvard:

"February

". . . Mother looks very well and is getting quite academic as she is taking some college courses.

". . . I am taking as my thesis for honors England's Foreign Policy since 1931. Am taking a course under Prof. Friedrich which is very interesting. I am still incognito but expect to go up and shake his palm and start discussing what a big impression he made on you when these papers start getting marked.

"Everyone is getting much more confident about our staying out of the war—probably because there is such a lull over there . . .

"Am getting along fine here—have been doing quite a bit of work as my courses are really interesting this year. That year is really standing me in good stead."

Joe Jr. to Father, from Palm Beach:

"April 5

"The Easter vacation is just about over and soon back to the law school for the last two months of the grind . . .

"Grandpa left today and looked very well but says that he doesn't feel very well. He had been feeling pretty well up until a couple of days ago when he took a look at the stock market and saw that one of his stocks had dropped four points and from then on his stomach started to go badly . . .

"Everyone has been very well and we have had plenty of sun. Teddy is fatter than ever and looks as healthy as it is possible to look. Jack finished his thesis.

"Primary election will be on the 30th of April . . . There was some criticism of me not being on the voting list but that was straightened out OK and the protester finally got his only consolation in stating that it was sending a child on a man's job.

"It looks like Dewey will get the Republican nomination OK, and it is still a mystery as far as the Democratic one goes. At the present time it doesn't seem that anyone could be elected except Roosevelt. The Republicans are rather afraid that Hull would be nominated for that would take a lot of the wind out of their sails. Farley has come out and said that his name will be presented at Chicago regardless of what happens. That's about all the news. . . ."

Jack to Father, from Harvard, mid-April:

"Just got back from the South. It was great down there—the weather was about the best I've ever seen. An awful lot of people were down—three girls to every man—so I did better than usual.

"Mother was in great shape and seems to be feeling fine. Bobby has increased in strength to such a degree that I seriously believe he will be bouncing me around plenty in two more years. He really is unusually strong and that school seems to have done him an awful lot of good as he has improved immensely as everyone has noticed— in every way. He looks 100% better too." (That "school" was Milton Academy).

"I am sending my thesis . . . Arthur Krock read it and feels that I should get it published. He thinks that a good name for it might be *Why England Slept* as sort of a contrast to Churchill's *While England Slept*. Krock felt it should be brought out in the spring—May or June—but it would depend on:

"1st When you resigned &

"2nd If you thought it was worth it—

"3rd If you stayed on thru the summer whether it could be published while you are in office. You can judge after you have seen it. . . .

"Please let me know what you think about the thesis as soon as you can—am sending it to an agent Krock gave me—and see what he thinks—the chief questions are:

"1. Whether it is worth publishing if polished up.

"2. If it can be published while you're still in office.

"Best to all,

> "Love,
> "Jack"

The professors at Harvard thought so highly of the thesis, in fact, that they suggested Jack expand it somewhat and interest a book publisher in it. The book came out that summer, with a foreword by Henry R. Luce, under the title *Why England Slept*. It got excellent reviews and sold extremely well.

Before the finished book could arrive in England, Joe had written to Jack that he had already heard good reports and:

"I am very anxious to read the final copy. I am sure if it reaches the problem as they now visualize it in England, the book will have quite a sale. Chamberlain, Halifax, Montagu Norman, and Harold Laski have all asked me about it. So, whether you make a cent out of it or not, it will do you an amazing amount of good, particularly if it is well received. You would be surprised how a book that really makes the grade with high-class people stands you in good stead for years to come. I remember that in the report you are asked to make after twenty-five years to the Committee at Harvard, one of the questions is 'What books have you written?' and there is no doubt you will have done yourself a great deal of good."

As usual, Joe was quite right. In addition to making a handsome amount of money for Jack (most of which he gave to repair bomb damages in England), it gave him an invaluable credential, as a young man wise beyond his years, when he later entered public life.

Joe Jr. to Father, from Harvard:

"May 4

"The only great excitement over here was the election and Grandpa thought I did quite well, so I guess the Kennedy name is a pretty good vote getter. I came in second by about 100 votes . . ." (This gave him a place on the delegation.) "It kind of looks like Roosevelt is going to run . . .

"People over here still feel the same way" (about the war). "However, every once in a while now you hear people talking about the need to go over now and not wait till it is too late.

"Grandpa is still making speeches and going strong. His latest remark is that Curley tried to sell the Boston Common but he stopped it. . . ."

Eunice to Father, from Manhattanville, early May:

"I made the tennis team. Last week we had our first match and we won. However, when I arrived at the court I had on white shorts, very respectable, and the nuns wouldn't allow me to play in them, so I was forced to wear a girl's skirt and shorts who must have had a size 64 waist. Both proceeded to fall off in the middle of the match. Such is life!

"I also bought a big lizard at the circus which jumped out of the box, and what a commotion! You would have thought I had let a lion out of his cage. Everyone started to shriek, one lady shrieked out, 'My heart, my heart,' and I was running like mad trying to catch him which I finally did. If looks or words could kill I would be 90 feet under. Anyhow I gave him back and got my money back. Now the nun is staring at me with fire in her eyes so I shall sign off. Please ask Rosie and the Moores to say a prayer for my exams and do say one, Dad, or else!"

Kick to Father, from Bronxville:

"May 21

"At the moment it looks as if the Germans will be in England before you receive this letter. In fact from the reports here they are just about taking over Claridges now. I still keep telling everyone 'the British lose the battles but they win the wars.'

"I have received some rather gloomy letters from Jane and Billy. Billy's letter was written from the Maginot Line. Daddy, I must know exactly what has happened to them all. Is Billy all right?"

("Billy" was young Lord Hartington, eldest grandson and heir of the Duke of Devonshire. He had been one of Kick's most attentive beaux while we were in London; and she liked him a great deal.)

"Jack just returned to Harvard after being home a week. He really is the funniest boy alive. He had the Irish maid in fits the whole time. Every time he'd talk to her he'd put on a tremendous Irish brogue. He still misses Cannon quite a bit."

(Frances Ann Cannon married John Hersey, who became both an excellent journalist and novelist. A few years later, when Jack had been through his harrowing war experiences in the Pacific and was back in Boston in a hospital recuperating, John Hersey, then a war correspondent for *Time-Life*, and having heard something about Jack's story from mutual friends—came to interview him. From their conversation, and details supplied by members of the crew, Hersey wrote a memorable article in *The New Yorker*, titled "Survival." That is how the saga of PT-109 came to public attention. The world is indeed small.)

"The house in Bronxville looks beautiful at the moment. All the trees and flowers are out . . . Mother came back from White Sulphur yesterday and looks very well.

"Teddy is very upset over the pictures of him in his birthday suit.

"Much love to Ed and Mrs. Moore and Rosie."

Jean to Father, from Bronxville:

"May 29

"How are you? . . . The nuns are all praying very hard for you.

"We are all very excited that Rosie is coming home. The house has been turned upside down with spring cleaning.

"Teddy now has to go on a diet. Miss Dunn has to get extra large size suits for him. We are all working very hard for the tests. I go to Mass every morning to pray that I pass them. Well, no very exciting news so I will close now.

"Oceans of Love and Kisses."

Joe Jr. to Father, from Harvard:

"June 12

"Well it's over except the shouting. I am confident I got through all right, however I would like to get some decent marks, as I really put in the time . . .

"It seems rather petty to talk about examinations when the whole world seems to be going to the devil. The country has gone through the most amazing change of public opinion." (This was after the Nazis had destroyed the French armies and two days before they entered Paris; the Petain government capitulated on June 22.) "All the professors around here are crazy with fright that America will not arm quick enough . . . There is a feeling around that we are going to get in before very long. No one has a reason for their feeling but they just have an idea that it is inevitable.

"I am going to investigate the possibility of joining the reserves of the Navy or Air Force, so that if anything happens I won't be a private. I think that compulsory military service is coming . . .

"I go to the Convention on the 15th of July . . ."

Jean to Father:

"June 20
"Hyannis Port
"We are all down at Hyannis Port now. Today Mother, Rose, Eu-

nice and Bob are all down at Harvard for Jack's graduation. Joe went on a trip on a boat so Teddy and I are the only ones in the house now . . . Teddy is learning to sail by himself now, he is going in some of the races with the skipper."

Teddy to Father:

"June 20–21?
"Hyannis Port
"We are down in cop-card [Cape Cod]. Mother has gone to jacks graduoin. joe is here. The weather is very dad. Would you get me the kings autograh for me. I will send you an other letter soon . . ."

Eunice to Father:

"June
"Hyannis Port
"The boats seem to be in fine shape, so here's hoping we take a few prizes this year. As yet there are only a very few people here and as for the Hyannis Port races it looks like the Tenovus will race the One More and nobody else but you can't tell." (We had a boat called *Tenovus* because there were the ten of us. Then Teddy was born. We needed another boat anyway, with a crowd our size, so we bought one and christened it *One More*.)

"I have been out in New York, Penn., and Cleveland, Ohio, visiting and playing in tennis tournaments. I received plenty of attention and I don't think it was because of my delightful personality (however I never know). I had my picture in the paper a couple of times and if I won a round it would be in big black type, and if I lost they put it in tiny small letters in the corner of the last page . . .

"The chief topic of conversation during the trip was your brains and what a wonderful job you were doing. Also how young looking Mother was. You can imagine how upset Mother was when I told her this. She almost jumped over the table in her excitement.

"Jack's graduation was really wonderful and we are sending you his picture in a cap and gown.

"Everyone is screaming for me to come as we are all going out with one another per us. . . ."

(Joe thought the children would never be married because they all enjoyed going out together so much. They were stimulated by each other's interests and plans, problems and ambitions.)

Jean to Father:

"June 24
"Hyannis Port

"To-day we went swimming and it was the coolest water I have ever been in . . . Rose wanted to go to the movies so I went with her. She is going to camp soon . . . Pat fell in the water a second time so she has been spending most of her vacation falling in the water . . . Mother went up to New Hampshire to see about Rose's camp.

"When Eunice went up to Cleveland she brought a newspaper article back with her that said she would give Hedy Lamarr a run for her money because she was so *beautiful*. I think she is going to send it to you. . . ."

Joe Jr. to Father:

"July 22
"Oshkosh, Wisconsin

"I am up here visiting Tom Schriber after the Convention and I thought I would give you some of my reactions.

"Even before the Mass. delegation left Boston there were arguments as to whom they would support, Farley or Roosevelt . . . We had a caucus the first night and it was the stormiest session that I have ever seen. They called each other liars and thieves . . . On the other hand there were those who felt that they had pledged themselves and they were bound by this pledge." (The delegation was pledged to Farley.) ". . . I had seen Krock previously, and he thought that I should stick with Farley . . . Of course someone demanded a poll of the delegation so I gave my vote orally. A lot of people came up to me afterwards and said that they thought I had done the right thing, and now I am more than ever convinced that it was the right thing."

(It was a complicated scene, but in Joe Jr.'s mind and conscience the issues were clear enough. He didn't like the idea of a "third term" for anyone. And, having run as a Farley delegate, he considered it morally dishonest to vote for anyone else unless and until Farley withdrew, which Farley did not. A lot of pressure was put on him by Roosevelt's managers; and pressure too on his father, by transatlantic telephone, to which Joe—even though he himself supported the third term—characteristically replied that the decision was up to Joe Jr.: "I wouldn't think of telling him what to do." Joe Jr. stayed steadfast with Farley all the way through.)

Joseph M. Patterson, president of the New York *Daily News*, wrote on that same date to Joe Sr. in London:

"Dear Joe:

"I was at the Democratic Convention in Chicago and wish to tell you what an excellent impression your son, Joe Jr., made on the delegates and spectators. When the Massachusetts delegation was being polled, he was kind of on the spot, as everybody knew, but he got up and said firmly, 'I was pledged to Farley and I vote for Farley.' He seemed to gain the respect of everybody there. I am sure he can have a political future if he wants one.

"With best wishes,
"Sincerely yours,
"J.M.P."

Joe's response to Patterson's letter shows his pride in his eldest son:

"One is always surprised—although I suppose one shouldn't be—when a busy man with lots on his mind has time to do as kind a thing as this.

"I judge that great pressure was brought to bear on Joe Jr., because Johnnie Burns called me from Chicago . . . Of course I told Johnnie that Joe Jr. would have to make his own decision and that I thought it would be manifestly unfair for me to mix in it one way or another. I thought that if he intended to go into public life, he might as well find out now if calling the play as he saw it was going to cause him difficulty. I wrote him a letter when it was all over and praised his stand. Jim Farley, from the thick of the campaign in Chicago, sent me a wire commending Joe for showing plenty of guts, so I was very happy. . . .

"Don't misunderstand me. There is nobody in the world who would rather see the Germans beaten than I would, but it strikes me that my job here is to keep as realistic as I can and to call the picture as I see it, which I am doing every day in my dispatches to Washington.

"It is rather dismal here with my entire family in the United States and I hate to have Mrs. Kennedy burdened with the whole responsibility, but . . . I felt I couldn't leave here until I had seen the bombing through. After that, we will see."

Two cables about that Chicago Democratic Convention of 1940 illuminate what the term "politics" has meant in our family. A cable from Jim Farley to Joe Sr. in London:

I WILL EVER BE GRATEFUL TO YOUR SON JOE FOR HIS MANLY AND COURAGEOUS STAND AT LAST NIGHT'S CONVENTION.

And Joe Sr.'s cabled reply:

. . . AS YOU CAN IMAGINE I HAD HEARD ABOUT THE STRUGGLE TO GET HIM TO CHANGE HIS VOTE AND WAS DELIGHTED HE TOOK THE STAND HE DID. AFTER ALL IF HE IS GOING INTO POLITICS HE MIGHT JUST AS WELL LEARN NOW THAT THE ONLY THING TO DO IS TO STAND BY YOUR CONVICTIONS. AM MOST HAPPY TO SAY HE NEEDED NO PROMPTING IN THIS RESPECT. MY BEST WISHES. . . .

Jean to Father:

"July 29
"Hyannis Port
"Jack's book has come out, he went to New York or someplace yesterday.

"Mother went up to Maine and she is going to go to camp for a week and get a rest.

"Teddy has gone out to race today. He is first in his series. He is learning to swim much better and . . . thinks he can do swan dives and everything. . . ."

"Grandpa and Grandma came down here yesterday afternoon . . .

"Everybody is very well and Teddy thinks he will go on a diet. He has been thinking that since he came down here although he has gotten a bit thinner.

"We all hope you will come home soon, Daddy.

"Well that's about all the news just now.

"Oceans of Love and Kisses. . . ."

Father to Jean:

"August 2
"London

"Your last letter, which arrived yesterday, was a nice newsy one and I was glad to hear about what's going on. I wish you would get hold of that Teddy and tell him to send me some news. All he says is, 'I am racing. Get me the King's autograph. I will write soon.'

"I am glad that you are sailing and doing so well. I think if you really got interested in it, with your good little head, you could make your sisters hustle. Also do keep after tennis because being proficient in sports helps you to get a lot more fun out of being with people . . .

"I have moved back into the embassy for five days a week, because there are so many things going on that I can't afford to take a chance on staying out at Windsor, but I have only opened my own bedroom and study, so the house looks pretty lonesome. . . . We are getting along very nicely, but I miss you all terribly. However, we had lots of fun when the going was good and one can't walk out on a job just because one wants to. Obligations must be fulfilled. Anyway I am hoping to have a few swims with you before you go back to school— if I am very, very lucky.

"Love to all and hugs and kisses to you."

Father to Eunice:

"August 2
"London

"I have had a lot of laughs at your observations re the members of the family.

"I have also been getting plenty of requests from Mother re your golf clubs. Where in the name of heaven did you leave them? Or, at what golf course did you use them, or to whose house did you ever take them on weekend parties? There is no sign of them at the embassy and we are sure we took everything away from Wall Hall. So, if you can give me any clue at all, I will get busy.

"I certainly was plenty homesick when I saw the picture in *Life* of you all sailing at Cape Cod . . . I still haven't given up hope that I may get the month of September there, or at least part of it, but that depends on Hitler. . . .

"Keep up your tennis and start playing golf. I am still going to make a champion out of you."

Jean to Father:

"August 5
"Hyannis Port

"Thanks loads for your nice long letter. It was awfully sweet of you to write all of us. It must have been an awful job.

"Mother arrived home last night from a camp in Maine which she stayed at for a week. She looks wonderful now.

"Jack's book seems to be a great success. All his friends wanted theirs autographed by him.

"Pat is on a diet and she has lost eight pounds and she really looks awfully well.

"Teddy says he is going to write to you more often and he is going to write you longer letters. He is getting bigger and broader every day. . . .

"Teddy has won one cup. I think I have won one but I have been protested so I won't know yet. We had a long distance race a couple of days ago. It was loads of fun. We brought our bathing suits and our lunch. We raced over and back and was it windy. Teddy steered going over and won by 3 mins and 8 secs. I steered coming back and won by 11 mins and 5 secs. We get a cup for that. Eunice and Bobby are doing quite well.

"I go to the Red Cross and make bandages every Monday and Thursday . . . It is really awfully nice . . .

"Kick is knitting a scarf for Billy and I am going to start knitting one for one of the soldiers . . .

"Eunice got a lovely painting from an elderly gentleman who came down one day with Condé Nast and he went crazy over Eunice. It is too bad nobody goes crazy over me.

"Don't forget to come home soon."

Joe to me:

"August 13
"London

"I have a chance to get this off again on the North Atlantic plane so am rushing it along. I went to see about your china and they haven't been able to give me much satisfaction yet. I have to get a sample of the plate and a sample of the color. They say they are still trying . . .

"I am also busy on the chintzes and I won't buy anything unless it meets all your requirements. Frankly, however, I am not at all taken with the one you sent me. I don't think it is sufficiently light and airy for that place . . .

"As to the situation here, there is little if any change. People are getting more confident that the home defense in the air is getting stronger. I am not prepared yet to make this judgment. If Hitler has the strength in the air he pretends he has, sooner or later it is bound to tell, and it is for that I am waiting.

"I read Jack's book through and I think it is a swell job. There is no question but that regardless of whether he makes any money out of it or not, he will have built himself a foundation for his reputation that will be of lasting value to him. Tell him I am taking the book today to Laski and I am going to have Laski give me some suggestions as to what people here might be helpful to get letters from for Jack, and I am also looking up who would be likely to do the best job publishing it.

"I am still taking very good care of myself and I am having surprisingly little trouble with my stomach considering the strain we are under . . .

"By the time the next letter is due we will know a great deal more about Germany's possibilities in the air. Until then, best love to you all."

Father to Eunice:

> "September 11
> "London

"I received your stories on Sunday and I sat myself right down on the porch and read them all.* You know, I think they are really wonderful . . . I knew you had a good sense of humor but I didn't know you could handle the descriptive part so well . . .

"There has been plenty of bombing going on . . . and they are still dropping them all 'round 14 Princes Gate. Last night they dropped one in the pool of Buckingham Palace . . . The prospect of bombing every night is driving them frantic. I don't know where it is all going to end but everything I see confirms what I always thought, that it ought never to have started. The unfortunate part of this war is that poor women and children are getting by far the worst of it. The soldiers aren't suffering in any such degree . . .

"I can't tell you what my state of mind would have been if any of you had been over here . . . I think I should have gone mad . . . The Germans are pursuing, I think, their usual methodical manner. I am not one of those who believe they are looking for maternity homes and hospitals to bomb. They are bombing their military objectives; and when you do that at night from fifteen or twenty thousand feet up in the air, you are bound to hit other things . . .

"Well, old darling, keep praying for civilization because heaven knows it needs it . . ."

Father to Jean:

> "September 11
> "London

"You have been one of my best little correspondents and I got another sweet letter from you yesterday. I certainly wish you could get that fat little brother of yours to write a little more frequently and tell me what he is doing. He was very good on the record,† but I

---

* Eunice had sent her father four essays.

† We sent a phonograph record, entitled *Voices*, for Joe's birthday. Each child recorded a birthday greeting.

think he should have a little more practice writing letters, because it looks to me as though the Kennedys are going to be good writers and I should hate to think that the Dude is not holding his end up, so will you see what you can do with him.

"The house at Windsor that I live in is such a bright color that the Air Ministry came in the other day and said it was such a perfect landmark for the German aeroplanes that it will have to be camouflaged, so they are trying to fix it up before the new moon. From this you can see all the problems that one has over here during the terrible war that this is." (As a matter of fact, bombs were dropped nearby. One of his staff aides, walking around the grounds, found a piece of bomb casing that bore the initials J.P.K. Probably a coincidence that Joe's initials were on it; nevertheless, they were.)

Father to Teddy:

"September 11
"London

"I certainly don't get all of those letters you keep telling me you write . . . your sisters do very well and you and Bobby are the worst correspondents I have in the family. It is very good practice for you to write, so I hope you will plan to send me a regular letter for so long as I am here. Incidentally, I certainly was thrilled to hear all your voices . . ." (The recording.)

"You are a great little cheer leader, and that Hip! Hip! Hooray! couldn't have been better . . .

"I was terribly sorry not to be with you in swimming at Cape Cod this summer, but I am sure you will know I wanted to be, but couldn't leave here while I had work to do . . .

"I thought you might be interested to know, and you might tell this to all your brothers and sisters, that the other night when I was going to the concert and afterwards to have dinner with Duff Cooper, the Cabinet Minister of Information, I dashed home to 14 Prince's Gate, put on my dinner jacket and left to go to the concert. When I got to Queen's Hall I found out the concert was canceled, and then I went back to my office, and after sitting there three-quarters of an hour I noticed by the merest chance that I had forgotten to shave for a couple of days, and I was going out to a dinner party without having shaved. So you can see how busy I am. I am sure everybody will laugh at this.

"I don't know whether you would have much excitement during these raids. I am sure, of course, you wouldn't be scared, but if you heard all those guns firing every night and the bombs bursting you might get a little fidgety . . .

"It is really terrible to think about, and all those poor women and children and homeless people down in the East End of London all seeing their places destroyed.

"I hope when you grow up you will dedicate your life to trying to work out plans to make people happy instead of making them miserable, as war does . . ."

Joe came back the next month, at his own insistence, for discussions with President Roosevelt about the war, American policy and—a matter that had been angering him—the State Department's penchant for working through special emissaries and otherwise operating behind his back without keeping him informed. The first evening after his arrival, he and I had dinner at the White House with the President and his personal secretary, "Missy" Le Hand, and Senator and Mrs. James Byrnes. Joe made his points in his most forthright way—which was *very* forthright. The President not only agreed with him about the State Department operations but went on to give the persons involved a verbal blistering. In fact, in describing his remarks I see that in my notes I have used the term "harangue."

The presidential election of 1940 was less than two weeks away and looked as if it would be a very close one; the "third term" issue was hotly debated, and the Republicans had an energetic and attractive candidate in Wendell Willkie. The President asked Joe that evening for his support and a public announcement. Joe agreed; he went on a national radio hookup of 114 stations (paying the expenses from his own pocket, as his personal contribution to the Democratic Party) and endorsed Roosevelt for re-election. His main point of emphasis was that he believed FDR could and would keep us out of the war. He closed by saying:

"My wife and I have given nine hostages to fortune. Our children and your children are more important than anything else in the world. The kind of America that they and their children will inherit is of grave concern to us all. In the light of these considerations, I believe that Franklin D. Roosevelt should be re-elected President of the United States."

At the request of Betsy Cushing Roosevelt, I too went on the radio and said I was sure the President would not lead my sons and their sons into war.

We had nagging doubts as to just how far, "short of war," FDR's policics could lead the country in safety. Yet Joe in all sincerity agreed with FDR at that point in history. Give England all the aid possible, while rearming this country to make it impregnable against attack in case England fell, as we were next on Hitler's list. Meanwhile, we should not fight unless attacked.

Peace was a continual theme in Roosevelt's campaign speeches. An evening or two after Joe's speech, FDR was in Boston—incidentally, welcomed there at the station by dignitaries including my father, with Jack in tow—and before a great crowd at the Boston Garden gave one of his most eloquent speeches, which included these memorable lines:

"And while I am talking to you mothers and fathers, I give you one more assurance. I have said this before, but I shall say it again and again and again: Your boys will not be sent into any foreign wars."

I must confess that I was as susceptible as most people to Roosevelt's charm and blandishments. He was undoubtedly a genius in his personal relationships. He knew that one of the easiest ways to get around me was to tell me complimentary things about my father. I knew what he was doing (later one of the Roosevelt boys told Jack it was true, and Jack told me). Nevertheless, even while I knew I was being charmed, the charm was difficult to resist.

The day after President Roosevelt's re-election, Joe sent in his resignation. The President wanted him to stay on, and in fact persuaded him to keep the title until a successor could be selected. Thus, his resignation was not formally accepted until February 1941.

He never re-entered government service again except as a consultant and, many years later, a member of the "Hoover Commission," set up to reorganize the executive branch of the government.

Yet he was never any less concerned with national and international affairs than he had been during the decade when he was helping to shape them.

Relaxing on an autumn day in the 1940s.

I christen the *Esso Richmond*.

Jean christens the *Joseph P. Kennedy, Jr.*

Caroline launches the carrier *John F. Kennedy.*

Joe at Jack's wedding.

The Duchess of Devonshire and Joe Jr., with Lord Hartington and Kathleen after their wedding in London, 1944.

Bobby and Ethel.

Wide World Photos

Pat and Peter.

Eunice and Sarge.

Harcourt-Harris, N.Y.C.

Jack and Jackie.

Jean and Steve.

Ted and Joan.

Eunice, Pat, Jack, and I before a "Kennedy tea."

Two congressmen—my father, John Francis Fitzgerald, and my son John Fitzgerald Kennedy. The desk shown is the one used by my father in Congress.

Chapter Fourteen

For most of the year following his resignation, Joe used his freedom from the strictures of public life to help organize sentiment against U.S. intervention in the war and the policies that could lead to it. He testified before committees of Congress, wrote articles, gave interviews, made speeches, and talked with influential friends. There were many of the country's leading citizens who felt as he did and undertook similar efforts. Yet, direct involvement became steadily more likely.

With the imminence of war and the feeling that it might be the last good time for a long time, I took a trip to South America. I had never been farther south than Panama. With Joe now back in the United States and able to cope with the children, I could travel with my mind at ease. It was a system we had always followed: As long as one of us was there, the other was free to go. I invited Eunice to come along. As soon as she finished her spring term at Manhattanville we cruised through the Caribbean islands and thence south to Rio de Janeiro. From there we traveled by air.

We were joined briefly by Jack. He was still having a hard time deciding on a career. He had thought of law school. Then, perhaps because Joe Jr. was to be a lawyer, he thought of becoming a businessman. Jack evidently figured that if the life of a businessman and financier was interesting enough for his father it should be interesting for him. Consequently, in the fall of 1940, he had enrolled in courses in economics, finance, and business administration at Stanford University. But he had no real appetite for it, so he left after the first semester. Then, impelled by the same urge to travel in the world and sharing my curiosity about South America, he had taken off by air about a fortnight after Eunice and I sailed, and met us in Rio.

After a time together he went on his own way alone, seeing whatever interested him, forming impressions of countries and their peoples. I daresay that his trip found echoes twenty years later when he was President and created the Alliance for Progress.

Eunice and I had quite a fascinating time. We learned a lot, we had fun and also a few thrills and chills, including flying over and between the towering snowy Andes in a plane bouncing wildly in the treacherous air currents. The windows frosted over completely and many people inhaled oxygen from overhanging tubes. I didn't need oxygen. I used my breath to clear a little space in the frost on the window so I could look out at the mountains.

I have diary entries from the trip.

"May 14, Barbados

"On our arrival at shore, we were delighted with the atmosphere of the town. The people are happy and gentle. Visited the cathedral which is as old as Plymouth, and found some graves in the church as old as any in Massachusetts, written in old English.

"Hired a car and visited a convent of Ursulines, where sisters were teaching children. Was struck by the cleanliness of all the children. They looked so scrubbed and immaculate, and I blushed when I thought of my little Teddy when he rushed to school some days. Happened to stop in at a class of the smaller ones just as they were saying their prayers, and I have seldom been so moved: to see those dark-skinned little faces, with those immense trustful, gentle brown eyes raised in prayer, convinced me for all time that there must be angels with dark faces."

"May 17, on board ship

"Talked to Chinese minister to Brazil, fellow passenger. From my own experience, I know diplomats shy away from women who seek information, because they are afraid of being quoted . . . He did say that China, although leaning toward communism at one time, was now veering away from it."

"May 21, Rio de Janeiro

"Jack and Eunice and I invited by Ambassador Jefferson Caffery to dinner at the United States Embassy. The first dinner in an embassy I have attended since I left London. Seemed reminiscent of many of my own in London. The china and glass at the U.S. embassies are the same world over. White Lenox china with gold crest; glassware is plain crystal with the coat of arms etched on. Menu cards, 4 inches by 6¼ inches, are ivory white with gold coat of arms at top.

"On my arrival I was presented to the papal nuncio and I chatted with him in French until dinner was announced. I sat next to Señor Aranha, the Brazilian Foreign Minister, whose family has been in politics five generations. We discussed the attitude of the Brazilian Government in the present world crisis, and he seems to feel it would be strongly influenced by which side won the victory abroad.

"It seems to me that the idea of a family serving in the government generation after generation, as is the case with so many English families as well, is one we might do well to think about and encourage in our own country."

Eunice and I traveled on to Argentina, across the Andes to Chile, thence to Peru, Ecuador, on then to Panama, and to Cuba. We arrived in Hyannis Port about June 20, full of stories of our adventures and just in time to get almost the full benefit of a Cape Cod summer.

At our house, the summers had some rather special qualities. For help in recalling them fully I wrote to Charles Spaulding, a friend of Joe Jr. and Jack's. He replied with a letter describing the summer of 1940, just after Jack's book was published, but the scene was essentially the same in earlier summers and again in 1941.

"Dear Mrs. Kennedy,

"Perhaps the best way for me to answer your letter is to recall the first time I met your family.

"George Means brought me to your house on the Cape at the end of a day in the summer of 1940. The two of us walked up on the porch. There was an uproar of voices, laughter, and insults pouring from every room—Billings' notes quite clear in the orchestration. Somebody yelled above the din that we should stay for supper.

"We walked into the house and I remember being startled to see so many young people—children then—who looked alike when they grinned and somehow managed to keep the atmosphere in the house at fever pitch even while involved in something as lackluster as getting ready for supper.

"George went into Jack's room, which was downstairs. There was a large inventory of *Why England Slept* stacked on the floor. 'They're going like hot cakes,' the author explained as we were introduced. I noticed a letter of praise from a very famous man in Europe lying on the floor, half under a bathing suit, and was about to pick it up when the former mayor of Boston entered. He carried a clipping from a Boston paper that made a flattering reference to himself, the justice of which he was at some pains to make clear to his grandson.

"Dinner followed shortly with the whole family and four guests present. A supermarket must have been cleaned out to supply the vegetables and the berries that were consumed at that sitting. The talk was about the Federal Reserve System and the argument lasted through the meal with the head of the house leading the company through a strenuous exercise on the subject.

"Afterward, there was a movie. When George and I left much later, the place was having difficulty calming down. Those who had gone to bed early were pounding shoes on the floor demanding a quiet that was coming with a grudging reluctance. A lot had gone into that day and it was dying hard, leaving behind a diary of activity that included a sailing race, an aggregate of twenty-three sets of tennis, a debate on the forces involved in the Spanish Revolution, some stories by the emperor about plungers of the twenties, a paper contributed by the girls listing the qualities that should be present in the ideal husband, the daily game of touch football, and, finally, a local war that broke out after the movie over the issue—would Ingrid Bergman go to fat.

"On the way home with George, I went over the evening in my mind and wondered about what had made it so good. There was the excitement of the unusual achievement of the house coupled at the same time with a complete lack of pretense. There was the constant spur of competition which brought out an intense appreciation of excellence. There was the feeling shared by everybody that anything was possible and the only recognized problem was that there would never be enough time. And this combined to produce the most heightened group of people, much less one family. I thought to myself—that's the best I've seen.

"All of this was many years ago. I have been close to the act off and on since. It's still the best I've seen. It never loses its fascination or inspiration for me. When one has stumbled and come back and been exposed again to your vivid point of view, one finds the energy to try again. When one sees how small his achievement has been and gets the impulse to start at once on something else much more demanding. All in all, it amounts to a considerable influence, I think the strongest I have known.

"This is as close as I can come in a few words to describing what I have found of value in your house.

"Chuck Spaulding"

Chuck Spaulding's letter about the ambience of our house at the end of summer in 1940 applies quite well to the summer of 1941, with a few additions and exceptions. Among them were radios and phonographs. I don't know how many we had in our house but certainly there were six or eight or so, including "portables." Several were operating morning, noon, and night around the house and grounds. During most of the daylight hours one could fairly well count on music coming from the directions of the tennis court, the beach, and the front porch—each according to the taste of the person running the machinery.

And then there were the telephones. There were several lines coming into the house, with instruments in nearly all the bedrooms and strategically placed in other areas. The telephones rang morning to night.

I mustn't neglect the barking of the dogs.

I have read someplace that I have an idiosyncratic dislike of dogs. Actually I grew up with dogs, in Concord and Dorchester. I think we always had a dog in the house. So I knew what a dog could mean to a child. When my children were old enough we began to acquire a series of dogs. There were so many through the years, including mutts from the pound as well as purebreds, that I can't begin to sort out their identities and eras. But we maintained a "house" dog until Jack was fourteen or so and began developing asthmatic troubles. He was apparently allergic to dog hair. It was sad because he loved animals, but it meant no house dogs so long as he was at home. It did not mean an absence of dogs: It merely meant that there would be "yard" dogs with occasional indoor privileges. One of these belonged to Jack.

Pat says:

"One of Jack's dogs was a Doberman Pinscher called Moe. Jack was in Arizona for his health and living in a rather remote place and bought the dog both for company and as a watchdog. Then he moved on someplace where he couldn't take the dog, so he shipped him home. It was supposed to be for Mother's birthday, or something like that. The dog arrived one day on the front porch in a big slatted, open crate with a big sign on it: MY NAME IS MOE AND I DON'T BITE. Everybody gathered around, and Teddy opened the door of the crate and the dog jumped out and bit him.

"He immediately sent a telegram to Jack:

'THIS DOG THAT DOESN'T BITE JUST JUMPED OUT
OF HIS CAGE AND BIT ME. TEDDY'

"Mother took the dog out for walks, and Moe became very attached to her. Only to Mother—a real one-woman dog. And Mother rather enjoyed him. For the rest of us it got to be terrifying. There were a couple of us old enough to go down to Hyannis to the movies at night. Daddy always made us put the car away in the garage when we got home. But after a few nights we couldn't do that, because to get from the garage to the house with Moe around was absolutely terrifying. Finally it got so we couldn't do anything, because he was so attached to Mother. He was biting everybody in sight. Except Mother. He adored her. But not the rest of us—if you kept all your limbs, or fingers, or toes, you were lucky. He lasted about five weeks and then Moe had to go. Mother, I'm sure, found a good home for him with someone who needed an insanely dedicated watchdog."

To summarize the sounds of summer: the bounce of the tennis balls, the splashings and belly flops and cannon balls in the ocean, the cacophony of the radios and phonographs, the cars "revving up" and backfiring, departing and arriving, the cries of welcome and farewell, the piano being tortured by someone learning to play, the yapping and barking of several involved dogs, the ringing of telephones and the maids' knocks on my door to ask, "Mrs. Kennedy, what should I . . ." I resolved to get away for an hour or two a day, but close by just in case something happened that I should know about.

I bought a little prefabricated one-room house and had it erected down at one corner of the beach. It was about the size of a tool shed —or of my little sewing room at our house on Beals Street—but big enough for a desk where I could take care of personal correspondence, an easy chair where I could sit and read, a cot on which I could nap, and space enough so that I could change clothes there if I felt like walking down to the water for a swim. Other "hermitages" have been grander, but this was perfect for me.

Imagine my horror when a summer or two later we had a hurricane and I watched my little house bob in the waves and then disappear toward the open sea. I was so sad that I had it replaced the following summer, at a higher and safer elevation from the shore. The children referred to it as "Mother's Little White House." I used it contentedly for a couple of years. But then came another and even bigger hurricane, and Little White House II also went out to sea without a trace. By then the Hyannis Port scene was quieter, and Joe and I had begun to spend part of each summer abroad. I didn't erect Little White House III. But I remember I and II with deep appreciation.

The summer of 1941 was the last one our family would ever have together.

Ordinarily Joe Jr. would have been returning to Harvard that fall for his last year of law school. However, believing the United States would be drawn into the war, he wanted to prepare himself for a role in active service. Accordingly, he volunteered for training as a Navy flyer; and in July, shortly before his twenty-sixth birthday, he reported for his primary training at the Squantum Naval Air Station near Boston. It was close enough so that he could come home for several weekends during the rest of that summer. Afterward he had advanced training at the big naval air station at Jacksonville, Florida. In the book *As We Remember Joe,* Jack wrote:

"As a cadet at Jacksonville, he was president of the cadet club, president of the Holy Name Society, and at the last, upon graduation, was awarded the Cutler Wings, given to that cadet as elected by his fellows who is best fitted for his duties as a United States naval officer.

"After being awarded his wings in May 1942 by his father at a graduation ceremony, he flew Caribbean patrols, and it was not until September 1943 that he finally realized his ambition and was sent to England with the first naval squadron to fly B-24s with the British Coastal Command . . ."

Jack had come to the same conclusion as Joe Jr., and on returning from his South American travels, soon after his twenty-fourth birthday, he volunteered for the Officers' Candidate School of the Army. Because of the back injury he had suffered in Harvard football, he failed the physical exam. He tried the Navy and was rejected for the same reason. During the rest of that summer he did all sorts of calisthenics and corrective exercises. In September he applied again to the Navy, and this time was accepted for the Navy's officer training course. Early that winter he received his commission.

At first he had a desk job in Washington, helping prepare a digest of relevant news and "intelligence" for the Navy's Chief of Staff, a duty he found dull. After Pearl Harbor, he quickly applied for sea duty. Nothing happened for some time. Then he was assigned to instruct recruits at a training base in South Carolina. His pal Lem Billings saw him "in action" there and told about it later—in *John Fitzgerald Kennedy . . . As We Remember Him*—in such a funny way that with Lem's permission I am including it here:

"He was stationed for a while in Charleston, South Carolina. My brother got married down South, and so I was there, and I went over after my brother's wedding just to see what was going on. He made, as far as I know, his first public speech. And I was there. He had to give a talk on incendiary bombs. He knew very little about the subject and did very, very well. I was impressed, because I had never heard him speak before. When we were at Choate, we both avoided public speaking—you could do that if you went into Dramatic Club. Neither of us was a good actor, but we avoided public speaking by doing that. After the speech was over, he was so pleased with himself that he said to the crowd, 'Now, are there any questions?' The first question was 'Well, you have told us about these two kinds of bombs; tell me, if one lands, how do you tell which is which?' Jack said, 'I'm glad you asked that question, because a specialist is going to be down here in two weeks and this is the kind of thing he wants to talk about.'"

He spent most of his first year and a half in the Navy in similar duties, which didn't appeal to him at all. He did manage to get home to Hyannis Port, on leave, during the summer of 1942. In the late fall of that year he was transferred to PT boats. He trained for about six months, and early in 1943 was sent off to the South Pacific, where by March that year he became skipper of PT-109.

Thus Jack, although he had been accepted into the Navy a couple of months after Joe Jr., was in a combat zone of the war, subject to all dangers of enemy action, six months or so before Joe Jr. arrived in England. As most spirited young men do in a national patriotic war, as this one became for all of us after Pearl Harbor, both had wanted to get away from routine military matters and into direct combat as soon as possible. In their long brotherly, friendly rivalry, I expect this was the first time Jack had won such an "advantage" by such a clear margin. And I daresay it cheered Jack and must have rankled Joe Jr.

One may wonder what I thought about all this. I detested it. War has always seemed to me "the ultimate insanity." Violence and war as the maximum demonstration of man's capacity for inhumanity to man were against my religious beliefs, my sense of morality, and my common sense. The future confirmed my beliefs in ways that in that period I could barely have imagined.

Yet, like nearly all mothers everywhere, I was caught in events and forces and circumstances utterly beyond my control. There was nothing I could do but to put on a cheerful face, to hope, and to pray.

The summer of 1941 was also the last one that Rosemary could be with us.

She had been making good progress for some time past, and Joe and I had every reason to be optimistic about her future. Not that she could be brought all the way up to the level of normality; this was an unrealistic hope. Yet there are many millions of people in the world with I.Q.'s below 100 who do useful work and have satisfactory lives. This was our ambition for Rosemary, and it seemed close to being achieved.

Yet, in the year or so following her return from England, disquieting symptoms began to develop. Not only was there noticeable retrogression in the mental skills she had worked so hard to attain, but her customary good nature gave way increasingly to tension and irritability. She was upset easily and unpredictably. Some of these upsets became tantrums, or rages, during which she broke things or hit out at people. Since she was quite strong, her blows were hard. Also, there were convulsive episodes. Manifestly there were other factors at work besides retardation. A neurological disturbance or disease of some sort seemingly had overtaken her, and it was becoming progressively worse. Joe and I brought the most eminent medical specialists into consultation, and the advice, finally, was that Rosemary should undergo a certain form of neurosurgery.

The operation eliminated the violence and the convulsive seizures, but it also had the effect of leaving Rosemary permanently incapacitated. She lost everything that had been gained during the years by her own gallant efforts and our loving efforts for her. She had no possibility of ever again being able to function in a viable way in the world at large. She would need custodial care. We searched for the proper place and found it in a convent in Wisconsin where the nuns were understanding of her condition and gave her all the care and compassion and cheerful loving kindness that her misfortune and her sweet nature deserved. She has been there for more than three decades. She has remained physically healthy and generally happy. I visit her every few months. Eunice goes about every six weeks. The other family members see her at least a few times a year. She functions on a childlike level but is able to have excursions in her motorcar, and to do a little personal shopping for her needs—always with an attendant—and to enjoy life to the limit of her capacities. She is perfectly happy in her own environment and would be confused and disturbed at being anywhere else. She knows us and is pleased to see us.

Rosemary's was the first of the tragedies that were to befall us.

In writing as I have, I have felt grief and pain hardly lessened despite the years. Yet there have been so many strange stories (for example, that Rosemary was present at Jack's inauguration) that I have felt obliged to relate the story as it really was.

That summer of 1941 was also the last one we had with Kathleen. She was twenty-one by then and, having finished her second year at Finch in New York that spring, spent much of the summer with us at Hyannis Port. She wasn't sure what to do next but liked the idea of journalism. That fall she got a job reporting for the Washington *Times-Herald*. As her father pointed out that would keep her in the thick of things in the most important capital in the world at one of the most important times in history.

She wanted to prove herself so she worked very hard and before long she won everyone's respect as a reporter and writer. She tried her best to avoid any attention or privilege that could come her way due to her father's fame. In fact, she strove so hard to blend into the staff and be just another cub reporter whose name was Kathleen Kennedy that one amusing incident is worth telling.

Joe gave each of the girls a fur coat, mink or her choice of some fine fur and in any style she felt was most becoming. Kick's, as I recall, was a long, lustrous mutation mink in a shade that would set off her glowing, lightly pink Irish complexion. Naturally she didn't wear it to the *Times-Herald* office. One evening she was supposed to attend a diplomatic reception and had put on an expensive dinner dress and her mink coat. Then she suddenly realized there was something she had forgotten to do at the office. On her way to the party she had her taxi wait while she hurried up to attend to it, and encountered a couple of her older female colleagues. They looked at her as though they couldn't believe their eyes and didn't want to. Later the grapevine had it that they feared their sweet innocent Kathleen had gone wrong, succumbed to the temptations of wealth, become a loose woman. She obviously couldn't afford such raiment on her wages as a cub reporter!

From her childhood Kick had been, in effect, our eldest daughter because of Rosemary's disability. She was small, quick, witty, and exceptionally bright. She was an enchanting child, girl, and young woman. She adored her two big brothers, and they in turn were delighted by her. When she was a teen-ager, and with Joe Jr. only five years and Jack only three years older than she, the three reached such near parity that they shared friends and experiences. During the embassy years, for instance, while Joe Jr. and Jack were becoming popular swains in London, Kick was becoming a rather spectacularly successful debutante and postdeb in the same set. They knew the same people, often went to the same places, heard the new songs, learned the new dance steps, listened to the latest jokes and youthful gossip, and talked about it together.

Consequently, when Joe Jr. and Jack went into the armed services expecting shortly to be sent to theaters of war, I think Kick felt rather left out. She too wanted to become directly involved in the war and to make her own contribution that would be constructive. Early in 1943 she left her newspaper job to join the Red Cross training program. She wanted to serve in a theater of war and hoped that this would be England.

She had developed a great fondness for that country and its people during our years there. She had many English friends. She was concerned about them, wanted to see them, and at least in some sense share their wartime ordeals. There was one young man especially who meant more to her than I realized at the time. This was William John Robert ("Billy") Hartington.

She got her wish. She was on her way to England by late June 1943, which was only a few months after Jack had arrived in the South Pacific and taken command of PT-109, and was actually close to three months before Joe Jr. arrived in England with his squadron to begin working with the British Coastal Command.

Her letters to us—and to Jack out in the South Pacific—form an interesting narrative.

To the Family:

> "June 27, 1943
> "On Board the *Queen Mary*

"After talking with you I went back to the hotel and got myself together. At 7:00 promptly, on one of the hottest days of the year, dressed in winter uniforms, raincoats, gas masks, wearing tin helmets, carrying 35-pound musette bags, not to mention the canteen and First Aid Kit strapped to the waist—we boarded the *Queen Mary*.

There are eight of us in a cabin and when I say on top of one another I do mean on top of one another! Nearly 18,000 troops are packed in all over the ship. They are sleeping in the hallway, decks, etc. It really is the most pathetic sight in the world . . .

"There are about 160 Army nurses and they are certainly a lot of tough babies. There are also about 300 officers of every nationality. Most of the Red Cross girls don't pay attention to them as it certainly isn't any compliment to be sought after when the ratio is so uneven . . . The girls are quite nice but you certainly get sick of a lot of giggling females and they still like to sit up until about 1:30 A.M. every night . . .

"We have had Mass every afternoon at 3:30—a wartime measure and guess where we have it—in the synagogue. I have been serving Mass as the soldiers don't seem to show up . . .

"I really am becoming quite excited at the thought of seeing England again and I am quite prepared for the changes. This arrival certainly is going to be different from our last one.

"I still haven't any idea about my assignment, but hope like anything it will be London for a while . . .

"About a half hour after each sharp swerve we are informed that this good ship has just missed a sub. There's another one. It was probably about nine miles to starboard.

"Tell Eunice I shall keep her constantly informed of all happenings as maybe she could join me (in the Red Cross) after graduation.

"Love to all and eat a lot of ice cream for me on Sunday."

To Jack:

"July 3
"Hampstead, England

"At the moment I am sunning myself in the Gores' garden. Still recovering from a rather hectic trip over . . .

"London seems quite unchanged. Food is very good. Blitzed areas are not obvious . . .

"Sissy and David Gore have two wee ones now. Lady Astor wrote me a note of welcome but she's at Plymouth at the moment. There are a great many in the country on maneuvers etc. . . ."

The Gores were Mr. and Mrs. David Ormsby-Gore, an attractive young couple. David* was just a year younger than Jack, and Sylvia ("Sissy") was, I suppose, about Kick's age; they had married only six months after our family had left England and had done well to produce two "wee ones," so soon. David and Sissy, Jack and Joe Jr. and Kick had been close companions during our time at the embassy. Kick's comment was a newsy note about old friends. David and Sissy, David particularly, would later have a conspicuous role in Anglo-American relations.

Some people resent the idea of a person other than a career diplomat being chosen for the important post of ambassador. But it seems to me an advantage. For instance, when Jack was President, Harold Macmillan sent over David Ormsby-Gore as England's ambassador to the United States. This choice was made because Jack and David Ormsby-Gore had been pals in England and understood each other.

The same principle applied to the appointment of General James Gavin to France in the early 1960s. General Gavin led our paratroopers into Paris to liberate the city, and Jack thought that a very pleasant relationship could be made between General de Gaulle and General Gavin.

From Kick:

"Dearest Little Kennedys,

"July 14
"London

"The job is going very well. I simply can't get over how nice everyone is. I must say that I expected old friends to be kind but they have exceeded all expectations. Anytime anyone ever says anything against the British in front of me they'll hear about it. Yesterday Lord Beaverbrook rang me up . . . I am going to dine with him next week even though he said, 'This admirer is the combined age of all your other admirers.'

". . . Billy and I went out together for the first time in London last Saturday. It really is funny to see people put their heads together the minute we arrive any place. There's heavy betting on when we are going to announce it. Some people have gotten the idea that I'm going to give in. Little do they know. It just amuses me to see how worried they all are . . ."

* The present Lord Harlech.

There were very great difficulties in the way of marriage between Kick and Billy, and I think I must make them clear.

Kick had, of course, been brought up in the Catholic Church and had been convent educated from early to late teens. Not only had she been thoroughly indoctrinated in her religious beliefs, but she had that "gift of faith" to which I have referred and to which I shall return. She also knew how much the Church meant to me, to most of her close relatives, and, historically, to her ancestors. It had, in fact, as I think historians of almost any persuasion would agree, been the main cohesive force, more important than language, custom, any circumstance that had enabled the Irish people to survive and in some ways prevail during the course of many centuries of domination by the English.

Billy's ancestors for generations had been occupants of highest offices in the English government of Ireland. As such they had done their best to suppress any sentiments for independence among or on behalf of the Irish. Indeed, in that regard, both sides of the family, the Cavendishes (Earls, Marquesses, and Dukes of Devonshire) and the Cecils (Earls and Marquesses of Salisbury), had been among the most conservative members of the ruling class. I think it would be fair to say that the Cavendishes and the Cecils deeply mistrusted the Irish people, and in turn were regarded as arch enemies by Irish patriots, who to a greater or lesser degree had been in a state of rebellion ever since the Norman-English conquest of Ireland a few centuries before.

Billy's grandfather, Marquess of Hartington and eighth Duke of Devonshire, had been Secretary of State for Ireland—that is to say, the British ruler or viceroy—in the 1870s, a post he hadn't wanted and from which he emerged with such bias that he later broke with his party, the Liberals, and defied Prime Minister Gladstone in order to form his own party to oppose Irish home rule. Meanwhile, his younger brother, Lord Frederick Cavendish, was appointed to the same post, Secretary of State for Ireland. He had been in office only a day when a gunman of the Irish independent movement shot and killed him in Phoenix Park, Dublin, in 1882.

To put it mildly, there was little in the family backgrounds to encourage a romance between Billy and Kick.

The Cavendish and Cecil families had always been among the strongest pillars of the Church of England. Moreover, Billy's father, the tenth duke, was a Freemason. And Freemasonry had been under condemnation by the Catholic Church for more than two centuries. Kick had said in her letter she wouldn't "give in": wouldn't leave her church to join Billy's, but it would have been equally unthinkable for Billy to leave the Church of England and become a Roman Catholic.

It was an apparently impossible dilemma. And Kick was realistic to have written, therefore, "It just amuses me to see how worried they all are."

To Jack:

"July 29
"London

"I have just returned from a day and a half spent in the country with Billy at Eastbourne. It has been blitzed quite badly, but the family continues to go there during the summer months. For twenty-four hours I forgot all about the war. It's the most lovely spot . . . Billy is just the same, a bit older, a bit more ducal, but we get on as well as ever. It is queer as he is so unlike anyone I have ever known at home or anyplace really. Of course I know he would never give in about the religion, and he knows I never would. It's all rather difficult as he is very, very fond of me and as long as I am about he'll never marry. However much he loved me I can easily understand his position. It's really too bad because I'm sure I would be a most efficient Duchess of Devonshire in the postwar world, and as I'd have a castle in Ireland, one in Scotland, one in Yorkshire, and one in Sussex I could keep my old nautical brothers in their old age. But that's the way it goes. Everyone in London is buzzing with rumors, and no matter what happens we've given them something to talk about. I can't really understand why I like Englishmen so much, as they treat one in quite an offhand manner and aren't really as nice to their women as Americans, but I suppose it's just that sort of treatment that women really like. That's your technique isn't it? . . .

"Well, take care, Johnny. By the time you get this so much will have happened. The end looks nearer now than ever.

Write to me . . . God bless you . . . Much love."

Kathleen's letter was prophetic. Four days later, PT-109 was cut in two by a Japanese destroyer. I did not know anything about his ordeal until after it was all over and he was safe. A message had come from the Navy Department that he was "missing in action" but it had been delivered to Joe, and he didn't show it to me. Joe did not want to torment me with uncertainty or give me bad news until it was absolutely necessary. Several days later, when Joe had gone riding at 8 A.M., as was his custom, I turned on the radio and heard the announcement that Lieutenant j.g. John F. Kennedy, earlier reported missing, had been found. I waited for more news about him, but there was none. I called Joe, who was twenty minutes' distance away. He came home immediately and confirmed the details, and he told me what he had known, and that he had been trying to spare me until the facts were established.

To the Family:

"August 24
"London

"Of course the news about Jack is the most exciting I've ever heard. There wasn't a very big piece in the English newspapers but quite enough for me to gather that he did really big stuff. I rang up Mr. Raymond Daniell at the New York *Times* and he told me where I could read all about it in last week's *Times* . . .

"They are keeping us very busy here at the Club and one does receive enormous satisfaction from doing lots of little things. The boys really crowd in here every night and most of them have gotten over the fear that I am some extraordinary being because I happened to have a father who really was (extraordinary, of course!) . . ."

To Jack:

"September 10
"London

"Goodness, I was pleased to get your letter. Ever since reading the news in all the newspapers over here I have been worried to death about you. All sorts of people have rung up about it and sent congratulations. I read the clippings from the New York *Times* but long to hear the whole story. Am sure Mrs. Luce is blaming your survival on 'her medal' . . ." (Clare Boothe—Mrs. Henry R.—Luce had become a Catholic convert and had given Jack a sacred medal when he went to war.)

"When the shouting and the tumult dies I don't know where we Red Cross girls will be. Very tired—of that I'm sure. It's a great joy, a great job but sometimes you don't know whether you are going to shoot yourself or that GI over there in the corner. However, there never was a job that was all milk and honey, was there?

". . . God bless you, much love."

To the Family:

"October 5
"London

". . . We had our big day last Saturday." (This was a carnival party at the Red Cross Club.) "Lord and Lady Astor dropped in and she had a remark for everyone, starting with me, 'You don't work in a Red Cross Club, you work in a lunatic asylum.' To a big tough top sergeant she'd make a remark, 'You don't need to be entertained. I should give you a lecture on temperance.' She kept looking for a boy from Richmond or any place in Virginia. Lord Astor just looked amazed, and I really don't blame him . . .

"Talked with Joe last night." (Joe Jr. had arrived at a Coastal Command base in southern England.) "He sounded very well but didn't have any idea when he could get up here. I'd go down there to see him on my leave but he says it would be silly as there's nothing to do and it probably wouldn't be a very good rest . . ."

To the Family:

"November 17
"London

"Haven't had a minute to write but there's lots to tell. The party went off very well, at least I think it did. . . . People swarmed in, it was the first party London had had for the young for two years. . . . Joe Jr. arrived with his entire squadron who were feeling no pain.

"Before dinner I was putting on my dress at Marie Bruce's when Irving Berlin rang her up . . . She told him I was giving a party and to come along. Then I spoke to him and told him he must come. . . . People don't pay much attention to celebrities over here and when he walked in he might have been Joe Snooks for all the glances he got. I planted him at a table with the Duchess of Devonshire, hoping she'd strike up a lively conversation. Sheila Milbanks suddenly appeared and as she had known Berlin on his honeymoon I knew he'd be well taken care of in her hands.

"I asked him to render us a few pieces and he finally agreed and got up saying he had known the family for years and he would do anything for any of us. (Please thank him again, Daddy, when he gets back home.) He played his new piece 'My British Buddy' and then a lot of his old ones. We all sang with him so it made everything go very well. The climax came when someone requested 'Over There,' which he said he didn't write but he'd finish up his performance with. . . .

"We wanted the band to stay on, but they refused past one. It was probably just as well . . . We had an incident before it was all over. A young Guardsman had rather too much to drink and set a match to Elizabeth Cavendish's new evening dress. She stayed on and told her mother, 'Before I was set on fire the boys didn't pay much attention to me, but afterwards I was very popular.' An American boy put the flames out. Angie Laycock said to her brave husband, General Laycock, 'Why didn't you do something about putting those flames out?' He replied, 'I thought it was a fireworks display.' . . .

"I have received lots of letters saying, 'Why aren't more parties like that given.' . . .

"Monday Joe and I did some shopping . . . Last night he and I dined with the Biddles, then went out to join some of his pals. We all went on to the 400 Club. Joe seems to be having a good time but no special girl friend. Goodness, it makes a difference having him over. He is in wonderful spirits. . . ."

To Mother and Daddy:

"November 26
"London

"First, if possible, could you get my typewriter over to me somehow. I am in awful need of it . . . I suppose Eunice or Pat have carried it off to school by this time. I am always borrowing somebody's, which I hate.

"Joe finished up his leave a bit tired. But I suppose that is the way with everyone. One feels one must pack all the fun possible in the shortest space of time. . . .

"David Ormsby-Gore and another couple came for dinner. We were praying that Lady Astor wouldn't ring up and find the house full, her food being eaten while she was taking a rest in Cornwall. . . .

"Got a letter from Joe yesterday. He was down with a cold like everyone else. People just don't get the right food here and they catch all sorts of diseases . . . I shall go down to see him before Christmas . . .

"Margaret Biddle's son has lost the sight of one eye, and one leg. Isn't it awful? Much love to all. . . ."

The romance between Kick and Billy continued and deepened greatly during this period and in the months ahead. So did their dilemma, one in which not only they but, naturally, the parents on both sides were painfully involved.

There were many transatlantic cables and telephone calls, and much correspondence. There was, I expect, enough material for a large novel. But the point of it all was simply—if that is the term—to find a way through innumerable complications to make possible a marriage that had everything sentimental in its favor. The two young people were much in love. Joe and I and the duke and duchess were friends. We were very fond of Billy. They were equally fond of Kick. This would have been "a marriage made in Heaven" except for the special and ironic circumstances of religious loyalties.

During the winter and spring of 1944, all of us—Joe and I, the duke and duchess, and of course Kick and Billy—tried to find some way by which, through some stretch of the rules, the marriage could be sanctioned or at least tolerated by both the Roman Catholic and Anglican churches.

One of our closest friends among the Catholic clergy in America was Francis Spellman, once bishop in the Boston archdiocese of Cardinal O'Connell and by then himself a cardinal and archbishop of the New York archdiocese. We enlisted him as our adviser and also as our friend at court, so to speak, with Pope Pius XII, the former Cardinal Pacelli. Since it was wartime and all letters, cables, and telephone calls were subject to censorship, we continued a code with Kick. His Eminence Cardinal Archbishop Spellman became "Archie Spell." So it was Archie Spell suggests this, or is doing that, or wants to know about the latest difficulty.

But, finally, it couldn't be worked out. The only way for Kick to marry Billy within the sacraments of the Catholic Church—and even this would be a civil ceremony—would be for Billy to agree that their children would be raised as Catholics; and, of course, he could not agree to that.

They decided to be married in a civil ceremony on May 6, 1944, at the Chelsea Registry Office, by an official who would correspond in our country to a justice of the peace. It was a very brief ceremony. The duke and duchess and a few other close kin were there for Billy, and Joe Jr. represented our family.

In *As We Remember Joe*, Kathleen wrote:

"Never did anyone have such a pillar of strength as I had in Joe in those difficult days before my marriage. From the beginning, he gave me wise, helpful advice. When he felt that I had made up my mind, he stood by me always. He constantly reassured me and gave me renewed confidence in my decision. Moral courage he had in abundance and once he felt that a step was right for me, he never faltered, although he might be held largely responsible for my decision. He could not have been more helpful and in every way he was the perfect brother doing, according to his own light, the best for his sister with the hope that in the end it would be the best for the family."

Another pillar for her was my friend Marie Bruce. Many years afterward while I was gathering my material for this book I asked her to send me her own direct recollections.

"Kick's dress was very pale pink crepe, dull surface, made quite plain. Little half hat was made of two pale pink ostrich feathers and one pale blue with a veil over it (pink). She carried my gold mesh bag with sapphires and diamonds, which I gave her for 'something

old and something new' and a new posy of pink camellias I made for
her from the camellias; Duke had sent a basket of them from Chatsworth that morning. . . . Best fitter in London, Miss Jarvis, sat
up all night to make the dress. There was no time for fittings, so she
copied one of Kick's American dresses. We did not have enough cou-
pons for material, so milkman gave us his. She looked enchanting.

"Charles Rutland (Duke of Rutland) was the best man. Only
others at marriage in the Registry were Devonshires, Anne, Elizabeth" (Billy's sisters) "Lady Salisbury" (from the Cecil side of the
family), "Lady Astor, young Joe, and me.

"Eddy and Moucher† gave her a diamond bracelet . . . Reception
was held at Lord Hambleden's house in Eaton Square. I gave five
pounds to the head waiter at Claridge's and had a chocolate cake
made for us without ticket! (Ration was one egg per week.) Carlton
House Terrace" (Devonshire's house) "was already bombed and they
lived in Mayfair Hotel.

"Kick went away in cherry colored coat and pink and white print
dress with a white hat made of white gardenias. For her trousseau,
I gave her all my Porthault underclothes. They were more feminine."
(Porthault is specially made French lingerie. During the war, brides
couldn't buy any, so their good friends would give them their own
new lingerie as wedding gifts.)

"Honeymoon was spent at Compton Place, Devonshire's house
at Eastbourne."

They had about three weeks together before Billy had to return to
his regiment. He was an officer in the Coldstream Guards and they
were in training for the Allied invasion of Europe that came a
month later.

Meanwhile, Jack, because of his injuries in the PT-109 episode,
had been in a naval hospital and then in the New England Baptist
Hospital in Boston. He continued his recuperation, during the first
seven months of 1944, partly in hospitals and partly with us at Palm
Beach and Hyannis Port. It was obvious he couldn't be on active
duty soon.

Bobby had become old enough to volunteer for the Navy, and had
entered the Navy's Officer Candidate School. Jack wrote him:

† The Duke and Duchess of Devonshire.

"The folks sent me a clipping of you taking the oath. The sight of you up there was really moving, particularly as a close examination showed that you had my checked London coat on. I'd like to know what the hell I'm doing out here while you go stroking around in my drape coat, but I suppose that's what we are out here for—so that our sisters and younger brothers will be made safe and secure —frankly, I don't see it quite that way. At least, if you're going to be safe and secure, that's fine with me, but not in my coat, brother, not in my coat."

In his introductory essay to *As We Remember Joe*—published in 1945, before the war was over, thus under restrictions of military security—Jack summed up briefly Joe Jr.'s war service from the time he arrived with his squadron in England in September 1943:

"This squadron, flying in the bitter winter over the Bay of Biscay, suffered heavy casualties, and by the time Joe had completed his designated number of missions in May" (the month of Kick's wedding) "he had lost his former co-pilot and a number of close friends.

"Joe refused his proffered leave and persuaded his crew to remain on for D-day. They flew frequently during June and July, and at the end of July they were given another opportunity to go home. He felt it unfair to ask his crew to stay on longer, and they returned to the United States. He remained. For he had heard of a new and special assignment for which volunteers had been requested which would require another month of the most dangerous type of flying.

"Now, this work that Joe did and which led to his death is still a Naval secret . . . It may be felt, perhaps, that Joe should not have pushed his luck so far and should have accepted his leave and come home. But two facts must be borne in mind. First, at the time of his death, he had completed probably more combat missions in heavy bombers than any other pilot of his rank in the Navy and therefore was preeminently qualified, and, secondly, as he told a friend early in August, he considered the odds at least fifty-fifty, and Joe never asked for any better odds than that."

It was not until several years after the war that we were able to know the circumstances of that "mission." Several accounts have been written. Probably the most accurate was that in 1948, the

"Tenth Anniversary Report, Harvard College Class of 1938," by a friend of Joe Jr.'s, who in the course of a long eulogy said:

"Joe, regarded as an experienced Patrol Plane Commander, and a fellow-officer, an expert in radio control projects, was to take a 'drone' Liberator bomber loaded with 21,170 pounds of high explosives into the air and to stay with it until two 'mother' planes had achieved complete radio control over the 'drone.' They were then to bail out over England; the 'drone,' under the control of the 'mother' planes, was to proceed on the mission which was to culminate in a crash-dive on the target, a V-2 rocket launching site in Normandy. The airplane . . . was in flight with routine checking of the radio controls proceeding satisfactorily, when at 6:20 P.M. on August 12, 1944, two explosions blasted the 'drone' resulting in the death of its two pilots. No final conclusions as to the cause of the explosions has ever been reached.

"Joe was posthumously awarded the Navy Cross . . . and also the Air Medal . . . In 1946 a destroyer, the USS *Joseph P. Kennedy, Jr.*, destroyer No. 850, was launched at the Fore River shipyards as the Navy's final tribute to a gallant officer and his heroic devotion to duty . . ."

"He left a lasting mark on the hearts of an extraordinarily large number of people, and his success and popularity indicated the promise of great achievements. That his progress should have been cut short is tragic, but in the words of Professor Laski he has entered 'that supreme immortality which belongs to all who proudly give their lives in the service of freedom.'

"Surviving Joe are his parents, Mr. and Mrs. Joseph P. Kennedy, Sr., of Palm Beach, Florida, and Hyannis Port, Massachusetts, and eight brothers and sisters . . ."

I remember that it was Sunday afternoon and we all had lunched outside, picnic style, on our big porch at Hyannis Port. It was about two in the afternoon, and Joe Sr. had gone upstairs for a nap. The younger children were in the living room chatting quietly so as not to disturb their father; I sat reading the Sunday paper. There was a knock at the front door. When I opened the door two priests introduced themselves and said they would like to speak with Mr. Kennedy.

This was not unusual: Priests and nuns fairly often came to call, wanting to talk with Joe about some charity or other matter of the Church in which he might help. So I invited them to come into the living room and join us comfortably until Joe finished his nap. One of the priests said no, that the reason for calling was urgent. That there was a message both Joe and I must hear. Our son was missing in action and presumed lost.

I ran upstairs and awakened Joe. I stood for a few moments with my mind half paralyzed. I tried to speak but stumbled over the words. Then I managed to blurt out that priests were here with that message. He leaped from the bed and hurried downstairs, I following him. We sat with the priests in a smaller room off the living room, and from what they told us we realized there could be no hope, and that our son was dead.

Joe went out on the porch and told the children. They were stunned. He said they must be brave: that's what their brother would want from them. He urged them to go ahead with their plans to race that day and most of them obediently did so. But Jack could not. Instead, for a long time he walked on the beach in front of our house.

There were no tears from Joe and me, not then. We sat awhile, holding each other close, and wept inwardly, silently.

Then Joe said:

"We've got to carry on. We must take care of the living. There is a lot of work to be done."

Kick asked for leave when she heard the news and hurried back home to be with us. Meanwhile, the Allied invasion of France had begun in June, and Billy and his regiment, in the tradition of the Guards, had been among the earliest units ashore, and had fought through France and into Belgium.

In mid-September, while Kick was still with us, the news came that Billy had been killed in Belgium. He died on September 10, a month after Joe Jr. died. We could scarcely believe it. It seemed too cruel that another tragedy had so soon befallen us. Kick then heard directly from the Cavendishes. It was true.

She left us then to be with them in their sorrow, and to continue with her duties in the Red Cross. We did not see her again until the war in Europe was over.

V-E Day was May 8, 1945, only months after the death of these two fine young men, each of them so beloved, each of whom had so much to give to the world.

Arthur Krock's *Memoirs* contains a paragraph that I quote without comment:

"The death of Joe Jr. was the first break in this circle of nine children, nearly all extraordinary in some way: handsome, intelligent, with a father and mother to whom they were devoted and who were devoted to them. It was one of the most severe shocks to the father that I've ever seen registered on a human being . . .

"He is, I'm sure, religious. At least we used to go to Sunday Mass together whenever and wherever I was visiting him. But his wife attended Mass . . . nearly every morning. At any rate, she bore up better than he did in the sense that he was truly stricken, whereas the philosophy of her religion clearly helped her. Joe Kennedy was so deeply distressed and hurt by the death of his boy, his eldest son, that when a number of us got together and wrote chapters in a little book called *As We Remember Joe*, each contributing some personal reminiscence, Kennedy looked at it, opened the cover, closed the cover, and, I am told, has never been able to read a line in that book."

Joe took his own advice that we should carry on, take care of the living, do a lot of work. He kept himself very busy with many things, some of which I shall have reasons to describe later on.

But one of the best ways to assuage grief, as I have said, which we first learned fully at this time—and would help us survive future tragedies—is to find a way to turn some part of the loss to a positive, affirmative use for the benefit of other people. I do believe that God blesses us for that and the burden is lightened.

In Teddy's volume of essays, that he collected and put into a book about his father, *The Fruitful Bough*, Eunice wrote:

". . . All my father's qualities were particularly alive to me when I watched him in the work of the Kennedy Foundation. Again, it was his great devotion to his children that brought him into this work. After my brother Joe's death in 1944, my father—still in grief —decided he wanted to build a memorial to his son. He had never believed much in building buildings. He wanted to invest in men. He asked us all at the table one day what could be done to best perpetuate Joe's memory.

"We gave him ideas: a gymnasium at Joe's school, an orphanage (Joe had spent much time in college working with underprivileged children). We all thought that since Joe, as our older brother, had taught us so many activities, his memorial should try to do something for young children.

"Dad then asked Sargent" (Sargent Shriver was a close and highly trusted staff assistant to Joe; he was just a few months younger than Joe Jr., and already we felt he was a member of our family—as in fact he became when he and Eunice were married later on) "to get judgments from around the country on what programs for children were most neglected by private foundations and the federal government. Sarge reported that foundation and federal efforts in the field of mental retardation were practically nonexistent.

"My father decided immediately to enter this field. He was particularly enthusiastic because my sister Rosemary was retarded, and he felt a great sympathy for parents who had suffered as much as he and my mother had over my sister . . .

"It was not surprising then that Dad wanted all his children to work together on the Foundation for retarded children. He believed that together we were almost unconquerable. Every major city in America needed a school for retarded. Since each of his children" (this of course came later) "lived in major cities—Pat in Los Angeles, Jean in New York, me in Chicago, the boys in Massachusetts, Dad established schools over a fifteen-year period in each of these cities, and encouraged each of us to take part in the school's development.

"Each of us served on the boards. Pat initiated the largest benefit for retarded children ever held in Los Angeles. My sister Jean and sister-in-law Ethel ran benefits in New York and in Washington to raise money for these homes. My mother supported all these benefits by attending them and giving wonderful talks.

"I asked Dad if we could sponsor a national conference on mental retardation. He listened and then said, 'Go to Jack. This movement needs the federal government behind it. The President can give it the prestige and momentum we can't give it if we work for one hundred years and had one hundred times as much money to put into the field.'

"Jack recognized the problem and the possibilities and the need immediately. 'That seems like a good thing for the country,' he said. 'Call Mike Feldman [one of Jack's senior staff assistants]. Let's get a meeting set. . . .'

"We had the meeting, and the President's Panel on Mental Retardation—the first of its kind in history—was launched. The result was the first federal legislation ever specifically directed at mental retardation."

It was funded by over four hundred million dollars, and the work went on.

It has been said that time heals all wounds. I don't agree. The wounds remain. Time—the mind, protecting its sanity—covers them with some scar tissue and the pain lessens, but it is never gone.

How can one endure in the face of tragedy? People have asked me. And surely I have often had reason to ask myself.

Joe was right in his words: "Carry on . . . take care of the living . . . there is a lot of work to be done." And right in his instinctive and immediate recognition that in sorrow we must look outward rather than inward, and thus can come peace of mind and peace of spirit.

Chapter Fifteen

When Jack was discharged from the Navy in the spring of 1945, he worked for the Hearst papers as a special correspondent, covering the British election, the Potsdam Conference, and the founding of the United Nations at San Francisco. He liked the work and he did well. In fact, Arthur Krock—who was certainly one of the best-informed journalists in the world—said in his *Memoirs* that Jack had been ". . . the only source of my expectation that Churchill would be turned out of office. This he strongly indicated in his dispatches, and more definitely in a private letter."

Many people think that his decision to enter politics was made for him by his father, that Joe practically forced him into it. That would have been completely out of character on both sides. Anyone reading Joe's letters to Jack and the others can see that giving orders to his children would have been contrary to the relationship he had with them. And Jack, quite as obviously, would not have submitted to such a parental command even if it had been given. (I can imagine his smiling agreeably and saying, "Yes, Dad," as he used to smile agreeably and say, "Yes, Mother," when I told him to put on a sweater—and then go off without it.)

It is true that the role he chose probably would have been different, and would have come later, had it not been for Joe Jr.'s death. Joe Jr. would have made a career in elective public office. That was his ambition and, I think, his destiny. Everyone thought so. And he had practically every asset for that role. As Jack wrote, "His success was so assured and inevitable that his death seems to have cut into the natural order of things."

Kick, in her essay about Joe Jr., finished with this paragraph:

"Without Joe there will be always a gap in the Kennedy family circle, but we are far, far luckier than most because there are so many of us. And I know Joe would always feel that Jack could easily take over the responsibility of being the oldest. I know the one thing Joe would never want is that we should feel sad and gloomy about life without him. Instead, he'd laugh with that wonderful twinkle shining out of his Irish eyes and say, 'Gee, can't you all learn to get along without me?' "

The period when Jack was confronting the fact his older brother was gone—and it took a while for all of us to emerge from a feeling of unreality, a bad dream—was a crucial time in events; in Jack's life, in the life of our family, and eventually in the political life of the country.

James Michael Curley, who had succeeded my father both as congressman and as mayor of Boston, and who was subsequently in and out of those two offices, and the governorship, during three decades, had run for mayor again in 1945 and had been elected. This left his congressional seat vacant; and, since Mr. Curley seemed to have no strong preferences about a successor, the way was cleared for a wide open race and a chance for the best man to win the Democratic nomination, tantamount to election.

Further, this congressional district, although its boundaries had been redrawn, was essentially the same region my father had represented when *he* went to Congress. It included the North End of Boston as well as the East End.

The combination of time, place, and circumstance made the idea of Jack's running for Congress attractive and reasonable, inexperienced in electoral politics though he was. I can say for certain they appealed enormously to my father, who at that time was a hale and healthy eighty-three. The idea that his grandson might be going to Washington to fill the same position that he had held filled my father with delight. Thank heaven, he lived to see it happen.

But if my father were directly associated with this campaign Jack would have been seen by many people as an heir to the old ways, which were of course inappropriate for his time. Moreover, my father, in his love and pride for Jack and thinking of him as torch-bearer of the Fitzgerald name and fame and achievements, would have thought of Jack as an incarnation of himself and would have tried to mold him to his own pattern. And that, frankly, would have been a disaster. They loved each other dearly but seldom were two people less alike.

Although Father wasn't asked to take the stump for his grandson in the campaign—as he would have dearly loved to do—that didn't prevent him from telling his innumerable friends about this marvelous young man. It didn't inhibit his appearances at campaign headquarters or stem his flow of stories about bygone campaigns. Nor did it deprive Jack of his advice. By then my parents had moved from the big house in Dorchester to an apartment suite at the Bellevue Hotel in Boston, a favorite place for political gatherings of all sorts, and thus a place where my father felt very much at home. It was also where Jack had his headquarters, on the same corridor. Joe and I had an apartment not far away. Other family members were also in town. So there were gatherings in Boston and also, from time to time during that busy campaign summer, at Hyannis Port. "Grampa" had plenty of opportunities to spin his tales of the past and to tell Jack what to do and how to do it. Some of the other descendants and relatives had begun to find my father's stories slightly tedious—but not Jack. He always listened with interest and respect, and with affection for Grampa shining in his eyes.

As John Henry Cutler relates in his biography of my father:

"On primary day he [Jack] went to the polls with his Fitzgerald grandparents, then went to see a movie, A *Night in Casablanca*. When the votes were counted, Honey Fitz hopped onto a table and danced a jig as he led the singing of 'Sweet Adeline.' . . . After the victory celebration, Billy Sullivan, a former assistant attorney general, patted Honey Fitz on the back.

" 'Congratulations, John F.,' he said. 'Some day—who knows?—young Jack here may be Governor of the Commonwealth.'

" 'Governor?' Honey Fitz smiled. 'Some day that young man will be President of the United States.' "

Jack found himself in a delicate situation. He had to campaign in an effective manner, yet he also wanted to be receptive to good advice. However, even at this time, the final decisions were his alone. At twenty-nine, Jack knew a lot about political science, government, diplomacy, national and international affairs. He had studied them at Harvard, had learned a good deal through his father's involvement in them, and had observed them as an author and journalist in these fields. He also knew something of "practical politics" from having read, observed, and listened to Grampa Fitzgerald. Jack always considered Grampa fabulous. He never tired of listening to him, and he soaked it all in.

So, he was by no means a naive youth. (He always, to the end, looked younger than his years, but during this time especially so because of his war injuries and a case of malaria, which cost him much loss of weight; at this point he looked like a nineteen-year-old who needed a lot of feeding up.) He understood that in this congressional district the names Fitzgerald and Kennedy were enough to get him off to a good start. In other parts of the district, notably Charlestown, where Irish ethnocentrism prevailed, the two names were held in some reverence.

One of Jack's assets was the fact that people laughed at the charge he was a "carpetbagger." Some of his rivals brought it up, on the grounds that he hadn't lived in the district since he was eleven and never had voted there and wasn't directly acquainted with the people and their problems and desires. This was absolutely true. Yet there is no Massachusetts law stating that a candidate has to live in the district he represents. But there is a law requiring that he be a registered member of his party twenty days before declaring his candidacy in that party's primary. Jack didn't know about this until a few days before the deadline. Jack hustled down to City Hall and quietly joined the Democratic Party.

While Jack knew about politics, he knew very little about the actual mechanics of organizing and operating a campaign.

For that matter, neither did my husband. Joe was wise in the fields of national and international political affairs, but his interest dwindled as the political unit grew smaller. Events at the level of district, city, town, and ward left him progressively bored. Particularly in

Boston. It was a life he had left long ago without regret. Yet he was keenly aware of the importance of the organization, strategy, and people in Jack's campaign. To this end, he asked his favorite, experienced realist, Cousin Joe Kane, to be Jack's adviser.

Cousin Joe was quite a rough diamond, with an abrasive style of thought and speech. My husband wasn't at all sure how he and Jack would get along, but they hit it off quite well. Jack was surprised, entertained, and informed. Having got into the race he was determined, of course, to win it, and Cousin Joe could tell him about the winds and tides, the shoals and channels in this particular form of navigation. He also had some good over-all ideas such as a slogan for the campaign: "The New Generation Offers a Leader." There were some echoes of that in Jack's inaugural address.

Obviously, to my father and to Cousin Joe Kane and to other relatives and close family friends, Jack looked like a promising neophyte and got the benefit of any doubts. It is worth asking how he looked to others who had no personal connection with us.

Some interesting answers have been supplied—from direct experience—by Dave Powers, who met Jack at the very beginning of this campaign but had no intention of joining it. He did so, however, and stayed with Jack afterward as a close associate to the end of the road in 1963.

"I was just out of the Air Force myself—a sergeant, mostly in China —and starting to look around and catch up on what was happening. Meantime I was on the 52–20—that was $20 a week for unemployed veterans up to 52 weeks—and living with my widowed sister and her eight children on the top floor of a three-decker tenement house in Charlestown.

"That day I'd been talking with John Cotter. He lived two streets away from me. A great, great guy. I'm having a beer with him and he's telling me about the fight. Curley is mayor, that leaves the seat in Congress open and there's going to be a battle royal for it. Mike Neville of Cambridge is running, and he's the number one 'tough guy' because he used to be mayor of Cambridge, is very strong there, and Cambridge has 30 per cent of the votes in the district. Cotter tells me he's going to run, too.

"Now mind you, Cotter has two things that give him great

strength. He was administrative assistant in Washington to Curley and before that to Congressman Joseph P. Higgins, which meant that all the requests and important matters back home in the district were channeled through him. He had helped do a lot of favors. And also, when Higgins left to take a judgeship, he had run for the spot himself and almost got it. So everybody in the district knew him, and he knew the district like the back of his hand. Cotter asks, 'Will you be with me?' And I agreed.

"At that point I don't know that Jack Kennedy is even thinking of being in there. Then I got this call from Bill Sutton who was working for Kennedy. I told him I was already with Cotter. And a few nights later—it was January 21, 1946—somebody knocked at the front door.

"In Charlestown in winter we shut off the front of the house and heat the kitchen. We don't have central heat, it's a stove here or there. People who know you come up the back way. Nobody comes up the front stairs—the front of the house is shut off. So, when somebody knocked at the *front door*—and I was baby-sitting for my sister that night—I went out there. And I saw this tall, thin, handsome guy. He introduces himself and says he's Jack Kennedy and could he talk with me a few minutes? I invited him in. We started talking and he said he was running for Congress. I said, 'Gee, John Cotter's running for that seat. I'm going to be with him. We grew up together and we stick together.'

"So, now he spends the next half hour picking my brains. He was sort of shy. But—I thought of the description of it later—he was 'aggressively shy.' He said, 'Well, what would you do if you were like me, a candidate running here for Congress?'

"Here's a millionaire's son from Harvard trying to come into an area that is longshoremen, waitresses, truck drivers, and so forth. I said, 'To start with, I'd get somebody on the waterfront for sure, somebody tied up with the labor unions and all that.' And he's writing this stuff down, and I'm thinking to myself, 'It won't do him any good. A millionaire's son from Harvard, they're going to laugh at him down there.'

"And he asked more questions. As he did the rest of his life. He wanted to know everything about everybody and everything. If you sold papers he wanted to know how many you sold and how much you made on a copy. He was interested in bootblacks, how many shoes they shined. He was incredible, this guy.

"As he was going out the door he said, 'Dave, will you do me a favor? I'm speaking to a group of gold-star mothers at the American Legion Hall next Tuesday. I don't know anyone in Charlestown. Will you come over with me?'

"Well, you'd do that: You'd do that for *anybody*. But can you imagine that—imagine feeling sorry for a millionaire's son? And I said, 'All right, all right, I will.'

"That Tuesday I met him at the Bellevue and he said, 'Shall we grab a cab?' I didn't know him that well—then—but thank God, I said, 'Let's take the elevated.' Because if we'd taken the cab I would have paid for it."

I said earlier Jack was absent-minded about carrying pocket money, and hence was often in difficulties about luncheon checks, taxi fares, and the like. In fact, I remember a time years later when I was in New York going in a taxi to the Plaza Hotel, and in the course of conversation the driver learned I was Jack's mother. "I'm glad you're in the cab," he said. "Your son rode with me a month ago and it turned out he didn't have any money with him. He said he'd make it good the next time he saw me. I haven't seen him since. He owes me $2.45." I promptly paid Jack's overdue taxi fare.

Dave Powers continues:

"We're on the el riding over and here he is looking around. We're coming from North Station to Charlestown and out the windows we're seeing Old North Church and East Boston and *Old Ironsides* and stuff like that—it's a long ride—and he's looking down at the longshoremen loading ships, and the neighborhood stores, and I said to him, 'This is almost a panoramic view of your district.' And solemn as hell he said, 'You know, this is the kind of district I would like to represent.'

"So we go over there and he's talking to these Charlestown gold-star mothers—we had an awful lot of boys die in the war, there was a National Guard unit and they were at Guadalcanal and places out there—and there were several hundred in the hall. And it seems to me he's making the world's worst speech. He's talking about the need for peace and the sacrifices of war, but he's certainly no orator. And I am getting nervous as hell. I'm the only other man there, they're all women. At the end he looked out at all those wonderful ladies, and in a kind of awkward way, sort of blurting it out from deep inside, 'I think I know how you feel because my mother is a gold-star mother too.'

"I could hear them—where I was sitting on the fringe—saying, 'He reminds me of my own': the John, Joe, Peter they had lost. When he finished his little ten-minute talk he was surrounded by these wonderful Charlestown ladies. In all my years in politics I've never seen such a reaction.

"We come out of there and he's solemn as hell. I said, 'Why don't we walk back over? It's still afternoon.' We're walking, and he's looking—in fact we stopped in at Faneuil Hall and Paul Revere's house in the North End.

"Along the way he said, 'How do you think I did?' And I said, 'You were great!'

"And he went on, 'Then you'll be with me?' And he put out his hand, and in the excitement of the ordeal I shook his hand and said, 'I will.'

"I walked back over the bridge thinking, 'What will I ever tell Cotter?' Luckily, the fight developed between Kennedy and Mike Neville, not Kennedy and Cotter. In the meantime I was getting a good deal of static from friends in Charlestown. Jack knew about it, and he'd cheer me up with one of his classical jokes: 'Just think, Dave,' he'd say, 'someday you can say you were with me from the beginning.'

" ' "We few, we happy few, we band of brothers;
For he to-day that sheds his blood with me
Shall be my brother; be he ne'er so vile,
This day shall gentle his condition:
And gentlemen in England now a-bed
Shall think themselves accursed they were not here,
And hold their manhoods cheap whiles any speaks
That fought with us upon Saint Crispin's day." ' " (Henry V)

With Joe Kane and other adepts such as Dave Powers involved, Jack's campaign had plenty of "professionalism." But also and at the same time it had a great supply of "amateur enthusiasm." It was a marvelous combination, a very effective one that continued throughout Jack's political career. Later, when Bobby and Teddy began running for office, it was characteristic of their campaigns too.

Friends began turning up from all over the area, and for that matter from all over the map. One of the first, naturally, would be Lem Billings. Lem has recalled:

"When I heard from Jack what he was doing I came over to Boston, mostly from curiosity but also thinking I might give him a little friendly encouragement in this amazing development. I never thought he'd go into politics. Neither had he. I figured he must be about as surprised as I was.

"He was living at the Bellevue Hotel, in two rooms there, bedroom and living room, and it was just beyond belief, because anybody could walk in. The rooms were filled with these old pols who had been connected with his grandfather, and they were always there, smoking cigars. He never turned anybody away; he wanted every vote he could get and every bit of help he could get. Slowly, young people began to be attracted. He needed some help over in Cambridge, where he had a headquarters, so I thought I'd run it for a week or two until he got somebody, and I ended up staying with him for the entire campaign."

Torbert Macdonald, his roommate at Harvard, was back there (after war service in another PT boat squadron) studying for his law degree. He did a lot of work for Jack in the Cambridge office and also in the one at nearby Somerville, where the head of the local headquarters was Timothy "Ted" Reardon, a Harvard classmate and roommate of Joe Jr.'s and also a very good friend of Jack's. Paul "Red" Fay, a PT boat pal, came on from his home on the West Coast and pitched in. There were many others—friends from the Navy, friends from school days and friends of no particular label; dozens of them, drifting in and out for long or short periods, and all pleased to do what they could for Jack. They were more or less his age, and their presence gave the campaign a look that matched the slogan "The New Generation Offers a Leader."

And then, too, of course, we of his family wanted to be helpful. By that campaign year of 1946 even Teddy, at age fourteen, was old enough to make himself useful doing office chores, running errands, bringing in coffee and sandwiches. Bobby, who would be twenty-one that November, had withdrawn from officers' training after Joe Jr.'s death and finished his military service as a seaman on the destroyer *Joseph P. Kennedy, Jr.* After his discharge that summer he came into the campaign full time and took over the East Cambridge section. Eunice, Pat, and Jean, did the innumerable office chores that are involved in a well-organized campaign, answered phones, made suggestions, kept tabs, pepped up rallies, and pushed a few thousand doorbells to tell householders they were Jack Kennedy's sisters and he would be a wonderful congressman, and to leave literature describing the reasons why.

Joe was intensely interested and active in the campaign, though he stayed behind the scenes. Because of his pre-Pearl Harbor position as a noninterventionist, which opponents twisted to label him an "isolationist" (which he was not), he had become a controversial public figure and he didn't want any of this to rub off on Jack's candidacy. Moreover, as Dave Powers indicated, there were always those who could be easily inflamed against Jack as a "millionaire's son" and a "spoiled rich kid." Therefore, Joe was as invisible as he could be, while knowing exactly what was going on, and why, and where, and how, and with hardheaded analytical judgments and prescriptions to offer when needed.

One of his favorite practical aphorisms which he had picked up from his friend Will Hays was "Things don't just happen, they are made to happen."

As for my own "role" in that campaign, Dave Powers has some stories to tell. I'm not sure I swallow all of them whole, because Dave is a raconteur and like all practitioners of the art he has a tendency to add flourishes for effect. On the other hand, he is famous for having a remarkable memory:

"She was important to Jack politically in 1946 because she made herself available for appearances anyplace, and because with the double-barreled name Fitzgerald and Kennedy she was better known than any in that Eleventh Congressional District. She had gone around with her father so much when he was in office or campaigning, and we were forever meeting people in Charlestown and East Boston and the North End and South and West who were Honey Fitz fans and they remembered her as the girl who had accompanied him; they were tied to Rose Fitzgerald Kennedy, they related to her.

"You have to grow up in politics to really know it. She wasn't 'in' politics—she wasn't running or seeking—but she was looking and listening. I remember one rally where she spoke, she was appalled that there wasn't somebody taking the names of everyone who showed up—because that's what her father used to do. She was always writing notes to us about things like that. In 1946, she had a greater understanding of precinct politics than anyone in our organization. And when you say 'precinct politics,' you only understand it by doing it or maybe, in her case, absorbing it by osmosis. She not only loved meeting people, but she cared about the people she met. This is the key.

"She didn't do a lot of speaking. We used her just at special times where it could count most, like with the Veterans of Foreign Wars. Remember, this is 1946, a great year for veterans. Each time, she was the star of the show. She must have been about fifty-six then, but she looked more like thirty-five. I recall when she was speaking to a VFW audience at Brighton—part of the district—and of course they all know she's a gold-star mother and that Jack almost got killed in the war. But she doesn't mention anything about how Joe Jr. died or how Jack's PT got cut in two. She talked about raising the family, with the index cards and all, and about living in England, and told some interesting little stories about the embassy. And that's one way I knew she was a real 'pro.' People want to hear about something different, and that's what she gave them. When she finished she got a standing ovation. Then she introduced her son, the candidate for the nomination in the Eleventh Congressional District.

"And Jack is slightly overwhelmed. Because he couldn't talk as well as his mother, then. I came up front with him as she was finishing and he stood there, listening to her—sort of overwhelmed that his mother could talk that well to an audience. As she was coming off the stage and he was going on, he stopped her and said, 'Mother, they really love you.'

"He didn't say anything like, 'Thank you, Mother.' The Kennedys are funny about saying things like that to each other, because there's so much loyalty they assume each one is going to *try* to help the others. They don't want thanks for trying, they want to be told if they've done it well. It would have been corny as hell for him to say, 'Thank you for making that speech.' He was saying more like, 'Mother, you did a great job. I admire you for such a great job.' A Kennedy would rather get applause from another Kennedy than from ten thousand other people."

Actually it was just a rather rambling talk I had put together—and for that matter I wasn't much of a speaker. I began with small groups and audiences who I knew were going to be friendly and later spoke to larger, more diverse and more sophisticated audiences. Gradually, I gained the confidence that comes with practice and experience. So by that time I was at ease and I spoke pretty well. Jack developed into a fine public speaker. But at that time he truly embodied the old saw "Unaccustomed as I am to public speaking . . ." He needed experience and also advice, which needless to say came from many directions, including some from me.

He spoke too fast, as I had also at first. When I was a child in school, if the teacher wanted a story read quickly in the class—if the bell was about to ring—I was the one always chosen because I could do it so fast. I expect I passed this on to my children. But staccato delivery is a handicap in a campaign. So I would often remind Jack of Churchill and Roosevelt—both of whom he had heard speak in person—and of their measured and effective pace.

Years later, when he was campaigning for the presidency, I would hear people say he spoke a bit too fast. And I would see him on television with a hand thrust into a jacket pocket. But by then those characteristics, along with the little repertory of gestures he developed—such as that short punch into the air with his forefinger to emphasize a point—had all blended into a personal style that was pleasing and effective. He was receptive to advice, but he used it in his own way. *If* he decided to use it.

But when he began running for Congress—hatless in a New England winter—it became Joe Kane's turn to worry. He explained that *all* politicians in the Boston region wore hats; that without a hat Jack looked like a college boy and nobody would take him seriously as a congressional candidate; that with a hat he could come closer to fitting the expected "image" and could gain many votes. Jack listened pleasantly and remained bareheaded. Losing all the battles, Joe Kane was determined still to win the war. He kept on mentioning the hat problem to Jack and enlisted allies who also mentioned it.

Dave Powers has contributed:

"Jack was the hardest-working candidate I ever saw. Nothing was ever too much if he figured it could help the cause. If he heard some other candidate had been to some benefit or church affair or something like that earlier and made an impression, he'd say to me, 'Dave,' —and this let's say is in the evening after already going that day for twelve, fourteen hours—'Dave, how about it, shall we go over and show them the *real* candidate?' And tired as you yourself could be feeling by then, you'd say, 'Sure, let's go,' even if it's half an hour away through traffic, because he was trying so hard, giving it everything he had, and with a guy like that—inside you're groaning for bed and sleep—you feel that you've got to do your best for him. And every place he goes, he makes votes. People warm up to him. Some days I'd go wake him up at the Bellevue around six-thirty in the morning, which would give time for us to get over to the shipyard or a factory to hit the incoming shift and for him to shake a few hundred hands. We'd have some breakfast and then start ringing doorbells in the three-decker neighborhoods, house to house, floor to floor, down the block. The mothers took one look, heard him say his name and mission and a few more words—and they loved him.

"We'd stop at some joint for lunch: This was always the same menu for him, a hamburger and a frappe, a frappe being a milkshake with ice cream in it. In the afternoon, more calls, maybe stopping in pool halls, grocery stores, taverns, anyplace the voters were; or maybe a special meeting someplace, a club, whatever.

"Back to the Bellevue for him to take a hot bath and rest his back and change clothes. And then go right through the evening. Lodge halls, VFW, Knights of Columbus, Knights of Pythias, name it, but the most usual thing was a string of what we called 'house parties.'

"I would arrange—somebody would arrange—for various women or young ladies in nearby neighborhoods to invite some friends over to their homes for refreshments and to meet John F. Kennedy. Who shook hands all around, had a Coke, and mingled around in a sociable way, then on cue made a few remarks about why he wanted to be elected to Congress and hoped for their votes; and thanked them and good evening—and on to the next place, maybe five or six in one evening.

"Now, with a guy like that—with that desire, and making votes everywhere he stops in—you tend to make a very full schedule. But here's something else. Jack has a funny sense of time and distance. He'd get interested in these people and he'd forget about time, and it was hard to disengage him and drag him away. And, anyway, he has the feeling that every place else is only fifteen minutes away. I've been with him in his apartment in the middle of Boston and he's soaking in his tub at a quarter of eight, and we're due in Worcester at eight, and he'd say, 'Dave, how far is it to Worcester?' And I'd say, 'Well, if we're driving, we're late already.' It would go like that.

"Now, I remember there was one of these big veterans' rallies someplace in the district and his mother was there, at our request, to say a few words and to introduce him as the candidate. We were running late. We got there late.

"Afterward, Jack and his mother were chatting with several of us in the campaign. Well, Joe Kane had that day evidently been pursuing his program to get Jack to wear a hat, because it's on Jack's mind. And he says, 'Mother, they're all telling me I should wear a hat, because it will make me look older.'

"And she looked him right in the eye and said, 'I think it's more important to be on time.'

"That's the same way she'd get her message across at a dinner or luncheon with family and friends. There would be a flow of discussion about something and she might not be saying much, but then she'd come in with just a word or two or a sentence that made them all blink.

"I saw this have an instantaneous effect that evening. Jack did a mental double-take and then he turned around to the fellows who were handling his schedule and said, 'How the hell do you happen to be scheduling me to be in Somerville at 8:00 and Charlestown at 8:30 and Brighton at 9:00? It's impossible.' So, through her remark, it brought them awake too, and the scheduling got looser, at least for a while. He kept on the fourteen-hour day. He never asked for anything but time, more time than it turned out he ever had. You know, he was so casual and easy and so interested and yet he was so hard-working. All he needed was a thirty-six-hour day."

I'm sure there's no such thing as a "women's vote." Women make up their minds individually and on the basis of numerous factors just as men do. Obviously, however, there are appeals that weigh more heavily with one sex than the other. For instance, men were much more likely to be interested in and impressed by Jack's war record. He didn't want to exploit it; in fact, it embarrassed him that it should be any factor in the campaign. Once when somebody brought it up and asked him how he happened to be "a war hero," he replied, "It was involuntary. They sank my boat." Nevertheless, the story was well known and it was a plus for him among men voters.

Bobby and I were wondering what could be done that might have a similar, special appeal for women. It has been said that the older women wanted to mother him and the younger ones wanted to marry him, a thought I find more than reasonable. However, for his youthful and manly charm to be effective, they had to meet him. Bobby suggested I give a reception and tea in his honor, and invite a lot of women and introduce them to the candidate.

It occurred to us that we already had a good model in the annual Fourth of July reception we held at the embassy in London. This was an open house. Everyone was welcome. There were refreshments, people strolled about and mingled, after meeting the ambassador and perhaps members of his family.

Where should we try out our idea first? Well, as Dave Powers has mentioned, Cambridge was the biggest ward and its favorite son Mike Neville was Jack's strongest rival. We rented one of the big public rooms at the Hotel Commander, and engraved invitations were sent to every registered voter in Cambridge.

That evening our receiving line consisted of me, as hostess, Eunice as my cohostess, and Jack between us. Jack was feeling dubious about the whole thing. Some of the seasoned politicos in the campaign had been more than dubious—openly and discouragingly skeptical. Jack, Eunice, and I waited expectantly to see what would happen.

What happened was that fifteen hundred people came to the reception. At times the line stretched all the way through the hotel lobby, through the entranceway, and outside and far down the block. For all of them there were handshakes, smiles, and some words from each of us. There were a few men there, but most were women, all of whom seemed to have had their hair done for the event. Jack was marvelous with them.

After the primary was over, Mike Neville's campaign manager was ruminating the results and was quoted as saying, "That reception was the clincher." I don't know about that. I hope it helped. Neville was supposed to take Cambridge by a landslide vote that would offset Jack's predictable strength in the North End and East End and other friendly territory. But it turned out to be a very close race there, with Neville just managing to win Cambridge.

As for the outcome of the district primary—in which, as I haven't mentioned, besides Jack Kennedy and Mike Neville and John Cotter, there were seven others, a grand melee of ten candidates—Jack won decisively with 42 per cent of the vote, about twice as many as Neville and well beyond three times more than Cotter.

Jack won the general election that fall, defeating the Republican candidate by better than 3 to 1, entering Congress at the age of twenty-nine, a year older than my father had been when first elected to the same Eleventh District seat.

It was a convincing victory, and subsequently Jack's performance as a congressman was difficult for anyone to fault. When he ran for re-election two years later, 1948, no one in either party bothered to make him run in the primary, and he continued in office by acclamation, so to speak. In 1950, he had five opponents in the Democratic primary, but he was renominated with five times the combined total of their votes, and then beat the Republican nominee by 5 to 1.

Presumably he could have gone on in the same way, in this same "safe seat," for the next thirty or forty years, rising by seniority through committee chairmanships and cloakroom camaraderie to become an extremely influential old man, perhaps Speaker of the House. The prospect of spending his life that way bored Jack intensely.

By the time his third term in the House would be over, Senator Henry Cabot Lodge, Jr., would be coming up for re-election again. It was difficult to imagine that Jack could win against him. Lodge was tall, handsome, charming, intelligent. He was a hard worker in government and an excellent campaigner. Although his ancestry and background were "Back Bay," he was one of the foremost liberals of the Republican Party in the state and nation. An "enlightened" Republican.

Lodge's ethnic appeal included the French-Canadians, many of whom had settled in the state, for he was fluent in French and thus could speak to them in their own language. Further, he had a beautiful sister-in-law who could accompany him to important meetings in Italian neighborhoods and introduce him, and translate for him in that language, for she had been born in Italy, a daughter of the noble family of Braggiotti. He had an excellent war record; a name known and respected everywhere; the prestige of his years in the Senate and party leadership in several of the important senatorial committees.

A factor of very great importance—he had been mainly responsible for persuading General Eisenhower to run for the presidency that year, a feat that endowed him with a share of the general's enormous popularity and prestige.

Thus, if ever there was such a thing as an "unbeatable" candidate, it seemed to be Senator Henry Cabot Lodge, Jr.

However, my husband believed Jack could win and encouraged him to make the race. At first I was taken aback by the idea. If anybody had asked me, I would have advised strongly against it. But in our thirty-eight years of marriage, I had seen his judgment vindicated so consistently that I didn't question it. If Joe said it was so, for me it was so. Jack took his time, weighing all the pros and cons carefully, sounding out opinions from people all over the state, then as usual made his own decision. He would run.

He was unopposed in the Democratic primary. No one else had any desire to take on the invincible Lodge, who also, of course, had no contenders in his own party for the nomination.

Kennedy vs. Lodge developed into one of the most famous battles in modern U.S. political history, and much has been written about it in many other books—easily available to anyone who wants a play-by-play account.

Suffice to say that in all essential features the pattern was the one developed in 1946 in Jack's first election except, of course, that by this time everyone was older and more experienced, and the scale of the effort was very much larger because this was not a district but a state. Joe and I took a comfortable apartment located conveniently in central Boston at 81 Beacon Street, and from there he kept a close supervisory eye on everything and did many things to smooth the way for Jack. He was aided by a secretary, by his lifelong friend and assistant Arthur Houghton, and by his much younger and equally trusted assistant Sargent Shriver.

Bobby, by then twenty-six and recently graduated from the University of Virginia law school, had an interesting job in the U.S. Department of Justice and was eager to get on with his own career. He and Ethel had barely settled in Washington, and he had no intention of taking part in the campaign. Nevertheless, when problems developed and he was needed, and was asked by his father and by Jack, he put aside his personal concerns and willingly came in as campaign manager. Some of the old politicians who had joined the troops were disgruntled by this, considering Bobby a politically innocent boy who had been sent to do a man's job. But Bobby already knew a good many of the ropes from the 1946 campaign. Further, he had as his "director of organization" Lawrence O'Brien, a man Jack's age and veteran even then of fourteen years' experience in local, district, state, and national politics. What Bobby didn't know about organizing a detailed campaign, Larry O'Brien did. And Bobby also brought in a number of his friends, notably the talented, tough-minded, loyal, and tireless Kenneth O'Donnell, who, with Larry, spent the next decade working in close rapport with Jack and Bobby in politics and government.

By this time some of the young relatives were old enough to have a part in Jack's exciting adventure. My niece Mary Jo recalls:

"I was between my sophomore and junior years in college and it was one of the greatest summers I ever had, because we had such a good time. I worked mostly in the Boston headquarters. Bobby was there, Kenny O'Donnell was there, Chuck Roach, my brother Joey, and a lot of others. Ted wasn't there that year because he was in the Army, in Europe. Uncle Joe would call the switchboard every morning. Freddy Fitzgerald was on the switchboard" (my nephew, son of my brother Fred) "which was unusual too, because he was only about fourteen or fifteen. Everyone told Uncle Joe he was a nut to have all these young people down in the headquarters. Finally, they did get a girl to run the switchboard but she was quite young too.

"Jack was out campaigning all over the state but most of the time he'd manage to get back to headquarters at night, get the latest word, and cheer us on.

"A bunch of us lived in the same rooming house on Marble Street.

Bobby, and Joey, and Jean McGarnigal, who was a secretary, and Pat came and stayed and then later she, Eunice, and Jean got an apartment. The woman who ran the rooming house couldn't figure out what was going on, because there were all these young men and girls coming in and out. But she looked **happy**. We always paid the rent on time. There were about eight of us there.

"We used to open the office early in the morning and work through until evening, sometimes later. There wouldn't be any cocktails afterward. Some of the men might have had a drink elsewhere, but nobody drank to my knowledge. Instead, we used to go over to the Ritz—and we would be covered with mimeograph ink and really not looking the 'Ritzy type'—and we'd all have a cream puff filled with ice cream with a lot of chocolate sauce over it. So that's what we'd do instead of having a drink.

"Kenny and Bobby would go out at night and make speeches. Eunice and Pat and Jean would be out making talks and showing sound films of a terrific interview Jack had given on the TV program 'Meet the Press.' All of us were doing something ten to fifteen hours a day. Usually everyone would be back and in bed by twelve. Then we were up again before eight. We just had a wonderful summer."

Jack campaigned harder than anyone else. He had been traveling around the state for several years, taking long weekends from the House, to meet people, make friends, seek allies, and, most important, to let voters see him and feel a personal relationship with him.

Soon his back was again causing severe and prolonged pain. Kenny O'Donnell has written about this:

"He traveled with crutches, which he concealed in his car when he arrived at the hall where the audience was waiting. Dave would notice him gritting his teeth when he walked with a determined effort from the car to the door where the chairman or the committee members were waiting to greet him, but then when he came into the room where the crowd was gathered, he was erect and smiling, looking as fit and healthy as the light heavyweight champion of the world.

" 'Then after he finished his speech, and answered questions from the floor, and shook hands with everybody, we would help him into the car and he would lean back on the seat and close his eyes in pain,' Dave says. 'When we got back to the hotel, out would come the crutches from the floor of the back seat and he would use them to get upstairs, where I would fill the bathtub with hot water, and he would soak himself in the tub for an hour before going to bed.'"

A list of people who helped Jack in that campaign would be the size of a city telephone directory. For instance, to get on the ballot in Massachusetts a candidate has to file nomination papers at the State House with the signatures of 2,500 people who are petitioning him to run. The signatures for Jack filled ten thousand pages and totaled 262,324. And getting these signatures was the work of local volunteers all over the state. Each political unit had a local leader or chairman; these chairmen were known as "Kennedy secretaries," a term that gave them a more personal tie to Jack and also indicated that this was a new kind of politics for a new era, remote from the old days of precinct, ward, and district "leaders" and their reputation of trading favors for votes.

The size of our family—and our "extended family" counting our numerous relatives—again turned out to be advantageous, since each of us had varied experiences and individual skills that could be put to use. We always checked to see which of us could do the best for Jack in a given situation—then that person did it. For instance, among the many ethnic groups that have come into Massachusetts on the tides of immigration over the years, there is a sizable portion of Lebanese; and, of course, like others, they have their clubs and associations. As it happened, Eunice had been to Lebanon, and furthermore had bought a beautiful shawl there. When there was a Lebanese meeting Eunice would put on her shawl and go and tell the people how much she had enjoyed visiting their country and why they should vote for Jack. I had been in Portugal and had pleasant memories of that country, so I was the logical one to speak in New Bedford, which has a large population of Portuguese descent. And so it went.

I had a few extra strings to my own bow. For one thing, I spoke French. I certainly never dreamed when I was a girl at the Blumenthal convent, studying French, and then working on it through the years, that someday I would be using it to help elect a son of mine U.S. senator. My French was not nearly as good as Senator Lodge's, but it was pretty good. I was interested and informed about French

Bobby Shriver, Bobby Kennedy, Jr., Joe Kennedy II, Maria Shriver, Christopher Lawford, Kathleen Kennedy, David Kennedy, and Courtney Kennedy with Grandpa and Grandma, 1957.

Caroline Kennedy and Grandpa.

Jacques Lowe

Dedication of the Joseph P. Kennedy, Jr. Hospital for Rehabilitation of Handicapped Children in Brighton, Massachusetts. To Joe's left is Cardinal Cushing (then Archbishop Cushing).

Joe's birthday, 1960. Standing are Stephen Smith, Jr., Bobby Shriver, Joe Kennedy II, Caroline Kennedy, Bobby Kennedy, Jr.; seated (left to right): Timmy Shriver, David Kennedy, Michael Kennedy, Courtney Kennedy, Joe, Maria Shriver, Kathleen Kennedy (holding Kerry Kennedy).

Joe with Joe II and Kathleen.

Jack's nomination, Los Angeles, 1960.

Paul Schutzer, TIME-LIFE *Picture Agency*

The morning after Election Day in Hyannis Port. Seated (l. to r.): Eunice, I, Joe, Jackie, Ted. Standing: Ethel, Stephen Smith, Jean, Jack, Bobby, Pat, Sargent Shriver, Joan, Peter Lawford.

The inaugural ball, 1961.

Schutzer, TIME-LIFE *Picture Agency*

Pablo Casals' concert at the White House.

Reception for Prime Minister Nehru; his daughter Indira Gandhi is at the far left.

Jack with John and Caroline.

White House reception for Haile Selassie.

Jackie and I chat with Madame de Gaulle upon Jackie's arrival at Orly Airport for the state visit in 1961.

Jack chats with Mrs. Khrushchev at state dinner in Vienna hosted by Austrian President Adolf Schaerf, 1961.

and French-Canadian history and culture. I bought French-Canadian newspapers, followed the news and opinions and various activities that were of special concern to these voters, and attended their fraternal and church meetings to say a few words about my experiences traveling in France. I said that Jack had worked and traveled there and greatly admired the French, so that he would be a good man both for Massachusetts and for the French heritage.

Dave Powers was talking about this not long ago:

"I remember we were having a great deal of difficulty in the French sections of Lowell. Father Morriset was very influential there. In fact, later on he was elected to Congress. Father Morriset endorsed Henry Cabot Lodge, Jr. Jack figured there was no one better to send up there than his mother. So Rose Kennedy went through the French-speaking sections of Lowell, talking French to them at meetings, and all. And, do you know, she pulled out the city of Lowell for us."

Remembering the surprising success of the reception and tea we had given in Cambridge in 1946, we decided to try the idea again. I would be the hostess, though assisted by two or three of the girls so it would be a family affair. The general purpose of the invitation would be "Come and meet the candidate and members of his family." At some point I would take the platform, say a few words of welcome, and introduce Jack, who would make a short, informal talk stressing the points of his campaign and, above all, giving the guests a chance to look him over and feel the warmth of his personality.

Polly Fitzgerald, the wife of my father's youngest brother, Edward, was in charge of the arrangements. I asked her to send me a few of her memories for this book:

"When Frank Morrissey" (Jack's aide) "called and asked me to see Jack about setting up some teas I learned that you were to be the attraction that would lure women to these events. Once they were there they would of course meet Jack, be impressed, and go on to work and vote for him . . .

"I remember saying to Jack that I didn't know anything about politics and he said, 'You don't have to. Just go about arranging the teas the way you would for any civic or charitable activity.' But Jack himself talked with me about all the little details when we were planning the format.

"We went out and found many, many women who knew nothing about politics, but who would like to serve on a committee to arrange a tea for the wife of the former ambassador to Great Britain. They were thrilled to be identified with you and your family. They even lent their silver services and lace tablecloths. They didn't cook proper meals for weeks and neglected their housework in their efforts on the committees for your teas.

"The first one was on May 18 in Worcester. Several thousand women turned out for it. Once we saw how it went there, we followed the same pattern everywhere. You were the one through whom we got the women to meet Jack. Those thirty-three tea parties in '52 ought to go down in history!"

And in fact they have. When it was all over and Jack had won, Lodge said: "It was those damn tea parties that beat me."

Later, Jack was amused when they were given so much credit; someone said that he had "floated into the Senate on an ocean of tea."

General Eisenhower took the presidency that year by a large majority, and he swept Massachusetts by a margin of 208,800 votes. Yet Lodge, who was so closely identified with Eisenhower and had his vigorous endorsement (in fact, Eisenhower came to Boston for the wind-up speech of his campaign, specifically to help Lodge), went down by 70,737 votes. At those thirty-three "Kennedy teas" we had about 70,000 guests, nearly all of them women. The close matching of the figures is, I daresay, coincidence. But I also think that the tea parties helped.

I have been asked if Jack was an emotional person. I suppose the reason for the question is that he always seemed so self-possessed, unruffled, equable, with a certain air of "detachment" as though he were in the scene and living it fully and yet observing the scene with himself in it. I think by and large this was true. He did have an even temperament, I think that in part it was a quality he acquired because of ill health. Some people could have given in to self-pity, but Jack inured himself against misfortune and lived his life to its fullest.

He chose to be optimistic. When he was going on a trip or had just won a race he would be excited and happy. When he was bedridden or had just lost a race he was not visibly depressed, just rather subdued. One of the few times I remember seeing him really nervous was election night of '52.

His headquarters were near our apartment on Beacon Street, so he spent time in both places. At his headquarters, according to O'Donnell, although "the vote was so close that as late as midnight the television and radio commentators were naming Lodge as the winner . . . Kennedy was so calmly sure of himself . . . that he remarked to Torbert Macdonald, 'I wonder what kind of a job Eisenhower will give Lodge.'" Back with us at the Beacon Street apartment, as the returns came in, changing every few minutes with Lodge ahead or Jack ahead, he kept pacing around from one room to another. I remember especially he kept taking his jacket off and then soon putting it on again, sometimes pulling it off in such a way that the sleeves were inside out, then putting it on that way, and doing the same motion again, so that part of the time the sleeves were right side and part wrong side. Torb Macdonald was with him, and my husband told him to help keep Jack calm. Jack calmed down.

In the morning, soon past eight, Jack and Torb came back to the apartment. Lodge had just conceded. Teddy was still doing his military service overseas, and the first words I heard Jack say were "Let's send a cable to Ted." Then he went to see his father, who advised him to have a Turkish bath and then go to bed.

Four years later at the 1956 Democratic Convention, Jack was called on to narrate a film history of the Party and to nominate Adlai Stevenson in Stevenson's second try against President Eisenhower. His words were so effective, and his platform manner and personality were so attractive to the delegates and to the public watching on television, that there was a spontaneous movement to put him on the ticket for the vice-presidency.

The reaction was a surprise to everybody concerned, and not least to Jack himself. Once he realized what was happening and that he actually had a fair chance for the nomination, his competitive nature took hold and he decided to go for it. Bobby, Kenny O'Donnell, and other loyal lieutenants went into action and worked furiously in the little time available, in about twenty-four hours.

Among the most surprised were my husband and I. We were spending most of that summer in a house we had leased on the Riviera. We had heard Jack's speech on short-wave radio and thought it extremely good, and Joe had kept up more or less with the convention news, but that was difficult because of the wide difference in time zones between the Riviera and Chicago. That Jack could be a candidate for the vice-presidential nomination was, so far as we knew, only a rumor. According to Kenny O'Donnell:

"Kennedy waited to get an idea of just how much support he could count on before declaring himself, particularly in the Protestant southern states. A delegate from Louisiana came to him and pleaded that he had to run. The Louisiana delegation had voted against their governor in favor of supporting Kennedy. 'We went out on a limb for you, and you can't leave us hanging there,' the Louisiana man argued. 'You've got to run.' That gave Jack the push that he needed. He turned to Bobby and said, 'Call Dad and tell him I'm going for it.'

"Bobby placed a telephone call to the ambassador's home on the French Riviera, by no means an enviable assignment. Jack disappeared . . . When the call came through, the ambassador's blue language flashed all over the room. The connection was broken before he was finished . . . Bobby quickly hung up the telephone and made no effort to get his father back on the line. 'Whew!' Bobby said. 'Is he mad!'"

Joe's remarks were not very "blue" but they were certainly emphatic. He felt sure President Eisenhower would be re-elected over Stevenson, and that Jack—in second place on a losing ticket—would damage his political future, since they might blame Stevenson's defeat on the fact that Jack was a Catholic. Jack was being very short-sighted, he said. He did say it vigorously.

But Jack, having made up his mind, went right ahead anyway. There was a tremendous battle for delegates between Jack and Senator Estes Kefauver. At the peak, Jack was within an eyelash, only 33½ delegate votes, of winning, and surely would have except for maneuvers by several senior members of the Party leadership. Kefauver won. Jack went to the Convention Hall from his command post at the Stockyards Inn and made a graceful acknowledgment and endorsement, and introduced a resolution that the nomination be made unanimous. It was so moved and passed.

Soon afterward, back at the Stockyards Inn, he called his father to tell him the sequence and the outcome. I remember my husband saying: *"That's one of the best things that could ever happen to you!"*

Again, he was right. For Jack, not being on that losing ticket, didn't suffer from its foreordained defeat and instead he had gained a great deal for the future.

The historian James MacGregor Burns, writing about Jack's role at the '56 Convention, said:

"He appeared as calm in defeat as in the prospect of victory. At the Convention Hall, he pushed his way to the rostrum: 'Ladies and gentlemen of this convention. I want to take this opportunity to express my appreciation to Democrats from all parts of the country . . .' Despite his grin, Kennedy looked wilted and disappointed. Yet as things turned out, this was his greatest moment—the moment when he passed through a kind of political sound barrier to register on the nation's memory. The dramatic race had glued millions to their television sets. Kennedy's near victory and sudden loss—the impression of a clean-cut boy who had done his best and who was accepting defeat with a smile—all this struck at people's hearts in living rooms across the nation. In this moment of triumphant defeat, his campaign for the presidency was born."

A year after the '56 Convention, Jack had arrived at a personal perspective that enabled him to say:

"Joe was the star of our family. He did everything better than the rest of us. If he had lived, he would have gone into politics, and he would have been elected to the House and to the Senate, as I was. And, like me, he would have gone for the vice-presidential nomination at the 1956 Convention, but unlike me, he wouldn't have been beaten. Joe would have won the nomination. And then he and Stevenson would have been beaten by Eisenhower, and today Joe's political career would have been in shambles . . ."

In 1958, Jack was up for re-election to the Senate. He won, this time, by almost a million votes, the biggest majority that any candidate in any campaign in the history of Massachusetts had ever received.

On that momentum he just kept on running for the presidency, which was two years away.

With my wildest hopes and dreams for him, I could hardly believe that, in a matter of only fourteen years, he would move from a rather shy, slightly embarrassed, sometimes awkward young candidate for Congress in 1946 to a still youthful-looking but mature President of the United States.

Chapter Sixteen

Meanwhile, from that first campaign of Jack's to the one for the presidency, we were concerned with a great deal else besides politics. In fact, except during election years, politics was rather far down the list of topics that occupied my thoughts. In the Kennedy family, as in all others, life and death went on happening. It is surprising to look back (I expect this happens to anyone who has lived a long time) and to feel that so much happened so quickly.

After the end of the war in Europe, when it was possible to travel freely again across the Atlantic, Kathleen would come to visit us, for a few weeks or more at a time, at Hyannis Port and Palm Beach. And of course that was always a blessing for us.

Her letters give some sense of her love for Billy and of her affection for the English people. In fact, she used to say that when she was here she spent most of her time explaining the British to the Americans and when she was there, explaining America to the British.

After recovering, outwardly, from the shock of Billy's death in the war, she went on to make a good life for herself in England. The duke and duchess and the other Cavendishes and Cecils took her with utmost affection into their family circle. She bought a little house in London. She found pleasure in the subdued, but still pleasant London "seasons" and in country weekends. She worked to do her part to bind up the wounds and dreadful damages of the war. She traveled in the British Isles and on the Continent. England became her home.

In 1948, she had taken a spring holiday on the Riviera and was flying in a private plane with a few friends to Paris, where her father was waiting to meet her. On the way—a route threading the edges of the French Alps—the weather went bad, navigation equipment was not adequate, and the plane crashed into a mountainside, killing all on board. Joe was notified and hurried to the scene. He watched as the body of his daughter was brought down the mountainside.

We lost our beloved Kathleen on May 13, 1948.

The duke and duchess wrote to us. A beautiful and heartfelt letter. I cannot bear to quote from it. They said how much they had loved Kathleen, and how grateful they had been to her because of the happiness she had brought to their son Billy. Kathleen was buried at Chatsworth, the Devonshire ancestral estate. The duchess suggested the epitaph on her gravestone: *Joy She Gave, and Joy She Has*. Billy was buried in Belgium, where he fell leading his troops during the war and where Kathleen once went to visit his grave.

My father remained hale and lively, full of wit and cheer and enthusiasm, well on into his eighty-eighth year. In his later years, he and my mother had a house at Hyannis Port, on Lighthouse Lane, about a ten-minute walk from our place. We saw them in those summertimes even more than we usually had.

While my father was growing old, Teddy was a boy growing up; and since my father was in semiretirement (the year of Teddy's birth he was sixty-nine), Teddy probably saw more of him than any of the other children had. He has some vivid memories:

"My first recollections of Grampa were at the Cape. He'd sit on that marvelous wall right outside the sun porch, sit for hours facing the southwest in the afternoon sun and sunset, enjoying the sea and salt air and sun. Or now and then he'd walk down to the sand and sit in all the seaweed and cover himself with it, because he thought the iron and the bromides from the seaweed could come into his skin.

"When I was in boarding school at Fessenden, I'd go into downtown Boston to the Bellevue Hotel and have Sunday lunch with him. In his and Grandma's apartment there he'd go around dressed very comfortably and informally. But by the time we went out he was spruced up, immaculate, a splendid sight. Downstairs on the way to lunch he'd take me through the kitchen and introduce me to any of the cooks or dishwashers I hadn't already met. Then the same in the dining room on our way to his table. He knew everybody because almost the same people came every Sunday, sat at the same place and ordered the same lunch; it was a sort of ritual.

"On a number of occasions Bob was there. He was in the Navy at the time, based nearby, and he'd join us.

"Afterward Grampa might take us for a walk through the Boston Common and point out where the British soldiers had been camping when they left to fight at Concord. Or we'd go down to the Old North Church and he would give us the story of Paul Revere's Ride again. Or down to the old well on Spring Street. Or maybe over to the *Constitution*, or out to Franklin Park. Each Sunday he had something different. Once in a while we'd start out and Grampa would run into old friends and they'd get wrapped up in conversation and telling stories and we'd never get there.

"He was a marvelous storyteller. I heard my first off-color story from Grampa. But he was laughing so hard while he was telling it that I don't think he ever got to the punch line. He enjoyed his own stories. He would start out telling a story, and start laughing, and pretty soon be laughing so hard he cried. It was very infectious. I can't remember any of them, but that's probably because they weren't such great stories—it was the way he told them.

"I do remember his talking on about 'Bigger, Better, Busier Boston' —and saying what was the matter with people that they didn't bring it about sooner? He'd say, 'My own daughter doesn't even have fish chowder. This is the trouble with the fishing industry, people just don't eat enough fish. They only eat it on Friday and they ought to eat it every day.' He'd go into Hayes-Bickford's and want pumpkin pie and they wouldn't be selling it that day. He'd say, 'Now you know up in Acton pumpkins are selling at three cents a pound. Why don't you buy pumpkins?' Also he'd try to get restaurants to serve squash. It was one of the things that was grown in some quantity in regions around Boston. He'd ask if they knew what a bargain squash was these days at the market. He was tremendously interested in the whole life and vibrancy of the city and everything that had to do with it.

"People seem to wonder how it happened that we as a family and especially perhaps in this generation—my brothers and sisters and I— became so much involved in public life. Obviously there were several influences, but Grampa surely had a part in it. He knew people's problems and motivations and needs, and what he talked about could easily be transformed into a current setting. And those little historical tours: I think that when you're a boy, you're going to be interested in the *Constitution* as a boat and as a fighting ship. But history, obviously, brings life into these monuments and characters and events. It's a reasonably easy transition to move from the issues of those times into the issues of these times."

My father's health began failing. I don't know the cause, if there was any precise cause; "circulatory troubles" mainly.

He passed away on October 2, 1950.

Joe had an office and a staff of perhaps a score of people in New York, and he had other trusted agents in other places where he happened to have large holdings on current operations (for instance, after Sarge and Eunice married they lived in Chicago, because Sarge was assistant manager of the Merchandise Mart). He also had a skilled full-time secretary and, nearby or quickly available, two or three trustworthy assistants who had worked with him through the years and who understood—without the need for detailed instructions—what he wanted done. Consequently, there was plenty of time for golf, swimming, walking (we again could have our long walks together), traveling, reading, talking, being with close friends, being with our children and then in due course with our grandchildren—enjoying the things that can make life so pleasant. What made it possible for Joe to conduct all sorts of intricate business while sitting in the solarium at Palm Beach with a beach towel around his middle and a straw hat when needed, or at Hyannis Port in equivalent ease and informality, was that fabulous invention, the telephone. I'm sure that if Joe had ever had to choose among all the marvels of modern technology the one thing to preserve from some holocaust, he would have discarded automobiles, airplanes, radio and TV, and all the rest including electric lights in favor of the telephone.

This predilection went back a long way. When we were courting he used to call me every evening. After we were married, whenever he was away, he would call me almost every day or evening. Eventually, it became a family habit and quite a wonderful one in a way, because of course it is marvelous to have a direct conversation instead of having to wait for the mails to get back and forth. Most letters leave questions unanswered or unasked anyway. Still, there are grounds for regret, for once a call is finished it's gone for keeps, whereas letters last. When Jackie became part of our family, the way the Kennedys used long distance appalled her. She said she had been brought up to think that a long-distance call was only for an urgent or special occasion.

As I have mentioned, Joe's various new ventures obliged me to keep adding to my vocabulary and knowledge, not to become expertly informed, but enough at least to keep up a conversation in case I found myself at dinner with people who were experts. In these later years I found this happening several times. An example that stays in my mind with vividness is that of horse racing.

Joe came home one night and told me he had just bought a large share in the Hialeah race track in Miami. It was the portion of the track ownership that had belonged to Colonel E. R. Bradley. I was used to surprises, but this was a rather extreme case.

Colonel Bradley had been one of the early entrepreneurs in the Palm Beach and southeast Florida coast area, and among other contributions to the landscape and entertainments had built a big restaurant and casino. It was quite a beautiful place. Dinners, with superb food, were about five dollars, and the service was swift and courteous. So, everyone turned up at Bradley's sooner or later, for luncheon or dinner, and afterward went into the casino and usually lost some money, enabling Colonel Bradley to recoup the losses on his delicious meals and pocket a profit besides. Everyone seemed to accept this as a fair arrangement for fine food in beautiful surroundings among friends and acquaintances. Bradley's, in fact, was a Palm Beach institution. Colonel Bradley himself felt so deeply about the place, regarding it as the fulfillment of his highest ideals, that he specified in his will that it not be sold as part of his estate but simply torn down. (And that is exactly what did happen.)

Joe and I used to go to Bradley's fairly often. Joe was not a gambler, except in the sense of taking closely calculated risks with the possibility of significant rewards. At Bradley's we would play roulette but seldom bet on a number, almost always on the red or black; and Joe would rely on "the law of probability," waiting for either red or black to come up in a long series of five or six in a row, and when that happened place a bet on the opposite color; and if we lost, then double the bet, and keep on doing that to the allowable limit. Usually, we came out a little ahead. Of course, we always kept the bets small. And it was fun.

During the years Colonel Bradley and Joe became good friends, partly, perhaps, because Joe, like himself, was a self-made man of Irish descent. Shortly before he died, he asked Joe to buy his interest in Hialeah, which he had helped found and developed into a beautiful place (especially famous for its ponds with flocks of flamingos) because, as he told Joe, he wanted it to go to an Irishman. I can't think of a more whimsical reason for buying substantial ownership of a race track, but I guess Joe was touched by the gesture. Besides, he thought it might be a good investment, which it did turn out to be. Meanwhile, he thought it could be an interesting sidelight to our Florida life, since the track is only about an hour and a half away from our house. Many people we knew went there.

We had a big box with one of the best views of the track and infield. There was a fine restaurant. Friends and interesting visitors were all over the place. As the largest stockholder, Joe had every facility at his disposal; the service to him and us and our guests couldn't have been better. I used to go down a couple of times a week for lunch and the afternoon.

It was up to me to learn the names of the leading racing stables and their owners (since they were likely to be mingling with us or visiting our box), the names and locations of other leading tracks around the country and something about their owners. And, of course, I had to master the form sheet and understand the tote board and how to place bets intelligently on the basis of past performance, track condition, and all the rest of the highly fallible information available to the bettor. I can't say that I became an expert handicapper, but my record wasn't so bad. And since I seldom ventured from the two-dollar window, my losses, if any, during an afternoon were bearable.

There was always something to do. In fact, there was a great deal to do, including the incessant dinner parties, cocktail parties, balls and galas of various sorts that dotted the winter season. Joe loathed big noisy cocktail parties, couldn't have cared less for the glittery charity balls (he would gladly send a check for the charity; but did he have to *go?*), and as for dinner parties, he would say: "The food is better at our house and the conversation is a lot better. All they want to do is to fight about Roosevelt and ask whether the stock market or real estate is going up or down, or what do I think about the fifth race on Saturday at Hialeah. . . ."

It has been said that Joe was a highly gregarious person who loved dining out, talking with many selected peers and enjoying all the social perquisites of his success. Nothing could be more untrue. His idea of a good time was to get up early and read the papers. Then he would swim, have a light lunch, and take a nap. In the afternoon he would play golf with me or a few close friends. He enjoyed having dinner at home with the family and perhaps two or three guests. Later in the evening he would read, listen to music, or screen a new film. He would set up the equipment on the patio of the Palm Beach house. It was lovely seeing the movies there in the tropical air under a starry sky. Joe rarely went to bed later than midnight. Meanwhile, of course, he would have dictated a lot of letters and had a dozen or two telephone conversations with people all over the country; but his heart and his real interests were always at home. He was actually —a strange term for a man of his tremendous vitality and interests— a homebody.

The children were with us during the Christmas holidays which stretched to various dates in January (why don't the schools learn to coordinate their vacation schedules?), and then again during the Easter holidays.

In any case, after they had gone back to school from their Easter vacations, and provided the weather was becoming mild by then in the North, Joe and I would go up to New York and stay for several weeks in a small apartment we owned facing Central Park.

Hyannis Port was our principal residence, our base of operations, as it were, for seven or eight months of the year from 1941 onward through all the years I have been describing. For all of us it became home. The children had their Christmas and Easter holidays in

Florida, but they had their summer vacations and all the spring and fall weekends they could manage at Hyannis Port.

It was a complicated household, especially during the late 1940s because by then the three Gargan children, Joey and Mary Jo and the youngest, Ann, were teen-agers and were spending the summers with us. So the age and circumstance of the inhabitants ranged from Jack, a U.S. congressman in his early thirties, to Ann, a girl in early adolescence. None of our older children was there all the time, because by then, like Jack, they had other things to do, but all were there for at least part of the summer and they tried to make their visits coincide or overlap. Moreover, they were likely to invite a friend or two along for a weekend or a week or so. It was a busy house and I was sometimes hard put to keep it passably well organized.

Evelyn Jones, who began working for us as a maid during that period, has recalled:

"Mrs. Kennedy always had so much on her mind. She was always going around with these notes. At the time I was first working there, they were wearing those twin sweater sets and she would have so many things to think of that she'd have all her sweaters pinned with notes. One day she ran out of space and tried to pin some on me. I wouldn't let her: It made me feel like a human bulletin board, but I sympathized with the problem."

I don't remember trying to enlist Evelyn as a message center, but I wouldn't be surprised.

Except for a few elementary rules and regulations such as being at meals on time, it was a very informal household. Joe and I wanted it that way. We wanted people to feel relaxed. Yet sometimes the relaxation got to be a bit extreme. For instance, there was a general tendency, especially among the boys, to leave towels and sweaters and sweatshirts and tennis racquets and tennis shoes strewn about. I remember that several times I came into the house and found tennis shoes parked anyplace from underneath the table in the entrance hallway to the top of the baby grand piano. I considered that to be extremely inappropriate, and I said so vehemently. One day they ganged up on me in the following way. This is a Lem Billings story and I can't guarantee it in all details, but it goes like this:

One of them, just to bait me, deliberately left a pair of very dirty white tennis sneakers on the dining-room table. I saw them and left a note sticking out from the top of one sneaker: "Bobby, are these yours?!"

Bobby came along, saw the note, and left another one with: "Dear Mother, no they're not mine. Jack's."

Jack came along, saw both notes, and left another: "Dear Mother, that's wrong. They belong to Teddy."

Teddy came along, saw and read the three notes, and left one of his own: "Dear Mother, that's a lie, they belong to Pat. . . ." And so forth, through several others. I never did find out whose dirty sneakers those were on the dining-room table. But in the dining room that evening, I noticed a lot of silly grins around the table, to which I paid no heed. (Lem Billings, by the way, was one of the worst at leaving things around. Was it Lem?)

As for the strewn towels, that reminds me that after showering the boys often used to go around anyplace in the house with one of our big bath towels knotted around their waists, sarong style. I made no objection; but, to say the least, it lent an informal touch.

When the cook was off, we'd gather in the kitchen and usually one of the girls, sometimes the boys too, would try cooking a dish, and then everybody would try it out. And comment on it. Some of them would be sitting on the table, or on chairs, or on the floor while the tasting went on. We would all sit around the kitchen table when everything was done, and there would be compliments—or razzing —about the food, and we would talk and gossip. They all enjoyed the experience and they also learned something: For instance, don't take an egg out of a cold refrigerator and expect it to be properly soft-boiled, even in rapidly boiling water, in just three minutes, because it won't be. I don't recall that any of them developed any specialties. Except perhaps Eunice, who was apt to be involved in telephoning or something when the dishes were to be washed or some other onerous kitchen task to be done. At least she was accused of that.

During the late 1940s, I still had a sizable population of teen-agers on my hands at Hyannis Port, and of course I felt obliged to keep track of them and, hopefully, to instruct them in good manners. My niece Mary Jo, whose age put her near the middle of this age group, has special memories of the time:

"There were Friday-night dances at the golf club, and Aunt Rose would drive over in her little blue car and look in on us, very unobtrusively, to see how we were doing. The next day some of us probably would get some coaching from her about dancing. I had my heels going in some funny way, and she'd give me a demonstration of how I looked and how to correct it. The boys would be pumping their dates' arms, and she'd show them how to dance smoothly. Bobby was a terrible dancer for a while. He not only pumped, he hopped. My brother Joey was probably even worse. He danced like a longshoreman. Aunt Rose tried to show him and then gave up and made him go to dancing classes. Teddy was a good dancer. He had a lot of rhythm, like Grampa Fitzgerald, who was a marvelous dancer.

"On Saturday nights there was a dance at the other club at Wianno Beach, which was a few miles away and practically all of us would go over there. Aunt Rose would dance with Bobby and Ted and my brother Joey to see how they were coming along.

"Uncle Joe was in on most of what was going on because he really cared so much about his children (and about nieces and nephews), and as he used to say, 'You'd better believe it.' Another of his expressions about his children was 'All my ducks are swans.' He really felt that way: His family was his life, Aunt Rose and the children.

For a man who valued domestic peace and quiet, Joe always showed remarkable forbearance. When the stream of traffic—friends and relations, Jack's continuing "surprises," those of others—grew even heavier than usual, I do remember his saying, more plaintively than complainingly, "This isn't a hotel. You don't have to have every room filled all the time." Actually, not only were all of them filled practically all the time during the summers but there often had to be double and triple occupancy. It was not at all unusual to have another "surprise" arrive in the driveway at eleven o'clock or so at night, and then we'd have to do some rearranging. If it was an extra boy and there were no vacant beds or cots left in any of the boys' rooms, we might have to start moving girls into other girls' rooms; or, of course, vice versa if the arrival was a girl; or if a boy and a girl arrived together it could become quite a checker game. We were, I expect, in the forefront of what now would be called "communal living."

Somehow we always managed to fit everybody in. Even if some of them might awaken next day with muscles a bit stiff or a crick in the neck from sleeping on a spare mattress or inflatable raft on the floor, they all seemed to have a very good time.

There were rules (largely implied) of manners and consideration which are part of civilized living. I assumed that people realized this was a large, involved, hospitable, but still personal household that took some thought and energy on my part to operate; otherwise, it was understood that everyone was to be himself or herself and have a fine time.

From Mary Jo:

"Aunt Rose kind of ran the whole show, I would say, in that she planned everything about how the house would be run, planned the meals, the schedules, coped with the help, directed and supervised that whole big enterprise, and yet it was really practically unbeknownst to us. At the time I never had the idea that anything was a big bother. It was all very gracious. Very happy, very easy."

It would have been somewhere around that time, with Teddy at about the age of eighteen—he was a freshman at Harvard—that Richard Clasby first came into our lives. Not many years later he and Mary Jo were married. I am told that he was one of the very few athletes in Harvard's history to have won nine varsity letters in football, hockey, and baseball.

Dick Clasby says:

"What really drew my attention first was that I was out for football, freshman football, and I kept getting hit and hit very hard. In athletics your greatest respect is for someone who really belts you, and even if you don't like the bruises you sort of have to like the guy, because he's good and he's playing hard, and that's the game. Well, this turned out to be Ted Kennedy. We happened to be walking the same way to and from football practice, and everything just seemed to fall into place and we became friends.

"Now, it's important to understand something about my personal circumstances. My dad was a cop, a good honest one but a cop, and my mother had to work most of her life to help make ends meet, so there was no money, and to me, a rich kid—I knew very few of them—was a spoiled sissy and was a kid I fought. Automatically, the first thing you do is fight them. The first one I ever liked or trusted was Ted, and it was sort of incredible to me, but we became close friends.

"It was sometime late that spring I first went to Hyannis Port and began to know the rest of the family. As I remember, Ted just said, 'How about taking a ride down to the Cape and get on the beach.' So we did that, except that was only part of it, a small fraction.

"When you arrived, there probably would already be a touch football game going on out on the front lawn, and before you even got your bag in the house you were playing football, and you might still be in the suit you'd gone to church in that morning.

"I looked at the game, the girls playing it along with the boys, and it didn't look like anything I would take seriously. You got tagged, so what? But they get you so involved, it's like Harvard versus Yale. Everybody is participating 100 per cent. If there's a little boy in the game and they throw the ball to him—and they do—and he doesn't try his best to catch it, that is considered bad. And if you're a big guy and another big guy has the ball and you are chasing him, you run as fast as you can, you do everything within your power to stop that ball. I think some of the guests were left slightly battered and bruised. There would be people from Washington, senators, high officials, and if you met them inside the house they would be dignified. But outside, they'd be running around in a pair of shorts and striving. It was like, 'I don't know what you can do for the country, but can you catch the ball, that's what's important right now.'

"The game they played wasn't the normal game. Ordinarily, in football you can't throw a forward pass except from behind the line of scrimmage, but they could throw it from anyplace. Then the person who caught it could forward pass again. So it became part football, part basketball. There was no blocking. You would change goals after each touchdown, but also you would change with the wind conditions —the yard is so close to the ocean. There were no kickoffs, you threw it to the other team. I don't know where the rules came from. I had never heard of them before, but I began thinking I've got to learn this wild game, if it's the last thing I ever do.

"It was an extremely competitive situation, but competition that was hard for me to understand. When you have young people in competition it often leads to hard feelings in the person or side that loses. They were out to win, but when the game was finished there wasn't anything from the winning side that would even hint 'Ha ha, you lost.' There was a great comradeship. They'd say, 'Great game, Bobby, or Ted,' or whoever it was. So you didn't feel you had lost, although five minutes before you could have thought—this is before I knew them that well—if you lost you were going to be ribbed about it all weekend.

"But they loved kidding and playing these rather fantastic jokes on each other. Again on football—and this would be a few years later on—we went down to Washington, and there was going to be a 'grudge' championship game between Bobby's team and Teddy's team. Well, there were guys I didn't know, but they were friends of Bobby's or Teddy's and it was 'Dick Clasby, I'd like you to meet Joe Somebody' and it was natural they both would have rounded up some of their best football-playing friends for 'the Big Game.' You wouldn't necessarily recognize their names or faces. It soon developed that they were *very* good football players. And that about three or four of Teddy's friends were members of the Baltimore Colts. But it also turned out that Bobby had had the same idea, and that three or four of his friends played for the Washington Redskins. It didn't take long for this double deception to come out into the open, and of course there was a riot on the field and on the sidelines among the rooters, and everybody had a hilarious time. In the end Teddy's fake-out team lost to Bobby's fake-out team, but I don't think anyone was really keeping much track of the score.

"Jack couldn't get into the rough action entirely because of his bad back—people did remember to be a little careful with him on account of that, but he participated."

Pat has a story about that:

"Jack was President-elect. He was forming his Cabinet and was having some of his meetings at Hyannis Port. The rest of us were out on the lawn playing football. A rainstorm came along—one of those sudden terrific storms—but we kept on playing anyway. From where Jack was, inside the house, he could look out and see us and it got to be too much for him to resist. During a break in his meetings he came outside, in this driving rain, and ran out for a pass. It was high, so he had to jump to catch it, and he came down hard. Bobby couldn't believe what he had seen and he yelled a typical compliment to the President-elect: 'Lots of guts, but no sense!' "

Dick Clasby continues:

"When you were with Jack there at Hyannis Port and if you weren't outside involved in something, you would soon find yourself involved in something that was going on inside such as various intellectual games which Jack organized and led. There would be, for instance, Categories. One category might be Shakespearean characters, and when you had to produce one beginning with 'M' you would have to think of Macbeth or Macduff or one of those or pass the question and lose the point."

I'm sure that Jack would have been attracted to such games in any case, as nearly all our children were, but one thing that fixed his and their interest, I believe, was the experience in England of taking "country weekends" in the English countryside at some of the great houses. Those were the late 1930s, the pre-Television Age, and although country life was bountiful in the daylight hours there were, at dinner and after dark, some hours when people were dependent on their own mental resources for entertainment. As a result, conversation was a highly developed art. Another result was the invention of amusing, intellectually stimulating and challenging "parlor games." I remember Kathleen talking about Anthony Eden and what a marvel he was at them. He was a weekend guest at a place she had in Ireland, and the group was playing a game involving historical names—persons, places, battles, and so forth—and he knew everything and always won.

Jack was great at keeping conversation going and bringing everyone into it, making it lively and humorous but interesting and worthwhile. I expect the experiences in England helped bring out that talent, and those English country-house games suited him exactly because of his background in history and literature and the endlessly curious nature of his mind. In turn and in due course, when Bobby was old enough, Jack's interest stimulated Bobby's interest, and he too became an inveterate inventor and organizer of parlor games. Ethel and I were talking about all this not long ago:

ETHEL: I remember that often after dinner you'd play the piano—always if there was a birthday—and everybody would gather around and sing with great gusto. Not in tune. You'd do old songs and newer and current ones; popular songs. People don't seem to do that much any more. And we'd play games afterward. Charades, and Murder, and Sardines, and Twenty Questions, and Ambassadors.

I: How did Ambassadors go?

ETHEL: Two people leave the room, and they decide who they are. They could decide to be people who weren't even of the same historical time: for instance, one could be Julius Caesar and the other could be Mrs. Roosevelt. So they come back into the room and carry on a dialogue, and the others try to guess who they are, and they do that by contributing to the conversation with remarks or questions which have to make sense to the historical personage—you know, something you really might say if you were having a chat with Julius Caesar or Mrs. Roosevelt. If you've guessed right, you don't announce it but the personage accepts you into the conversation and is friendly toward you. But otherwise he or she just ignores you, which is a terrible put-down. The one who first gets accepted into the conversation by both personages wins the game. It's a marvelous game, just great fun.

I: Jack must have been good at it.

ETHEL: Yes, he was very good. Another one he liked was Indirect Questions. It's like Twenty Questions but it's more fun. The same as in Ambassadors you decide who you are, let's say you're Charlemagne, and we try to guess, but the way we do it is through indirect questions. We'd say to you, "Are you a seventh-century Irish poet?" and you have to think of one and answer with, for instance, "No, I'm not Caedmon," and if you couldn't you'd say, "I pass," and then the one who asked would be entitled to a direct question such as "Are you living?" or "Are you an American?" or "Are you an astronaut?" and get a direct Yes or No answer. It would go on that way and finally get winnowed down to where somebody'd guess "Are you Charlemagne?" and be the winner.

I: Which ones did Bobby like best?

ETHEL: He liked those, and Categories and Charades and Sardines.

I: You were good at those games. I remember you and I had a discussion about Paul Revere's ride and I was quoting the poem that goes "Listen, my children and you shall hear, of the midnight ride of Paul Revere. On the nineteenth of April in Seventy-five . . ." and you said it was the eighteenth of April. I said, "Ethel dear, one of my brothers was born on the nineteenth of April and it's been a big celebration half my life, so you're wrong." And you said, "Do you mind if I get the book?" And you got it, and of course it was the evening of the eighteenth of April that Revere started the ride and the battle took place on the day following—the nineteenth.

About this time, Joe and I began to wonder when we were going to have grandchildren.

Bobby blazed the trail. Ethel was Jean's roommate and best friend at Manhattanville; and that's how Bobby and Ethel met. Their romance flowered, they married in 1950 and their first child, Kathleen Kennedy, was born in 1952 during Jack's run for the Senate against Lodge.

Eunice and Sarge married in 1953, Pat and Peter in 1954, Jean and Steve in 1956, Ted and Joan in 1958. Once the idea took hold it became a veritable processional down the aisle, and with our children, our nieces and nephews, and the children and nieces and nephews of our friends, Joe and I could count on a wedding every few months during that decade.

Jack was the oldest to marry. By the time he was approaching his mid-thirties his father and I had really begun to wonder if he was going to remain a bachelor for several years more and then marry late in life. We knew that for us marriage had brought such great satisfactions, that a good marriage is one of the happiest conditions of life, and of course we wanted this for him. And so, while not worrying, we were in a sense waiting and wondering.

The first I ever heard of Jackie was sometime during the winter of 1951. She—and her younger sister, Lee, as I recall—were vacationing with their family in Hobe Sound, up the coast from Palm

Beach. Jackie worked in Washington on one of the newspapers and knew several of our children, since by that time Jack, Eunice, and Bobby were working in Washington. She was invited to spend a few days at our Palm Beach house while some of them were there. I wasn't there myself at the time; I was detained on other matters and arrived a little later that year. Soon afterward, however, I received a thank-you letter. It was signed "Jackie." I thought it was from a boy, and how extraordinary for a boy to write such a charming letter. I wondered, who is Jackie? It turned out Jackie was a girl, and I began hearing all sorts of good things about her from members of the family, and that Jack was taking her out often and liked her a great deal.

I didn't meet her until the next year, in the summer of 1952, at Hyannis Port. I liked her at once. Jackie, of course, has her own special memories of coming there for the first time, and meeting her potential mother-in-law, and what the general ambience of our household was like.

"The first time I met her was about a year, a little more than a year, before I married Jack, when I came that summer for a weekend. I remember she was terribly sweet to me: For instance, I had a sort of special dress to wear to dinner—I was more dressed up than his sisters were, and so Jack teased me about it, in an affectionate way, but he said something like 'Where do you think you're going?' She said, 'Oh don't be mean to her, dear. She looks lovely.'

"She did everything to put one at one's ease. She was so friendly . . . everything. So that was really nice. Because I expect I was nervous. It was the first time I'd seen all of Jack's family together. I'd met him in Washington when he was in Congress, and he used to come to Bobby and Ethel's house, so I knew him with Bobby and Ethel well, and I knew Eunice, but I'd never seen the whole group together. Obviously, if you really liked the elder brother and were rather shy you might have been a little nervous. So that's it: She went out of her way to put me at ease, and I liked her enormously. I had already met Jack's father when I'd gone for a weekend at the Palm Beach house. He was the same—so welcoming and kind. I adored him.

"It was a marvelous weekend. How can I explain those people? They were like carbonated water, and other families might be flat.

They'd be talking about so many things with so much enthusiasm. Or they'd be playing games. At dinner or in the living room, any-where, everybody would be talking about something: They had so much interest in life—it was so stimulating. And so gay and so gen-erous and so open and accepting to outsiders. I thought they were wonderful."

I must now explain that when the children married, Joe and I—and of course their spouses too—faced the problem of what we should be called: "Mother and Father, Mom and Dad," any variation on those? My feeling, in which Joe concurred, was that both we and our in-laws would find this slightly uncomfortable. We weren't their parents: To my ear it sounded artificial. But then what? When they began to have children, who would be calling us "Grandpa and Grandma," it seemed both simple and seemly if we were known that way by our in-laws as well as our grandchildren. And that became the general principle. When someone refers to "Grandma" or "Grandpa" in the next pages the references are to me or to Joe.

However, two additional notes on this note. For some reason, it didn't seem appropriate to Jackie to call me "Grandma" and she used the expression "Belle Mère," a French colloquialism for a mother-in-law one really likes. And needless to say, I have always liked that.

I wish there were some equivalent expression in English. "Grandma" has its perils. Before a recent party, I was fresh from the beauty parlor, had put on a new Paris gown, and when the ensemble was complete, my maid exclaimed, "Oh madam, you don't look a day over fifty!" Sarge, in his late fifties, with his portion of gray hair, was at the party and when I entered, he greeted me from across the room in loud clear tones: "Hello, Grandma!" I was immediately deglamor-ized and very conscious of my eighty years.

Jackie and Jack became engaged in the early summer of 1953, and the announcement set off various festivities, including an engage-ment party given by friends of ours, the Harringtons, in a big house they had in Hyannis Port at the edge of the golf course. The party involved—for the younger element—a "scavenger hunt," which be-came rather famous, or perhaps the better term would be notorious, in our family.

Ethel and I were talking about this:

I: There was something about taking the policeman's hat.

ETHEL: Yes. That was the night Pat "borrowed" a bus. One of the things we were supposed to hunt for was "the longest object," and so Pat found the bus. I guess the driver had disappeared into the station for a minute or two. And the next thing he knew . . .

I: Where was the bus?

ETHEL: In Hyannis. And she drove it right to the Harringtons' and parked it in the driveway.

I: A big bus like that?

ETHEL: Yes. I can't remember who, but one of them appropriated a policeman's hat. By the time they got home there were three squad cars of policemen talking to Grandpa.

My nephew Joey has some illuminating memories about that scavenger hunt:

"Bobby, Pat and I were part of a team. You had to get different things like 'a monster from the sea,' and I remember we went in and got one of Uncle Joe's frozen salmon from a refrigerator. Another one of the things on the list was 'a menu from a famous restaurant.' There was a place called Charlie's, so we drove there and I went in to get the menu. But also on the list was 'a show of courage,' and at Charlie's in those days they had a police officer on duty. Somehow I decided that as 'a show of courage' I should take the policeman's hat. I grabbed it, ran out the door, leaped into Bobby's car— Pat had the bus—and down the street we went. We went around picking up more items.

"When we got back to the house at Hyannis Port that evening, there looking for us were some of the maddest-looking policemen I've ever seen.

"Uncle Joe came up from the movie room as this confrontation was taking place. The policemen were quite upset, naturally, but Uncle Joe was fit to be tied. Bobby and I got the royal dickens. We heard him very clearly in no uncertain terms.

"The next morning Uncle Joe was sitting in the sunroom and I went in and said, 'I'm sorry about last night, we just got carried away,' and he said, 'Well, Joey, don't worry about it but I certainly expect it's *not* going to happen again'—and he kind of smiled. And I said, 'No, I'm sure that won't happen again.'"

There were many preparations for Jack and Jackie's wedding. Jackie says:

"We got engaged in June and the wedding was going to be in September at Newport, so I remember one day my mother invited Jack's mother over to Newport for lunch and to discuss the plans. Jack was there for the weekend. And the situation amused me so much. Because here was Jack, he was thirty-six at the time and he was grown up and he was a senator. And his mother was coming to have lunch with my mother, and we were going to the beach and he and I would have a swim first. The two mothers were dressed up—Bailey's Beach was dressy then—and I remember she had on a beautiful light blue silk dress and a big hat. Jack had on some undershirt and a pair of bedroom slippers, and I expect she was rather mortified at the sight her son presented. I remember that on the way over, the two mothers were in the front of the car and we were sitting in the back seat, sort of like two bad children.

"Anyway it was, I'm sure, one of his least favorite days—the two mothers sitting there in their hats and pearls and white gloves chattering away about the wedding. So we went swimming. I came out of the water earlier; it was time to go for lunch, but Jack dawdled. And I remember she stood on the walk and called to her son in the water, 'Jack! . . . Ja-a-ck!'—and it was just like the little ones who won't come out and pretend not to hear their mothers calling— 'Ja-a-ck!' but he wouldn't come out of the water. I can't remember whether she started down or I went down to get him, but he started coming up, saying, 'Yes, Mother.'"

It was a splendid wedding, with all the traditional ceremonials and a large group of attendants. Numbers of Jack's schoolboy, college, and Navy "surprises" such as Lem Billings, Torb Macdonald, and Red Fay, and newer ones such as Charles Bartlett, were on hand in cutaways and striped trousers, as were Teddy and Joey, as was Sarge, who by then was a brother-in-law. Bobby was best man. Jackie was perfectly beautiful in ivory silk taffeta and rosepoint. Her matron of honor was her sister Lee. Ethel and Jean were bridesmaids. Archbishop (later Cardinal) Cushing presided at the ceremony and also read a special blessing on the marriage from the Pope. There were eight hundred in the church including all sorts of notables and more than twelve hundred at the reception. I read in one account that: "So great was the traffic that cars were backed up nearly half a mile and it took almost two hours for the guests to pass through the reception line to greet the couple." I daresay Jackie must have got a little tired smiling and shaking hands, but I can't think of a more appropriate introduction to her new life as the wife of a political figure.

Jack loved her and was proud of her and appreciated her. And it would be hard to imagine a better wife for him. She brought so many things that helped round out and fulfill his character. She developed his interests in art, music, and poetry—especially poetry, in which he had had only a mild interest before. He learned to delight in it because she had such pleasure from it. In fact, she wrote a poem about him, inspired by *John Brown's Body*, a play they had seen on their honeymoon. It is dated October 1953, a month after their marriage.

So far as I know this has never been seen except by those of us in the family and by a few good friends and associates. It is a treasure in several ways, and I include it here, in its entirety.

Meanwhile in Massachusetts Jack Kennedy dreamed

Walking the shore by the Cape Cod Sea
Of all the things he was going to be.

He breathed in the tang of the New England fall
And back in his mind he pictured it all,
The burnished New England countryside
Names that a patriot says with pride
Concord and Lexington, Bunker Hill
Plymouth and Falmouth and Marstons Mill
Winthrop and Salem, Lowell, Revere
Quincy and Cambridge, Louisburg Square.
This was his heritage—this his share
Of dreams that a young man harks in the air.
The past reached out and tracked him now

He would heed that touch; he didn't know how.
Part he must serve, a part he must lead
Both were his calling, both were his need.

Part he was of New England stock
As stubborn, close guarded as Plymouth Rock
He thought with his feet most firm on the ground
But his heart and his dreams were not earthbound
He would call New England his place and his creed
But part he was of an alien breed
Of a breed that had laughed on Irish hills
And heard the voices in Irish rills.

The lilt of that green land danced in his blood
Tara, Killarney, a magical flood
That surged in the depth of his too proud heart
And spiked the punch of New England so tart
Men would call him thoughtful, sincere
They would not see through to the Last Cavalier.

He turned on the beach and looked toward his house.

On a green lawn his white house stands
And the wind blows the sea grass low on the sands
There his brothers and sisters have laughed and played
And thrown themselves to rest in the shade.
The lights glowed inside, soon supper would ring
And he would go home where his father was King.
But now he was here with the wind and the sea
And all the things he was going to be.

> *He would build empires*
> *And he would have sons*
> *Others would fall*
> *Where the current runs*
>
> *He would find love*
> *He would never find peace*
> *For he must go seeking*
> *The Golden Fleece*

All of the things he was going to be
All of the things in the wind and the sea.

> Jacqueline Kennedy
> October 1953

Jackie is a rather quiet and shy person and soft-spoken—at least in comparison with most of our brood—and there may have been doubts about her among one or another of Jack's brothers or sisters or cousins at first, but that marvelous poem, which they read, immediately resolved them. Here indeed was an admirable new member, someone who could contribute a new dimension, who had insights and sensitivities challenging to them, and a fascinating person to know.

I admired the fortitude and courage she showed when Jack had to have his back operations. The first one, when he almost died, was in October of 1954, and there she was, still a young bride, deeply in love with her husband and faced with being widowed. When he was brought down—still on a stretcher—to Palm Beach to recuperate, we had a nurse with him the first few weeks, but then the doctor said she wouldn't be needed any more provided there was someone else to change the dressings. Jackie took that on: The doctor taught her how to do it. The incision was very large, it was still draining, and the dressings had to be changed several times a day. She did this skillfully and gently and calmly, and made no comment about it to anyone.

From the very beginning, Jackie and I always got along quite well. When there is friction between a mother-in-law and a daughter-in-law, I expect that two main reasons would be that the mother-in-law feels possessive and protective about her son, as if she can't quite accept the fact he's not a little boy any more but a grown-up man with a life of his own to lead; and also that she simply doesn't have enough to do to occupy her thoughts. Our situation was quite different. Joe and I always encouraged our children to take responsibilities; we loved them and they always knew it, but there was no clinging on our part. And I had so many things to do, so many interests, that I couldn't have found the time to make a nuisance of myself to my daughters- or sons-in-law even if I had been so disposed.

Jackie was remembering:

"We spent every Christmas and Easter vacation with them, until the White House. We spent the first four summers with them at Hyannis Port. During Jack's convalescence from the operations we spent the whole time with them in Florida, and I had every meal with them. So for long periods I really lived with them.

"And I think it's so sick when you hear those mother-in-law jokes on the radio or any of the media. They used to make me sad even before I had a mother-in-law. They really used to make me almost angry when I heard them; because I'd think, are people really like that? And then this woman, my mother-in-law, she just bent over backwards *not* to interfere. If she gave a suggestion, it was in the sweetest way. She sort of set you—set Jack and me—up as an entity.

"I think it's doubly extraordinary coming from that strong family where all the ties were so centripetal.

"And so: everything. I loved her very much. And I do now. She was just the most extraordinary mother-in-law, Belle Mère."

As the tribe increased, we began to have a housing crisis. It never was really solved—still isn't—at the Palm Beach house, because there was only so much space and it seemed foolish to build on or to buy another nearby house just so that everybody could be there at the same time for only a few weeks of a year.

Evelyn Jones, who worked for us a lot during that period, has some vivid memories of the logistical situation:

"There were always people waiting to get into rooms—there were always more people than rooms. Once Teddy was in a room, it was next to Mrs. Kennedy's, and somebody else was arriving. I think it was Mrs. Jack and the baby, Caroline. There was no other place to put them but that room—we knew that Teddy was leaving sometime that afternoon or evening, but he hadn't said when. Among the help we used to say, 'It's a military secret around here when something's going to happen.' So Teddy came back from wherever he'd been in the afternoon and all of his things were out in the hall. He came downstairs and was mumbling to Jean, 'Who put my things out in the hall?' Well, after all . . . And then another time, one day when

Mr. and Mrs. Jack were here—he was President—and they were leaving, Mrs. Shriver had been renting a house nearby and she couldn't wait. She had all their bags out and put them in the front hall downstairs, even before they were really out of the room. But all that was quite frequent."

Our house at Hyannis Port had only about the same number of bedrooms, but there the problem soon began to solve itself, for they could take a much longer cumulative time—the summer vacations, and weekends all the way through from after Easter to Thanksgiving —and this made it sensible for them to buy their own houses, especially as their families increased. Bobby and Ethel rented a place the first two or three years; then a house next door to ours came on the market, and they bought it. And that was the beginning of what came to be known as "the Kennedy compound"—though that is a misnomer if I ever heard one. A few years after Bobby and Ethel bought their house, another came on the market: It is catty-corner from ours and directly back to back with Bobby and Ethel's, and thus the three back yards adjoin, separated by some shrubs and outbuildings. This one became Jack and Jackie's house. It was a spacious and congenial arrangement—everyone in any of the three houses being able to walk back and forth through the back yards.

Actually, that group of three is bounded on the street side by a tall, split-picket, closely nailed fence—enough to give us a modicum of privacy from people driving past. The other two sides are open: the beach and also the lane coming into the properties where Jean and Steve had a house. Eunice and Sarge have a house a ten-minute walk from these, below the golf course, facing the ocean. Teddy and Joan have a house another ten minutes away, with an even better ocean view, near the top of a high hill known as Squaw Island.

By 1960 there were houses galore, with plenty of space for Pat and Peter and their children whenever they came to visit, and for friends and everyone's "surprises," and we were all close enough to see one another as easily and often as we wished.

Joe and I by then were seventy-two and seventy. Both of us were healthy, active, enjoying life fully. We had suffered grievous losses but we rejoiced in our children who remained and in our grandchildren. And we had the excitement, the drama, the pride, the great thrill that our eldest surviving son was running for the presidency of the United States.

Chapter Seventeen

❦❦

Public life is the crown of a career and to a young man it is the worthiest ambition. . . . Politics is still the greatest and most honorable adventure.

> John Buchan, Lord Tweedsmuir
> 1940

Some men give up their designs when they have almost reached the goal. Others, on the contrary, obtain a victory by exerting, at the last moment, more vigorous efforts than before.

> Polybius
> circa 150 B.C.

There were a number of reasons why, supposedly, Jack couldn't win the Democratic nomination in 1960, and even if he did why he would be unable to win the election.

First, he was too young. In 1960, he would be forty-three, and no one so young had ever been elected President.

Second, he had had no experience in the executive branch of government, either state or national, whereas the presumed Republican nominee, Richard Nixon, had two terms in the vice-presidency and could claim to have been closely involved in many of the major undertakings of the Eisenhower administration.

Third, he had little or no support among the Party's established national leaders: former President Truman, Mrs. Roosevelt, Sam Rayburn, and Lyndon Johnson, and others.

Most important, he was a Catholic. A good many of the more influential state and city leaders were Catholics. But they knew how important anti-Catholic bias had been in defeating Al Smith for the nomination in 1924, and in his loss to Herbert Hoover in the election of 1928. True, there was now a new generation, and religious tolerance had grown. But how much, how far, and how effectively was debatable. There were strong feelings, and in some cases strong convictions, among Catholic as well as Protestant and Jewish leaders that Jack's Catholicism would prove to be too severe a handicap. Political leaders dislike backing losers.

Nevertheless, after thinking the matter over and talking with his father, among others, Jack decided to run.

From the moment of the decision, everybody went to work. It wasn't until after Jack made his formal declaration of candidacy—January 2, 1960—and the state primaries began that I had any direct role in the campaign. But there had been a great deal of preparation that went before, and naturally one couldn't be the mother of the candidate and the wife of Joseph P. Kennedy without knowing something about those preliminaries.

It was understood that when Jack ran, Bobby would be his campaign manager. And so, after Adlai Stevenson's nomination in 1956 and when that campaign got under way, arrangements were made for Bobby to travel along in Stevenson's entourage of helpers and advisers and press during the rest of that summer and fall. (For people who haven't been involved in a big campaign, I'm sure it would be rather amazing to see the sheer "logistics," of getting the candidate and his staff from point to point, fed and sheltered, besides arranging for the conferences with local leaders, for speeches, for radio and television appearances, and for shaking hands up and down Main Street.) Joe wanted Bobby in on all this so he could observe how a national campaign is run, to understand the problems, and benefit from any lessons that could be learned. Jack was very much in favor of this. For much of the summer and fall of 1956 Bobby traveled with the Stevenson campaigners. It was a rich experience and Bobby did learn a great deal, including some mistakes to avoid, all of which was put to good use later.

Joe believed that experience was the best teacher and he was always alert to ways in which the children could be trained for public life.

If he made a donation for a hospital, school, or charity it was not he who was photographed and applauded and who made the presentation speech, but one of the children. When he gave a new gymnasium to Manhattanville in memory of Kathleen and it was ready for dedication, it was Teddy who represented the family, went through the ceremonies, shook the hands, and made the speech, though at the time he was barely into his twenties.

Teddy was wearing a dark suit, which was proper for the occasion, but had tan shoes. His father was as quick to notice as I was, and he said, "We must tell him about that."

I don't know why Jack, Bobby, and Teddy were so hard to educate about such simple rules of dress—*black* shoes with any shade of gray or black or dark blue suits. Among many reasons for my admiration of Jackie, Ethel, and Joan is that they did manage to get their husbands to pay attention to clothes, even to the extent that eventually they became known as being quite well dressed. It was something the wives could do, while I seemed doomed to frustration.

Jack was making speeches throughout the country during the late 1950s, and Dave Powers usually accompanied him, doing all sorts of things, from telling jokes and giving political advice to carrying and unpacking his baggage to save strain on Jack's bad back, and Dave remembers:

"She was great for notes. I might be going somewhere with the candidate and I have his bag and I'd be opening it to unpack and get his things put away. And if we had left from Florida or Hyannis Port or someplace his mother was, there inside could be a note to me: like make sure he doesn't have holes in his socks. You know, when you're in politics and you're on a stage, sitting up there and the audience looking you over and you begin to feel a sock slipping down, you have to go for that sock and pull it up. Well, evidently one time when this happened and she was there she noticed a hole in one sock—not a big one, but big enough to notice, so that was the message: 'Make sure the socks Jack wears do not have holes in them.'"

I felt that if he were going to take the time to travel and prepare a good speech, why have people distracted by a hole in his sock?

I have always felt that appropriate dress and grooming are part of good manners, and that good manners are important—as I freely reminded the children from time to time.

Ethel and Bobby began saving my notes and letters on that topic; and not long ago, while Ethel was going through papers at her house that might help with this book she came across a round-robin letter from me that she considers a good example. I defer to her judgment and am putting it in. The date, June 19, 1958, would place it near the hole-in-the-sock period.

"Dear Children:

"This letter which I am sending to all of you may be of some help to you in the future.

"When there is a clergyman present at luncheon or at dinner, the hostess asks him to say grace and no one is seated until after he has done so. The same thing applies at the end of a meal. . . .

"When traveling abroad, bring calling cards with you. Send them around to the embassy by courier or leave them yourself with the corner turned down and possibly the address of the hotel. You then will probably get a phone call for luncheon or tea. A lady is supposed to leave a card for every lady of the embassy. A man leaves them for every man, as well as for the ladies. For instance, last year when I was in London, I went to the embassy and left two cards: one for Mrs. Whitney and one for her daughter Sara Roosevelt. If your father had been with me, he would have left three. However, you know your father.

"Also, when you have gone to a luncheon or dinner at the home of an important person, it is well to write a note of thanks immediately. For instance, when the Cardinal gave a luncheon for Grace Kelly, she wrote a note of thanks that very afternoon and it made a tremendous impression.

"I am just giving you these few hints. Perhaps, if you follow them, you will be more of a success socially.

"Much love,
"Grandma"

Ethel has unearthed another note from those times, and although it doesn't deal with proper manners as such, it does have to do with respect for the value of one's personal possessions—which for most people in the world have always been hard won. It is dated November 17, 1959, and so fits in here:

"Dear Ethel,

"Bobby took me to the top floor of your house the other evening and I noticed a Jaeger Le-Coultre clock in one of the maid's rooms. Since these sell for $50 or $60 in Switzerland—probably $90 here—I would think that you would like to keep it for traveling. It is very easy to get a good electric clock for $4.95 and this would be most suitable. . . .

"The Jaeger clock is sometimes difficult to set because it has just the one knob; but if you like, I will show you how to operate it . . . when you come for Thanksgiving.

"We are already stuffing the turkey and cooking the cranberries.

"Much love to all,
"G. Ma"

Another item from Ethel's collection that probably belongs here simply because of my belief that attention to details, even the minor gestures that are part of human communication, is important in all human relationships. Sometimes it may be inconvenient to give them one's attention, as I daresay it was for Bobby when he received my note dated March 7, 1960, addressed to him at Kennedy Campaign Headquarters, Wisconsin Avenue, Milwaukee:

"Dear Bobby,

"Will you autograph a copy of your book for the Duke of Windsor and then send it to me here in Palm Beach? I will then see that the Duke receives it.

"I believe that the inscription should read: 'To H.R.H. the Duke of Windsor.'

"Much love.
"G. Ma"

I'm sure that Bobby did sign and send the book as soon as he could, although probably not that day or week, because Wisconsin was a terribly important primary and Bobby had a lot on his mind.

There are vivid memories from that time, especially during the winter of 1959–60, of Joe's activities behind the scenes on behalf of

Jack's candidacy. He would be in the solarium—the "bull pen" as it came to be called by the children—at the Palm Beach house, with a hat, a towel, a cool drink, and a telephone, contacting influential leaders all over the country. He worked especially hard on Governor David Lawrence of Pennsylvania who, a Catholic himself, was unable to believe that a Catholic could be elected President and therefore why sacrifice the Democratic Party by giving Jack the nomination. And often Joe would go to Hialeah (and often I would be with him) not for the races really but because some influential political leader or editor or someone able to exert leverage at the Convention would be there that day, and Joe would want to talk with him.

Jack and his father were in almost daily communication. There would be long conversations. If Jack had some bad news to report I would hear his father saying—as usual—"You know, that may be one of the best things that could have happened to you. . . ." After putting down the telephone he might sit a minute or two looking dejected, or start pacing the floor muttering denunciations of someone. Then, quite likely, he would sit down and start making some more telephone calls.

My active participation in the campaign began in the Wisconsin primary on March 15, a date I would not be able to give with precision, except for another letter that Ethel saved. It was dated March 14, from Palm Beach, and was from me to Bobby and Ethel's eldest daughter, Kathleen (namesake of our beloved Kathleen, "Kick"), a little girl of only about eight or nine. She was and always has been a delight to me. The letter shows that, for us, politics had become a normal part of life:

"Dear Kathleen,

"I was very glad to hear from you. I wish you were not so far away because I would love to have you come over here often for luncheon or dinner. It would be nicer still if I could read you a story every night.

"I have not forgotten about our date for the ballet. The next time I see you I will tell you the story about the *Nutcracker Suite*, for that is the name of the ballet we will see, either this year or next year.

"The weather has been quite cool down here, but we go in swimming just the same. And then, we all yell because it's so cold. But after a while we get used to it and then we like it.

"I am on my way to Wisconsin to make speeches for Jack. I hope you will be able to take a trip with me some day, but right now, it is very important that you work and study hard in school. When Jack was a little boy, he studied very hard and so he knew all about Paul Revere and George Washington. And when he was older, he studied a lot of European history. I hope that you too will work hard in school.

"Grandpa has gone to a ball game, but I know that he would want me to send you his love.

"I had some oranges shipped to you last week. I think you and your brothers and sisters will enjoy them. Tell them I send them all a kiss and hope to see them soon. And much love to you, dearest Kathleen.

"Affectionately,
"Grandma"

I spent eight days in Wisconsin. My schedule began around 8:30 A.M.—with a talk to a breakfast club, or a radio or TV appearance, and ended in mid-to-late evening, time enough for seven or eight hours' sleep. There were comments about my stamina, but actually that's all the rest a mature person is likely to need. Of course, as one grows older one needs less sleep, and at the time I was seventy.

The general design of Jack's 1960 campaign was mainly an extension and elaboration of the ideas that had been effective in 1946, '52, '58. It was marked by great effort and attention to details on the part of everyone: friends, supporters, allies, recruits and draftees, volunteers, cousins and cousins-in-law in our extended family, and above all the immediate family. Again there were tea parties and "house parties," with Polly Fitzgerald coming on again, as she had before and always would, tirelessly and gallantly, to make so many necessary arrangements. There are too many people to thank. I can't put all their names in here, and I hope they will understand. Everything was handled so efficiently that I was never exhausted in spite of a rather hectic schedule—a schedule that was made for me, without my advice but with my consent, by Bobby and his campaign associates, who decided where and how and when I could help most effectively.

I remember I did have one bright idea that was vetoed. Although it had been many years since I learned German at Blumenthal, I had kept up at least a fair proficiency in it. I knew that Wisconsin had a large population of German descent and I thought this was a situation made to order for me. I could address some German social and community organizations, *Geselleschaft* and perhaps introduce some German expressions into my radio and television interviews, thus capitalizing on my German as I had on my French in the 1952 Senate campaign. But apparently memories of the war were still too strong and the German language was out of fashion, even in Milwaukee, so my idea was turned down. I accepted this with disappointment (all those years of study!), but with good grace.

The point was, what could we do for Jack. This was true for all of us. Even at peril. Teddy's ski jump was an example. Here is his own account:

"It was rather like Jack saying, when someone asked him about being a war hero, 'It was unintentional. They sank my boat.' I went to a ski-jump event near Madison because there was a big crowd there, eight or ten thousand people, and the idea was that somebody would introduce me on the public-address system and I would say a few words about the election and vote for my brother, and then go around and shake hands. Someone in charge said I should go to the platform at the top of the jump and be introduced from there. So up I went and there were several people waiting and one fellow with an official's badge introduced me and ended by adding, 'Maybe if we give him some encouragement, he'll jump.' The crowd applauded.

"I had on ski clothes, more or less, so I would blend into the scene of the day. I could ski pretty well. I should've by that time because my parents, Mother in particular, started me out when I was six or seven, and Dad was in the embassy and Mother took us over to Switzerland for the Christmas and New Year holidays. And I remember seeing my brother Joe go down that dangerous one-man bobsled run, and skiing with him and Jack—they were trying to teach me—and I twisted my knee, and they took me down to the hospital, and I was laid up for a while. But I had done a lot of skiing later and

I was pretty good at the usual things, though I hadn't jumped. I knew the principles.

"This was an Olympic-size jump, but I thought I'd try. Somebody was kind enough to offer to lend me a pair of skis. So down I went. In the circumstances, it seemed I should. I didn't show the grace of an eagle, but I managed to keep everything going in the right direction and landed upright about seventy-five feet or so away and skied on down the slope and was very happy still to be alive. There was applause. Maybe there were some extra votes for Jack. . . .

"I certainly never went around looking for things like that. But I did find myself involved in a similar situation later on during the general election. They put me in charge of the campaign in the mountain states, so one day I was at a big rodeo in Miles City, Montana. I was there with the same idea, to be introduced and say something about my brother and shake some hands. But they said no political figures were going to be introduced. They said, 'If you want to ride, you'll be introduced like everybody else.' Which would be like, 'Ted Kennedy, now comin' out of chute 4.'

"I knew how to ride a horse. I never had been on a bronco. But if that's the way it had to be . . . so I got on the bronco and we went out the chute, and I think I may have lasted six seconds—it seemed like an hour before I was thrown. No real damage, no broken bones. People seemed to think I had done all right for an amateur. They like to test you in that part of the country. Possibly I had conveyed something about our family—about Jack—that resulted in a few more votes.

"Jack called me shortly after that to say that he had just talked with the state chairman in Wyoming, who told him I was coming to Rock Springs the next Saturday night. They were arranging to have a sharpshooter shoot a cigarette out of my mouth at twenty yards. Jack said, casually, that he didn't think I had to go through with that if I didn't want to, but . . ."

Teddy was always stalwart, and optimistic from the time he was a little child. I think none of us were greatly surprised by his ski jumping and bronco riding. If anyone among us was surprised about any of us, I suppose it would have been about Jackie. This was her first experience in hard campaigning. She had been out with Jack a few times in the 1958 senatorial campaign, but there had been no question about his winning, only about winning a landslide victory that would help establish him for 1960. We knew she had plenty of spunk and courage, but we also knew she was a rather shy person who found a lot of public attention uncomfortable. She was not a natural-born campaigner.

But there she was traveling with Jack in motorcades, standing in receiving lines, shaking hands along Main streets, and even taking off on her own now and then into supermarkets to announce herself as the wife of John F. Kennedy, presidential candidate and urging the shoppers to give him their votes. All of us were newly impressed. She was a wonder.

There were numerous candidates for the Democratic nomination that year. Among them were Senator Lyndon Johnson, Senator Stuart Symington, and former Governor and twice nominee Adlai Stevenson, who was being encouraged by many admirers such as Mrs. Roosevelt to seek the presidency again and who found that prospect pleasing. The only candidate, however, who was willing to contest the primaries with Jack in "neutral" states (those uncommitted to a "favorite son" or other leader) was Senator Hubert Humphrey of Minnesota. Thus, he was Jack's opponent in Wisconsin.

He seemed to have all the advantages. His state and Wisconsin are neighbors; both predominantly rural; both noted for their Progressive, Farmer-Labor sentiments. Senator Humphrey was almost as admired in Wisconsin as in his own constituency, and deservedly so. He is a fine public servant. Jack liked and respected him, and this was reciprocated by Senator Humphrey. In fact, there weren't any essential points of disagreement between them except one: Who was going to be the Democratic nominee? Jack came into this natural "Humphrey territory" as an Easterner, the son of a well-known "capitalist," and with little or no record to offer as a champion of the agricultural interests and special concerns of the Midwest farm belt.

Consequently, when Jack won against such odds it seemed to me that it should have been a cause for celebration. Yet, somehow, the loser seemed to be in the position of being the winner, or at least the presumed winner in the next primary. Political chess of this sort has always baffled me. I quote Kenny O'Donnell, Bobby's friend and assistant and later Jack's assistant at the White House, who was there:

"Kennedy won in Wisconsin with more popular votes than any candidate in the history of the state's primary, carrying six of the ten congressional districts and getting two thirds of the delegate votes. That seemed good enough to me, but it was not good enough to satisfy the experts, because Kennedy failed to carry the three so-called Protestant districts in the western part of the state and lost to Humphrey in the Second District, around Madison, where we had expected to win. In the hotel room at Milwaukee, Eunice Shriver was puzzled to see her brother glancing at the impressive popular vote figures with a glum expression on his face. 'What does it all mean, Johnny?' she said to him.

" 'It means that we've got to go to West Virginia in the morning and do it all over again,' Jack said. 'And then we've got to go on to Maryland and Indiana and Oregon, and win all of them.' "

As older readers may remember, West Virginia attained fame in national politics in 1924 when its delegates at the Democratic Convention steadily, through dozens of ballots, voted for Oscar W. Underwood in order to prevent the nomination of Governor Alfred E. Smith of New York, primarily because Smith was a Catholic. The population of West Virginia was almost wholly Protestant and it was still suspicious of "Catholic influences" in the United States Government and thought that a Catholic President might "take orders from the Pope." To all of us, and probably most of all to Jack, this would be about as sensible as to say that American members of the Episcopalian Church would "take orders" from the Archbishop of Canterbury about secular matters. But illogical as it was, "the Catholic issue" had to be faced against almost the worst odds imaginable, and with Catholic political leaders such as Governor Lawrence of Pennsylvania waiting to take their cue from the outcome and filled with pessimism about Jack's chances in West Virginia.

A public-opinion poll had been taken in the state a few months earlier and showed Jack winning against Hubert Humphrey—if they ever ran against each other there—by 70 per cent to 30 per cent. But a similar poll taken after the campaign was actually under way reversed the figures, showing 70 per cent for Humphrey. Kenny

O'Donnell has described the welcome that he, Bobby, and Larry O'Brien received when they arrived from Wisconsin and went to a meeting of West Virginia campaign workers:

"'Well,' Bobby said to them pleasantly, 'what are our problems?'

"A man stood up and shouted, 'There's only one problem. He's a Catholic. That's our goddamned problem!'

"The room broke into an uproar with everybody yelling at us that nobody in the state would vote for a Catholic in a contested presidential primary. . . . All over West Virginia, they were getting abuse and ridicule from their friends and neighbors because they were supporting a Catholic. I began to gather that apparently Kennedy's Catholicism was not well known to most West Virginians until the recent reports of his religious problems in the Wisconsin primary were given widespread coverage by local newspapers and television news shows. Overnight our whole situation in West Virginia had changed. . . . I looked at Bobby. He seemed to be in a state of shock. His face was as pale as ashes.

"When we left the meeting, Bobby went to a telephone booth and called Jack in Washington. . . . Jack was taken aback by Bobby's discouragement. 'It can't be that bad,' he said, and reminded Bobby of the precampaign poll. Bobby said, 'The people who voted for you in that poll have just found out that you're a Catholic.' "

In 1952, I had been made a papal countess by Pope Pius XII. In the terms of the scroll, which was delivered to me by Francis Cardinal Spellman, this was in recognition of an "exemplary life and . . . many charities." Understandably, I considered this a tremendous honor, especially as it was the only such conferred by Pius XII during his long reign. I had used the title very seldom, only at special events and ceremonies of the Church; and only in Italy or France or other predominantly Catholic countries. But in West Virginia, with "Popery" suddenly the big issue, the media there surely would bring it up in interviews and feature articles if I came into the state to campaign. I would have been, to say the least, "counterproductive."

So I wasn't invited. I don't recall any discussion of the fact that I might be a problem. Bobby just said something like "Mother, after you worked so hard in Wisconsin, go on back to Palm Beach and get some rest for a few days. Then we're booking you into Indiana, and

Nebraska, and Maryland, and maybe some other places . . . we'll work it out and Polly will have the list."

I was entirely used to this procedure. I never knew—and it never bothered me—who decided my itinerary. They were places where the committee thought I could attract a group and be effective with it.

Although I wasn't involved in the West Virginia campaign, I do have one vivid memory of it. Franklin D. Roosevelt, Jr., had been visiting us at Palm Beach earlier that year. We all had dinner and then went out to the patio, in the tropical moonlight, and the talk went on. Of course it turned to politics, and then to West Virginia and the questions as to whether Jack should contest the primary there and, if so, whether FDR, Jr., would go into the state to campaign for him.

This scene, the conversation and situation, stays in my memory because I felt that young Franklin had so many qualities and assets that almost no elective office seemed beyond his reach. He had a marvelous personality. He had the smile, the voice, the facility and vocabulary, the stature and bearing and stalwart good looks, "charisma," and, above all, in terms of practical politics, he had the magic that was associated with his name. I remember feeling thankful that evening that FDR, Jr., was not a candidate in the primaries or the election against our son, because I thought Jack or anyone would have had a hard time winning any election against him.

I quote Kenny O'Donnell:

"Kennedy's most valuable campaigner in West Virginia was Franklin D. Roosevelt, Jr., whose famous name is held in reverence in the coal-mining state. Roosevelt's father pushed NRA legislation that gave coal miners the right to organize and to get decent living wages. . . . Recruiting Franklin Roosevelt for duty in West Virginia was Ambassador Kennedy's idea. The ambassador" (this, of course, had become an honorary title: just as anyone who has been a governor or senator or general is usually addressed by that title thereafter) "also saw to it that letters to voters in West Virginia, praising Senator Kennedy and signed by Roosevelt, were shipped to Hyde Park, New York, to be postmarked and mailed from there. . . . Roosevelt spoke for Kennedy all over the state and was mobbed by admirers wherever he went. Appealing to the militant patriotism of the West Virginians, he heavily emphasized the senator's war record, sometimes making it seem as if his own destroyer and PT-109 had fought in the same battles. . . . One of his often-used and most effective lines, holding up two fingers tightly pressed together, he said, 'My daddy and Jack Kennedy's daddy were just like that!' "

Jack decided that the only way to deal with the religious issue was to face it head on, bring it up himself in his speeches, invite questions from everyone about any and every aspect of it. To the great credit of the people of West Virginia they listened, understood, and responded to the man and the real issues. They voted for Jack by such a majority that Senator Humphrey withdrew from the race in the remaining primaries. The significance of the victory was that the religious issue could be surmounted and thus Jack's candidacy was still alive, and it was possible to glimpse ultimate success.

I kept diary notes during that time. Here are a few dated June 23, 24, and 25:

"Jack and Jackie, Jean and the children down at Hyannis this weekend for the summer. Went for dinner Friday and Saturday nights at Jackie's house, but Jack looked tired and went to bed early. Saturday he played golf in the morning with Jean, and later when I went over they all were playing croquet. Caroline was out there, too, and the dog Charlie racing back and forth chasing Jack's ball. Whereupon, Jack harangued the dog at the top of his lungs. . . .

"Jack on the phone and particularly incensed because Governor Meyner of New Jersey will not come out for him. After dinner, we called up Dad. As usual he was reassuring, said it was 'in the bag,' and that everyone got nervous about these things near the end.

"As Jack's mother, I am confident that Jack will win because his father says so, and through the years I have seen his predictions and judgments vindicated almost without exception. And so, I believe it. He also says, and has said all along, that if Jack gets the nomination he can beat Nixon.

"We are all furious at Governor Brown of California and Governor Lawrence of Pennsylvania because they will not come out for Jack now. Their support would clinch the nomination for him. Joe has worked on Lawrence all winter but he still can't believe a Catholic can be elected. He has been one of the most exasperating and tantalizing forces. . . ."

This was only about two and a half weeks before the Convention opened at Los Angeles, and Jack had been campaigning actively as a declared candidate for nearly six months, and as an undeclared one for almost four years.

The Convention itself is rather blurred in my memory. I was excited. We all were in or near Los Angeles except for Jackie, who by then was in mid-pregnancy and Jack didn't want her exposed to the tumult of Los Angeles, so she stayed home. Jack had two places, a hotel suite and a small apartment, which was far from the Convention scene where he could relax. Joe and I and other members of our family stayed at Marion Davies' house. Joe said he would much rather remain there on the evening of the balloting, away from the crowds and the photographers. The rest of us were at the Convention Hall. Pat was a member of the California delegation. Teddy was a floor manager. Bobby was at his command post. Steve, Sarge, the girls—everybody was someplace doing important work. I went to Convention Hall and sat in one of the boxes with Eunice, my niece Ann Gargan, and a few of the older grandchildren.

Jack won the nomination on the first ballot. There was joyful, ear-shattering pandemonium. Pat and I were called to the platform to stand with him as everyone cheered and waved. It was a very proud moment.

I was on the road during a good deal of that summer and fall, campaigning in the general election, and when it was all over Jack gave me a map of the United States which he had marked to show the places I had gone to and signed it, "For Mother—With Thanks." The map shows that I was in fourteen states and made forty-six appearances, significant enough to be put on the record. Somewhat to my own surprise I found myself turning into a regular "politician." I didn't miss a chance to ask anyone to vote for Jack. I talked with taxi drivers, elevator operators, waitresses, porters, manicurists and anyone with whom I could strike up a conversation.

Taxi drivers are, of course, proverbially great conversationalists, and on the way from the airport to my hotel the dialogue might begin with my remark: "Well, how's business? Probably it will be better when a Democrat gets in." Some of them seemed suspicious. They would size me up in the rearview mirror and perhaps decide I was too well dressed to be a Democrat and was a Republican *agent provocateur.* Their replies would be cagey. Others would respond readily, but often had objections to Jack, such as that he was too young for the job. "He's young in years," I would say, "but not in experience, and isn't that what's most important?" Or I would hear, "We always have a war with the Democrats in office." I would reply that John Kennedy had had tragic deaths in his own family in the last war. He had seen good friends killed or maimed, and had himself been severely wounded. Surely this had given him a horror of war. Often, the problem of his Catholicism would arise. I remember hearing variations on the theme "I don't want any Pope running things over here." I would answer that the Pope lives in Italy but certainly doesn't run things there, even though it's a Catholic country; and that France is mainly Catholic and De Gaulle is a Catholic, but the Pope certainly did not give any orders to De Gaulle; and that Catholics in the U.S. Congress never voted as a bloc; and therefore the whole "Catholic issue" was nonsense. If, by the end of the trip, the driver hadn't figured out that I was related to Jack I would tell him who I was; in which case, usually, his face would light up, he would say he was glad to meet me, and he was certainly going to vote for Jack. The same thing generally happened with waitresses, baggage porters, and others: They might have a rather uninterested look at first but would end up assuring me Jack would get their votes. I remember sitting next to a woman on an airplane. We got into a conversation, which I drew around to my favorite subject, and by the time we landed she asked me to send her a large supply of campaign buttons.

Teddy was asked recently about what I added to the campaign:

"Mother is superb in talking with a group. She puts out; she turns on right away; she works at it. She knows what the audience's interests are likely to be. She has a feel for these things and also she has done her homework and is very much aware, plugged in, and she has been thinking.

With Konrad Adenauer, December 1964.

With Arthur Rubinstein, Florence, Italy, June 1961.

Jackie snapped Joe holding John Jr., on the White House grounds, 1961.

Joe at the White House in 1961 with Stephen Smith, Jr. (Another photo by Jackie.)

One hour after this photograph was taken Joe suffered the stroke that left him paralyzed, December 19, 1961.

Toronto Star Syndicate

The Canadian Association for Retarded Children presented me with the International Award of Merit for Distinguished Service to the Mentally Retarded.

In Canada, a visit with retarded children.

The late King Gustaf of Sweden received me at Drottningholm Palace, 1966.

I visited Rickombergaskolan, a home and school for handicapped children, Sweden, 1966.

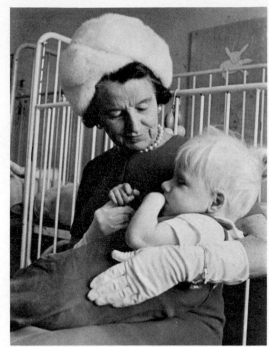

Roland Andersson

Niagara Falls, 1969.

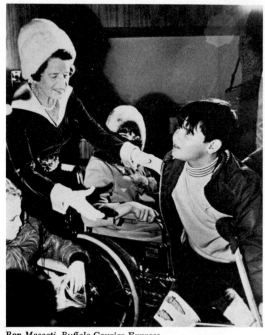

Ron Moscati, Buffalo Courier-Express

Ron Moscati, Buffalo Courier-Express

At an outing for handicapped children, I accepted a Girl Scout calendar from Liz Scotland.

"But where she comes through best is in a person-to-person relationship. She's interested in people, genuinely interested in them as individual human beings, and I think this is a very important part of her success, not only in campaigning but in all the aspects of her life. People feel the interest she has in them: She is able to communicate that to them.

"Time and again people say about Jack that even when he was President he had this very personal interest in anyone he was with. He was listening, responding, communicating fully. And it came from her."

Here are some other diary notes of the late summer and fall of 1960 at Hyannis Port:

"Jack is home today. We all went to his house last night, Ethel, Joan, and I. He eats ravenously of lobster and corn on the cob. According to Dr. Jordan of the Lahey Clinic, corn and lobsters are the worst things for a tummy like I have and Jack has. The roses are so beautiful now at the Cape. The fogs and the climate here seem exactly right for them. In the paper this morning there was an article about the superb Kennedy organization. The efficiency—the results —all this because it is a family team at the center, with Jack, his brothers, his sisters and brothers-in-law, and the over-all strategy of their father, who I doubt will ever get credit for the constant, unremitting labor he has devoted to making his son President."

"October 7, 1960
"Jacksonville, Florida
"It was our anniversary today but I almost forgot it this morning when I telephoned Joe . . . as I am campaigning now. Had planned to take a plane but ran into an electric storm just before Jacksonville so decided to stay here all night. I went to headquarters this morning and photos were taken. As they were last night on arrival, although I had not expected them and I was in flat shoes and a tweed coat. With my hair windblown, after having been matted down half the day by perspiration from the television lights and from the humidity which seems to pervade the South at this time of the year.

"I have been thinking all day of Jack and his debate with Nixon and praying, praying, praying. It must be such a strain with all the world watching, waiting, and then reacting, and discussing, criticizing.

"The immediate reactions, I suppose, depend upon the community. Like Hot Springs" (I was there during the first debate) "where most people said the debate was even because Hot Springs has a strongly Republican audience who did not discuss it in an analytical way.

"But so many women in the reception lines in the days since then seem to regard Jack almost like a new Lincoln. 'Thank you for giving us someone like your son,' or 'I am praying for your son every night,' or 'I heard his speech and I just know that he is going to save this country,' or 'I am a Presbyterian (or Methodist, or Baptist) and I'm for your son.' Others might say with a giggle, 'I love your son,' or 'I touched him. He is so good-looking.' "

"October 8

"I watched Jack last night on the debate, praying through every sentence. As I had prayed during the day. He looked more assured than Nixon and looked better physically. Jack seemed to have all the initiative and once or twice rose to inspiring heights of oratory. . . . Jack really looks, sounds, and acts like young Lincoln . . ." (A mother's reaction, a mother's pride.)

"October 9

"The policeman came into the hairdresser's and said comment was that Jack had won the debate, or rather people had liked him better.

"People think that Jack speaks too fast. I agree and have already told him, because the audience has to become accustomed to his Boston accent as well as to the inflections and the modulations of his voice. The newspapers have also commented on this."

It has often been said that the series of debates tilted the election in Jack's favor and were the crucial factor of the campaign. If so, it was an odd turnabout. For Mr. Nixon had been the star of his college debating team, a lawyer trained in presenting evidence and making rebuttals, a naval intelligence officer trained in the art of gathering and presenting information, a Vice-President, and an extremely skillful as well as long-seasoned speaker in national campaigns. Jack had avoided public speaking during his school years. He began his career as a speechmaker in 1946 as a congressman. He learned to speak effectively through constant practice. I think this is another reason why Jack's career—his development and his victories in the face of challenge—should be an inspiration to young men who have had years of perplexity and self-doubt before deciding who they are, and what they want to become.

While I was watching the debates and was hoping and praying for Jack at every point or riposte he made, I found myself wondering about Richard Nixon's mother, who was watching and listening somewhere and was just as involved emotionally as I was. From everything I had heard she was a fine woman and devoted mother—who had suffered the tragic loss of a child—and was firm in the faith and principles of her Quakerism. Of course she had the same love and hopes for her son as I had for mine; and, as I saw Jack doing so extremely well, my sympathies were also with her.

The evening of Election Day we were all at Hyannis Port waiting for the returns to come in. Bobby's house had been converted into election headquarters. It looked and often sounded chaotic—teletype machines clattering, telephones ringing, television sets going, typewriters clicking, and people walking around with pencils and pieces of paper in their hands and talking with other people earnestly about something that was happening someplace around the country and what that might mean. There were lots of people. The whole top echelon of the campaign staff; the expert analysts, newspaper reporters, photographers, stenographers, telephone operators, and many others. Bobby was in the middle of it all. Jack was in and out. Teddy, Steve, Sarge, Peter, the girls, the cousins, friends; everybody was working and not interfering with anybody else. For once there wasn't much kidding or much gaiety. The race was extremely close, and there was tension in the air. Now and then people came over to our house for a sandwich or a drink or a change of scene. Jack would come in to tell his father about a new development. And Joe and I would be wandering in and out of Bobby's house. He and I had very little conversation that evening. He was trying to get the latest exact figures and to project from them how the counts in critical districts were likely to develop. I didn't want to interrupt his train of thought. I went over to see Jackie a couple of times because she was rather alone at her house, out of the melee because she was in the eighth month of pregnancy. Jack was deeply preoccupied.

I was moving around a lot. For me, movement and activity have always been necessities in times of stress. People have asked me if I prayed. I'm sure I did, even though it was a little late for that after the polls had closed. But I pray instinctively—instead of talking to myself or burdening others—it's my natural reaction.

I couldn't bear to think that Jack would lose. In spite of the uncertainties, the figures that shifted back and forth all that evening and into the night I kept thinking, he'll win, of course he will. Finally, late that night, after the tide seemed to have swung in his favor, I went to bed in order to be rested enough to be somewhat prepared for the outcome, whatever it would be.

I'm sure everyone who was there has a store of special memories. Eunice:

"It was very long. Everybody would be walking back and forth from house to house. Jack was over at our father's house a lot, and back to Bobby's to see what was on there, and now and then over to his house to check there, and to sit and rest awhile.

"There were a lot of people and a lot of discussion of votes in each state. We were behind in Illinois, and everybody was waiting for Chicago. Returns from the West Coast came in sometime early the next morning (because of the time difference). There were a few hours of sleep for most people, but we were still walking around—I ran into Jack and asked him if he had won and he said, 'We don't know yet, we haven't heard from California'—or maybe it was still Chicago—'so it's not over yet.' And made some funny remark. He had his walking stick and was going for a walk on the beach.

"There was a general air of confidence. Of course, you're never sure of anything. But we always thought we were going to win."

I think the outcome must have been decided sometime toward daybreak because it was around four-thirty, as I learned later, that the Secret Service men closed in around our adjoining properties and particularly around Jack's house, taking over the protection of the presumed President-elect.

Pat (in a letter, much later):

"I remember that around 3 A.M., when it looked good for Jack—later reversed, but then reversed again—we all went into the kitchen for something to eat. Jack left later by the kitchen door and I can see him now, crossing into Bobby's back lawn in the dark, walking to his own house, and the Secret Service closing in right behind him. A couple of us said (hardly able to believe it): 'Good night, Mr. President.'"

Later that morning, when it was clear that Jack was indeed the President-elect, it was, of course, essential that he address the nation through the press and television. Arrangements had been made at the U.S. Armory in Hyannis. Cars assembled to carry Jack, his family, and his staff members there.

Pat remembers:

"We all got into the caravan of cars in the circle in front of the house—everybody but Dad, who was on the front porch, back a little in the shadows, looking very happy. He never wanted even to imply any credit to himself for Jack's successes, and he had decided to stay at home out of the range of photographers and reporters. Jack suddenly realized what was happening. He got out of the car, went back up to the porch, and told Dad to come along and hear his speech. Jack insisted on it. And finally he talked Daddy into getting into our car."

At the armory, Jack's audience consisted of the press, TV crews, and a small crowd of townspeople.

Toward the end of perhaps the busiest, most exciting months of our lives, we closed the house in Hyannis Port for the winter and made the annual migration to Palm Beach.

We had Thanksgiving at Palm Beach and needless to say it was a day of very special thanksgiving. Jack and Jackie and Caroline couldn't be with us because by then the new baby was due to arrive at almost any time, and Jackie remained near her own doctor and hospital in Washington. John Fitzgerald Kennedy, Jr., was born early in the morning of November 25, to the great relief and joy of all, especially Jack, who adored Caroline, but also wanted a son.

Jack stayed on in Washington through early December, busily occupied in selecting his Cabinet and other high officials for his Administration. Yet he also found time to pay attention to Caroline and visit Jackie and baby John two or three times a day. The baby had been delivered by Caesarean operation, which of course meant that Jackie's recovery from childbirth took longer than usual. However, by December 9 she was well enough to travel, and he brought her and the baby and Caroline, and a nurse and nursemaid aboard the family plane, the *Caroline*, to stay with us during the Christmas and New Year's holidays and until we all went back north for the inauguration. He was at the house for a long weekend, then had to return to Washington, then came back, and was back and forth several times (with flocks of Secret Service men and swarms of journalists) during the next four or five weeks.

I have an extraordinarily vivid memory of Jack visiting the White House on an official courtesy call and being advised by President Eisenhower about current important matters of state. The retiring President met the new one at the White House steps. They shook hands, smiled, stood together, and chatted a minute or so for the photographers and then President Eisenhower—looking, I thought, rather like a kindly uncle turning over the keys of the manor to a bright and well-favored nephew—escorted Jack inside.

It was then at last, in that one small episode seen on television, that I really realized fully that Jack was going to be the President.

This may seem strange, but Joe, who was somewhere else, saw the same news program and told me later he had had exactly the same reaction. The almost impossible dream had come true.

During the intervals with us at Palm Beach Jack was almost as busy as in Washington, meeting and talking with all sorts of people, putting his government together, working on his inaugural address, issuing announcements, and answering questions at daily press conferences. Often he conducted the latter almost anyplace around the house or grounds, but if it were a formal conference with a large group from various media it would most likely be held on the spacious patio at the back of the house—where so often, in earlier, quieter times we had enjoyed dining al fresco at a few small tables and staying on, with a few guests and the household staff, to watch a film. One of these big conferences took place late in December at the time of Senator William Fulbright's visit. He was chairman of the Senate's Foreign Relations Committee, and there had been a lot of speculation that he might be the new Secretary of State. I have some diary notes:

"After a game of golf, Jack and Senator Fulbright came in through the back door, showered, and then went out to the patio, which was bright with klieg lights and full of cameramen and reporters, about fifty of them. The camera people kept moving around and the reporters asked a lot of questions which Jack and Fulbright, looking showered and spick-and-span, answered with poise and good humor. Ann Gargan was visiting us. She and I stayed in the upper balcony, hidden in the dark, and watched.

"I had met Senator Fulbright earlier in the day, found him charming, relaxed, easy to talk to, and very interesting. Mrs. Fulbright joined us for dinner. Looks attractive, conservative, middle-aged, and intelligent. Liked her, as she was pleasant and natural and contributed to the conversation without intruding." (I have always felt that men have expert knowledge of their jobs and a grasp of the factors that influence them. But women can be invaluable in bringing a fresh viewpoint to a conversation.)

There was a continual stream of guests, all of them notables of some degree, which kept me in a state of hyperactivity. I'm sure I went around much of the time covered with notes from myself to myself. It was a hectic time for the help. They all bore up bravely and cheerfully, showing initiative and gallantry under fire. Evelyn Jones recalls some episodes:

"One day Mr. Johnson, who was going to be Mr. Jack's Vice-President, and Mr. Sam Rayburn and several others were coming. Mr. Johnson and Mr. Rayburn would be in the house; that was an understanding already made, but the question became, which rooms?

"We were working on this the day before, and Mrs. Jack wanted Caroline next to her, in an adjoining room in that suite. But we had already discussed and decided the only way was to put Rayburn in Mrs. Kennedy's room and put Mr. Johnson in the next one—Mrs. Kennedy insisted he go in the next one and share the bath with the nurse and the baby—and you know how that would have been. The other alternative was to move Caroline and the nurse up to the adjoining bath with the other nurse and the baby, but she didn't want that.

"The next morning when I came to work everything was in a furor. I said, 'What's going on?' The cook, Matilda, said, '*The Johnsons are at the airport and they'll be here for breakfast!*' Not he, but the Johnsons. So I said, 'Well, all right, you take care of breakfast, and I'll see what I can do.'

"Well, after quite a few other complications we finally did get everyone arranged or rearranged, and Mr. Jack said to me, 'Oh, that's fine. Good. Good, and thank you, Evelyn, very much.'

"But then guess what happened? Senator Mike Mansfield flew down later that day to join in the meetings with the others, and Jack invited him to spend the night at the house.

"There was no place to put him except in one of those small rooms in the back, the area the architect designed as servants' quarters in the early days when people at Palm Beach used to have a lot of live-in help. He didn't mind at all. They're nice rooms. But the layout of the house is confusing to someone who doesn't know it. And after the meetings, when he came back into the house late that night, and one of the Secret Service boys showed him the way through the back entrance and through to the back stairway, he went on up from there in the dark, not wanting to disturb anybody, and opened the first door on his left, which he remembered was the one to his room. He lit a match to find the light switch and heard a woman's tense voice calling, 'Who's there?' Mrs. Jack's Swedish masseuse was sitting up in the bed with the covers drawn up around her and a frightened look on her face.

"As I heard the story next day he said something apologetic and got out of there as fast as he could, into the room next door, which was his room. I expect that's one of the first events of the Kennedy administration that Senator Mansfield has always remembered."

The house was in a state of happy chaos. Here are a couple of other diary notes of mine that will help demonstrate both the happiness and the chaos:

"January 4, 1961

"The photographer from *Harper's Bazaar*, Richard Avedon, has been here to take pictures of Jackie. Also with him two young women, one of whom I heard later was the sister of Leonard Bernstein, the young conductor of the New York Philharmonic. Kenneth, the hairdresser from New York, came down to do Jackie's hair. A fitter from Cassini, the dressmaker, appeared, carrying long boxes containing Jackie's dresses, most of which were not yet finished but were advanced enough for photos.

"She is still convalescing and rests in between. She looks marvelous, as her figure is much better than previously, I believe.

"Jack came in—freshly shaven, handsome, well-groomed, poised. The next thing I knew Caroline was romping about, all dressed up in an adorable white organdy dress and a pink ribbon in her hair. She had been outside with her nurse awaiting the call for pictures. The most precious addition was yet to come—John F. Jr., who looked infinitely adorable as he lay cuddled in his mother's arms being photographed. As it was rather a cool day I worried that he would get cold, because his head was exposed for a long time in the living room, which has no heat and which may be drafty, although the photographer's big screen probably cut off a lot of the draft.

"It seemed that the house was full of dressmakers and photographers and assistants. A lot of milling around.

"LeMoyne Billings is here. I heard Jack say to him afterward, 'Well, that was certainly a morning wasted.' "

"January 5

"I was going to make an appointment for myself with the hairdresser downtown when Joe told me that Kenneth was here again, and Avedon and the same screen and same personnel appeared all over again, much to my surprise, as no one told me they were coming.

"Jackie and Jack have the bedroom downstairs in the extreme corner of the house, which is Jack's old room. She has to rest. She is reading all these books from the Library of Congress on the White House. She has just written a very good article, 'How to Bring Up a Child to Be Happy.' One thing that she suggested was the merit of learning a piece of poetry for the mother's birthday present or drawing a picture, no matter how crude. Both ideas stimulate the child and encourage its interest and please the mother, and they are simple pleasures that can be developed in any home. A marvelous idea and one which had never occurred to me.

"Well, anyway, I dashed downstairs, found Kenneth in Jackie's room just setting her hair on mammoth-sized rollers. He said for me to shampoo my hair upstairs, and then he would set it. Which he proceeded to do. It looked very well until I played golf in the afternoon. Meanwhile, I had to sit under the dryer in the guest room, next door to where Jack and Lem were staying; so while I sat, the maid packed Jack's clothes, LeMoyne dashed in and out opening doors, and Kenneth dashed in to see if I was dry.

"After my hair had been set and combed out I had to walk back through the living room in my long blue bathrobe. I nodded to one of the photographer's assistants and warned her about the loose neckline on Jackie's half-finished velvet dress. I looked out the window to the front lawn and saw someone was swinging Caroline, of which I disapproved, as I thought she would be too tired for the photographers. Then I took a quick look at John F. Jr., wrapped in blankets and awaiting his turn to be photographed. And I caught a glimpse of the Secret Service men on the beach outside on the ocean front.

"Boxes are piled galore in the back part of the house, presents for Jackie and the baby, mostly for the baby, and everything had to be opened first and examined by the Secret Service. None very expensive but all appreciated as sincere tokens.

"If I go into the study, Jack probably is in there in conference. If I want to go out the front door to the street, the door is locked behind me almost before I get out. There are policemen and Secret Service men there, and often a crowd of fifty to a hundred people gathered in hopes of seeing Jack.

"The back door is also always locked now. None of this makes too much difference to me except I am a bit confused as to where I should come and go. If I go out my front door, there are people there having their pictures taken. Last night I went out the back way through the help's dining room, and there was a hairdresser from the town delving into a bowl of salad. Evidently, she had waited quite a while to do somebody's hair and was hungry, and the salad bowl was on the maids' table, and they had disappeared to their respective duties. I was dumbfounded, and she was doubly so at seeing me, and seeing me exiting through the servants' quarters. She just threw up her hands and I gave a laugh and she gave a laugh and out I went."

Not long afterward, Jack and Jackie and their family went back to their house in Georgetown. Bobby and Ethel lived about half an hour away in McLean, Virginia. The rest of us, when we assembled at the scene a few days before Inauguration Day, which was January 20, lived in Steve and Jean's house in Georgetown or in another house nearby which we rented. Joe and I had Teddy and Joan and Ann Gargan with us at our house.

It began to snow the afternoon before the inauguration. And it snowed and snowed and turned into one of the worst snowstorms in the history of Washington. By evening, traffic was hopelessly snarled, cars were sliding and struggling through the drifts, and many were stalled, immobilized and abandoned.

Pat and Peter and some of their friends in the entertainment world had worked long and hard to organize a preinaugural variety show—a "gala"—directed by Roger Edens that had celebrated performers, including Sir Laurence Olivier, Alan King, Helen Traubel, Leonard Bernstein, Ella Fitzgerald, Sidney Poitier, Ethel Merman, and many others, who would be contributing their names and services to honor the new President. Obviously, Joe and I wanted to be there and should somehow manage to despite the incredible weather. I have a vision of Joe and me and Ann Gargan (Teddy and Joan were off in another car) in a big, powerful, official car being driven through the black January night and enveloped in great, white, fluffy snowflakes, which were quite beautiful but limited visibility to a few yards and progress to a few miles an hour. In the front seat, with the driver, was a man with a snow shovel. Every now and then, when the drifts and the churned-up snow slush had us in jeopardy, he would put on his gloves, hunch his coat collar up, seize the shovel, and go out and extricate us. I was so amused by the situation and preoccupied with wondering whether we would actually get to our destination that I didn't learn his name or anything else about him. Yet in my memory he remains one of the heroes of the evening.

The gala was excellent, though a bit disjointed because half the performers had been stuck or delayed in the snow and arrived at random times. The show continued until early morning, and Jack and his father stayed through the final number. I left around midnight, knowing I would be getting up for early Mass and that the day was sure to be a long one. An after-theater party had been arranged by Joe at one of the Washington restaurants. Jack felt he ought to attend, with the result that he couldn't have been home in bed for some sleep until after 4 A.M. Not the amount of sleep I recommended for his Inauguration Day.

By daylight that morning the storm was spent, or nearly so, but had left a thick blanket of snow and a cold, wet wind. Our rented house was only half a mile or so from the nearest Catholic church, and since I am accustomed to walking, except when the weather is really impossible, I decided to walk to Mass, though one look outside showed me that the sidewalks were buried and I would have to trudge up the middle of the street. I put on galoshes and a heavy coat and thick gloves and a couple of woolen scarves, including one tied over and around my head, babushka style, and took off for church.

As I approached I noticed a great many policemen outside, police cars, and other unmarked cars occupied by anonymous-looking men, whom I automatically thought of as Secret Service agents. Suddenly it occurred to me that Jack must be coming there for Mass.

I asked one of the policemen if President-elect Kennedy was expected, and he gave me a kind but guarded look and said he didn't know, maybe so. I went inside and sat near the rear in a side aisle. A few minutes later Jack came in and sat in one of the middle aisles toward the front.

I hadn't suggested to him that he go to Mass that morning. Jackie wasn't with him, because she was still convalescing from the birth of John Jr. I realized that he was there of his own volition: that he wanted to start his presidency by offering his mind and heart, and expressing his hopes and fears, to Almighty God, and asking His blessing as he began his great duties. He didn't know I was there and I didn't want to go and sit with him, bundled up as I was in my scarves and galoshes. I just followed the Mass and, from a distance, looked at him very happily.

Nor did I come to him after Mass, because I knew there would be photographers ready to pop pictures of any personal encounter, and I wanted no picture taken of him with me in my regalia. However, since I had already come plowing through the snow and it was an hour later and I had many things to do that morning to get ready for the ceremonies, I thought it would be an advantage if I could get a ride back to my house. I went over to one of the Secret Service men and said, "I am Mrs. Kennedy, the President's mother. Will you please have someone come with a car and pick me up and take me to my house?" He nodded. But no car came. Evidently he thought I was either an impostor or demented—because I certainly didn't look like a President's mother.

After waiting awhile, I walked home. It was no hardship, accustomed as I had been to New England winters, although I would have welcomed a ride.

The rest of that day is somewhat blurred in my memory because so much was happening, with one stupendous scene following another. My emotions were deeply involved because it all centered on my son. It was overwhelming. The scenes need no description here—they were photographed and written about endlessly. What I can add are some personal notes and thoughts, and some details that may be interesting or amusing.

I have already described Jack's steadfast aversion to hats. There had been a long tradition for more than a century that the men involved in the inaugural ceremonies, except for the military, wear some version of the "top hat." General Eisenhower, for his two inaugurations, wore a black Homburg. For his inaugural, Jack changed back to the top hat. Whether because of his respect for history and for the dignity of the event and the degree of formality it implied, or influenced by Jackie's sense of style and decorum, it was part of the costume of the day. The assortment of top hats that turned up was extraordinary. (Mrs. Eisenhower, seeing the former President in his top hat, remarked that he looked like Paddy the Irishman.)

As for Jack, I later saw photographs of him in which he was wearing or waving his own top hat, and I have fleeting memories of scenes in which he actually kept it on his head for a while, but nearly all the time he either carried it at his side, or stuck it under a chair, or turned it over to somebody to take care of until the next unwelcome moments when it would be necessary to put it back on.

In the inaugural seating arrangements at the Capitol Plaza, Jack and Jackie were, of course, front and center with President and Mrs. Eisenhower and flanked by the Johnsons and Nixons, the two vice-presidential couples, and surrounded by the leaders of the Court, the Congress, the military services, and the diplomatic corps. Although Joe and I and our niece Ann Gargan were in the front row on the Kennedy-Johnson side, we were at the end, and since the photographers were focusing on the middle we were left out of everything except the panoramic pictures. I have never seen one in which I am recognizable; in fact, some friends asked me later where I had been during the ceremonies. I have always wished I had a picture of me with my son when he was being inaugurated President.

Joe and I were close enough so that we could have exchanged some words with Jack in the minutes after he came down the Capitol steps, under escort of notables, and took his place. But we didn't do that. We stood and applauded him, as everyone else did, and as we took our seats we gave each other a squeeze of the hand, with no need or desire for words because everything was understood in this moment.

My mother, who was in her mid-nineties, was living with my brother Tom's family, and was too frail for the trip from Boston to Washington. Her eyesight had begun to fail but she could see well enough to watch television, and I knew what a thrill and satisfaction it must have been for her as she saw her grandson with his right hand upraised, his left resting on the Fitzgerald family Bible (Jack had sent two Secret Service men to get it), which contains the records of her and my father's marriage and forebears and descendants. One of the few sad thoughts I had during that day was that my father had not lived long enough to rejoice with her and with us. How immeasurably pleased he would have been.

Joe had been a little apprehensive about the inaugural address, not because he doubted Jack's ability to create and deliver one that would be memorable, but because he had so admired the speech Jack had given only a fortnight earlier to a joint session of the Massachusetts legislature, dealing with the same basic ideas that he was bringing to the presidency. Joe wondered if Jack could equal his own eloquence on the same themes so soon afterward, speaking to the nation. Because the speech was delivered to a state audience, it is not as widely remembered as it deserves to be. Next to the inaugural address, it is my favorite among Jack's speeches.

". . . I have been engaged in the task of constructing an Administration. It has been a long and deliberate process. Some have counseled greater speed. Others have counseled more expedient tests. But I have been guided by the standard John Winthrop set before his shipmates on the flagship *Arbella* 331 years ago, as they, too, faced the task of building a government on a new and perilous frontier. 'We must always consider,' he said, 'that we shall be as a city upon a hill— the eyes of all people are upon us.'

"Today, the eyes of all people are truly upon us, and our government, in every branch, at every level, national, state and local, must be as a city upon a hill, constructed and inhabited by men aware of their grave trust and their great responsibilities.

". . . History will not judge our endeavors, and a government cannot be selected, merely on the basis of color or creed or even party affiliation. Neither will competence and loyalty and stature, while essential to the utmost, suffice in times such as these.

"For of those to whom much is given, much is required. And when at some future date the high court of history sits in judgment on each of us, recording whether in our brief span of service we fulfilled our responsibilities to the state, our success or failure, in whatever office we hold, will be measured by the answers to four questions:

"First, were we truly men of courage, with the courage to stand up to one's enemies, and the courage to stand up, when necessary, to one's associates, the courage to resist public pressure as well as private greed?

"Second, were we truly men of judgment, with perceptive judgment of the future as well as the past, of our own mistakes as well as the mistakes of others, with enough wisdom to know what we did not know, and enough candor to admit it?

"Third, were we truly men of integrity, men who never ran out on either the principles in which we believed or the people who believed in us, men whom neither financial gain nor political ambition could ever divert from the fulfillment of our sacred trust?

"Finally, were we truly men of dedication, with an honor mortgaged to no single individual or group, and compromised by no private obligation or aim, but devoted solely to serving the public good and the national interest?

"Courage, judgment, integrity, dedication—these are the historic qualities of the Bay Colony and the Bay State . . . which, with God's help, this son of Massachusetts hopes will characterize our government's conduct in the four stormy years that lie ahead."

I remember their conversation after the Massachusetts speech, with Jack back in Florida and his father complimenting him and saying it was so good he should have saved it for the inaugural address; or, since he hadn't done so, that he might well incorporate some of the best parts of it in the inaugural, because the time was short and Jack would have to have a truly excellent speech ready. And Jack said, "Yes, Dad, I will have," and nodded. His father said, "Well, I hope you're working on a good one, because it should be good—it should be your best." Jack had said, "Yes, Dad." His father took his word for it and didn't ask to see a draft, nor did Jack volunteer to show him; and this, I suppose, was mainly because he kept on revising and polishing it, and was still at it the morning of the inauguration. Hence when he stepped to the rostrum neither his father nor I had more than a general idea of what he would be saying.

As we all know now it was one of the great inaugural addresses in the history of the Republic. Several people reported that when it was over they saw tears glistening in Joe's eyes. Perhaps so. I had been rapt in my own feelings. I was proud, thankful, and humble that I, among the millions of American women of my generation, was the mother of the new President—this confident young leader in whom so many had placed their trust. I thought to myself, what a glorious opportunity he has to mold his country and to influence the whole world. I found myself thinking of those words of St. Luke I had often recited to him: "Of those to whom much has been given, much will be required." I said to myself, drawing on Cardinal Newman's words, "He will do good, he will do God's work."

I felt that Joe and I had given our country a young President whose words, manner, ideas, character, everything about him bespoke future greatness.

After the ceremonies Jack and Jackie, and Lyndon and Lady Bird

Johnson, went into the Capitol to the old Supreme Court Chamber—a most handsome room that had been refitted for such occasions as this—where they were the guests of honor at a luncheon given by the Joint Congressional Inaugural Committee. The guest list was, of course, limited to "official" personages, so Joe and I were not there. (I can understand the nicely considered diplomatic geographical balance between New England boiled stuffed lobster and prime Texas ribs of beef; I can imagine that the dessert *pâtisserie bateau blanche* was a symbolic gesture to Jackie's French ancestry. But what, I wonder, is the political meaning of the first course, cream of tomato soup with crushed popcorn?) Joe and I, and Jackie's family, and various relatives and friends lunched together in a private room at the Mayflower Hotel, and afterward went out to the reviewing stand to watch the inaugural parade.

A few personal notes about that:

The weather continued bitter cold and, in fact, became worse. The reviewing stand was roofed and enclosed on three sides, but, of course, was open across most of the front—ample space for the frigid breezes to sweep in. If we, bundled in our coats, were chilled I hated to think of what must be happening to the marchers: the boys from the service academies, the bandsmen and fife and drum corpsmen, the patriotic and fraternal societies, all those hundreds of groups from near and far. But at least they could keep moving. Worse off were the thousands of spectators lining the streets—especially those who had been lucky enough, they had thought, to have seats in the stands—whose blood must have been slowly congealing. Nevertheless, the parade went on as planned, about three and a half hours, and every unit that came along stepped smartly, looked lively, performed whatever stunts or formations they had practiced and looked as cheerful as on a day in May. Even most of the spectators along the way and in the stands stayed on, risking frostbite. In all, it was a triumph of mind over matter and, I thought, an extraordinary testimonial to the enthusiasm—the warmth, so to speak—that Jack inspired in them.

Jack had given the inaugural address not only hatless—which I suppose could be considered a seemly gesture of respect for the occasion—but also coatless, which struck many people as being far beyond the call of duty or any need to demonstrate "vigor" and dauntlessness. However, since the speech lasted only fourteen minutes it was unlikely he would freeze. Later, during the parade, he was again without an overcoat most of the time. He would slip it on now and then, wear it for five or ten minutes, then off it would come again. I think this was a quite unconscious response to his feeling of excitement. I was reminded of that evening back in 1952 when the returns from the Senate election were coming in and he kept taking off his jacket, then putting it on a bit later, sometimes with the sleeves inside out.

I don't know what the reasons might be, but extremes of heat and cold didn't seem to bother him as much as they did most people. As he stood there in the frigid wind, with no hat, no overcoat, reviewing the great parade, I thought of that boy who in late fall, when the weather was really getting cold, would start out of the house in thin trousers and no sweater; and if I intercepted him and suggested a sweater or jacket he would look back with that disarming smile and say, "Yes, Mother, I'll do that later"—and be on his way.

Bobby was in the reviewing stand as Attorney General. Jack wanted him in that office, their father thought it was a perfect idea; Bobby had resisted for weeks because he feared it would be misunderstood and criticized as nepotism (and criticized it was), but had submitted to the arguments of his brother and father. In any case, I found myself in the position of being the mother of both the President and the Attorney General, which I found rather overwhelming.

That night there was the inaugural ball. In fact, there were five balls at different locations. The big one, at the armory, had a throng of about a thousand people; including Joe and me, other members of the family, and good friends waiting for Jack and Jackie in the presidential box at one end of that great arena. Everyone turned and applauded as they arrived and took their places and smiled at the crowd, and everyone was smiling back at them: There was such a feeling of admiration and warmth that one could almost literally feel a wave of love and pleasure.

Jackie looked perfectly beautiful, and Jack had never looked more handsome. During the grueling months of the campaign and pre-inaugural, tired and often exhausted as he was, he had somehow put on ten or fifteen pounds. I thought of how I used to save the steak juice and any extra portions for him, and stuff him with custards and other healthy desserts; and of how he used to drink rich milk shakes at school and college, hoping to fill out—and now despite all the stress and labor that should theoretically have worn him down he had been built up instead. The life of presidential candidate, President-elect, and now President apparently agreed with him very well. He had lost that lean, Lincolnesque look I had liked, but had gained something I liked better: He looked entirely healthy.

Joe wore the white tie and tails he had seldom worn since the ambassadorship, and had found to his satisfaction that they still fit quite well, nearly twenty years later. I had saved the gown I wore when I had been presented at court and was delighted to find I had not changed in any dimension and I could wear it without alteration; and I did so, in confidence, because it was a classic, timeless design and thus as much "in style" as when Molyneux had made it for me more than twenty years earlier. There were many compliments about it that evening. It is now part of the Smithsonian collection of gowns worn by American women during special events in history.

After the ball, Joe and I returned to our quarters in Georgetown. Jack and Jackie, the President and First Lady, went home to the White House.

We left the next day. We didn't stop for a visit or farewells at the White House. We knew that Jack would be involved in his new duties and obligations; and that Jackie, too, would have a lot to do, and we didn't want to take up any of their time. And so, quietly and happily, we returned to Florida.

Chapter Eighteen

A great tradition can be inherited
but greatness itself must be won.
Winston Churchill

I am a man and therefore whatever
concerns mankind is my concern.
Terence
circa 150 B.C.

"The exercise of vital powers along
lines of excellence in a life affording
them scope" is an old Greek definition
of happiness. It is a conception permeated
with energy of life . . . It led along many
an untried way.

Edith Hamilton

Joe was so determined to avoid any appearance of influencing Jack that he did not set foot in the White House except once during the rest of that year, and even then only for part of a day and evening and at the personal insistence of Jack and Jackie. There is a memorandum to him from his secretary, in advance of the date, which has a couple of charming and evocative little touches:

"Mr. Kennedy:
"Tish Baldridge called to confirm the following:
"Jackie is most anxious to have you visit all the grandchildren at

the White House down by the duck pond. All the children will have had their naps, and she is bringing Caroline in from Glen Ora.

"President JFK would be delighted if you would lunch with him.

"They also confirm dinner with Robert and President Jack for 7:30. Jackie asks if she could possibly sit quietly in the corner—and be included for dinner."

If the world were as logical a place as one would hope, Joe's reluctance to be seen in Washington in those times seems illogical. After all, both the U.S. mails and the telephone system still functioned, and anything his father wanted to say to Jack could be said by those means. And, in fact, there was a lively correspondence between the President and his father, and they talked by telephone several times a week and sometimes several times a day; though mostly the calls were about personal or family matters, or matters of information that Jack knew his father could provide. There was also, now and then, advice that Jack solicited, or his father felt was really worth offering about matters of state. But if we had taken a house in Washington (there had been rumors, totally unfounded, that we would) each time Joe went to the White House to see his grandchildren there would have been speculative news reports that he had gone to give Jack advice about how to run the government. So his absence from the scene was probably necessary.

But I suffered no such strictures. Indeed, I suppose my absence would have been a cause for comment. In any case I was lucky enough (an unforeseen additional blessing of motherhood) to be at the White House now and then.

When I was there I often used to walk on the lawn, pausing occasionally to peek at Jack at his desk in his study, which was located in a bright sunny corner on the ground floor. On two sides it has long window doors. He could look out and see Caroline, and later baby John, playing close by; and when he had a few minutes he could go out and join them.

Mrs. Paul Mellon, encouraged by Jackie, donated the large and lovely rose garden. Jack could see this from his windows, too, and would go outside when he felt like a breath of air and stroll among the scented plants. Wherever we lived we had always had

gardens: from zinnias and marigolds and the hardiest annual back-
yard garden flowers at Beals Street, to the tropical exotics at Palm
Beach and the fine roses and old-fashioned beds of colorful mixed
annuals at Hyannis Port (the source of those bouquets that Ethel
mentioned as one of her first memories of us). Jack took both pride
and interest in the rose garden. He wanted to know the varieties. He
also had ideas about the juxtaposition of colors, and if there were
yellow leaves or other signs of distress he wanted to know what
ought to be done and who would take care of it. I must say I was a
bit surprised, for I never had heard nor seen him demonstrate any
interest in horticulture at home.

When I visited the White House I stayed the first few times in
the Queen's Room, but then later on usually in the Lincoln Room.
Each had its interesting and attractive qualities, along with a few
disadvantages. Both are suites of sitting room, bedroom, and bath.
In the Queen's Room there is—or was when I was there—a four-
poster canopied bed done in lovely chintz and taffeta, with the other
furniture and the drapes mostly in chintz also: everything in harmonious colors and designs, and comfortable and feminine. The
ideas carried through also, in a somewhat more formal way, into the
sitting room or reception room, which gave this room a sense of
spacious ease and comfort along with just the right degree of elegance. As I recall, all this was largely Jackie's idea. The sitting room
also had a quite good-looking convertible couch, or day bed, which
in need could be folded out to accommodate a child or nursemaid
or extra family guest.

On the other hand, it gets very little morning sun, and since I am
an early riser that was not to my liking. Further, the view from the
windows is of Pennsylvania Avenue, a most noble name with many
historic associations but, I'm sorry to say, visually rather drab.

The Lincoln Room—which I daresay is just the same now as it was
then and had been—received a lot more sun, but even so always
seemed a bit damp, probably because the ceilings were so high it was
difficult to heat; while also, in the warm weather, it was not easy to
get air because the windows were so long and heavy they were hard
to raise or lower. The furniture is dark, austere, and rather massive,
the style of those mid-nineteenth-century times. I remember, for

instance, the bed being so high that I, being short, had first to mount a bedside stool, and from there levitate up onto the bed, and that it was something of an adventure every time. The dressing tables included what apparently were some of the first electric lights ever installed. This wouldn't matter to a man but did for a woman; so every time I wanted to put on my make-up for the evening and inspect my coiffure and decide on a necklace or brooch I would do so in the bathroom, where the lighting was twentieth century.

But I preferred the Lincoln Room for my own reasons, which mainly involved the view. Any time I looked out those long and heavy windows I could see the Washington Monument; simple, straight, pointing directly to the sky. I could see also the children's playground down below just beyond the rose garden and I often watched them and some of their little playmates on the swings and slides; or, in the winter, watched as Jackie drove them around that part of the grounds in a sleigh pulled by Caroline's pony Macaroni. Then too in any season—away from the rose garden and the children's play area but still in view—there was the frequent drama of the presidential helicopters. One of Jack's innovations was to have distinguished visitors such as heads of foreign governments met by protocol officers at the Washington airport and then transferred to helicopters and flown directly to the White House grounds. An honor guard would be drawn up there in smart formation and full-dress uniforms. Passing through this corridor of splendid-looking young men, the visitor would come to the front entrance of the White House where Jack would be waiting on the steps to greet him.

The first time the drama was put on it turned into something of a comedy, because the strong air currents from the helicopter blades blew off a lot of the hats of the honor guard and there was a scramble of guardsmen chasing hats and trying to get back into line. From then on they were held at a discreet distance until the machine landed, and everything went as it was supposed to; always an impressive and exciting scene.

As I mentioned, the Lincoln Room is actually a bedroom and sitting-room suite. I spent a good deal of time in the sitting room, reading the papers, taking breakfast and often other meals, and writing notes and cards to friends and relations who, I knew, would treasure a personal communication from the White House.

Of course I was at family meals when the White House schedule of the day allowed simple, informal family meals to occur. And if I happened to be there at the time of a state dinner of formal entertainment I would always be included if I wished to be. Apparently this raised a matter of official protocol, which I had never even thought about until I began doing this book.

At an official function, or even a private one where dignitaries are present, there has to be some order of precedence in entering, leaving, seating, and so forth; otherwise there would be confusion and embarrassment; and, thus, protocol is, so it seems to me, just an extension of such a useful amenity as putting place cards at a luncheon or dining or bridge table—it makes life really far more simple for everyone involved.

People in official positions soon learn to take the whole thing for granted. There are staff assistants who know who is coming to an official luncheon or state banquet, let us say, and who communicate with other assistants or secretaries who pass on to you the necessary information such as that Mrs. Joseph P. Kennedy is to be escorted to dinner by Ambassador So-and-So from Someplace, and in the order of procedure will follow HRH the Crown Prince of Something; and on the scene there will be somebody to introduce the ambassador and point out the crown prince in case you haven't met them, as probably you haven't. I was so used to all this, from our time at the embassy in London, and from much else I have related, that I simply followed the instructions and didn't bother to wonder about my exact rank in protocol as the President's mother. And I believe that the protocol people had to burrow back through the archives to find precedents and decide what to do about me because not many mothers of Presidents had been alive when their sons took office and fewer still had been at formal White House functions. But they finally decided they would have to give me some position because I was or might be there. I have now inquired and discovered where I belonged: where the mother of a President belongs—at least until they change the rules:

She belongs behind the President and the First Lady, behind the

Vice-President and his wife, behind the Justices of the Supreme Court and their wives, behind the Speaker of the House and his wife, but ahead of all the members of the Senate and House, the Cabinet, the military establishment, the diplomatic corps, and all the rest, and their respective wives.

Twice (when Jackie was unable to be there because she was expecting their son Patrick, and after his death), Jack asked me to substitute for her as his official hostess at state dinners. One was for President and Señora Arosmena of Ecuador; the other was for Emperor Haile Selassie of Ethiopia. On those occasions, escorted by my son, the President, I was automatically advanced to first in precedence. Needless to say, I felt aglow with honor and pride and excitement—along with feeling slightly like Cinderella, knowing that my high and glamorous position would vanish with the end of the party and I would be reduced in rank from First Lady to mother-in-law of the First Lady.

Incidentally, the Emperor and I discovered that not only were we contemporaries, but had birthdays within a day of each other. We decided that sometime we must arrange to celebrate our birthdays together. And actually—unlike most such socially inspired spontaneous great ideas—we later did.

Another rather odd matter of official manners: When your son is President, how do you address him and how do you refer to him in conversations with others, and under what circumstances would you change from one mode of nomenclature to another?

Obviously, this is not a common problem but it was one that Joe and I suddenly found ourselves encountering; as did his brothers and sisters and relatives and friends and associates, in some degree. The dignity of the office is such that there is an automatic mental shifting of gears, so to speak, and people who had been on first-name, nickname terms with him felt constrained to address him as "Mr. President" and mention him even in conversations among themselves as "the President." Dave Powers says that even when they were splashing around together in the White House pool and Dave was entertaining him with his endless supply of jokes and anecdotes, it was still the same: It was "Mr. President." For the family, however, there were a few complications which were resolved—more or less —as follows.

Whenever we were with him in any official or public setting we addressed him as "Mr. President," just as everyone else was supposed to do. In a conversation with anyone in such a setting we spoke of him as "the President" or "President Kennedy." (Bobby would do the same, by the way, at Cabinet meetings.) We would do this also with members of his staff and official family and leaders of Congress and other dignitaries, public and private.

When it was just the family, or family and very close friends, he was still "Jack" or the family's favorite nickname for him, "Johnny."

I'm sure he couldn't have cared less except insofar as nomenclature might affect the honor of the presidency as an institution. He did care about that. Otherwise, he took it all in stride, with his usual humor and modesty.

One reason for my bringing up this topic is that all of us, and I too—I who used to whack him on the britches when he was a naughty little boy—became so used to referring to him in public as the President or as President Kennedy that I still do now and then, even in family and personal correspondence in my diary.

One hears about the burdens of the presidency.

It seemed to me that—most of the time—Jack enjoyed his presidency enormously. I think the challenges of the office excited him, and that he was exhilarated by the opportunities it could give him to do what he could for his country. He increased in eloquence, wisdom, poise, and confidence, and—to my special satisfaction—in physical health. Not since earliest childhood had he been so robust as he was in those last three years; a factor that made his death not only so tragic but so ironic.

But, of course, there were burdens, and are and always will be so long as the country and the office exist. They can be terrible; and, of course, Jack was fully sensitive to them. But by the time he was President he had developed such poise that he could not be overwhelmed and bore his trials with the same determination and grace as he had borne his illnesses. I was an inadvertent witness to this quality on the very day of the first crisis of his presidency:

"April 19, 1961
"The White House
"Phoned Joe, who said Jack had been on the phone with him much of the day, also Bobby. I asked him how he was feeling and he said 'dying'—result of trying to bring up Jack's morale after the Cuban debacle.

"That night, anyway, Jack and Jackie and I went to dinner at Greek embassy as previously arranged. Many people outside the embassy. Greek ambassador came down steps to meet the President, much as we had come outside to meet the King when he came to London embassy. Many photographs. I wore pink chiffon dress made by Greek designer Dessès. Jackie in white satin sheath by Cassini. Hairdresser had come to White House before the dinner to give combing out.

"After dinner, Jackie and I chatted with women awhile. Then joined the men for a short time as Jack wanted to leave. Throughout dinner and evening, and way there and back, he had seemed his usual self, quite composed, gave no hint of worries until back at the White House when he said, 'Good night' to me in car and rushed to his office.

"Jackie walked upstairs with me and said he'd been so upset all day. Had practically been in tears, felt he had been misinformed by CIA and others. I felt so sorry for him. Jackie so sympathetic and said she had stayed with him until he had lain down that afternoon for a short nap. Said she had never seen him so depressed except at time of his operation . . ."

It happened that I was present, on the sidelines, at the first great triumph of his presidency. This came soon, only about ten weeks later, in early June of that year, in Paris and then Vienna at the time of his meetings with President de Gaulle and Chairman Khrushchev.

When I say "happened" I mean it literally since a U.S. President is not under obligation to have his mother nearby while consulting with other heads of states. Yet, ever since the late twenties and early thirties, I had been going to Paris in the spring almost every year, the war years of course excepted. I went because I love the city especially at that season, and because I wanted to look at the spring collections at the fashion houses and pick out a few things that I felt becoming, and thought Joe would like, to wear on special occasions during the season ahead. Usually I would go over around the middle of May and, since it takes several fittings for a dress to be perfect, would stay on through early June.

Jack knew from boyhood that this was part of my yearly schedule, which I would not like to change, especially as I was now the mother of the President and would be making appearances at the White House and diplomatic receptions and would want to look my best. So there it was. He and I would be in Paris during part of the state visit. So the State Department had to find some way to involve me in the festivities, even though I would not be officially part of the presidential party.

I almost missed seeing Jack and Jackie's arrival at Orly Airport. Inasmuch as I was unofficial it was explained to me that there seemed to be no way to work me into the official reception committee—headed by President and Mme. de Gaulle, which would be driving to Orly in a fleet of cars. I asked if I could go along, unofficially, and sit and wait in one of the cars so I could see and hear the welcome and reception of my son. This was permitted. But the concession apparently upset the precision of the French official logic, because at the airport I was invited to the pavilion where the others had assembled.

General and Mme. de Gaulle arrived and I was presented to them. I sat on the presidential divan a few minutes with Mme. de Gaulle, and we exchanged the usual pleasantries about the impressive ceremonies attending Jack's arrival, and my excitement and pleasure at his being in Paris, and about children.

It was a beautiful morning. At about 10 A.M.—on time—the gleaming, graceful form of Air Force One glided down from the sky and taxied to the mark at the end of a long red carpet. Jack came down the steps first and was greeted by De Gaulle and a delegation of other high officials. As the honor guard saluted, they strode to the pavilion followed by Jackie and the presidential group. Jack made a short, eloquent speech expressing his pleasure at being in France. Then he and Jackie circulated among the welcoming party, being introduced and exchanging greetings with those they knew. I thought he looked a little surprised when he spotted me, but he gave me a big grin. Yet I expect he wasn't very surprised, even when three chairs were brought forward and I was asked to sit with Mme. de Gaulle and Jackie while the photographers and television crews clicked and popped and whirred away at us together.

On the way from the airport, as soon as we entered Paris we found the streets lined with throngs of people—shopkeepers, factory workers, housewives, people of all sorts including a great many children waving little American flags; nearly all of them looking very friendly and rather excited. I will always remember those thousands of faces full of welcome and those miles of smiles. Apparently—so I was told—there had been few times, if any, when the Parisians had demonstrated such a spontaneous friendly interest in visitors from abroad. I rode in a car with Mrs. Gavin, the wife of our ambassador to France, and with Mme. Alphand, the wife of France's ambassador to the United States.

That evening there was a dinner for a hundred and fifty at Versailles, which with its furnishings and courtyards and sweeping balustrades and fabulous fountains and perfect grounds is undoubtedly the most beautiful and most impressive of all great palaces in the world. The banquet was in the Hall of Mirrors, which again was an extraordinary tribute to Jack and Jackie—and Franco-American friendship—for it is very rare in these times that it is used for state entertainments. I knew in advance that I would be invited to this grand event so I had prepared myself with a new evening gown, which of course was French. Jackie, in her new role as a leader of American fashion, had been wearing only clothes from American designers (winning the adoration of the American fashion industry), but tactfully this time broke her rule by having a gown designed and made for her by the French designer Givenchy. She looked absolutely stunning that evening—and never less than marvelous during the whole visit—and with her French maiden name, her command of the country's language, and familiarity with its customs and civilization and appreciation for all the French virtues from *couture* to *cuisine* to *courage* to *culture* she was, it seemed, adopted by the French people almost instantly as an exquisite expatriate daughter.

Her own excitement at being in France, the country she loved most next to her own, seemed to add to her beauty, and the more beautiful she became, the more enthusiastic the French became.

It has been said that success in any milieu involves a combination of the right person at the right place at the right time. Jackie was the woman; Paris was the place; spring was the time. She was indeed a *succès fou*. Jack was delighted, both with her and for her. And he said at an event the next day: "I think I should introduce myself—I am the man who accompanied Jacqueline Kennedy to Paris."

Despite the glamour and beauty of dinners of state, I found myself wondering, once again, what useful purpose such events really serve. They cost the treasury a lot of money. They require a great amount of planning and effort, attention to fine details. But it has always seemed to me that they are rather a waste of time for the statesmen involved, both hosts and guests, for they have important matters on their minds and yet must spend hours chatting away with the wives of state functionaries and listening to speeches.

At least speeches are shorter than they used to be. Years ago, my father was speaking somewhere, my mother was sitting in the audience, and the person next to her didn't know who she was, and when the speech ended my mother turned and said something like, "Well, what do you think about him?" The person said: "He's OK. But he talks too long." We used to tease my father a little about that.

Between ceremonials, however, President Kennedy and President de Gaulle did have a series of long, private, friendly and very frank talks—cumulatively about eight hours, I understand—ranging over all the mutual concerns of the two nations. The informal young President and the monolithic old President evidently got along very well together. Each liked and admired the other. They found a great deal to agree upon and established a rapport that would enable them to deal with points of difference amicably and productively.

I was allowed to go on to Vienna, where Jack expected to hold meetings with Chairman Khrushchev of the U.S.S.R.

I have diary entries written in Vienna:

"June 3 & 4, 1961
"Here in Austria again after about fifty years. The last time was

with my father and sister Agnes. Father was Mayor of Boston and we came with the Boston Chamber of Commerce to visit different European cities.

"I had remembered, though vaguely, the magnificent palace of Schönbrunn and the art galleries. But what had stayed in my mind most was remembrance of the thrill I had when I went on a small steamer one night down the Danube and waltzed joyfully as the orchestra played "The Blue Danube" waltz. I wonder to myself as I write this if the young man with whom I waltzed has ever come back, and if he too has remembered the night in 1911 when, young and gay and carefree, we danced the hours away. Nowhere do the waltzes sound quite the same as when they are played here, and no matter how often they are played one does not tire of them. The thought crosses my mind every night when I listen to the little three-piece orchestra in this small hotel.

"I have had so little opportunity to speak German in later years that I am no longer fluent, but it is fun to try it again now. The two Austrian government officials between whom I sat at the big state dinner given in honor of Jack and Khrushchev did not speak English—so at last, at least for once, I found my German very useful.

"Met Mrs. Khrushchev for the first time at the evening (first evening) reception at the Schönbrunn Palace. She has a very pleasant, welcoming smile when she meets people and it is quite disarming. Figure looked strong, sturdy, capable of hard physical exertion. Wears her hair drawn straight back. No make-up. After introduction, she told me immediately she knew a lot about me as she read an article about me in *McCall's Magazine*, which surprised me.

"The following day I saw her again at the concert given by the Vienna Philharmonic Orchestra. Von Karajan conducted. The Russian violinist David Oistrakh played and was superb. Afterward he and his wife came up to the box and were received by Mrs. Khrushchev. She wore plain dark gray tailored suit."

During the stay in Vienna I chatted with her several times. The diary continues:

"I had hoped Mrs. Khrushchev might speak German. But she spoke English. We discussed our children, etc., always a safe subject.

Her daughter-in-law was with her. Mrs. Khrushchev does not smoke, nor does her daughter-in-law, nor do they drink vodka. This was brought to light during a good-natured discussion of our respective daughters-in-law. I powdered my nose and she watched me and said, 'I must learn your beauty secrets.' "

Mrs. Khrushchev was one of the special surprises and delights of that trip.

Her English was quite good, and I learned later she had been a schoolteacher for many years and had been teaching English to others. I was surprised that she had read an article about me, in an American magazine. She had little or no prior notice that I would be in Vienna—because I hadn't known myself until I asked Jack in Paris. Whereas I had known well in advance that if the Kennedy-Khrushchev talks took place in Vienna as scheduled, she would be there as her husband's hostess. Yet I had not bothered to read up about her, and I was a little annoyed at myself for not having had equal foresight.

I had the impression that had Mrs. Khrushchev and I lived in the same town, I would find her a reliable friend in any emergency. She was sturdy, capable, and had great charm. I was impressed by how well informed she was.

Later on when people asked me about meeting the Khrushchevs, I would often work in the fact that Mrs. Khrushchev had learned English and had read up on me, whereas her daughter-in-law had not; and I would add, "This shows that although some daughters-in-law are smarter than their mothers-in-law, there are some mothers-in-law who are smarter than their daughters-in-law." People's expressions would become interested. But I thought it better to leave them in suspense.

Ethel says, "Well, we're not going to put that to the test, I hope. Which one is she talking about?"

One other thought about Mrs. Khrushchev. Her husband was the leading communist of the time and my husband was one of the leading capitalists. Yet she and I understood each other and got along very well.

I had begun collecting autographs as a girl. Later, as the children arrived and grew and Joe became increasingly prominent, I would ask various leading personages—such as President Hoover and President Roosevelt—to autograph copies of their books, and I would pass those out to the children at Christmas or birthdays, as souvenirs of the times and as a way to encourage their interest in current history. When Jack became President I decided to continue with the custom but in a special way, by getting autographed books by people who were outstanding in many fields—the arts and sciences as well as government—during the years of his presidency. Such a collection would be particularly treasured by Caroline and John Jr. when they grew up. I had accumulated quite a few, from Sean O'Casey to the Duchess of Windsor and including some chiefs of government such as Prime Minister Macmillan and Prime Minister Nehru. I was rather surprised to find that Generalissimo Franco had not written a book, and even more surprised that by that time, 1961, neither had Chancellor Adenauer. However, Adenauer's office had copies of his speeches, some of which they bound in book form, and he autographed that and sent it to me.

On inquiry, it turned out that Premier Khrushchev had not written a book either.

But, of course, there had been many photographs taken of him and Jack together during the Vienna meeting. And so as the next best alternative I decided to send some of those to him and ask him to sign them; then I would have Jack do the same, and probably return one to Premier and Mrs. Khrushchev and distribute the others among our family.

Premier Khrushchev signed the photographs and returned them to me and I sent them on to Jack with a note about my plan.

I received the following letter from him:

"Dear Mother:

"If you are going to contact the heads of state, it might be a good idea to consult me or the State Department first, as your gesture might lead to international complications.

"Love,
"Jack"

To which I replied:

"Dear Jack:

"I am so glad you warned me about contacting the heads of state, as I was just about to write to Castro.

"Love,
"Mother"

Jack and I had many amusing moments recalling this exchange of letters.

Joe and I spent most of that summer on the Riviera. After he went back to Hyannis Port I stayed on in France for some weeks more, partly because I wanted to see the fall fashion collections in Paris and also because I realized that with Jack and Bobby in high office and so much attention in the media about our family, our enclave at Hyannis Port would be a tourist attraction right through the months of fine fall weather at the Cape. The scene had been noisy enough with the children and grandchildren without tourist traffic. I had always needed times of peace and quiet and by then had reached a stage in life when I needed them more; so I thought it behooved me to stay away until near Thanksgiving, which I did.

Meanwhile, the telephone and postal systems had continued to work quite well. And meanwhile, too, all through the year, despite the dramas that occurred, our family life went on. I won't suggest that it went on altogether normally because, naturally, it was complicated by the official positions of Jack and Bobby—and Sarge, as director of the Peace Corps—and Jackie and Ethel and Eunice as their wives; and further by the fact that Teddy was preparing to run for Jack's old Senate seat from Massachusetts, and that in Joan he had a strikingly beautiful wife who caused heads to turn wherever she went; and that Pat was married to Peter, a movie and TV star; and that all of us, as a family, consequently were under continual public scrutiny, which does not make for a placid existence. But the public and private portions of our lives merged in a seamless way, really.

"January 24, 1961
"Palm Beach

"Mrs. John F. Kennedy
"The White House
"Washington, D. C.
"Dear Jackie:

"I have enclosed a few items for Jack's diet. I tried to get a few ideas from Dr. Travell that were constructive. There are copies enclosed in case you want to leave one at the other house.

"Just discovered *Never on Sunday* is on the condemned list.
"With love,

"Affectionately,
"G'Ma"

"February 23
"The White House

"Dear Grandma,

"We went to the White House after having dinner at Daddy's office. We had lots of fun. I wish you had been with us. We saw lots of rooms.

"Love,
"Kathleen, Joe, Bobby, David,
"Michael, Courtney"

(These were six of Bobby and Ethel's children, and the office was the Attorney General's. It must have been a picnic in more ways than one.)

"March
"Boston

"Dear Dad,

"Frankie is keeping me on the go day and night. I think that the reaction has been quite good except for a few cynical old pros. I have found some old Irish stories that Grampa used to tell which have really helped out during the activities of St. Patrick's Day.

"Enclosed is a comment from the Worcester paper after we were up there last week . . . Everything else is going well.

"Love,
"Ted"

"Frankie" was Frank Morrissey, a widely experienced Massachusetts political figure who had helped Jack in his campaign and who had been enlisted now to help Teddy in his first bid for elective office. There was still some testing and decision-making to do as to whether this should be for the governorship or the Senate. Extracts from the article, by John F. Battles in the Worcester *Telegram*, follow:

"One of Central Massachusetts most astute politicians says 'Ted Kennedy will run for governor next year!' This Democratic leader made his private prediction at the Emerald Club's big St. Patrick's Day party at the Auditorium where young Kennedy was the featured speaker—a smash, by the way . . . He says the only thing that can stop Ted Kennedy from running for governor is if he decides instead to run for U.S. senator . . . Hardly a day or night goes by that doesn't see the handsome, personable brother of the President speaking before some group somewhere in the Bay State. . . . Those who came in contact with him at the Auditorium were struck by the warmth he generates . . ."

"April 13

"Dear Dad,

"Thanks so much for shipping Smiths, Shrivers, and Charlie Bartlett all the way to New York. It was a great luxury to ride on the *Caroline* during the campaign but to ride in it now without any 'Cause' was just too marvelous—really too much. We had to keep our seat belts on the whole way and Jean retired immediately to the bedroom . . . she says from fear. It didn't stop the rest of us from enjoying a very good dinner and toasts galore to you, the biggest-hearted leader on the New Frontier.

"Love,
"Eunice"

"July 13
"Beverly Hills

"Dearest Mother and Daddy,

"Well it finally arrived. Five and a half pounds, red hair and the longest fingers I have ever seen. So maybe she'll have Dad's brains too! She was born Sunday the 2nd and we had the christening last

Saturday as Bobby was out that weekend. He's the godfather . . . Talked to Jack today and he asked me to hostess the end of the month as Jackie can't be there . . . should be fun. I will then go to the Cape and leave there August 7th, arriving the 8th at Nice, where I will see you . . .

"Love + xxx
"Pat"

"She" was Robin, the only grandchild until then to have inherited Joe's coloring. Later on there would be another, Teddy and Joan's third child, Patrick. But only those two out of all the twenty-eight grandchildren, which rather surprises me.

(Cablegram to me from Hyannis Port, July 22:)

GRANDMA THE GOATS ARE NOT ENJOYING EATING IN YOUR DINING ROOM HALF AS MUCH SINCE THE GOOD TABLE IS GONE. HAPPY BIRTHDAY. ALL THE GRANDCHILDREN.

The dining-room table is a beautiful old piece which had begun to show signs of wear, so I had sent it out for repairs. Knowing there would be a lot of small grandchildren and playmates around that summer, I thought it just as well not to have it brought back to the house until I returned.

"July 25
"The White House

"Dear Dad:

"Many thanks for your letter.

"I must say Macmillan has an even tougher time with the British press than we do with ours. It is difficult to understand Lord Beaverbrook . . .

"Things seem to be going reasonably well here. I will call you this weekend.

"Love,
"Jack"

"Late July
"Aboard airliner

"Dear Mother & Dad,

"Recently saw Dr. Sidney Farber who is the head of the Children's

Hospital and Jimmy Fund and really well regarded, and he said he would help out preparing some position papers on medical care and some other programs.

"We visited the Kennedy Home in Brighton, the Catholic Guidance Center where we gave the gym, the Massachusetts General Hospital to see the progress in the Kennedy Laboratories. So you can see we have been keeping busy in your absence.

"Last week Eddie McCormack told Hal Clancy" (former publisher of the Boston *Herald-American*) "that he definitely was going to run for the U.S. Senate. He said that he doubted whether I would, because about a week before at a luncheon in Washington the Attorney General congratulated him on his brief on the school desegregation cases and said some nice words about him. When I heard this I ran down brother Bob, and he said what's so bad about that and he would say some nice things about me, too. . . .

"Jack is in good shape in spite of the fact that I cleared his clock in backgammon, taking 7 out of 9 games from him. . . . The final game we played he said he would never play again unless he licked me and a good thing for all of us he did.

"Eunice had a birthday party and is still trying to figure out why the dining-room table has disappeared, since Bobby Shriver doesn't dance on it this year.

"Caroline still is looking for Grampa and asking her father where Grampa got his ice cream and why can't he do as well.

"Joan and Kara send their love.

"The *Marlin* is still afloat and everyone is fine.

"Love
"Ted"

"July 26
"Hyannis Port

"Dear Mother and Dad,

"This summer is passing like no other summer. The weather has been great, the children are all fine and the help is fantastic. Jack is feeling the best he has felt in six months. We went out in the *Marlin* yesterday over to Cotuit and he swam like mad and is in fantastically good humor and so is Jackie. We are all told to build air-raid shelters but otherwise he has no startling news!

"Pat comes next Saturday with her children. She will stay one week and then leaves for Europe and cruising, heading in your direction.

"Tommy is working the gray pony so that he is going much more smoothly.

"All is great—for today.

"Love & hugs,
"Eunice"

"July 28
"The White House
"Dear Grandpa,

"Caroline dictated this letter. In case you don't understand Snapdragon Swallow, she never says her name now. This week it is Lilac Birdie & last week Daffodil Horse. People are rather surprised when they ask her name. . . .

"She says your birthday is in September and she will give you a tie and a red dog.

"All love,
"Jackie"

(Caroline's letter follows:)

"Dear Grandpa,

"You know what Stephen did to me? He wiggled me and I didn't like it.

"Give my love to Grandma & Anne & Peppy's down there so give him this letter. When the whirley-birds came in he was fast asleep.

"It was raining today rainy rainy. I think it was quite a storm. I'm sick and tired of this weather.

"Next week I'll be Snapdragon Swallow."

"Early August
"Hyannis Port
"Dearest Mother & Daddy,

"Everything is going splendidly at the Cape. It is just like a health camp—tennis, golf, water skiing every day. Stephen told me he wants to live here forever and so do we all. Jackie is talking of staying here till October. . . . Jack is in splendid form . . . swimming last week-end and seems very relaxed and cheerful. . . . Pat arrives tonight for a week. . . . Bobby & Ethel are going to Africa next week for 2 days for Independence Day on the Ivory Coast. . . . The Secret Service men spend most of their day entertaining the children and driving the motorboat. So see what you are missing. . . . How's the Riviera??

"Love & xxx
"Jean"

"August 21
"Hyannis Port

"Ambassador and Mrs. Joseph P. Kennedy
"Villa Vista Bella
"Cap D'Antibes
"France
"Dear Gramma and Grampa,

"Things were supposed to simmer down here at the Cape with all the troops moving out, scattered all over Poland and Yugoslavia. Tho we really miss the contingent in the south of France an awful lot and it is sad you're so very far away, when I think of Gramma's 'tummy' and what's going on here maybe 3,600 miles is about the right distance.

"I think roughly the whole attitude of the Secret Service down here is about the same as Casey Jones when he said so determinedly, 'We're gonna reach 'Frisco but we'll all be dead.' . . .

"The tales about the Secret Service are endless: sitting and slurping their popsicles with the children every afternoon at 2:45 when the Dairy Maid Milk Bar truck drives in—or this very afternoon when one who has never heard of Metrecal, but should have, simply wrapped his arms about the mast of the (Wianno) Senior and re-fused to budge during the 2 hour sail returning from Great Island in the teeth of a nor'easter. . . . Of course the children kept shouting to him that Seniors hardly ever tip over—only when there's a storm or something like if the centerboard hits the bottom too hard or if water comes rushing in (you couldn't see the gunwale the en-tire afternoon for all the water that was pouring in). . . .

"Thank you for the wonderful time you gave all of us at Bella

Vista. . . . Those fantastic meals & that relaxation which you cooked up in the Waring blender. . . . Hugs to all of you. . . .

> "Kisses & love,
> "Ethel"

Several notes on this. Eunice and Jean, escorted by Lem Billings, had gone touring in Poland and Yugoslavia and places between. The contingent in the south of France were Joe and I. Ethel and Bobby had visited us there. The blended "relaxation" was a rum cocktail, Joe's favorite.

Joe was seventy-three that September 6. Jean, who was still traveling in Yugoslavia with Lem, sent him a cable:

HEPPY NIRSKEY LOVE FUMSKY JEANSKY LENNSKY

Birthdays always were gala events in our family, and for Joe's in particular the children were inspired to all sorts of inventive lengths: theatricals written, costumed, and performed by themselves; musical numbers in which they set lyrics about him to the tunes of popular songs; and much doggerel versifying. The humor was always full of "inside jokes" which don't translate well without extended footnotes, which I want to avoid since nothing kills a joke like having it explained.

Here are excerpts from a poetic masterpiece Jean sent to her father for his birthday:

> *There once was a gruff old bear*
> *Who summertimes left his lair.*
> *While he was away*
> *Do you think we would say*
> *What went on in that very chair?*
>
> . . . .
>
> *Daddy we had a great time in Hyannis*
> *And only dreamt of living like Landis*
> *So here's to dear Pappy*
> *Have a real happy, happy—*
> *For you Vivas, Hurrahs and Hosanna.*

And here are examples of verses the children had made up for his seventieth birthday:

To the music of "Santa Claus Is Coming to Town"
> *Oh, you'd better watch out*
> *You'd better take care*
> *We're just like honey to a certain old bear*
> *Gram Papa is coming to town.*
> (and four more verses in that vein)

To the music of "Yankee Doodle"
> *He's the famous bear of Wall Street*
> *Just a grizzly in his house*
> *Old J. P. he went away*
> *And left his family all to play*
> *But he's come back for this big day*
> *And he's our Happy Birthday Boy.*

To the music of "Peg of My Heart"
> *Mart of my Heart*
> *It stands there by the sea*
> *Mart of my Heart*
> *It makes money money for me*
> *When we were kids*
> *In the middle of the block*
> *We had lots of fun you know*
> *But, oh, those trusts were coming in slow*
> *So that's why we love*
> *That Mart of my Heart.*

To the music of "California, Here We Come"
> *Dear Old Daddy, here we come*
> *Right back where we started from.*
> *With husbands and children and nurses galore,*
> *With Hackett, and Billings, still plunked at the door.*
> *Dear Old Daddy, here we stay*
> *Where we saw the light of day,*
> *You may have to go away*
> *But where else can we live*
> *Where we don't have to pay?*
> *Hip, Hip, Hurray . . . !*

"September 19
"Paris

"Joe Dearest,
"How can I have all this—and you—And still have Heaven, too!

"Love to all,
"Rosa"

"November 20
"Hyannis Port

"Dear Ethel:
"I think it would be a good idea if the children learned to bring in their bicycles at night, as it really is a pity to have them outside in the dampness.

"It would be quite easy to make them do this by just forbidding them to ride the following day after not putting their bicycles away the night before.

"Much love,
"G. Ma"

The next month both Joe and I were at the Palm Beach house as usual and making our preparations for Christmas. My niece Ann Gargan was staying with us at the time. She had been in training to be a nursing nun, in one of the orders that specialize in the care of the sick, and was nearing the time for her vows when she herself developed symptoms of multiple sclerosis, a disabling disease, and hence had to give up her plans. That was in 1959, and since then she had been living much of the time with us, while undergoing medical treatment. This was extraordinarily successful. By late 1961 practically all signs of nerve impairment were gone and she could take part in life fully, including sports. Joe was as pleased about this as I was. Ann was the youngest of the Gargan children, and Joe had made a special pet of her. And of course she adored him. He liked to play golf early in the morning, whereas I preferred the mid-afternoon, so Ann was often his golfing companion.

In Teddy's book *The Fruitful Bough*, Ann wrote:

"Uncle Joe always wanted to keep life interesting and moving—maybe he kept on the move too much. On the morning of December 19, 1961, we were on the move again. We generally played golf about 8:30 but Jack was down in Palm Beach and was leaving for Washington that morning. Uncle Joe rode to the airport with him. I followed in another car, so that I could bring Caroline and 'Grandpa' back home from the airport. We dropped Caroline off at home and went directly to the Palm Beach Country Club to play nine holes. Being later than usual, the front nine was crowded. So we played the back nine. We finished the sixteenth, and as Uncle Joe picked up his ball, he said he felt rather faint. But he told me to tee off the seventeenth, as there were people waiting behind us. I did. He was sitting on the bench. I asked if he wanted his ball teed up. He said no—he would just walk along.

"So we started out. His balance was all off. I asked his caddy to run and get a golf cart. With some difficulty, Uncle Joe asked if we had gotten Caroline home all right. I assured him we had. This seemed to ease his mind. The golf cart arrived. I got the car and we drove home. Upon reaching the house, he felt better. He was delighted to find Jackie and Caroline waiting to have a swim with him. No one made him happier than his grandchildren. He went upstairs right away to change for his swim. I persuaded him to rest. . . . He fell fast asleep, then awoke about five minutes later, coughing and unable to speak, or to move on the right side. . . ."

That morning I had been at Mass. Then I had a few errands to do, so I was home a bit later than usual, which didn't bother me because I had kissed Jack good-bye and knew that Joe and Ann would be going with him to the airport and then would be playing golf. Perhaps it was around eleven-thirty that I arrived back at the house. Ann came to me and, looking rather worried but not too worried, told me that Uncle Joe was not feeling well at all and she had managed to get him to take a nap. None of it registered much on me at the time. After all, everyone feels giddy or weak from time to time, and if there is someplace to lie down, in that case one sensibly lies down, rests, naps, waits for Nature to take the healing course it usually does. It barely occurred to me there could be anything seriously wrong with him. True enough, he was seventy-three, yet he had always been vital, active, alert, and such a strong central presence in all our lives that in my own mind, I suppose, I had thought of him just going on and on to some indeterminate time, getting older but meanwhile immune to any serious physical impairments.

And so, when Ann told me about his not feeling well, I was concerned but not alarmed, and went on with my usual schedule at that time of the day. Ann soon came down to tell me this did not seem to be just a temporary upset but needed the attention of a doctor; who was called and came out quickly, and after examining Joe sent for an ambulance, in which he was taken to St. Mary's Hospital, about fifteen minutes from our house, on the other side of Lake Worth.

I followed to St. Mary's, and while the medical examinations were going on—a number of doctors involved—I was most of the time in the hospital chapel, praying, praying.

After the examination the doctors told us that Joe had a blood clot and partial hemorrhage in one of the arteries of his brain—a "stroke"—and his chances of living were problematical; and that if he lived his chances of being restored to anything near his customary level of activities were not good.

Jack was still on his way back to the White House when his father was taken ill, and had barely arrived at his office when it was realized that he was seriously ill. Meanwhile, Bobby had been notified—he in turn called Jack—and a few hours later, that same afternoon, Jack was back in Palm Beach on Air Force One bringing Bobby and Jean with him. Eunice couldn't get on that plane, but came down on a commercial flight that afternoon or evening. Pat came in from California, and Teddy down from Boston.

In other words, Joe was not expected to live; though no one then, or in the next days, wanted to tell me.

That was the nineteenth of December. By the twenty-fourth, Christmas Eve, which for so many years had been a time of joyous expectation in our house, he had developed pneumonia and had such difficulty in breathing that the doctors had to make an incision in his throat and insert a tube through which he could receive oxygen.

He survived the crisis, began to gain, and a few weeks later was off the "critical" list and strong enough to be brought home.

From that time on, Ann entered into a life of devotional care that could not have been more complete had she taken her vows. Her uncle Joe had done everything possible for her during her illness and recuperation; she now dedicated herself wholehcartedly and single-mindedly to helping him. He needed nursing care around the clock, so of course she couldn't do it all, and there were other nurses and assistants, but it was Ann who interviewed and hired them and remained in charge. This was a wonderful comfort for Joe, for he loved and trusted her as if she were a daughter. And of course I loved and trusted her, too, and knowing that she had been well trained in nursing I was sure I could count on her to do or cause to be done everything that could help him toward recovery.

The blood clot and neurological damage had left Joe unable to speak and with almost complete paralysis of his right arm and leg. His mind, however—his comprehension of things said and seen and sensed and in short of all the life around him—apparently had been only moderately impaired. By springtime his general physical condition had improved to such a degree that his doctors said he was ready to begin the long, laborious process of exercises and other therapies through which, hopefully, he might regain the powers of speech and movement. Accordingly we—Ann and I, and Joe on a stretcher, with medical personnel and special equipment—flew to New York, where Joe entered the Institute of Rehabilitation Medicine, whose director was—and is—Dr. Howard Rusk. There Joe's full-time attending physician was one of Dr. Rusk's most trusted assistants, Dr. Henry Betts, a brilliant young man who subsequently became head of a similar institute, the Rehabilitation Institute of Chicago. Dr. Betts was in charge of Joe's case at the New York institute and later on attended him also at Hyannis Port and other places. At Teddy's request, he contributed some memories of that period to *The Fruitful Bough:*

"The most pervading characteristic he exhibited was that of a gigantic and natural commanding presence. At no time was he a pitiful or passive invalid. There was no question for even a second of who was the dominant force when he was around. With his eyes, facial expression, and strong left hand, he could convey any reaction from tremendous disdain to the most poignant and feeling expression of affection and appreciation. He had an uncanny comprehension and . . . noticed the most meticulous details of the manner in which the staff performed their duties and always expressed his evaluation, either positive or negative, leaving no doubt as to his opinion . . . his displeasure at lack of perfection . . . his satisfaction with a job well done.

"For probably the first time in his life, he was dependent on the planning of another individual. This was not an easy adjustment to make. . . . He vacillated from complete cooperation and appreciation of my efforts to total dissatisfaction . . . (but soon) there was never the slightest problem between the two of us.

"He showed gigantic strength of character. . . . There was a difficulty in maintaining himself as the symbol of strength and the family leader in such a relatively passive state, but he did it by just his presence, and the indefinable qualities still so evident in him, that convey strength and leadership in all great men . . .

"Mr. Kennedy learned to walk quite soon and put tremendous effort into this with great satisfaction. . . .

"The greatest pleasure in his leisure time was, of course, his family. In the evenings, Mrs. Kennedy would come (to the Institute) for a quiet dinner, then both would sit peacefully and watch television until it was time for bed. He was always especially relaxed with his wife and, even though he could say no words, they seemed to communicate completely.

"Probably the most moving moment during his stay in New York was when the President visited. Dr. Rusk had suggested he demonstrate the walking he had just learned to do, which he could manage then only between two parallel bars with assistance.

"Mr. Kennedy refused to agree to this, but greeted the President in the little house assigned to him (on the Institute grounds). After the visit, the President wheeled his father to the garden and indicated that he must leave. Mr. Kennedy anchored his progress in the chair with his good and very strong left foot, locked the chair, and indicated that he wanted to stand, which he had previously not been able to do alone. Some assistance was offered, but he shunned it angrily.

"Then, with incredible effort, he forced himself to an erect, dignified, and normal-appearing standing position. He then fixed the President with his piercing eyes and extended his left hand to say good-bye. The President, obviously moved, quickly turned and disappeared to the street and out of sight. We could hear loud applause

Flame of Hope project.

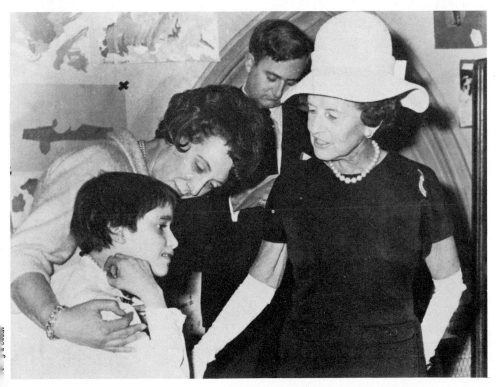

A visit to a school for the mentally retarded, Paris, 1966.

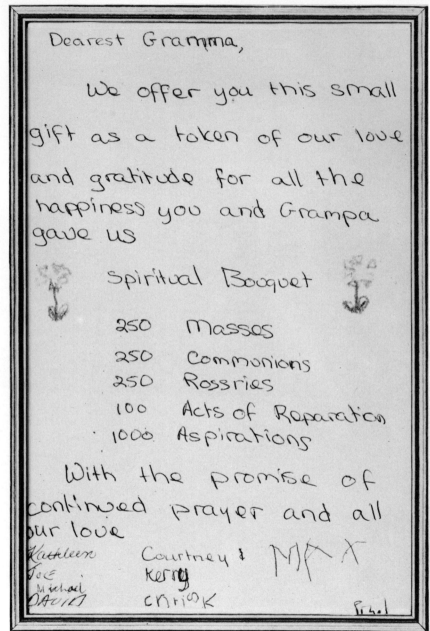

Dearest Gramma,

    We offer you this small gift as a token of our love and gratitude for all the happiness you and Grampa gave us

Spiritual Bouquet

250	Masses
250	Communions
250	Rossries
100	Acts of Reparation
1000	Aspirations

With the promise of continued prayer and all our love

Kathleen   Courtney &   MAX
Joe   Kerry
Michael
David   Chris K

Bobby and Ethel's children have given Grandpa and me a Spiritual Bouquet. They have recited Rosaries and have gone to Mass for our intentions. A very moving and deeply appreciated tribute.

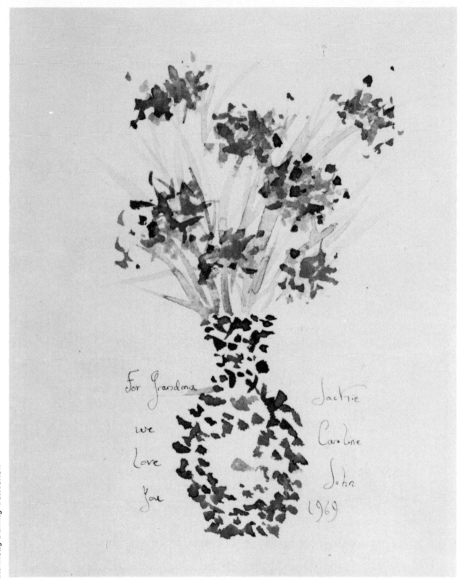

For Grandma
we
Love
You

Jackie
Caroline
John
1969

Jackie's painting of a Spiritual Bouquet.

Poem for Grandpa

Love Caroline

Christmas 1967

Once there lived a little blue mouse.

Who wasn't scared of cats

He lived in a tiny shocking pink house

With his friend the sparrow, Ignatz.

They went on long walks and had long talks

In mostly the month of May.

They would picnic by a laughing brook

And spend a pleasant   day.

The only thing they didn't have

For which they used to pray

Was someone as nice as Grandpa

Who they missed more every day.

Caroline's poem to Grandpa.

The opening of the John F. Kennedy Center for the Performing Arts in Washington, D. C., September 1971.

Marc Chagall and I in September 1964, on the Riviera.

Teddy and I with the Duke and Duchess of Windsor, Palm Beach.

Joe II and I.

My twenty-eight grandchildren and I.

Photography by I

and shouts, then the roar of motorcycles. Until their din was entirely gone, Mr. Kennedy stood, his eyes fixed straight ahead to where his son had disappeared. He sat down then and slowly wheeled away into the garden . . .

"When we were in Hyannis Port he seemed most happy, though the pleasures there were simple. He loved to go to movies" (in our little theater and projection room) "and enjoyed being in a boat" (the *Marlin*, skippered by "Captain" Frank Wirtanen, a wonderful man) "and he reveled in the company of his many grandchildren, to whom he was extremely gentle and affectionate. He often went for (automobile) rides, always stopping to greet familiar faces. . . . He loved to sit quietly, even alone, and watch the sea from his chair, strategically placed for the view.

"On weekends, the President usually arrived and, as soon as we knew his jet had landed at a nearby air force base, Mr. Kennedy would go to the center of the front porch, in any weather, and await the arrival of the helicopter. . . . The number-one helicopter always landed on the lawn directly in front of him. Right after greeting his wife and children, the President would stride, with his energy echoed by the tremendous roar and force of the jet helicopters, to pay homage to his father, who seemed to dominate it all. These were touching moments; even more so when the President departed, when Mr. Kennedy would be left with his thoughts as the helicopters disappeared into the Cape Cod fog. He sometimes cried, but even that somehow never destroyed the image of strength he projected . . ."

Joe had always disliked self-pity for any reason, and overt displays of grief made him uncomfortable. He used to tell the children, and later the grandchildren, that tears accomplished nothing. Instead of thinking about a hurtful present they should think about better times tomorrow, and how to bring those about.

His secretary for several years before his stroke had been Diane Winter, who in *The Fruitful Bough* wrote of him as he had been:

"Despite . . . tragedy, Mr. Kennedy was unshakably positive and optimistic about the future. I remember hearing him clap his hands in steady rhythm to accentuate the admonition, said in mock sternness to his grandchildren, 'No—crying—in—this—house! No—crying—in—this—house!' "

His tears afterward were of course entirely involuntary and uncontrollable—a side effect, I suppose, of the neurological damage—but anyway there they were, and made his situation all the more heartbreaking for those who loved him.

Joe's stroke had occurred in a part of the brain that was inaccessible to surgery, so the major hope for him, as Dr. Betts has indicated, was a retraining process in which the intact parts of his nervous system would take over the functions of the damaged parts. This required not only courage and determination, which he always had and still had in abundance and applied to his problem of recovery, but also a long time spent in repetitious and laborious exercises for the benefit of a daily or weekly almost imperceptible gain. And, of course, this was completely against his nature. He was, in Dr. Betts's term, "massively frustrated." And it was so contrary to everything about him that I had known—known for some fifty-five years by then—that I think I underwent a certain degree of emotional paralysis for a time. I find that one of the very few diary notes I took was in midsummer of 1962 and was this:

"Joe's illness. The grief when I see him cry and the pity when I see one who was so strong and independent lie helpless in bed, saying 'no, no, no.' Sometimes when he means, 'yes.'"

Slowly, with good care and his indomitable will, and supported by prayer and by the love and encouragement which surrounded him, he came back as far as it was possible physically. He was able to stand, with the aid of a cane, and with the cane, and someone's arm for balance on the other side, to walk a few steps. He had been an athlete, had loved exercise. We built an enclosed swimming pool at Hyannis Port, heated and with the sprays and bubblers and other fixtures of a health spa (and enclosed and heated the pool we had at Palm Beach), so that he could swim every day, as part of his therapy. Going up or down stairs, even with assistance, remained beyond possibility, hence elevators were installed at both houses. Mainly—aside from the considerable time every day he would have to rest in bed—he was confined to his wheel chair, or favorite easy chairs at our houses, or a chair on a boat, because standing for more than a few minutes was a great strain on his strength.

His speech improved somewhat but the few words he acquired

were slurred and hard for others to understand. I'm sure this embarrassed him, and after a while he settled back on the two words he could say with some distinctness, "yes" and "no." Sometimes he would not even try those and would rely wholly on the expressive language of his face and good left arm and hand.

The learned skills gained and faded, came back and increased and then went again, for physiological and psychological reasons that were beyond my knowledge and probably beyond that of the medical specialists.

He and I had always talked with each other a lot. That was not so much because we were verbal people (though I suppose we were, comparatively) as because there was just always so much to talk about. Yet, in so many ways, we had understood each other with no need for words: a gesture, an expression, a look, a nod, a cue, or, as I believe possible, that harmonious meeting of minds that is empathy, the unspoken understanding. In his distressed condition I couldn't count on it but most of the time it was still there. In the midst of his tragedy this was one blessing.

As he made progress, minute and sometimes evanescent though it was, and as his general health became fairly stabilized, he could again take part in life. The limits of his participation were of course severe. He came to family meals, occupying his usual position at the head of the table and followed the conversation attentively and, so far as possible for anyone who was speechless, took part in it. He was amused by the family banter that went on (though he couldn't speak he could laugh; and that marvelous grin of his was intact) and was as receptive as ever to any badinage or infra dig humor that they might direct at him. For instance there was a series of "souvenir pillows" (this had started before his illness, but continued) printed with one of his characteristic expletives such as *Applesauce!* or admonitions such as *You're dipping into your capital!* Or familiar sayings such as *You have just made a political contribution*—an "inside joke" that deserves explanation. He had given the children trust funds, but the income was still administered by his business office. When one of them was involved in a campaign and needed funds a tithe was levied on the others, which they would hear about in a letter from him beginning, "You have just made a political contribution . . ."

And so it was with everyone: everyone trying to give him the support and reassurance that he had always given us.

Evelyn Jones was with us during some of those times and remembers:

"When I'd be going by near his chair I'd always talk to him as if he were just the same, and he was the boss and he was the king of the ship, and that's all there was to it and just the same. My husband, Tom, and I had bought a place. I took pictures of it and showed them to him. He was so interested. Once in a while he'd put his good hand on your arm as if he were trying to say thank you. Which of course you knew. And one of his smiles when you fixed him up in his chair was worth all the money in the world—you couldn't pay for it. He knew that you knew he was handicapped and yet was still Mr. Kennedy; and that was it.

"One thing I insisted on doing, though the girl working with me used to get a little upset once in a while. When Mr. Kennedy was quite ill he would often change his mind. So I had a place set for him in the dining room, I had a tray set in the butler's pantry to take into the library, and if they were eating out on the patio I had a place set for him there. Because if he thought he wanted to eat in the library by himself, by the time I was serving he might be out on the patio—and I would *not* not have had a place for that man for the world. The other girl said, 'Why don't you wait and find out?' I said, 'It would be too late.' And I said, 'Just don't fret about it because if he suddenly decides he wants to go someplace to eat there's going to be a place for him. And he's not going to find somebody in his place.' It would break his heart to find somebody sitting in his place. So you did these things for him and you did them because you loved him.

"Mrs. Kennedy was wonderful with him. They all were. They did anything and everything they could think of to do for him, in any and every way, all the details. Mrs. Kennedy went over the linens with me after he became ill, and she ordered new linens. She said, 'Because I want him to have the best.' And Mrs. Shriver said one day, 'You know, I think the fact that Daddy still dresses and has his clothes come from Sulka's just the same as if he were well is *important*.' And he felt so too, because he'd come down the elevator to the library and would be dressed so nicely and would be so proud and everyone would be complimenting him. They were passing "t.l.s" around the place but in those days especially for him. Often they'd come to the table and say, 'I've got a t.l. for you.' And then they'd tell him something that someone else had said to them about him that was a compliment. . . ."

Fairly soon, sooner than one could reasonably expect, we were able to resume in a general way the annual pattern of our lives: spring, summer, and fall in Hyannis Port, winter in Palm Beach, with intervals in New York. Joe, with Ann and the medical attendants, would make these trips in the *Caroline*. I would leave about a fortnight earlier, to get the houses opened and everything in readiness; and to do some personal shopping and perhaps see a few old friends; and also, in that interval, to go out to Wisconsin to visit Rosemary.

When we were in New York, there were always friends and distinguished former associates who wanted to see Joe to pay their respects, wish him progress and, I suppose, by their attention, reassure him that he was still a very important person. One day, for instance, General Douglas MacArthur came to the apartment. I have a diary note:

"I was amazed at his diction, wonderful command of English and felicity of expression. He stayed about half an hour and talked all the time, which was wonderful as Joe does not talk, but during the General's remarks nodded his head in assent occasionally."

Another time we were invited to lunch with former President Herbert Hoover at his apartment in the Waldorf Towers. A diary note:

"It was wonderful to see the delight on both faces when they met. Though of different political allegiances they were old friends. And I remembered Joe saying once that Mr. Hoover was one of the few people in the world who really did enlighten him with knowledge and experience and wisdom. I had met him a couple of times and found him rather withdrawn and aloof, but on this day he was amiable, seemed in a very expansive mood, talked a great deal, and seemed anxious to put us at our ease and make our visit a happy one. But he had been very sick himself. His nurse, whom he had had for a long time, was near to help him if he needed anything and she sat with us at luncheon. He obviously was frail. Moreover he was very deaf.

"So here was Joe, who cannot speak, and Mr. Hoover, who cannot hear, trying to communicate. The two men, friends, both with great achievements to remember; each aware of his own and the other's crippling infirmities now, trying to make the best of it. And so poignant, inexpressibly sad, when each of them from time to time through the meal wept silently."

I expect that these occasional weeping spells were associated with the neurological damage he had suffered; but I think also they were a manifestation of the "massive frustration" that Dr. Betts mentioned. André Malraux once wrote: "Man is not made for defeat. He may be vanquished but not destroyed." Joe absolutely, resolutely, and even furiously refused to accept any idea of defeat and he could barely tolerate the idea of having been temporarily vanquished. A few of my diary notes of the time:

"Joe wants and tries to do things like he did in the past. I keep thinking what a pity that such a superior person dedicated to good- ness and efficiency should be so crippled—through no fault of his own. . . .

"It was so sad and nerve-racking to see him try to tell me some- thing which I could not understand, or complain about something which I could not fathom. He is still very vital and vigorous about expressing his wishes and gets cross and impatient if we cannot un- derstand him. . . . Sometimes he uses his left arm or leg to push or whack the nurses. . . .

"The nurses work only eight hours at a time and sometimes I do not think they coordinate very well. For instance, one says that Joe has slept well, while the night nurse has told me his breathing was irregular or heavy. Then the first one says, 'The night nurse is new and is not accustomed to his breathing.' Often one goes on vacation or says she has to take a few days off, and then the substitute doesn't know the routine or perhaps even how to work the wheel chair properly. . . . One night, a nurse got him into the elevator and then didn't know how to operate the release pedal on the chair, so the chair was too extended and the elevator door could not close. Also, once they did get down, she had difficulty getting the chair out of the elevator. And so Joe sat for five or six minutes bursting with rage. . . .

"Naturally, all these times fill me with annoyance and sadness for his sake, and with frustration because I can do so little about them. . . ."

Nevertheless, it was because of this tremendous determination that he was able to keep going and to take part in such a number of his former activities. In New York we continued to dine out: dinner usually at La Caravelle, which he enjoyed and where the manager Robert Meyzen and the headwaiters knew his table and our tastes, and could arrange everything gracefully. And Joe continued to go to his New York office—not long at a time, perhaps an hour or two, a few times a week—to look over the books and operations of the office.

Sometimes on these journeys or stopovers he and I would go to Washington and spend a few days in the White House. This was another rather strange blessing: For by then not even the most cynical persons could suppose that Jack was being directed by his father; and so at last Joe could feel free to visit and take a father's pride and pleasure in the fact his son was the President. Whenever he was there, Jack made sure to be with him several times a day, give him the news of government and, in the most respectful and tactful way, solicit his advice, so far as he could give it.

Bobby and Ethel would come to the White House for dinner or, if everything seemed propitious, Joe and I, and Ann, and perhaps the night nurse, and Jack and Jackie would converge at their house in the countryside near Washington; probably would be joined there by Eunice and Sarge, who lived in the same area; and perhaps by Pat and Peter, and Jean and Steve, and Teddy and Joan, if they happened to be around at the time. We seldom lacked a quorum.

The year that Teddy ran for the Senate was also the first year of Joe's illness; and, of course, this put Teddy under extra pressure, not only because he loved and revered his father and was worried about him, but because he knew that Joe had very much wanted him to make the race. Teddy would have worked extremely hard in any case. But if there is anything beyond "going all out" that's where Teddy went because he knew how much a victory would mean to his father.

It was quite a memorable campaign and attracted much national attention in the various media, for it had intrinsic elements of drama. If Teddy won, our family would have the President, the Attorney General, and a member of the Senate at the same time, which was unprecedented. The contest involved a collision of some of the strongest political forces in the state, and some of the best-known names in U.S. politics—with a lot of evocative political history in the background. Teddy's opponent for the Democratic endorsement, at the state convention, was Eddie McCormack, who not only was attorney general of Massachusetts but was the nephew and protégé of John W. McCormack, the Speaker of the U.S. House of Representatives, who of course was backing him with all the influence at his command. (The Fitzgeralds, Kennedys, and McCormacks had had many encounters in Massachusetts' political life: usually as friends, sometimes as foes, sometimes friendly enemies.) The prospective, and actual, winner on the Republican side was George Cabot Lodge, son of Henry Cabot Lodge, Jr., whom Jack had defeated for the Senate in 1952, and great-grandson of Henry Cabot Lodge who had defeated my father for the Senate in 1916. Making matters even more interesting, there was an Independent candidate, H. Stuart Hughes, professor of history at Harvard, grandson of Chief Justice Charles Evans Hughes (whose house, by the way, we had rented when we moved down from Boston to Riverdale), who had run against Woodrow Wilson for the presidency in the election of 1916.

A considerable confrontation, to be sure.

I was involved very little in that campaign, for I felt that Joe needed me, and I wanted to be with him. Furthermore, Teddy apparently was feeling a bit oppressed by this time at being the "kid brother" in the family and was out to show that he could win on his own merits as a candidate. He made this well known in the family. Jack was very pleased with him and also rather amused. Teddy recalls:

"He knew that when I was running in Massachusetts I told the voters I wanted to be judged on my own and not on the family name. So in a speech he made in 1963, he said, 'Teddy wants to be judged on his own; so he is thinking of changing his name . . . from Teddy Kennedy to Teddy Roosevelt.'"

As I recall, I did go on radio or television a couple of times, gave some interviews about Teddy, helped Joan with a few special contacts such as my friends in the French-Canadian communities, and also played the piano several times at meetings; really only a "stunt" because despite my lessons and years of playing in the circle of friends and family I was only an amateur, whereas she was accomplished enough to be a concert pianist.

Joan had been out a few times before with Teddy and the others when Jack was running, but this was her first time as the wife of a candidate—a special and difficult and delicate role for anyone. Like Jackie, Joan is a rather private, reserved, and shy person for whom the public appearances, with the receiving lines and handshaking and motorcades and speechmaking and interviews and all the rest, would not be at all easy. In fact, all this was almost crushingly difficult at times; we women in our family had plenty of reason to know, having done such a lot to set the pattern. But again like Jackie, Joan proved herself to be made of iron when the needs were put upon her. She was a great campaigner. And at this point in my story, I think it can be understood—in all dimensions—that this is a great compliment.

I'm sure that every mother wonders about the "right girl" for her son and deeply hopes that somehow he and she will meet and have a fulfilling life together. I have been fortunate in all three of my daughters-in-law. Earlier in this book, Jackie and Ethel reminisced about their impressions when they encountered us and began to think of joining the family. I asked Joan to do this too, and here is what she says:

"The Kennedys and my family, the Bennetts, lived only about three blocks from each other in Bronxville, so it would sound wonderful if I could say Ted and I were childhood sweethearts. But what happened really was that when I was four years old and Teddy was seven, going on eight his father became ambassador to England and the family moved to London. Afterward they came back to Bronxville but not for very long. Ted and I have no memories at all of each other from those years. We've often asked each other, trying to find anything like 'We *must* have been buying ice-cream cones at the same time in the same drugstore some Sunday after church,' but it's a complete blank. And that's the way it went for the next fifteen years or so, until October of 1957, the beginning of my senior year at Manhattanville.

"Jean's the one who has to take the responsibility. She and Ethel had been roommates at Manhattanville. She had introduced Ethel to Bobby and that turned out to be a great success, and maybe that gave her a sense of power as a supermatchmaker. Anyway, what happened was that Ethel's family lived in Greenwich, Connecticut, and that summer there was a party at her house and I went with a boy who used to be engaged to Jean. Jean was there. Naturally she was curious to meet this blonde who had turned up with her former beau. We chatted awhile, mostly about Manhattanville, and liked each other, and she more or less took me under her wing at the party.

"Then, that October, Jean was back at Manhattanville for an afternoon with her parents and some other members of her family, including Teddy. They had many associations with the college and with the Sacred Heart schools in general. They had given a new gymnasium in memory of Kathleen and were there for the dedication. Ted was a second-year law student at the University of Virginia, but he was on hand for the ceremonies and was the one who made the speech.

"I didn't hear it. I had come back early from a Yale weekend because I had an important paper to type, and I was feeling bored enough with school duties without having to hear somebody make a speech. There was a reception and tea afterward, to meet the Kennedy family and Cardinal Spellman, and I had no intention of going to that either. My roommate Margot Murray urged me to be sensible and go because, as she reminded me, only seniors were invited, attendance was taken, nonattendance meant demerits, and those meant I could be "campused," a fate worse than going to the reception. So, over to the prom room I went for the reception. Jean spotted me and said, 'I want you to meet my little brother.'

"I'll never forget that moment. I expected to see a small boy. Instead I found myself looking up at somebody 6 feet 2 inches and close to 200 pounds. And, I must say, darn good-looking.

"We've talked about that, too, and agree there was something instantaneous, almost a shock of recognition as if each of us realized 'This is it, this is the one' though, of course, it took a while to believe it.

"We saw each other as often as possible, which wasn't very often. A Sunday brunch in New York. A ski trip to Stowe with mutual friends. In the spring, a weekend with others at Charlottesville, where Ted and his friend and fellow law student John Tunney (now a senator from California) shared a small house near the university campus. That June, after I was graduated from Manhattanville, Ted invited me to Hyannis Port for the weekend. I asked who would be there, and he said so far as he knew it would be only his mother. His father was in the south of France then; other members of the family wouldn't come until late June when all schools were out.

"Suddenly it dawned on me that I was going to meet the mother! And it would be just the three of us staying at her house. I was a bit apprehensive. I wanted to please her.

"My first and really all-pervading memory of her at the Hyannis Port house was that she immediately put me at my ease and in a very short time I liked her enormously. She was delighted that we shared Manhattanville as an alma mater and wanted to know about the school activities and the personalities such as Mother O'Byrne. She had a lot of questions that weekend. Not that she bombarded me with them; not at all, but she was very warm, very alive, very interested in what I thought. When we talked I felt she was giving me her undivided attention, and of course that is the best kind of compliment.

"Later on, I learned that she called Mother O'Byrne to inquire about 'Joan Bennett's grades and behavior' at school. Luckily I had a good record.

"I was invited back to Hyannis Port twice more that summer, and met nearly all the rest of the family. I am a good swimmer and a pretty good sailor, but I remember feeling terribly unathletic. However, Ted taught me, watched out for me, and everything went well. I was asked back for Labor Day weekend. Ted and I were walking on the beach and had got from his parents' house to just about where our own house is now, when he said, 'What do you think about our getting married?' I said, 'Well, I guess it's not such a bad idea.' Ted sat right down in the sand. Then he said, 'What do we do next?' I said I thought it should be up to him to decide about plans. He decided we should be married as soon as the arrangements could be made.

"It happened that his father arrived home from France that very night, and of course I would be meeting him the next day. I had heard terrifying stories about him (not from Ted or anyone in the family, of course, but here and there), and I was scared to death. I'll never forget it. He sat in a big wing chair at the far end of the long living room. He was a very imposing man. I walked in, by myself, approached and sat at his feet on an ottoman. The first thing he asked me was:

" 'Do you love my son?'

"I thought at the time it was a rather needless question. But, looking back now, I can agree that after all it was the fundamental one. When the interview was over (and it was an interview), he said simply that if Ted and I wanted to be married we had his blessing.

"There were many preparations, of course; many close consultations between my mother and Ted's mother, as well as conversations between my father and his father. Without my going into all that, it is enough to say that everyone got along very well, and that all the Kennedys and Bennetts and hordes of friends turned out for the wedding, which was performed by Cardinal Spellman in Bronxville at St. Joseph's Church, where Ted and I both had attended as children.

"Ted's mother, who is now grandmother to our three children and 'Grandma' by her choice to me too (and Ethel, Sarge, and Steve), later on paid me the highest compliment I can imagine. She said: 'When I was saying my rosary at night I used to be praying also that Teddy would find the right girl. You were the answer to my prayers.'

"I love her and admire her for many, many reasons, but what may be even more important in a mother-in-law and daughter-in-law relationship is that I *like* her. We are friends, we get along, we are at ease. We can tease each other without hurting each other, and that is because we have love, understanding, and trust."

Teddy won in the state convention against Eddie McCormack, who refused to accept that decision and took the matter to the state primaries, where Teddy won in the popular vote by a very big margin.

This left him "eyeball to eyeball," so to speak, with George Lodge, the Republican nominee, in the general election, with Stuart Hughes, the Independent, in nominal contention.

Meanwhile, many people—local "Kennedy Secretaries" and others, sometimes the younger relatives of those who had helped in the early campaigns—had rallied to Teddy's cause, or were on their way, or said they would be ready whenever needed. Members of the family, and of Jack's circle of assistants and friends, were in the scene from time to time. Bobby came up from Washington, as did Ted Sorensen. Polly and her group arranged teas and receptions. Joey Gargan was there. Steve Smith became so effective that he was lassoed to manage all the boys' subsequent campaigns. So again it was a matter of loyalty, organizational effort with attention to all details, devoted family participation and guidance—and, needless to say, a hardworking, intelligent, and attractive candidate.

Teddy won. As soon as he could be certain of his victory Teddy called his father. Joe couldn't speak, but he listened as Ted told him the news and all that he knew his father would want to know. Joe smiled delightedly, which in Evelyn's true perception "was worth all the money in the world—you couldn't pay for it."

Not long ago I came across an article about Joe that appeared in the September 7, 1957, issue of the *Saturday Evening Post*, in which he was quoted as predicting that someday one of our sons would be President, another would be Attorney General, and another would be a U.S. senator—all this simultaneously. I suppose I had seen the article when it came out and perhaps had read this forecast, but if so I had put it out of my mind because it seemed such an implausible idea. Nevertheless, it had happened. And once again I was amazed at Joe's almost preternatural ability to judge people and events and discern the shape of the future.

I must say also that when Teddy was elected, when all three of our surviving sons were in positions of leadership and great responsibility in the nation's government, then I—looking back over all the years to when they had been children, little boys on their way to youth and manhood, those impressionable years when "the twig is bent"—thought to myself that I must have done something right.

And so we entered a golden time. It was shadowed by Joe's illness; yet, as I have said, he was still able to enjoy a good many of the pleasures of life; and his spirit was comforted by the manifest affection that surrounded him—surrounded would be a literal term when the grandchildren were visiting—and, above all, by the accomplishment of the grand design he had for his sons, and by their love and respect for him.

He delighted in hearing from the grandchildren and received reams of mail from them, sometimes in their own scrawls if they were old enough to write, otherwise dictated to their mothers. From this large trove, here are a few samples.

"February 5, 1962
"The White House

"Dear Grandpa,

"We rode on the sleigh and there was no snow—but there was no snow—but there was some and we rided all the morning.

"Macaroni tried to get in front and he tried to kick Buster too and we rode on the leadline. . . .

"Daddy is sitting with Mummy and me and not John a bad squeaky boy who tries to spit in his mother's Coca Cola and who has a very bad temper.

"I hope to meet you soon. Antoni lives in London but he's here now and he likes you and he wants you to be his Grandpa.

"I love you so much. Twenty hundred yards I love you.

"From Caroline"
(As told to her mother)

"September 25
"Peace Corps
"Office of the Director
"Washington

"Dear Grandpa,

"I hope you are feeling better. And I hope that I will be coming up to see you soon. And I whant to tell you what I have to do evry week. I have to do reading and writing and Arithmetic. Some day I am going to get sick of school work too. Oh! I ment to tell you. I've been in school for two weeks . . . I'm in the third grade. And I am working very hard. . . . I hope you will feel better.

> "Your loving child
> "Bob Sargent Shriver"

> "1962" (undated)
> "The White House

"Dear Grandpa,

"Come back to the White House and throw all the horses out of the President's office.

> "With all our love.
> "Jack—Jackie—John—
> Caroline"
> (Dictated to her mother)

> (Undated)
> "Washington

"Dear Grampa and Granma,

"I will be at the cape in a week. how are you feeling? I have a giant turtle. I will see you soon.

> "xxxxxxxxxxxxxxxxxx
> "Bobby
> "Robert Francis Kennedy Jr."

> "April 6, 1963
> "Rockville, Maryland

"Dear Grandpa and Grandma,

"My sister Maria made her first confession on Thursday. Now she wants to go to confession every minut, hour, and day. Plus go to communion. Whitch she will do on April 28, 1963. Whitch is my birthday. She is looking forward to this day very much. She sends her love to you and Grandma.

"I am now an Altar boy and I serve Mass. I have a partner. . . . He is a nut. Because his makes mistaks when we serve. He is so nutty. Well Good by now I hope I will see you soon.

> "Your loving child
> "Bobby Sargent Shriver"

And of course the children and their spouses wrote him often, always keeping him informed of what they were doing or about to do out there in the wide world he could no longer reach. Here, for instance, is one from Jackie, from the White House, in 1962:

"Dearest Grandpa,

"You were taking a nap when I left. I am off to Italy with Caroline for 2 weeks—to stay with Lee and Stas. We will send you lots of postcards & pictures & miss you very much. We will see you soon when we get home & bring you some marvelous present. . . .

"Please put the picture of Jack & me & Caroline & John right by your favorite chair where Eunice will see it—& nail it down so she can't take it away & put Timmy there instead.

"I love you—
"Jackie"

A characteristic scene that seldom varied much and I remember so well would be when Jack and the presidential party would come up to the Cape for summer weekends. Dr. Betts has mentioned this, but I can supply some details and from another viewpoint, and from another point in time. These are diary notes that I made in 1964, when it was all over and I was trying to remember what it had been like when. . . .

"Jack was here with all of the excitement of the helicopters arriving on Friday evenings in front of our house. The Secret Service would set up a telephone in front of the porch an hour or two in advance, in order to keep track of the exact time of arrival, because there could be a change of a few minutes to half an hour. The children would gather in the driveway—fifteen or twenty or thirty of them with their friends. The dogs would be there barking, the maids would stand a bit in the background, and probably a few close friends would also have gathered. The fire trucks were at the end of the driveway. The voice of the Secret Service man could be heard discussing the time and the weather conditions for landings.

"Then at a distance we could hear the sound of the motors. Joe would be wheeled out on the porch with a robe over his knees. A wave of excitement would sweep over the group as we watched the

first helicopter approach, then slow down, then balance itself gracefully, expertly, precisely to land exactly on the small yard in front of
Joe's chair where he was waiting on the porch. The door of the helicopter would open, officers would step out, then the President.

"Caroline and John would run and jump into his arms. He would
lean over ever so affectionately and hug and embrace them. I always realized he was a little wary as to how he bent, so as not to hurt
his back; and, of course, he never lifted them up into his arms. But
the casual onlooker would never have detected any difficulty.

"Then Bobby's children would run to him, or the Shrivers' or
Lawfords' or Smiths' or Teddy and Joan's—whoever was there. They
would all be laughing, joking, about the sunburns or the races won
or lost.

"Jack then would come up onto the front porch where his father
was sitting so proudly in his wheel chair. They would embrace, say
a few words; then Jack would come and hug me too and let me kiss
him on the cheek. And Jack would always have a big, all-embracing
smile.

"Then, after a few minutes, everyone would separate, going to
their own various houses but to come together later, for dinner, at
our house and perhaps—depending on how many people were on
hand—at one of the other houses.

"The presidential yacht—the *Honey Fitz*—usually was anchored
here during those summers. Often the next day Jack would go out in
it with some of the family, friends, and staff. Joe usually would go out
in the family cruiser, the *Marlin*, and one or two of the boys would
take turns being with him. Jackie and some of the other girls did a
lot of water skiing, pulled by a speedboat. Sunday, after Mass, was
more of the same, mixed in with golf and tennis and other sports
and lively conversation.

"Then on Monday morning the same scene, the same excitement,
as the helicopters took off for the airport and the trip back to Washington."

Jack's administration had its rough times, its share of crises, but
as he settled into the presidency, it seemed that he gained increasing confidence and momentum, and that soon he proceeded from

triumph to triumph. Among the most remarkable were those of June 1963, on official travels that took him to Germany, Ireland, England, and Italy. I wished that I could go along, as all four countries have special associations for me, and I thought in particular I might be helpful in Germany as Chancellor Adenauer spoke very little English and my German might at last come in handy. "Mac" Bundy told me later it really would have, that my interest in the language and country would have eased the way with the Chancellor.

Alas, it was not to be. First, because Joe was not feeling very well and I hesitated to leave him; also because Jack had already invited Eunice and Jean, and Jackie's sister, Lee, for most of the trip, and I really felt it would be unfair to the poor boy to have his mother along too—otherwise I might have hitched my way to Germany as I had to Austria in 1961.

However, Jack seemed to get along quite well without my linguistic assistance. He had tremendous and enthusiastic crowds everywhere he went in West Germany; and this was the time, too, when he went to West Berlin and was greeted by perhaps the biggest crowds ever seen, more than a million people, and gave that famous speech that closed with the words: "All free men, wherever they may live, are citizens of Berlin, and therefore as a free man, I take pride in the words *Ich bin ein Berliner!*"

He flew then to Ireland. Not really for matters of state—Irish-American relations couldn't have been more cordial—but as a brief, sentimental journey to the land of his ancestors. Jack delighted in his Irish heritage. And, perhaps, took a more than ordinary interest in it because of stories he had heard from his grandparents, handed down to them by their parents, about the miserable conditions under which the immigrants of the 1840s and '50s had arrived in Boston, and the poverty and social disdain they suffered there as "muckers" and the like, a condition from which they could rise only by hard work and ingenuity.

Jack believed fully, devoutly, in America as a land of opportunity. He took to heart the ideal of America as a land of liberty and the words inscribed on the pedestal of the Statue of Liberty: "Give me your tired, your poor, your huddled masses yearning to breathe free . . ." For some years he had been making notes for a book he intended to write, someday, about the migrations of the many national, ethnic, political, and religious groups to this country, the problems they fled and those they had to face, the processes of their assimilation here: The title he had in mind was *A Nation of Immigrants.*

And so I'm sure his heart was in it fully when he spoke on the quayside at New Ross and said: "When my great-grandfather left here to become a cooper in East Boston he carried nothing with him except two things, a strong religious faith and a strong desire for liberty. I am glad to say that all of his great-grandchildren have valued that inheritance."

The people of Ireland already felt a proud affinity for him as one of their own. But when they saw him in person and heard him speak and sensed his special feeling for them, they went all but berserk with joy. The whole island—as those with him told me later—appeared to be a tumult of admiration and celebration.

Later on, after he was gone from this life, Sybil Connolly, the Irish designer, who was there at the time, mentioned a certain remark she heard and I asked her to write it out for me:

"I promised you that I would send you the remark made by the then Dutch ambassador to Ireland, commenting on the visit of President Kennedy there in the spring of 1963.

"On the fantastic reception which the President received and the way the Irish people took him to their hearts, he said: 'It is the conquering Alexander returning to his people.' And there is a ring of truth in this.

"I wish that you could see for yourself, over the hearth of almost every cottage in Ireland—a picture of the Sacred Heart, of the Blessed Virgin, and of President Kennedy—it is extremely moving."

Jack loved poetry. And there remained a special place in his heart and mind for that delicate, dew-drenched, and musical poetry that seems characteristic of Ireland. Among the Irish poems he cherished most was one that was recited for him by the Irish Ambassador Thomas Kiernan, in honor of John Jr., when John was still a baby:

> "*We wish to the new child*
> *A heart that can be beguiled by a flower*
> *That the wind lifts as it passes*
> *Over the grasses after a summer shower,*

A heart that can recognize
Without aid of the eyes
The gifts that life holds for the wise.
When the storms break for him,
May the trees shake for him their blossoms down.
In the night that he is troubled
May a friend wake for him
So that his time be doubled,
And at the end of all loving and love,
May the Man Above
Give him a crown."

Jack, I am told, was so moved that he found it difficult to speak. But then said, "I wish it had been written for me."

I think that in a way it was.

He went to England for talks with Prime Minister Macmillan. But this too was in part a sentimental journey, for on the way he went privately, with Jean, Lee, and Lem, accompanied by the Duke and Duchess of Devonshire, to Chatsworth, to visit Kick's grave. They prayed by the graveside and left a bunch of fresh-picked Irish roses at the headstone.

In Italy, his last stop, he conferred not only with the leaders of government but with the newly crowned Pope Paul VI at the Vatican. The Pope told him he remembered our family very well from the time, twenty-five years earlier, we had come to the coronation of Pope Pius XII and then Pius had confirmed little Teddy in the Church in a private ceremony. Pope Paul sent his greetings to all of us, with special ones for Teddy.

Then Jack was back in Washington, and cleared his desk enough so that he was able to come up and have the long Fourth of July weekend with us, and tell us about his rather fabulous experiences. Afterward, he was with us for most of the summer and fall weekends.

The last of these visits was on Sunday, October 20, 1963. Kenny O'Donnell and Dave Powers have described the Monday-morning departure:

"Ambassador Kennedy was on the porch in his wheel chair. The President went to him, put his arm around the old man's shoulder and kissed him on the forehead. He started to the helicopter, turned, looked at his father for a moment, and went back and kissed him a second time. . . . It almost seemed as if the President had the feeling that he was seeing his father for the last time.

"When the President was inside the helicopter waiting for the take-off, he looked out at the figure in the wheel chair and his eyes filled with tears.

" 'He's the one who made all of this possible,' the President said to Dave sadly, 'and look at him now.' "

He had to be in Texas several days during mid-November, to smooth some political problems in the Democratic Party there, and would be taking Jackie with him. But then they planned to come back, with Caroline and John, for the annual family reunion and Thanksgiving at Hyannis Port.

I remember Friday, November 22, began as one of those perfect late autumn days at the Cape. At that time of year the air is crisp but not cold, just cool enough to make some warmth from fireplaces most welcome even if not entirely needed, and it has such freshness from the sea that one's spirits are lifted up. There is a special quality to the light then too: It is golden, pure, making everything stand out in clear relief and with a peculiar and lovely luminosity—every white clapboard house and every tree and autumn-colored leaf or bare branch, every bayberry and sumac and wild beach rose with its red pips and valiant remaining blossoms, seem to come to special life, as if to assert their qualities and beauties and reasons for being just before the frosts and snows. Many of the garden flowers are still in bloom, too: the asters and chrysanthemums and calendulas and black-eyed susans and marigolds and other old-fashioned blooms that we always planted abundantly in our gardens and that made such a show of color through the fall. By then, also, the tourists and "summer people" had gone and the village, though not deserted, was somnolent.

And so on that beautiful morning, after I had been to Mass and we had had breakfast, Joe and I went for a ride in the station wagon, simply enjoying the weather, the scenery, and the serenity; then went back to the house; then I went over to the golf course. Usually I liked to play in the afternoons, but at this season on the Cape the afternoons become short and dusk soon falls, so I played in the mornings: played the usual nine holes, then came back to have lunch with Joe.

After lunch, Joe had his nap. I was feeling rather tired and went to my room to lie down for a while. Soon, I heard Ann's radio set blaring so loudly in her room down the hall that I got up and went to tell her to please tune it down, or better yet just turn it off. Ann said the volume was up because she had just heard from one of the staff, who had been listening to a favorite program that was interrupted by a news bulletin, that along the route in Dallas someone had taken some shots at the President and he had been wounded.

I had a mixture of reactions. Worry about Jack, of course, instinctively. But then a rejection of the idea that it could be something terribly serious because, after all, he had been through so much, from the time he was in danger of death from scarlet fever as a little child to the time he nearly died from his back operation, and so many things in between, so that almost automatically I had in the back of my mind the thought "Jack is having some more hard luck, another problem about his health but he'll surmount it." Further, I had trained myself through the years not to become too visibly upset at bad news, even very bad news, because I had a strong notion that if I broke down, everybody else in the household would.

I went back to my room and paced the floor, trying to think that Jack was going to be all right; that soon the news would come that he had not been wounded badly. After a while I went back to Ann's room and found that the news was worse. My heart sank. But I still couldn't realize that what seemed to be happening was really happening. Then, a few minutes later, Bobby telephoned from Washington and said Jack was in extremely serious condition and was not expected to live. And then, soon, the news came that Jack was gone.

At any such time of shock and grief I suppose that most people fall back for some support on familiar patterns of behavior that can be followed automatically. In our household, many long years before, Joe and I had adopted as a general principle that if there was bad news to be faced it should be given in the morning, not late in the day, for otherwise there would be a sleepless night which would only make the debility worse. Hence, I made a spontaneous decision that Joe should not be told of the tragedy when he awakened from his nap, and that if it were at all possible he should not know of it until the following morning. This would also allow time for his physician, then Dr. Boles, to come down to the Cape from Boston, and for Teddy and Eunice to come up from Washington, as they had called and said they wanted to do so, with Bobby staying in Washington to take care of Jackie and supervising all the things that would need to be done there. Sarge, Jean, and Steve were also in Washington; Pat, on her way from California. I told Ann and the nurses that Mr. Kennedy was not to be informed of anything about this until the children had arrived and we could decide how and when he would be told.

They all, the household staff and everyone, entered into a conspiracy of kindness. Shocked and grief-ridden though they were, they acted their parts superbly well. For example, Joe was in the habit of looking at television after his nap or of seeing a movie in our basement projection room. The TV screen was filled with news of the tragedy; Ann was working on him to see a movie that day instead. He agreed. But he lost interest in the film after a while and wanted to come back up to see his programs. Ann had unplugged all the sets so that none of them worked, and of course he was irritated, but then he seemed to accept this as one of those coincidental freakish defects of modern technology and contented himself as much as he could by reading a magazine. Now and then, one or another or several of us would go into his room to chat about something, almost anything that would have been an ordinary thing to talk about. Joey Gargan heard the news and hurried down from Boston to help in any way he could—one way being to enter into these apparently casual and rather aimless conversations during which everyone was inwardly anguished except Joe, who may have suspected something was wrong but didn't know. Ann was supposed to have left that day to visit Mary Jo and Dick Clasby and their family, who lived in Detroit at that time. Joe realized this, but Ann explained by telling him that Wilbert Marsh, the gardener and caretaker of our Hyannis Port place and of whom Joe was very fond (he was the brother of Evelyn Jones, who has contributed some memories here), had been in an accident and she wanted to stay to be sure that everything was all right with him. Joe accepted this well-meant fabrication.

Meanwhile, as that afternoon wore on, I spent much time in our front yard or on our beach, and walked and walked and walked, and prayed and prayed and prayed, and wondered why it had happened to Jack. He had everything to live for: a lovely and talented wife, a perfect partner for him, and two beautiful little children whom he adored. He had made such a glorious success of his life and of his presidency, and at last, for the first time since early childhood, he had become really healthy. Everything—the culmination of all his efforts, abilities, dedication to good and to the future—lay boundlessly before him. Everything was gone. And I wondered why.

I heard and read later that most of the nation, and even much of the world, was in a state of suspended animation after the tragedy: some mixture of incredulity, outrage, shock, and immense grief, and that this was true wherever the news came and among all groups and ages, but especially among the young, because so many young people looked to Jack as a hero and model for their lives. A friend of mine told me later that his young son, a boy then of about thirteen, came home from school looking taut and almost ashen and went at once to his room. And when the father, knowing the news and knowing how the boy Kevin had idolized Jack, went up and touched him on the shoulder and started to try to say something that would make it bearable, the boy began sobbing "It's not fair! . . . It's not fair! . . . It's just *not fair!* . . ."

I walked on the beach and I thought, "Why?"

In the afternoon the day had turned quite cold and the fogs and mists had begun coming in, as often happens at that time of year, and on one of my trips to the house I had bundled up in warm clothing. I think I put on the same old but warm coat I had worn through the snows when I went to Mass the morning of Jack's inauguration. It was then, or somewhere around that time, about four in the afternoon, that someone came out to tell me President Johnson was calling us on the radio telephone from Air Force One, on the way back to Washington.

When I picked up the receiver and said, "Hello," I heard his voice, full of recognizable anguish, saying, "Mrs. Kennedy, I wish to God there was something I could do." I don't remember what I said, but I thanked him for calling with his sympathy; then I heard Lady Bird's voice. She and I had done some campaigning together in 1960, and had liked each other. I had found her to be intelligent, warm, and understanding. She said a few words first—I don't remember— and then, "We must all realize how fortunate the country was to have your son as long as it did." And I said, "Thank you, Lady Bird." And that's all either of us felt like saying just then.

I went back to the yard and the beach.

My reaction to grief takes in part the form of nervous activity. I have to keep moving, walking, pulling away at things, praying to myself while I move, and making up my mind that I am not going to be defeated by tragedy. Because there are the living still to work for, while mourning for the dead.

Dr. Boles arrived. There were many telephone calls, all of them so wonderfully well meant. Dr. Boles went to check on Joe's general condition, on the acceptable grounds that he would be leaving for Florida soon after Thanksgiving and this was therefore a routine checkup. Dr. Boles told us that Joe could, physically, withstand the emotional shock, though he agreed it would be better if it came not that evening but in the morning. Ted and Eunice arrived together and went in, as casually as they could manage, to see their father. Perhaps Joe was surprised by this conjunction but there was no reason to be very surprised: After all, he was due for a checkup from Dr. Boles. Joey had a holiday house at Hyannis Port. Both Ted and Eunice traveled a lot, because of their public interests and responsibilities and therefore might drop in on us most anytime.

After dinner—Joe having a tray in his room, which was not unusual, I having a cup of broth or something in mine, the others having something downstairs—we all assembled, as casually as possible, in Joe's room and chatted there for a while until he was ready for sleep.

It was decided among us, with Ted really deciding to take it on himself, that he should be the one to tell his father the next morning.

I went to the morning devotions at the beautiful little church, St. Francis Xavier's, in Hyannis—where all four sons had served as altar boys—and stayed on for the first Mass of the day, to which Ted and Eunice came. I had called the pastor the night before and asked him to say this Mass for Jack. It was one of the first things I had thought to do. There were reporters and photographers, some of whom even tried to talk to me within the church, but I could do nothing but ignore them.

After Mass we went home to breakfast. And, as usual, after breakfast Joe went back to his room for a rest. It was very soon then that Ted—with Eunice, Ann, the doctor, a nurse, perhaps one or two others; not I, for I couldn't stand it—went in and told him, as gently yet as straight-out as he possibly could, what had happened and that Jack had passed away.

As I heard from them afterward, Joe not only took the tragic news bravely but seemed to want to comfort them.

The doctor had already given him a sedative, and soon he went back to sleep.

The doctor said that it would be feasible for Joe to go to the funeral in Washington that Monday, but he rejected the idea. One of his old friends, Father John Cavanaugh, the former president of Notre Dame University, came to stay at the house for such aid and comfort as he could give. The two of them sat together and watched the ceremonies on television.

It was far easier for me to travel, and I felt I should be there. And I was. I did not walk with the others in the procession from the White House to the Cathedral because I felt queasy, quite unwell, that morning. Nor did I take Communion at the Cathedral, as some others did, because I had already been to an early Mass and had received it then. I was at the graveside in Arlington, of course, for the final ceremonies. Afterward, with the others, I went to the White House to help express our family's appreciation to the numerous heads of state, other dignitaries, and many friends who had traveled from far places to pay respects; among those friends, the Duke and Duchess of Devonshire.

Then, that evening, I came back to Hyannis Port to be with Joe.

Chapter Nineteen

❦

For I have promises to keep
And miles to go before I sleep
And miles to go before I sleep
                    Robert Frost

We in the family reacted to our common grief in our own ways. But we could all be reasonably steady because of the faith, hope, and love we shared. And because we knew quite well what Jack would want from us: He would want courage, he would want as many smiles as we could manage, and he would want his death to be an affirmation of life. He would want us to think of him with love, but to live for the living, and to cherish such happiness as we could find and give, and any bit of light and hope and example of fortitude that might help us and others. We all realized this, and it needed no discussion, and we all did our best.

Everyone knows the bravery and dignity with which Jackie conducted herself during the ceremonies. Afterward, at the White House, she had received the many eminent visitors from abroad, and did so not only with composure but with some appropriate word or gesture of thanks for each of them. As General de Gaulle remarked, "She gave an example to the whole world of how to behave."

Thanksgiving was three days later. I think it was well understood —with only a few words passed around in confirmation—that we would go ahead with it as usual at Hyannis Port. And so during Tuesday and Wednesday the children and in-laws and cousins and grandchildren began arriving. We didn't know whether Jackie would come. After everything she had been through in Dallas and Washington it would have been entirely understandable if she had wanted a time of seclusion. But on Wednesday evening she too arrived, bringing Caroline and John. And on Thursday we had the Thanksgiving celebration, with every one of us hiding the grief that gnawed at us and doing our best to make it a day of peace, optimism, and thanks for the blessings that were still left to us.

Not long ago Jackie was thinking back to that time—and to times of hard misfortune or tragedy that came later—and she said:

"Something so incredible about them is their gallantry. You can be sitting down to dinner with them and so many sad things have happened to each, and—God!—maybe even some sad thing has happened that day, and you can see that each one is aware of the other's suffering. And so they can sit down at the table in a rather sad frame of mind. Then each one will begin to start to make this conscious effort to be gay or funny or to lift each other's spirits; and you find that it's infectious, that everybody's doing it. They all bounce off each other.

"They all have a humor that's my favorite kind. It's a little bit irrelevant, a little bit self-mocking, a little sense of the ridiculous, and in times of sadness of wildly wicked humor of irreverence. I don't mean they're laughing when they shouldn't be. But to make a real effort to use the light touch when everybody's sad—I think it is wonderful.

"They have been such a great help to me. My natural tendency is to be rather introverted and solitary and to retreat into myself and brood too much. But they bring out the best. No one sits and wallows in self-pity. It's just so gallant that it really makes you proud. And you think, look at these people and the effort they are making, and you think that's a lesson you want to take with you."

Early that December, Joe and I went back to the Palm Beach house. We had Christmas in the usual way—the big tree and all the trimmings—and some of the children and grandchildren were able to be there. They all came for visits that winter and spring as often as they could, to cheer our lives.

There was much for me to do, especially during those first few months. Many thousands of letters of sympathy and condolence came to us: far more than I could possibly reply to personally, so most had to be taken over by the girls, or near relatives, or people in the New York or Washington offices who knew our minds and would know what to say. However, there were hundreds from personal friends and others whom I felt ought to hear directly from us; and, of course, that was up to me, since it was impossible for Joe.

His general health seemed about the same as before. But, whereas when the President came to visit he had often been able to move around somewhat in a walker, or even with a cane and some help, soon after Jack's passing he seldom tried this and spent most of the rest of his days in a chair.

There are some lines from Tennyson's "Ulysses" which Jack had especially liked:

> *I am part of all that I have met:*
> *Yet all experience is an arch wherethrough*
> *Gleams that untravelled world, whose margin fades*
> *For ever and for ever when I move.*
> *How dull it is to pause, to make an end,*
> *To rust unburnished, not to shine in use!*
> *As though to breathe were life.*
> *Life piled on life were all too little.*

And I thought sometimes to myself how aptly and how sadly more than ever those words could apply to Joe, who now seemed doomed, mainly, "To rust unburnished, not to shine in use," whereas we others had at least the solace of being able to move about and do things useful to Jack's memory and ideals.

There were so many memorials for Jack that even we in the family were surprised—as well as deeply appreciative—for bereaved as we felt, we could not have anticipated the sense of bereavement that was felt apparently by most Americans and indeed by vast numbers of people all over the world. I was often invited to take part in the programs and ceremonies; and when I could, I did.

The first major one, as I remember, that I felt I could and should and really wanted to attend was in January, in Boston, when Cardinal Cushing offered a solemn high Mass for Jack at Holy Cross

Cathedral and Erich Leinsdorf conducted the Boston Symphony Orchestra in Mozart's *Requiem in D Minor.*

Boston, Jack's birthplace and associated with so many memories of him and such intimate, almost infinite memories of our family . . . The cardinal, who married Jack, who had given benediction at his inauguration and now so recently had buried him, and who was such a very dear family friend . . . the Boston Symphony, with all it had meant to Joe and me when we were courting and as young marrieds . . . the beauty of the Mass, of the cathedral, and of the music and the special poignancy that Mozart had died leaving it an unfinished work . . . all these elements together had a nearly over-powering effect. I managed with difficulty to keep a grip on myself and show outward composure.

The next month I went north again, to New York, to attend a benefit dinner for the Joseph P. Kennedy, Jr. Foundation (for Mental Retardation). Eunice had organized it. Bobby and Ted were there also. President Johnson was the speaker. In the course of an eloquent address, in which he pledged his Administration to continue the government's support for work in mental retardation, initiated by Jack, he also paid what I'm sure was a deeply felt tribute to Jack as a man and a statesman, and to our family, saying: "Our generation is proud and blessed to have known the Kennedys."

Soon afterward the Johnsons came to Florida for a Democratic fund-raising dinner in Miami. I have a diary note:

"February 27, 1964

"President and Mrs. Johnson stopped at Palm Beach to see Joe, on their way to Miami. He had mentioned to Bobby the possibility of coming here, and the hour was arranged. Strange to say, I was a little excited as well as sad. About an hour before their arrival they called up from Air Force One to see if I was going to be home. In that case, Lady Bird would come over with him. They arrived about 4:45, saw Joe in the study. The President told his plans for the Miami meeting. I showed Mrs. Johnson our living room, with the beamed ceilings and old Spanish tiles, which are characteristic of the early Palm Beach houses built by the architect Mizner. Then we joined the men for a glass of orange juice. Pierre Salinger, the press secretary who used to work for Jack, was with the President; also a military aide in uniform. After about twenty minutes they departed. There were a few people outside on the street who applauded them, and they waved back.

Easter came early that year. Jean came down to Palm Beach with Steve and their children to stay two weeks and see her father. This was convenient for me because I had been invited to attend ceremonies in Paris where one of the principal avenues was to be renamed for Jack. This was late March and early April.

An entry in my diary:

"First, I went to Boston to see my mother before going abroad, spent the night there, and was glad of it. I put my head in her room in the morning and I saw a shaft of light directly across her face. It crept in through a space between the wall and the curtain. I do not know why the nurses do not do something about such things. The same way when I came to lunch with her one day and found her scrambled eggs cold on a cold plate.

"The same principle as for nurses and governesses with the children. I always used to walk up the beach in the summer to see that a new governess was not flirting with the swimming instructor while the children sat around in wet bathing suits. Or I would go to the children's dances and walk around to see how they were dancing, a very easy thing to do in the summertime when you could stand outside and look through the windows. Also, I was always present during the children's meals. Perhaps the cook gave them the same soup every night because she did not have enough imagination, or did not want to bother giving them a different one. Or a different dessert. The nurse would not want to complain about it because she would not want to get in wrong with the cook. So it was a good idea for me, as a mother, to keep an eye on all these things, which I tried to do.

"Mother 98 now. I have tried to see her every few months. Sight and hearing are failing and I think she knows nothing about Jack's passing. When I see her she is quiet, sitting always in the same chair, and weeping a little when she sees me."

In Paris:

"Arrived in Paris at midnight, their time, and unpacked my bags to be ready for the ceremony in the morning. Ambassador Bohlen met me at the plane and explained all details. In the morning about 9:30 stopped at the ambassadorial residence for coffee, then drove to the site of ceremony, on the Seine, where Ambassador Bohlen & André Malraux, the French Minister of Culture, escorted me. The president of the Parisian city council, Aubertin, made some brief but eloquent remarks renaming the Quai de Passy to Avenue du President Kennedy. It is a beautiful street, going along the right bank, and had many memories for me; many more now . . . In numerous French towns and villages, streets are being renamed for Jack. And also in other countries.

"At the Paris ceremony the people looked grim and sympathetic. As they do every place if I go out and am recognized. My old acquaintance M. Zembrzuski, manager at the Ritz, said he really dreaded to see me because his grief was so deep and he would not know what to say.

"Much as I appreciate these sentiments they make it more difficult for me, because of the constant reminders."

Loel and Gloria Guinness are friends of our family. They have a house down the coast from us in Florida and also (among other places, for they move around a lot) a house in Normandy where they spend the spring. Knowing I would be in France that season, they had invited me to drop in on them. After my time in Paris, I wanted to get away from people who wished to commiserate with me. Since the Guinnesses are always lively and cheerful, I went to see them.

Later they were recalling that visit for my book, and Gloria said:

"It was the coldest Easter I have ever known in my life. We wanted to send a car and driver to Paris to bring her because, you know, with the train there is a big waiting room, the confusion, the luggage. But she said, 'Thank you, don't bother at all. I would prefer to take the train.' Then some hours later she arrived at our station in Normandy, and Loel went with a car and driver and got her and her luggage and she arrived at our house. The first thing she said was, 'How can I find out what time Mass is and where?'

"She found out there was a Mass at 7 o'clock in the morning every day in different churches, which would take turns. Now, this woman never, but never once in the three or four days she was there, talked about pessimism, about tragedy, or that she was in mourning.

"Now, staying with us at the house were my niece who was seventeen and my son who was twenty-six—Freddie Brisson was there too. She suppered with the young people, talked with them, made them laugh, found out that my niece was a heretic who didn't like church, so she dragged her to church right away and said it doesn't make any difference if you don't believe—you come with me because I don't want to be alone. So then the girl began to go to church again because she liked it. She is still going to church in Mexico where she lives.

"My husband had terrible backaches in those days, and the day before Rose left we were sitting and suddenly she said, 'You know, Loel, what you should do is try these pads that one sticks on the back. Because, you know, Jack had this terrible problem with his back, and I told him about those plasters and they helped him.'

"At that moment she cried. Then recovered immediately and said, 'Terribly sorry,' and she dried her tears and changed the conversation. And that is the only time in the years I have known Rose Kennedy I have ever seen her cry, and I think it was only because she was thinking of her boy as a young boy being hurt, that was what made her cry. We were good friends and from then on we became the greatest friends."

I should add a note of explanation about the "plasters." They are thin but strong adhesive bandages made of an elastic fabric that can be applied across the back to give extra support. I had suggested to Jack that he try them, and he took a supply along on that last trip of his to Europe. And when he came back and—that July Fourth weekend—helicoptered onto the front lawn at Hyannis Port, and after greeting the children, then his father, and coming to me, he said, "Mother, those plasters of yours really helped. I only wish I had known about them sooner." To my mind this was an example of his demeanor and attitude in so many ways: He was open to advice, and when it worked he was open in his thanks.

Back home in the United States there was much to do and think about: memorials, dedications, grand projects conceived in Jack's honor, particularly the Kennedy Center for the Performing Arts, in

Washington, and the John F. Kennedy Library in Cambridge, near the Harvard campus.

It has become customary, in modern times, for American Presidents to collect speeches, state papers, correspondence, and documents of their administrations and bring them together in a place where they can be accessible to historians, scholars, and students. Jack had chosen the site he wanted for his library, on property owned by Harvard but on the other side of the Charles River; overlooking the river and with a view of the main campus. He planned to spend a great deal of his time there after his presidency. Assuming that he would be elected to a second term he would be only fifty-two years old when he left the White House, with many years ahead in which to apply his experience, energy, and talents to the good of the nation and of the world. This location would give him access to the tremendous intellectual facilities and personnel of the Boston area, with its distinguished universities and colleges, and also to the minds of the thousands of students whom he could hope to inspire and inform and encourage toward the ideals he held. The library, as he had envisioned it, would have been of fairly modest proportions: big enough for a few offices and reading rooms, for his archives, and for books about or relevant to his presidency—including the history of it that he intended to write himself.

After his death the idea seemed to grow spontaneously that it should be much enlarged to include all the facilities, programs, and staff to make it a major center for the study of political science and statecraft. As well as a library, it would become a school of government and, especially through its adjunct Institute of Politics, would seek to further one of President Kennedy's deepest concerns—increasing the understanding and cooperation between the scholarly community and the political world—conceiving politics not only as the search for public power but also as its use for public purposes: in short, the whole of government. There would also be room for the personal memorabilia of his life such as his childhood letters, some of which have been quoted here; the coconut shell on which he wrote the message that the natives took to the nearest Allied base after the PT-boat episode and that resulted in his rescue with his surviving crew members; and a few thousand other items. (Dave Powers is curator of the collection.) And the archives would be broadened to include family and other materials that could shed light on his life. (The materials for this book will eventually go there.)

This much bigger enterprise needed a great deal of money. Hence, fund-raising committees came into existence all across the country. It also needed enabling legislation on the part of several government bodies, in the first instance by the Massachusetts legislature. One of the things I did after returning from France was to give testimony to the joint legislative committee, explaining why a library of this sort would be such an appropriate memorial to him and why I felt he would have appreciated it.

Others in the family were out doing the same sorts of things— making appearances, giving talks, helping to raise funds, helping to make plans, doing affirmative things—and I'm sure it was a helpful catharsis for them, especially for Jackie. Her sister, Lee, to whom she always was extremely devoted, stayed with her for a time, but then of course had to return to her home and husband and children in London. Fortunately, Jackie enjoyed the company of her sisters-in-law, and they all rallied to her with love and affection and with all the time they could find free from their husbands, families, and other responsibilities.

Jean, who had the smallest family and also was the nearest in age, was probably her closest companion—especially after Jackie moved with the children from Washington to New York, where Jean and Steve and their family live. Jackie and Jean went around the country a lot, looking at libraries and cultural centers, and at drawings and scale models, talking with architects, trying to plan what should be done in memory of their husband and brother. And surely this was good for both of them, and all of us.

Early that summer, on June 19, there was very nearly another tragedy within our family. Ted and another young senator, Birch Bayh of Indiana, and Mrs. Bayh, and Ed Moss, a close friend and aide of Ted's, were due at a meeting in Springfield, Massachusetts, and had taken a charter flight—through a foggy night—and the plane crashed during the approach to the landing field. The pilot was killed. Later, Ed Moss died. Senator and Mrs. Bayh were bruised and cut and had fractures, and were hospitalized, but did escape without long-range serious effects. Ted was very badly injured. As we learned later, he had sent all the others ahead in the first ambulance that arrived —while he lay stretched out on the ground with no more than first aid—and waited for the second one to take him to the emergency ward. Once in the hospital, it was touch and go for a while as to whether he would live; and after that, if he lived, whether he would be able to walk and lead a normal life again, since several of his vertebrae were fractured and there was a possibility his spinal cord had been damaged.

He was bedfast for six months—most of them in traction—but with his rugged constitution he was able to progress to a wheel chair, to crutches, and finally to walk and run and even engage in sports; although for years afterward, until fairly recently, he had to wear a back brace. He seems to be in perfect health now.

Meanwhile, during his convalescence, he was able to take care of the important business of his Senate office by telephone, mail, and courier, as Jack had done while recovering from his back operations. And again like Jack, who had used the months while he was laid up to write *Profiles in Courage*, Ted turned his physical incapacity to constructive use by collecting and editing the essays about his father that became *The Fruitful Bough*.

Here are a few diary entries made during the early summer of 1964, following Ted's accident:

"Ted is in the hospital, and Joan is with him most of the time. And if she can't be there, Jean, Pat, Eunice, or others try to go up. I have not been yet. The day I was planning to go, Teddy had been scheduled to make a speech in Philadelphia at a memorial for Jack and I substituted for him. Then, the next time I planned to go turned out to be the day of dear Mary Moore's funeral.

"I try to keep myself very busy all the time, as it is the only way I can keep normal and not think about what might have been. I read and study French continually, although at times I think it is foolish as in Paris everyone at the hotel and at the couturiers speaks English, and I know few French people socially. I am reading a lot of books on art, and especially the seminars issued by the Metropolitan Museum. We go around here to the different houses of the family for dinner, and often there are guests, many of them friends of Jack's.

"President and Mrs. Johnson have called to tell us how sorry they were to hear of Ted's accident and to wish him full recovery. They spoke highly of him, as also in the past they had of Bobby. They have seemed most thoughtful and solicitous about our family. Have called us a number of times and also have called Jackie often. I have written them and thanked them, and told the President how much these attentions have meant, particularly to Joe: a boost to his morale.

"Bobby is here, but seems to be distracted by the confusion and uncertainty surrounding his own plans. He feels that he should do nothing to prevent his being chosen by President Johnson to run as Vice-President, although he thinks it unlikely that will happen. Sometimes he talks about going abroad for a year to write a book or just to get away from it all."

Bobby had been very close to Jack; had felt united with him. Not so much in the earlier years because there were eight years between them, and that is a big gap when children in a family are young. In maturity the difference lessens, and soon they discover one another as equals and contemporaries with the same interests. And so it was with Jack and Bobby. Bobby had worked in the 1946 congressional campaign, had managed the first Senate campaign, had managed the presidential campaign, had been in Jack's Cabinet and at his right hand through every problem that arose during the presidency. And as brothers they shared ties of loyalty, sentiment, memory.

No wonder, then, that Bobby at first acted as if he had been cut adrift and did not know quite what to try to do in the years ahead. However, automatically and instinctively and very deeply, he wanted to do what Jack would have wanted of him, which in the first urgent priority of things would be to help Jackie and the two children.

It was Bobby who met Air Force One when it arrived back from Dallas the night of the assassination with Jack in his coffin and Jackie in her bloodstained suit and who took charge of everything and stayed in charge, acting for the family and for himself and for her. He stayed with Jackie through most of the waking hours of those next days, went out with her to Arlington at midnight to pray at Jack's grave and leave a little, personal bouquet of flowers there. Stayed on in support or nearby until she was on the plane with Caroline and John Jr. to fly up to us on Thanksgiving Eve.

Bobby, whose life had been so much involved with Jack's, did not himself come up for Thanksgiving. It was something he could not quite do. He had reached a state, I suppose, of almost insupportable emotional shock. He and Ethel and their older children went down to Florida for a few days, where I daresay he walked the beach and thought and thought, as Jack had done when he heard of Joe Jr.'s death.

In any event, during those next months—and indeed for the next years—Bobby was a main pillar of strength in Jackie's life: adviser, protector, confidant, and good, cheerful companion whenever he was needed. Ted, of course, did everything he could for her too, but he was younger than she, whereas Bobby was four years older and thus suited by age as well as temperament for the role of protective older brother. She had no really close male kin of her own. Her father was dead. There was a much younger half brother, only a boy. So it was natural and fitting that she should turn to Bobby in this time of sorrow and reconstruction in her life.

We were at Hyannis Port when Teddy's airplane accident happened. Jean had tuned in the eleven o'clock news: Just then a bulletin came through. She ran across the lane and told Bobby. The two of them, without disturbing their father and me at the big house, began driving and arrived at the hospital around four in the morning. After assuring himself that his brother was still alive and might pull through, Bobby found Mrs. Moss, whose husband was dying, and spent a long time walking and talking with her to give her any comfort he could.

He went back to check on Ted, who was encumbered with all the tubes and tents and medical paraphernalia of the desperately ill, but who was able to summon a small smile and in a muffled voice say, "Is it true that you are ruthless?" It was a typical Kennedy brotherly joke, and I expect that at that moment Bobby felt things were really going to be all right for Ted.

Ted was up for re-election that year. Obviously, campaigning in person was out of the question, but he had an able and devoted staff, headed by Steve Smith. I made a few appearances for him to help out. But it was Joan who was the star of that campaign. She was all over the state, doing all the chatting and speaking and handshaking and all the rest that a hard-working candidate must do, and which did not come naturally to her but which she performed tirelessly and superbly. A lot of others, Steve especially, were certainly doing something right because Teddy was re-elected with more than 75 per cent of the votes.

It became apparent, as that summer of 1964 went on, that President Johnson preferred to have someone other than Bobby on the ticket with him for Vice-President. I suppose that was a natural reaction on his part, not involving unfriendly feelings necessarily but rather that if he were elected to his own term of office he would want to start afresh on his own, without the continual reminder of Jack's presidency, which Bobby's presence in White House councils and events and as presiding officer in the Senate inevitably would bring. I was disappointed for Bobby because I knew he wanted the nomination. But I felt that the Johnsons had behaved toward us with tact and kindness and good will in a situation that, difficult as it was for us, was difficult for them also. I liked President Johnson, admired him for his qualities, and I could understand his position. And I certainly could sympathize with Lady Bird, who has her own wonderful qualities. (Mrs. Johnson is a very warm, sympathetic person. I campaigned with her a few times in 1960 and found her always co-operative and eager to help in every possible way. She never hurried away after the speeches at the receptions but always inquired about the transportation of guests. We all thought she was a very gracious First Lady.)

In any case, Bobby had to decide what to do; and having reached the conclusion that he wanted to stay in public life, that he had "promises to keep," he decided to run for the Senate in the New York State elections. He won the Democratic nomination without too much trouble—just a great deal of organization and effort, to which he was well accustomed—but the general election was something else indeed, for his opponent was the Republican incumbent Kenneth

Keating, a distinguished man in record and appearance, and with a polished platform manner and well-demonstrated appeal to voters.

Although by this time Bobby knew all the ins and outs and behind-the-scene techniques of politics, he had never himself run for public office, never been a candidate in a way that would oblige him to come through to the general public as a personality. And he was not overly endowed by nature and temperament for that different role. It hadn't been his style, and he had never had reason until then to develop it. He took on the challenge but not entirely happily and not easily. (But I remembered that Jack too had been ill at ease at first meeting strangers and asking for their votes. I recall the story that at the very beginning of the 1946 congressional campaign Joe happened to be standing chatting with some friends on a corner in South Boston when suddenly Jack appeared across the street and started introducing himself to people who came along. Joe looked on in pleased amazement and commented: "I never would have thought he had it in him!")

By this time I was, to say the least, an experienced speaker and campaigner. So I was in Bobby's campaign quite a bit. Previous campaigns had shown that I could attract an audience. Also, I realized Bobby could stand a little coaching, and further that if he and I were on the platform together I could make him feel somewhat more at ease. I had a special utility also, as his mother, in meeting the charge that he was a "political carpetbagger," an out of stater who had no business running in New York State.

We had a little routine worked out about this, originating in a meeting at the auditorium of the Riverdale School. He brought up the charge that he was an outlander, then turned to me and said, "Tell them, Mother." Which I would do, chapter and verse, about moving from Brookline to Riverdale and to Bronxville when Bobby was only two years old, and this was home to us for the next four-teen years; and then even afterward we always had a residence in New York City, and that the city had always remained the head-quarters for my husband's business interests, and Bobby and all the others had gone for some years to schools in New York, and so forth —and what more identification with the state could anyone want? All of which seemed to soothe people's fears that Bobby, as senator from New York, might not have the state's interests fully at heart. Again the family helped, particularly Jean Smith who spoke throughout the state.

On request, Polly Fitzgerald and several of her loyal helpers came down from Boston to organize the teas, receptions, and handle a few thousand details. I asked her for her recollections:

"There was one incident in Bobby's Senate campaign I'll always remember. He was such a reluctant candidate in those days—still bereft after Jack's death the year before.

"There were telephone calls to us, 'Tell Bob he's got to look at the people when he meets them!' Or 'Tell Bob to smile—he looks as if he hates campaigning!' I used to wish the people could know the real Bobby. One night we had a reception in a hotel in New York City. You were there with him. The plan was for you to say a few words and then introduce him. His speech, which was being typed at headquarters, had not been delivered to the hotel—and we were all a little frantic.

"You were on the platform speaking. He turned to me and said, 'What will I talk about?' I said to him, 'Just go out with your mother and talk and be yourself—it will be better than any speech.'

"He did just that. You kidded him and he relaxed—he teased you—you both chatted about politics as you knew them through your father when you were young. You talked with him about his childhood. You were superb. And he was so warm. The people loved it and I always felt that evening was the turning point in him as a campaigner."

Bobby won the election by more than 700,000 votes.

Teddy had been discharged from the hospital in mid-December.

And so, when Congress reconvened that January of 1965 there were two Kennedy brothers present in the U.S. Senate for roll call.

A little later *Time* did a long article about the two of them and the extraordinary circumstances that had brought them to the Senate at the same time; and they were shown on the cover of the magazine, facing each other in quarter profile with the Capitol dome in the background. We had the cover glassed and framed, and their father indicated he wanted it put up on the wall, in his bedroom at the Palm Beach house, directly opposite his bed, so it would be in his view every time he was in bed. Facing it, hanging above his head-board, he wanted a portrait—a soft pastel, charming and true—of Caroline at the age of three or four. The bed is gone now, a few things in the room have been changed, but the two pictures still hang in the same place.

Joe's condition was about the same as it had been in times of crisis when it seemed he might be nearing the end. But he recovered at those times and felt so well that he was determined to stand on his feet and take a few steps. It was mostly a slow, grueling process of attrition, yet with a spirit never less than valiant.

Ever since his stroke we had needed a strong man to help him because he had to be lifted in and out of the car, boat, or bath; the same man would also drive him, help with the nursing care such as turning him in bed (Joe still weighed about 180 pounds, so that wasn't easy). There had been several, in a series (from the time of "Captain" Frank), but the last one—a strapping young fellow named John Ryan, 6 feet 2 inches or so, and with a gentle, witty, and optimistic outlook—came on in 1966.

(I would like to say something about the *Marlin* and its faithful captain, Frank Wirtanen. "Captain" Frank came with the *Marlin* when Joe bought it in 1952. From then until 1962 [Joe used it only in the summers in Hyannis Port but after he became ill he brought it to Palm Beach for the winter], Captain Frank became a permanent fixture of the household. The grandchildren adored him, and he guarded and watched over them whenever they came on the *Marlin*.)

John Ryan stayed through the time of my husband's death in 1969, then stayed to help me until 1973. I asked him to give some of his memories of the years he helped my husband. He recalled:

"I had heard through a friend that the family would be needing an aide for Mr. Kennedy, because the one they had was leaving to go to law school. I had an interview with Ann Gargan—she hired anyone who had anything to do with her uncle—and got the job. So one day, with Frank Saunders, the fellow who was driving for Mrs. Kennedy and the family at the time, I went up to Boston to meet Mr. Kennedy, because he'd had a relapse and was in the New

England Baptist Hospital. That was *the* hospital for the family. President Jack had spent most of his recovery there after the war. Ted did most of his convalescing there after the airplane accident. And so forth. Never mind about 'Baptist,' they wanted good medical care, and this was one of the very best hospitals in the country. Mr. Kennedy was in bed, and Frank said to him, 'Mr. Ambassador, this is John Ryan and when you get out of here, sir, he'll be working for you.' The ambassador looked up at me, and Frank said, 'He's a big one, isn't he?' The ambassador smiled a little bit.

"Frank and I drove back to Hyannis Port and went to the house to report to Ann Gargan. She said that since the time I had been hired the doctors had told her it didn't look as if the ambassador was going to live much longer, and of course in that case there was no job. A day or so after that I was introduced to Mrs. Kennedy: 'John Ryan, who has come to work for the ambassador.' I said, 'But I have been let go, because I guess I won't be needed.' She said: 'I don't believe that the ambassador is going to die in the hospital and I believe that he will come back—he'll be back here in Hyannis Port. So why don't you just stay around? If you want to get another job go ahead, but I would like to have you here.' I said: 'Well, if I'm going to be on the payroll I want to be doing something useful.' There are always a lot of odd jobs to do around the compound, so I kept busy. Then just a few weeks later, around the first of December, the ambassador came home from the hospital.

"Knowing him—as I came to know him during the three years after that—I would say it was because of determination that he came home. Every time he seemed to be dying he was probably thinking to himself, 'I don't care what your prognosis is, and the hell with you, I'm going to *do* it.' There were several times he would have these drastic seizures and become unconscious—out for an hour or hour and a half at a time, totally out. The nurse would have started cardiac massage, I would start the oxygen. The priest would be called and come and give him the Last Rites. And then Mr. Kennedy would wake up. And want to go out on the boat. And we would try saying, 'Sir, why don't you just rest now and we'll go out tomorrow?' But he really felt like going. We'd go, and he'd be all right."

I remember such episodes, and one in particular when he seemed so near the end that we called the children in Washington to say they should hurry home at once. We weren't able to reach them easily because, as it happened, they had gone up to New York to attend a big political dinner. By the time we could talk with them their father had recovered from the attack and was sleeping soundly. Next day he was alert, had a good color, and was expecting to go for his usual morning drive in the car.

John Ryan continues:

"Many people outside the family and staff assumed by this time he must be sort of a 'vegetable' but that was wrong. Mrs. Kennedy made sure he got the New York *Times* and the Boston papers every day, and *Time*, *Life*, and *Look* every week. He couldn't hold them well because he had only the one good hand, but when he'd finished a page he'd signal, and you'd turn the page; and he'd go right through a whole magazine.

"He loved sports. So now and then we'd go off to a baseball or football game. We would discuss players and strategies, I giving my opinions, and he with a Yes or No or a whole range of comments he could get across with his facial expressions and his gestures. He didn't like pills or shots, in fact he didn't like medication because he didn't want to be dependent on medicines, or on people for that matter. He wanted to do for himself as much as he possibly could. Like in the mornings in the swimming pool. Because of the buoyancy of the water Ann Gargan would be the one to help him in. We had bars all around the side of the pool and he'd go along the bars. He'd move his right leg and he'd take his left leg and kind of give a little kick or hop with it and move himself along.

"To him it would be a bad morning—and it was an exceptional morning—if he got only half or three quarters of the way around and became too tired and had to come out. Then he'd be mad at himself because he didn't have enough energy. We'd tell him it was really great, but he never accepted our compliments unless he went the complete way. Then it was fine.

"He didn't like having to be helped but he appreciated help. He would do little things that expressed his gratitude. On several occasions, riding with him in the elevator, he'd just . . . I'd be alone with him in the elevator riding downstairs . . . and he would just take my hand and kiss it. As his expression of gratitude. In other words, he wanted to let you know that he knew what was happening. . . .

"Mrs. Kennedy was there, basically, all the time. She was there with him and around him."

"Basically" is an apt word for it. I was there most of the time; and when I was, I saw him often during the day and evening. We always had breakfast, lunch, and dinner together. I would talk to him, tell him news of the family or of friends or other matters I thought would interest him. Sometimes I would read to him from letters I had received, or newspaper items I had clipped out, or passages that had struck me in some book I might be browsing in for my continuing education and as a help for insomnia. Often, after dinner, we would look at television together until his bedtime, which was quite early because he tired easily.

I had luncheon and dinner invitations rather often, and also there were a few traditional social events—the big charity balls at Palm Beach—that were organized for good causes and to which everyone subscribed and turned out in finery and fine spirits. It was a way to see old friends; the atmosphere was always rather exciting; I enjoyed it; so I went to them, perhaps three or four a winter season. None of this, however, interfered with my times with Joe.

If I had a luncheon or dinner engagement I would tell my hostess I might be a bit late. Since Joe lunched punctually at noon and dined punctually at six, I could have a light meal with him and still usually arrive in time for another light meal there. The galas and concerts and such seldom began before eight in the evening, and by that time he was in bed. He always knew my plans because I always told him. He was interested. There was never any sign from him of anything but approval. He did not want me to be tied to his sick bed; he did want me to have some life of my own and to enjoy life. The circumstances had changed drastically, but we still had the same complete understanding that we had had during more than fifty years of marriage. From the beginning of his illness I never dressed for an evening out until after dinner, when Joe was in his room asleep. There was nothing of subterfuge; it was simply that I thought the sight would remind him of the irretrievable past and that it would be kinder if I dressed and then went on my way.

With Ann in charge, with an efficient and devoted nursing staff, and stalwarts such as John Ryan on hand, and with excellent doctors who would always respond quickly in any emergency, I felt that I could be away from time to time for periods of days or weeks. There were things that were needful and that I wanted to do. I wanted to visit Rosemary every few months. I wanted to encourage and participate in the programs for the mentally retarded and the numerous works in other fields that had been developed by the Joseph P. Kennedy, Jr. Foundation. I wanted to take part in and help to move along the memorials to Jack—the library, the cultural center, so many others. For instance, toward the end of 1964 and in early 1965, I was abroad several times to lend my presence and a few words to an exhibit of photographs, documents, and memorabilia of Jack's life and presidency. It went to England, France, Germany, a number of other countries, and each time I tried to be there, at least briefly, and it was inspiring to see and sense the great interest, the deep affection and admiration that were shown by such vast numbers of people of so many nations about Jack.

So, in those years there were many demands, opportunities, reasons to be active. And the more so, naturally enough, in 1968 when Bobby decided to run for the Democratic nomination for the presidency.

His father didn't want him in that race; but, in his condition, was not able to explain to Bobby why it was not a good idea at that time.

I had profound misgivings of my own about it. I felt that Bobby had so many responsibilities to his family and within our general family; and that he was still young enough—at the age of forty-three—that there would be later opportunities for him to try for the presidency; and that meanwhile he shouldn't take the burdens of the nation on his shoulders and instead should try to relax a little bit.

Polly Fitzgerald has recalled:

"In December 1967, I was in Washington for a meeting. I called Bobby the day I was leaving and he said that he too was going to Boston and would go on my flight so we could have a visit. We had a very philosophical talk all the way home and at one point he spoke of you and said, 'My mother says I'm too serious and that I should do more things that I'd like to do—have more fun, and not always do what I think I should do or must do.'"

But Bobby, once having made up his mind about the right course for him, balancing everything together—everything, I daresay, from his childhood through all that had happened to this time, in his full maturity—was not going to be deflected from what he believed he "should do or must do." People have talked about the streak of "romanticism" in Jack. But Bobby, for all his supposed ruthlessness —such a mistaken term for him—really was a romantic idealist. By this expression, I mean that with faith and effort one can do great good in the world. I have mentioned that Tennyson's "Ulysses" was an inspiration to both my sons. Bobby took its second line as the title of one of his books (*To Seek a Newer World*):

> *Come, my friends,*
> *'Tis not too late to seek a newer world.*
> *Push off, and sitting well in order smite*
> *The sounding furrows: For my purpose holds*
> *To sail beyond the sunset, and the paths*
> *Of all the western stars, until I die.*
> *It may be that the gulfs will wash us down;*
> *It may be we shall touch the happy isles,*
> *And see the great Achilles, whom we knew.*
> *Though much is taken, much abides; and though*
> *We are not now that strength which in old days*
> *Moved earth and heaven; that which we are, we are.*
> *One equal temper of heroic hearts,*
> *Made weak by Time and Fate, but strong in will*
> *To strive, to seek, to find, and not to yield.*

And so once again "the troops rallied": the loyal cadres that Bobby and Ted and Jack himself, and Steve and others had built all over the country. Polly Fitzgerald came out again, accompanied by some of those same wonderful, selfless women who had helped set up the "Kennedy teas" during Jack's campaigns. And I, of course, prepared to take to the road again to help wherever and however I could. I was seventy-seven then, and it seemed to surprise people that I should be out stumping for my son, leading the demanding life entailed by a big campaign. It didn't seem at all odd to me: By then it had come to seem perfectly natural.

I find that people who have not been in politics are often curious about some of the "how-to" aspects of campaigning: How to shake hands with a thousand people without having your right hand become sore and your arm ache. How to stand in a receiving line for two or three hours without having your feet begin to kill you. As for handshaking, I was fortunate because my audiences were largely women, and they do not press one's hand very hard. Men, on the other hand, seem to think that a powerful handshake is a mark of cordiality. Thus, it is not unusual for a male candidate, after a hard day's campaigning—I know this has happened with Jack, Bob, and Ted—to end the evening with a sore right hand.

As for being on one's feet for hours at a time, there is nothing so unusual about that—salespeople, production-line workers, postal employees, many others are obliged to be—but even so there is a difference; in a receiving line one has no chance to move around and keep the blood circulating and the muscles functioning more or less normally. One is fairly rooted to the spot. Hence, I learned, in case of a long reception, to have a chair or couch directly behind me so I could half sit against one of its arms from time to time. With a little practice at this, you can look as if you're practically standing. And, of course, people are kind. They realize you may be a little tired. If you seem to be perched just a bit to relieve your aching back, they understand.

In a national campaign, I found, one should try to avoid being in a receiving line with local candidates, or for that matter even state candidates, unless that is necessary, because the people in line include so many of their friends or close associates who want to stop and chat with them, thus delaying everyone else, adding an extra hour or so—like traffic backing up on a busy highway when one car has a blowout—which could be an hour one couldn't spare because one had an appointment to be someplace else just then.

It is bad politics—and basic bad manners—to keep an audience waiting, and the speaker who does so begins with an initial disadvantage that he has to overcome before he can get his message across. Hence, when meetings are closely scheduled, ways have to be devised to disengage the candidate or speaker from one place to get him or her to the next place on time. Yet in almost any receiving line there will be people who want to have a personal talk, others who want to stand with you while a friend with a flash camera focuses and takes aim and snaps some pictures including the proverbial "just one more, please." And at the end of the meeting, while you are on your way out, there are likely to be those who come up to you to add a few footnotes about something.

Now, all this not only is pleasant in its way but also can be useful, for the essence of campaign politics is to establish personal rapport with the voters. One must be tactful and patient, and make sure that no one's feelings are hurt. But this takes some planning. One evening, early in Jack's campaign for the presidency, he was waiting in the car after a meeting and feeling irritated with Jackie because she was still inside the hall or vestibule in conversations with people. I said to him, "The girl can't just rush away from people; it would make a very bad impression. You ought to have an aide with her who will be primed in these situations to say, 'Excuse me, Mrs. Kennedy, but your husband is waiting for you,' or 'You have another engagement and I'm afraid you'll be late if you don't leave now.'" Jack agreed, and from then on it was done that way; though I don't know why I had to be the one to remind him, for this is only sensible. Polly Fitzgerald, Dave Powers, Frank Morrissey are among those whom I remember with special gratitude because they could always keep things moving nicely. In anything, there is only a certain amount of time.

I was almost never on the same platform at the same time with Bob during that 1968 campaign. He had hesitated a considerable while before going into the primaries and came in late, not until mid-March. There was a lot of time to make up. He had become a fine speaker, an iridescent personality, a national figure of great stature in his own right, and could attract huge audiences. I, for my part, could by then count on having audiences of considerable size. So the best idea was that we should go our own ways—as should others in the family—and cover as much ground and contact as many people as possible in the time available. The only advice I gave him was about a few personal details. I heard some of his speeches and realized he was lapsing into the family habit of talking too rapidly, so I sent him a note about that. I noticed also he was letting his hair grow awfully long, perhaps because he was racing around the country so fast with so much on his mind that he didn't think about getting to a barber shop. Anyway, I began to hear comments such as "Why the dickens doesn't he get a haircut?" and I told him. He got a haircut.

I made an absent-minded mistake myself in that campaign. Perhaps I made several, but this one landed in the newspapers. Bobby had just won in Indiana, and as usual there were interviews—I must have been interviewed a few thousand times in the course of my life— and a reporter commented that the Indiana campaign had cost a lot of money, and it must be nice to know the Kennedys could afford it; something to that effect.

I had heard such comments so many times during the years, ranging from the complete malice of reports that Jack had won in West Virginia because Kennedy agents were out buying votes (investigated and found to be without a grain of truth) to the slightly funny cartoon showing Jack with his father and Joe saying to him, "Don't worry, son. If you lose the election I'll buy you a country." All this struck me as unfair, for although Joe did contribute substantially to the financing of the campaigns, the amounts were almost trifling compared to those he gave to schools, charities, medical research, and so forth. And further, that the secret of the Kennedy successes in politics was not money but meticulous planning and organization, tremendous effort, and the enthusiasm and devotion of family and friends. Apparently my irritation had reached a flash point, because I was quoted as saying: "It's our money and we're free to spend it any way we please. It's part of this campaign business. If you have money, you spend it to win . . ."

During Jack's candidacy in 1960, a main purpose of my talks for him had been to show that he was not too young for the presidency: this because of lifelong interests in history and government, his family background, and his long and varied experiences in matters of political science. When I campaigned for Bobby in 1968, I tried to dispose of his image of "ruthlessness." I pointed out that he had had many tough assignments in government and had accepted them willingly, committing himself with a whole heart, with all his great energy and determination. When he was Attorney General, his probes into labor racketeering and organized crime were marked by his idealism and courage. He was often threatened with cruel reprisals against his family. I emphasized that, above all, he was kind. His heart often ruled his intellect. He was open and honorable and selfless.

As his mother, I suppose my testimony can be considered biased. I would like now, therefore, to quote some passages from the book that Pat did about him posthumously, *That Shining Hour*.

Averell Harriman:

"Robert F. Kennedy was one of the most gallant men I have ever known. He was fearless. He faced facts squarely. It was impossible for him not to tell the truth as he saw it. I think that is why some people thought he was ruthless. At times the truth is ruthless. He supported the causes he believed in regardless of the enemies he knew that he would make. But few men have won the deep respect and affection of so many. Negroes and other minorities knew that he had accepted their cause as his own.

"If he had been elected President, he would have been a great President . . . He understood the problems of our time . . ."

Sandy Vanocur:

"Bobby was the most vulnerable human being I have ever known. He was also the most outraged. I now believe that the two go together, and that it was his sense of outrage that made him so vulnerable. He was outraged that there was poverty, sickness, war, and evil, and all he asked was that we respond to all that is wrong in this world . . . He was a conscience in our midst, and now we have come to understand how little some people wish to understand conscience. . . . But there is simply no sense in being a Kennedy if you do not keep asking yourself and others to try to do better. He kept telling us this or that was unacceptable. And, ultimately, this is what so many people could not abide and that which so many of us cherished, that he only asked that we try to do better, that we try to love each other a little more. He asked only that we try to be more than we are."

Dame Margot Fonteyn:

"He was a man of great compassion and intelligence. He loved people but not in any muddle-minded or sentimental way. He was as intolerant of fools as anyone. Clearly his family took first place in his life. This alone represented a considerable number of people with whom he was constantly in touch; and this gave him his strength. Then there were his many friends. He never spoke of them superficially but seemed always to know what they were doing and to be concerned about their problems.

"Then there were just people. He really cared about millions of people: about children, young people, poor people, American people, and people all over the world. . . . Somehow he found time for everyone. Compassion for people was the motivation of all his life."

Benno Schmidt (financier, lifelong Republican; and the topic here, Bedford-Stuyvesant, is a grievously depressed area in New York City):

"I was surprised and slightly curious when I arrived at my office on December 8, 1966, to find a note that Senator Robert Kennedy wanted me to call him in Washington. I had never met nor even seen Senator Kennedy at that time. I returned the call and he said he would like to see me . . . 'today, if possible.' 'I will be in my office all day,' I answered, perhaps a bit curtly. 'Good,' he replied very gently. 'I would like to fly up on the four o'clock shuttle, if I may. This should get me to your office slightly before six, and I will try to be through in time not to disrupt your dinner. Thank you so much. . . .' Where, I thought, was the arrogance I had heard about?

"He arrived on schedule, and I liked him enormously from the time he set foot in the office. After very brief initial amenities, he outlined with simple eloquence and great persuasiveness his program for Bedford-Stuyvesant and concluded by asking me to serve as a director.

"Commencing with that first meeting . . . I was to be increasingly aware of how incredibly inaccurate the widespread impressions of Bob were, both as a person and a politician. He was a man of enormous compassion, the highest principles, essentially shy and somewhat reticent, with one of the greatest senses of humor I have ever encountered (usually with himself the victim of the joke). He was great fun to work with. He not only accepted, but he sought views which differed from his own, and one of the wonderful things about working with him was the extent to which one could differ with him and part company feeling so clearly that friendship had not been touched. . . ."

Harold Macmillan:

"My relations with Bobby were certainly a case of friendship at first sight. . . . Bobby's magic was inherent in his character. It was part of him; inherited, not acquired. Nor was it always connected with a happy mood. For he could be angry; especially angry with selfishness and folly, and with the wicked neglect of pressing and urgent cries for help going out both from his own country and from all the world. He could be savage as well as smiling. For what he felt, he felt deeply, even passionately. But he had taught himself to acquire a trained mind to serve his generous heart. . . . He had reached an intellectual as well as moral maturity."

Arthur Schlesinger, Jr.:

"It was obvious, first of all, that he had a direct, fresh, and unconventional intelligence of a high order. He had, in addition, what Eliot somewhere calls an 'experiencing nature'—that is, exceptional powers of curiosity and sympathy which enabled him to see problems from the viewpoint of the other fellow and which in time led to his extraordinary identification with the outcasts, victims and casualties of our society. One had always supposed him to be tough and courageous. But the readiness and warmth of his friendship made it impossible ever after to accept the then prevalent theory of him as an unyielding man . . . one was increasingly impressed by his rare gentleness and consideration and increasingly enchanted by his wonderful, wry, sardonic humor.

"For a long time these remained private qualities. What was exciting in the last decade was to watch Bobby, almost in spite of himself, become a public man and to see how, somewhat to his embarrassment, he became the vital hope for so many millions of Americans . . . For a shy man, he eventually achieved a remarkable rapport with his audiences. I will never forget whistle stopping with him through the central valley of California at the end of May 1968. It was a clear, sunny, joyous day. Great crowds streamed out to see him—the weatherbeaten faces of old farmers, rapt Mexican-Americans, ardent young men and women, excited boys and girls. He beguiled and exhorted his hearers with a marvelous mixture of banter and intensity—kidding them, kidding himself, then talking with great seriousness about poverty or racial injustice or the war in Vietnam.

"He was always growing and would never have stopped. He had become the voice of American reason and conscience. . . . His powers as leader, thinker, and orator seemed to be coming into rich maturity all at once . . . at last, one felt, people were beginning to understand what Robert Kennedy was really like.

"No one offered a greater promise of superb public service for our country."

Theodore Sorensen:

"That Bob Kennedy was regarded as a ruthless 'hater' by those who did not know him was a bitter irony bordering on absurdity. For I never knew a man with more capacity for love.

"He truly loved his fellow men . . . and could be deeply, visibly moved by both individual and mass demonstrations of human good will and generosity. He truly loved his country, while simultaneously trying to improve it, and was willing to serve it in any post . . . provided it offered him an opportunity to make a genuine contribution to this nation's advancement.

"Above all, he loved his family—openly, unashamedly, and uncritically—and it was this love which seemed to many of us outside the family to illuminate his life and to enrich his spirit more than anything else. His love for his brother Jack was special and fierce. . . . After the President's death, he showed it by showering affection upon Jackie, Caroline, and John. Like many others whom he rallied after the Dallas tragedy, I will always remember how deeply moved and greatly helped I was by his visit to my White House office a few days later, still wearing sunglasses to conceal his puffed and reddened eyes, but there to talk about our future instead of the past.

"His love for his father was redoubled, not strained, by the latter's tragic illness that might have discouraged a less determined son. Bob's campaign schedule for May 9, 1968, was incredibly heavy and hectic . . . Yet he insisted on adding in the middle of that schedule a flight to the Cape for a farewell lunch with his father. . . . At lunch, I saw Bob—as I had so many times before—tell his father how the campaign was coming, how much the old warhorse's advice and assistance were needed, where the campaign trail had been and was headed. . . . On the plane returning to Washington, he fell fast asleep in his seat, content that his exhausting effort had made possible this brief and not easy visit that sadly turned out to be his last.

"His love for his mother shone through on that same visit. Her strength renewed his, her concern for his well-being warmed him. I chose not to remind either of an evening many years earlier when Mrs. Kennedy vowed to us both that she would campaign once more for Jack in 1964 but never for Bob. They had teased each other about it that night, and when I asked him the reason (she had simply said to him, 'You know why'), he told me it was because he had not kept his clothes neat as a teen-ager. Whatever the reason, he was in 1968 lovingly grateful that she had relented. . . ."

If Ted Sorensen says Bobby said that to him it must be true. But it must have involved some "inside" family humor, because Bobby had been comparatively well organized—for a teen-ager—whereas, as Lem Billings said that he and Jack had the messiest room at the Choate School, and Jack's teen-age inclinations had been much the same at home.

In any case, having made a number of appearances for Bobby in the eastern and midwestern states, I did go out to help in those western primaries, especially the one in California, which of course has become one of the crucial factors in a national nomination.

Having then done what I could I wanted to get home again to check on things there. I flew back to Hyannis Port to await the California primary returns on radio and TV. It seemed to be a close race at first, as we had expected, with Bobby ahead, then behind, pulling ahead again. But by eleven that night, eastern time, he was ahead substantially and it seemed fairly certain he was the winner. Feeling thankful but also a bit tired after my travels, I went to bed.

The next morning I awakened around six, in time for early Mass, and turned on the television for news of the final results, and instead heard that Bob was being taken to the hospital.

Again, I couldn't believe—my mind somehow would not allow me to think—that it could be anything really serious. There had been an accident of some sort, perhaps during a victory celebration. I went on dressing, listening distractedly; then Ann came in, saying he had been shot.

It seemed impossible that the same kind of disaster could befall our family twice in five years. If I had read anything of the sort in fiction I would have put it aside as incredible. I still wanted to go to

Mass—urgently wanted to go to Mass—though Ann told me the phones had been ringing and reporters and photographers would be at the church.

On the way out of the house we met our pastor, Monsignor Thomson, who had heard the news and had come up from Hyannis. He rode back down to the church with me. I really don't remember what was said or much of what I was thinking, except that I was praying. *Lord have mercy!* And thinking, *Oh, Bobby, Bobby, Bobby*.

Later, back at the house, I kept busy in my room, sorting, rearranging, doing *anything* to keep busy, because I had to keep moving. And I prayed. And I wondered. I still couldn't believe it, although I knew it was so.

The next morning, Thursday, June 6, Bobby passed away.

The funeral plane arrived from California that evening, and Bobby lay in state at St. Patrick's Cathedral in New York, where great throngs came to pay their respects. I have read that a hundred thousand people were there that night and through the next day and night.

At the service, on Saturday, Ted delivered the eulogy and did so, in some of the most demanding minutes of his life, with dignity, simplicity, eloquence, and grace. His three brothers were gone. His father would go soon, as he knew. And he was a credit to all of them.

His summary of Bobby's character was perfect in truth: ". . . a good and decent man, who saw wrong and tried to right it, saw suffering and tried to heal it, saw war and tried to stop it." And of Bobby's idealistic aims:

> *"Some men see things as they are and say, 'Why?'*
> *I dream things that never were and say, 'Why not?'"*

There were some comments later in the press about my "composure" and "self-possession" and "bravery," and it was remarked that from time to time I gave a wave of the hand to people who had gathered in the cities and towns and hamlets—some even on rooftops—to watch the funeral train pass. I don't know now whether the waving was a good idea or not. Apparently there were those who thought it inappropriate. But I did this, and encouraged the children and grandchildren to do so as most of them did, because I felt that if people cared enough to come out and pay their respects we ought at least to give them some sign of appreciation. As for my being composed—I had to be. If I had broken down in grief I would only have added to the misery of the others and possibly could have set off a chain reaction of tearfulness. But, in fact, it was not just I who set an example of fortitude. They all set it for one another. For example, young Joe II, who adored his father and who was barely seventeen, went through the cars where various elder friends, official dignitaries, colleagues and staff assistants of Bobby's, and some of the press were riding and introduced himself and thanked them on behalf of the family for being with us.

Ethel was most admirable of all. She and Bobby loved each other deeply—they loved being together, sharing everything; they had a perfect life. Much as I would grieve for Bobby and miss him, I knew she would miss him even more: not only for all they meant to each other but as the father of her ten children, with the eleventh to come posthumously a few months later. I knew how difficult it was going to be for her to raise that big family without the guiding role and influence that Bobby would have provided. And, of course, she realized this too, fully and keenly. Yet she did not give way: She was calm and courageous, and I was very proud of her.

Bobby had a consuming passion to do what he thought was right and the will and the vigor to pursue that goal regardless of physical fatigue or difficulties.

In government service, he espoused tough assignments, the criminal segment, the gangster element, and he had an unflagging zeal for trying to correct some of the inequalities of life among the disadvantaged, the handicapped, the aged. The Vietnam war he viewed as a tragic episode in our history. In all his endeavors, he was indifferent to either fatigue or adverse criticism.

He adored with a passionate devotion Ethel and his little children with whom he laughed and played in his happiest moments. On his holidays, they always accompanied him—whether it was climbing mountains, skiing on the snowy slopes, or shooting the rapids on river boats. Even when I advised Ethel and him to be free—to be relaxed, to be concerned with only their own personal comfort, he never wanted to spare himself of added responsibilities.

He accepted life's challenges and he welcomed the opportunities for work which opened before him. He rejoiced in life's gifts and laughed and sang and played, too, with zest and enthusiasm. He was a deeply religious man, a fact for which his father and I were very grateful.

How sad are our hearts when we realize that we shall never see Bobby again, with his tousled, windblown hair, his big, affectionate smile, carrying one child piggyback and leading another by the hand—his dog close behind them. What a joy he brought us. What an aching void he has left behind, which nothing in the world can ever fill. We admired him, we loved him, and our lives are indeed bleak without him.

A devoted husband, a beloved son, an adored brother—I know that I shall not look upon his like again.

After Bobby's death there were so many messages of sympathy from all over the country and most of the world, from people of every station in life, that—until such time as they could be acknowledged individually, which would take months—I felt I ought to do something to express our gratitude. Accordingly, I went on television on a national broadcast. This is the substance of my message:

"May I extend my sincere thanks to all of you who offered your prayers, affection, and condolences. . . . We know that this tribute came from your hearts and our hearts responded with deep appreciation. . . .

"We cannot always understand the ways of Almighty God. The crosses which He sends us, the sacrifices which He demands of us. . . . But we accept with faith and resignation His Holy Will, with no looking back to what might have been, and we are at peace. We have courage, we are undaunted and steadfast, and we shall carry on the principles for which Bobby stood. . . .

"We know his heart's hopes and so we shall honor him not with useless mourning and vain regrets but with firm resolutions. . . . Acting now to relieve the hungry, working now to aid the disadvantaged for whom he felt so deeply and for whom he worked long hours.

"And in our thoughts of him and in our prayers we shall remember Ethel. And their little children, with whom he laughed and played. May they remember their father not only as one who gaily shared their childhood sports and triumphs but also as one who pledged his heart, soul, and strength to the betterment of humanity, and to the spiritual enrichment and honor of our great country."

After Bobby's death, Joe's condition declined until by the fall of that year he was approaching helplessness, not even able to feed himself the greater part of the time, suffering all the annoyances and discomforts and indignities of hopeless infirmity. With his remarkable physical stamina and his remarkable will, he stayed on until November 18, 1969. Then, surrounded by those who remained of his family, and quite peacefully, he passed away. I was kneeling by his bedside, holding his hand. Next to Almighty God, I had loved him—do love him—with all my heart, all my soul, all my mind.

With the deaths of his brothers and then the death of his father, Ted was the only surviving male member of our immediate family. Ninth and last child, youngest son, it was now up to him to be "the head of the family." And he responded magnificently.

Chapter Twenty

In perfect honor, perfect truth,
And gentleness to all mankind,
You trod the golden paths of youth,
Then left the world and youth behind.
Ah, no! 'tis we who fade and fail—
And you, from Time's slow torments free,
Shall pass from strength to strength and scale
The steeps of immortality.

The lines are from John Buchan's "Fratri Dilectissimo" (Dearest Brother), and I found them a few years ago and transcribed them in my notebook, for, to me, they signified my lost children.

From the same author, in another book, *Pilgrim's Way*, I drew other words and adapted them and made them my motto:

I know not age, nor weariness nor defeat.

In the resurrection of Christ we find our sure hope in the immortality of the individual soul, as well as the promise of a resurrection of our own bodies, to enjoy forever the presence of God in heaven, above the grave. This faith and assurance give life, with all its struggles and earthly disappointments and frustrations, a sublime meaning and are a source of wonderful strength and constant guidance.

So my life went on, with both an overwhelming sense of loss and a determination to remember with dearest love, yet to meet the future with my head into the wind.

I thought, during this period, a good deal about Jacqueline. I think that all of us felt that after a suitable time of mourning, and such time as it might take her spirits to mend, she would be able to participate fully again in life.

After a while, when she did feel like going out to the theater and some events in New York City, and having a few dinner parties at her apartment, and needed escorts, the men were either members of the family—Bobby particularly at that time—or close family friends and associates.

I had known Aristotle Onassis for some years. I used to see him here and there when I was traveling in Europe. We would be at some of the same parties and receptions and be having lunch or dinner at some of the same restaurants, so we would chat a bit about this or that and became friendly acquaintances. Once or twice, as I recall, he stopped in to visit us for a day or evening at Hyannis Port. I have a memory of him one summer day on our front porch sitting rather scrunched up in one of our tall, fanback white wicker chairs. Several of us were in white wicker chairs too, and others were seated, reclining or sprawled out on cushions which were somewhat the worse from the summer sun and wet and fogs and hard use from grandchildren. The white paint on the wicker was beginning to flake, as it always does. Everything was pleasant, attractive, practical, but far from elegant. And knowing of Onassis' fabulous wealth and style of life—islands, yachts, and villas with retinues of servants—I wondered if he might find it a bit strange to be in such an informal environment as ours. If so, he showed no sign of it. He was quietly companionable, easy to talk with, intelligent, with a sense of humor and a fund of good anecdotes to tell.

I liked him. He was pleasant, interesting, and, to use a word of Greek origin, charismatic.

Even so, when Jean called me one morning in October 1968 and said Jackie was going to marry him—and would be calling me later in the day to tell me about it—I was completely surprised. In fact, I was rather stunned. And then perplexed. I thought of the difference in their ages. I thought of the difference in religion, he being Greek Orthodox; and the fact he had been divorced; and I wondered whether this could be a valid marriage in the eyes of the Church. I thought of Caroline and John Jr. and whether they could learn to accept Onassis in the role of stepfather so that he could give them the guidance that children need from a man. There were many things on my mind—my thoughts were awhirl—but I began trying to sort them out, give the various factors some order of priority.

And, with contemplation, it seemed to me the first basic fact was that Jackie deserved a full life, a happy future. Jack had been gone five years, thus, she had had plenty of time to think things over. She was not a person who would jump rashly into anything as important as this, so she must have her own very good reasons.

I decided I ought to put my doubts aside and give Jackie all the emotional support I could in what, as I realized, was bound to be a time of stress for her in the weeks and months ahead. When she called I told her to make her plans as she chose to do, and to go ahead with them with my loving good wishes. I was reassured when during our talk she said she had consulted Cardinal Cushing who spoke out for her, through the press, with this statement: "My advice to people is to stop criticizing this poor woman. She has had an enormous amount of sadness in her life and she deserves whatever happiness she can find." Jackie seemed relieved by my attitude and afterward, when she saw Ted, told him she was greatly cheered by my congratulations and my confidence in her.

The wedding would be in Greece. Jackie invited me, but I felt that I shouldn't be that far away because of my husband's declining health. Pat and Jean, the girls nearest Jackie in age, did go to represent our family and our regard for Jackie in every circumstance.

Jackie recently was remembering that time and said:

"When I married Ari, she of all people was the one who encouraged me. Who said, 'He's a good man.' And 'Don't worry, dear.' She's been extraordinarily generous. Here I was, I was married to her son and I have his children, but she was the one who was saying, if this is what you think is best, go ahead. It wouldn't surprise anyone who has really known her; but anyway, how extraordinarily generous that woman is in spirit. I always called her 'Belle Mère'—I still call her that.

"She comes and visits us. It's wonderful for Caroline and John. And Ari adores her. The first Easter after we were married she came to spend a few days with us in the Caribbean. That next summer she stopped over in Greece. She was on her way to Ethiopia to have a joint birthday celebration with Haile Selassie. Then, after Grandpa died late that year—I was there in the room with the others when he died—she was feeling sort of shaky. She came and spent New Year's with us.

"If I ever feel sorry for myself, which is a most fatal thing, I think of her. I've seen her cry just twice, a little bit. Once was at Hyannis Port, when I came into her room, her husband was ill, and Jack was gone, and Bobby had been killed . . . and the other time was on the ship after her husband died, and we were standing on deck at the rail together, and we were talking about something . . . just something that reminded her. And her voice began to sort of break and she had to stop. Then she took my hand and squeezed it and said, 'Nobody's ever going to have to feel sorry for me. Nobody's ever going to feel sorry for me,' and she put her chin up. And I thought, God, what a thoroughbred."

I have a diary note dated February of that new year, 1970, when I was back home:

"Jackie sent me an album of photos taken while I was in Greece and wrote amusing captions under them. One on the Acropolis— where I went with Ari and a historian—shows me in a black midi with cock feathers and she wrote, 'Me like Circe.' Another of me going to church the following Sunday, and she captioned it, 'Demure like Heidi with a kerchief on her head.'

"Along with the album she sent a letter which quite overwhelmed me, with her really heartwarming expressions of the pleasure all of them shared in my visit at New Year's. And how utterly unexpected was life's chain of events—that she and I, after all our experiences together, should now start to share new experiences in an extremely different environment and atmosphere, and it all happened so unexpectedly.

"I am thrilled by her assurances of welcome because this way I shall always be able to contact Caroline and John, and to know that all enjoy having me with them, including Ari and his relatives. And New Year's was possibly a little less foreign to the children because I was there.

"Jackie has often quoted the words in the biblical Book of Ruth in which Ruth declares to her mother-in-law Naomi: 'Whither thou goest, I will go.' And I too feel that the bonds of loving understanding between Jackie and me are just as strong as those between Ruth and Naomi."

I've always admired Jackie's courage, and I remember the difficult time she had when her son John was born.

Jackie had a premature Caesarean birth with John. It was necessary for him to be placed in an incubator for a number of days as he was suffering from the same lung affliction which caused the death of her second son, Patrick, a number of years later. Jackie was very weak when she finally left the hospital, and her activities were totally restricted. Mrs. Eisenhower invited her to the White House for a tour, and Jackie requested that a wheel chair be waiting as it was impossible for her to walk any distance. No wheel chair was there, and Jackie was given a full tour, which included walking up and down the stairs and posing for photographers. When she returned to her house in Georgetown she became quite ill and decided to take the baby and nurse to Florida. John's health was not very good when he arrived in Palm Beach, but due to the care of a brilliant pediatrician he began to improve slowly.

There was still tremendous confusion and activity surrounding Jackie in those days—all of which made convalescence most difficult. Jack would sit in their bedroom preparing his inaugural speech and Pierre Salinger and others would come in the room for conferences.

It was also a trying time for Jackie as so many reporters were asking for interviews. One reporter, Laura Berquist of *Look*, wanted to do an interview about which First Lady Jackie admired most. The day of the interview, Jackie was too ill to see her, so Jack gave the interview for her. He told Miss Berquist that Jackie most admired Mrs. Truman because she kept her family together in the White House regardless of the limelight that suddenly hits a President. Jackie felt Mrs. Truman kept her own values as before. That was what Jackie wanted to do more than anything: Keep her family together in the White House.

By Inauguration Day, Jackie was still suffering from physical and nervous exhaustion. (The month after the baby's birth had been the opposite of recuperation.) Jackie missed all the gala events she had wanted to share with Jack. She did go to the inaugural gala, but had to go home in the first intermission. She could not go to Mass with Jack Inauguration Day. I know Jackie really felt sad that she could not participate more in those first shining hours of Jack's.

Now I want to say some things about Ted. My thoughts turn to a time recently when Eunice and I were invited to lunch with the editors of this book and someone proposed the question to us: "Would you rather be a senator or the mother of a senator?" Eunice with alacrity said she'd rather be a senator. Very well, each to his own. But I began to think about my answer, and later I wrote a note to myself:

"I would much rather be known as the mother of a great son or a great daughter than the author of a great book or the painter of a great masterpiece."

Ted is like his brothers in many ways, yet different from them, just as they differed from each other: each of them a unique personality; each child a product of the fascinating and mysterious equation of "nature and nurture." As for nurture, I suppose his position in the family had some bearing. Being the last child and a robust, handsome little boy, I expect that in our family he received the most affection from the most people at the earliest age, and that this helps to account for his cheerful and outgoing character, his expectation of liking people and of being liked. In a rather old-fashioned but good term, he always had a "sunny disposition."

Further, quite considerably more than the other three boys, he had the wonderful advantage of having sustained attention and influence from his father. He was not quite nine years old when his father resigned the ambassadorship and went into semiretirement. True, it was only semi, for Joe remained active both in business and in public affairs, as I have related here earlier. True, Ted would soon be in boarding school. But during the school holidays, during the long summer vacations at Hyannis Port, Joe was at home with the family (Ted, in fact, has the boyhood impression that "he was at home with us all the time"), and also, at last, he could take time to go to any event, school or otherwise, in which his young son Ted was involved. It was not a qualitative matter, because as anyone who reads this book will realize, Joe was very closely concerned with all of them. But it was a quantitive difference of large order. Joe spent a great deal more time with Ted than with the other boys, and that counted.

In conversations for this book Ted discussed various influences, as he saw them, that his father and I had in the family's life and his own life in particular:

"Mother and Dad's characteristics balanced remarkably well. He was a motivating, dominating, powerful force with very high expectations—especially for his sons. She had the softness and gentleness and understanding that made his standards livable and reachable. From him you felt powerful demands on you. From her you felt compassion, encouragement, and support.

"Of course, it wasn't that well defined, because my father was kindhearted and understanding and my mother could be quite exacting. She wanted excellence. She always strove for it herself. Even now, when I visit her, I'll find her listening to those French records. Or walking up and down the lawn reading that notebook of hers with all the quotations she's clipped from someplace and Scotch-taped in. She still sends me copies of them. And all those little drills —how to use 'I' and 'me'—which she'll bring out even now if she hears you make a grammatical slip.

Ted had three older brothers to take as his models and to strive to please. I have mentioned earlier that his faith in them was so great that at the age of seven or eight he would jump off the cliff at Eden Roc down to the water while Joe Jr. and perhaps Jack would be yelling at him to make the effort, but ready to save him in case he was stunned on impact and sank. He has some other memories of that era—when our home was still in Bronxville—that no doubt added even more admiration for his brothers.

"I remember their teaching me how to ride my bicycle, and coaching me how to jump off the garage roof with a parachute. And then Bobby had a pig. He was interested in making money, to supplement his allowance, and somebody had convinced him there was money in raising pigs, so he had bought a shoat and had it in a pen and was feeding it up—it was a medium-size pig by then. One day it got loose. Bobby must have been away from the house at the time, because I remember Joe and Jack chasing the pig around the lawn. Pigs are very hard to catch, but they finally got it, and I thought that was really great. Bronxville is a respectable place and we lived in a nice neighborhood and what the neighbors thought must have been something. This was probably about the same year that they got an alligator and put it in our swimming pool down in Florida to surprise us."

Yes, and it was also about that year that both of them went off to boarding school.

Since they were all individuals, I don't know who among the brothers most resembled whom, but I expect there was a special bond between Jack and Ted, if only for one reason. With our large family, and the spread in ages, it occurred to me when Jean was born to nominate the eldest, Joe Jr.—who was old enough, let's say, to be her uncle—as her godfather. He was honored. Thus, from some odd inspiration, in this case mine, traditions can be born. For when Ted arrived there was a letter from Jack, a very sweet letter asking if he could be the godfather of the new baby. And he was. Thus Ted, as he grew old enough to understand and appreciate the ideas involved —and Joe Jr. being gone—could see Jack in that extra dimension, not only as the admired elder brother but as the godparent whose words, ideas, inspirations, examples, attitudes—really, everything about Jack —were bound to be respected.

The two surviving older brothers both had their influences, as Ted was recalling in conversation:

"When I was young I had two different types of relationship with my brothers. I suppose the relationship with Jack in the early years was as much as an older friend as a brother. You know, there were fourteen years between us. And he was not going to be too interested for a while in me. Not, say, when I was six and he was twenty. Or I was ten and he was twenty-four. Or when he was a congressman and I was fourteen.

"I did more things with Bobby. He kept track of me more when I was in the lower school at Milton—sixth, seventh, eighth grades, along in there—because he had gone to the same school and knew about it and because he was that much closer in age. He was only seven years older than I was. That put him out of reach in any possible sense as a contemporary in those years—but it did mean that he could be my big brother.

"Jack was always interested but I think it was when I was around tenth-eleventh grade in school that he began to take a more direct personal interest, and he would give me encouragement about school. He could look at situations in a way that made things look not so grim as the headmaster might have reported.

"He was almost a combination of father and brother, but as a brother would be he was more approachable and better able to look at the lighter side of situations."

Obviously this is not the place, nor would there be the space, to describe Teddy's development from kid brother to statesman. However, there are a few points I do want to mention.

After Jack and Bobby's deaths he made it his responsibility to work toward the goals that had been most important to them. As one example, Jack had proposed abolishing the discriminatory parts of our immigration laws. It was Ted who guided the bill through the Senate. He took over Bobby's interest in the poor and the hungry and expanded it into the international field with the war victims in Biafra and Bangladesh. Bobby had campaigned to end this country's military involvement in Vietnam. Ted was one of the most effective leaders in mobilizing the congressional and public sentiment that finally brought that about. It wasn't a matter simply of following his brother's footsteps, however. He brought his own judgment and skills to bear and developed his own themes and programs. Ted has made his voice heard effectively in such fields as defense policy, better health care, arms control, reform of the Selective Service Act, voting rights for the eighteen-year-olds, and other important legislation.

What few people would have any way of knowing, however, was that at the same time he was doing everything needful, everything generous and thoughtful, on my behalf and on behalf of Jackie and Ethel and their children. With Jackie's two and Ethel's eleven there were thirteen children for whom he was *in loco parentis*; and with his own three, that made sixteen for whom he felt a close responsibility. He was at the hospital with Ethel when the last baby was born, and again when she was ready to come home, and when they left the hospital he was the one who carried the baby. There were all sorts of responsibilities, most of them simply implicit in the role that devolved on him as the only surviving son, and he took them wholly and cheerfully and carried them along, busy as he was. With his extraordinary thoughtfulness and understanding, Ted has been a loving, guiding influence for all the grandchildren. No one outside the family can ever know how much his efforts have meant to the shaping of their lives.

The Edgartown Regatta weekend is always one of the gala times at the Cape, with people coming in from all directions and mixing into all festivities besides those having to do directly with the race. My children have participated in it for many years, and 1969 was no exception. I knew that Ted was flying up from Washington to Martha's Vineyard on Friday, the eighteenth, to skipper Jack's old boat the Victura in a race that afternoon, with Joey Gargan to crew for him.

I had heard also, probably from Joey—since it was his idea and he was the host, organizer, and chef—that after the race they would be going to a cottage Joey had rented on nearby Chappaquiddick Island. That is one of many islands in the Cape region. It was only vaguely familiar to me, and Ted had never been there before. Joey had planned a "cookout" with some of the men and women who had worked with Bobby during his presidential campaign. Politics is built on personal loyalties, and the people who work so hard with such devotion in a campaign need the personal thanks and appreciation that a get-together of this sort provides. I had been to many with my father.

One of the young women invited was Mary Jo Kopechne. She had been one of Bobby's most dedicated staff assistants in Washington and during his 1968 campaign for the presidency. She had high intelligence, and was a loyal and hard-working and wonderful person. Ethel knew her well, of course, as did several of the others in the family. She and most of the others had been guests at Hyannis Port the previous summer for a cookout and a sailboat ride, and they had had a reunion in Washington during the winter.

The events of that tragic night have been thoroughly reported in the world press and in the hundreds of pages of inquest proceedings. All of that material has been made public, and tells how Ted drove over a narrow bridge and the car plunged into the water upside down and Mary Jo was drowned; how Ted managed to get out of the car himself, although he nearly drowned; how he repeatedly dived to find Mary Jo, and went back to the cottage for help from Joey and his friend, Paul Markham; how the efforts of all three failed; and how Ted did not report the accident until the following morning.

I first saw Ted when he returned to Hyannis Port the afternoon after the accident. Tragedies were no new experience to Ted. With the rest of his family, he had suffered the premature losses of a sister and three brothers. And with God's grace, he escaped the same death which his close friend Eddie Moss met in the plane crash in Massachusetts in 1964, although Ted suffered a broken back, which healed but which still bothers him today. During the tragic experiences our family had, Ted's own faith and fortitude had been an inspiration to the rest of us.

This occasion was different and, to me, terribly distressing when I saw him. He was so unlike himself it was hard to believe he was my son. His usual positive attitude, which he displayed so clearly at other times of difficulty, had vanished. He was disturbed, confused, and deeply distracted, and sick with grief over the death of the young woman.

From my own impressions of him during the days following, his actions and ideas were those of a person in a state of shock. His own near death from drowning, the physical trauma and pain of his own injuries, the despair and emotional turmoil—these terrible events surpassed the limits of human endurance.

I was deeply distressed, especially in the wake of all the tragedies which preceded this one. The impact was on all of us. (It was all the more grim because for so many years the Edgartown regattas had been the high point of our summers, times of special happiness and relaxation. I remember we used to set the table when we saw the sails coming back.)

In the days after the accident, I watched, as did my daughters, with apprehension as Ted tried to recover from this terrible shock. With the continuing good care of Dr. Robert Watt and his own natural resiliency and reserves of strength, he started to pull himself together. I have a diary note: "Ted improves every day." A good many friends came to show support and friendship, even though he really needed peace and rest.

At the end of the week, after he had appeared in court to answer the charge of leaving the accident, he went on television to address the voters of Massachusetts, to explain what had happened, to admit the seriousness of his actions and to accept full responsibility for the tragedy. In view of his plea of guilty and the ugly and destructive gossip that was being spread about the accident, he said he had to decide whether it was proper for him to remain in public life. I thought he spoke truly from his heart.

The public response—over one hundred thousand telegrams and letters—the opinion polls, editorial comment, and more or less the whole spectrum of means for judging public sentiment without actually going to the length of a general referendum—was quite favorable and helped persuade him that the criticism could be overcome, that he could still be an effective voice for his constituents, and he should therefore stay on in the Senate and in public life.

There is not a great deal on this earth that one can do to relieve grief except to let the bereaved know that one does understand, care, and feel; and to try to add to hope and faith, in any possible way. There is a quote I remember which says that "in this way, we turn our heartaches into constructive efforts and lighten the sorrows of others." I think letters help.

I wrote to Mr. and Mrs. Kopechne, trying to say that I, having suffered the loss of one of my own daughters, Kathleen, at the same early age of twenty-eight, could realize what a suffering this was for them; and how badly I felt that my son was in any way involved in their loss; and that my sympathy and prayers were with them. Later when I was in New York and learned they also were there, I asked them over to the apartment, and we talked about the joys and sorrows that life brings to all of us.

In the months following the tragedy, Ted worked extremely hard in the Senate and in his campaign in 1970 for re-election. The voters of Massachusetts gave him a fine vote of confidence.

By the time of the primaries for the 1972 presidential nominations, the opinion polls showed that Ted was one of the "most admired" men in the United States, and that among both Party leaders and voters around the nation he was at or near the top as the choice for the Democratic nomination.

I did not want him to run. No one who really cared about him wanted him to—the family and the old friends and the close members of his staff; I'm sure it was practically unanimous. Even strangers would approach me and say, "Don't let him, Mrs. Kennedy." The reason was altogether too obvious in view of what had happened in our family, and I won't say more except that there seemed to be a certain number of deranged people wandering around. I could not bear another such loss. And there were all those sixteen children, Jack and Bobby's and his own, for whom he had a responsibility and who needed him.

There was a great deal of pressure on him, from many leaders and supporters of the Democratic Party, to run for the presidential nomination. And after Senator McGovern was nominated, there was great pressure to get him on the ticket for the vice-presidency, as I was in a position to know since he spent most of the Convention time at Hyannis Port with the family, sailing every day, accompanied by his children and various nieces and nephews.

It may seem strange, but he and I never had a full discussion and examination of the situation. No sitting down together on the davenport in the living room and, "Teddy, what I think is . . ." and "Well, Mother, this is how I feel . . ." We wouldn't do that. It would be, for us, clumsy and would go against the grain of our relationship, which doesn't need that sort of dialogue for us to understand each other. He knew I didn't want him on the ticket in either place that year, and it soon became clear to me that he had no intention of seeking or taking either one.

Someday, perhaps, Ted may decide to seek the presidency. When the time and circumstances are right, I would like to see him President, because I know he would be a credit to that high office and do wonderful things for the country. But as for the immediate future, he has plenty of important work to do in the Senate, particularly just now, programs to raise the national level of health care and to create a system of national health insurance. As for our family situation, most of the grandchildren are still young. And there are still too many risks, as anyone who reads the daily newspapers knows well.

Ted, of course, will decide for himself, just as his brothers did. But if anyone wants to know whether I think he should run for President in 1976, my answer is: "I hope he will not."

Meanwhile, during these past few years, life for me has been quite full enough without having another President in the family. In fact, it has been so full that I must schedule my time carefully in order to accomplish a large portion of the things I want to do. I am active from early morning to fairly late at night (except for a nap after lunch), and since I am well into my eighties now, people seem surprised that I keep going as I do, appearing at various events and on television, and manage to hold my own.

I believe in keeping interested, growing and learning. Sedentary people are apt to have sluggish minds: A sluggish mind is apt to be reflected in flabbiness of body and in a dullness of expression that invites no interest and gets none. Vivacity, intelligence, curiosity, receptivity to ideas, true interest in other people have special relevance as one gets on in years.

I try to take my own advice. I am busy with many projects, especially for the mentally retarded. Eunice is the one who is really in charge, for the family, of the large range of on-going programs created by the Joseph P. Kennedy, Jr. Foundation, but I serve in any useful way I can. For instance, when I accept invitations to appear on commercially sponsored television shows—David Frost and Dinah Shore's are recent instances—it is always with the proviso that I can take part of the time to describe the great need for programs to aid the mentally handicapped, discuss some of the programs that have come into existence, and encourage people to take an interest and to make contributions to expand the work.

As for politics, I daresay I have long since acquired a conditioned reflex. When Sarge accepted the 1972 Democratic vice-presidential nomination I felt the same old excitement and volunteered to help in any way I could. I was quite busy with several things at the time—particularly, this book—but I did go out a few times that summer and autumn to make appearances and some short speeches on behalf of the McGovern-Shriver ticket.

Meanwhile, I respond to politics, to the demands and opportunities of public life and service. Evidently I have acquired a certain status—I wouldn't know how to describe it, except perhaps as a position of "respect"—and there is no point in having that advantage unless one uses it for good causes. I don't take to the stump, I don't head up committees, I don't join demonstrations, I don't do any of those things, and I don't assert my ideas and hopes in didactic ways.

Teddy says:

"Mother is especially good in a one-to-one relationship, and that's because she not only cares about people in general but as individuals. She and I might be out walking together in the dusk at Hyannis Port and a carful of people, usually parents and children, would pull up, lost, and ask directions to the Kennedy compound. Tourists, citizens, people from all over. I used to accuse her of always looking at the license plate first to see if the car was from a state with a presidential primary. But that was entirely a joke, because invariably she would not only give them directions but point out one or two sights of special interest. Now, most of these people probably had seen her at some time on television when she was all dressed up in one of her Paris creations, so that probably would be their idea of her, which didn't match at all with this woman who was walking down Scudder Avenue or one of those roads in flat heels, a sweater and skirt, maybe a scarf, a golf cap, probably a pair of dark glasses she still had on because the evening sun had bothered her eyes. But they would start recognizing her voice and way of speaking; and ask her, 'Is it . . . ?' and she would say, 'Yes it is' . . . and they would smile, and thank her, and drive off in a state of complete captivation and rapture. All right. That's part of Mother.

"Then there is another aspect which is her one-to-one relationship with people in government. I can talk with Mother in the political sense about how to get a bill passed or a government program going, for instance, to help the mentally retarded because she has been so interested in that. I could tell her what we were doing, working with the key figures in the House and Senate, and she'd make the suggestion 'Well, I wonder if I'd write to them and tell them how interested our family is, and how interested I personally am . . . because of Rosemary and our experience. . . .' And then she writes an absolutely beautiful letter. She really takes the time. These are personal letters. And they really have a tremendous impact on the key committee members of the Appropriations Committee and so forth. They have been exposed to testimony from all directions, yapped at by interest groups and disagreeing experts with reputations and positions to guard, and here comes a letter from someone they know of and respect, who cares because of personal experience, and who has studied and thought about it from that point of view. This is what I mean by person to person.

"She has lived that way, with the idea 'If it's worth doing, it's worth doing well.' She communicates that in raising children, meeting people, writing to congressmen; she exemplifies it, and this is political in the fine sense."

I was at dinner at a friend's house, and the conversation had taken a slightly morbid turn, which caused me to remark: "But I'm sure God wants us to be happy and take pleasure in life. He doesn't want us to be sad." The man sitting opposite looked at me as if he had discovered a miracle and said, "Mrs. Kennedy, that is one of the most inspiring statements I ever heard." I remember the incident because of his rather thunderstruck reaction and the fact that all I said was something I have always believed.

I see no reason still to doubt it. God made the world and made us to live in it for a while. We owe Him infinite thanks and obligations and duties. Surely among these is the appreciation of the delights of life: the beauties of nature, the places and people of this earth, the pleasures of good company, the grace of laughter, the scent of a flower, the sounds of music, the rhythm of dancing, the infinite satisfactions of true love—all those joys that are there for us to claim as human beings created by God's will and endowed by His wisdom with capacities to enjoy this life. Birds sing after a storm; why shouldn't people feel as free to delight in whatever sunlight remains to them? If more people were more thankful for what they have, instead of mournful for what they have not, much good would come to the world. Pessimism feeds on itself. So does optimism.

In some aspects of living I want and need stability and certainty. I have found that a daily schedule, with regular hours assigned to certain activities in a customary pattern, not only enables me to accomplish much more than I could otherwise but lends structural support to living. Because there it is, you know what you will be doing or at least intend to do the next day. In fact, I seem to be rather famous or notorious, at least well known, within the family for budgeting time.

Although in the day-to-day course of events I like predictabilities, I couldn't stand spending my life that way all the time. I would hate having to be rigid. Life is too full of things waiting to be seen. When I was a girl I used to pause and stare at the windows of steamship or travel agencies, with their displays of posters, and wonder what it would be like to *be* there: actually to *be* in Rome and Paris and London and St. Petersburg and Constantinople and Athens and Cairo and Addis Ababa and Hong Kong and Shanghai and all those other imagined places.

I have never recovered from that wanderlust. I have seen much of the world now, but there is much more, and I want to keep refreshing my mind for as long as I live with new places and new experiences.

I feel much the same way about people. There are those I love dearly and whose welcome could never wear out. There are friends whom I cherish and want to see often; and, of course, friends whom I don't see often—because of distance or other complications—but still cherish.

I would dislike spending my time with people who are always tremendously serious and take up one cause after another. And I would be bored to distraction if I had to spend a great deal of time with people who think the good life consists of luncheons and teas and golf games and bridge parties. I have always felt that if drawn out a little and given an opportunity most people will have something worthwhile or even remarkable to say.

I suppose that the apotheosis of the idea of traveling to far and unusual places and meeting fascinating people in the shortest period of time came in the summer of 1970. Late that June I flew to Switzerland and spent a little time in an Alpine health resort; then flew to Greece to visit Jackie and Ari; and from there went to

Ethiopia to visit the Emperor. I took diary notes and when I was back at Hyannis Port I wrote them up. These are excerpts:

"Took the plane to Athens where I was met by Mr. Kindel of the embassy and his wife who kindly accompanied me in an airport car to the location of Ari's seaplane. There I met Mr. and Mrs. Emil Mosbacher. He—known as 'Bus'—is the great yachtsman, defender of the America's Cup, and State Department's chief of protocol. We were joined by Franklin Roosevelt, Jr., and his wife. We would be flying for about an hour to Ari's island, Skorpios, where his yacht the *Christina* was anchored.

"All the others sensibly fastened their seat belts but I left mine loose. We landed at Skorpios with a tremendous bump and I, in my loose belt, flew into the air and came down on my back a little strongly. By the end of three or four bumps I was really rather lame. Which taught me that I must secure my seat belt firmly in the future.

"I had been on the *Christina* several times before, and the life was, as I remembered, really quite casual. All the guests did just about as they wanted. Lee and Stas Radziwill were there, with their children, who are close contemporaries of Caroline and John Jr. Maria and Timmy Shriver were there too, and both are near Caroline's age. So they all played merrily together on the beach and went swimming and diving and snorkeling and fishing.

"Maria is regarded as quite a beauty, with her regular features, rather piercing blue eyes, and, for a young girl of twelve, showing promise of having quite a good figure, now that she has lost weight. Years ago when I was young there was no discussion of weight, we just lost it automatically when we grew older and fell in love with a beau and wanted to be thin.

"Caroline is, of course, a beautiful child too. She resembles Jack a great deal. She looks at you like Jack used to. Listens, thinks, and feels out the situation in her mind, then goes on to act but with certain reservations unspoken.

"But, to get back to the adults. FDR Jr. and I reminisced about the old days . . . when my husband was such a close colleague of his father and campaigned for him . . . when Franklin Jr. visited us at

Palm Beach and went campaigning for Jack in West Virginia . . . time had passed, much had happened . . .

"Ari's main headquarters are in Athens, so he is there generally through the week and then joins Jackie and the guests at Skorpios on weekends. Hence I saw little of him this time. But when I did he was very congenial, considerate, a perfect host. And Jackie, of course, is a perfect hostess. It seems to be a good marriage.

"In the evenings we would leave the yacht and go up the high hill —some in cars, some of us walking—to the house at the top, to have a leisurely dinner. Food would be sent up from the yacht. We had delicious hors d'oeuvres as we sat outside on the main terrace. Then went inside and dined at the long table in the spacious dining room, simply and comfortably furnished. Later, clustering near the fireplace if it was a cool evening. Or strolling outside, exclaiming over the beauty of the moon on the sea and the neighboring islands. It was quite lovely. At about eleven we would start down the hill again, most of us walking because it took only six or seven minutes going downhill. Then a few minutes' boat ride back to the *Christina* and a sound sleep.

"Left Skorpios July 20, and I went to Mass in Athens, dined alone in my hotel room and went to bed until about 1:30 A.M. Took the plane at 2:30 in the morning. I was going economy class, finally went to sleep and thought I was safe from interruptions until I would arrive in Addis Ababa. The plane stopped at the other main city, Asmara, and Bus Mosbacher or someone had sent word I would be on that flight, so there was a group from the U.S. consulate waiting for me. They greeted me and brought me flowers. It was 8:30 in the morning, and I had had very little sleep—dozing or half asleep for a few hours—and my dress was all wrinkled and my hair was disorderly, so I was rather embarrassed. I appreciated the trouble they had taken and I thought they were charming to do it.

"I arrived then at Addis Ababa, and was met by the Emperor's representative, whose name I was told was pronounced "Martha," which was simple enough, and by Ambassador Hall and his wife, and was brought to the Emperor's guesthouse."

This adventure had begun years earlier, during Jack's presidency, when the Emperor paid a visit of state to the United States and— as I have mentioned—Jackie was indisposed and Jack asked me to substitute for her as his official hostess at the White House. I had read that his birthday is July 23, and since mine is July 22, I brought this up in the course of the chatter one engages in to take the stiffness out of these official events. One remark led to another, and the Emperor declared that since we were practically twins we must celebrate our birthdays together sometime, and invited me to Ethiopia. This is the kind of opportunity that, for me, is impossible to resist: Everything I had ever heard about Ethiopia, the name itself, made it seem fascinating. I had found the Emperor to be congenial. So I had kept the thought in the back of my mind ever since; and with the approach of my eightieth birthday I decided to take him up on his invitation.

Another reason to go at that time was that Jean would be in East Africa that summer with her two young sons, on safari to photograph the wild game, and on their way back from Kenya they would be stopping in Ethiopia at the same time I would be there; so I thought it would be fun to see them there and share an interesting experience. Further, in Jack's honor and memory, the Emperor—through his own charitable foundation, His Imperial Majesty Haile Selassie I Foundation—had built a new library for the university, the John F. Kennedy Library, and this would be ready for dedication.

Sarge, with all his contacts in the world of diplomacy, took a keen interest in the plans, and in conversation with the Ethiopian ambassador found out that whereas I would be eighty on my birthday, Haile Selassie would be only seventy-eight. I had somehow got it into my mind that he and I were born the same year. I felt some chagrin to learn he was younger than I. But not enough to interfere with the trip.

From my diary:

"The state guesthouse is a large and comfortable house at the end of a long garden with many flowers, trees, and shrubs that were strange to me, but most of them colorful and attractive. Everything well kept. No elevator but a wide and easy flight of stairs up to my room, and a large and well-appointed bathroom-dressing room, most welcome to me.

"I relaxed most of that first day, not only from the fatigue I felt from the long flight and lack of proper sleep but because of an advance cable from Dr. Hansford, the State Department's regional medical adviser, with 'advice regarding health precautions' which included this: 'Altitude of guesthouse 8,500 feet. Necessitating slower pace of activity, good cardio-vascular reserve.'"

High altitude never really has bothered me. I have mentioned a flight over the Andes many years ago. However, I preferred not to tempt fate that first day, not before I had been to my birthday party at the Imperial Palace and had the chance to see something of the city and the country.

The Emperor put his car, a dark red Cadillac, at my disposal, and after Jean and the two boys arrived the next day, as scheduled, we did a lot of sight-seeing; mostly she and I, as the boys would be much more interested in such features of palace life as the large enclosure full of lions. The Emperor traces his genealogy to an alliance between the Queen of Sheba and King Solomon, as related in the Old Testament. Hence, one of his principal titles is Lion of Judah, and hence, also, the lion as a symbol of his throne and the tradition of keeping lions in the park of the royal palace. Indeed, I was told that the tamer ones used to be allowed to roam free in the grounds, or even in the palace itself. Although I could sympathize with the lions, I was personally relieved this was no longer the case.

And, again, from my diary:

"When we were out for a drive in the Emperor's car, it was a very odd sensation to see how people along the boulevards and streets— probably knowing nothing at all about who was in the car but recognizing it as the royal conveyance—would stop in their tracks and bow reverently as it passed. Another disconcertment: The middle of the back seat had been elevated several inches, because the Emperor is small, not much taller than I, and when he rode, this would enable his subjects to view him. But Jean is several inches taller than I, so when she sat next to me, perched on this special throne, she truly looked down on me and I felt like a midget.

"We thought the Ethiopian people were good looking and many of the women quite beautiful, with large luminous eyes and almost classic features; well built, poised, erect, confident, with pleasant and friendly smiles and white teeth that seemed to glisten in contrast to their dark brown skin. The governing class dresses in European fashion, but I was most intrigued by the sight of average women moving along the streets with such natural grace and dignity clad in immaculate white cloth, draped in something between a toga and a sari, and with the hems and borders done in three or four inches of embroidery in beautiful colors and designs."

I had rested and aroused and refreshed myself enough by the afternoon to go to the palace to be received by the Emperor. He sat at the head of a table at the end of a long room. I approached, stopping to make a deep curtsy, and he greeted me in the most hospitable way, and we reminisced for a few minutes; then I took my leave.

The next day was my birthday, and the Emperor gave a dinner in my honor at the palace; or, more precisely, at the modern new palace; the much older and slightly crumbling but more traditionally palatial one is still used also. We dined at a long table in a quite pleasant dining room, with the Emperor, of course, at the head of the table:

"I was on the Emperor's right. He said he preferred speaking French, as we had in Washington.

"Jean was there and American Ambassador Hall and Mrs. Hall, but otherwise the guest list of perhaps twenty-five or thirty was made up of the Emperor's immediate family.

"The Emperor was cordial. We chatted about this and that. He had two small dogs with him, as apparently he almost always has: the mother and one of her male offspring. The male dog was much bigger than his mother, which led to a few humorous exchanges, inasmuch as my sons all have been considerably taller than I am. However, I would not describe this as a festive occasion. The women were more or less grouped together, except for Jean and Mrs. Hall and me, and there was a certain air of constraint. I had heard that the family and nobility and officials were deeply in awe of him. He has great dignity and sits unusually straight. Afterward Jean said that the little dogs and I seemed to be the only ones that were not afraid of the Emperor.

"The next day, the birthday of the Emperor, there was a luncheon for hundreds of people in the tremendous banquet hall of the old palace. Again I was at the Emperor's right, with his sister and sister-in-law opposite on the left. The most noticeable thing, for me, about the Emperor's birthday 'party' was the solemnity. No one spoke loudly, nearly in whispers; few people spoke at all. There were no toasts to the Emperor's health and happiness, so far as I recall, no humorous attempts, no slightest word directed to or about the head of the state—the sort of thing we would do in America, and would happen in most countries of the Western world."

During the next couple of days, Jean and I had the opportunity to see some of the countryside—and it is magically beautiful, with its flowering vegetation and lush green hills and valleys, with mingled clouds and mists and sunshine and thin and brilliant air. We visited many places of special interest in Addis Ababa such as the rehabilitation center for girls handicapped by accident or disease, including blindness, a common affliction in that part of the world. The girls are taught to lead useful lives by weaving silks and other fabrics, especially rugs, which are done mostly in tones of beige and brown and are quite attractive.

I arrived back at Hyannis Port in early August, after being away about six weeks, having traveled twenty-five thousand miles or so. Surely, whatever the distance, travel is one of the essences of vitality. Moving, seeking, learning, enjoying being alive.

I continue to make rather extensive trips—to France, Greece, other places on the Continent—three or four times a year, and also travel a lot in the United States on personal and charitable matters. But so far as possible, I prefer to keep my time free during the summer months, because that is when the children come to Hyannis Port, bringing their children, and this is a time of family reunion.

Of course, since all the adults and for that matter the older grandchildren are always busy with many things in many places, there is a continual ebb and flow, but they all get there at some point, and they try to coordinate so that as many as possible can be there together at the same time.

The summer of 1972 was especially hectic because of Sarge's vice-presidential candidacy, which meant that he and Eunice had to be on the go most of the time. So were Ted and Joan. Ted was out campaigning all over the country for the national ticket, and also for state and local candidates. He was in and out from time to time. Pat, Ethel, and Jean were there most often, but they too had their projects that took time and travel, one in particular being the first of the now-annual Robert F. Kennedy Celebrity Tennis Tournaments for programs that reflect Bobby's ideals, especially his wish to help the disadvantaged children.

Somehow, despite all the comings and goings of that unusually busy summer, it happened—partly by planning but mostly by lucky coincidence—that for two days all twenty-eight grandchildren were in Hyannis Port at the same time. Such a thing had never happened before, and the odds would be long indeed against its happening again. So I did what was obviously the thing to do: I managed—with intricate complications and maneuvers, and imprecations and persuasions, such as I can leave easily to the imagination—to corral all of them and had their picture taken with me.

When Jackie remarried, some wondered whether she would keep the house she and Jack had at Hyannis Port. But she soon said she was going to, because it meant so much to her and to Caroline and John Jr., and she wanted them always to be able to come back to it. And, save for some intervals, that is the way it has worked out. Jackie wrote the following account and gave it to me:

"We spent the first four summers of our marriage with Jack's parents at Hyannis Port. We didn't have our own house here until Caroline was born, or what I mean to say is that's when we moved into it. Grandpa wanted to keep everyone together here. He had this house for us before we lived in it after Caroline was born. I fought against the idea, I thought it was too close, I wanted to be away from the compound.

"But now I am glad. I was reading about a Harvard study of what makes for happy families. Especially what would count most in this age of uncertainty. There were many factors, of course, but close to the top would be a situation in which a number of families knew each other well and had ideas and values they shared, and the children could play at one another's house and sometimes be invited and welcomed for meals. That could happen in a village or small town or a neighborhood, and it's kind of what happens here with the cousins. They're separated more or less most of the year, they live in different cities or different areas of big cities, but they all know one another; and this is the place where they get together, and I think that's awfully important for them.

"The first two summers after I married Ari I wasn't here with the children. Though they were here at times for visits. Then I came back with them for about half the summer.

"And sometimes I think that time heals things . . . and you forget certain things . . . I mean, I can't remember Jack's voice exactly any more . . . but I still can't stand to look at pictures of him and I don't have any around here except in the children's rooms . . . and when I came back everything just hit me, because this was the only house where we really lived, where we had our children, where every little pickle jar I had I found in some little country lane on the Cape . . . and nothing's changed since we were in it . . . and all of the memories came before my eyes.

"So anyway, after I had looked around and unpacked and all that, the first thing I did was walk over to see her. And we were sitting and talking about a lot of things, and I said, 'It really hits, doesn't it' . . . something like that . . . and that evening she called me and said, would I like to take a little walk around nine-thirty or ten because she didn't want me to be here and alone and be sad. And I thought: 'That woman who has so many reasons to be sad—for her to be thinking about calling me.' It shows you what else she's like. Then the next morning she called and asked me to come and swim with her at such and such a time and . . . you know, as if she's sort of taking care of me because she thinks I'm in this house by myself with too many memories. So that's what she's like really.

"And I found myself becoming so happy here. The children are happy, and the cousins are here, and all the grandchildren adore her. She's their grandmother and they love her, they're touched by her, they're amused by her, and they respect her. And she does something so clever with them: She sees them in little groups . . . she'll ask my two over for a lunch or she'll ask herself here for lunch, or she'll see all the Lawfords, or see the three teen-age girls, or the little boys who will be interested in fishing, or the college and precollege ones—and talk with all of them on the level of what interests them —instead of in some great mass scene where they're all tangled little bodies.

"She has the food they like, which is the same food she gave to her children . . . creamed chicken and Boston cream pie and apple jelly and . . . in all the years I've known her she's always had the same kind of food, which is the most wonderful, best food there is in the world, sort of American home-cooking food . . . always the apple jelly and the carrot and celery sticks and the wonderful roast chicken and the acorn squash and the ice cream and cake and all those things that are so good and children love. I think you always like to know that all the best kinds of things are at your grandmother's house."

I don't know. Sometimes I'm not sure what I should talk with them about, because so many years have passed, times change, ideas change as the generations come along, and it is hard to keep up with what they are thinking and what the "in thing" may be that season. But the daughters and daughters-in-law tell me just to keep going in the same ways I did in raising my own children.

Pat says:

"I think she had a great influence on the way we brought up our children. (I don't know whether she'd appreciate credit for that or not—maybe not *all* twenty-eight of them.) But even in little things —like I keep my own card index on my four, due to her example. And her interest in historical places and history in general . . . and conversation at the table about events . . . I've always tried to do something like that too. I have maps in my dining room—countries, states, capitals, and all that. I think she influenced us a lot that way, the girls and the boys too. And the idea of public life. My children are very much interested, which I think is marvelous. Of course, they have heard so much about politics, campaigns; they've lived through so much of it, so it seems natural, but most of it comes down to them through us from Mother and of course from Daddy."

Ethel says:

"I've never met a woman like her. She's constantly thinking about how to get others to think. I mean, it's really extraordinary. And certainly it's because of her that our children at the dining table and in the car pools have something to say about current events, instead of all that same stuff children usually talk about. It makes the conversation so much more interesting. I try to start it off with some of the newspaper clippings and all that, which I never would have thought about on my own. I think, to some extent, we've all taken over some of those things she did.

"And then, too, it was really at Grandma's strong suggestion that we began to separate the family at supper hour into two or three groups. Otherwise, you'd just have been trying to spoon pablum into Rory and not paying much attention to Kathleen or Joe or the others' problems."

Several of the grandchildren—on sufficient encouragement from fathers or mothers, aunts, uncles, others—have given their own opinions about life as it is these days in our family, and about me, and about Hyannis Port, and indeed about quite a number of matters that may be interesting to others as they have been to me. *For everything there is a season,* and they of course were speaking from the season of life they had reached. That would have been eleven and getting close to twelve for John Jr. Some of what he has said—and what others have said in other "oral histories" that follow in the next pages—may make me beam a bit, some may make me blush a bit. But never mind, this is what was said:

John Jr.:

"She really likes me to learn a lot. And every time you go over there she asks you all about math and history and languages, or who were the Pilgrims and when they came and asks you who everyone is. And like, do you know this and do you know that. And she talks about the church and talks about learning things, and she tries to teach you things. She talks a lot, but it's interesting what she talks about. Sometimes she talks about my father and she'll maybe tell a story about how bad he was when he was little, or when she was little and some of the bad things she did. She laughs and then you laugh. Every time we go she tells a few of the same stories. Most of the things are pretty funny.

"She has very good food. She has really good Boston cream pie. She has millions of cakes all of the time and she has good custard.

"I'd like to come back here every year. I love it."

Caroline:

"She wants everybody to be as happy as they can and stuff like that. If she can do anything about it. I mean, if they can be happier because of something she can do, then she does it.

"She makes such an effort over everybody. She wants everybody to have a chance.

"I saw her in New York when she was on the David Frost show—I was in the audience. The people sitting behind me thought she was terrible. They were a little bit older than me, and they said she was dead to the world and so on because she was saying everybody should get out and work and help everybody else because she did it for the retarded. They didn't like being told they should go out and work. But I thought she was really good.

"Grandmothers don't have to get mad at you for a lot of things like mothers do, but Grandma only gets mad at stuff you do that's not nice to other people—if you're rude or mean or something. Even then she does it nicely. She doesn't get really mad—she just says something in a way that you can see that it wasn't nice to somebody else.

"She's always trying to bring out the best things. If she sees some picture of me she'll say things like, 'You should always remember to stand with your hands away from your sides because it makes you look thinner.' Or like, I shouldn't put my teeth over my lip because it might give me buck teeth. She really goes out of her way to see if you have anything that could help you and then she encourages you to develop it. I like to draw and paint and write verses. It's pretty bad, it's really pathetic, but now and then when I write to her I send a verse, and she'll write back something like, 'We know you're not only an artist, but also a poet.'

"I guess all grandmothers are supposed to be good, and I could say something like that: 'All grandmothers are good but Grandma is the best'—but that would sound really stupid. It would be really gross.

"But she is good. I know that if I ever really needed her for anything, she'd always be there."

I cheerfully admit to bias in the matter, but I do think that Caroline shows a lot of talent in her verses. For Christmas 1971, she sent me a poem about her little brother. She had illuminated each verse with a water-color drawing in the margin, so that it was as much a painting as a poem. With her special permission I am putting it here:

JOHN

He paints his bathroom walls in the middle of the night,
He comes into my room and unscrews every light,

Swinging on a door smeared with Crazy Foam
Singing to himself, "Consider Yourself at Home," *

At four in the morning you can find him making glue
In the back hall near his guinea pig zoo.

He is trying to grow sea monkeys in his toothbrush
glass,
You can see it on his teeth which bear a coating like
grass.

He comes spitting in my room jabbing left and right
Shouting, OK, Caroline, ready for a fight.

He is trying to blow us up with his chemistry set,
He has killed all the plants but we've escaped as yet.

He loves my mother's linen sheets and hates his own
percale.
He can imitate the sounds of the humpback whale.

I love him not just because I oughter
But also because blood runs thicker than water.

> Signed: For Grandma
> Merry Christmas, 1971
> Lots of love,
> Caroline

In September of 1972 Caroline went off to boarding school at Concord Academy. I was on one of my excursions to Paris just at that time. I wrote her a letter from there. Recently she sent it back to me for use in this book, with a note saying, "You have to use it even if there's no room because it's so good and it's so 'you' and it made such a difference. . . ." Therefore:

> "September 22, 1972
> "Paris

"Dearest Caroline,

"This is just a little note to tell you I am thinking about you and

---

* Jackie has supplied an explanatory note: "This is a song from *Oliver*, which was John's school show that year. He was in the cast as a member of Fagan's gang of pickpockets and thieves."

hoping all goes well and that you are not too lonely, etc. The first few weeks in a new environment are always the most difficult ones so do not be too discouraged, but meet the challenge with determination and the realization that this new school is your particular commitment this year, and that you are going to make it a happy year and a successful one. Life is really so wonderful for you all, dearest Caroline, because you have new and exciting experiences constantly under such pleasant circumstances. Learn all you can about Concord and New England, the part of the world which your dear father cherished so deeply and to which he referred nostalgically in several of his speeches.

"Have fun, too, because I know God has given us many opportunities to be gay and happy and we should enjoy them to the utmost.

"When you pass the Concord Library, the Concord High School or the Catholic church, think of me almost seventy years ago driving my horse and carriage to the library in the summer, searching the Louisa Alcott books—studying my Latin (The Aeneid) in high school—going to Mass at the Catholic church; and if you are near say a little prayer for me, as I pray for you here in Paris—that all may go well.

"I am sure you will be happy as I was, my dear granddaughter.

"My deepest affection and love and hugs and come to Hyannis whenever possible.

"Grandma"

Kara, Ted and Joan's daughter, wrote me not long ago:

"Dear Grandma,

"I have been practicing my French for you to quiz me about and have been extremely careful to put the article in front of the word, as you taught me on your last visit.

"In religion, we are studying the Old Testament and I am giving an oral report on the Last Supper.

"Teddy is enjoying all his presents and Patrick sometimes tries to sneak in to play with them.

"I hope you have a nice Christmas and I look forward to seeing you soon.

"Love,
"Kara"

I had a note recently from Maria Shriver, Eunice's daughter:

"Dear Grandma:

"When I was little I used to yell every time I had to go to the dentist's. My mother mentioned this to you, and you wrote me a letter about it. Mother had me keep the letter and reread it every time before I was to see the dentist, so I would be more courageous.

"It really did help. I still didn't like going to the dentist, but I stopped yelling.

"Since I have practically memorized it by this time I am returning it to you, because I think it belongs in your book.

"Love,
"Maria"

In that case, here it is:

"October 15, 1965

"Dear Maria:

"Your mother just told me how nervous and upset you were at the dentist's office. I was so surprised, dear Maria, because I always think of you as being very brave about everything. . . .

"Usually in this family, we try not to complain and try to cooperate with the doctors and the dentists. You know, Uncle Jack had a pain in his back so severe he never could lift his children up in the air those last few years, but he never said, 'I feel terrible' or 'I cannot stand this backache.' He just let the doctors do their best to help him.

"Your mother and all our children had such good dental care and cooperated so well that now everyone speaks of the Kennedy smile and the Kennedy teeth. They even ask what kind of vitamins I used to give the children. All of them had to wear braces on their teeth for years. . . .

"So, dear Maria, the next time you go to the dentist, say a little prayer, smile, and make up your mind that no one is going to say that you are a baby but rather they will say that you are a courageous girl, willing and eager to help your mother and the doctor do what they think is best for you.

"Much love,

> "Affectionately,
> "G. Ma.

"P.S.: Be an example to the younger ones. If you squeal, they will squeal. If you say it is OK, they will say OK.

> "Love again,
> "G. Ma."

Most of what I was saying to Maria, of course, in effect was simply that there really is such a thing as "mind over matter," and that the principle can enable one to disregard present pain in the hope of future gain. For instance, I daresay not even the most confirmed devotee of cold showers would maintain that the first impact of the frigid water is pleasant; rather it is the pleasant aftereffect that makes that cold shock worthwhile. There are innumerable analogies of all kinds and degrees, including in my case a direct one that my grandson Steve Smith Jr., Jean and Steve's eldest son, brought up when he was talking about me for this book.

Steve Jr.:

"One of the things I've always thought was really amazing about Grandma was that she'd go swimming out in the Sound every day like up to and through Thanksgiving. It'd be fifty degrees out. I mean in the air, and the water could be colder, and Grandma would have her towel over her shoulder and would be going down the dune to go swimming. It would just freak out all the kids, all these tough little kids throwing footballs and climbing all over the roof and stuff. They wouldn't dream of going into that cold water. They couldn't *believe* it; but there goes Grandma, eighty-something years old, right into the ocean."

There are certain practical limits, of course, and I don't press my luck by going in when the water is really cold or when there are actual storm conditions, for I am not that skilled a swimmer and I have full respect for the waves and tides and undertows. But, while abiding by common sense, I have found through many decades that there are few activities that so improve the circulation and the general sense of vitality and optimism as a swim in brisk water, preferably salt water. I try to schedule a session of about fifteen minutes at least once a day.

My liking for regular exercise seems to have made a particularly keen impression on a number of grandchildren, because here is Christopher Lawford, with a few more athletic notes.

Chris:

"I walk with her every now and then, and she'll go back and forth on her front lawn where her children, our parents, used to play the touch games, and she'll keep going and I get tired. Her energy never ceases to amaze me. It's just phenomenal. I play golf with her. What she does, she hits the ball and she always hits it in a straight line. No hooks, no slices. Always straight all the time. She doesn't hit it very far, an average of maybe seventy-five yards, but straight. And then she walks rapidly after it. We'd do that for six, seven, eight holes. She's in her eighties and I'm not even twenty and I am exhausted. I wanted to take a golf cart but she wouldn't hear of it. And I said, 'Grandma, how in heck do you do this?' Bad weather or anything, nothing stops her.

"There are all kinds of aspects to Grandma, but when you begin thinking about them you start realizing that practically all of them are facets of the same character and the same entity. Like she keeps her strength and energy going by self-discipline. There's no baloney with Grandma. She often reminds me that life is not a bowl of cherries, and that you have to do a lot of things you don't really want to do. And that often you don't get to do what you want when you want. And there are plenty of times when you're going to have to put your head down and just get through it. And she's right. I think her basic philosophy, or purpose, in raising her children, and now in influencing her grandchildren, has been to try to teach them to teach themselves.

"She doesn't push her ideas on you, not even in religion. It's an exchange of ideas. She wants to know what you are thinking. Most older people talk your ear off. They don't want to hear about you, they want to tell you about themselves and *tell* you generally. With Grandma it's totally the opposite. Totally. What she cares about is *you*, what's on your mind, what are your interests, and for that matter what are your problems if any, and if you feel like saying something about them, although she won't pry. And then she might make a remark about how Jack did something in a situation, or she did when she was a girl of about your age, or something will remind her of a conversation at the dinner table in the earlier days. She very often relates back to scenes and conversations at the dinner table when everybody was still pretty young and the family was together. We took a walk one summer night around ten-thirty, and we walked an hour or so all over Hyannis Port, in the middle of the road, just talking. But as I think back about it now, it was really mostly about me. Nothing much in particular sticks in my mind about it, but I'm sure I got some of my own ideas worked out and absorbed some of hers.

"Ever since I can remember, Grandma has been instilling in me the idea that I was lucky to have been born with advantages and I should use them to help people who are less lucky. I have grown up with that belief. It's something so much a part of me I don't have to think: It's what I have done and expect to do.

"I was part of a low-cost housing program in a deprived section of Boston. I have worked on behalf of underprivileged people in several other localities during my teen-age years. I have worked with the mentally retarded both in schools and at the Shriver Day Camp, where I was a counselor for two summers. Whatever I achieve or fail to achieve in my efforts to make the world a better place for those who are afflicted or underprivileged, Grandma will have to take some of the responsibility, because she had such a great deal to do with setting the direction of my life.

"Experience has shown me why she and others in my family have encouraged me to help the needy. I know now that I as an individual, as someone who cares and will take the time, can really make a difference, and that to be able to help others is actually one of the most exhilarating and satisfying experiences anyone can possibly imagine."

Bobby and Ethel's children are the eldest among the twenty-eight grandchildren; in fact, among them the span runs from eldest to youngest grandchild. Kathleen—known in the family as Kathy—is the eldest granddaughter. She is a wonderful girl: highly intelligent, interested in public service—she has worked, for instance, among the Indians—and has decidedly a mind of her own. Which means, naturally, that she and I do not agree about some things that I consider important. But that's all right. I defend her right to disagree, and, besides, I think that as she gets older she will come more to my way of thinking. Be that as it may be, here is a segment of "oral history" from her viewpoint.

Kathleen:

"I arrived in Paris with this friend of mine, and we had our backpacks on because we had this great idea we'd bicycle through the Loire Valley. It was raining in Paris and we really had no place to stay, and so Anne said, 'Why don't you call your grandmother?' Because we knew she was in Paris and she always stayed at the Ritz. So we trekked over to the Ritz, after marching about fifteen blocks because we got off at the wrong subway station. We asked for her at the Ritz and the man at the desk said in low tones of regret that Mrs. Kennedy is not staying here this year, she's at the Plaza Athéné. So we arrived over there.

"First of all, they'd hardly let us in the door, because I had blue jeans on that hadn't been washed, as usual, and the backpack and a floppy hat and sort of half of a raincoat, and did not look like the material you would want. But we got through to her from the lobby phone and she was totally surprised because she didn't know we were going to be in Paris then; and we went up, and she could hardly believe it when these two dirty kids arrived in her hotel room. But she was terrific. She sort of gasped and said well, ah, go over and do this and sit down and didn't know exactly what to do with us. (Like she'll say, 'When my children were growing up we all liked nice clothes. You don't like those sort of clothes. What can I give you?') She always wants to help out but she doesn't know exactly how to do it. So she was terrific, you know. She gave us a big tea and suggested we might want to use her bathroom to bathe and clean up and make ourselves more comfortable.

"She wanted to get us a room at her hotel, but we didn't think we'd fit in too well in the long run. We began making telephone calls and reached some friends and they told us about a good cheap place on the other side of town. She was very nervous about that. So we all went down and she asked at the concierge desk about it, and of course they had never heard of it at all and they were totally disdainful about it. Grandma said she wondered if it was all right for boys to stay there—but not girls? She took us over to the Left Bank in a taxi, and with her long Dior gown on walked into this halfway shabby hotel and interviewed the concierge there. 'Will these girls be safe? Is there a shower?' And trying out her French. Because that's what the man at this hotel spoke. But she was terrific about it, and she was keeping her sense of humor throughout. Anne and I stayed there the next few days while we were in Paris.

"She always tries to keep that sense of humor going. She wants to know what's going on and is really interested. And always wants to ask questions, making sure we're learning. Like we're going by a landmark building like Notre Dame or Les Invalides or the Louvre and it's 'Do you know the differences among the Doric, Ionic and Corinthian columns?' And seems a little surprised when you do. And then this thing of saying a little plaintively, 'Can I give you a Dior dress? I don't know, Kathleen, what exactly do you *like*?' . . .

"There's that thing about the grandmother and the grandchildren always get along and the parents have to be the disciplinarians, and I can see how it could be partly true. She'll write these Mummy and Eunice and Jean and Pat and Joan letters suggesting they tell us where to put the bicycles and what to do with the dogs and so forth, but with the grandchildren—well, she wants to teach us but she wants to side with us, in a lot of ways.

"And she has this amazing ability to sort of step outside herself for a while and realize that though you're this proper person and you like to speak French and to do everything properly, on the other hand now and then in the 1970s being proper can be slightly absurd. But always *knowing*. It always strikes you when somebody has a sense of humor about themselves, especially older people. You think they've grown wise because they're older. Not realizing that the sense of humor goes with it, and if they didn't have that they wouldn't have become wise. And that's one of the best things about her."

Well, it is pleasant to be credited with a quality that one had always assumed about oneself, even though it may have been hidden from time to time from public or even private view by what I might call the avalanches of events. But as for being such a "proper" person, I have never thought of myself that way, and I think I can refute the charge with one recent incident that landed me in the Palm Beach newspaper.

I had stopped in at Mrs. Wrightman's house because she was giving a luncheon honoring my friend Mary Lasker, but I had to leave early because there was something else I had scheduled, and John Ryan was supposed to come and pick me up in the car. But there was a misunderstanding about the time, or somebody's watch was wrong, so after waiting for him on the porch I walked down the driveway to wait for him at the road. He still didn't come, so I started walking home. But it is quite a long distance, and it was a hot day, so I decided the sensible thing was to try to get a ride with one of the passing motorists. I raised my thumb in the way I had seen hitchhikers do.

I was well dressed in a white suit, with a good scarf and hat, and I was sure I looked respectable and I thought I looked attractive. I was therefore rather mortified when car after car went by, at least a dozen of them, until finally a man did stop and I got in.

Lest there be any misinterpretation of my motive, I told him who I was and what the problem was. He looked a bit amazed and very kindly drove me to my front door. As it happened, later that afternoon I was in the Bonwit Teller shop and saw him with his wife helping her pick out a few things, so I went over to thank him again and introduce myself to her and also to tell her how it happened that I had been riding with her husband. She said he had already told her. We all smiled and I shook hands and that was the end of the story except that a day or two later the press got hold of it, and it became a feature article with a cartoon drawing of me and words to the effect that "Rose Kennedy, although now in her eighties, has taken up hitchhiking. . . ."

Most of my grandchildren are still too young to be thinking much about what they want from life except the next allowance and the penny candies they are going to load up on at the News Store. Or being allowed to crew in races. And dolls and footballs. Ice-cream sodas and going to the movies. Dreams of glory and Boston cream pies.

Even the older ones are still too young to know what they really want.

I don't and will not try to impose my ideas and values on them (not that it would do any good if I did), and I don't pry into their lives. I don't have the opportunity to see them enough in a directly personal, relaxed, and conversational way to know what they are doing most of the time, or what they are thinking about most things. Although we do sometimes have religious discussions I often find that their ideas about the Church, about faith, about God are groping, tentative, skeptical, and thus, to me, rather difficult to understand. When I have talked with them about Holy Week they were interested, but there was little knowledge about it even among those who had attended Catholic schools and even though some had been to the Holy Land. And the idea of going to church because it's Lent didn't seem to occur to some of them.

But of course the Church has changed too. The ancient rule of no meat on Fridays—which I remember so well my father, in public life, had to be so careful about at official luncheons and banquets— and the rule of fasting after midnight before taking Communion (now it's only one hour) and such things were based on the idea of self-sacrifice. So, in my lifetime, life has changed on every level. I daresay that at the present pace of events in the world the rate will become even rather more dizzying than it has been.

And so, in this world of change, in which it is very easy for anyone to become confused, I think naturally of my grandchildren, and perhaps the great-grandchildren that I may be lucky enough to see, and of those even beyond that generation, and I wonder what I can say that will be meaningful.

The best I can do is to pass on to them some of my own ideas and a few special hopes. Again calling on the insights of others past and present for extra perspectives.

I hope they will realize where they came from and how they happen to be where they are. They came—on the Kennedy-Fitzgerald side—from ancestors who were quite poor and disadvantaged through no fault of their own but who had the imagination, the resolve, the intelligence, and the energy to seek a newer, better world for themselves and their families. And had the willingness to work as hard as they had to, and suffer whatever had to be suffered, and to look to the future and plan for whatever could be planned, and to seize gratefully on any piece of good luck that came their way. If none came, to look for it, look for opportunity.

In a short time, just a few generations, these beleaguered Irish immigrants had produced a family to whom many in the world looked in admiration. It was an inspiring story. They are the continuing part of it, and I hope they will try always to be worthy of it.

I hope they will realize and remember that the United States of America was one of the few places—perhaps almost the only place—in the world where this saga could have happened. I hope they will always feel a deep sense of gratitude toward this country, and deep pride in it, and deep obligation to preserve, protect, and defend it. If they choose to take the means of political life and public office, so much the better, for this has been so much a part of our family tradition, and it would please me to think of its being continued. But there are other careers, other ways and means, full time or part time or spare time as the case may be and circumstances may permit. Everyone should do something for the common good of this country and all its humanity.

I hope they will have courage. And my definition of the term would be similar to that given by Socrates (I believe):

"We are capable at the same time of taking risks and of estimating them beforehand. Others are brave out of ignorance. When they stop to think they begin to fear. But the man who most truly can be accounted brave is he who most knows the meaning of what is sweet in life and of what is terrible, then goes out undeterred to meet what is to come."

I hope they will have strength to bear the inevitable difficulties and disappointments and griefs of life. Bear them with dignity and without self-pity. Knowing that tragedies befall everyone, and that although one may seem singled out for special sorrows that is not really so; that worse things have happened many times to others in the world, and that it is not tears but determination that makes pain bearable.

I hope they will comprehend that the span of any life is short and all the days and hours are precious. I hope they will live life fully while they are alive, in all the dimensions of both its duties and its beauties. Here are some lines from Cardinal Newman:

"God has created me to do Him some definite service. He has committed some work to me which He has not committed to another. I have my mission. I have a part in a great work; I am a link in the chain, a bond of connection between persons. He has not created me for naught. I shall do good. I shall do His work."

Very often I am asked about what people like to call my "philosophy of life." When it is put that way it always seems to me to be a rather formidable expression, and one too profound to respond to in simple terms. All the same, like everyone else, I am sure I do have certain principles and values which have always loomed large in my approach to life and the problems we all face in living it to the best of our abilities. Now, as I approach my eighty-fourth year—it seems even older when I see it in print—I find it interesting to reflect on what has made my life, even with its moments of pain, an essentially happy one.

I have come to the conclusion that the most important element in human life is faith.

If God were to take away all His blessings, health, physical fitness, wealth, intelligence, and leave me but one gift, I would ask for faith— for with faith in Him, in His goodness, mercy, love for me, and belief in everlasting life, I believe I could suffer the loss of my other gifts and still be happy—trustful, leaving all to His inscrutable providence. When I start my day with a prayer of consecration to Him, with complete trust and confidence, I am perfectly relaxed and happy regardless of what accident of fate befalls me because I know it is part of His divine plan and He will take care of me and my dear ones.

For me, faith means the continuing awareness of the existence of God, not in some far-off and unrelated manner, but as an object of a spiritual experience in which I am personally involved. I am as confident of God's existence as I am of my own, and I see Him as Lord and Savior relating lovingly to all who are created by His hand. He reveals Himself in His Word and for Catholics especially He reveals Himself also in His Church, and both of these must be experienced in faith to comprehend the riches they enfold.

We must guard against the thought that faith is mere credulity or that we can simply talk or reason ourselves into possessing it; the truth is that just as it centers upon God, so too it comes from Him to those who seek it. Nor should we think of faith either as something we are born into, a kind of family legacy in the spiritual realm. Although we teach our children very early in life what we call the truths of faith, each one of them at some time in his or her development as a human being must pray for the gift of faith, must personally accept the gift of faith and cherish it as his or her own.

What I want to make clear is that from faith, and through it, we come to a new understanding of ourselves and all the world about us. It puts everything into a spiritual focus, if I may say it that way, so that love, and joy, and happiness, along with worry, sorrow, and loss, become a part of a large picture which extends far beyond time and space.

I often hear from people who have been stricken with some kind of overwhelming tragedy, and at the time that they write they are often very close to desolation. Naturally, I feel very strongly for such people, and I try to console them as best I can, although this is difficult when one knows them only by the few words of a brokenhearted letter.

Then I tell them that out of my own experience I feel that one must turn to God in faith, knowing that His loving-kindness is never far from us and that His providence never allows us to be tested beyond our strength. If we can truly believe in His presence and goodness to us, we are never alone or forsaken.

During my long lifetime I have found three devotions which were of special spiritual inspiration to me. The Rosary has helped me to lead a happy life devoted to the love of God and for the benefit of my family and my friends, and the welfare of my neighbor. The rosary may be a silly symbol for some people, but for me if I cannot sleep, if I am worried on a plane, if I am pacing the floor overwrought in thinking of my husband's illness and I hold the rosary in my hand, it gives me comfort, trust, serenity, a sense of understanding by the Blessed Mother because as I have talked and prayed to her all my life, in happy, successful times, I know now she will understand and comfort me and bring me solace in my anxious troubled moments—and sometimes I have given a rosary to my friends when they are exhausted and baffled by their problems—and so many times I have heard them say, "Oh, Rose, if only I had your faith. If only I could have the trust and confidence in the Almighty which you have." And so I have urged my children and grandchildren to embrace this faith bequeathed to them, to foster it, to try to strengthen it by prayer, reading, and study, seeking information on dogma that they cannot understand.

Another favorite is the *Meditations* by Cardinal Newman, which always brings me consolation when I am discouraged and find myself in an inexplicable dilemma—some turn of events that seems to be unexpected and unnecessary.

And my third great source of inspiration is my devotion to the Stations of the Cross. As we know, the fourteen pictures represent events in the last three hours of our Lord's life just before His death. I follow this journey often, in church, kneeling before each one as I knelt in Jerusalem on the Via Dolorosa. I see Jesus, silent, in the early scenes of the false accusations against Him. I see His mother meet Him in the fourth station uncomplaining about His cruel fate, and I ask her to help me and my children, too, to carry our crosses. I see Jesus fall three times on this journey, bowed down by fatigue and the weight of the cross but continuing the journey undaunted, unlamenting, and I recall His words in the Garden of Gethsemane to His Heavenly Father, "Not My Will but Thy Will be done." I repeat His words again and again. Finally, the twelfth station when He died, and I think of my three sons in their last moments—on their final missions, undertaken for the benefit of humanity—and I bow my head in silent resignation to God's Holy Will. I think of my eldest son, Joe, when his airplane exploded over the English Channel. I recall kneeling heartbroken at Jack's catafalque in the Rotunda at Washington, and I weep again at the remembrance of Bobby's funeral cortege, in New York, led by Ethel and his ten children.

At the fourteenth station, I see the Blessed Mother view, for the last time, her Son placed in the tomb. I think again of my beloved ones. I take renewed strength and courage in the thought that as Jesus Christ rose from the dead, my husband and I and our sons and daughters will one day rise again and we all shall be happy together, never more to be separated. My spirits are lightened and my heart rejoices, and I thank God for my belief in the Resurrection. "I am the resurrection and the life; he who believes in me, even if he die, shall live; and whoever lives and believes in me shall never die."

This promise has been a steady source of guidance and inspiration throughout my life, and I hope and pray that all who read this book may find renewed peace and strength and joy in these thoughts.

Index

Adams, Charles Francis, 232
Adenauer, Konrad, 406, 438
Alcott, Louisa May, works of, 16–17, 47, 209, 510
Alexandra, Czarina, 207–8
Ambrose, Margaret, 219
Anderson, Mrs. *See* Dunn, Elizabeth
Aranha, Señor (Brazilian Foreign Minister), 279
Arosmena, President and Señora (Ecuador), 398
Astor, Lady Nancy, 233, 245, 250, 294, 296, 298; described, 245, 294
Astor, Lord, 233, 294, 296
As We Remember Joe (John F. Kennedy), 121, 126–27, 170–71, 173–74, 284, 297, 299, 302
Avedon, Richard, 380–81

Baker, Newton D., 195
Baldridge, Trish, 393
Baldwin, Stanley, 253
Barkley, Alben, 235
Barkley, Mrs. Alben, 235
Bartlett, Charles (Charlie), 350, 409
Baruch, Bernard, 194, 199
Battles, John F., article on Ted Kennedy in politics, in Worcester *Telegram* by, 409
Bayh, Senator and Mrs. Birch, injuries suffered in plane crash with Teddy Kennedy by, 455–56
Beaverbrook, Lord, 290, 410
Bennett, Constance, 190

Bennett, Joan (Mrs. Edward M. Kennedy). *See* Kennedy, Joan
Bennett family, and marriage of daughter Joan to Ted Kennedy, 429–30, 432
Berlin, Irving, 294–95
Bernstein, Leonard, 381; at inauguration "gala," 383
Berquist, Laura, 485
Bessborough, Lady, 227, 228
Betts, Dr. Henry, 419–21, 422, 426, 436; description of his patient Joseph P. Kennedy by, 419–21
Biddle, Margaret, 296
Billings, LeMoyne (Lem), 165, 178, 180–83, 201, 215–16, 280, 284–85, 338–39, 350, 381, 382, 414, 415, 440, 475; descriptions of Jack Kennedy by, 165, 180–81, 182–83, 215–16, 475; and Jack Kennedy's congressional campaign and victory, 312–13; *John Fitzgerald Kennedy . . . As We Remember Him* by, 182, 284–85
Bingham, Robert Worth, 212
Bohlen, Charles E., Ambassador, 452
Boles, Dr., 443, 445
Boothe, Clare. *See* Luce, Mrs. Henry R.
Bradley, Colonel E. R., Joseph Kennedy's purchase of part ownership in Hialeah race track from, 335–36
Braggiotti family, 321

Brown, Edmund G., and Jack Kennedy's presidential nomination campaign, 370–71

Bruce, Marie, 294–95; recollection of Kathleen (Kick) Kennedy at her London party by, 297–98

Buchan, John (Lord Tweedsmuir), quoted, 357; lines from his "Fratri Dilectissimo" (Dearest Brother) quoted, 481

Bullitt, William (Bill), 206, 207, 208, 235, 240, 246, 247; and Rose Kennedy's trip to Moscow, 206, 207, 208

Bundy, McGeorge, 438

Burgess, Thornton, 111; Adventures of Reddy Fox by, as favorite of Jack Kennedy as a small child, 111

Burke, Margaret (sister-in-law), 186, 189

Burns, James MacGregor, quoted on Jack Kennedy's role at 1956 Democratic Convention, 329

Burns, John (Johnnie), 267

Burns, Robert, quoted, 201

Byrnes, Senator James, 274

Byrnes, Mrs. James, 274

Cabot family, 49. See also specific individuals

Caffery, Jefferson, 279

Cannon, Frances Ann (later Mrs. John Hersey), 256–57, 263

Cassini, Oleg, 138, 381, 400

Cavanaugh, Father John, 446

Cavendish, Duke and Duchess of, 30, 291–92, 301, 338

Cavendish, Elizabeth, 295

Cavendish, Lord Frederick, 291

Cavendish, Lord Frederick Charles, 30

Cavendish family, 30, 301, 331. See also specific individuals

Cecil, Duke and Duchess of, 291–92, 331

Chamberlain, Neville, 221, 223, 233, 236, 237–45 passim, 250, 251, 252, 253, 261; and negotiations prior to Second World War, 236–45, 252

Chamberlain, Mrs. Neville, 221, 233, 245; described, 233

Chaplin, Charlie, 186

Child, Brigadier-General Sir Hill, 221

Churchill, Winston S., 261, 305, 316, 393; quoted on greatness, 393; While England Slept by, 261

Clancy, Harold (Hal), 411

Clasby, Richard (Dick), 341–44, 443; description of Kennedys and football games at Hyannis Port by, 341–44

Clasby, Mrs. Richard. See Gargan, Mary Jo

Cole, Charles, 51

Colum, Mary (formerly Mary Magiore), 35

Colum, Padraic, 35

Connolly, Sybil, description of President Kennedy's trip to Ireland by, 439

Copeland, Professor Charles ("Copey"), 74

Cotter, John, and Jack Kennedy's race and victory for congressional seat, 309–10, 312, 320

Coughlin, Father Charles E., 194

Curley, James Michael, 306, 309, 310

Cushing, Betsy (Mrs. James Roosevelt), 197–98, 275

Cushing, Harvey, 197

Cushing, Mary, 197

Cushing, Richard Cardinal, 129, 350–51, 449–50, 483; offers solemn high Mass for President Kennedy at Holy Cross Cathedral, 449–50; on Jackie's marriage to Ari Onassis, 483; presides at wedding of Jack and Jackie Kennedy, 350–51

Cutler, John Henry, 43; biography of Rose Kennedy's father, Honey Fitz: 3 Steps to the White House, 307

Daniell, Raymond, 293

Davies, Marion, 371

De Gaulle, Charles. See Gaulle, Charles de

De Mille, Cecil B., 95

Derby, Lord, Joe and Rose Kennedy as guests at Epsom Downs of, 230

Devonshire, Duke and Duchess of, 234, 263, 291, 295, 296, 298, 332, 440, 446

Dewey, Thomas E., 260

Dietrich, Marlene, 234

Donnalley, Reverend Mother, 128

Donovan, Joseph, as best man at wedding of Joseph P. and Rose F. Kennedy, 69

Duncan, Mary. *See* Sanford, Mary

Dunn, Elizabeth (*later* Mrs. Anderson), 159–60, 219, 236, 244, 257, 259, 265; description of Kennedy family life at Hyannis Port by, 159–60

Eden, Anthony, 234

Edens, Roger, 383

Edward III, King of Great Britain, 222

Edward VII, King of Great Britain, 42

Einstein, Albert, 243

Eisenhower, Dwight D., 321, 326, 327, 328, 357, 378, 385, 386, 485; greets the new President, John Kennedy, at the White House, 378; at inauguration of President Kennedy, 385, 386; and Kennedy vs. Lodge in senatorial contest, 321, 326

Eisenhower, Mrs. Dwight D., 385, 386; at inauguration of President Kennedy, 385, 386

Elizabeth, Princess (*later* Elizabeth II, Queen of Great Britain), 220, 223, 224, 238

Elizabeth, Queen (consort of George VI), 220, 221–24, 225, 226, 231, 238, 239, 246–49; described, 220, 221–24

Elphinstone, Lord and Lady, 221

Emerson, Ralph Waldo, 209; quoted, 3, 17

Ena, former Queen of Spain, 231

Fairbanks, Douglas, 186

Falaise de la Coudraye, Marquis Henri ("Hank") de la, and Gloria Swanson, 186, 188–89, 190

Farber, Dr. Sidney, 410–11

Farley, James A. (Jim), 44, 260, 266–68; and Joseph P. Kennedy, Jr., and his nomination contest with FDR, 266–68; quoted on politics, 44

Fay, Paul ("Red"), 313, 350; and Jack Kennedy's congressional campaign, 313, 350

Feldman, Michael (Mike), 304

Finnegan, Margaret, 32

Finnegan, Miriam, with Rose F. Kennedy at the Blumenthal convent in Holland, 32, 34, 35, 40, 153–54

Fisher, Robert (Bob), and Joseph P. Kennedy's love of Harvard football, 74

Fitzgerald, Agnes (sister, *later* Mrs. Joseph F. Gargan), 11, 29, 31–32, 33–34, 35–36, 41, 42, 43, 54, 55, 61, 67, 69, 93, 94–95, 127–28, 155; death of, 128; described, 33–34, 128; as maid of honor at sister Rose's wedding to Joseph P. Kennedy, 69; with Rose in Europe, 29, 31–32, 33–34, 35–36, 41, 42, 43, 54, 55–56

Fitzgerald, Edward (brother), 325

Fitzgerald, Mrs. Edward (Polly), and Kennedy family political campaigns and "tea parties," 325–26, 363, 369, 433, 467, 469; on Bobby Kennedy, 466

Fitzgerald, Ella, 383

Fitzgerald, Eunice (sister), 14–15, 40, 90, 96; described, 96

Fitzgerald, Frederick (brother), 23, 322

Fitzgerald, Frederick, Jr. (nephew), 322

Fitzgerald, John Francis (Honey Fitz, father), 5, 6–13, 15, 16, 29–31, 90, 92–93, 106, 107, 136, 194, 216–17, 232–34, 237, 259, 260, 262, 269, 271, 280, 306–9, 314, 315, 320, 332–34, 340, 386; background, family, marriage of, 5, 6–13, 15; death of, 334; described, characteristics, 6–13, 22–26, 31, 52–54, 332–34, 403; elected mayor of Boston (1905), 24–26, 27; founds City Club, 51; and marriage of daughter Rose, 57–65; and politics, 12, 19–26, 27, 29, 40–41, 43–45, 47, 51, 52–55; publishes *The Republic* (weekly newspaper), 21–22; and Rose's debut, 48–49

Fitzgerald, Mrs. John Francis (Mary Josephine Hannon, mother), 5, 6–11, 23–24, 38–39, 42, 54, 63, 89–90, 103, 232–34, 237, 259, 269, 307, 386, 403, 451; character, description of, 13–15, 54

Fitzgerald, John Francis, Jr. (brother), 14–15

Fitzgerald, Polly. *See* Fitzgerald, Mrs. Edward

Fitzgerald, Rose Mary Murray (paternal grandmother), 5, 8

Fitzgerald, Thomas (brother), 11

Fitzgerald, Thomas (paternal grandfather), 5, 6, 8, 20

Fonteyn, Dame Margot, quoted on Bobby Kennedy, 471–72

Forrestal, James, 129

Franco, Generalissimo, 406

Frankfurter, Justice Felix, 170, 251

Frankfurter, Mrs. Felix, 251

Frost, David, Rose Kennedy's appearance on television show of, 494, 508

Frost, Robert, quoted, 447

Frothingham, Louis, defeat by John Francis Fitzgerald in Boston mayoralty race of, 25

Fruitful Bough, The (Edward M. Kennedy), 141–43, 144, 302–4, 416–17, 419–22, 456

Fulbright, J. William, 379

Fulbright, Mrs. J. William, 379

Gage, Viscount, 224

Galsworthy, John, quoted, 115

Gargan, Ann (niece), 128–29, 160, 338, 371, 379, 383, 386, 416–19, 442, 443–44, 446; and religion, 160; and Uncle Joseph P. Kennedy's stroke and illness, 416–19, 425, 446, 462, 463, 464, 465

Gargan, Joseph F. (brother-in-law), 128, 132

Gargan, Mrs. Joseph F. *See* Fitzgerald, Agnes

Gargan, Joseph F., Jr. (Joey, nephew), 88, 127–32, 140–41, 322–23, 338, 340, 349–50, 433, 443, 445, 490, 491; and Chappaquiddick, 490, 491; description of family life with the Kennedys by, 127–32, 140–41, 349–50

Gargan, Mary Jo (niece, *later* Mrs. Richard Clasby), 128–29, 131–32, 137–38, 139–40, 141, 322–23, 338, 340, 341, 443; description of family life with the Kennedys by, 137–38, 139–48, 340–41; description of Jack Kennedy's senatorial campaign by, 322–23

Garner, John Nance, 195

Gaulle, Charles de, 400–2, 447

Gaulle, Mrs. Charles de, 400–2

Gavin, General James, 290

George V, King of Great Britain, 251

George VI, King of Great Britain, 221–23, 224, 226, 231, 239, 244, 246–49

Gloucester, Duchess of, 231

Goldsmith, Arthur, 68

Good, Dr., and birth of Rose Kennedy's first child, Joseph, Jr., 78

Goulding, Edmund, 191

Grace, Peter, 256

Grace, Princess, 360

Guinness, Gloria, 452–53

Guinness, Loel, 452, 453

Haile Selassie, Emperor, 398; and visit of Rose Kennedy to Ethiopia, 484, 498, 499–500, 501, 502–3

Halifax, Lord and Lady, 221, 222, 229, 248, 249, 261

Hall, Ambassador and Mrs. (to Ethiopia), 502
Hamilton, Edith, quoted, 393
Hammarskjöld, Dag, quotations from *Markings* by, vii, 145
Hannon, Mary Josephine. *See* Fitzgerald, Mrs. John Francis
Harlech, Lord and Lady. *See* Ormsby-Gore, Mr. and Mrs. David (*later* Lord and Lady Harlech)
Harriman, Averell, quoted on Bobby Kennedy, 471
Harringtons, the, 348, 349
Hartington, Marchioness of (Kathleen Kennedy), 30, 200, 256–57, 263–69, 271, 306, 331, 344, 359, 430; activity in Second World War, 287–302 *passim*; *As We Remember Joe* on, 297; birth, childhood, early years, 30, 75–76, 83, 84, 85, 92, 119, 121, 153; death in plane crash of, 332, 440; debut of, 225; described, 287–88; in Europe as daughter of ambassador to Great Britain, 213–14, 216, 217, 220, 225, 227, 234, 235, 239, 246, 250, 252, 256, 287–98 *passim*; marriage and death of husband, 287–302; at school in Europe, 200–1, 206–8
Hartington, Marquess of, William John Robert Cavendish (Billy), 30, 263, 271, 288–98 *passim*, 332; killed in Belgium, 301–2, 332; marriage of Kathleen Kennedy to, 30, 291–92, 296–98
Hartington, Marquess of (eighth Duke of Devonshire), 291
Hays, Will ("Hays Office"), Joseph P. Kennedy and, 190–91, 314
Hearst, William Randolph, 195–96, 203, 218–19; and Roosevelt/Smith nomination stalemate and Joseph P. Kennedy, 195–96
Hennessey, Luella, 164–65, 219, 236, 244, 257; description of Bobby Kennedy as "people-minded" by, 164–65

Hersey, John, 263
Hersey, Mrs. John. *See* Cannon, Frances Ann
Higgins, Joseph P., 310
Hitler, Adolf, 236–37, 239–40, 241, 243, 245, 253, 270
Holden, William, 191
Hoover, Herbert, 194, 406, 425–26; Joseph P. Kennedy on "Hoover Commission" with, 194
Houghton, Arthur, 321
Howe, Louis McHenry, 196
Hughes, Charles Evans, 166, 428
Hughes, H. Stuart, 428, 433
Hull, Cordell, 260
Humphrey, Hubert, 366, 367–68, 370

I'm for Roosevelt (Joseph P. Kennedy), 203

John Fitzgerald Kennedy . . . As We Remember Him (Lem Billings), 182, 284–85
Johnson, Lyndon B., 357, 366, 379–80, 386, 388–89, 444–45, 450–51, 457, 459; on death of President Kennedy, 444–45
Johnson, Mrs. Lyndon B. (Lady Bird), 380, 386, 388–89, 450–51, 457; on death of President Kennedy, 445
Jones, Evelyn, 338, 354, 379–80, 424–25, 433, 443; description of Rose Kennedy and Kennedy family life by, 338, 354, 379–80, 424–25
Jones, Thomas (Tom), 424
Juliana, Princess (*later* Queen of the Netherlands), 40

Kane, Joseph (Joe), 309, 312, 316, 318; and Jack Kennedy's congressional campaign, 309, 312, 316, 318
Karajan, Herbert von, 404
Keating, Kenneth, defeat by Bobby Kennedy for Senate seat from New York of, 459–60
Kefauver, Estes, 328–29
Kelly, Grace. *See* Grace, Princess

Kennedy, Caroline (granddaughter), 101, 113, 354, 370, 377–78, 379–80, 381, 382, 394, 396, 406, 411, 412, 417, 434, 435, 436, 437, 441, 448, 462, 482–83, 484, 498; described, 498; relationship and correspondence with grandparents, 412, 417, 434, 435, 436, 462, 484, 504–6, 507–10

Kennedy, Edward M. (Ted), 76, 141–43, 150, 155, 339, 341–42, 343, 350, 359, 383, 427–33, 443, 445–46, 467, 468, 479, 483, 486–96, 503–4; airplane accident and injuries, 455–57, 458–59, 463, 491; birth, childhood, early years, education, 89, 102, 106, 108, 123–28, 129, 132, 133–34, 141–43, 159, 167, 210–11, 213, 216, 219, 227, 234–37, 239–41, 244, 257, 259, 260, 264–73 passim, 278, 282, 486–89; and brother Jack's political career, 313, 322, 364–65, 371, 372–73, 375; campaign and election to Senate from Massachusetts, 407, 408–9, 427–33, 458–59, 461; and Chappaquiddick, 490–92; and death of brother Jack, 450–58; description of father by, 141–43; descriptions of, 123–28, 147–48, 489–90; and The Fruitful Bough, book on his father, 141–43, 302–4, 416–17, 419–22, 456; at Harvard, 141, 147–48; marriage to Joan Bennett, 429–32; and mother's discipline, 133–34; physical attributes of, 125–26, 147–48; re-election to Senate (1970), 492–94; relationship with brothers, 486–89; and religion, 162, 163

Kennedy, Ethel (Mrs. Robert F. Kennedy), 3, 44, 108–9, 138, 188, 322, 347, 349, 350, 355, 360–61, 362, 383, 395, 405, 407, 408, 413–14, 416, 427, 429, 430, 432, 458, 477–78, 489–90, 504, 514; and death of husband, 477–78, 479, 489–90, 522; description and recollections of

mother-in-law and Kennedy family life by, 108–9, 138, 360–61, 395, 506–7; at Hyannis Port, 344–46, 349, 373; and the Joseph P. Kennedy, Jr. Foundation, 303

Kennedy, Eunice. See Shriver, Eunice Kennedy

Kennedy, Jacqueline. See Onassis, Jacqueline Kennedy

Kennedy, Jean. See Smith, Jean Kennedy

Kennedy, Joan (Mrs. Edward M. Kennedy, formerly Joan Bennett), 44, 355, 373, 383, 407, 410, 427, 429–32, 459, 503; courtship and marriage of, 429–32; described, 407, 429, 432; and husband's plane accident, 456, 459

Kennedy, John F. (Jack), 75–76, 80, 83, 84–85, 87, 101, 141, 150, 154, 155, 165, 173, 200–3, 210, 233, 235, 243, 244, 251–52, 256–57, 259–62, 263, 280, 303, 331, 338, 339, 343–44, 359, 460, 463, 466, 468, 485–89, 493, 498, 500, 510; ailments and illnesses of, 84–85, 93–94, 120, 145–46, 153, 176, 201, 202–3, 214, 215–16, 282, 284, 298, 343, 352, 453; "Appeasement at Munich" (Harvard thesis) by, 253; As We Remember Joe (book on his brother) by, 121, 126–27, 170–71, 173–74, 284, 297, 299, 302; aversion to wearing hats, 316, 318, 385–86, 389; birth, childhood, early years, 75–76, 80, 83, 84–85, 88–89, 93–94, 97, 100, 102, 110–14, 116–17, 119, 125–26, 129–30, 132, 135, 151, 153, 154, 162–63, 166, 170, 174–83; and brother Ted's Senate campaign, 429; and Camelot, 112; campaign and election to Congress, 306–20; campaign and election to Senate, 320–27; at Choate, 174–83; courage of, 145–47; death of, 441–46, 447–48 ff., 522; and dogs, 282; descriptions of, 111–12, 118–

22, 129–30, 145–47, 174–83, 215–16, 305–6, 310–11, 316–18, 326–27, 330, 390–91; education of, 110, 174–83, 200–3, 214–16, 277; entry into politics of, 21, 305–30, 331; European trip as President, 438–40; and father, 144, 284–85, 418, 420–21, 427, 436–37, 440–41; favorite childhood reading (list of books), 112; at Harvard, 214–16, 253, 261, 265; inaugural address by, 386–88; and inaugural ball and parade, 389–91; inauguration as President of, 382–91; *John Fitzgerald Kennedy . . . As We Remember Him* on, 284–85; John F. Kennedy Library and, 454–55; and the Joseph P. Kennedy, Jr. Foundation, 303, 304; Kennedy Center for the Performing Arts in honor of, 453–54; and love of poetry, 439–40, 449; marriage of, 346–55; Massachusetts legislature speech by, 386–88; money habits and attitudes of, 113–15, 118–19; and "Muckers Club" at Choate, 180–83; *A Nation of Immigrants* (proposed book) by, 438–39; and Nixon debates, 373–75; as President, 393 ff., 437–46 *passim*; and presidential campaign and election (1960), 356, 357–77 ff., 469, 470; and President's Panel on Mental Retardation, 304; at Princeton, 201–3; *Profiles in Courage* by, 145–47, 456; reaction to death of, 447–55; reading habits of, 110–14; and re-election to Senate (1958), 330; relationship with brother Joe Jr., 119–22, 126; and religion, 162–63, 165; and religious issue in presidential campaign and election, 357–58, 367–72; and South American trip, 277–79; speaking ability of, 106–7, 284–85, 315–16, 374–75; swimming ability of, 135; and tardiness, 102; and vice-presidential nomination contest (1956), 327–30; and war service as

skipper of PT-109, 263, 284–85, 288 ff., 293; writing ability of, 113–14, 145–47, 456; and White House rose garden, 394–95; *Why England Slept* by, 239–40, 261–62, 268, 271, 279, 280

Kennedy, Mrs. John F. *See* Onassis, Jacqueline Kennedy

Kennedy, John Fitzgerald, Jr. (grandson), 101, 113, 377–78, 380, 381, 382, 384, 394, 406, 434, 435, 437, 441, 448, 482–83, 484, 498; birth of, 377–78, 384; description of grandmother by, 101, 507; poems on, 439–40, 508–9

Kennedy, Joseph P., 2, 5–6, 7, 18, 80, 123, 124, 165, 166, 285–86, 287, 296, 300–4, 332, 334 ff., 349–50, 358–59, 433, 457, 461–62, 478, 486–87, 504; as ambassador to Great Britain, 2, 84, 198, 212, 213–53, 254–76; background, family of, 5–6; and banking, 65–66, 71, 80; birthday poems to, 414–15; characterized, described, 7, 17, 57, 71, 139–45, 302–4, 337, 340, 347, 416 ff., 448–49, 462–64; and children's striving for excellence, 143–49; courtship and marriage of, 47, 57–69; death of, 479; and death of son Jack, 442–46, 448–49; and death of son Joe Jr., 301–2; devotion to, and love and concern for, his children, 138–49, 151–59, 161–62, 164, 168, 169–74, 179–83, 202–3, 214, 256 ff., 340, 355–56, 486–87; and election of son Ted to Senate, 433; as father of the President, 393–94, 400, 401, 407, 427, 436–37, 440–42; and FDR and the New Deal, 80, 194–97, 199–200, 201, 203–5, 211–12, 213, 241–42, 243–44, 253, 258, 274–75; *The Fruitful Bough*, book on, 141–43, 144, 302–4, 416–17, 419–22, 456; and Hialeah race track part ownership, 335–37, 362; and "Hoover Commission," 275–76; *I'm for Roo-*

sevelt by, 203; and the Joseph P. Kennedy, Jr. Foundation, 302–4; and "Kennedy plan" (aid to German Jews), 243; and Maritime Commission, 211–12; and movie industry, 185–92, 203; and political career of son Jack, 308–9, 314, 321, 322, 328–29, 358–59, 361–62, 369, 373, 375–76, 377, 378, 383–84, 386, 388–89, 390–91, 461, 466, 470; and politics, 118, 194–205, 211–12, 213–53, 254–76 (see also specific individuals); and rearing of children (early years as parent, family life), 101–4, 113–14, 116–18, 124, 125, 127, 128, 131–32, 136–37, 169–98 passim; and Second World War, 241–53, 255–77 passim; and Securities and Exchange Commission, 199–201, 211, 213; and stock market, 192–94, 199–200; stroke and illness of, 416–28, 433–46, 449, 462–66, 479; Trafalgar Day speech by, 242–43
Kennedy, Mrs. Joseph P. See Kennedy, Rose Fitzgerald
Kennedy, Joseph P., Jr. (Joe), 106, 119–22, 137, 202, 210, 214, 234, 235, 243, 244, 250, 265, 277, 279, 288, 293, 298, 299–303, 329, 365, 487–88; As We Remember Joe on, 121–22, 126–27, 170–71, 173–74, 284, 297, 299–302; birth, childhood, early years, 75–76, 77–79, 80, 83, 84–85, 88–89, 91, 92–93, 97, 98, 106, 116–17, 119, 125–26, 137, 151, 162–63, 166, 169–74; death of, 299–303, 522; described, 119–22, 126–27, 171–74, 284, 297, 299–302; education of, 169–74, 177, 233, 264; graduated from Harvard, 233, 264; as Navy flier in Second World War, 283–84, 285, 288, 293, 294, 295–96, 297, 299–302; and politics, 259, 260, 262, 266–68; relationship with brother Jack, 119–22; and religion, 162–63; USS Jo-

seph P. Kennedy, Jr. named for, 300
Kennedy, Joseph P., Jr., Foundation, The, 302–4, 450
Kennedy, Joseph, II (grandson), 477
Kennedy, Kara (granddaughter), 510–11
Kennedy, Kathleen (Kathy, granddaughter), 362–63, 514–16
Kennedy, Kathleen (Kick). See Hartington, Marchioness of
Kennedy, Patricia. See Lawford, Patricia Kennedy
Kennedy, Patrick (grandfather of Joseph P. Kennedy), 5, 19–20
Kennedy, Mrs. Patrick (formerly Bridget Murphy), 5, 20
Kennedy, Patrick (grandson, son of Edward and Joan Kennedy), 410, 510
Kennedy, Patrick (grandson, son of Jack and Jackie Kennedy), 398, 485
Kennedy, Patrick Joseph (P.J.), 5, 17, 19–21, 25, 29, 62, 65–66, 93; and banking (Columbia Trust Co.), 65–66, 80; death of, 191; and politics in Boston, 19–21, 25, 29
Kennedy, Robert F. (Bobby), 75–76, 108, 150, 333, 339, 340, 347, 350, 355, 359, 360–61, 383, 410, 411, 415, 427, 430, 433, 437, 442, 469–79, 482, 493, 504, 514; as Attorney General, 390, 407, 408; birth, childhood, early years, education, 75–76, 83, 102–4, 110, 116, 121, 123, 128, 132, 140, 147–48, 159, 163–65, 202, 210, 213, 216, 219, 220, 227, 234, 236, 237, 256, 257, 259, 260–61, 263, 487–89; and campaign and election as Senator from New York, 459–61; and campaign for presidential nomination (1968), 466–76; death of, 475–79, 489–90, 522; and death of brother Jack, 450, 457–58, 461, 474, 482; described, 103–4, 147–48, 165, 467–68, 469–75, 476, 477–79; description of father by, 144; and games at Hyannis Port, 343–46, 349; as "people-minded,"

165; political campaign personality and speaking ability of, 469–70; and political career of brother Jack, 313, 319, 322–23, 324–28, 358, 361–62, 363–64, 368–69, 371, 375–76, 383, 394, 399, 400; and promptness at family table, 102–4; reading habits of, 110; refutation of his "ruthlessness," 470–75; relationship with older brothers, 487–89; and religion, 163; and Second World War, 298–99; sense of humor in, 473, 475; *That Shining Hour* (book) on, 103–4, 147–48, 161–65, 471–75; *To Seek a Newer World* by, 467; writing ability of, 113

Kennedy, Mrs. Robert F. *See* Kennedy, Ethel

Kennedy, Robert Francis, Jr. (grandson), 435

Kennedy, Rose Fitzgerald (Mrs. Joseph P. Kennedy), and Abbotsford Club, 52; and Ace of Clubs, 47–48, 73, 80; and autograph collecting, 406–7; Beals Street house, 71–75, 82, 84–85, 114, 119–20, 395; birth, background, childhood, early education, parents, 5–17, 19–26, 27–45 (*see also* Fitzgerald, John Francis; Fitzgerald, Mrs. John Francis); at Blumenthal convent in Holland, 31–43; Bronxville home, 100, 103–17, 166 ff., 185, 190–212, 256, 487–88; California trip (1923), 94–95; and care of children's teeth, 135–36; and Cecelian Club, 52; and child rearing, 77–85, 87–98, 99–183 *passim*; and children's education, 104–83 *passim*; and children's "learning experiences," 99 ff., 149; and children's physical training and activity, 135, 143, 159, 166; and children's promptness, 101–4; and children's reading, 109–13; and children's smoking and drinking, 136–38; and children's striving for excellence, 143–50; and clothing (fashion sense), 186–88; at Convent of the Sacred Heart (Boston), 28; courtship and marriage of, 47, 57–63; and death of son Bobby, 475–79; and death of son Jack, 442–46, 447–55, 466; debut into society of, 48–56, 62; described by her family, 483–84, 487–88, 495–96, 503–16; description of Boston society by, 49–50; description of White House by, 394–95; diary (1923) of, 87–98; and disciplining of children, 132–36, 139–40; and dogs, 281–82; and early years of marriage (parenthood, family life), 71–76, 77–85, 87–98, 99 ff. (*see also* specific aspects, family members); and Ethiopian trip, 497–503; in Europe (1908), 29–31 ff.; in Europe (1933), 197–99; in Europe (1935), 200 ff.; in Europe as President's mother, 400–16; and family Christmas, 97–98, 106; on family clannishness, 122; and family conversations and games, 104–8 ff., 337–56; and family picnics, 100–1; favorite food of, 505–6; first meeting with husband, 17; on the French Riviera, 328, 407–16; gives dinners for King and Queen of Great Britain, 246–49; and golfing, 192; and grandchildren, 101, 108, 139, 164, 346, 348, 356, 362–63, 408 ff., 498, 504–16 (*see also* specific children); and Hialeah race track, 335–37; Hull cottage, 77–78; and husband's movie connections, 185–92; and husband's stroke and illness, 416–46 *passim*, 462–66; at Hyannis Port (Cape Cod), 87, 101–31 ff., 185, 197, 279–83, 337–56, 370, 373–77, 395, 421–34 ff., 447–48, 458, 463, 482, 490–95, 503–16; interest in, and love of, music, 28–29, 32, 47, 73–74; and "Little White House" at Hyannis Port, 283; and love of travel, 497–503; made papal countess by Pius XII, 368; as mother of the President, 339–46; Naples Road home, 75, 83; at New England Conservatory of Music, 28, 47; in Palm Beach, Florida, 59–61, 197, 210, 214, 258, 335–37, 346–47, 353, 354, 361–62, 368, 371–91, 416–19, 448 ff.; in Panama with father, 54–55; in Paris, 186–90, 515–16; and political campaigning and speaking ability, 257, 314–16, 318, 324–25, 362, 368–69, 371–73, 459–61, 466–76, 494–95 (see also specific campaigns, elections, individuals); and reading, 16–17, 47; relationship with Jackie, 353–56, 481–86, 497, 499, 504–6; and religious faith and philosophy, 14, 160–65, 481–82, 496–97, 512, 517–22; Riverdale home, 166; on the Rosary and the Stations of the Cross, 521, 522; at Sacred Heart Convent in Manhattanville, 43–45; and Second World War, 229, 236–53, 255–76, 283–305; and sons' political careers, 305–30, 331, 357–58, 368–91, 459–61, 466–76, 494–95 (see also specific campaigns, elections, family members); and son Ted's plane crash and injuries, 455–57; and South American trip, 277 ff.; in Soviet Union, 205–10; as wife of ambassador to Great Britain, 213–53, 255–76; at Windsor Castle, 221–25; as youngest member of Public Library Investigating Committee, 47

Kennedy, Rosemary, 75–76, 83, 84–85, 90, 119, 149, 150–59, 214, 287; birth and mental retardation of, 150–59, 161; custodial care in Wisconsin convent for, 285–86, 425, 466; at school in Europe, 213, 225, 227, 235, 236, 252, 257, 258, 264, 266, 303

Kent, Duchess of, 231

Kent, Duke of, 231, 250

Kent, Frank, Great Game of Politics by, 21

Khrushchev, Nikita S., 400, 403–5, 406–7

Khrushchev, Mrs. Nikita S., 403–5, 406–7; described, 404–5

Kiernan, Thomas, poem on John Kennedy, Jr., by, 439–40

King, Alan, 383

Kopechne, Mary Jo, 490–92

Krock, Arthur, 129, 195–96, 211, 212, 261, 266; description of Joseph P. Kennedy, Jr., on his death by, 302; Memoirs, 195–96, 302, 305

Lasker, Mary, 516

Laski, Harold, 170–72, 180, 200, 269, 271, 300; Jack and Joseph P. Kennedy, Jr., as students of, 170–72, 180, 200, 261, 300

Lasky, Jesse, 185

Lawford, Christopher (grandson), 164, 513–14

Lawford, Patricia Kennedy, 150, 164, 188, 192, 211, 216, 234, 236, 282, 323, 383, 410, 412, 418, 443, 483; birth, childhood, early years, 75–76, 87, 103, 117, 119, 124–25, 131, 138, 163–69, 211, 216, 257–58, 266, 339, 349; and brother Jack's political career, 323, 371, 377; described, 138, 167–69; description of mother by, 506; and the Joseph P. Kennedy, Jr. Foundation, 303; marriage to Peter Lawford, 355, 407; That Shining Hour, on brother Bobby, by, 103–4, 147–48, 164–65, 471–75

Lawford, Peter, 164, 355, 375, 383, 407

Lawford, Robin (granddaughter), 410

Lawrence, David, 362, 367, 370–71

Laycock, Angie, 295

Le Hand, "Missy," 274

Leinsdorf, Erich, 450

Lelong, Lucien, 187, 227

Lindbergh, Charles, 229

Lindbergh, Mrs. Charles (Anne Morrow), 229

Lipton, Sir Thomas, 41–42, 49, 67, 72, 160, 207–8; friendship with Kennedy family, 41–42, 49, 160; "proposal" of marriage to Rose Fitzgerald, 67

Lloyd, Harold, 186

Lodge, George Cabot, defeat by Ted Kennedy for Senate seat of (1962), 428–29, 433

Lodge, Henry Cabot, Jr., defeat by Jack Kennedy for Senate seat of (1952), 320–21, 324, 325, 326–27, 428

Lodge family, 49. See also specific individuals

Lomasney, Martin, 21, 24, 25

London, Jack, 209

Luce, Henry R., 230, 261

Luce, Mrs. Henry R. (Clare Boothe), 230, 293–94

MacArthur, Douglas, 425

McCormack, Edward (Eddie), 411, 428, 432

McCormack, John W., 428

Macdonald, Torbert (Torb), 215, 251, 313, 327, 350; description of Jack Kennedy by, 215; and Jack Kennedy's congressional campaign and election, 313

McGarnigal, Jean, 323

McGovern, George, 493, 495

McKinley, William, 33–34

Macmillan, Harold, 290, 406, 410, 440; description of Robert F. Kennedy by, 473

Magiore, Mary (later Mrs. Padraic Colum), 35

Maher, Mr. (housemaster at Choate), on Jack, 177–78

Malraux, André, 426, 452

Mansfield, Michael J. (Mike), 380

Margaret Rose, Princess (of Great Britain), 220, 223, 224, 238

Markham, Paul, 491

Marlborough, Duchess of, 250

Marlborough, Duke of, 250

Marsh, Wilbert, 443–44

Mary, Dowager Queen of Great Britain, 225, 233, 247, 251; described, 225; "receives" the Kennedys, 225

Mary, Queen of Scots, 223

Maxwell, Elsa, 234

Mayer, Louis B., 185

Means, George, and Kennedy family life at Hyannis Port (1940), 279–81

Meditations (Cardinal Newman), 519, 521–22

Mellon, Andrew, 218

Mellon, Mrs. Paul, 394

Memoirs (Arthur Krock), 195–96, 302, 305

Merman, Ethel, 383

Meyner, Robert, 370

Meyzen, Robert, 427

Milbanks, Sheila, 295

Mix, Tom, 116–17

Moley, Raymond, 199–200

Molyneux (British dress designer), 227, 228, 391

Monk, Sir John, 231, 247

Moore, Edward (Eddie), 88, 89, 91, 93, 97, 120, 155, 166, 216, 244, 258

Moore, Mrs. Edward (Mary), 88, 89, 93, 94, 97, 155, 216, 244, 258; death of, 456

Morgan, J. P., 217

Morgenthau, Henry, 195, 197, 211–12

Morgenthau, Mrs. Henry, 211

Morriset, Father, 325

Morrissey, Frank, 325–26, 408, 409, 469

Morrow, Mrs. Dwight, 229

Mosbacher, Emil ("Bus"), 498, 499

Mosbacher, Mrs. Emil, 498

Moss, Edward (Eddie), 455, 458, 491

Moss, Mrs. Edward, 458

Murphy, Bridget. See Kennedy, Mrs. Patrick

Murray, Margot, 430

Nast, Condé, 271

Nawn, Harry, 55

Nawn, Hugh, 55–56, 64

Neville, Mike, 309, 312, 319–20
Nicholas, Czar, 207–8
Nixon, Richard M., 357, 370, 373–75, 386; Jack Kennedy's televised debates with, 107
Nixon, Mrs. Richard M., 386
Noonan, James, 104
Norfolk, Duke of, 244
Norman, Sir Montagu, 201

O'Brien, Lawrence (Larry), 322, 368
O'Byrne, Mother, 431
O'Casey, Sean, 406
O'Connell, Joseph (Joe), 90–91
O'Connell, Mary. See Ryan, Mary O'Connell
O'Connell, William Cardinal, 69, 91, 244, 296–97
O'Donnell, Kenneth (Kenny), 147–48, 322, 323–24, 327–28, 367–68, 369–70, 440–41
Oistrakh, David, 404
Olivier, Sir Laurence, 383
Onassis, Aristotle (Ari), 44, 482–84, 497, 498, 499, 505
Onassis, Jacqueline Kennedy (Jackie, Mrs. John F. Kennedy, later Mrs. Aristotle Onassis), 44–45, 101, 145, 153, 335, 346–55, 370, 371, 376, 377–78, 379–80, 381–83, 384, 386, 388–89, 390–91, 469, 489, 509; described, 346–55, 402–3, 429, 447, 458, 481–86; as First Lady, 393–98, 400, 402–3, 407, 408, 410, 412, 429, 434, 435, 436, 437, 438, 441, 485–86; "How to Bring Up a Child to Be Happy," article by, 381–82; and husband's death, 443, 444, 447–48, 455, 457–58, 481–83, 489; and husband's political career, 365–66; marriage to Jack Kennedy, 346–55; marriage to Onassis, 44–45, 482–84, 497, 499, 504–6; poem on Jack Kennedy by, 351–53; relationship with mother-in-law, Rose Kennedy, 353–56, 481–86, 497, 499, 504–6
Ormsby-Gore, Mr. and Mrs. David

(later Lord and Lady Harlech), 290, 296
Pacelli, Eugenio Cardinal (later Pope Pius XII). See Pius XII, Pope
Patterson, Joseph M., 251, 267
Patterson, Mrs. Joseph M., 251
Paul VI, Pope, 440
Pickford, Mary, 95, 186, 216
Pius XI, Pope, 198–99; death of, 243–44
Pius XII, Pope (formerly Cardinal Eugenio Pacelli), 204–5, 244, 297, 440
Poitier, Sidney, 383
Polybius, quoted, 357
Powers, David F. (Dave), 161–62, 309–12, 314–15, 316–18, 319, 323–24, 325, 359, 398–99, 440–41, 469; as curator of Jack Kennedy's memorabilia collection, 454–55
President's Panel on Mental Retardation, 304
Profiles in Courage (John F. Kennedy), 145–47, 456

Radziwell, Lee, 346–47, 350, 436, 438, 440, 455, 498
Radziwell, Prince Stanislas (Stas), 436, 498
Rajpipla, Maharajah of, 231
Rayburn, Sam, 357, 379
Reardon, Timothy ("Ted"), 313
Revere, Paul, 6, 312, 333
Rockefeller, John D., III, 137
Rockefeller, Nelson, 137
Roosevelt, Eleanor (Mrs. Franklin Delano Roosevelt), 197, 205, 211, 345, 357, 366
Roosevelt, Franklin Delano (FDR), 53, 80, 118, 170, 194–97, 199–200, 201, 203–5, 211–12, 213, 243–44, 249, 253, 258, 260, 262, 266–67, 274–75, 316, 337, 369, 370, 406; described, 275; and Second World War, 237–38, 241–42, 274–75
Roosevelt, Franklin D., Jr., 369–70, 498–99
Roosevelt, James (Jimmy), 197–98

Roosevelt, Mrs. James (Betsy Cushing), 197–98, 275
Roosevelt, Sara, 360
Roosevelt, Sara Delano, 205
Rush, Dr. Howard, 419, 420
Rutland, Charles, Duke of, 298
Ryan, John, 462–65, 516
Ryan, Mary O'Connell, 90, 91, 153–54

St. John, George, 175, 177, 179–80, 181, 182, 183
St. John, Mrs. George, 175–76
Salinger, Pierre, 450–51, 485
Saltonstall, Leverett, 9
Sanford, "Laddie," 124
Sanford, Mary, 123–24
Sarnoff, David, 203
Saunders, Frank, 462–63
Scanlon, Michael (Mike), 238
Scanlon, Mrs. Michael, 246
Schenck brothers, 185
Schiller, Johann Christoph Friedrich, 39
Schlesinger, Arthur, Jr., quoted on Bobby Kennedy's intelligence and humor, 473–74
Schmidt, Benno, quoted on Bobby Kennedy, 472
Selassie, Haile, Emperor. *See* Haile Selassie, Emperor
Shakespeare, William, 30
Shore, Dinah, Rose Kennedy's appearance on television show of, 494
Shriver, Eunice Kennedy (Mrs. Sargent Shriver), 7, 9, 81, 90, 133, 148–50, 165, 213, 234, 235, 236, 271, 289, 319, 323, 339, 347, 407, 409, 411–12, 413, 414, 418, 424, 438, 443, 445–46, 456, 486, 511; birth, childhood, early years, 75–76, 91–92, 99–100, 122, 126, 135–36, 143, 148–50, 167–68; and brother Jack's political campaigns, 323, 324, 367, 371, 376; correspondence with parents, 210–11, 216, 256–57, 262–63, 265–66, 269–70, 272; debut party of, 249–50; described, 149–50; de-

scribes her father, 302–4; and the Joseph P. Kennedy, Jr. Foundation, 151, 302–4, 450; marriage to Sargent Shriver, 303, 334, 355; on mother's taste in clothing, 187–88; and President's Panel on Mental Retardation, 304; and religion, 163, 165; and sister Rosemary, 151, 152–53, 155, 286; and South American trip, 277–79
Shriver, Maria (granddaughter), 435, 498, 511–12
Shriver, Robert Sargent (grandson), 434–35
Shriver, Sargent (Sarge), 149–50, 303, 321, 334, 348, 350, 355, 371, 375, 407, 409, 432, 443; and the Joseph P. Kennedy, Jr. Foundation, 303; and vice-presidential nomination and campaign (1972), 494–95, 503–4
Shriver, Timmy (grandson), 498
Smith, Alfred E. (Al), 53, 194, 195, 358, 367
Smith, Jean Kennedy (Mrs. Stephen Smith), 193, 213, 220, 234, 236, 257, 264–65, 266, 268–69, 270, 323, 350, 354, 356, 383, 409, 412–13, 414, 418, 427, 430–31, 438, 440, 443, 456, 461, 482, 483, 488, 504; in Africa, 500, 501–3; birth, childhood, early years, 76, 102, 108–9, 123, 125, 135, 159, 167; and death of brother Jack, 451, 455; and the Joseph P. Kennedy, Jr. Foundation, 303; marriage to Steve Smith, 355, 383
Smith, Stephen (Steve), 355, 371, 375, 383, 409, 412–13, 427, 432, 433, 443, 451, 455, 459, 467; and campaign and election of Ted Kennedy to Senate, 433, 459; and election of Jack Kennedy as President, 371, 375, 383; and home in Hyannis Port, 355, 412–13
Smith, Stephen, Jr. (grandson), 512–13
Sorensen, Theodore (Ted), 433; de-

scription of Robert Kennedy by, 474–75

Spaulding, Charles (Chuck), recalls Cape Cod summer with the Kennedys, 279–81

Spellman, Francis Cardinal, 204, 296–97, 368; officiates at marriage of Ted Kennedy to Joan Bennett, 432

Steele, Mr. (director, summer school at Choate), on Jack, 177

Stevenson, Adlai E., 147, 327, 329, 358, 366

Storrow, James Jackson, 43, 45, 51

Strauss, Richard, 32

Sullivan, William (Billy), 307

Sutton, William (Bill), 310

Swanson, Gloria, Joseph P. Kennedy's movie industry ventures and, 117, 186–92; in Queen Kelly, 190–91; in Sunset Boulevard, 191; in The Trespassers, 186–90; in What a Widow, 192

Swope, Herbert Bayard, 194

Symington, Stuart, 366

Taft, William Howard, 53

Tennyson, Alfred, lines from his "Ulysses" quoted, 449, 467

Terence, quoted, 393

That Shining Hour (Patricia Kennedy Lawford), 103–4, 147–48, 164–65, 471–75

Thomas, Norman, 194

Thompson, Fred, 185; and his horse, Silver King, 185

Thoreau, Henry, 16, 209

Toscanini, Arturo, 74

To Seek a Newer World (Robert F. Kennedy), 467

Traubel, Helen, 383

Travell, Dr. Janet, 408

Tregaskis, Richard, 215

Truman, Harry S, 357

Truman, Mrs. Harry S, 485

Tunney, John, 431

Tweedsmuir, Lord. See Buchan, John

Underwood, Oscar W., 367

Vanocur, Sandy, quoted on Bobby Kennedy, 471

Vaughan, Cardinal, 48

Vaughan, Reverend Bernard, 48

Victoria, Queen, 50, 221–22

Von Stroheim, Erich, 190–91

Watt, Dr. Robert, 491

Wilhelmina, Queen of the Netherlands, 222

Willkie, Wendell, 274

Wilson, Woodrow, 54, 68, 428

Windsor, Duke of, 361

Winter, Diane, 421

Wirtanen, "Captain" Frank, 421, 462

Woodin, William H., 197

Why England Slept (John F. Kennedy), 239–40, 261–62, 268, 271, 279, 280

Zukor, Adolph, 185